Critical Incident F
Active Shooter at
Robb Elementary School

Uvalde, Texas

United States Government

Content Advisory

The team took great care to be intentional about the words used in this report to convey the facts. Nevertheless, the descriptions may be activating for some readers due to the explanations of this mass casualty incident, including the age of the victims.

The team deliberately does not name the subject to avoid glorifying the subject's actions and out of respect for the victims' families.

For resources, including free and confidential emotional support, please visit https://988lifeline.org/ or call/text 988 to reach the Suicide & Crisis Lifeline, available 24 hours a day, 7 days a week, 365 days a year.

Dedication

This report is offered to honor the memories of the innocent victims—young students and teachers—who were senselessly killed on May 24, 2022, at Robb Elementary School in Uvalde, Texas. To memorialize those whose lives were taken, we created remembrance profiles to capture the spirit of each victim and to amplify their voices, which were silenced. These can be found in "Appendix A. Remembrance Profiles" and online at https://cops.usdoj.gov/uvalde.[1]

This report is also dedicated to the survivors—those who feared for their lives and the lives of their loved ones—who selflessly risked their own safety to call for help and to try to protect others and who witnessed the horror, watching in anguish as the event unfolded. To hundreds of survivors in this community, we know the negative impacts, including physical, mental, and emotional injuries, will not end and that your grief remains very heavy. Many of you continue to bear the scars and pain you suffered from the loss of your loved ones and the loss of your sense of safety in your own community.

It is our intention to honor all of you by remembering your loved ones and representing your stories, sharing them here with the rest of the country. We hope that our review of the events of May 24, 2022, can provide answers to the remaining questions and lessons that may help others in the future.

The country mourned with the Uvalde community on that tragic day. While we remain heartbroken by your loss, we are driven by the need to provide an authoritative accounting of the days and months leading up to that day, the response that transpired on May 24, and the events and actions that followed.

The following page lists the names of the victims.

---

[1] Placement of the Remembrance Profiles is based on requests from some of the families of the victims.

Below are the names of the innocent lives lost that day:

Nevaeh Alyssa Bravo, 10

Jacklyn "Jackie" Cazares, 9

Makenna Lee Elrod, 10

Jose Flores Jr., 10

Eliahna "Ellie" Amyah Garcia, 9

Irma Linda Garcia, 48

Uziyah Sergio Garcia, 10

Amerie Jo Garza, 10

Xavier James Lopez, 10

Jayce Carmelo Luevanos, 10

Tess Marie Mata, 10

Maranda Mathis, 11

Eva Mireles, 44

Alithia Haven Ramirez, 10

Annabell Guadalupe Rodriguez, 10

Maite Yuleana Rodriguez, 10

Alexandria "Lexi" Aniyah Rubio, 10

Layla Marie Salazar, 11

Jalilah Nicole Silguero, 10

Eliahna Cruz Torres, 10

Rojelio Fernandez Torres, 10

Contents

Acknowledgments

The U.S. Department of Justice extends appreciation and thanks for the commitment and support of the leaders of the Uvalde community, especially former Uvalde Mayor Don McLaughlin for reaching out to the Associate Attorney General to request this review. It takes courage to voluntarily undergo an assessment, especially one of this magnitude.

The Justice Department thanks the City and County of Uvalde. In the midst of this tragedy and pain, the people of Uvalde demonstrated kindness, hospitality, and openness.

The Justice Department extends deep appreciation to the family members, victims, responders, and community members who agreed to speak with the review team through their discomfort and pain. The candid and often vulnerable conversations were invaluable to this report.

The Justice Department also acknowledges the agencies and organizations that were responsive to requests for documents and data, in particular, the officials and personnel of the Uvalde Police Department; the Texas Department of Public Safety; the Bureau of Alcohol, Tobacco, Firearms and Explosives; the Federal Bureau of Investigation; and U.S. Customs and Border Protection for their responsiveness.

The Justice Department acknowledges with gratitude the important contributions of the Critical Incident Review (CIR) subject matter experts who contributed to this review.

On behalf of the Office of Community Oriented Policing Services (COPS Office) team who led this review, we extend our appreciation to the COPS Office personnel who supported us throughout this project. In particular, we acknowledge and thank the leaders and staff in the following divisions: Resources and Technical Assistance; Communications; Management Services; Finance; Budget; Information Technology; Facilities; Legal; and Publishing. We also thank the staff and contractors who provided transcription and interpretation services throughout the project and the translation services for the report. We also share our appreciation for the staff of the Associate's Office, Justice Management Division, DOJ Library, Bureau of Justice Assistance, Office for Victims of Crime, Office of Justice Programs Publishing Team, Office of Privacy and Civil Liberties, Office of Information Policy, Office for Access to Justice, and particularly the U.S. Marshals Services Evidence.com Team for their substantial support and assistance.

Executive Summary

On May 24, 2022, a mass shooting at Robb Elementary School in Uvalde, Texas, shook the nation. With just two days left in the school year, a former student armed with an AR-15 style assault rifle took the lives of 19 students and two teachers, physically injured at least 17 others, and left countless families, friends, and a community grief-stricken for their unimaginable loss. In the aftermath of the tragedy, there was significant public criticism of the law enforcement response to the shooting. At the request of then Uvalde Mayor Don McLaughlin, the U.S. Department of Justice (DOJ) announced on May 29, 2022, that it would conduct a Critical Incident Review (CIR) of the law enforcement response to the mass shooting. Recognizing that "[n]othing can undo the pain that has been inflicted on the loved ones of the victims, the survivors, and the entire community of Uvalde," the Attorney General stated that the goal of the CIR was to "assess what happened and to provide guidance moving forward."

A full understanding of the response of local, state, and federal law enforcement agencies and personnel is critical for addressing many unanswered questions, identifying crucial lessons learned, enhancing prevention initiatives, and improving future preparation for and responses to mass shootings in other communities. In providing a detailed accounting and critical assessment of the first responder actions in Uvalde, and the efforts since to ameliorate gaps and deficiencies in that response, the CIR is intended to build on the knowledge base for responding to incidents of mass violence. It also will identify generally accepted practices for an effective law enforcement response to such incidents. Finally, the CIR is intended to help honor the victims and survivors of the Robb Elementary School tragedy.

The CIR was led by the Office of Community Oriented Policing Services (COPS Office) with the support of a team of subject matter experts with a wide variety of relevant experience, including emergency management and active shooter response, incident command, tactical operations, officer safety and wellness, public communications, and victim and family support (see "About the Team"). The CIR team collected and reviewed more than 14,100 pieces of data and documentation, including policies, training logs, body camera and CCTV video footage, audio recordings, photographs, personnel records, manuals and standard operating procedures, interview transcripts and investigative files and data, and other documents. The CIR team visited Uvalde nine times, spending a total of 54 days on site. The team conducted over 260 interviews of individuals from more than 30 organizations and agencies who played a role in or had important knowledge or information about areas related to the review. Those interviews included personnel from the law enforcement agencies involved in the response to the mass shooting, other first responders and medical personnel, victims' family members, victim services providers, communications professionals and public information officers, school personnel, elected and appointed government officials, survivors and other witnesses, and hospital staff.

Organization of the Report

This report provides the results of the independent, comprehensive assessment conducted by the CIR team. The period for collecting documents and data through this CIR was June 2022 until June 2023, defined throughout the report as the review period. To organize this comprehensive review, the team established the following areas of focus:

- **Incident Timeline Reconstruction.** This chapter provides an authoritative account of pertinent facts leading up to, during, and immediately following the tragic mass shooting.

- **Tactics and Equipment.** This chapter examines tactical approaches and availability of special tools and equipment during the critical 77 minutes between the arrival of first responders on scene through the classroom entry and killing of the shooter.

- **Leadership, Incident Command, and Coordination.** This chapter examines the leadership, incident command, decision-making, and coordination actions that took place across responding agencies and law enforcement leaders.

- **Post-Incident Response and Investigation.** This chapter assesses the establishment of post-incident investigative command and activities, victim identification, and crime scene management, as well as administrative investigations and after-action reviews.

- **Public Communications During and Following the Crisis.** This chapter examines communications activities and approaches with and between government entities (including law enforcement) and the general public, family members, professional media, social media, and others.

- **Trauma and Support Services.** This chapter analyzes support and resources provided to survivors, victims, responders, and other stakeholders.

- **School Safety and Security.** This chapter documents the school safety planning and assesses the security apparatus of the Uvalde Consolidated Independent School District (UCISD).

- **Pre-Incident Planning and Preparation.** This chapter assesses the training, agreements, and procedures for law enforcement, other first responder agencies, and other relevant stakeholders in the critical areas of active shooter response, incident command, emergency management, and other significant areas.

Terminology and Treatment of Names

Names are important. The team deliberated on the treatment of names and decided on the following:

- The subject's name is not used to avoid glorification.

- Only elected officials and chief executives of agencies are named where appropriate. All other individuals are left unnamed.

Additionally, this report refers to "victims" and "survivors" interchangeably to respect that some people prefer to be referenced as survivors and others as victims. The CIR team was also cognizant of and attempted to avoid terminology like "triggered," "targeted," and other gun-related language as well as time frame references (which typically convey celebrations, such as "anniversaries"), out of respect for the fact that these terms are often activating for some victims, survivors, responders, and family members.

Overview of CIR Factual Observations

At 11:33 a.m. on the morning of May 24, 2022, the subject entered Robb Elementary School equipped with a high-powered AR-15 rifle. He immediately started shooting and within a minute entered classrooms 111 and 112, which were connected via an interior door.

Within 3 minutes of the subject's entry into the school, 11 law enforcement officers from the Uvalde Consolidated Independent School District (UCISD) and Uvalde Police Departments (UPD), including supervisors, arrived inside the school. Hearing continued gunfire, five of the responding first on scene (FOS) law enforcement ran toward classrooms 111/112. The other six FOS did not advance down the hallway, including UPD Acting Chief Mariano Pargas, who was in the best position to start taking command and control, and to start coordinating with approaching personnel. One of the officers said to "line up to make entry" and within seconds shots were fired from inside one of the rooms. Two officers were hit with shrapnel, and all responders retreated to positions of cover.

After three attempts to approach the classrooms, the focus of the responders shifted from entering classrooms 111/112 and stopping the shooting to evacuating other classrooms, attempting to negotiate with the subject, and requesting additional responders and equipment. With this shift from an active shooter to a barricaded subject approach, some responders repeatedly described the subject over the radio as "barricaded" or "contained." Yet within four minutes from FOS arrival, 911 dispatch confirmed that class was in session and reported that they had received calls from victims.

Chief Pete Arredondo of the UCISD Police Department (UCISD PD) directed officers at several points to delay making entry into classrooms 111/112 in favor of searching for keys and clearing other classrooms. Occupants of other classrooms were at risk of further injury as a result of the high-powered nature of the shooter's AR-15 style rifle and from possible crossfire once classrooms 111 and 112 were entered. At several points, UCISD PD Chief Arredondo also attempted to negotiate with the subject. Others called out over the radio for additional resources and indicated that they were waiting for a tactical team to arrive, such as Uvalde special weapons and tactics (SWAT), the Texas Department of Public Safety (TXDPS), and the U.S. Border Patrol Tactical Unit (BORTAC). Chief Arredondo, who became the de facto on-scene commander, was without his radios, having discarded them during his arrival, and communicated to others either verbally or via cell phone throughout the response.

Over the course of the incident, overwhelming numbers of law enforcement personnel from different agencies self-deployed to the school. Leadership on scene, however, had not established command and control, to include an incident command post (ICP), staging area, or clear perimeter around the hallway or the school. Thus, arriving personnel did not receive accurate updates on the situation or direction for how to support the response efforts. Many arriving officers—based on inaccurate information on the scene and shared over the radio or from observing the lack of urgency toward entering classrooms 111/112—incorrectly believed that the subject had already been killed or that UCISD PD Chief Arredondo was in the room with the subject. As leaders from additional law enforcement agencies arrived, including Uvalde County Sheriff Ruben Nolasco, the lack of clear communication and command structure made coordination difficult. Emergency medical responders faced similar challenges as they deployed. They struggled to identify who was in charge, and ambulances encountered streets blocked by law enforcement vehicles.

Concerned families were also arriving at the school. They likewise had difficulty obtaining information about their loved ones' status. Incorrect and conflicting information was also being shared on social media with the UCISD posting that all students and staff were safe in the building and later posting messages about reunification that conflicted with the UPD posts.

At 12:21 p.m., 48 minutes after the subject entered the school, the subject fired four additional shots inside classrooms 111/112. Officers moved forward into formation outside the classroom doors but did not make entry. Instead, presuming the classroom doors were locked, the officers tested a set of keys on the door of a janitor's closet next to room 112. When the keys did not work, the responders began searching for additional keys and breaching tools. UCISD PD Chief Arredondo continued to attempt to communicate with the subject, while UPD Acting Chief Pargas continued to provide no direction, command, or control to personnel.

After another 15 minutes, officers found a second set of keys and used them to successfully open the janitor's closet. With working keys in hand, the officers then waited to determine whether a sniper and a drone could obtain sight of and eliminate the subject through the window. Those efforts were unsuccessful.

At 12:48 p.m., 27 minutes after hearing multiple gunshots inside classrooms 111 and 112, and 75 minutes after first responders first entered Robb Elementary, officers opened the door to room 111. A team composed of BORTAC members, a member of the U.S. Border Patrol Search, Trauma, and Rescue Unit (BORSTAR), and deputies from two local sheriffs' offices entered the rooms, and officers killed the subject when he emerged shooting from a closet. The subject was killed at approximately 12:50 p.m., 77 minutes after the first officers entered the school and after 45 rounds were fired by the shooter in the presence of officers.

There were 587 children and many other teachers and staff members present at Robb Elementary School that fateful day. In the end, 19 children and two staff were killed, with at least 17 survivors physically injured. Since not all the children and staff present at Robb Elementary at the time of the shooting were brought to the hospital or otherwise assessed for any medical concerns, it is unknown how many in total sustained physical injuries as a result of this incident.

Wounded and deceased victims were transported to Uvalde Memorial Hospital, while the majority of other victims were transported to the Uvalde Civic Center, where the Reunification Center was eventually established. At the hospital and the center, some families were reunited with their children. But other families received incorrect information suggesting their family members had survived when they had not. And others were notified of the deaths of their family members by personnel untrained in delivering such painful news.

In the days, weeks, and months following the tragedy, survivors, families, and responders received varying levels of support services. Many organizations arrived in Uvalde in the days that followed to assist survivors and families in accessing mental health and other victim support resources. But since then, difficulties with tracking victims and transitioning service providers have meant that some victims, family members, and community members have not received services.

Public communications challenges continued throughout the response and in the aftermath of the tragedy. Both impromptu and scheduled news conferences and media engagements contained inaccurate and incomplete information. Victims, families, and community members struggled to receive timely and accurate information about what occurred on May 24. And although government officials and school administrators hosted several family briefings and school board meetings over the weeks and months after the shooting, those events offered limited information and few substantive responses from officials and, in some cases, exacerbated the distress of the families.

Overview of CIR Team Analysis

Based on these facts, the CIR team identified several critical failures and other breakdowns prior to, during, and after the Robb Elementary School response and analyzed the cascading failures of leadership, decision-making, tactics, policy, and training that contributed to those failures and breakdowns. From the facts and analysis, the CIR team has been able to identify generally accepted practices for an effective law enforcement response to similar mass shootings and offer recommendations in hopes that in the future, law enforcement would be able to act quickly, save lives, and prevent injuries to the greatest extent possible.

The most significant failure was that responding officers should have immediately recognized the incident as an active shooter situation, using the resources and equipment that were sufficient to push forward immediately and continuously toward the threat until entry was made into classrooms 111/112 and the threat was eliminated. Since the tragic shooting at Columbine High School in 1999, a fundamental precept in active shooter response and the generally accepted practice is that the first priority must be to immediately neutralize the subject; everything else, including officer safety, is subordinate to that objective. Accordingly, when a subject has already shot numerous victims and is in a room with additional victims, efforts first must be dedicated to making entry into the room, stopping the subject, and rendering aid to victims. These efforts must be undertaken regardless of the equipment and personnel available to those first on the scene.

This did not occur during the Robb Elementary shooting response, where there was a 77-minute gap between when officers first arrived on the scene and when they finally confronted and killed the subject. Several of the first officers on scene initially acted consistent with generally accepted practices to try to engage the subject, and they moved quickly toward classrooms 111/112 within minutes of arriving. But once they retreated after being met with gunfire, the law enforcement responders, including UCISD PD Chief Pete Arredondo—who we conclude was the de facto on-scene incident commander—began treating the incident as a barricaded subject scenario and not as an active shooter situation.

As more law enforcement resources arrived, first responders on the scene, including those with specific leadership responsibilities, did not coordinate immediate entry into the classrooms, running counter to generally accepted practices for active shooter response to immediately engage the subject to further save lives. Instead, law enforcement focused on calls for additional SWAT equipment (which should not delay the response to an active shooter), requests for delivery of classroom keys and breaching tools (which may not have been necessary to gain entry), and orders to evacuate surrounding classrooms prior to making entry into classrooms 111/112.

In addition to the overall failure to appreciate the active shooter nature of the situation, responders also failed to act promptly even after hearing gunshots around 12:21 p.m., which should have spurred greater urgency to confront the subject but instead set off a renewed search for keys.

There were also failures in leadership, command, and coordination. None of the law enforcement leaders at the scene established an incident command structure to provide timely direction, control, and coordination to the overwhelming number of responders who arrived on the scene. This lack of structure contributed to confusion among responders about who was in charge of the response and how they could assist.

Communications difficulties exacerbated these problems. Per UCISD policies, Chief Arredondo was the on-scene incident commander, but he lacked a radio, having discarded his radios during his arrival thinking they were unnecessary. And although he attempted to communicate with officers in other parts of the hallway via phone, unfortunately, on multiple occasions, he directed officers intending to gain entry into the classrooms to stop, because he appeared to determine that other victims should first be removed from nearby classrooms to prevent further injury.

These failures may have been influenced by policy and training deficiencies. For example, recent training that UCISD PD provided seemed to suggest, inappropriately, that an active shooter situation can transition into a hostage or barricaded subject situation. And while many of the FOS had sufficient active shooter and incident command training, other key FOS responders lacked any active shooter training or incident command training. The vast majority of the officers from different law enforcement agencies had never trained together, contributing to difficulties in coordination and communication on the day of the incident. The lack of pre-planning hampered even well-prepared agencies from functioning at their best.

Chapter by Chapter Summary

As noted above, the CIR team organized the review of the Robb Elementary School response by focusing on particular topics. A summary of the CIR team's observations and recommendations for each of these chapters is provided below.

Chapter 1. Incident Timeline Reconstruction

This chapter provides an authoritative account of pertinent facts leading up to, during, and immediately following the tragic mass shooting.

Chapter 2. Tactics and Equipment

Police active shooter response tactics have undergone significant changes and evolution over the years. Throughout most of history, the police response to an active shooter incident was to secure a perimeter and call out a SWAT team and, in some cases, negotiators. Most officers lacked specialized, advanced training and preparation to handle such situations. The watershed moment in tactical changes occurred following the Columbine massacre in 1999. Following Columbine, law enforcement expert tacticians and associations testified that the new paradigm for responding to crises like Columbine is rapid deployment. Rapid emergency deployment puts significant responsibility on the first responding officers, who may not be fully equipped or trained as a SWAT team member. First responders are instructed to go toward the violent offender, if necessary, bypassing injured victims and placing themselves in harm's way.

"Chapter 2. Tactics and Equipment" examines the tactics and pieces of equipment that were contemplated, sought, and deployed over the course of the incident response at Robb Elementary School, beginning with the initial officers' approach from outside the school and ending approximately 77 minutes later when the medical triage of victims inside classrooms 111/112 began.

Selected Observations

To see the full list of Observations, see "Chapter 2. Tactics and Equipment."

- The first officers on scene immediately moved toward the sound of gunfire and into the West Building of Robb Elementary to stop the shooter, which was in adherence to active shooter response generally accepted practices. Once inside the building, five of the first officers on scene continued to press down the hallway and toward a barrage of gunfire erupting inside of rooms 111/112. (Observation 1)

- After officers suffered graze wounds from shrapnel, the first officers on scene did not penetrate the doors to rooms 111/112 and repositioned to a barricaded subject situation. This mindset permeated throughout much of the incident response, even impacting many of the later responding officers. Despite their training and despite multiple events indicating the subject continued to pose an active threat to students and staff in the building, including the likelihood and then confirmation of victims inside the room, officers on scene did not attempt to enter the room and stop the shooter for over an hour after they entered the building. The shooter was not killed until approximately 77 minutes after law enforcement first arrived. (Observation 3)

- The effort to clear and evacuate the entire West Building was intentional and directed by Chief Arredondo, to preserve and protect the lives of the children and teachers who remained in the hot zone, while the shooter remained an active threat with multiple victims in rooms 111/112. This was a major contributing factor in the delay to making entry into rooms 111/112. The time it took to evacuate the entire building was 43 minutes, beginning at around 11:38 a.m., when Chief Arredondo realized there were occupants in room 109 that he could not access, and ending at 12:21 p.m., when four shots were fired, and that same room was finally evacuated through the windows. During this time and prior to 12:21 p.m., there were multiple stimuli indicating that there was an active threat in classrooms 111/112—including: the barrage of gunfire during the initial response; the children and teachers observed when evacuating the classrooms; the single shot fired at 11:44 a.m.; the notification that class was in session; the notification from an officer on scene that his wife, a teacher, was inside classrooms 111/112 and shot; and multiple radio broadcasts of a 911 call from a student inside the classroom. (Observation 6)

- Some officers on scene believed that they were waiting for more assets to arrive, such as shields and a specialized tactical team, to make entry. (Observation 7)

Selected Recommendations

To see the full list of Recommendations, see "Chapter 2. Tactics and Equipment."

- Officers responding to an active shooter incident must continually seek to eliminate the threat and enable victim response. The shooter's immediate past actions and likely future actions serve as "triggering points" that indicate the appropriate response should be in line with active shooter response protocols.[2] An active shooter with access to victims should *never* be considered and treated as a barricaded subject. (Recommendation 3.1)

- Law enforcement training academies and providers should ensure that active shooter training modules include the factors in determining active shooter versus barricaded subject situations. (Recommendation 3.3)

---

[2] IACP, *Model Policy on Active Shooter.*

- Officers responding to an active shooter incident must first and foremost drive toward the threat to eliminate it. In the event there are resources available and an opportunity to evacuate bystanders and victims from the hot zone, officers must balance the risk posed by evacuation versus the risk posed by remaining in lockdown and potentially in the crossfire. Evacuations in such circumstances must be conducted in the most expeditious manner, limited to those immediately in harm's way, and not at the expense of the priority to eliminate the threat. In the case of Robb Elementary, the CIR team concludes that the effort to evacuate was protracted and should not have caused such significant delay in the eventual entry into rooms 111/112. (Recommendation 6.1)

- Officers responding to an active shooter incident must be prepared to approach the threat and breach or enter a room using just the tools they have with them, which is often a standard-issue firearm/service weapon. (Recommendation 7.1)

Chapter 3. Leadership, Incident Command, and Coordination

Leadership in law enforcement is absolutely critical, especially in moments of a dire challenge, such as the active shooter incident at Robb Elementary School. It requires courageous action and steadiness in a chaotic environment. Leadership can arise regardless of rank or title. Such moments require steady and commanding actions and based on facts gathered for this report, this leadership was absent for too long in the Robb Elementary School law enforcement response.

"Chapter 3. Leadership, Incident Command, and Coordination" describes key principles related to leadership in an active shooter incident, including the need to direct an immediate response to the active shooter threat and to establish a coordinated and collaborative command and control system. The chapter analyzes the actions of leaders from several law enforcement agencies, including UPD, UCISD PD, UCSO, TXDPS, and CBP in responding to the shooting at Robb Elementary School. The chapter discusses incident command and management; coordination with other law enforcement agencies, including mutual aid; self-deployment by other local, state, and federal law enforcement personnel; and emergency medical services/fire medical response.

Selected Observations

To see the full list of Observations, see "Chapter 3. Leadership, Incident Command, and Coordination."

- Leadership from UPD, UCISD PD, UCSO, and TXDPS demonstrated no urgency for establishing a command and control structure, which led to challenges related to information sharing, lack of situational statuses, and limited-to-no direction for personnel in the hallway or on the perimeter. (Observation 4)

- Failure to establish a unified command led to limited multiagency coordination. (Observation 5)

- There was no uniformly recognized incident commander on the scene throughout the incident. (Observation 8)

- UCISD PD Chief Arredondo was the de facto incident commander on the day of the incident. Chief Arredondo had the necessary authority, training, and tools. He did not provide appropriate leadership, command, and control, including not establishing an incident command structure nor directing entry into classrooms 111 and 112. (Observation 9)

- On the day of the incident, no leader effectively questioned the decisions and lack of urgency of UCISD PD Chief Arredondo and UPD Acting Chief Pargas toward entering classrooms 111/112, including within their respective agencies and agencies with concurrent/overlapping jurisdiction (e.g., Uvalde County Sheriff Nolasco, Uvalde County Constable Zamora, Uvalde County Constable Field, TX Ranger 1). (Observation 12)

Selected Recommendations

To see the full list of Recommendations, see "Chapter 3. Leadership, Incident Command, and Coordination."

- Agency leaders must immediately determine incident status and the appropriate command structure for the event. Leadership must continually assess and adjust as the threat and incident evolve. (Recommendation 4.1)

- As soon as possible and practical, the lead agency should establish a unified command that includes a representative from each primary first responder agency to facilitate communication, situational awareness, operational coordination, and allocation and delivery of resources. (Recommendation 5.1)

- The ICP should provide timely direction, control, and coordination to the agency leadership, other agencies, and other critical stakeholders before, during, and after an event or upon notification of a credible threat. The ICP must also serve as an intelligence collection and dissemination node. (Recommendation 7.4)

- Agencies should create and train on a policy, and set an expectation that leaders will act in a manner consistent with that policy during critical incidents. (Recommendation 12.1)

- A memorandum of understanding (MOU) or memorandum of agreement (MOA) needs to be developed among agencies within a county or region that provides clarity on who is in command, taking into consideration an agency's training, experience, equipment, and capacity to take the lead during a multiagency response to a critical incident. (Recommendation 12.2)

- Agencies should use the Incident Command System (ICS) for more than large-scale tactical events. They should incorporate as many of the ICS principles as possible in response to varying levels of emergencies or planned events, so ICS becomes a regular component of the agency's culture. (Recommendation 13.1)

Chapter 4. Post-Incident Response and Investigation

Establishing investigative command after a multiagency response to a mass casualty incident is critical to ensuring effective control and coordination of the scene and responsive resources, assignment of investigative assets, collection of information and intelligence, and external and internal communication. In the wake of a critical incident involving a law enforcement response, multiple investigations and reviews will often occur. In addition to a criminal investigation of the subject, critical incidents often result in one or more administrative investigations of officer conduct during the incident.

The "Post-Incident Response and Investigation" chapter centers around criminal and administrative investigations and associated activities and processes that took place at Robb Elementary School, such as management of the crime scene, evidence collection, and interagency coordination in such efforts. Additionally, it describes several critical incident reviews that were initiated following the tragedy.

Selected Observations

To see the full list of Observations, see "Chapter 4. Post-Incident Response and Investigation."

- The involvement of local agencies in the hallway during the incident led the district attorney, in consultation with the TXDPS, to assign Texas Rangers to solely investigate the incident. (Observation 1)

- Body-worn camera (BWC) video captures officers walking into the crime scene without an investigative purpose or responsibility in the immediate aftermath of the incident. Furthermore, in the days that followed, crime scene preservation was compromised, and the crime scene team had to continually stop and start their important work when non-investigatory personnel entered the hallway and classrooms 111/112 for the purpose of viewing the scene. (Observation 4)

- The Texas Rangers Crime Scene Team processed and exhaustively documented an incredibly challenging crime scene that put their training, policies, and procedures to the test. The team conducted an after-action review to examine their efforts and learn as an organization. (Observation 9)

- Among the agencies with the most involved personnel, most have not completed administrative investigations into their officers' actions on May 24. (Observation 11)

Selected Recommendations

To see the full list of Recommendations, see "Chapter 4. Post-Incident Response and Investigation."

- Agencies should have a formal agreement or understanding on investigative command after a multiagency response. (Recommendation 1.1)

- Leaders must respect the integrity of the crime scene and only access it with a declared and documented legitimate purpose. Crime scenes need to be held without contamination until completed. The crime scene team should be permitted to do their methodical work without continuous interruptions by VIPs who want to enter the crime scene but have no probative need to do so. (Recommendation 4.1)

- Agencies in regional proximity to each other should conduct multiagency tabletop exercises for complex investigations that may necessitate mutual aid and support from each other. Doing so will build greater interagency coordination in activities like evidence collection as well as understanding of jurisdictional boundaries, capabilities, processes, and expectations among partner agencies. The tabletop exercises should include local, state, and federal agencies, as appropriate, and be designed to exploit weaknesses, uncover strengths, and develop solutions. (Recommendation 7.1)

- Agencies should adopt parallel investigations policy for criminal and administrative investigations, including for major incidents, while taking diligent steps to ensure that information derived from compelled administrative interviews are completely walled off from any criminal investigation into the officer's or agent's actions. (Recommendation 11.1)

- Agencies that engage in after action/critical incident reviews should adequately resource the effort to ensure high-quality and timely reports of lessons learned and areas for organizational improvement. (Recommendation 12.1)

Chapter 5. Public Communications During and Following the Crisis

Public communications during and after a disaster, emergency, or mass violence event is itself an intervention that can help victims and community members prepare and respond effectively. Communications from trusted leaders who exude a sense of calmness, competency, control, and compassion that integrate trauma-informed information can also help those impacted manage their stress and distress reactions to these events. Thus, both internal and external communications are vitally important in every disaster, emergency, and mass violence incident. These communications must be timely and accurate and provide as much information as appropriate at any given time, providing the community with a sense of trust and confidence during a time in which many are learning the most devastating news that anyone can receive.

The "Public Communications During and Following the Crisis" chapter describes critical components for coordinated communication during and after a tragedy, including the identification of a public information officer (PIO) and the establishment of a Joint Information System (JIS), housed by a Joint Information Center (JIC). The chapter canvasses the public communications in the days, weeks, and months following the shooting at Robb Elementary School and describes how inaccurate and untimely information combined with inconsistent messaging created confusion and added to the victims' suffering.

Selected Observations

To see the full list of Observations, see "Chapter 5. Public Communications During and Following the Crisis."

- Inaccurate information combined with inconsistent messaging created confusion and added to the victims' suffering, both on the day of the incident and in the days after the mass shooting. (Observation 1)

- Family members encountered many obstacles to locating their loved ones, getting access to the hospital, and getting information from leadership, law enforcement, and hospital staff in a timely manner. This includes initial information posted by UCISD on the reunification site followed by a series of contradictory posts between UPD and UCISD on reunification. This added to the confusion, pain, and frustration. (Observation 5)

- Spokespersons for UCISD and TXDPS, the only agencies speaking publicly, did not coordinate their messaging during the afternoon of the incident. Some conflicting information was shared by the two agencies. (Observation 11)

- All social media public messaging was posted only in English. The one exception to this was the FBI San Antonio Field Office's messaging starting on May 25. (Observation 15)

- The extent of misinformation, misguided and misleading narratives, leaks, and lack of communication about what happened on May 24 is unprecedented and has had an extensive, negative impact on the mental health and recovery of the family members and other victims, as well as the entire community of Uvalde. (Observation 18)

Selected Recommendations

To see the full list of Recommendations, see "Chapter 5. Public Communications During and Following the Crisis."

- To establish leadership and a sense of order, the lead agency must be swift, proactive, accurate, and transparent in its messaging. Relevant information that is not law enforcement-sensitive should typically be released as soon as it is confirmed. However, speed must be balanced with the need for accuracy. It is critical that information is verified before it is released even when there is tremendous pressure to release information quickly. (Recommendation 4.3)

- When reunification is complete and the victims' families have been notified, the lead agency should release that information to the community. This is a crucial step in unifying the community to start the healing process. (Recommendation 6.2)

- The lead agency should institute incident command and establish a JIC for coordinating the release of all public information, including victim information from all medical facilities that can be incorporated into coordinated news briefings. (Recommendation 7.1)

- When an organization recognizes that an error has occurred, it should admit the mistake and share what actions it is taking to rectify the problem and prevent it from happening again. Even when the mistake is egregious, an agency can maintain or seek to regain public trust by being open and holding itself accountable to the community. In these moments, a law enforcement agency can build community trust by holding itself to the highest possible standard. (Recommendation 13.1)

- In a community with a large population with limited English proficiency, officials should post emergency information in English and in other predominant languages. This inclusive approach will help ensure that critical public safety messages reach a larger audience and will help boost trust. (Recommendation 15.1)

- Intentional transparency is needed for the victims, survivors, and loved ones who are seeking answers about what happened; however, authorities need to provide information in a trauma-informed, victim-centered, and culturally sensitive manner. (Recommendation 24.1)

Chapter 6. Trauma and Support Services

Support services for individuals who are exposed to tragedies like a mass casualty incident, including victims, family members, the broader community, and responders, are essential. Helping those affected understand that they can access crisis counseling, learn good coping skills, reach out to social supports, and access their innate strengths to build their resilience, can protect against people developing a mental illness as a result of their exposure to a traumatic event and its aftermath. Adequate support, services, and resources all contribute to recovery and healing.

"Chapter 6. Trauma and Support Services" assesses the support and resources provided to survivors, victims, responders, and others involved in the shooting at Robb Elementary School. This chapter describes the acute services provided in the first 24–72 hours following the shooting, including during the evacuation process and the establishment of the Reunification Center for families and survivors. It also describes intermediate and long-term survivor and victim family support; support services for law enforcement and other responders; and management of emotional/trauma support for the broader Uvalde community following the tragic incident at Robb Elementary School.

Selected Observations

To see the full list of Observations, see "Chapter 6. Trauma and Support Services."

- Once the children and adults were rescued from their classrooms during the evacuation process, they received limited instruction and direction on where to proceed. Due to the chaotic nature of the evacuation, children and school personnel were not adequately evaluated medically prior to being transported to the Reunification Center. As such, injured victims had delayed medical care and were at risk of further injury. (Observation 1)

- The establishment of a Reunification Center was delayed and chaotic. Families and next of kin received conflicting instructions on the location of the center. (Observation 6)

- The death notification process was disorganized, chaotic, and at times not conducted in a trauma-informed manner. (Observation 9)

- Responders were not provided timely, immediate access to trauma and support services, and many reported feeling abandoned and unsupported in the weeks and months following the critical incident. Others reported being aware of the services but electing not to use them. (Observation 14)

- Shared trauma is a concern for the Uvalde community due to compounding factors, including the size of the community and its interrelatedness. For the hundreds of law enforcement, medical, behavioral health, and government personnel who responded to this incident, shared trauma can make what happened even more overwhelming. Law enforcement's trauma is also exacerbated by the backlash from the community—as the community's trauma is exacerbated by the lack of an adequate response from law enforcement. (Observation 16)

- The Uvalde community continues to need support and guidance as it struggles with the negative impacts of the failed response, a lack of accountability for those implicated in this failure, and remaining gaps in the information about what happened to their loved ones. (Observation 43)

Selected Recommendations

To see the full list of Recommendations, see "Chapter 6. Trauma and Support Services."

- Officials should ensure all victims of a mass violence incident are screened medically and assessed for mental health concerns soon after evacuation and no later than 24-48 hours post-incident. (Recommendation 2.1)

- In the weeks and months following an incident, victims and family members should receive follow-up or continued monitoring to ensure they are receiving the necessary mental health care and other services. (Recommendation 2.2)

- Victim advocates should be assigned to communicate with and assist families. Each family member of a deceased person and each injured victim should be assigned a victim advocate who works with that family/victim consistently throughout the treatment and recovery period, having frequent communications to ensure the family/victim is aware of and able to access needed services and supports. (Recommendation 9.4)

- Local officials engaging in trauma and death notifications should consult national resources and ensure best practices are followed when providing these notifications. Preparedness and planning can help a locality identify areas where they have fewer trained or experienced staff, thus the areas where they need mutual aid supports. (Recommendation 11.1)

- Leaders from responder agencies need to provide services to all personnel involved in a mass casualty incident (MCI), which for some agencies means everyone on their staff. These services should include resources on post-disaster behavioral health and secondary traumatic stress, referrals to health care providers, and peer support. (Recommendation 14.5)

- As part of disaster preparedness planning, communities—including law enforcement—need to plan for the aftermath of a critical incident. This planning should include generally accepted practice processes, education and training, support, and resources. A trauma-informed, culturally sensitive approach should be applied to the victims, survivors, and impacted community members, as well as responders and their families. (Recommendation 16.3)

- A family assistance center(FAC) should be established within 24 hours of an incident with a security plan that includes external law enforcement presence and a process for internal vetting of providers and those seeking services. (Recommendation 18.1)

- The definition of responders should be expanded, consistent with generally accepted practices, to include disciplines other than law enforcement, fire, and rescue staff, such as dispatchers, EMTs, health care providers, ambulance drivers, behavioral health providers, and faith-based leaders. This should be reflected in all support services provided by resiliency centers, nongovernmental and governmental entities, and other support service providers. (Recommendation 31.2)

Chapter 7. School Safety and Security

While the primary goal of school districts across the United States is to educate, they must also prepare for myriad threats to school safety and security, ranging widely in scale and seriousness. In addition to certain safety functions maintained at the school district administration level, such as threat assessment teams, school safety committees, student counseling services, and physical security maintenance and upgrades, many school districts throughout the nation partner with local law enforcement agencies to establish school resource officer programs, and some create their own police departments. Among the 1,207 independent school districts in Texas, 309 (about 26 percent) have their own police department, including the UCISD.

"Chapter 7. School Safety and Security" reviews the safety and security apparatus of UCISD on May 24, 2022, including UCISD policies and procedures on active shooter response and incident command and their policies on locked doors, use of an emergency alert system, history of drills and exercises, establishment of its police department, and district-wide and campus planning processes around school safety.

Selected Observations

To see the full list of Observations, see "Chapter 7. School Safety and Security."

- UCISD's campus safety teams met infrequently, and annual safety plans were based largely on templated information that was, at times, inaccurate. (Observation 5)

- UCISD had a culture of complacency regarding locked-door policies. Both exterior and interior doors were routinely left unlocked, and there was no enforced system of accountability for these policies. Door audits were conducted, but not done systematically, nor were they documented. On May 24, all of the exterior doors and at least eight interior doors of the West Building, where the incident took place, were unlocked. (Observation 8)

- Law enforcement arriving on scene searched for keys to open interior doors for more than 40 minutes. This was partly the cause of the significant delay in entering to eliminate the threat and stop the killing and dying inside classrooms 111 and 112. (Observation 10)

- Four years into its existence, the UCISD PD was functioning without any standard operating procedures. A range of UCISD employees, including administrators, faculty, support staff, and police officers, told the CIR team they had no knowledge of, nor had they been informed about, their school police department's policies and procedures. The UCISD PD has recently drafted standard operating procedures. (Observation 18)

Selected Recommendations

To see the full list of Recommendations, see "Chapter 7. School Safety and Security."

- School district police departments should enter into MOUs that establish mutually agreed upon clear jurisdictional responsibilities with other neighboring agencies that are likely to respond to a critical incident on school property. The MOUs should account for not only routine criminal activity, but also critical incidents. The MOU should address the issue of unified command, in addition to incident command, and account for the capacity and capabilities of the respective agencies. (Recommendation 2.1)

- Law enforcement, first responders, emergency management, and other municipal government agencies should coordinate with school districts to conduct multiagency preparedness exercises on at least an annual basis. Exercises should operate in accordance with the state and local regulations regarding active threat exercises. The exercises should be incorporated into the emergency operations plans and Campus Safety Plans. (Recommendation 3.1)

- Communities should adopt a multidisciplinary approach to school safety that includes school police, law enforcement, school officials, mental health professionals, and other community stakeholders. It is especially important that all voices in the school community be heard, including faculty, staff, administrators, counselors, nurses, resource officers, parents, and students. Every stakeholder must feel empowered to play a role in reducing fear and raising the level of safety in and around schools. Each campus should establish and train school safety committees that will meet at least monthly for this purpose. (Recommendation 4.2)

- School districts should invest in upgrading or replacing all doors (or locks) throughout its campuses to remedy this issue, so that doors can be locked from the inside. (Recommendation 9.1)

- School districts should implement universal access boxes. A universal access box refers to a locked box that contains master keys, located near the entry points of school buildings, that can be accessed by authorized emergency first responders and school district staff. (Recommendation 10.1)

- School districts should ensure that emergency alert systems are well-understood by all staff. In the case of UCISD, district leadership should issue a district-wide clarification on the use of PA systems in conjunction with Raptor emergency alerts. (Recommendation 11.1)

Chapter 8. Pre-Incident Planning and Preparation

Pre-incident planning is crucial in preparing for and responding to mass violence incidents, as it enables agencies and organizations to develop strategies and procedures to respond quickly and effectively to such incidents. The planning process involves identifying potential risks and hazards, assessing the likelihood and potential impact of incidents, and creating plans and procedures to respond to them. When a mass violence incident occurs, a community's response is not limited to one agency, but falls to multidisciplinary stakeholders, including law enforcement, fire, emergency medical services, hospitals, victim service providers, prosecutors, emergency management, government and civic leaders, media, businesses, and individual community members. The planning process—coordinating routinely among all relevant stakeholders, developing agreements, and conducting multidisciplinary trainings, exercises, and drills—is foundational, as are relationship- and trust-building.

Most failures in response can be traced back to failures in pre-incident planning and preparation, and this is true of the mass casualty incident at Robb Elementary School. "Chapter 8. Pre-Incident Planning and Preparation" describes the policies and procedures, training, mutual aid agreements, and other formal coordination efforts in Uvalde prior to May 24, 2022, and explains how those pre-incident processes impacted the response at Robb Elementary School.

Selected Observations

To see the full list of Observations, see "Chapter 8. Pre-Incident Planning and Preparation."

- Responding agencies lacked adequate related policies and, in most cases, any policy on responding to active attackers. (Observation 1)

- The Uvalde emergency operations center (EOC) developed an adequate emergency management plan. However, not all the relevant agencies and organizations actively participated in the process, drills, and exercises which ultimately contributed to a failed emergency response on May 24, 2022. (Observation 2)

- The MOU between UPD and UCISD PD that was active the day of the incident failed to adequately outline the expectations and authorities for a response to a mass violence event. The agencies failed to exercise the MOU, nor cross-train in preparation for a critical incident. (Observation 3)

- Responding agencies had minimal exposure to incident command system (ICS)/National Incident Management Systems (NIMS). Of those serving in top leadership positions within the primary responding agencies, only UCISD PD Chief Arredondo and the TXDPS regional director had taken training in ICS/NIMS. (Observation 6)

- Responding officers had levels of active shooter training that varied in terms of their length of time and quality, leading to failures in operationalizing the training. (Observation 7)

- Personnel from responding agencies rarely trained and exercised in a multiagency environment. (Observation 8)

Selected Recommendations

To see the full list of Recommendations, see "Chapter 8. Pre-Incident Planning and Preparation."

- Every agency must have a clear and concise policy on responding to active attacker situations. (Recommendation 1.1)

- Agencies should regularly review after-action reviews (AAR) with other regional agencies to plan as a region for a coordinated and collaborative response to possible similar events. (Recommendation 1.2)

- Agencies should consider obtaining state- or national-level accreditation to adopt and maintain standardized policies and procedures. This process also ensures accountability and transparency that can enhance confidence and trust in law enforcement among the communities they serve. (Recommendation 1.3)

- Regional public safety partners should plan, train, and exercise unified command for complex incidents. This includes federal, state, and local law enforcement, fire, EMS, and emergency management as well as other governmental and non-governmental agencies that would respond to a critical incident. (Recommendation 2.9)

- Elected officials should establish a Multi-Agency Coordination (MAC) Group to provide policy guidance to incident personnel and support resource prioritization and allocation. Typically, these groups are made up of government agency or private sector executives and administrators whose organizations are either impacted by, or provide resources to, an incident. MAC Groups enable decision-making among senior officials and executives, and delegate command authority to the incident commander to cooperatively define the response and recovery mission and strategic direction. Additionally, MAC Groups identify operational priorities and communicate those objectives to the Emergency Operations Center and the pertinent functions of the Incident command system and the joint information center. (Recommendation 2.11)

- Interagency training, drills, and exercises help to build relationships at the front-line officer level and, if attended by law enforcement supervisors, can further strengthen relationships and the efficacy of a multiagency response to a mass casualty incident. Though policies may differ slightly among agencies, overarching commonalities are the same in an active attacker incident. (Recommendation 8.1)

- Each PIO should draft a crisis communication plan and practice it at least four times a year with smaller events. This will help identify problem areas and solutions and ensure everyone is familiar with the plan and knows their role instead of trying to figure that out during a crisis. (Recommendation 12.2)

We hope the observations and recommendations in this report will improve the preparation and response by those law enforcement agencies assessed during this review, as well as other law enforcement agencies throughout the country. We also provide this independent review of what transpired as a measure of dedication not only to those who lost their lives on May 24, but also to the surviving victims, family members, and others deeply and forever affected by this tragedy.

Introduction

"Help!" "Help!" "Help!" "I don't want to die. My teacher is dead." "One

of my teachers is still alive but shot." "Officer!" "Officer!" "Are they

[officers] in the building?" "There is a lot of dead bodies."

These were the words of nine- and ten-year-old children at Robb Elementary School in Uvalde, Texas, on May 24, 2022, during a call with 911. At this point in time, these students and three teachers had been trapped in classrooms 111 and 112 with an active shooter for 37 minutes. This call lasted for nearly 27 minutes. Even though law enforcement were in the hallway, just outside the classrooms, it was another 13 minutes after the call ended before law enforcement rescued the survivors. In fact, for 77 agonizing, harrowing minutes, children and staff were trapped with an active shooter. They experienced unimaginable horror. The survivors witnessed unspeakable violence and the death of classmates and teachers. Tragically, 19 students and two teachers perished.

An active shooter not only took their lives, but also physically and mentally injured survivors, families, Robb Elementary staff and students, and the Uvalde community. There were multiple failures that contributed to the extent of the tragedy at Robb Elementary.

At the direction of Attorney General Merrick Garland, under the leadership of Associate Attorney General Vanita Gupta, this Critical Incident Review (CIR) Report identifies and assesses the factors that contributed to the failures. It provides a comprehensive accounting of what happened on May 24, 2022, and assesses the systems in place in the weeks leading up to that day. It not only examines the actions of law enforcement, but those of all responding agencies. It assesses school safety measures, emergency management, and the myriad systems designed to promote safety. The Report also assesses the communications provided to survivors and families immediately after the shooting began, including the inaccurate narrative told to the Uvalde community and the country in the hours and days afterwards. Additionally, it assesses the trauma and support services provided to the victims, survivors, and family members as well as responders.

Answering the call of former Uvalde Mayor Don McLaughlin for an independent, objective assessment of what happened on May 24, 2022, the Attorney General established this CIR. Sadly, the families and Uvalde community continue to have so many unanswered questions. The first goal of this report is to provide information to those most affected by the tragedy. It is our hope that it will aid in their healing. In providing a detailed accounting and assessment of what transpired in the days and months leading up to the shooting, the immediate first responder and other actions taken, and the efforts since to address and improve upon gaps and deficiencies, we also hope to build on knowledge regarding how to best respond to incidents of mass violence.

The attorney general pledged to provide an assessment that would be fair, transparent, and independent. A CIR team was established that included DOJ's Office of Community Oriented Policing Services (COPS Office) and subject-matter expert members with both extensive experience in conducting these reviews and a deep knowledge in relevant areas including emergency management and active shooter response, incident command and management, school safety, tactical operations, crisis communications, and trauma services. The COPS Office has previously conducted a variety of independent, objective assessments of responses to other critical incidents, including mass shooting tragedies, and brings that experience to this CIR as well.

CIR Areas of Examination

To organize this comprehensive review, the team established the following areas of focus, each of which is presented in a separate chapter in this report:

- **Incident Timeline Reconstruction.** This chapter provides an authoritative account of pertinent facts leading up to, during, and immediately following the tragic mass shooting.

- **Tactics and Equipment.** This chapter examines tactical approaches and availability of special tools and equipment during the critical 77 minutes between the arrival of first responders on scene through the classroom entry and killing of the shooter.

- **Leadership, Incident Command, and Coordination.** This chapter examines the leadership, incident command, decision-making, and coordination actions that took place across responding agencies and law enforcement leaders.

- **Post-Incident Response and Investigation.** This chapter assesses the establishment of post-incident investigative command and activities, victim identification, and crime scene management, as well as administrative investigations and after-action reviews.

- **Public Communications During and Following the Crisis.** This chapter examines communications activities and approaches with and between government entities (including law enforcement) and the general public, family members, professional media, social media, and others.

- **Trauma and Support Services.** This chapter analyzes support and resources provided to survivors, victims, responders, and other stakeholders.

- **School Safety and Security.** This chapter documents the school safety planning and assesses the security apparatus of the Uvalde Consolidated Independent School District (UCISD).

- **Pre-Incident Planning and Preparation.** This chapter assesses the training, agreements, and procedures for law enforcement, other first responder agencies, and other relevant stakeholders in the critical areas of active shooter response, incident command, emergency management, and other significant areas.

CIR Methodology

The period for collecting documents and data through this CIR was June 2022 until June 2023, defined throughout the report as the review period. Given the topics described above, the assessment primarily focused on the actions of the law enforcement agencies that responded at Robb Elementary on that day of tragedy, including:

- Uvalde Police Department (UPD)

- Uvalde Consolidated Independent School District Police Department (UCISD PD)

- Uvalde County Sheriff's Office (UCSO)

- Texas Department of Public Safety (TXDPS)

- U.S. Customs and Border Protection (CBP)

- U.S. Marshals Service (USMS)

- Bureau of Alcohol, Tobacco, Firearms and Explosives (ATF)

- Federal Bureau of Investigation (FBI)

Where relevant, however, the assessment also examined the planning, preparation, and response of other entities, including the Uvalde Consolidated Independent School District (UCISD), other responder agencies, government entities, victim services providers, and other key stakeholders.

To gather and analyze documentation, information, and data, the CIR team used the following methods:

- **Research and Data Analysis** of data sources, training records, timeline deconfliction, and collected evidence and documentation. Also, the team researched open source media; national standards, best practices, and generally accepted practices and standards in relevant areas of policing policy and practice; research literature; and any other relevant issues identified in the review to provide a foundation from which to conduct gap analysis.

- **On-Site Data Collection** was conducted in Texas locations including Uvalde, Austin, San Antonio, Hondo, Del Rio, Eagle Pass, Dilley, Cotulla, San Marcos, and Maxwell.

- **Introductory Meetings** with senior officials from law enforcement, government, school, hospital, and other responder agencies were conducted to discuss the CIR, call for full cooperation, and identify specific needs.

- **One-on-One Interviews** were conducted with individuals with a role in the areas of focus with critical knowledge about an area under review (including adult victims and family members), as well as those impacted by this tragic event.

- **Group Meetings and Interviews** were also conducted with those with a role in the areas of focus.

- **Two Family Forums** were held with family members of the victims and survivors of this tragedy to provide information on the CIR and status updates on the review, and to provide an open forum to collect feedback and answer questions.

- **Walkthroughs of Robb Elementary** were conducted to fully understand the physical layout of the school via first-hand on-site analysis, including the West Building in particular.

To gather and analyze data sources, training records, timeline deconfliction, and collected data and documentation, the team employed a variety of extensive review methods. Over the span of 11 months, the CIR team collected over 14,100 pieces of documentation related to the areas of focus. These included policies, training logs, body camera and CCTV video footage, audio recordings, photographs, personnel records, manuals and standard operating procedures, interview transcripts and investigative files and data, and other documents.[3]

In the course of its work, the CIR team visited Uvalde nine times over the span of 11 months and has spent a total of nearly 54 days on site. It conducted more than 260 interviews of individuals who played a role, or had important knowledge or information, related to the areas of examination (see table i-1 on page 5). More than 30 organizations and agencies were represented through these interviews, including personnel from the law enforcement agencies involved in the response to the mass shooting; other responders and medical personnel; victims' family members; victim services providers; communications professionals and public information officers; school personnel; elected and appointed government officials; survivors and other witnesses; and hospital staff.

CIR team members also observed five nationally recognized active shooter training course deliveries[4] in order to review generally accepted practices and standards that are referred to throughout this report and were used in validating certain observations and recommendations.

The recommendations rely on the expertise of the CIR team, generally accepted practices and standards, including relevant literature and past critical incident reviews, and pertinent policies and trainings.

The CIR will be essential for recounting the response of nearly 400 officers in response to the mass shooting. It will also be crucial for describing and accounting for the elapsed 77 minutes before law enforcement stopped the subject and rescued survivors and the 21 murdered students and teachers. The full scope of the report will include a detailed accounting and assessment of what transpired in the days and months leading up to the shooting, the immediate first-responder and other actions taken, and the efforts since to address and improve upon gaps and deficiencies. As with any after-action assessment, there is no "one-size fits all" formula. Resulting recommendations are grounded in the facts specific to the response at Robb Elementary but provide valuable insights for the field.

---

[3] To protect the confidentiality of individuals who participated in this CIR, report statements derived from primary, secondary, and tertiary source documents, evidence, and interviews will be denoted within footnotes as "CIR Fact Finding." Similarly, "CIR Document and Data Request" is used for any documents and data provided by responding agencies to the CIR team.

[4] See "Appendix B. Report Methodology" for the full list of training courses.

Table i-1. Interviews conducted by CIR team, broken out by stakeholder type

Stakeholder	Number of interviews
Community/Faith-Based/Businesses	5
Federal/Agency (Non–Law Enforcement)	6
Federal/Law Enforcement Agency	31
Hospital/Medical	9
Local/Campus Agency	4
Local/Emergency Management	2
Local/Government Agency	12
Local/Non-Governmental Organization	3
Local/Police Department	37
Local/School District	35
Local/School Law Enforcement Agency	5
Local/Sheriff's Office	6
National/Non-Governmental Organization	21
Paramedics/Regional Transportation	19
State/Association	3
State/Law Enforcement Agency	39
State/Non-Governmental Organization	7
Training Provider	8
Victim/Family/Witness	15
Grand Total	267

Terminology and Treatment of Names

Names are important. The team deliberated on the treatment of names and decided on the following:

- The subject's name is not used to avoid glorification.

- Only elected officials and chief executives of agencies are named where appropriate. All other individuals are left unnamed.

Additionally, this report refers to "victims" and "survivors" interchangeably to respect that some people prefer to be referenced as survivors and others as victims. In addition, the CIR team was cognizant of and attempted to avoid terminology like "triggered," "targeted," and other gun-related language as well as time frame references (which typically convey celebrations, such as "anniversaries"), out of respect for the fact that these terms are often activating for some victims, survivors, responders, and family members.

For a more detailed description of the CIR methodology, refer to "Appendix B. Report Methodology."

Organization of the Report

The report begins with an incident timeline reconstruction that recounts key facts before, during, and immediately following the tragic incident. This report is then organized around the topical chapters outlined above, within which relevant events and activities are reconstructed; law enforcement and other stakeholder actions are described; decision-making by key leadership is analyzed and assessed; and other related activities are documented. Each chapter includes:

1. an introduction to the issues under review;

2. a description of generally accepted principles and standards for those issues

3. an analysis of the preparation, response, and post-incident response activities viewed from the lens of that particular issue;

4. observations based on the evidence and documentation obtained throughout the CIR process;

5. lessons learned and recommendations for improvements that align with generally accepted practices and standards for those agencies and stakeholders included within this review, as well as for global application for law enforcement and stakeholders assessing their own plans for preparing for and responding to mass violence events.

Also included are important appendices that are valuable supplemental resources to understanding the full scope of the review and in providing additional context for the descriptions, observations, and recommendations contained in this report. These include

- **Remembrance Profiles**;

- A full set of **Observations and Recommendations**;

- A detailed description of the **CIR Methodology**;

- **Leadership, Incident Command, and Coordination Supplemental Materials**;

- **Public Communication Supplemental Materials**;

- **Trauma and Support Services Supplemental Materials**;

- **Pre-Incident Planning and Preparation Supplemental Materials**;

- Descriptions of team members in **About the Team**;

- Lists of **Abbreviations and Acronyms** contained within the report.

On behalf of the U.S. Department of Justice, we express our sincerest condolences to those impacted by the tragic events of May 24, 2022. Our hope is that this report will aid in the healing process for the Uvalde victims, survivors, families, and community, and provide important guidance to the law enforcement field and to other stakeholders moving forward.

Chapter 1. Incident Timeline Reconstruction

Introduction

Precisely reconstructing the timing and sequence of events was critical in assessing the public safety response to the shooting at Robb Elementary. This Incident Timeline Reconstruction provides a comprehensive account of pertinent facts leading up to, during, and immediately after the tragic mass shooting. The Critical Incident Review (CIR) team relied on voluminous primary and secondary sources, including body-worn camera (BWC) and closed-circuit television (CCTV) footage, radio communications, and 911 call logs and audio, in addition to analytic products produced and provided by U.S. Customs and Border Protection's (CBP) Office of Professional Responsibility (OPR), the Federal Bureau of Investigation (FBI), and the Texas Department of Public Safety (TXDPS).

Importantly, the various recording systems involved in this incident—such as officers' BWCs, security footage from the nearby funeral home's CCTV, and radio communications—were not synchronized and therefore had different timestamps, inadvertently recording the same event or action as occurring at different times. To resolve this issue, the CIR team conducted a careful analysis to align all actions in this Incident Timeline Reconstruction with one true, synchronized time.[5] The CIR team analyzed the times down to the second and, in instances where possible, the fraction of a second.

Organization

This chapter is organized into two sections. The first contains a high-level, narrative summary of the Incident Timeline Reconstruction. The second contains a minute-by-minute list of key actions and events and the locations in which they occurred. Each timeline entry describes all actions that occur within the 60 seconds that compose that minute. For example, an action that occurred at 12:01:01 p.m. and one that occurred at 12:01:59 p.m. would appear in the same timeline entry for "12:01 p.m."

In both sections, the reconstruction is organized into five phases, each of which represents a span of time that conceptually captures a series of de facto related events and actions. Notably, the phases *are not intended to represent* predetermined response operations by any of the law enforcement agencies on scene.

Phase I (11:21 a.m.–11:39 a.m.) comprises the time period from when the subject shoots his grandmother through the end of the first responding officers' initial approach toward the classroom doors.

---

[5] All times, unless otherwise noted, are in Central Time.

Phase II (11:40 a.m.–12:21 p.m.) comprises the time period following the officers' initial approach through a series of four shots fired at 12:21 p.m.

Phase III (12:22 p.m.–12:49 p.m.) comprises the time period following the 12:21 p.m. shots fired through the entry into rooms 111 and 112.

Phase IV (12:50 p.m.–1:15 p.m.) comprises the time period following the entry into rooms 111 and 112 though the completion of medical triage and evacuation.

Phase V (1:16 p.m.–3:15 p.m.) comprises the time period from the beginning activities of the investigation and establishment of investigative command of the scene, through a secondary threat at the high school.

Figure 1-1. Map of locations in the West Building of Robb Elementary

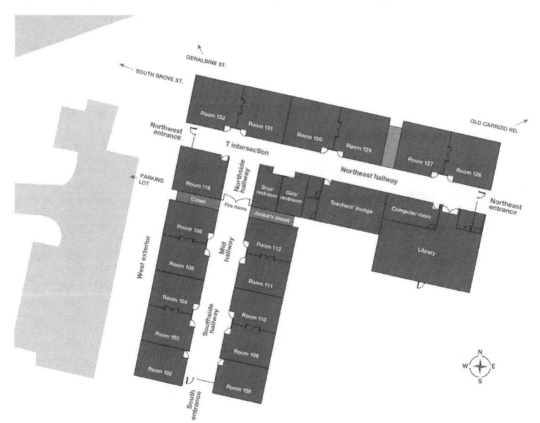

Robb Elementary West Building Locations

Figure 1-1 illustrates the West Building of Robb Elementary where the mass shooting occurred. The locations noted in the figure represent specific locations called out throughout the incident reconstruction in the pages that follow. Note that some classrooms are joined by an interior door. Although adjoining classrooms share a recessed doorway, they each have their own entry door.

High-Level Incident Summary

Phase I: 11:21 a.m.–11:39 a.m.

Phase I of the incident begins when the subject shoots his grandmother at her residence at approximately 11:21 a.m., and ends after the first arriving officers' initial approaches to classrooms 111 and 112, at approximately 11:39 a.m.

After shooting his grandmother, the subject messages an acquaintance about the crime he just committed and his plan to "shoot up an elementary school" next. He steals a vehicle from the residence and crashes it just a few blocks away, into a ditch near Robb Elementary. Multiple 911 calls are placed in response to the crash. Meanwhile, the subject exits the vehicle and begins shooting a high-powered, AR-15-style rifle at workers from a nearby funeral home before entering the school grounds and heading toward the West Building of Robb Elementary.

UCISD Staff 1, who is still on the phone with 911 about the crash, witnesses the gunfire and notifies the 911 operator. The UCISD Staff 1 then reenters the West Building and begins lockdown procedures. They completely close the exterior door through which they entered. The door is not propped open but, unbeknownst to them, it is not locked as it should be.[6] 911 dispatch alerts all units to respond. Multiple Uvalde Consolidated Independent School District (UCISD) employees use the school's emergency alert system, Raptor™, to send an alert as the subject reaches the West Building.

As the subject reaches the West Building, he initiates multiple barrages of gunfire along the exterior west wall. Children and teachers are outside on the playground at the time, as the subject then approaches the building. At 11:33 a.m., the subject enters through the northwest door of the West Building via the closed, unpropped, and unlocked exterior door. The subject enters the building approximately five minutes after he crashes into the ravine and 11 minutes after shooting his grandmother. The subject walks directly to adjoining rooms 111 and 112 and begins shooting toward their recessed doors. The subject walks into the vestibule while shooting and appears to try to access and may enter room 112. Approximately 10 seconds later, the subject steps back into the hallway, continuing to shoot, and then appears to enter room 111. The subject then accesses both rooms 111 and 112 through the connecting doors between them.[7]

---

[6] The exterior doors to the Robb Elementary West Building are required by policy to be set to lock. However, the only way to confirm that they are locked is by opening the door and testing the handle from the outside.

[7] Rooms 111 and 112 connected internally through an adjoining door on the shared wall, and each had a separate door accessible from the hallway. Due to the placement of the closed-circuit television (CCTV) camera in the hallway combined with the recessed doorways, there is limited footage of what occurs when the subject enters the vestibule. However, looking at the footage slowed down and zoomed in, the team analyzed the subject's foot patterns and movement of the firearm. Combining this analysis with interviews conducted and observed from those in rooms 111 and 112, the CIR team believes there is a possibility that the initial assault included entering each of the classrooms from the hallway.

Within three minutes of the subject entering the building, first responding officers enter from both the south and northwest side entrances while the subject is actively shooting inside rooms 111 and 112. In addition to hearing gunfire, the officers experience smoke from recent gun fire and dust from sheetrock and see shell casings on the floor. Officers quickly identify where the shooting is occurring and run toward rooms 111 and 112.

Responding officers are hit with shrapnel from the shooter's gunfire from inside the classrooms. After initial approaches toward the doors, the officers retreat, not approaching the doors again until entry is made more than an hour later.

Upon arrival, responding officers also learn of intermittent radio difficulties when inside the hallway. Some officers go outside of the hallway and request a special weapons and tactics (SWAT) team and additional resources over the radio, including shields, flashbangs, and for all units to respond starting at 11:37 a.m. An active school shooting is called out over the radio early on during the incident, but then the terms "contained" and "barricade" are used multiple times to describe the conditions of the incident during Phase I of the event, including over the radio to dispatchers and officers en route (starting at 11:37 a.m.). Also, at 11:37 a.m., Uvalde Consolidated Independent School District Police Department (UCISD PD) Ofc. 1 identifies the room the shooter is in as his wife's classroom.

Phase II: 11:40 a.m.–12:21 p.m.

Phase II of the incident begins at 11:40 a.m., after the initial response has ended, defined as the last time the first officers on scene retreat from the doorway of classrooms 111/112. Phase II ends when multiple shots are fired again from inside the classrooms at 12:21 p.m. and officers move down the hallway and toward the classrooms.

During this 41-minute period of time, many more officers from a multitude of agencies arrive on scene. There is a great deal of confusion, miscommunication, a lack of urgency, and a lack of incident command. Analysis of how the lack of an incident command structure impedes the overall response is in "Chapter 3. Leadership, Incident Command, and Coordination."

Figure 1-2. West Building room clearing and evacuation status as of 12:21 p.m.

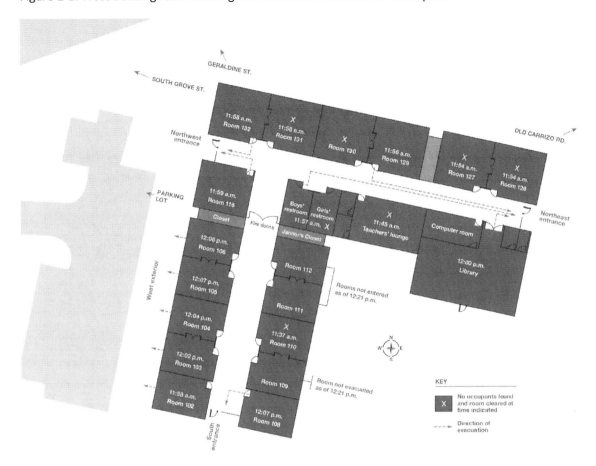

At 11:40 a.m., UCISD PD Chief Pete Arredondo, who tossed his radios because he stated that he wanted his hands to be free and indicated there were reception and transmission issues inside the building, calls the emergency communications center from inside the West Building and says that he is inside the building with the subject, who is armed with an AR-15. Chief Arredondo says he "needs a lot of firepower" and that he wants "the building surrounded." As he is on the phone with dispatch, he learns about a call occurring at the same time from a teacher in the building, who states they believe another teacher has been shot. Chief Arredondo asks whether the teacher is with the shooter, but dispatch does not know. He shares the room number of the shooter's location with dispatch, then asks for SWAT to set up by the funeral home (which is across the street). He states that he needs more firepower because "all we have" in the hallway at that time are handguns.

The scene continues to be largely a bifurcated response on the north and south ends of the hallway. There is some effort to communicate across each side of the hallway, primarily by phone calls between Chief Arredondo and Uvalde County Precinct 1 Constable Johnny Field. Chief Arredondo and Constable Field coordinate the evacuation of rooms in the West Building; however, at no point is there a common operating plan among officers on scene. Inside the building, intermittent radio issues continue, with radios sometimes working and sometimes not. Chief Arredondo is on the south side of the hallway, and many—but not all—officers on both sides of the hallway view him as the incident commander.[8]

As more officers respond to the scene, families and local community members also begin to gather near the school and funeral home, many of whom express concern and fear for their children. As time passes, bystanders grow increasingly upset and even angry about the tragedy unfolding at the school and the lack of information available to them.

There is ongoing discussion among officers on scene about negotiating with the subject in classrooms 111/112. The discussion is often marked by confusion, including the incorrect information that Chief Arredondo is in the room with the subject. This is broadcast over the radio and conveyed in person among officers on scene. Although the misinformation is corrected by some officers, it persists and continues to spread inside and outside the hallway. This misinformation is first stated at 11:50 a.m. and repeated over the radio. At 12:10 p.m., 20 minutes later, the misinformation is still being shared when a TXDPS trooper on scene misinforms TXDPS dispatch. Attempts to begin a dialogue with the shooter by phone and from outside of the room in the hallway are unsuccessful in both English and Spanish.

At approximately 11:56 a.m., UCISD PD Ofc. 1 informs Constable Field, in the presence of several other officers at the T-intersection of the West Building hallway (see figure 1-1 on page 8), that his wife, a teacher in classroom 112, says she has been shot. Uvalde Police Department (UPD) Acting Chief Mariano Pargas guides UCISD PD Ofc. 1 out of the hallway via the northwest door.

Classroom 110 has already been cleared by Chief Arredondo at the onset of the response. Rooms 127 and 126 in the northeast hallway of the building are cleared and evacuated beginning at approximately 11:54 a.m. The classrooms on the west side of the building are cleared and evacuated between 11:58 a.m. and 12:07 p.m., and each evacuation is completed in approximately two minutes or less. Officers on scene break the exterior windows to rooms 102, 103, 104, 105, and 106 to evacuate children and teachers.

Students and a teacher in room 108 are evacuated directly out into the hallway and south doorway. One teacher is evacuated from room 116 directly through the hallway and out the west entry door. Room 129 is also found to have one teacher inside, who is evacuated out the east entry door. One child is found inside the boy's restroom and evacuated out the east entry door. One adult is evacuated from room 132. One adult is evacuated from the library sometime around 12:00 p.m.;[9] however, the exact time is unknown. Evacuated children and staff run to the funeral home, where families also begin to converge. Other rooms in the West Building are cleared and found to be vacant. Some doors are locked, and some are not.

---

[8] CIR Fact Finding.

[9] CIR Fact Finding.

As children and teachers are evacuated from classrooms, there is growing realization that, in addition to the teacher inside classrooms 111/112 with the subject, there are likely children present in these rooms. Chief Arredondo, in attempts to negotiate with the subject, states "these are innocent children."[10] A TXDPS sergeant comments to another TXDPS agent on scene that the subject "shot kids." While assisting with evacuations, UPD Sgt. 1 comments that "there has to be kids everywhere."[11]

By approximately 12:09 p.m., all classrooms in the hallways have been evacuated and/or cleared except rooms 111/112, where the subject is, and room 109. Room 109 is found to be locked and believed to have children inside.

At the south end of the hallway, the focus on evacuating room 109 sets off a search for master keys and calls for any entry team from the north end of the hallway to wait until that room is evacuated. Uvalde County Precinct 6 Constable Zamora goes to the north side of the hallway and obtains a set of keys from a UCISD PD lieutenant. Concerned about crossfire into room 109, Chief Arredondo says that the team presumed to be entering classrooms 111/112 from the other side of the hallway needs to wait until they are able to evacuate room 109.[12] He says, "Time is on our side right now. I know we got kids in there, but we gotta save the lives of the other ones."[13] At approximately 12:10 p.m. a child calls 911 from inside classroom 112, stating they are in a room full of victims. The call lasts approximately 16 minutes, through the shots that are fired at 12:21. Dispatch broadcasts over the radio information about the call at approximately 12:12 p.m., and this information is received and disseminated through both sides of the hallway.

Around this time, the CBP Border Patrol Tactical Unit (BORTAC) commander arrives on scene. The BORTAC commander speaks on the phone with a TXDPS sergeant, who relays Chief Arredondo's direction to wait for entry. Soon after the call started from the child inside classroom 112, word continues to spread to the law enforcement group at the T-intersection that there are victims in room 112. A law enforcement officer states that "an officer heard from his wife who is in the room dying."[14]

---

[10] Uvalde Police Department Body-Worn Camera Footage.

[11] Uvalde Police Department Body-Worn Camera Footage.

[12] At this time, there is not an entry team formed and ready to enter the classrooms. Chief Arredondo is referring to the arrival of the BORTAC Commander and likely entry thereafter.

[13] Uvalde County Constables Body-Worn Camera Footage.

[14] Texas Parks and Wildlife Body-Worn Camera Footage.

Figure 1-3. Aerial view of Robb Elementary School, Hillcrest Memorial Funeral Home, and adjacent streets

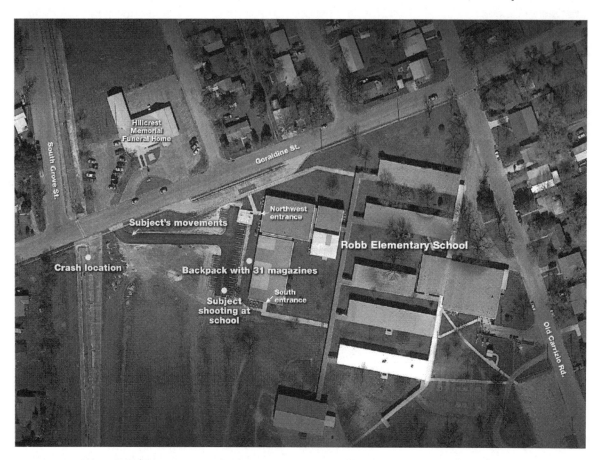

Image source: Airbus, CNES/Airbus, Maxar Technologies. Map data source: Google Maps. Event details source: CIR Document and Data Review; Investigative Committee, *Robb Elementary Shooting Interim Report*.

At 12:21, while Constable Zamora is re-trying keys on room 109, the subject fires four shots inside classrooms 111/112. Officers on both sides of the hallway quickly take cover. Some in the T-intersection immediately move into formation without a word. A Zavala County deputy and a CBP agent advance down the hallway toward the shots fired, followed by the CBP BORTAC commander, another CBP agent, a TXDPS special agent, and others trailing behind. The other law enforcement personnel remain at the T-intersection without advancing. At this point, there is an understanding on both sides of the hallway that an entry team has been formed and they are about to make entry into rooms 111/112.

Phase III: 12:22 p.m.–12:49:58 p.m.

Phase III of the timeline begins at 12:22 p.m., immediately following four shots fired inside classrooms 111 and 112, and continues through the entry and ensuing gunfight at 12:49 p.m. During this time frame, officers on the north side of the hallway approach the classroom doors and stop short, presuming the doors are locked and that master keys are necessary. Also during this time, UCISD PD Chief Pete Arredondo calls off the directive to evacuate room 109 through the door using master keys and instead orders that the evacuation be conducted through the windows. When classroom 109 is evacuated, it is discovered that the room has in fact been occupied by numerous students, including a teacher who has been shot in the abdomen and a child who has been hit in the face by shrapnel. They have been inside room 109 bleeding and muffling their cries to avoid detection by the subject.

Chief Arredondo, who is on the phone with another responding officer on the north side of the hallway, gives the go-ahead to make entry into classrooms 111/112. Chief Arredondo states, "What team? Got a team ready to go? Have at it."[15] He then begins explaining aspects of the building and classroom, stating that the door is probably locked and that he is going to try to find some keys to test.

Law enforcement medics arrive and begin establishing a triage area outside of the restrooms on the north side of the hallway.

The CBP BORTAC commander tries one set of presumed master keys that do not work. After waiting for approximately nine minutes, the BORTAC commander goes to retrieve breaching tools. Shortly after he returns, working master keys arrive at approximately 12:36 p.m. With working keys in hand, officers in the hallway wait to find out whether a sniper can obtain a visual and eliminate the subject through the window. This is unsuccessful.

At around 12:48 p.m., the entry team enters the room. Though the entry team puts the key in the door, turns the key, and opens it, pulling the door toward them, the CIR Team concludes that the door is likely already unlocked, as the shooter gained entry through the door and it is unlikely that he locked it thereafter. The entry team is composed of three BORTAC members, a CBP Border Patrol Search, Trauma, and Rescue Unit (BORSTAR) member, and deputies from two local sheriffs' departments— Uvalde and Zavala counties. There is one shield in the stack, which had been provided by the U.S. Marshals Service (USMS) and is rifle-rated. As the entry team prepares to move in, the door begins to swing closed. One team member attempts to move a chair against the door to prop it open, but the door is too heavy, and eventually another member of the entry team simply holds it open as the team makes entry.

After a brief pause in action, gunfire erupts from inside the classrooms. The subject is killed by the entry team at approximately 12:49:58. A BORTAC member receives a graze to their head and leg.

Phase IV: 12:50 p.m.–1:15 p.m.

Phase IV of the incident entails the immediate aftermath in classrooms 111/112, the medical triage and evacuation, and the beginnings of the establishment of a command post at the funeral home.

Within a minute of the subject being killed, officers in the hallway begin entering rooms 111 and 112. Some are held off by a CBP medic at the T-intersection on the north side of the hallway, while others crowd the hallway and classrooms. Multiple officers are shouting to make room for medics and for the victims to be evacuated. There are 33 children and three teachers inside.

---

[15] Uvalde Police Department Body-Worn Camera Footage.

One victim is carried out toward the south door. All others are either moved or escorted toward the north side of the hallway. Officers and medics carry out a total of 16 victims, many of whom are quickly determined to be deceased and brought to classrooms 131/132. Nine child victims walk or run down the hall, escorted by law enforcement. Two go down the northeast hallway and seven exit through the northwest door.[16] Some of these children are injured, including at least one with a gunshot wound.[17]

As more officers continue to enter classrooms 111/112, a TXDPS ranger states that everyone inside the room who is not a medic needs to clear out, and some officers begin exiting in response.[18]

By 12:53 p.m., just three minutes after the room was entered and the subject killed, a CBP medic declares all remaining victims in room 112 deceased.

By 12:55 p.m., UCISD PD Chief Pete Arredondo asks for the rooms in the building to be cleared again, and soon after, at 1:00 p.m., he calls for all entrances to be blocked off.

Phase V: 1:16 p.m.—3:15 p.m.

Phase V of the incident entails the beginning activities of the investigations, the establishment of investigative command at the scene, and the response to a secondary threat at Uvalde High School.

After 2:00 p.m., the crime scene investigation is underway. Although there is no official time of record, at some time around 1:00 p.m., and after consultation with the Texas Rangers, the Uvalde County District Attorney determines that the investigation should be conducted solely by the Rangers and not in conjunction with any of the other local agencies, including UCISD PD (see "Chapter 4. Post-Incident Response and Investigation").

At 2:12 p.m. there are unconfirmed reports of a secondary threat at Uvalde High School, which turn out to be false. Multiple agencies respond to the high school, as it is locked down. The Civic Center is also locked down as a protective measure at around 2:25 p.m. Officers also are stationed at all UCISD campuses at this time.

At Uvalde High School, responding officers form a perimeter around the campus as parents begin to gather, many of whom are expressing concern and anger.

By 3:15 p.m., schools begin to release kids upon realizing that the secondary threat has not surfaced.

The documentable timeline of the incident and the immediate aftermath for this analysis concludes at 3:15 p.m.

---

[16] Robb Elementary School CCTV Footage.

[17] CIR Fact Finding.

[18] Uvalde Police Department Body-Worn Camera Footage.

Minute-by-Minute Timeline

The incident and response unfolded across various locations inside and outside of the Robb Elementary campus. Each entry in the minute-by-minute timeline is coded with the location. Additionally, "radio traffic" and "911 communications" are coded as locations. When these communications occur *from* a specific, known location that is pertinent to understanding their context, both pieces of information are provided.

The CIR team identified 33 events within the incident response, representing key thematic activities that recurred over the course of the incident and response. For more information on the timeline synchronization, locations and events, please see Appendix B: Report Methodology.

Phase I: 11:21 a.m.–11:39 a.m.

Phase I comprises the time period from when the subject shoots his grandmother through the end of the first responding officers' initial approach toward the classroom doors.

11:21 a.m.–11:27 a.m.

Grandparents' Residence

The subject shoots his grandmother around 11:21 a.m., subsequently sending a message to an acquaintance that he had done so and informing the acquaintance that he is going to "shoot up an elementary school" next.[19] Shortly after, the subject steals a vehicle from his grandparents' residence on Diaz Street and drives toward Robb Elementary via Grove Street (see figure 1-3 on page 14).

Events: Shooting at Grandparents' Residence

11:28 a.m.

Robb Elementary: Perimeter

The subject arrives at Robb Elementary and crashes the vehicle he is driving into a ditch, approximately 100 yards from Robb Elementary (see figure 1-3 on page 14).[20] Meanwhile, outside the school, UCISD Staff 1 witnesses the crash and runs inside to their classroom in the West Building to retrieve their cellphone, call 911, and report the crash.[21]

Events: Vehicle Crash Next to Robb Elementary

---

[19] CIR Document and Data Review; Investigative Committee, *Robb Elementary Shooting Interim Report.*

[20] Hillcrest Memorial Funeral Home CCTV Footage.

[21] Robb Elementary School CCTV Footage.

Funeral Home
Communications: 911

Multiple funeral home employees also observe the crash. Two employees walk toward the crash site to assist, when the subject, having now exited the vehicle, appears with an AR-15-style rifle and fires multiple rounds at them. One of the funeral home employees calls 911 and is on the phone as shots are fired. They report that the subject is "jumping the school yard."[22] None of the funeral home employees are struck by gunfire.[23]

Events: Vehicle Crash Next to Robb Elementary; Shots Fired

Robb Elementary: West Building Northwest Entrance
Robb Elementary: West Building Exterior, Parking Lot
Communications: 911

UCISD Staff 1, still on the phone with 911 and now back outside of the West Building, observes the gunfire and reports it to the 911 operator.[24]

Around the same time, the subject approaches Robb Elementary and enters school grounds by climbing over the fence on the west side of the campus.[25]

Events: Subject Enters School Grounds and Approaches West Building

Robb Elementary: West Building Northside Hallway
Communications: 911

UCISD Staff 1 reenters the West Building and notifies UCISD Staff 2 of a man with a gun outside. Still on the phone with 911, UCISD Staff 1 advises that the shooter is on campus and "the kids are running." UCISD Staff 1 then yells to students down the hall toward the south entrance of the building to get in the classrooms, in effect initiating lockdown procedures in the West Building.[26]

Events: Subject Enters School Grounds and Approaches West Building; Shots Fired; Robb Elementary Lockdown

---

[22] Uvalde Police Department 911 Call.

[23] Hillcrest Memorial Funeral Home CCTV Footage.

[24] Uvalde Police Department 911 Call.

[25] Hillcrest Memorial Funeral Home CCTV Footage.

[26] Uvalde Police Department 911 Call; Robb Elementary School CCTV Footage.

Communications: Radio Traffic

UPD dispatch calls out over the radio that a white truck (note: the truck was gray) has crashed and the occupant of the vehicle is armed with a gun.[27]

Events: Vehicle Crash Next to Robb Elementary

11:30 a.m.

Communications: Radio Traffic

UPD radio traffic calls out "several shots fired" and asks all units to respond.[28]

Events: Shots Fired

11:31 a.m.

Robb Elementary: West Building Exterior, Parking Lot

Around the same time, a UCISD PD officer is responding to radio traffic about the male subject from the car wreck having a gun.[29] The officer enters the West Parking Lot through the open gate in a white patrol vehicle. The officer does not appear to see the subject, who is nearby in between vehicles in the parking lot.

Events: Subject Enters School Grounds and Approaches West Building; Officer Arrivals

Communications: Radio Traffic

En route to Robb Elementary, UPD Sgt. 1 advises over UPD radio to shut down the school, while the subject continues his approach toward the school and reaches the school parking lot.[30]

Events: Subject Enters School Grounds and Approaches West Building; Robb Elementary Lockdown

11:32 a.m.

Robb Elementary: West Building Exterior, Parking Lot

The subject walks along the outside of the West Building and fires three barrages of gunshots into the exterior wall of the West Building.[31]

Events: Subject Enters School Grounds and Approaches West Building; Robb Elementary Lockdown; Shots Fired

---

[27] Uvalde Police Department 911 Call; Uvalde Police Department Radio Traffic.

[28] Uvalde Police Department Incident Call Log.

[29] CIR Fact Finding.

[30] Uvalde Police Department Incident Call Log; Hillcrest Memorial Funeral Home CCTV Footage.

[31] CIR Document and Data Review; Robb Elementary School CCTV Footage; Hillcrest Memorial Funeral Home CCTV Footage.

Robb Elementary: Perimeter

The first UPD patrol vehicles arrive at the intersection of Geraldine and Grove Streets (see figure 1-3 <u>on page 14</u>).[32]

Events: Officer Arrivals

Robb Elementary: West Building Northside Hallway

UCISD Staff 1 and UCISD Staff 2 reenter their classrooms (132 and 116, respectively). UCISD Staff 2 then goes back into the hallway and shouts for children and teachers to get into their rooms. UCISD Staff 2 then returns to their room.[33]

Events: Robb Elementary Lockdown

Communications: UCISD Raptor Alert

UCISD's emergency alert system, Raptor, sends out a lockdown alert reading, "[EMERGENCY] Lockdown - has been initiated at Robb Elementary School. Log into Raptor Emergency Management now for your immediate tasks."[34] (Multiple UCISD employees later report using their phones to initiate the alert.)

Events: Robb Elementary Lockdown

11:33 a.m.

Robb Elementary: West Building Northwest Entrance

The subject reaches the northwest door of the West Building and enters through a closed and unpropped but unlocked door, immediately making his way down the hallway toward rooms 111 and 112.[35]

Events: Subject Enters West Building and Classrooms 111 and 112

---

[32] Hillcrest Memorial Funeral Home CCTV Footage.

[33] Robb Elementary School CCTV Footage.

[34] CIR Document and Data Review.

[35] Robb Elementary School CCTV Footage.

Robb Elementary: West Building Hallway, Outside Classrooms 111 and 112

The subject begins shooting into classroom 111 or 112, a barrage that lasts approximately six seconds. The subject walks into the vestibule while shooting and appears to try to access and may enter room 112. Approximately 10 seconds later, the subject steps back out into the hallway again, continuing to shoot, and then appears to enter room 111. The subject then accesses both rooms 111 and 112 through the connecting doors between them.[36]

Events: Subject Enters West Building and Classrooms 111 and 112; Shots Fired

Robb Elementary: West Building Northside Hallway

A Robb Elementary student exits the bathroom and looks around the corner, retreating back when they see the shooter in the hallway and hear gunfire.[37]

Events: Subject Enters West Building and Classrooms 111 and 112; Shots Fired; Robb Elementary Lockdown

Communications: Radio Traffic

Around this time, UPD radio traffic indicates that the subject has made it into the building, that he is shooting inside the building, and that there is a "school shooting."[38]

Events: Subject Enters West Building and Classrooms 111 and 112; Shots Fired

11:34 a.m.

Robb Elementary: West Building, Inside Classrooms 111 and 112

Shortly after entering the recessed doorway for the last time, the subject initiates more gunfire lasting approximately 3 seconds, during which the pace of gunfire changes from rapid fire to single action.[39]

Events: Subject Enters West Building and Classrooms 111 and 112; Shots Fired

---

[36] Robb Elementary School CCTV Footage. Rooms 111 and 112 connected internally through an adjoining door on the shared wall, and each had a separate door accessible from the hallway. Due to the placement of the closed-circuit television (CCTV) camera in the hallway combined with the recessed doorways, there is limited footage of what occurs when the subject enters the vestibule. However, looking at the footage slowed down and zoomed in, the team analyzed the subject's foot patterns and movement of the firearm. Combining this analysis with interviews conducted and observed from those in rooms 111 and 112, the CIR team believes there is a possibility that the initial assault included entering each of the classrooms from the hallway.

[37] Robb Elementary School CCTV Footage.

[38] Uvalde Police Department Radio Traffic.

[39] Robb Elementary School CCTV Footage.

Communications: UCISD Raptor Alert

UCISD Flores Elementary enters lockdown.[40]

Events: UCISD: Other Campus Lockdowns

11:35 a.m.

Robb Elementary: West Building, Inside Classrooms 111 and 112

Inside the classrooms, the subject engages in another barrage of gunfire lasting approximately 19 seconds.[41]

Events: Subject Enters West Building and Classrooms 111 and 112; Shots Fired

Robb Elementary: West Building Northwest Entrance

Responding officers approach and enter the doors on the northwest side of the hallway. Three UPD officers (UPD Lt. 1, UPD Sgt. 2, and UPD Det. 3) enter the building. UPD Lt. 1 and UPD Sgt. 2 immediately advance down the hallway toward classrooms 111 and 112.[42]

Seconds later through the northwest entry, four more officers arrive and enter the building from the west door. They are UPD Acting Chief Mariano Pargas, UPD Det. 1, UPD Ofc. 1, and UCISD PD Ofc. 1.[43]

Events: Officer Arrivals; Officers' Initial Approach to Classrooms 111 and 112

Robb Elementary: West Building South Entrance

As more gunfire erupts inside the building, UPD Sgt. 1 approaches the south doorway and transmits over radio, while running toward the building, "Shots fired! Get inside! Go, go, go!"[44] Around this time, UPD Sgt. 3, UCISD PD Ofc. 2, and UCISD PD Chief Arredondo enter the south entrance of the hallway, while UPD Sgt. 1 is still approaching.[45]

Events: Officer Arrivals; Shots Fired

Communications: Radio Traffic

A TXDPS aircraft unit radios to request more information on a school shooting in Uvalde and states they will be in the area and can assist.[46]

---

[40] UCISD Raptor Data Export.

[41] Robb Elementary School CCTV Footage; Uvalde Police Department Body-Worn Camera Footage.

[42] Robb Elementary School CCTV Footage; Uvalde Police Department Body-Worn Camera Footage.

[43] Robb Elementary School CCTV Footage.

[44] Uvalde Police Department Body-Worn Camera Footage; Robb Elementary School CCTV Footage.

[45] Robb Elementary School CCTV Footage.

[46] Texas Department of Public Safety Radio Traffic.

Uvalde County Sheriff's Office (UCSO) Sheriff Ruben Nolasco advises over radio of a woman shot on Diaz Street.[47]

As the active shooter event unfolds at Robb Elementary, the shooting at the subject's grandparents' residence is reported over the radio, indicating a woman has been shot in the head on Diaz Street.[48]

Events: Shooting at Grandparents' Residence; Air Support

Robb Elementary: West Building
Communications: 911

Someone from inside the West Building calls 911 and whispers "help me." Dispatch asks the individual to stay on the line with them and asks where they are. The caller does not respond.[49] The call ends after 44 seconds. This information is never reported out over the radio.

Events: Presence of Victims: Acknowledgment and Discussion

11:36 a.m.

Grandparents' Residence

UCSO Dep. 1 arrives on scene at Diaz Street; Sheriff Nolasco is already on scene.[50]

Events: Shooting at Grandparents' Residence

Robb Elementary: West Building Northside Hallway

A teacher is seen entering their classroom, room 130, on the northeast side of the hallway.[51]

Events: Robb Elementary School Lockdown

Robb Elementary: West Building Southside Hallway

UPD Sgt. 1 enters the building and sees UCISD PD Chief Arredondo, UCISD PD Ofc. 1, and UPD Sgt. 3 inside, further up toward classrooms 111 and 112. There is mention of an AR-15 being used. UPD Sgt. 1 experiences intermittent radio break failures for approximately 30 seconds while in the hallway.[52]

Events: Officer Arrivals

---

[47] Uvalde Police Department Radio Traffic.

[48] Uvalde Police Department Body-Worn Camera Footage; Uvalde County Sheriff's Office Radio Traffic; Uvalde County Sheriff's Office Body-Worn Camera Footage.

[49] Uvalde Police Department 911 Call.

[50] Uvalde County Sheriff's Office Body-Worn Camera Footage.

[51] Robb Elementary School CCTV Footage.

[52] Uvalde Police Department Body-Worn Camera Footage.

Robb Elementary: West Building, Outside Classrooms 111 and 112

UPD Lt. 1, UPD Sgt. 2, and UPD Sgt. 3 are outside of doorway. UPD Lt. 1 and UPD Sgt. 3 have handguns drawn on the door. An officer in the vicinity instructs officers to line up and make entry. Another officer is overheard saying that they cannot see inside.[53]

The subject initiates a barrage of gunfire inside the classroom. UPD Lt. 1 and UPD Sgt. 3 are struck with shrapnel from the gunfire. Officers retreat down the south and north directions of the hallway.[54]

Events: Shots Fired; Officers' Initial Approach to Classrooms 111 and 112

Robb Elementary: West Building, Inside Classrooms 111 and 112

The subject fires more rounds from inside classrooms 111 and 112, including a barrage of 11 shots fired over the course of approximately 53 seconds.[55]

Events: Shots Fired

Communications: 911

A teacher calls, stating she is in the closet in the fourth grade building (i.e., the West Building).[56]

Events: Presence of Victims: Acknowledgment and Discussion

Communications: Radio Traffic

TXDPS Lt. 1 communicates with TXDPS Communications, confirming the location of the shooting and requesting that Communications dispatch troopers in the vicinity to Robb Elementary.[57]

Dispatch broadcasts that there is a teacher in a closet and that someone is banging on the door where they are hiding.[58]

Events: Officer Arrivals; Presence of Victims: Acknowledgment and Discussion

---

[53] UCISD lockdown protocol requires the classroom lights be turned off. However, since the hallway lights remained on, visibility into the classroom was likely significantly compromised.

[54] Robb Elementary School CCTV Footage; Uvalde Police Department Body-Worn Camera Footage.

[55] Robb Elementary School CCTV Footage.

[56] Uvalde Police Department 911 Call.

[57] Texas Department of Public Safety Radio Traffic.

[58] Uvalde Police Department Radio Traffic.

Robb Elementary: West Building Southside Hallway

After the subject fires shots inside classrooms 111/112 and officers are retreating, UCISD PD Chief Arredondo stops at classroom 110.[59] This is the same room that Arredondo will later claim he cleared shortly after entering the West Building at 11:35 a.m.[60]

Events: Room Clearings and Evacuations

Robb Elementary: West Building South Entrance

UPD Sgt. 1 exits the hallway to use his radio and broadcasts, "He is inside the building, we have him contained. Building on west side of property. Careful with windows facing east. Male subject with AR."[61]

Events: Callout of Containment and Barricade

Robb Elementary: West Building Northside Hallway

UPD Lt.1 advances alone toward the classrooms and takes up a position of cover in the hallway by the fire doors, which are north of the classroom doors and adjacent to the janitor's closet, as the subject fires approximately three more shots.[62]

Events: Initial Approach to Classrooms 111 and 112; Shots Fired

Robb Elementary: West Building Northwest Entrance

UPD Sgt. 2 exits the building and encounters the TXDPS sergeant, who says that TXDPS is sending more people.[63] This is the first time that UPD Sgt. 2 gets on the radio and reports shots fired. UCISD PD Ofc. 1 conveys that the incident is unfolding in his wife's (Adult Victim 1) classroom. This information is shared in the presence of multiple officers, though it is not clear from the video evidence whether the information is received and acknowledged.[64] UPD Sgt. 2 repeats several times that they have "got to get in there" while just outside and inside the door at the northwest end of the hallway.[65]

Events: Officer Arrivals; Presence of Victims: Acknowledgment and Discussion

---

[59] Uvalde Police Department Body-Worn Camera Footage.

[60] CIR Fact Finding.

[61] Uvalde Police Department Body-Worn Camera Footage.

[62] Robb Elementary School CCTV Footage.

[63] Uvalde Police Department Body-Worn Camera Footage.

[64] Uvalde Police Department Body-Worn Camera Footage.

[65] Uvalde Police Department Body-Worn Camera Footage.

Robb Elementary: West Building Northside Hallway

CBP Border Patrol Agent (BPA) 1 arrives and positions along the wall at the T-intersection of the north end of the hallway.[66] He is the first BPA on scene.

Events: Officer Arrivals

Robb Elementary: West Building South Entrance

UPD Sgt. 3 is overheard outside of the south door saying, "We have him contained in this office."[67]

Events: Callout of Containment and Barricade

Communications: Radio Traffic

The first request to activate Uvalde SWAT is made over the radio by UCISD PD Ofc. 1. There is also more chatter that a male subject has an AR, in addition to an "officer down" call in response to UPD Lt. 1 and UPD Sgt. 3, who were struck by shrapnel while at the doorway.[68]

Events: SWAT Callout

Grandparents' Residence

UCSO Dep. 2 arrives at Diaz Street residence and runs to the back of the home, where he links up with Sheriff Nolasco, UCSO Dep. 3, and UCSO Dep. 1.[69] Deputies request emergency medical services (EMS).[70] When asked, the grandmother identifies her assailant as her grandson and tells UCSO personnel on scene his name.[71]

Events: Shooting at Grandparents' Residence; Subject Identification

Robb Elementary: West Building South Entrance

UPD Sgt. 1 radios to request any available units to respond and to bring shields.[72]

Events: Request for Shields

---

[66] Robb Elementary School CCTV Footage.

[67] Uvalde Police Department Body-Worn Camera Footage.

[68] Uvalde Police Department Radio Traffic.

[69] CIR Fact Finding; Uvalde County Sheriff's Office Body-Worn Camera Footage.

[70] Uvalde County Sheriff's Office Body-Worn Camera Footage.

[71] Uvalde County Sheriff's Office Body-Worn Camera Footage.

[72] Uvalde Police Department Body-Worn Camera Footage.

Robb Elementary: West Building Northside Hallway

UPD Lt. 1 retreats down the hallway to the T-intersection.[73]

Events: Initial Approach to Classrooms 111 and 112

Robb Elementary: West Building Northwest Entrance

UPD Sgt. 2 is outside of the building and on the phone with a member of the USMS task force of which they are a part,[74] explaining "shots fired at the school . . . guy's inside the classroom right now . . . he's in a classroom, actively shooting" and asking for assistance, saying "the more help the better."[75]

Events: Officer Arrivals

Communications: Radio Traffic

UPD Acting Chief Pargas calls out on the radio for "any agency available" to come out and help.[76]

Another request is made for air operations over the radio, but the requestor is not identified.[77]

EMS are requested and dispatched to the grandparents' residence.[78]

Events: Officer Arrivals; Air Support

Grandparents' Residence

UCSO Dep. 2 and UCSO Dep. 3 depart Diaz Street and head toward Robb Elementary, while Sheriff Nolasco and UCSO Dep. 1 remain at the Diaz Street location.[79]

Events: Shooting at Grandparents' Residence

Phase II: 11:40 a.m.–12:21 p.m.

Phase II comprises the time period following the officers' initial approach through a series of four shots fired at 12:21 p.m.

---

[73] Robb Elementary School CCTV Footage.

[74] CIR Fact Finding.

[75] Uvalde Police Department Body-Worn Camera Footage.

[76] Uvalde Police Department Body-Worn Camera Footage.

[77] Uvalde Police Department Radio Traffic.

[78] Uvalde Police Department Radio Traffic.

[79] Uvalde County Sheriff's Office Body-Worn Camera Footage; CIR Fact Finding.

Robb Elementary: West Building Northside Hallway

UPD Lt. 1 takes steps again toward classrooms 111/112 but ultimately returns to the T-intersection. This third retreat by UPD Lt. 1 ends all forward momentum toward the door during the initial approach.[80]

Events: Initial Approach to Classrooms 111 and 112

Communications: Radio Traffic
Robb Elementary: West Building South Entrance

UPD Sgt. 1 requests numerous assets over the radio, including air support, ballistic shields, flashbangs, and for TXDPS to be notified. They also provide an update on the situation, communicating that a male subject is inside the school, still shooting, contained, and barricaded in what UPD Sgt. 1 currently believes to be an office.[81]

Events: Callout of Containment and Barricade; Request for Shields; Air Support

Communications: 911

A teacher calls 911 from inside room 102, stating that they are locked down in their classroom and that they believe someone is shot inside another classroom in the building.[82]

UCISD PD Chief Arredondo uses his phone to call dispatch from inside the West Building and says that he is inside the building with the subject, who is armed with an AR-15-style rifle. Chief Arredondo says he "need[s] a lot of firepower" and that he wants "the building surrounded." As he is on the phone with dispatch, he learns about the call occurring at the same time from the teacher in classroom 102, who is stating they believe another teacher has been shot. Chief Arredondo asks whether the teacher is with the shooter, but dispatch does not know. He tells dispatch that the shooter is in room 111 or 112, then asks for SWAT to set up by the funeral home across the street. He says that he needs more firepower, because all they have are handguns and they "need to surround the building."[83] Then he tells the dispatcher, "I need you to be my radio for me."[84]

Events: Presence of Victims: Acknowledgment and Discussion; SWAT Callout

---

[80] Robb Elementary School CCTV Footage.

[81] Uvalde Police Department Body-Worn Camera Footage.

[82] Uvalde Police Department Incident Call Log.

[83] Uvalde Police Department Dispatch Landline.

[84] Uvalde Police Department Dispatch Landline.

Robb Elementary: West Building Northwest Entrance

UPD Sgt. 2 calls out on the radio that the subject is in Adult Victim 1's classroom and says to check if class is in session.[85]

UCSO Dep. 2, UCSO Dep. 3, and UCSO Dep. 4 arrive at the north side of the West Building and inquire about the situation. Each of them initially positions themselves at the entryway. They learn the subject has fired multiple rounds inside the classroom and that it is unknown whether any children are inside.[86]

Events: Presence of Victims: Acknowledgment and Discussion; Officer Arrivals

Robb Elementary: West Building South Entrance
Communications: Radio Traffic

UCISD PD Ofc. 2 relays UPD Sgt. 2's request to check whether Adult Victim 1's class is in session.[87]

Events: Presence of Victims: Acknowledgment and Discussion

Communications: Radio Traffic

Dispatch notifies over radio of a possible gunshot victim in the classroom across from room 102 and adds that a teacher is in room 116 barricaded inside a closet.[88]

Events: Room Clearings and Evacuations

Robb Elementary: Perimeter

Family members and community members are on scene near the funeral home, while the first EMS arrive in front of Robb Elementary.[89]

Events: Crowd Control; EMS Arrivals and Actions

---

[85] Uvalde County Sheriff's Office Body-Worn Camera Footage.

[86] Uvalde County Sheriff's Office Body-Worn Camera Footage.

[87] Uvalde Police Department Body-Worn Camera Footage.

[88] Uvalde Police Department Radio Traffic.

[89] Hillcrest Memorial Funeral Home CCTV Footage.

Robb Elementary: West Building Exterior West

The TXDPS sergeant is at the northwest entry and requests UCSO Dep. 3 and others to walk down the west side of the building because another unknown law enforcement officer (LEO) identified a black backpack on the ground at the exterior of the building, by the windows of room 102 (see figure 1-3 on page 14). After approaching the bag, the TXDPS sergeant appears to call off the recovery of the backpack, stating it is "too risky," and returns to the north entryway. It is later discovered that the bag belongs to the subject and contains dozens of loaded magazines.[90]

Events: Subject's Backpack: Observation and Recovery

Robb Elementary: West Building South Entrance
Communications: Radio Traffic

Dispatch confirms that "the class should be in session right now . . . the class should be in session right now."[91] Upon learning of the status of classrooms 111/112, UCISD PD Ofc. 2 relays over the radio that the class is in session. This information is transmitted and picked up on LEO radios on both sides of the hallway.[92]

Uvalde dispatch advises over the radio that UCISD PD Chief Arredondo "has stated he got the shooter in room 111 or 112. He's gonna be armed with a rifle." Uvalde dispatch also states Chief Arredondo is requesting SWAT by the funeral home, south of the building.[93] This transmission is picked up on LEO radios on both sides of the hallway.

Events: Presence of Victims: Acknowledgment and Discussion; SWAT Callout

Robb Elementary: Perimeter

More parents and family members arrive on the scene near the funeral home.[94]

Events: Crowd Control

---

[90] Uvalde County Sheriff's Office Body-Worn Camera Footage.

[91] Uvalde Police Department Radio Traffic.

[92] Uvalde Police Department Radio Traffic; Uvalde Police Department Body-Worn Camera Footage; Uvalde County Sheriff's Office Body-Worn Camera Footage.

[93] Uvalde Police Department Radio Traffic; Uvalde Police Department Body-Worn Camera Footage.

[94] Hillcrest Memorial Funeral Home CCTV Footage.

Communications: Radio Traffic

More radio communications broadcast that the subject is "barricaded" in one of the "offices" and also advise that he is still shooting.[95]

An officer requests assistance with crowd control at the funeral home.[96]

Events: Callout of Containment and Barricade; Crowd Control

Robb Elementary: West Building Northwest Entrance

Outside of the northwest doorway, UCSO deputies inquire whether there are kids inside classrooms 111/112 and an unknown LEO (off camera) responds that "class is in session."

Events: Presence of Victims: Acknowledgment and Discussion

11:44 a.m.

Robb Elementary: West Building, Inside Classrooms 111 and 112

The subject fires a single shot inside the classroom.[97]

Events: Shots Fired

11:45 a.m.

Robb Elementary: West Building Northside Hallway

UPD Ofc. 2 is outside the doorways of rooms 129/130 and asks the Uvalde County fire marshal whether there are any students in the rooms. The fire marshal responds that there is a teacher inside and they should not evacuate at that time. The fire marshal and UPD Det. 1 then clear the teacher's lounge on the other side of the northeast hallway.[98]

Events: Room Clearings and Evacuations

---

[95] Uvalde Police Department Radio Traffic.

[96] Uvalde Police Department Radio Traffic.

[97] Uvalde Police Department Body-Worn Camera Footage; Uvalde County Sheriff's Office Body-Worn Camera Footage.

[98] Uvalde Police Department Body-Worn Camera Footage.

Robb Elementary: West Building Northwest Entrance

As UCSO deputies and other unknown LEOs discuss the situation, UCSO Dep. 3 asks whether the subject is in a classroom and how the room is configured. An unknown LEO responds, "Yeah, with kids."[99]

Events: Presence of Victims: Acknowledgment and Discussion

Communications: Radio Traffic

TXDPS dispatch advises all Val Verde County units and TXDPS Criminal Investigations Division to respond to the scene of the Robb Elementary school shooting as quickly as possible.[100]

Events: Officer Arrivals

11:46 a.m.

Robb Elementary: West Building T-Intersection

Twelve LEOs are at or near the T-intersection deliberating tactics. Some officers note the crossfire with the other side of the hallway. Uvalde County Precinct 1 Constable Johnny Field asks whether a window is present for them to do negotiations through, and another officer says they need a bullhorn. UPD officers identify UPD Ofc. 3 (not among the officers present at the time) as a negotiator. An officer in the hallway also states that more shields are needed.

Events: Negotiations; Requests for Shields

Robb Elementary: Perimeter

Parents and family members gathered around the school shout at LEOs on the other side of the fence on the north side of the building. Some say that their kids are in the building. One person says, "Either you go in or I'm going in."[101]

Events: Crowd Control

11:47 a.m.

Communications: Radio Traffic

Dispatch states CBP is sending all units to respond.[102]

Events: Officer Arrivals

---

[99] Uvalde County Sheriff's Office Body-Worn Camera Footage.

[100] Texas Department of Public Safety Dashboard Footage.

[101] Uvalde County Sheriff's Office Body-Worn Camera Footage.

[102] Uvalde Police Department Radio Traffic; Uvalde Police Department Body-Worn Camera Footage.

Communications: UCISD Raptor Alert

UCISD Uvalde High School enters lockdown.[103]

Events: UCISD: Other Campus Lockdowns

11:48 a.m.

Robb Elementary: West Building T-Intersection

Multiple LEOs are at the T-intersection. Constable Field asks whether UPD has a team that they can stack and a shield. UPD Ofc. 2 responds that they have one shield.[104]

Events: Request for Shields

Communications: Radio Traffic

UPD Sgt. 1 requests UPD communications to contact all UCISD schools and have them lock down. Communications confirms it will contact schools to lock down. UPD Sgt. 1 also communicates over radio that multiple agencies are on scene and that they are trying to secure the outer perimeter because families are arriving on scene.[105]

Events: UCISD: Other Campus Lockdowns; Crowd Control

11:49 a.m.

Robb Elementary: West Building T-Intersection

UPD Lt. 1 states that they "gotta get in there," and Constable Field replies that "There is no active shooting. Stand by. Someone can be hurt, but stand by." Other officers in the hallway reaffirm the decision to wait. One officer states they are waiting for shields. Constable Field points out that they have one shield right there with them.[106]

Events: Request for Shields

Robb Elementary: West Building South Entrance

UPD Cpl. 1 states to UCSO deputies that the backpack (referencing the subject's backpack) needs to be picked up in case the subject makes it out of the room and is able to pick it up.[107]

Events: Subject's Backpack: Observation and Recovery

---

[103] UCISD Raptor Data Export.

[104] Uvalde Police Department Body-Worn Camera Footage.

[105] Uvalde Police Department Body Worn-Camera Footage; Uvalde Police Department Radio Traffic; CIR Document and Data Review.

[106] Uvalde Police Department Body-Worn Camera Footage.

[107] Uvalde Police Department Body-Worn Camera Footage.

Communications: Radio Traffic

UPD officer en route states that they have shields but cannot get through traffic.[108]

Unknown officer states that they are "coming up with a game plan."[109]

Events: Request for Shields

11:50 a.m.

Robb Elementary: West Building South Entrance
Communications: Radio Traffic

An unknown officer inaccurately states that UCISD PD Chief Arredondo is in rooms 111/112 with the subject. This is repeated by UCISD PD Ofc. 2 over the radio.[110] UPD Sgt. 1 and UPD Cpl. 1 open the south door, and an unknown LEO says to get out of the hallway because they believe BORTAC is there and will be stacking up to make entry.[111] No members of BORTAC are on scene at this time. UPD Sgt. 1 rebuts the unknown officer, stating that Chief Arredondo is in charge and in the room. Another officer points out that Chief Arredondo is right across from the door.[112]

Events: Negotiations

Robb Elementary: West Building Northside Hallway

Upon hearing radio communication about 401 (Chief Arredondo radio code) is in the room with the shooter, officers on the north side of the hallway point out that he is not with the shooter and is on the other side of the hallway.[113]

Events: Negotiations

Communications: UCISD Raptor Alert

UCISD Batesville Elementary enters lockdown.[114]

Events: UCISD: Other Campus Lockdowns

---

[108] Uvalde Police Department Body-Worn Camera Footage; Uvalde Police Department Radio Traffic.

[109] Uvalde Police Department Radio Traffic.

[110] Uvalde Police Department Radio Traffic.

[111] Uvalde Police Department Body-Worn Camera Footage.

[112] Uvalde Police Department Body-Worn Camera Footage.

[113] Uvalde Police Department Body-Worn Camera Footage.

[114] UCISD Raptor Data Export.

Robb Elementary: West Building Northwest Entrance

Three BPAs arrive on scene and enter the West Building through the northwest doorway.[115]

Constable Field says, "We need a stack, with that shield."[116]

Events: Officer Arrivals; Request for Shields

Communications: Radio Traffic

An officer on scene requests assistance from a unit that can manage the crowd growing on the school perimeter, which is relayed by dispatch over radio to a UPD officer arriving on scene.[117]

Events: Crowd Control

Robb Elementary: West Building T-Intersection

A UCSO deputy brings a shield to the T-intersection, noting that it is not rifle-rated.[118]

Events: Request for Shields

Robb Elementary: West Building South Entrance

Officers outside the south doorway discuss BORTAC. UPD Sgt. 1 states they are coming, and another officer states they are already there and on the other end of the hallway.[119] CBP personnel have arrived on scene, but no members of BORTAC have arrived.

Events: Officer Arrivals

Communications: Radio Traffic

An unknown officer radios a request to have EMS "come prepared," and for them to wait at the funeral home.[120]

Events: EMS Arrivals and Actions

---

[115] Robb Elementary School CCTV Footage.

[116] Uvalde Police Department Body-Worn Camera Footage.

[117] Uvalde Police Department Radio Traffic; Uvalde Police Department Body-Worn Camera Footage.

[118] Uvalde Police Department Body-Worn Camera Footage.

[119] Uvalde Police Department Body-Worn Camera Footage.

[120] Uvalde Police Department Radio Traffic.

Robb Elementary: West Building T-Intersection

Constable Field is on the phone with UCISD PD Chief Pete Arredondo; officers on the north side of the hallway appear to be waiting for instruction from the outcome of the phone call. Some officers inquire about the status of the negotiator.[121]

Events: Negotiations

Robb Elementary: West Building South Entrance

UPD Sgt. 1 asks for confirmation from UPD Sgt. 3 that Chief Arredondo has made contact with the subject. UPD Sgt. 3 denies this and says no one has made contact with the subject.[122]

Events: Negotiations

Communications: UCISD Raptor Alert

UCISD Morales Junior High School goes into secure status.[123]

Events: UCISD: Other Campus Lockdowns

Robb Elementary: West Building Northeast Hallway

Officers clear classrooms 126 and 127, which are not occupied.[124]

Events: Room Clearings and Evacuations

Robb Elementary: Perimeter

EMS arrive on scene near the funeral home.[125]

Events: EMS Arrivals and Actions

---

[121] Uvalde Police Department Body-Worn Camera Footage.

[122] Uvalde Police Department Body-Worn Camera Footage.

[123] UCISD Raptor Data Export.

[124] Uvalde Police Department Body-Worn Camera Footage.

[125] Hillcrest Memorial Funeral Home CCTV Footage.

Robb Elementary: West Building T-Intersection

Constable Field ends his call with Chief Arredondo and announces that they are going to clear the room next to classrooms 111/112 and start negotiations.[126]

Events: Negotiations; Room Clearings and Evacuations

Robb Elementary: West Building Northeast Hallway

Officers clear room 129 on the northeast side of the building, evacuating a teacher out of the building and through the east doorway.[127]

Events: Room Clearings and Evacuations

Robb Elementary: West Building T-Intersection

UCISD PD Ofc. 1 conveys to Constable Field that his wife says she's been shot. He says this in the presence of multiple officers who appear to quietly acknowledge what he says. UPD Acting Chief Pargas escorts UCISD PD Ofc. 1 out of the northwest door.[128]

Events: Presence of Victims: Acknowledgment and Discussion

Robb Elementary: West Building South Entrance

Officers on the exterior of the south entry discuss the status of victims, whether there are any children present, and if they can have the information confirmed with the school. UCISD Ofc. 2 states that they think the subject is in the classroom of UCISD PD Ofc. 1's wife.[129]

Events: Presence of Victims: Acknowledgment and Discussion

Communications: Radio Traffic

An unknown officer on the radio advises that more civilians are approaching the school perimeter. Then an unknown officer responds, "let PD take point on this."[130]

Events: Crowd Control

---

[126] Uvalde Police Department Body-Worn Camera Footage.

[127] Uvalde Police Department Body-Worn Camera Footage.

[128] Uvalde Police Department Body-Worn Camera Footage.

[129] Uvalde Police Department Body-Worn Camera Footage.

[130] Uvalde Police Department Radio Traffic.

Robb Elementary: West Building Northside Hallway

Officers clear and evacuate the boys' and girls' restrooms. The boys' room is occupied by one child, who is evacuated through the northeast door.[131]

There is continued discussion about making entry, and UPD Ofc. 2 responds that they are waiting for a negotiator and shields. Another officer in the hallway asks who is in charge, and UPD Ofc. 2 indicates it is UCISD PD Chief Pete Arredondo.

Events: Room clearings and evacuations; Negotiations; Request for shields

Robb Elementary: West Building Southside Hallway

UCSO Dep. 2 enters room 102 and observes children inside. He instructs the children to exit out the window and alerts other officers in the hallway.[132]

Events: Room Clearings and Evacuations

Robb Elementary: West Building Northside Hallway

Officers clear room 131 and 132 through an adjoining door.[133] UCISD Staff 1 is evacuated from room 132 via the northwest entrance,[134] and no one is present in room 131.[135]

There is more discussion among officers on the north side of the hallway. A TXDPS special agent inquires whether children are inside the classroom with the subject and an officer responds that they do not know. He says that "if there are kids in there, then you go in."[136]

Events: Room Clearings and Evacuations; Presence of Victims: Acknowledgment and Discussion

Robb Elementary: West Building West Exterior

Officers evacuate students and a teacher from room 102 through the window, out to the west side of the building and toward the funeral home.[137]

Events: Room Clearings and Evacuations

---

[131] Texas Department of Public Safety Body-Worn Camera Footage.

[132] Uvalde County Sheriff's Office Body-Worn Camera Footage.

[133] Uvalde Police Department Body-Worn Camera Footage.

[134] Robb Elementary School CCTV Footage.

[135] Uvalde Police Department Body-Worn Camera Footage.

[136] Texas Department of Public Safety Body-Worn Camera Footage.

[137] Uvalde Police Department Body-Worn Camera Footage.

Communications: Radio Traffic

Dispatch notifies over radio that BORTAC is en route.[138]

Events: Officer Arrivals

11:59 a.m.

Robb Elementary: West Building Southside Hallway

Chief Arredondo is in the hallway and attempts to establish contact with the subject, who remains inside rooms 111/112. There is no audible response from inside the classrooms.[139]

Events: Negotiations

Robb Elementary: West Building Northwest Entrance

Officers evacuate UCISD Staff 2 from room 116 and out the northwest entrance.[140]

In the east corridor, an officer repeats the misinformation that Chief Arredondo is in the room with the subject.[141]

Events: Room Clearings and Evacuations; Negotiations

Robb Elementary: West Building West Exterior

TXDPS Texas Ranger (TX Ranger) 1 is on scene at the west parking lot, toward the south end of the building, and receiving information from UPD Sgt. 3 about the location of the subject.[142]

Events: Officer Arrivals

Communications: UCISD Raptor Alert

UCISD Dual Language Academy goes into secure status.[143]

Events: UCISD: Other Campus Lockdowns

---

[138] Uvalde Police Department Body-Worn Camera Footage; Uvalde Police Department Radio Traffic.

[139] Uvalde County Sheriff's Office Body-Worn Camera Footage.

[140] Robb Elementary School CCTV Footage.

[141] Texas Department of Public Safety Body-Worn Camera Footage.

[142] Uvalde Police Department Body-Worn Camera Footage.

[143] UCISD Raptor Data Export.

Robb Elementary: West Building Southside Hallway

Chief Arredondo continues negotiation attempts, stating that "These are innocent children" and that law enforcement does not want anyone else to be hurt.[144]

Events: Negotiations: Presence of Victims: Acknowledgment and Discussion

Funeral Home

The first large group of evacuated children arrives at the funeral home, along with a teacher. Three more groups arrive shortly after.[145]

Events: Room Clearings and Evacuations

Communications: Radio Traffic

Dispatch advises that air operations is en route and almost on scene.[146]

Officers request positive ID on the subject.[147]

Events: Air Support; Subject Identification

Communications: UCISD Raptor Alert

UCISD Crossroads Academy goes into secure status.[148]

Events: UCISD: Other Campus Lockdowns

Robb Elementary: West Building Southside Hallway

Chief Arredondo continues his attempts to make contact with the subject.[149]

Events: Negotiations

---

[144] Uvalde County Sheriff's Office Body-Worn Camera Footage.

[145] Hillcrest Memorial Funeral Home CCTV Footage.

[146] Uvalde Police Department Radio Traffic.

[147] Uvalde Police Department Radio Traffic.

[148] UCISD Raptor Data Export.

[149] Uvalde County Sheriff's Office Body-Worn Camera Footage.

Communications: Radio Traffic

An officer requests assistance with crowd control on the east side of the building, stating there are only two officers there.[150]

Events: Crowd Control

Communications: UCISD Raptor Alert

UCISD Dalton Early Childhood Center goes into secure status.[151]

Events: UCISD: Other Campus Lockdowns

12:02 p.m.

Communications: Radio Traffic

Dispatch provides over radio the name and approximate age of the subject, and advises that a witness saw him approaching the school with a rifle and two backpacks.

Events: Subject Identification; Subject's Backpack: Observation and Recovery

Robb Elementary: West Building West Exterior

Officers evacuate children from the window of room 103 out onto the west side of the building and toward the funeral home.[152]

Events: Room Clearings and Evacuations

Robb Elementary: West Building

A TXDPS helicopter arrives on scene.[153]

Events: Air Support

Robb Elementary: West Building Northwest Entrance

The TXDPS sergeant is outside of the northwest entrance as children are being evacuated from room 103 and comments that the subject shot kids.[154]

Events: Presence of Victims: Acknowledgment and Discussion

---

[150] Uvalde Police Department Radio Traffic.

[151] UCISD Raptor Data Export.

[152] Uvalde Police Department Body-Worn Camera Footage.

[153] Uvalde Police Department Radio Traffic; Uvalde County Sheriff's Office Body-Worn Camera Footage.

[154] Texas Department of Public Safety Body-Worn Camera Footage.

Robb Elementary: West Building T-Intersection

UPD Ofc. 2 obtains two shields from outside the doorway and brings them into the hallway.[155] There are now a total of three shields at the T-intersection of the hallway.

Events: Request for Shields

Robb Elementary: West Building West Exterior

After helping evacuate children from multiple classrooms, UPD Sgt. 1 says, "There has to be kids everywhere."[156]

Events: Room Clearings and Evacuations; Presence of Victims: Acknowledgment and Discussion

Robb Elementary: West Building, Inside Classrooms 111 and 112
Communications: 911

A child calls from inside Robb Elementary, stating there is a school shooting. The call lasts less than one minute. The call information is not shared over radio, but dispatch determines the call is coming from inside the school and calls the number back.[157, 158]

Events: Presence of Victims: Acknowledgment and Discussion

Robb Elementary: West Building West Exterior

Officers break out the windows from room 104 and evacuate children through the window onto the west side of the building, sending them toward the funeral home.[159]

Events: Room Clearings and Evacuations

Communications: Radio Traffic

Dispatch advises that three buses will be lining up near the funeral home to provide transport.

Events: Room Clearings and Evacuations

---

[155] Uvalde Police Department Body-Worn Camera Footage.

[156] Uvalde Police Department Body-Worn Camera Footage.

[157] CIR Fact Finding.

[158] CIR team could not definitively determine whether this is the same call that was later placed to a child inside the room at 12:10 p.m.

[159] Uvalde Police Department Body-Worn Camera Footage; Uvalde County Constables Body-Worn Camera Footage.

Funeral Home

More evacuated children and teachers arrive at the funeral home.[160]

Events: Room Clearings and Evacuations

12:05 p.m.

Robb Elementary: West Building Northeast Hallway

The misinformation that UCISD PD Chief Pete Arredondo is in the room with the subject continues to be shared, this time by a UCSO deputy to a game warden on scene.[161]

Events: Negotiations

12:06 p.m.

Communications: Radio Traffic

An officer requests information about the location of the command post. The response back is that officers are having trouble establishing a command post and that they need officers to keep parents and family members at bay, as they are trying to push their way into the funeral home.[162]

Events: Crowd Control; Establishing Incident Command Post

Robb Elementary: West Building West Exterior

Officers evacuate children from room 106 out of the window onto the west side of the building and send them toward the funeral home.[163]

Events: Room Clearings and Evacuations

Funeral Home

More evacuated children and teachers arrive at the funeral home.[164]

Events: Room Clearings and Evacuations

---

[160] Hillcrest Memorial Funeral Home CCTV Footage.

[161] Texas Parks and Wildlife Body-Worn Camera Footage.

[162] Uvalde Police Department Radio Traffic.

[163] Uvalde Police Department Body-Worn Camera Footage; Uvalde County Constables Body-Worn Camera Footage.

[164] Hillcrest Memorial Funeral Home CCTV Footage.

Communications: Radio Traffic

TX Ranger 1 requests TXDPS to send all troopers available to assist with crowd control.[165]

An officer inquires over radio whether there is a location set up for reunification but does not receive a response.[166]

Events: Crowd Control; Reunification

12:07 p.m.

Robb Elementary: West Building Southside Hallway

Officers discover children and a teacher inside room 108, which is unlocked, and evacuate them through the hallway and out the south door.[167] Law enforcement has been staged near the door of room 108 for more than 25 minutes.

Events: Room Clearings and Evacuations

Robb Elementary: West Building West Exterior

Officers break out the windows of room 105, evacuate children onto the west side of the building, then send them toward the funeral home.[168]

Events: Room Clearings and Evacuations

Communications: Radio Traffic

An officer advises over radio that a large number of parents and family members are heading toward the northwest corner of the school and some are armed.[169]

Events: Crowd Control

Robb Elementary: Perimeter

A UCSO deputy and UCSO Sheriff Ruben Nolasco speak with a person who says they are a family member of the subject. This person is very distressed and says that their child, who attends Robb Elementary, is in the building.[170]

Events: Crowd Control

---

[165] Texas Department of Public Safety Radio Traffic.

[166] Uvalde Police Department Radio Traffic.

[167] Uvalde County Sheriff's Office Body-Worn Camera Footage.

[168] Uvalde Police Department Body-Worn Camera Footage; Uvalde County Constables Body-Worn Camera Footage.

[169] Uvalde Police Department Radio Traffic.

[170] Uvalde County Sheriff's Office Body-Worn Camera Footage.

Robb Elementary: West Building Southside Hallway

UCISD PD Chief Pete Arredondo asks UPD Sgt. 3 to find a master key from one of the school officials.[171] Arredondo is seeking the key to access room 109, which is locked and has children and a teacher inside. This is the first documented request for a master key.

Events: Search for Keys; Room Clearings and Evacuations

Robb Elementary: West Building West Exterior

UPD Sgt. 3 walks around toward the west side of the building, asking whether anyone has a master key. Uvalde County Precinct 6 Constable Zamora says that he thought the other side had master keys.

Events: Search for Keys

Funeral Home

More evacuated children arrive at the funeral home.[172]

Events: Rooms Clearings and Evacuations

12:09 p.m.

Robb Elementary: West Building Southside Hallway

Chief Arredondo tells Constable Zamora to have the helicopter switch locations, as it is "too loud." Zamora goes outside and asks the law enforcement officers, "if you can have the copter redirect, it's too loud for communication."[173] Chief Arredondo tells UPD Sgt. 1 that they are waiting for a master key and that room 109 needs to be cleared and vacated before they do any kind of breaching. He says, "Time is on our side right now. I know we got kids in there, but we gotta save the lives of the other ones."[174] An officer then informs Chief Arredondo of radio traffic indicating that BORTAC has just arrived. Chief Arredondo responds that BORTAC needs to wait—"Tell them to calm the [expletive] down for a minute."[175]

Events: Air Support; Presence of Victims: Acknowledgment and Discussion

---

[171] Uvalde County Sheriff's Office Body-Worn Camera Footage.

[172] Hillcrest Memorial Funeral Home CCTV Footage.

[173] Uvalde County Constables Body-Worn Camera Footage.

[174] Uvalde Police Department Body-Worn Camera Footage; Uvalde County Sheriff's Office Body-Worn Camera Footage.

[175] Uvalde County Sheriff's Office Body-Worn Camera Footage.

Communications: Radio Traffic

Radio traffic from officers on scene advises that shields are up, multiple agencies are on scene, and BORTAC has arrived. There is also a request for the helicopter to move because it is hard for officers to hear inside and outside of the school building.[176]

Events: Request for Shields; Air Support; Officer Arrivals

12:10 p.m.

Robb Elementary: West Building Southside Hallway

An officer suggests breaking the window out to evacuate room 109, instead of waiting for the master key. Chief Arredondo declines, indicating he does not want to create any noise that may cause the subject to shoot in that direction as they are evacuating.[177] Chief Arredondo then calls Constable Field, talking about the need to get a master key and to verify that the hallway is vacated.[178] UPD Cpl. 1 continues attempting to communicate with the subject.[179]

Events: Room Clearings and Evacuations; Search for Keys; Negotiations

Robb Elementary: West Building T-Intersection

Officers discuss BORTAC's arrival being 30 minutes away. An officer asks if they are going to push or if they want to hold.[180] It is not clear which officer is asking and to whom, and there is no audible response captured in any BWC footage.

Events: Officer Arrivals

Robb Elementary: West Building Northwest Entrance

Officers are outside the northwest doorway. One officer, addressing UPD Acting Chief Pargas, asks if they are just waiting for BORTAC. UPD Ofc. 3 walks over and says that BORTAC is on the way and he needs an officer in charge to make decisions. Acting Chief Pargas refers to TX Ranger 1, stating that Rangers have a team coming out.[181]

Events: Officer Arrivals

---

[176] Uvalde Police Department Radio Traffic; Uvalde Police Department Body-Worn Camera Footage.

[177] Uvalde County Sheriff's Office Body-Worn Camera Footage.

[178] Uvalde Police Department Body-Worn Camera Footage; Uvalde County Sheriff's Office Body-Worn Camera Footage.

[179] Uvalde County Sheriff's Office Body-Worn Camera Footage.

[180] Texas Parks and Wildlife Body-Worn Camera Footage; Uvalde Police Department Body-Worn Camera Footage.

[181] Uvalde Police Department Body-Worn Camera Footage.

Communications: Radio Traffic

A TXDPS trooper on scene provides an update to TXDPS dispatch, repeating misinformation that the chief of UCISD PD is in room 111 or 112 with the active shooter. The TXDPS trooper also relays that they have learned the name of the subject and provides it to TXDPS dispatch.

Events: Negotiations; Subject Identification

Robb Elementary: West Building, Inside Classrooms 111 and 112
Communications: 911

911 dispatch calls back the child who had previously called and hung up from inside classroom 112, stating they were in a room full of victims.[182] The call lasts approximately 16 minutes, through the shots that are fired at 12:21, and ends at 12:26.[183] Dispatch broadcasts the call information over the radio at approximately 12:12 p.m., and this information is received and disseminated through both sides of the hallway.[184]

Events: Presence of Victims: Acknowledgment and Discussion

12:11 p.m.

Robb Elementary: West Building Northwest Entrance

Sheriff Nolasco is with TX Ranger 1, UPD Ofc. 3, and others discussing the situation. TX Ranger 1 has a map provided by a UCISD PD lieutenant. It is a basic map and does not include features of the building and rooms, such as windows, closets, or the doors that connect classrooms from within their interiors. UPD Ofc. 3 states that BORTAC is still 45 minutes away and that just one member of BORTAC is on scene now, referring to the BORTAC commander who has just arrived.[185] Sheriff Nolasco asks questions and provides direction regarding the evacuations and reunification location.

Events: Officer Arrivals; Room Clearings and Evacuations; Reunification

Robb Elementary: West Building, Inside Classrooms 111 and 112
Communications: 911

The child from room 112 remains on the phone with 911. They state that their teacher is dead. Dispatch asks if the door is locked but there is no audible response.

Events: Presence of Victims: Acknowledgment and Discussion

---

[182] Uvalde Police Department Dispatch Landline.

[183] Uvalde Police Department Dispatch Landline.

[184] Uvalde Police Department Body-Worn Camera Footage; Uvalde County Sheriff's Office Body-Worn Camera Footage; Uvalde Police Department Radio Traffic.

[185] Uvalde County Sheriff's Office Body-Worn Camera Footage.

Robb Elementary: West Building Southside Hallway

UCISD PD Chief Pete Arredondo tells Constable Zamora he is waiting for a master key and that he told UPD Sgt. 3 to get him one. Zamora conveys that there is one on the other side of the hallway.[186] A stack composed of TXDPS troopers (including the TXDPS sergeant), a BPA, and a UCSO deputy is at the south doorway. Chief Arredondo approaches them, stating that they need to hold so room 109 can be evacuated first.[187]

Events: Search for Keys; Room Clearings and Evacuations; Stack Formation

Communications: Radio Traffic

Dispatch advises over radio that a child called and is in a room full of victims. This communication is transmitted on both sides of the hallway and the exteriors of the building.[188]

Events: Presence of Victims: Acknowledgment and Discussion

Robb Elementary: West Building, Inside Classrooms 111 and 112
Communications: 911

The child from 112 remains on the phone with 911. Dispatch advises the child that they will tell them when it is ok to open the door.

Events: Presence of Victims: Acknowledgment and Discussion

Robb Elementary: West Building T-Intersection

The BORTAC commander enters the building through the northwest door. They approach the T-intersection, begin receiving information from officers on scene, and learn that there are victims inside rooms 111/112.[189]

---

[186] Uvalde County Constables Body-Worn Camera Footage.

[187] Uvalde County Constables Body-Worn Camera Footage.

[188] Uvalde Police Department Body-Worn Camera Footage; Uvalde County Sheriff's Office Body-Worn Camera Footage; Uvalde Police Department Radio Traffic.

[189] Texas Parks and Wildlife Body-Worn Camera Footage; Uvalde Police Department Body-Worn Camera Footage; Robb Elementary School CCTV Footage.

Around the same time, UPD Ofc. 4 carries in a crate of what they believe to be flashbangs but learns shortly after are stinger grenades, which disperse small rubber pellets to disorient and temporarily incapacitate individuals in a specific area. The BORTAC commander asks about gas and UPD Ofc. 4 replies that gas is coming.[190]

Events: Officer Arrivals; Presence of Victims: Acknowledgment and Discussion

Robb Elementary: West Building South Entrance

Constable Zamora reiterates Chief Arredondo's direction that there should be no entry until Arredondo gives permission.[191] After asking UPD Sgt. 3 about the status of the master keys, Constable Zamora then goes to the other side of the hallway, via the exterior west side of the building, to obtain master keys.[192]

Events: Search for Keys

Robb Elementary: West Building West Exterior

UPD Lt. 1 and other officers locate the subject's backpack at the west exterior of the building, uncover dozens of fully loaded magazines and hundreds of rounds of ammunition, and transmit this information over the radio.[193]

Events: Subject's Backpack: Observation and Recovery

Robb Elementary: West Building, Inside Classrooms 111 and 112
Communications: 911

The child from 112 remains on the phone with 911. The child asks the 911 dispatcher to send help for their teacher, whom they say is still alive but shot.

Events: Presence of Victims: Acknowledgment and Discussion

12:14 p.m.

Robb Elementary: West Building T-Intersection

UPD Ofc. 4 reenters with a crate full of CS gas (commonly known as "tear gas"). The BORTAC commander asks about masks, then exits the building to get their own mask.[194]

Events: Tools and Equipment: CS Gas

---

[190] Robb Elementary School CCTV Footage.

[191] Uvalde County Constables Body-Worn Camera Footage.

[192] Uvalde County Constables Body-Worn Camera Footage.

[193] Uvalde Police Department Radio Traffic; Uvalde County Constables Body-Worn Camera Footage.

[194] Uvalde Police Department Body-Worn Camera Footage.

Robb Elementary: West Building Northwest Entrance

Constable Zamora, having come from the other side of the building to find a master key, obtains a set of keys from UPD Det. 2. They are a large set of keys with a big ring attached to a red lanyard. He sees a UCISD PD lieutenant, who stops to help him look through the keys. The lieutenant breaks off a portion of them and hands them to Zamora, saying one of them will open all of the doors.[195] These keys are later discovered not to work on room 109.

Events: Search for Keys

Communications: 911

The child from 112 remains on the phone with 911. Dispatch asks how many children are in the room and the child estimates up to eight. The child is also advising others around them to try to keep quiet, as some are crying or moaning.

Events: Presence of Victims: Acknowledgment and Discussion

12:15 p.m.

Communications: Radio Traffic

Dispatch advises there is one teacher who is still alive, with wounds, in the classroom with eight or nine children. Dispatch is "not too sure" about the number of wounded.[196] Dispatch adds that their information is coming from a student inside the classroom.[197]

There is also communication over radio between two officers indicating that buses are on scene, parents should go to the rear of the funeral home, and UCISD needs to be there to release the kids.[198]

Events: Presence of Victims: Acknowledgment and Discussion; Reunification

Robb Elementary: West Building, Inside Classrooms 111 and 112
Communications: 911

The child from 112 remains on the phone with 911. They ask dispatch to please hurry and state that their teacher is about to die.

Events: Presence of Victims: Acknowledgment and Discussion

---

[195] Uvalde County Constables Body-Worn Camera Footage.

[196] Uvalde Police Department Dispatch Landline.

[197] Uvalde County Constables Body-Worn Camera Footage.; Uvalde Police Department Radio Traffic.

[198] Uvalde Police Department Radio Traffic; Uvalde County Constables Body-Worn Camera Footage.

Robb Elementary: West Building Northwest Entrance
Communications: Radio Traffic

Outside the northwest entrance, an officer stresses to UPD Acting Chief Pargas that "the room is full of victims."[199] Acting Chief Pargas grabs the radio and walked away to make a phone call to dispatch. Acting Chief Pargas asks dispatch if there are enough EMS on standby, then asks about the call from the child.[200]

Events: Presence of Victims; Acknowledgment and Discussion

Robb Elementary: West Building T-Intersection

The BORTAC commander returns to the hallway. They are on the phone with the TXDPS sergeant, stating that "these guys are about to make entry on this side," then ends the call by saying they will stand by.[201] The BORTAC commander then continues to receive information from officers on scene. The discussion revolves around who is in the room with the subject and whether there is active killing happening. The answers are affirmative regarding the presence of a teacher and children in the room with the subject; however, there is no specific reference to the injured teacher or any injured children inside the room.

Events: Room Clearings and Evacuations; Presence of Victims: Acknowledgment and Discussion

Robb Elementary: West Building Southside Hallway

Constable Zamora arrives back at the south hallway with a set of keys. UCISD PD Chief Pete Arredondo tries them on room 109 and they do not appear to work.[202] The TXDPS sergeant says that the BORTAC unit is going in, and Chief Arredondo responds that they need to secure room 109 first. The TXDPS sergeant relays to the BORTAC commander that they need to clear classroom 109 first.[203]

Events: Search for Keys; Room Clearings and Evacuations

Robb Elementary: West Building, Inside Classrooms 111 and 112
Communications: 911

The child from 112 remains on the phone with 911. The child asks if they should open the door, and someone inside the room with them responds "no." The dispatcher asks the child to stay quiet, and the child responds that their teacher will not stay quiet.

Events: Presence of Victims: Acknowledgment and Discussion

---

[199] Uvalde Police Department Body-Worn Camera Footage.

[200] Uvalde Police Department Dispatch Landline.

[201] Uvalde Police Department Body-Worn Camera Footage; CIR Fact Finding

[202] Uvalde County Constables Body-Worn Camera Footage; Uvalde Police Department Body-Worn Camera Footage.

[203] Uvalde County Constables Body-Worn Camera Footage.

Robb Elementary: West Building Southside Hallway

UCISD PD Chief Arredondo, UPD Sgt. 1, and Constable Zamora continue to work on the door to room 109, trying the keys multiple times and then trying to breach it with a knife.[204]

Events: Search for Keys: Room Clearings and Evacuations

Robb Elementary: West Building Northwest Entrance

TX Ranger 1 advises UPD Acting Chief Pargas to establish a command post, stating that they need to bring together the senior officers from each of the law enforcement agencies on scene to get a handle on assets and resources and begin relaying information from inside the building. Acting Chief Pargas assigns UPD Lt. 2 to establish a command post.[205]

Events: Establishing Incident Command Post

Communications: Radio Traffic

An officer requests over radio for an opening to be made on Perez Street, to make way for school buses that are being used for transport.[206]

Events: Room Clearings and Evacuations; Reunification

Robb Elementary: West Building, Inside Classrooms 111 and 112
Communications: 911

The child from 112 remains on the phone with 911. Dispatch asks if there is anyone behind the door and the child replies "no."[207] Dispatch states they are getting officers there.

Events: Presence of Victims: Acknowledgment and Discussion

---

[204] Uvalde Police Department Body-Worn Camera Footage; Uvalde County Constables Body-Worn Camera Footage.

[205] Texas Parks and Wildlife Body-Worn Camera Footage.

[206] Uvalde Police Department Radio Traffic.

[207] Uvalde Police Department Dispatch Landline.

Robb Elementary: West Building Northwest Entrance

An emergency medical technician (EMT) from BORSTAR approaches the northwest door and asks about the location of room "12," where victims are. There is initial confusion about the status of victims in classrooms 111 and 112. One officer at the doorway states affirmatively that there are victims inside the room. The BORSTAR EMT enters the hallway and continues to the T-intersection.[208]

Events: Officer Arrivals; EMS Arrivals and Actions; Presence of Victims: Acknowledgment and Discussion; Negotiations

Robb Elementary: West Building Southside Hallway

Still unable to open the door to room 109, officers continue trying to breach it with a knife. Constable Zamora also tries speaking through the door, announcing himself and the other officers as law enforcement.[209] However, the children and teacher inside the room do not respond.

Events: Search for Keys; Room Clearings and Evacuations

Robb Elementary: West Building, Inside Classrooms 111 and 112
Communications: 911

The child from 112 remains on the phone with 911. The child continues to talk with dispatch, who is relaying guidance to stay quiet. Someone else inside the classroom is heard in the background stating that they need to come in immediately.[210]

Events: Presence of Victims: Acknowledgment and Discussion

Robb Elementary: West Building T-Intersection

The BORTAC commander is on the phone, while simultaneously asking officers in the hallway about the status of the door to classrooms 111/112. UPD Sgt. 2 responds that they do not know if the door is locked. The BORTAC commander seems to hear that the door is locked, as they say on the phone, "They're saying the door is locked."[211] UPD Sgt. 2 repeats that they do not know the status of the door.

---

[208] Texas Parks and Wildlife Body-Worn Camera Footage.

[209] Uvalde Police Department Body-Worn Camera Footage.

[210] Uvalde Police Department Dispatch Landline.

[211] Uvalde County Sheriff's Office Body-Worn Camera Footage; Texas Parks and Wildlife Body-Worn Camera Footage.

It is not clear from this exchange whether the BORTAC commander receives the correct information. An officer asks for a set of master keys, and another informs them that the keys already went to the other side of the building.

Events: Search for Keys

Robb Elementary: West Building Southside Hallway

Constable Zamora asks another officer either over the phone or in the hallway to have the UCISD PD lieutenant bring the whole set of keys, because the ones they previously obtained are not working.[212]

UCISD PD Chief Pete Arredondo calls Constable Field and reiterates that there is a classroom full of children that he needs to evacuate. Constable Field says that there is an entry team on the north side of the hallway, and Chief Arredondo explains that he also has a team on his side.[213]

Events: Search for Keys; Room Clearings and Evacuations

Communications: Radio Traffic

UPD Acting Chief Pargas requests UPD Lt. 2 to start setting up a command post; UPD Lt. 2 reports back affirmatively.[214]

An unknown officer makes a request for assistance at the funeral home, where parents and family members are converging and children are being evacuated.[215] Another officer states that they have four buses behind the funeral home, and a third officer advises them not to release any children to parents without accounting for the children.[216]

Events: Establishing Incident Command Post; Room Clearings and Evacuations; Reunification

Robb Elementary: West Building, Inside Classrooms 111 and 112
Communications: 911

The child from 112 remains on the phone with 911. Another child gets on the phone. Dispatch asks their name but their response is inaudible. Dispatch continues to state that officers are there and that the child should not open the door until dispatch tells them to.

Events: Presence of Victims: Acknowledgment and Discussion

---

[212] Uvalde County Constables Body-Worn Camera Footage.

[213] Texas Department of Public Safety Body-Worn Camera Footage; Texas Parks and Wildlife Body-Worn Camera Footage; Uvalde County Sheriff's Office Body-Worn Camera Footage.

[214] Uvalde Police Department Radio Traffic.

[215] Uvalde Police Department Radio Traffic.

[216] Uvalde Police Department Radio Traffic.

Robb Elementary: West Building Southside Hallway

Chief Arredondo explains to officers in the hallway that he wants to evacuate room 109 to avoid more victims, acknowledging the victims already in rooms 111/112.[217]

Still unable to open the door to room 109, UPD Sgt. 1 asks if anyone in the hallway has breaching tools available, but none of the 15 officers on the south side of the hallway respond that they do.[218]

Events: Presence of Victims: Acknowledgment and Discussion; Tools and Equipment: Breaching

Robb Elementary: West Building Northwest Entrance

Another shield arrives and is brought in through the northwest door of the building.[219]

Events: Request for Shields

Robb Elementary: West Building, Inside Classrooms 111 and 112
Communications: 911

The child from 112 remains on the phone with 911.

Events: Presence of Victims: Acknowledgment and Discussion

Robb Elementary: West Building, Inside Classrooms 111 and 112
Robb Elementary: West Building Northside Hallway
Robb Elementary: West Building Southside Hallway

The subject fires four shots inside the classroom. Officers on both sides of the hallway quickly take cover.[220] Officers on the north side of the hallway advance toward the classroom doors, stopping short of the doorway, near the janitor's closet adjacent to the classrooms. On the south side of the hallway, Constable Zamora is heard saying "he's communicating," followed by UCISD PD Chief Arredondo shouting "can you hear me, sir? Can you hear me, sir?"[221]

Events: Shots Fired

---

[217] Uvalde Police Department Body-Worn Camera Footage; Texas Department of Public Safety Body-Worn Camera Footage.

[218] Uvalde Police Department Body-Worn Camera Footage; Texas Department of Public Safety Body-Worn Camera Footage.

[219] Uvalde Police Department Body-Worn Camera Footage.

[220] Robb Elementary School CCTV Footage; Uvalde Police Department Body-Worn Camera Footage; Texas Parks and Wildlife Body-Worn Camera Footage.

[221] Uvalde County Constables Body-Worn Camera Footage.

Robb Elementary: West Building, Inside Classrooms 111 and 112
Communications: 911

The child from 112 remains on the phone with 911. They state "he's shooting." The dispatcher reiterates that the child should make sure everyone stays quiet.

Events: Presence of Victims: Acknowledgment and Discussion

Phase III: 12:22 a.m.–12:49:58 p.m.

Phase III comprises the time period following the 12:21 p.m. shots fired and ends with the entry into rooms 111 and 112.

12:22 p.m.

Robb Elementary: West Building Southside Hallway

UCISD PD Chief Pete Arredondo calls for the windows to classroom 109 to be broken out to start evacuation.[222]

Events: Room Clearings and Evacuations

Communications: Radio Traffic

Dispatch calls out over the radio: "Student on line just heard three shots fired."[223]

Events: Shots Fired

Robb Elementary: West Building, Inside Classrooms 111 and 112
Communications: 911

The child from 112 remains on the phone with 911.

Events: Presence of Victims: Acknowledgment and Discussion

12:23 p.m.

Robb Elementary: West Building Northside Hallway

The officers who approached classrooms 111/112 at 12:21 p.m. start inquiring about master keys and calling out the need for a master key.[224] A BPA tosses a set of keys to the BORTAC commander, who pauses and briefly discusses a plan to deploy CS gas into the rooms through the exterior windows.[225]

---

[222] Uvalde Police Department Body-Worn Camera Footage.

[223] Uvalde Police Department Radio Traffic.

[224] Texas Parks and Wildlife Body-Worn Camera Footage; Robb Elementary School CCTV Footage; Uvalde County Sheriff's Office Body-Worn Camera.

[225] Robb Elementary School CCTV Footage; Uvalde County Sheriff's Office Body-Worn Camera.

This plan is eventually called off on account of the children in the classroom;[226] the exact time when it is called off is unknown.

Events: Stack Formation; Search for Keys; Tools and Equipment: CS Gas

Robb Elementary: West Building Southside Hallway

Officers hear faint cries coming from a nearby classroom, saying they "hear children." It is not clear which classroom the cries are coming from.[227] UCISD PD Chief Pete Arredondo resumes his attempt to communicate with the subject, who remains inside classrooms 111/112.[228]

Events: Presence of Victims: Acknowledgment and Discussion; Negotiations

Robb Elementary: West Building South Entrance
Communications: Radio Traffic

Evacuation of room 109 begins through the window and is announced over the radio shortly after.[229]

Events: Room Clearings and Evacuations

Robb Elementary: West Building, Inside Classrooms 111 and 112
Communications: 911

The child from 112 remains on the phone with 911.

Events: Presence of Victims: Acknowledgment and Discussion

12:24 p.m.

Robb Elementary: West Building Northeast Hallway

BORSTAR and CBP medics begin establishing a triage area outside the restrooms in the northeast hallway. A BORSTAR medic notes that "the victims have been bleeding for a while so be prepared."[230]

The BORTAC commander tests the set of keys on the janitor's closet next to classroom 112 and learns that they do not work.

Events: EMS Arrivals and Actions; Room Clearings and Evacuations; Search for Keys

---

[226] CIR Fact Finding.

[227] Texas Department of Public Safety Body-Worn Camera Footage.

[228] Uvalde Police Department Body-Worn Camera Footage.

[229] Uvalde Police Department Radio Traffic.

[230] Uvalde Police Department Body-Worn Camera Footage; Robb Elementary School CCTV Footage.

Robb Elementary: West Building Southside Hallway

An officer inside the hallway asks whether there any children inside the classroom with the shooter, and Chief Arredondo acknowledges that there are.[231]

Events: Presence of Victims: Acknowledgment and Discussion

Robb Elementary: Inside Classrooms 111 and 112
Communications: 911

The child from 112 remains on the phone with 911.

Events: Presence of Victims: Acknowledgment and Discussion

12:25 p.m.

Robb Elementary: West Building Southside Hallway

UCISD PD Chief Pete Arredondo is on the phone, asking for confirmation when "the room" is cleared. He is likely referring to classroom 109, which is the final room evacuated before law enforcement makes entry into classrooms 111/112.[232]

Uvalde County Precinct One Constable Johnny Field reports to officers in the hallway that "the teacher's shot in there," referring to Adult Victim 2, who has suffered a gunshot wound to the torso from one of the shooter's bullets.[233]

Events: Room Clearings and Evacuations; Presence of Victims: Acknowledgment and Discussion

Robb Elementary: Inside Classrooms 111 and 112
Communications: 911

The child from 112 remains on the phone with 911.

Events: Presence of Victims: Acknowledgment and Discussion

---

[231] Uvalde Police Department Body-Worn Camera Footage.

[232] Uvalde Police Department Body-Worn Camera Footage.

[233] Uvalde County Constables Body-Worn Camera Footage.

Robb Elementary: West Building Northside Hallway

Officers discuss the layout of the classrooms, specifically whether they are connected. One officer indicates that the classrooms do in fact connect via an internal adjoining door, which is acknowledged by the BORTAC commander.[234]

Events: Discussion of Classrooms 111/112 Layout

Robb Elementary: West Building Southside Hallway

Chief Arredondo is on the phone, explaining that they are "trying to preserve the rest of the lives first" as the rationale for evacuating the building before entering classrooms 111/112.[235]

The evacuation of classroom 109 is complete. The entire West Building has been evacuated, with the exception of classrooms 111 and 112.[236]

Events: Room Clearings and Evacuations; Presence of Victims: Acknowledgment and Discussion

Funeral Home

Five children evacuate to the funeral home, likely from classroom 109.[237]

Events: Room Clearings and Evacuations

Communications: Radio Traffic

An unknown officer advises over the radio that there is one shooting victim in an ambulance.[238]

Events: Presence of Victims: Acknowledgment and Discussion; EMS Arrivals and Actions

Robb Elementary: West Building, Inside Classrooms 111 and 112
Communications: 911

The child from 112 remains on the phone with 911.

Events: Presence of Victims: Acknowledgment and Discussion

---

[234] Uvalde Police Department Body-Worn Camera Footage.

[235] Uvalde Police Department Body-Worn Camera Footage.

[236] Uvalde Police Department Body-Worn Camera Footage; Texas Department of Public Safety Body-Worn Camera Footage.

[237] Hillcrest Memorial Funeral Home CCTV Footage.

[238] CIR Document and Data Review; Uvalde Police Department Body-Worn Camera Footage.

Robb Elementary: West Building Northside Hallway

The BORTAC commander reviews the map with the game warden.[239] This map is later found to omit some details, including the adjoining doors between classrooms 111 and 112.

Events: Discussion of Classrooms 111/112 Layout

Robb Elementary: West Building Southside Hallway

Chief Arredondo is on the phone with another responding officer who is on the north side of the hallway. Arredondo gives the go-ahead to make entry into classrooms 111/112, stating, "What team? Got a team ready to go? Have at it."[240] He then begins explaining aspects of the building and classroom, stating that the door is probably going to be locked and that he is going to try to find some keys to test. At this point, the need for keys is the focal point of entry into classrooms 111/112 for the first time during the response.

Events: Search for Keys; Stack Formation

Robb Elementary: West Building, Inside Classrooms 111 and 112
Communications: 911

The call with the child inside room 112 drops.

Robb Elementary: West Building Northside Hallway

Officers wait for another key to arrive.[241] A USMS deputy marshal calls out over their radio to bring a Halligan tool.[242]

UCSO Sheriff Ruben Nolasco states that there needs to be just one person making calls or radio communication from inside, and that right now there are too many.[243]

Events: Search for Keys; Tools and Equipment: Breaching

---

[239] Robb Elementary School CCTV Footage.

[240] Uvalde Police Department Body-Worn Camera Footage.

[241] Uvalde Police Department Body-Worn Camera Footage.

[242] Uvalde Police Department Body-Worn Camera Footage.

[243] Uvalde County Sheriff's Office Body-Worn Camera Footage.

Robb Elementary: West Building Southside Hallway

UCISD PD Chief Pete Arredondo calls someone and relates that the master keys he obtained earlier are not working, stating that a custodian may have a set that works. He then relays the information to Constable Zamora and directs him to go obtain the keys, describing whom to look for.[244]

Events: Search for Keys

12:29 p.m.

Robb Elementary: West Building Northside Hallway

The BORTAC commander discusses plans to use CS gas, stating they just need breachers. They discuss with another BPA that the master keys are not working and that the subject is shooting at the door every time someone gets close to it, repeating what they heard from other officers on the scene.[245]

Events: Tools and Equipment: CS Gas; Tools and Equipment: Breaching; Search for Keys

Robb Elementary: West Building Southside Hallway

Chief Arredondo communicates with officers in the hallway, stating that they have cleared all of the rooms except for the one where the shooter is. He points out that there are two doors and that the room they need to go into is 111 (referring to it as "the south door"). Someone asks if the rooms are adjoining, and Chief Arredondo replies that it is just a wall between them.[246]

Events: Room Clearings and Evacuations

Robb Elementary: West Building South Entrance

Constable Zamora speaks with the UCISD PD lieutenant, and both of them say that they have someone bringing them keys.[247]

Events: Search for Keys

---

[244] Uvalde Police Department Body-Worn Camera Footage; Texas Department of Public Safety Body-Worn Camera Footage.

[245] Uvalde County Sheriff's Office Body-Worn Camera Footage.

[246] Uvalde Police Department Body-Worn Camera Footage.

[247] Uvalde County Constables Body-Worn Camera Footage.

12:30 p.m.

Robb Elementary: West Building South Entrance

A rifle-rated shield arrives at the south entrance with another USMS deputy . They bring the shield inside the building.[248]

Events: Request for Shields; Officer Arrivals

12:31 p.m.

Robb Elementary: West Building Southside Hallway
Robb Elementary: South Entrance

UCISD PD Chief Pete Arredondo is on the phone and relays to others around him that the entry team on the north side is getting breaching tools.[249] Chief Arredondo refers to the entry team as BORTAC. Although there are BORTAC members included, the entry team is composed of officers from multiple agencies.

UPD Sgt. 3 comes up to Constable Zamora and says that the officers grouped up outside were talking about distracting the shooter by banging on the window to help the entry team (see "Chapter 2. Tactics and Equipment" for more on this tactic).[250] Constable Zamora comments "stand by."[251] He goes in and conveys the idea to UCISD PD Chief Arredondo, who says with a phone to his ear that they are "waiting on the breacher first."[252]

Events: Tools and Equipment: Breaching

12:32 p.m.

Robb Elementary: West Building Northside Hallway

The BORTAC commander exits the hallway to retrieve a Halligan tool[253] from their vehicle.[254]

Events: Tools and Equipment: Breaching

---

[248] Texas Department of Public Safety Body-Worn Camera Footage.

[249] Uvalde Police Department Body-Worn Camera Footage.

[250] Uvalde County Constables Body-Worn Camera Footage.

[251] Uvalde County Constables Body-Worn Camera Footage.

[252] Uvalde County Constables Body-Worn Camera Footage.

[253] A Halligan tool, or Halligan bar, is a multifunctional tool used for forcible entry through a doorway. It can also be used to rip through walls, floors, or other surfaces.

[254] Robb Elementary School CCTV Footage.

Robb Elementary: West Building Southside Hallway

Chief Arredondo is on the phone discussing with someone on the north side of the hallway the need for master keys and the possibility of using flashbangs, breaching through the window, and utilizing a sniper.[255]

Events: Search for Keys; Tools and Equipment: Breaching; Tactics: Sniper

12:33 p.m.

Communications: Radio Traffic

An unknown officer advises over the radio that EMTs from Brackettville are arriving, asking where they should stage.[256]

Dispatch advises over the radio that San Antonio Police Department SWAT is en route and 30 minutes away.[257]

Events: EMS Arrivals and Actions; Officer Arrivals

12:34 p.m.

Robb Elementary: West Building Southside Hallway

Officers discuss the nature of the situation. One asks whether there are any victims in the room with the shooter, which is confirmed by UPD Sgt. 1 and another officer.[258]

Constable Zamora inquires about the location of UCISD PD Ofc. 2, who is bringing the keys, and learns that the officer is on the other side of the hallway.[259]

Events: Presence of Victims: Acknowledgment and Discussion; Search for Keys

Communications: Radio Traffic

CBP EMTs advise that they have arrived and ask where they should go.[260]

Events: EMS Arrivals and Actions

---

[255] Uvalde Police Department Body-Worn Camera Footage.

[256] Uvalde Police Department Radio Traffic.

[257] Uvalde Police Department Radio Traffic; Uvalde Police Department Body-Worn Camera Footage.

[258] Uvalde Police Department Body-Worn Camera Footage.

[259] Uvalde County Constables Body-Worn Camera Footage.

[260] Uvalde Police Department Radio Traffic.

Robb Elementary: West Building Northside Hallway

The BORTAC commander reenters the north hallway with a Halligan tool and heads toward classrooms 111 and 112.[261]

Events: Tools and Equipment: Breaching

Robb Elementary: West Building Northside Hallway

TX Ranger 1 enters the hallway and hands a new set of keys to the BORTAC commander, who tests the keys on the janitor's closet, then on rooms 131 and 132, and confirms they work as master keys on multiple doors.[262]

Events: Search for Keys

Robb Elementary: West Building Southside Hallway

Officers on the south side of the hallway can see the key that arrived on the north side being tested on the janitor's closet and working.[263] One officer, acknowledging this, says, "Looks like they're about to breach."[264]

Events: Search for Keys; Stack Formation

Robb Elementary: West Building Northwest Entrance

Two additional BORTAC members arrive through the west entrance, one of whom is a sniper.[265] The BORTAC commander meets them near the T-intersection and they discuss the situation.[266] According to interviews, around this time, the BORTAC commander decides to see if the sniper can get a visual on the subject and potentially eliminate the threat. Additionally, a drone operated by a TXDPS member is used to try to observe inside the classroom. Neither of these efforts is successful. These actions likely occur during the gap in time between the retrieval of working keys and the eventual entry into rooms 111/112.[267]

Events: Officer Arrivals; Tactics: Sniper

---

[261] Robb Elementary School CCTV Footage.

[262] Robb Elementary School CCTV Footage; Uvalde County Sheriff's Office Body-Worn Camera Footage.

[263] Uvalde Police Department Body-Worn Camera Footage.

[264] Texas Department of Public Safety Body-Worn Camera Footage.

[265] Robb Elementary School CCTV Footage.

[266] Uvalde County Sheriff's Office Body-Worn Camera Footage.

[267] CIR Fact Finding.

Robb Elementary: West Building Southside Hallway

Chief Arredondo is on the phone stating that the keys should be tested on other doors before using them to enter classrooms 111/112. He then continues attempts to communicate with the subject, this time using the subject's name.[268]

Events: Negotiations

12:38 p.m.

Robb Elementary: West Building Southside Hallway

Constable Zamora tells Chief Arredondo that TX Ranger 1 has the keys on the other side of the hallway.[269]

Events: Search for Keys

12:39 p.m.

Robb Elementary: West Building Northside Hallway

Law enforcement medics continue setting up medical triage. Multiple stretchers have been brought into the hallway.[270]

Events: EMS Arrivals and Actions

12:40 p.m.

Communications: Radio Traffic

An unknown officer states over the radio that they are going to need help for security at the Civic Center, which is being set up as the reunification/notification center.[271]

Events: Reunification

---

[268] Uvalde Police Department Body-Worn Camera Footage.

[269] Uvalde Police Department Body-Worn Camera Footage; Texas Department of Public Safety Body-Worn Camera Footage.

[270] Robb Elementary School CCTV Footage.

[271] Uvalde Police Department Radio Traffic.

Robb Elementary: West Building Northside Hallway

Officers are calling for masks, with the expectation that gas is going to be used for the entry.[272]

Events: Tools and Equipment: CS Gas

Robb Elementary: West Building Southside Hallway

Chief Arredondo is on the phone, asking if anyone is able to see through the windows. He says, "We do understand there are some injuries in there . . . So we cleared off the rest of the building so we wouldn't have more than what's in there."[273]

Constable Zamora obtains a phone number that he believes to be the subject's and dials it. The call does not go through.[274]

Events: Presence of Victims: Acknowledgment and Discussion; Negotiations

Robb Elementary: West Building Northside Hallway

A CBP medic directs another medic to go to the other side of the hallway, in case victims need to be evacuated out of the south entry.[275]

Events: EMS Arrivals and Actions

Robb Elementary: West Building Southside Hallway

Chief Arredondo continues talking on the phone. During the conversation, he makes a statement about getting the door open and says, "We can't get the door open." He continues the phone conversation, describing the building layout and where the shooter is. He then says that he is looking for a sniper and asks if they could get a sniper on the rooftop.[276]

Meanwhile, there is general confusion among officers on the south side about whether the other side is making entry and if the door is locked. The conversation continues for approximately three minutes.[277]

Events: Tactics: Sniper

---

[272] Uvalde County Sheriff's Office Body-Worn Camera Footage; Texas Department of Public Safety Body-Worn Camera Footage.

[273] Uvalde Police Department Body-Worn Camera Footage.

[274] Uvalde County Constables Body-Worn Camera Footage.

[275] Texas Department of Public Safety Body-Worn Camera Footage.

[276] Uvalde Police Department Body-Worn Camera Footage.

[277] Texas Department of Public Safety Body-Worn Camera Footage.

Communications: Radio Traffic

UPD Lt. 2 advises that a command post has been set up at the funeral home.[278]

Events: Establishing Incident Command Post

12:43 p.m.

Robb Elementary: West Building Northside Hallway

One of the rifle-rated shields is passed down the hallway toward the stack outside of the doors to rooms 111/112.[279]

Events: Stack Formation

Robb Elementary: West Building Southside Hallway

The conversations among officers continue. Someone asks about the key and UPD Lt. 1 notes that the entry team has it, gesturing down the hallway toward the north side. Someone refers to approaching the doors to rooms 111/112 as a "death sentence."[280]

Chief Arredondo states, "That door I bet you was unlocked . . . we tell 'em, we tell 'em, we tell 'em."[281] Although the focus on both sides of the hallway is the doors to classrooms 111/112, it is not certain whether he is referring to interior or exterior doors in that moment.

Events: Search for Keys

Communications: Radio Traffic

Unknown officers indicate that they cannot observe the classroom through what they describe as a tinted window. Another officer indicates the window screens are down.[282]

Events: Tactics: Sniper

---

[278] CIR Document and Data Review; Uvalde Police Department Radio Traffic.

[279] Texas Department of Public Safety Body-Worn Camera Footage.

[280] Texas Department of Public Safety Body-Worn Camera Footage.

[281] Uvalde Police Department Body-Worn Camera Footage.

[282] Uvalde Police Department Radio Traffic.

Robb Elementary: West Building Northside Hallway

CBP and TXDPS medics continue to coordinate triage at the northeast hallway.[283]

Events: EMS Arrivals and Actions

Robb Elementary: West Building Northwest Entrance

Multiple officers and EMTs are staging at the northwest entrance door.[284]

Events: EMS Arrivals and Actions

Robb Elementary: West Building Southside Hallway

Chief Arredondo continues to speak on the phone, stating that they need to breach and they need a key. UPD Sgt. 1 and UPD Lt. 1 inform him that the keys on the other side. Chief Arredondo learns from the person on the phone that the key works and then says, "If you are ready to do it, do it," while also suggesting a distraction be created via the window.[285]

Events: Search for Keys

Robb Elementary: West Building Northside Hallway

Officers on the north side of the hallway observe and call out that the entry is occurring.[286]

Events: Entry into Classrooms 111/112

Robb Elementary: West Building Southside Hallway

Chief Arredondo says "Doors open," while another officer in the hallway says "They're going in."[287]

Events: Entry into Classrooms 111/112

---

[283] Uvalde County Sheriff's Office Body-Worn Camera Footage; Texas Department of Public Safety Body-Worn Camera Footage.

[284] Uvalde County Sheriff's Office Body-Worn Camera Footage.

[285] Uvalde Police Department Body-Worn Camera Footage.

[286] Uvalde County Sheriff's Office Body-Worn Camera Footage; Texas Department of Public Safety Body-Worn Camera Footage.

[287] Uvalde Police Department Body-Worn Camera Footage.

Communications: Radio Traffic

An unknown officer advises over the radio that TXDPS SWAT is on scene at the southeast corner of the campus.[288]

Another unknown officer states, "All copy, we are going to attempt to open the door."[289]

Events: Officer Arrivals

12:47 p.m.

Robb Elementary: West Building T-Intersection

CBP and TXDPS medics continue to prepare law enforcement around them for the triage that is about to occur.[290]

Events: EMS Arrivals and Actions

Robb Elementary: Outside Classrooms 111 and 112

There is no definitive evidence as to the exact time the entry team opens the door to room 111. However, based on interviews with officers in the stack, there is a minute or more between when they open the door and enter the room, and when they engage the subject. Based on the reactions of other officers in the hallway, we estimate the time the door is opened to sometime during the minute of 12:48 p.m.

The entry team is composed of three BORTAC members, a BORSTAR member, and deputies from two local sheriff's departments—Uvalde and Zavala counties. There is one shield in the stack, which has been provided by USMS and is rifle-rated. The first officer in the stack, the BORTAC commander, puts the key inside the door and turns it, pulling the door toward them and opening it.[291] As the entry team prepares to move in, the door begins to swing closed. One team member attempts to move a chair against the door to prop it open, but the door is too heavy, and eventually another member of the entry team simply holds it open as the team makes entry.

A second entry team, also composed of officers from multiple agencies on scene, is initially stacked up on the opposite side, outside of the door to room 112. However, when the first stack enters, sees that there is a door joining the two classrooms and it is open, like one big room, the second entry team is called off due to concerns over crossfire. Instead, the second stack moves in directly behind the first stack through the door of room 111, but never makes entry due to the door closing behind the first stack.[292]

Events: Stack Formation; Entry into Classrooms 111/112

---

[288] CIR Document and Data Review.

[289] Uvalde Police Department Radio Traffic.

[290] Uvalde County Sheriff's Office Body-Worn Camera Footage.

[291] This is not an indication that the door was locked; it simply describes the actions taken by the officer.

[292] CIR Fact Finding.

Robb Elementary: West Building Southside Hallway

Chief Arredondo speaks on the phone, explaining that the door is open but he does not know what is going on inside.[293]

Events: Entry into Classrooms 111/112

Communications: Radio Traffic

Constable Zamora advises over the radio: "all units, they're making entry."[294]

Events: Entry into Classrooms 111/112

12:48 p.m.

Robb Elementary: West Building Southside Hallway

In response to the confusion over the lack of activity after the entry team enters classrooms 111/112, Chief Arredondo speculates that the subject could have escaped onto the roof. UPD Sgt. 1 advises over the radio for air units to keep an eye on the roof.[295]

Events: Entry into Classrooms 111/112

12:49:58 p.m.

Robb Elementary: West Building, Inside Classrooms 111 and 112

The subject emerges from the closet in classroom 111 and engages the entry team with gunfire, striking a BORTAC member from the entry team. Officers on the entry team return fire.[296] A BORTAC member receives a graze to their head and leg.

Events: Entry into Classrooms 111/112

Phase IV: 12:50 p.m.–1:15 p.m.

Phase IV comprises the time period following the entry into rooms 111 and 112 though the completion of medical triage and evacuation.

---

[293] Uvalde Police Department Body-Worn Camera Footage.

[294] Uvalde County Constables Body-Worn Camera Footage; Uvalde Police Department Radio Traffic.

[295] Uvalde Police Department Body-Worn Camera Footage.

[296] Uvalde Police Department Body-Worn Camera Footage; Robb Elementary School CCTV Footage; CIR Fact Finding.

Robb Elementary: West Building, Inside Classrooms 111 and 112

A barrage of gunfire continues from inside the classrooms and the subject is killed.[297]

Events: Shots Fired; Subject Killed

Robb Elementary: West Building Hallway, Outside Classrooms 111 and 112

More than 20 officers are on both sides of the hallway. Many of them begin moving toward the doorway, and some enter the rooms. Officers near the T-intersection begin moving forward but are stopped by a law enforcement medic.[298]

Many officers crowd the doorway and hallways, preventing egress.[299]

Officers throughout the hallway call for EMTs, yell that kids are coming through, and ask for help to get them out.[300]

Events: Presence of Victims: Acknowledgment and Discussion; Medical Triage and Evacuation

Robb Elementary: West Building Northside Hallway
Robb Elementary: West Building Northwest Entrance

The first victim is carried out of the classrooms and brought up the north side of the hallway and out the northwest door.[301]

Events: Medical Triage and Evacuation

Communications: Radio Traffic

A radio callout states that the subject is down and EMS are needed in room 112.[302]

A UPD lieutenant calls out over the radio that a law enforcement vehicle is blocking the roadway and needs to be moved to clear the way.[303]

Events: EMS Arrivals and Actions

---

[297] Robb Elementary School CCTV Footage; Uvalde County Sheriff's Office Body-Worn Camera Footage; Uvalde Police Department Body-Worn Camera Footage.

[298] Robb Elementary School CCTV Footage.

[299] Uvalde Police Department Body-Worn Camera Footage.

[300] Robb Elementary School CCTV Footage; Uvalde County Sheriff's Office Body-Worn Camera Footage; Uvalde Police Department Body-Worn Camera Footage.

[301] Robb Elementary School CCTV Footage.

[302] CIR Document and Data Review.

[303] Uvalde Police Department Radio Traffic.

Robb Elementary: West Building Southside Hallway

One victim is carried out toward the south door.[304]

Events: Medical Triage and Evacuation

Robb Elementary: West Building, Inside Classrooms 111 and 112

Officers pick up victims, remove them from the room, and carry them into the hallway.[305] Officers continue shouting for EMTs and for the room to be cleared.[306]

Events: Medical Triage and Evacuation

Robb Elementary: West Building T-Intersection
Robb Elementary: West Building Northeast Hallway
Robb Elementary: West Building Northwest Entry

More law enforcement medics positioned at the T-intersection rush toward the classrooms, where there are 33 children and three teachers inside.[307]

A total of nine child victims are carried and moved out by law enforcement to the T-intersection. Four are brought toward the northwest door and positioned outside of rooms 131/132, and five are brought over to the triage area in the northeast hallway.[308]

Nine child victims walk or run down the hall, escorted by law enforcement. Two go down the northeast hallway, and seven exit through the northwest door.[309] Some of these children are injured, including at least one with a gunshot wound.[310]

Events: Medical Triage and Evacuation

---

[304] Uvalde Police Department Body-Worn Camera Footage.

[305] Uvalde Police Department Body-Worn Camera Footage.

[306] Uvalde County Constables Body-Worn Camera Footage.

[307] Robb Elementary School CCTV Footage.

[308] Robb Elementary School CCTV Footage.

[309] Robb Elementary School CCTV Footage.

[310] CIR Fact Finding.

12:52 p.m.

Robb Elementary: West Building, Inside Classrooms 111 and 112

As more officers continue to enter classrooms 111/112, a TXDPS ranger states that everyone inside the room who is not a medic needs to clear out, and some officers begin exiting in response.[311]

Events: Medical Triage and Evacuation

Robb Elementary: West Building T-Intersection

Four more child victims are brought to the T-intersection by law enforcement. Two are positioned near the east hallway, close to the intersection, and two are brought outside of classrooms 131/132.[312]

Events: Medical Triage and Evacuation

Communications: Radio Traffic

An unknown officer advises, "Remember, all the children need to go to the bus unless they are injured."[313]

Constable Zamora calls out for more EMTs over the radio.[314]

Events: Medical Triage and Evacuation

12:53 p.m.

Robb Elementary: West Building, Inside Classrooms 111 and 112

A BORSTAR medic leaves room 112 and announces that all victims remaining in that room are deceased.[315]

Events: Medical Triage and Evacuation

Robb Elementary: West Building Northwest Entry

Another victim is carried out through the northwest doorway.[316]

Events: Medical Triage and Evacuation

---

[311] Uvalde Police Department Body-Worn Camera Footage.

[312] Robb Elementary School CCTV Footage.

[313] Uvalde Police Department Radio Traffic.

[314] Uvalde Police Department Radio Traffic.

[315] Uvalde Police Department Body-Worn Camera Footage.

[316] Robb Elementary School CCTV Footage.

Communications: Radio Traffic

Constable Zamora says over the radio to ensure the perimeter is clear with no families.[317]

An unknown officer advises that EMS are approaching the southeast corner of the campus.

Radio traffic advises that Alamo EMS are en route.[318]

Events: EMS Arrivals and Actions; Medical Triage and Evacuation

12:54 p.m.

Robb Elementary: West Building Hallway East

Two deceased child victims are covered with a mylar blanket in the east hallway, close to the T-intersection.[319]

Events: Medical Triage and Evacuation

12:55 p.m.

Robb Elementary: West Building Hallway, Outside Classrooms 111 and 112

UCISD PD Chief Pete Arredondo asks for tactical units to help clear rooms one more time.[320]

UCSO Sheriff Ruben Nolasco, approaching the area, announces the need to start securing the exterior doors to keep people from coming in.[321]

EMTs approach the doorways with a stretcher and are informed that they will not be needed inside the classrooms.[322]

Events: Room Clearings and Evacuations

Robb Elementary: West Building Northwest Entry

A child victim is carried from the east hallway over to the west side and out the northwest door.[323]

Events: Medical Triage and Evacuation

---

[317] Uvalde County Constables Body-Worn Camera Footage.

[318] Uvalde Police Department Radio Traffic.

[319] Robb Elementary School CCTV Footage.

[320] Uvalde Police Department Body-Worn Camera Footage.

[321] Uvalde Police Department Body-Worn Camera Footage.

[322] Uvalde Police Department Body-Worn Camera Footage.

[323] Robb Elementary School CCTV Footage.

Robb Elementary: West Building Hallway, Outside Classrooms 111 and 112

Chief Arredondo asks who has the master keys, and some individuals in the hallway indicate that the BORTAC commander does.[324] A UCISD PD officer tells Chief Arredondo that they have the master keys and hands them to a BPA to conduct room clearings, as requested by Chief Arredondo.[325]

Officers on scene use master keys to open and clear classrooms 105/106, which are directly across from classrooms 111/112.[326]

Events: Room Clearings and Evacuations

Robb Elementary: West Building Northwest Entry

A child victim previously positioned in the northeast hallway is put on a stretcher and brought out the northwest door.[327]

Events: Medical Triage and Evacuation

Communications: Radio Traffic

Radio traffic advises that BORTAC will assist in double-checking rooms.[328]

An unknown officer states, "They can egress on Geraldine Street, north of Perez."[329]

Events: Medical Triage and Evacuation

12:57 p.m.

Robb Elementary: West Building T-Intersection

The two deceased child victims near the T-intersection are moved into classrooms 131/132.[330]

Constable Zamora starts telling officers in the hallway and those near the northwest door that the hallway needs to be cleared.[331]

Events: Medical Triage and Evacuation

---

[324] Uvalde Police Department Body-Worn Camera Footage.

[325] Uvalde Police Department Body-Worn Camera Footage.

[326] Uvalde Police Department Body-Worn Camera Footage.

[327] Robb Elementary School CCTV Footage.

[328] CIR Document and Data Review.

[329] Uvalde Police Department Radio Traffic.

[330] Robb Elementary School CCTV Footage.

[331] Robb Elementary School CCTV Footage.

Robb Elementary: West Building South Entrance

Officers are with a victim outside of the south door, performing chest compressions.[332]

Events: Medical Triage and Evacuation

Communications: Radio Traffic

An unknown officer advises that more officers are needed to come help with parents and family members and provide crowd control at the perimeter.[333]

Another unknown officer inquires about air evacuation, stating the helicopters need to start landing at the school.[334]

Events: Crowd Control; Room Clearings and Evacuations; Air Support

12:58 p.m.

Robb Elementary: West Building Southside Hallway

UPD Sgt. 1, now with the master keys, opens the door to classroom 104. Officers from various agencies clear classrooms 103/104.[335]

Events: Room Clearings and Evacuations

Robb Elementary: Perimeter

Two TXDPS troopers are on a school bus brought in to assist with evacuation. Six child victims have been evacuated to the bus, two of whom have gunshot wounds. The bus brings all six of the children to the hospital.[336]

Events: Medical Triage and Evacuation

12:59 p.m.

Robb Elementary: West Building Southside Hallway

Officers enter and clear classrooms 108 and 102.[337]

Events: Room Clearings and Evacuations

---

[332] Texas Department of Public Safety Body-Worn Camera Footage.

[333] Uvalde Police Department Radio Traffic.

[334] Uvalde Police Department Radio Traffic.

[335] Uvalde Police Department Body Worn Camera Footage.

[336] Texas Department of Public Safety Body-Worn Camera Footage.

[337] Uvalde Police Department Body-Worn Camera Footage.

1:00 p.m.

Robb Elementary: West Building Southside Hallway

Chief Arredondo calls for all entrances to be blocked off, giving this direction to UPD Sgt. 1. Chief Arredondo is on the phone with an unknown individual, discussing taping off the entirety of school grounds for the crime scene. Chief Arredondo reiterates that no one should be entering.[338]

Events: Closing off the Crime Scene

1:01 p.m.

Robb Elementary: West Building Hallway, Outside Classrooms 111 and 112

Sheriff Nolasco calls Chief Arredondo over to introduce him to a TXDPS captain, who states, "We are here to help." Chief Arredondo replies, "Thank you."[339] Chief Arredondo tells Nolasco and the TXDPS captain that they are closing off the crime scene.[340] They continue discussing the status of the building and room clearings. Sheriff Nolasco mentions a room that may not yet be cleared, and Chief Arredondo responds that Constable Field is clearing rooms.

Events: Closing off the Crime Scene

1:02 p.m.

Robb Elementary: West Building Hallway, Outside Classrooms 111 and 112

Officers attempt to walk through fire doors from the north side of the hallway. Chief Arredondo meets them at the fire doors and asks if they are done clearing the building.[341]

A TXDPS captain, speaking to an unknown officer on the other side of the fire doors, instructs the officer to start a crime scene log—"anybody comes in, write their name down"—but then insists that the officer should not let anybody in.[342]

Events: Room Clearings and Evacuations; Closing off the Crime Scene; Investigative Activity

Robb Elementary: West Building T-Intersection
Robb Elementary: West Building Northwest Entry

Three Texas Rangers are observed on scene at the T-intersection.[343]

---

[338] Uvalde Police Department Body-Worn Camera Footage.

[339] Uvalde Police Department Body-Worn Camera Footage.

[340] Uvalde Police Department Body-Worn Camera Footage.

[341] Uvalde Police Department Body-Worn Camera Footage.

[342] Uvalde Police Department Body-Worn Camera Footage.

[343] Uvalde Police Department Body-Worn Camera Footage.

At the northwest entry door, an unknown officer states that the Rangers want the door closed and entry closed off.[344]

Chief Arredondo introduces himself to one of the Rangers at the T-intersection.[345]

Events: Officer Arrivals; Closing off the Crime Scene

Communications: Radio Traffic

UPD radio traffic indicates "one in custody," seemingly referring to the subject.[346] This is followed up shortly after with "Shooter male subject detained and in custody."[347]

Events: N/A

1:03 p.m.

No reportable data.

1:04 p.m.

Communications: Radio Traffic

Updated radio traffic states that there are multiple deceased victims and multiple injured, and that EMS are working on the scene. It also states that the shooter is deceased.[348]

Events: Presence of Victims: Acknowledgment and Discussion; EMS Arrivals and Actions

1:05 p.m.

Robb Elementary: West Building T-Intersection

Chief Arredondo approaches the Texas Rangers and inquires about obtaining assistance with resources. One Ranger replies that a captain and a lieutenant outside of the northwest door are establishing a command post and that Chief Arredondo can address his request to them.[349]

An EMT enters through the northwest door and confers briefly with a Ranger, before entering classroom 131 to confirm the deceased. Shortly after, a second medic is requested to the same room.[350]

Events: Establishing Incident Command Post; EMS Arrivals and Actions; Investigative Activity

---

[344] Uvalde Police Department Body-Worn Camera Footage.

[345] Uvalde Police Department Body-Worn Camera Footage.

[346] Uvalde Police Department Radio Traffic.

[347] Uvalde Police Department Radio Traffic.

[348] Uvalde Police Department Radio Traffic.

[349] Uvalde Police Department Body-Worn Camera Footage.

[350] Uvalde Police Department Body-Worn Camera Footage.

1:06 p.m.

Communications: Radio Traffic
Robb Elementary: Perimeter

An unknown officer calls out that multiple vehicles are blocking Geraldine and Grove Streets, which are needed for ingress and egress.[351]

Events: Medical Triage and Evacuation

1:07 p.m.

Communications: Radio Traffic
Funeral Home

UPD Lt. 2 calls out for all agencies on scene to send a representative to the command post at the funeral home.[352]

An unknown officer requests BORTAC over the radio, asking that one of their vehicles be moved so buses can get through. The BORTAC commander confirms they will move the vehicles.[353]

Events: Establishing Incident Command Post; Medical Triage and Evacuation

1:08 p.m.

Robb Elementary: West Building Southside Hallway

EMTs are escorted through the fire doors to rooms 111/112 to confirm the deceased.[354]

Events: EMS Arrivals and Actions

1:09 p.m.

No reportable data.

1:10 p.m.

Robb Elementary: West Building South Entrance

Chief Arredondo confers with the UCISD PD lieutenant, the TXDPS captain, and Sheriff Nolasco. They discuss the status of the crime scene, location of the command post, location of the Reunification Center, and press conference.[355]

---

[351] Uvalde Police Department Radio Traffic.

[352] Uvalde Police Department Radio Traffic.

[353] Uvalde Police Department Radio Traffic.

[354] Uvalde Police Department Body-Worn Camera Footage.

[355] Uvalde Police Department Body-Worn Camera Footage.

Multiple other officers convene at the location, including two Texas Rangers, one of whom was on scene during the incident. There is a deceased victim on the ground outside the doorway on the exterior of the building, and Chief Arredondo expresses the need to cover the victim up.[356]

Events: Establishing Incident Command Post; Reunification

1:11 p.m.

Funeral Home

Law enforcement personnel from multiple agencies, including UPD, TXDPS, and USMS, begin to establish an incident command post (see "Chapter 3. Leadership, Incident Command, and Coordination").[357]

Events: Establishing Incident Command Post

Communications: Radio Traffic
Robb Elementary: Perimeter

More radio traffic requests CBP to move their vehicle, which is blocking an ingress/egress route; shortly after, radio traffic states that a BPA has arrived and is moving the vehicle.[358]

Events: Medical Triage and Evacuation

1:12 p.m.–1:13 p.m.

No reportable data.

1:14 p.m.

Robb Elementary: West Building South Entrance

A Texas Ranger states that the Rangers are setting up the command post at the funeral home. They ask Chief Arredondo if he is ok with that, to which Arredondo responds, "That's fine. Let's do it."[359]

Events: Establishing Incident Command Post

---

[356] CIR Fact Finding.

[357] Hillcrest Memorial Funeral Home CCTV Footage.

[358] Uvalde Police Department Radio Traffic.

[359] Uvalde Police Department Body-Worn Camera Footage.

1:15 p.m.

Communications: Radio Traffic

Radio communication states that no additional ambulances are needed at the location of Robb Elementary.[360]

Events: EMS Arrivals and Actions.

Phase V: 1:16 p.m.—3:15 p.m.

Phase V comprises the time period from the beginning activities of the investigation and establishment of investigative command of the scene, through a secondary threat at the high school.

1:16 p.m.

Communications: Radio Traffic

An unknown officer asks where kids should be taken for reunification and is told to take them to Uvalde High School rather than the Civic Center.[361]

Events: Reunification

1:17 p.m.

Communications: Radio Traffic

An unknown officer asks who is the lead for the investigation, referencing the vehicle at the ditch, which contains a weapon and ammunition. The officer is told by a UPD officer that the Texas Rangers will be leading the investigation.[362]

Events: Closing off the Crime Scene; Investigative Activity

1:18 p.m.

No reportable data.

1:19 p.m.

Communications: Radio Traffic

EMS unit reports it has arrived on scene.[363]

---

[360] Uvalde Police Department Radio Traffic.

[361] Uvalde Police Department Radio Traffic.

[362] Uvalde Police Department Radio Traffic.

[363] Uvalde Police Department Radio Traffic.

UPD Lt. 2 requests white boards for the incident command post at the funeral home.[364]

Events: EMS Arrivals and Actions; Establishing Incident Command

1:20 p.m.

No reportable data.

1:21 p.m.

Robb Elementary: West Building South Entrance

UCISD PD Chief Arredondo receives a phone call from an unknown individual, to whom Arredondo conveys that they are establishing incident command at the funeral home. He further states that TXDPS has everything it needs and is helping, and that UCISD PD is going to work the investigation in conjunction with TXDPS. Chief Arredondo departs shortly after stating to the individual on the phone that he will walk to them.[365]

Events: Establishing Incident Command System

1:22 p.m.

Funeral Home

Law enforcement personnel at the command post begin to implement Incident Command System (ICS) protocols (see "Chapter 3. Leadership, Incident Command, and Coordination").[366]

Events: Establishing Incident Command

1:23 p.m. –1:24 p.m.

No reportable data.

1:25 p.m.

Communications: Radio Traffic

UPD Lt. 2 states that the suspect's vehicle at the ditch needs to be secured and wrapped up in police tape.[367]

Events: Closing Off the Crime Scene; Investigative Activity

1:26 p.m.–1:30 p.m.

No reportable data.

---

[364] Uvalde Police Department Radio Traffic.

[365] Uvalde Police Department Body-Worn Camera Footage.

[366] Hillcrest Memorial Funeral Home CCTV Footage.

[367] Uvalde Police Department Radio Traffic.

Robb Elementary: West Building Southside Hallway

A Texas Ranger moves a deceased victim from outside the south door back into the school building.[368]

A Texas State Trooper takes a statement from UPD Sgt. 1.[369]

Events: Closing Off the Crime Scene; Investigative Activity

Funeral Home

Law enforcement personnel at the incident command post begin to establish a unified command system (see "Chapter 3. Leadership, Incident Command, and Coordination").[370]

Events: Establishing Incident Command

Communications: Radio Traffic

A UPD sergeant advises that 40 children still need to be transported.[371] An unknown officer responds that they can escort one of the buses to the children.

Events: Reunification

Communications: Radio Traffic

A UPD sergeant requests contact with UCISD, advising they have a bus with 40 students who need transport.[372]

Events: Reunification

Communications: Radio Traffic

UPD Acting Chief Mariano Pargas requests the address on Diaz Street where the subject is believed to have been residing. Uvalde dispatch reports back with the address.[373]

Events: Investigative Activity

---

[368] Uvalde Police Department Body-Worn Camera Footage.

[369] Uvalde Police Department Body-Worn Camera Footage.

[370] Hillcrest Memorial Funeral Home CCTV Footage.

[371] CIR Document and Data Review.

[372] CIR Document and Data Review.

[373] CIR Document and Data Review.

1:34 p.m.–1:39 p.m.

Grandparents' Residence
Communications: Radio Traffic

A UPD detective unit reports being at the location on Diaz Street.[374]

Events: Investigative Activity

1:40 p.m.–1:45 p.m.

No reportable data.

1:46 p.m.

Communications: Radio Traffic

The FBI's Evidence Response Team Unit is reported to be en route.[375]

Events: Investigative Activity

1:47 p.m.

No reportable data.

1:48 p.m.

Grandparents' Residence
Communications: Radio Traffic

A UPD unit is on scene at the residence of the subject's grandparents and reports it to be unoccupied.[376]

Events: Investigative Activity

1:49 p.m.–1:53 p.m.

No reportable data.

---

[374] CIR Document and Data Review.

[375] CIR Document and Data Review.

[376] Uvalde Police Department Radio Traffic.

Robb Elementary: Perimeter
Communications: Radio Traffic

Uvalde dispatch advises that buses containing Robb Elementary children are getting ready to depart and will head to the Civic Center.[377]

Events: Reunification

1:55 p.m.–1:59 p.m.

No reportable data.

2:00 p.m.–3:15 p.m.

After 2:00 p.m., the crime scene investigation is underway. Although there is no official time of record, at some time around 1:00 p.m., and after consultation with the Texas Rangers, the Uvalde County district attorney determines that the investigation should be conducted solely by the Rangers and not in conjunction with any of the other local agencies, including UCISD PD (see "Chapter 4. Post-Incident Response and Investigation").

At 2:12 p.m. there are unconfirmed reports of a secondary threat at the Uvalde High School, which turn out to be false. Multiple agencies respond to the high school, as it is locked down. The Civic Center is also locked down as a protective measure at around 2:25 p.m. Officers are stationed at all UCISD campuses at this time.

At the high school, responding officers form a perimeter around the campus as parents and family members begin to gather, many of whom are expressing concern and anger.

By 3:15 p.m., schools begin to release kids upon realizing that the secondary threat has not surfaced.

Events: UCISD: Other Campus Lockdowns; Crowd Control; Investigative Activity

---

[377] Uvalde Police Department Radio Traffic.

Chapter 2. Tactics and Equipment

Introduction

Police active shooter response tactics have evolved and changed over the years, driven by a variety of high-profile incidents and a growing understanding of these unique situations. Throughout most of history, the police response to an active shooter incident was to secure a perimeter and call out a special weapons and tactics (SWAT) team and, in some cases, negotiators. Most officers lacked specialized, advanced training and preparation to handle such situations.

The watershed moment in tactical changes occurred following the Columbine (Colorado) High School massacre in 1999. The first call to 911 from Columbine High School was received within one minute of the first shot being fired. While the first law enforcement officer arrived on-scene within five minutes, it took 47 minutes for the first law enforcement officer to make entry into the high school, even though shooting by the two subjects ended just 13 minutes after the first shot was fired. From the first shot fired, each passing minute robbed innocent students and staff who had been injured in the attack of the opportunity to be located, triaged, and evacuated by first responders to a higher level of trauma care.

In January 2000, Colorado Governor Bill Owens established the Columbine Review Commission to review the aftermath of the tragic Columbine High School mass shooting that resulted in the murder of 12 students and one teacher.

The Commission's proceedings revealed that traditional training for officers responding to major incidents, like Columbine, emphasized that the task of first responders was to contain and control until the arrival of a SWAT team.[378] Several law enforcement experts noted that prior to Columbine, in most emergencies, time was on the side of the responding officers. Past practice and training counseled the first responding officers on the scene of a crisis, such as a hostage scenario, to contain and control the scene until a SWAT or tactical team arrived. Those specialized units would have the proper equipment and training to resolve the situation. However, with Columbine, time was not on the side of the police because the suspects controlled a large public building with numerous victims. Moreover, it was an active situation.

During one of the Commission's 15 public hearings, law enforcement expert tacticians and associations, such as the National Tactical Officers Association (NTOA), testified that the new paradigm for responding to crises like Columbine is "rapid deployment." This training paradigm focuses on "preparing responding officers—not SWAT teams—for immediate entry into structures under the circumstances similar to Columbine, i.e., active perpetrators in control of a school or other large public building where many potential victims are present."[379]

---

[378] *Report of Governor Bill Owens' Columbine Review Commission.*

[379] *Report of Governor Bill Owens' Columbine Review Commission.*

After hearing from the law enforcement experts, the Governor's Commission recommended that "all first responding law enforcement officers, and especially all school resource officers, receive training in the concepts and skills of a rapid emergency deployment."[380] Rapid emergency deployment puts significant responsibility on first-responding officers, who may not be fully equipped or trained as a SWAT team member. First responders are also instructed to go toward the violent offender, if necessary, bypassing injured victims and placing themselves in harm's way. When seconds count, the ability to quickly and effectively get to the assailant and stop the violence is paramount.

The Commission made no specific proposals regarding the weaponry and protective gear that responding officers in such a situation should have. However, it did recommend that if responding officers are trained in rapid deployment tactics enabling them to pursue and apprehend armed perpetrators in large public buildings like a school, they should have weapons and protective equipment available for such a situation.[381] The tactic of surrounding the school and waiting for a SWAT team was criticized for the prolonged response time.

Active shooter incidents required new response tactics to be researched, developed, tested, trained, and implemented across the law enforcement profession. What was previously an incident for SWAT to respond to was becoming recognized as a front-line patrol officer responsibility. Tactics for response to an active attacker incident could no longer rely on the tools, expertise, personnel, and specialized training of a fully assembled SWAT team. Instead, the profession needed to develop actionable guidance, direction, and training that enabled a patrol officer to respond to an active shooter as quickly and safely as possible, by moving toward the threat, stopping the killing, and stopping the dying. In the active attacker incident, time is not on law enforcement's side.

Training needed to be focused on quickly neutralizing the threat with the tools routinely carried by the first responding patrol officer, or readily available, in their patrol vehicle. Training also needed to focus on law enforcement triaging of the injured, providing basic life-saving medical aid to stabilize their condition, and rapid evacuation to a higher level of medical care.

Today, training officers in active shooter response generally includes the following concepts and tactics:[382]

- Gathering intelligence while en route

- Seeking out intelligence upon arrival on scene

- Communicating the location of the threat, conditions of the scene, actions of on-scene law enforcement, and needs from follow-on responders (L-CAN)

- Moving toward the threat efficiently and effectively

---

[380] U.S. Fire Administration, *Fire/Emergency Medical Services Department Operational Considerations*.

[381] *Report of Governor Bill Owens' Columbine Review Commission*.

[382] The CIR team reviewed training curricula and observed several training deliveries for active shooter response training from three national-level training providers: ALERRT, LSU NCBRT, and NTOA. For analysis of training needs, see "Chapter 8. Pre-Incident Planning and Preparation."

- Eliminating the threat

- Identifying locations of victims and assessing for physical injuries

- Triaging injured victims for evacuation to a higher level of medical care

- Evacuating injured to a higher level of medical care

Since Columbine, law enforcement has continued to learn from these incidents, identify lessons learned, and refine training and tactics accordingly. Although there is little data or research specifically on law enforcement training and policies *prior* to Columbine, it is widely recognized that law enforcement policies, training, and response has evolved since that time to incorporate the need to immediately address the threat and differentiate barricade situations from active shooter scenarios. First and foremost, there has been the consistent recognition that law enforcement needs the training and tools to immediately identify and neutralize the threat. This was the principal finding from the Columbine tragedy. Active shooter incidents at Virginia Tech (2007), the Washington Navy Yard Building (2013), Route 1 Harvest Festival in Las Vegas (2017), Marjory Stoneman Douglas High School in Parkland, Florida (2018), and others have all highlighted the importance of this in saving lives.[383] Additionally, as described in the Advanced Law Enforcement Rapid Response Training (ALERRT) Center's courses, developed in conjunction with the Federal Bureau of Investigation (FBI), the "priority of life scale" shifted post-Columbine so that innocent civilians were at the top of the scale, followed by law enforcement, and, last, attackers.[384]

Post-Columbine, rapid deployment in a crisis is predicated on the first four or five responders forming an active shooter response team and making entry. In a situation where seconds count, any delay in response could be detrimental to potential victims. However, due to the different response times to an active shooter situation, the hard-and-fast recommendation of having a four-to-five-member rapid deployment response team has been reduced to where some agencies authorize a single officer to enter an active shooter location.[385] Recent tactical training also emphasizes solo officer response when the situation demands. These tactics have arisen due to incidents where immediate action by a lone officer could have helped save lives.

The establishment and proper use of an incident command structure has also been a common lesson learned across incidents, as was prominently the case in the active shooter response at the Washington Navy Yard Building in 2013. Though law enforcement entered the building within minutes, it took over an hour to locate and kill the shooter, due to the size of the building. Among the key lessons learned was the value of establishing an incident command structure early on to coordinate resources. Incident command is discussed more fully in "Chapter 3. Leadership, Incident Command, and Coordination."

---

[383] ALERRT, Active Shooter Response Level 1 Version 7.2; MPD, After Action Report, Washington Navy Yard; Virginia Tech Review Panel, Mass Shootings at Virginia Tech; LVMPD, 1 October: After-Action Review.

[384] ALERRT, Active Shooter Response Level 1 Version 7.2.

[385] Martaindale and Blair, "The Evolution of Active Shooter Response Training," 342–356.

Another common theme in lessons learned from past active shooter incidents is the need for timely medical triage and evacuation. Incidents at the Century 16 Theater in Aurora, Colorado (2012), Washington Navy Yard Building (2013), Pulse Nightclub in Orlando, Florida (2016), and Route 91 Harvest Music Festival in Las Vegas, Nevada (2017) highlighted the need for law enforcement responders to be equipped with tourniquets, have basic training to immediately treat and triage victims, and deploy tactics that will get victims to medical professionals as soon as possible in order to save lives.

The importance of civilian actions during an active shooter incident came to light in the wake of the Virginia Tech mass shooting, when a student murdered 32 individuals on campus in just 11 minutes. Some students barricaded doors and effectively denied the shooter's entry into their rooms. After the Route 91 Harvest Music Festival shooting, civilians were essential in assisting with medical application to the injured and helped mitigate lives lost as a result.

The school shooting at Marjory Stoneman Douglas High School brought to light the need for a solo officer response to such incidents, following criticism of the single school resource officer on duty for not confronting the shooter. Just recently, the effectiveness of a quick, solo response to an active shooter situation was evident in the May 6, 2023, shooting at a mall in Allen, Texas, where a lone police officer at the mall on an unrelated assignment heard the gunfire and rushed toward the suspect, killing him.[386] Tragically, using an AR-15–style rifle, the assailant killed eight innocent victims and injured at least seven others. But this shooter was stopped by a lone officer.

Twenty-four years have passed since the tragic events at Columbine High School, and yet our nation and law enforcement continue to grapple with the persisting problem of mass shootings, highlighting the need for consistent training and preparation.

Scope

This review examined the tactics and pieces of equipment that were contemplated, sought, and deployed over the course of the incident response, beginning with the initial officers' approach from outside Robb Elementary and ending approximately 77 minutes later with the medical triage of victims inside classrooms 111/112. The assessment that follows was based on primary and secondary interview data with involved officers, analysis of body-worn camera (BWC) and closed-circuit television (CCTV) footage, and, where applicable, agency policies and training on various tactical responses, equipment, and tools. In preparing this chapter, the Critical Incident Review (CIR) team benefited from the expertise of subject matter experts, who assisted in developing the observations and recommendations for this chapter. Where not otherwise cited, the practices identified in this chapter derive from the experts' collective knowledge and experience.

Throughout the incident response, there were at times much discussion and deliberation among officers on scene—making it sometimes difficult to hear and understand what was being said and by whom. At other times, there was silence and the mindset of officers in the hallway at that time was unclear.

---

[386] "What to Know about the Allen, Texas, Mall Shooting."

Relatedly, there were at times some direction and coordination happening and at other times none. When it is clear that a particular tactic or piece of equipment was deliberated or its use was directed by an individual or group on scene, we make note of that in the analysis below.

This chapter reviews major tactical responses and deployments, including tools and equipment, over the course of the law enforcement response to Robb Elementary.

- Active Shooter Tactics—this section describes fundamental principles of active shooter response, room clearing and evacuations, and stack formation room entry; it then provides an analysis of the tactics deployed during the law enforcement response at Robb Elementary.

- Equipment Use and Deployments—this section describes the fundamentals of select types of equipment used or considered during the law enforcement response at Robb Elementary; it then provides an analysis of the equipment deployed during the law enforcement response at Robb Elementary.

Each section discusses the general principles and best practices related to the particular topic and any relevant background before analyzing what occurred on the ground at Robb Elementary. The chapter concludes with observations and recommendations.

Before delving into the review of each of the topics listed above, it is important to emphasize that officers on scene should have recognized the incident as an active shooter scenario and moved and pushed forward immediately and continuously toward the threat until the room was entered, and the threat was eliminated. That did not occur. Instead, officers, including leadership on scene, treated the incident as a barricade situation, which resulted in significant delay before the shooter was actively engaged by law enforcement. This is the single most critical tactical failure in the incident response. Nothing offered in the assessment below should be construed to mitigate or justify that failure of action.

Active Shooter Tactics

Active Shooter Tactical Principles

When a law enforcement officer responds to an active shooter event, the lessons learned from Columbine are that first responders should react quickly and confront the shooter to prevent further killing and to render first aid to victims. The difficulty confronting first responders is balancing the goals of officers' safety with engaging the shooter to save innocent lives. Police academy training emphasizes preservation of life, officer safety, and the use of force commensurate with the situation. However, in an active shooter event, officers should be trained to confront and stop the subject's actions immediately.[387] This immediacy of action mitigates the risk to potential victims. ALERRT trains officers on

---

[387] Martaindale and Blair, "The Evolution of Active Shooter Response Training," 342–356.

the priority of life scale, which lists victims (injured and uninjured) first, followed by law enforcement, and then the subject(s).[388] The following subsections outline some of the key aspects of tactical responses to an active shooter incident.

Active Shooter versus Barricaded Subject

Barricade and active shooter situations require different procedures, tactics, and mindset for a law enforcement response.

In an *active shooter* situation, there is an ongoing, dynamic scenario unfolding wherein the subject is targeting and killing people. Priority concerns of law enforcement are the neutralization of the threat, the prevention of more injuries and death, and beginning to triage and provide appropriate medical aid to the injured. As described in the introduction to this chapter, an active shooter requires immediate response, even if that means entry by a single officer, as the primary goal is to stop the shooter as quickly as possible. Quick and clear communication with other first responders is essential in active shooter situations, as they need to rapidly assemble into a response team using sound tactical formation, assessing their environment, and moving rapidly toward the threat. The International Association of Chiefs of Police's (IACP) model policy for active shooter defines "active shooting" as "an incident in which one or more armed persons have used, or are reasonably likely to use, deadly force in an ongoing manner, and where persons have been injured, killed, or are under imminent threat of death or serious bodily harm by such persons."[389] Notably, as per IACP's model policy, active shooting is inclusive of a subject's past actions (i.e., "have used") and presumed imminent actions (i.e., "are reasonably likely to use") regarding the use of deadly force in an ongoing manner. An individual that has engaged in active shooting and *has access to victims* should *never* be considered anything other than an active threat and the law enforcement response to such circumstances should align with active shooter response principles.

A *barricaded subject*, on the other hand, generally involves a subject or suspect who is being sought by law enforcement, has placed themselves in a physical location that is not immediately accessible, and has refused orders to exit.[390] In such situations, the law enforcement response includes operational containment of the subject while attempting to negotiate a peaceful resolution. In a barricade situation, there is typically communication between an officer (often times a negotiator) and the subject. Unlike active shooter situations, time is on the side of law enforcement, who can marshal resources such as negotiators, SWAT teams, and specialized equipment and tools, and continually assess options to resolve the situation. As described by IACP's advisory board, a "triggering point" in a barricade situation is whether the subject engages in hostile actions toward victims, bystanders, or officers, which "justifies the initiation of direct law enforcement action" to prevent or stop such behavior.[391] Like many situations in law enforcement, the nature of the threat can evolve over the course of an incident and, therefore, a

---

[388] ALERRT, *Active Shooter Response Level 1 Version 7.2*.

[389] IACP, *Model Policy on Active Shooter*.

[390] IACP, *Model Policy on Response to Barricaded Individuals*.

[391] IACP, *Model Policy on Response to Barricaded Individuals*.

barricaded subject can become an active shooter incident and necessitate an entirely different response, such as whichever officers are on scene at that moment transitioning into an immediate tactical solution.

In summary, an active shooter rarely ceases to be an active shooter and always remains an active shooter so long as the shooter has access to victims. Active shooter response protocols indicate that an active shooter's immediate past actions and reasonably assumed imminent actions, along with the presence of victims, all determine what actions law enforcement should take.

Room Clearing and Evacuation

During an active shooter incident, the first priority of responding officers is to eliminate the threat. The first responding officers will not be in a position to aid and facilitate in the evacuation of other victims who are locked down in or within the vicinity of the building/location.

If there are officers or others on scene that can assist with evacuations, to the extent that can be done safely and not at the expense of eliminating the active shooter threat, evacuations should begin as soon as possible.[392] Evacuations of victims and others who remain within the hot zone of a mass violence area are a priority action for responders. A hot zone is a hazardous area that is usually considered unsafe and only designated responders are authorized to remain for reasons of rescue, recovery, and containment. A warm zone is usually a transition space leading to a cold zone, which is a safe area.[393]

Victims should be guided to a designated safe and secured location outside of the hot zone to receive medical triage, emotional support, and basic needs such as water and restrooms.

Other important practices for evacuations from an active shooter incident include:

- Identify safe routes that are not in the line of active shooter or law enforcement fire, which may or may not be those that have been exercised and predetermined by school safety plans[394]

- Communication among all first responders on the status, direction, and destination for evacuees, while not broadcasting such information to the active shooter

- Clearly mark rooms and buildings which have been cleared, secured, and evacuated; this can be done using items such as tape, markers, chalk, or things found within the building that can clearly distinguish that a room is cleared

---

[392] IACP, *Active Shooter Model Policy.*

[393] McGee and Reilly, "Terrorism and Homeland Security."

[394] IACP, *Model Policy on Active Shooter.*

- Quickly assess the physical structure of the building including walls and doors, for their penetrability to gunfire

- Gather any intelligence from evacuees that can be ascertained about the building, the shooter, or other facts and circumstances of the location and incident

- Ensure medical triage and transport is established for any injured evacuees

On average, an active shooter incident is over within approximately 12 minutes from first notification, whether ended by the shooter dying by suicide, law enforcement responders killing or apprehending the shooter, or civilians/bystanders on scene restraining or, in some rare cases, killing the active shooter.[395] If civilians on scene have not self-evacuated, it is likely that evacuations will occur after the shooter is neutralized. However, in more extended response situations where the shooter is being searched for or, in the case of the Robb Elementary active shooter incident, inside a classroom, there may be a limited window of opportunity to quickly assess and balance the risk posed by crossfire that would put victims in harm's way—whether by remaining locked down or evacuating—while officers on scene approach the classroom where the shooter is and make entry, likely engaging in a gunfight as a result. This should never detract from the priority goal of eliminating the threat, for which action should be immediate. The interior walls in the West Building, as is the case in many school buildings throughout the country, were sheetrock and easily penetrated by gunfire. Rounds from the shooter's rifle penetrated multiple walls throughout the West Building. Given the configuration of the building and location of the subject, any person remaining inside the building was a risk for lethal injury from either the subject or law enforcement rounds.

Stack Formation and Room Entry

Dynamic room entries are among the most dangerous operations in law enforcement, where a team of officers enter a room and must engage in close-quarters combat with an armed assailant, who may be in a tactically advantageous position.

While there are some different schools of thought on the officers' patterns of movement upon entering the room, trainers and practitioners generally acknowledge that it is often a matter of preference and officers should use the tactics they have been trained on. The key to successful stack formation and room entry is seamless coordination and synchronization between the team members in any condition. This can be challenging with an entry team composed of officers from various agencies, especially if they have not trained together and may use different tactics and communication (i.e., verbal and non-verbal).

Ideally, the entry team wants to enter the room with an element of surprise, speed, and violence of action. These fundamentals of a successful room entry can be compromised if a doorway is not properly assessed and breached, as needed.

---

[395] FBI, Active Shooter Incidents: 20-Year Review.

Checking the doorknob to see if it is unlocked should be the first immediate approach. This is not only the easiest method, but also enables the entry team to maximize the surprise and speed with which they enter, putting them in a tactically advantageous position. If a door is found to be locked, there are various breaching tactics that may be deployed, dependent upon the tools available, experience and expertise of officers on scene, type of door, and urgency of the situation. Some examples include mechanical breaching (i.e., with a Halligan tool or sledgehammer), ballistic breaching (i.e., with a firearm), and explosive breaching. Training also teaches officers to seek alternate entry points (i.e., windows, doors, etc.) and to use distraction as a tactic.

As previously discussed in this chapter, in an active shooter situation, law enforcement has been trained to respond and immediately confront and stop the threat. There is no need to wait for special tactical units to breach a room.

An Uvalde Police Department (UPD) SWAT team, however, existed on the day of the incident. UPD Policy 8.3 Special Weapons and Tactics Team, effective date: 12/18/2013, established the governing regulations in the selection, training, equipping, and use of the UPD SWAT team. This policy establishes a UPD SWAT team. The policy requires one supervisor, one hostage negotiator, one tactical medic, one designated marksman (sniper), and a "sufficient number of officers" of any rank to carry out the responsibilities of the team. Additional officers could serve as "alternates" for the team and "are not permanently assigned" to the team. Additionally, the policy states that the alternates would be chosen by the same selection process as the "full-time SWAT members." The 10/24/19 UPD SWAT Inventory Sheet contained, among other equipment, the following:

- Sledgehammer
- Battering ram
- Halligan bar
- Two police entry shields

Based upon the 10/24/19 UPD SWAT Inventory Sheet, there were 10 members of the team. Notably, UPD is a police department of approximately 26-30 officers. As per the 2023 NTOA Tactical Response and Operations Standards for Law Enforcement Agencies, the recommended minimum staffing for a Tier 1 SWAT team is 34 personnel; Tier 2 SWAT team is 25 personnel; Tier 3 Tactical Response team is 16 personnel; and for a Tier 4 Perimeter Control and Containment team is 15 or less personnel. The NTOA standards state that Tier 4 teams are *not* SWAT teams. Moreover, the standards delineate that Tier 4 teams are not capable of having a designated sniper, negotiator, or tactical medic.[396]

As recommended by the most recent NTOA standards,[397] the UPD, with its limited staffing, should not be considered a SWAT team; rather, it falls in the range of a Tier 4 Perimeter Control and Containment

---

[396] NTOA, Tactical Response and Operations Standard.

[397] These standards were promulgated and published in 2023 and were not in existence at the time of the incident.

team. However, as per the NTOA standards, a Tier 4 team may have the capabilities to conduct crisis entries in hostage rescue operations and active assailant situations.

The UPD SWAT team, with their limited personnel and capabilities, is not an anomaly in law enforcement agencies. Most agency/department SWAT teams do not align with the 2023 NTOA Tactical Response and Operations Standards for Law Enforcement Agencies recommendations. Many agencies/departments have units that they called SWAT but lack the requisite capabilities, which can undermine the confidence of its community.

Tactics Used at Robb Elementary

From the onset of the law enforcement response to Robb Elementary through the medical triage and emergency evacuation of victims, officers initiated several tactical movements and responses, many of which incorrectly aligned with a barricade situation as opposed to an active shooter response.

Initial Response

The officers who arrived first on scene and made entry into the West Building initially acted in accordance with active shooter response principles. They did not wait outside as gunfire continued to erupt from inside the building, they immediately moved toward the threat and inside the West Building. Four officers entered through the south entrance, including two UPD sergeants, an Uvalde Consolidated Independent School District Police Department (UCISD PD) officer, and UCISD PD Chief Arredondo. Three UPD officers, including one lieutenant, one sergeant, and one detective entered through the northwest entrance. They were followed shortly after by four more officers through the northwest entrance, including Acting Chief Pargas from UPD. In total, 11 officers from two agencies, including the chief and acting chief for those respective agencies, arrived on scene within three minutes of the subject entering the building.

From the north side of the hallway, the first three officers entering immediately moved toward the sound of gunfire coming from classrooms 111/112. On the south side of the hallway, the first two officers entering also immediately approached the doorway to 111/112. In their interviews, a majority of officers who arrived first on scene reported the smell of gunfire and observed spent shell-casings on the ground, bullet holes in the walls, and a hazy fog in the hallway. Officers bypassed closed doors, quickly looking through the classroom door windows to gain information as to the whereabouts of the shooter. Efforts were made to see inside the broken door window of room 111, however, due to the lights being out and the blinds being shut, the room was dark, and officers could not see inside.

Although officers moved rapidly toward the gunfire, this approach was not coordinated and officers did not establish a tactical formation, which created potential issues with crossfire as they neared the doorway.

The first officers on scene approached the doors to 111/112 with the intent to enter, not knowing the status of the doorway or exactly what or who was on the other side. As they arrived at the doorway at 11:36 a.m., they observed two closed doors side-by-side and darkened rooms. The doorway was set back in a vestibule that measured approximately three feet in depth. One of the officers said to "line up to make entry,"[398] and within seconds, shots were fired from inside one of the rooms. Two of the officers were struck with shrapnel and all tactically retreated to positions of cover. UPD Lt. 1, who was hit with shrapnel, reengaged shortly after, while the other officers remained in a position of cover. Given the initial injuries sustained by the two officers, it would typically be reasonable for law enforcement to retreat, creating an opportunity for a "tactical pause."[399] This is expected and trained in all basic police officer training levels. When officers have distance, cover, and time, they create the opportunity for options, evaluation, and an informed approach; however, the exception is in an active shooter situation. In this situation the first officers on the scene (FOS) experienced three different volleys of fire, which should have alerted them to engage the active shooter immediately by penetrating the classroom door. Considering the visual, audible, and other sensory activations at the scene of the hallway, generally accepted practice would have been for the law enforcement to immediately and without hesitation penetrate the classroom with the objective of stopping the shooter. See the "Stimuli Throughout the Incident" in "Appendix D. Leadership, Incident Command, and Coordination Supplemental Materials."

Transition to Barricaded Subject Response and Evacuations

Instead, this is the point at which the active shooter response effectively ceased and officers on scene transitioned to a barricaded subject response. Shortly after, some officers called out that the subject was "contained" and "barricaded," which was then repeated over the radio. This terminology persisted over much of the remainder of the incident. From approximately 11:38 a.m. until 12:47 p.m., close to the time law enforcement made entry, the subject was wrongly described as "barricaded" or "contained" at least 26 times. In half of these instances, this was broadcasted over police radio and received by other officers both on scene and en route. Some officers were also communicating this information with others via text or phone calls. Although most references to a barricaded or contained subject also included the "triggering point" that the subject was either still shooting or had injured an officer, there were at least nine occasions in which this key piece of information was not shared. In those nine instances, the receiver of the information only heard that there was a barricaded or contained subject, likely adding substantial confusion to the overall response, as more and more officers converged on scene with a fundamentally different understanding of the situation. As more officers arrived on scene, those who entered the West Building mostly remained positioned down the hallway, either on the south or north sides. Figure 2-1 on page 97 illustrates the "barricade" and "contained" references, along with the modality of communication. These should be understood as the least number of references, as it represents what was available in the records and files provided to the CIR team.

Other actions taken on both sides of the hallway comport with the decision to treat the incident as a barricaded subject. On the north side, officers were seeking UPD's negotiator, who eventually attempted to contact the subject via phone and was unsuccessful. There is also discussion about negotiations among officers and a request for a bullhorn. Throughout the response, officers on scene, including leaders, also were indicating that a tactical team such as Uvalde SWAT, Texas Department of

---

[398] Uvalde Police Department Body-Worn Camera Footage.

[399] ACS, *ATLS: Advanced Trauma Life Support*; PERF, "ICAT: Integrating Communications, Assessment, and Tactics."

Public Safety (TXDPS), or Border Patrol Tactical Unit (BORTAC) was en route, implying room entry was their responsibility. Although requesting more resources, including tactical teams, may have been a prudent decision, tactical teams are *not* a requirement for responding to an active shooter. Tactical teams take time to deploy, arrive on scene, get briefed, and develop a tactical solution for the situation. One of the key lessons learned from Columbine over 20 years ago was that officers can no longer wait for SWAT deployments when responding to an active shooter, as closing the gap in time it takes to address the threat can save lives.

Figure 2-1. References to "barricaded" or "contained" subject

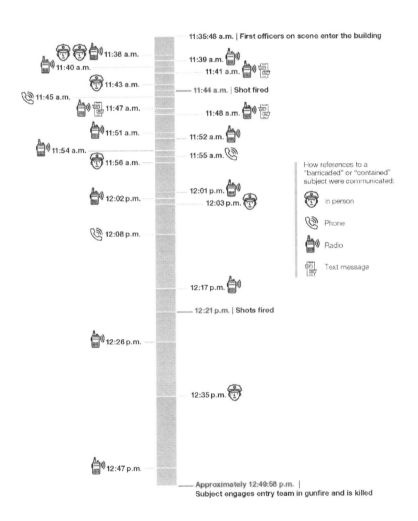

On the south side of the hallway, there were numerous attempts by Chief Arredondo, throughout the response until shortly before the subject was neutralized at 12:49:58 p.m. to establish communication and negotiate with the subject through the walls, from his (Chief Arredondo's) position in the hallway.

In addition to attempting to negotiate with the subject, Chief Arredondo also began coordinating evacuations of other classrooms in the West Building. After the initial approach toward rooms 111/112 was abandoned, Chief Arredondo cleared room 110 and found it unoccupied at approximately 11:37 a.m. The clearing and evacuation of the rest of the West Building did not begin until 11:45 a.m., when officers on the north side of the hallway cleared the teacher's lounge, which was unoccupied.

According to Chief Arredondo, he directed the clearing and evacuation of the entire building, coordinating the effort on the north side through Uvalde County Precinct 1 Constable Johnny Field, in an effort to preserve the life of the children and teachers in the hot zone. He acknowledged the likelihood that there were victims and deceased in the room with the shooter and intentionally prioritized the evacuations over immediate breach and entry into the room.[400] This is counter to active shooter response principles, which state the priority is to address and eliminate the threat.[401]

By noon, all rooms by the T-intersection and in the northeast hallway were cleared and evacuated, locating four UCISD personnel and one student. These room clearing and evacuations included seven classrooms, two restrooms, the teacher's lounge, and the library.

As the last rooms were being cleared and evacuated in the northeast hallway, officers on the south side hallway began to clear rooms on the south side, north side, and mid hallway, which are on the western side of the building, primarily through the windows and into the west exterior of the building. A Uvalde County Sheriff's Office (UCSO) deputy opened an unlocked door to room 102 and observed children and a teacher inside. He advised them to evacuate out the window, and they were met on the outside by officers. The windows to rooms 103, 104, 105, and 106 were each broken out, as teachers and students were not responsive to officers knocking on, and in some cases, shouting into windows, to have them opened from the inside. The teachers and students denied access to the rooms, in adherence to lockdown protocols. Rooms 105 and 106 were in the line of fire from the shooter's location in rooms 111/112.

Room 116 was evacuated through the hallway and out the northwest entrance, due to its doorway facing north and proximity to the exit. Between 11:58 a.m. and 12:07 p.m., all rooms on the west side of the hallway were evacuated. Shortly after, at approximately 12:09 p.m., a UCSO deputy observed children and a teacher inside room 108 and coordinated with other officers in the hallway to evacuate them out into the hallway and through the south entrance. All evacuated teachers and children ran to the funeral home across the street from Robb Elementary.

At this point, all but three rooms in the West Building were cleared and evacuated—rooms 111/112, where the subject remained with dozens of victims, and room 109, which was on the same (east) side of the hallway, adjacent to room 111, with one classroom in between (see figure 2-2 <u>on page 99</u>).

---

[400] CIR Document and Data Review.

[401] ALERRT, *Active Shooter Response Level 1 Version 7.2.*

Room 109 was locked and believed to have occupants inside. Chief Arredondo directed officers on the south side of the hallway to search for master keys to open the door so they could evacuate and clear the room. He also communicated to the north side of the hallway, via Constable Field, that the plan was to evacuate the final room (109) before any attempt to enter rooms 111/112 was made. On the south side, a stack composed of officers from multiple agencies entered the doorway and Chief Arredondo told them the same—specifically to wait before entering the room with the shooter until room 109 was evacuated.

Figure 2-2. West Building room clearing and evacuation status as of entry into classrooms 111 and 112

At approximately 12:12 p.m., dispatch advised over the radio that a child had called 911, stating they were in room 112, and said they were in a room full of victims. This communication was transmitted on both sides of the hallway and exterior of the building.[402] Chief Arredondo continued to insist that room 109 be cleared before any further effort to make entry into classrooms 111/112 even though he stated that he knew there were children in there around 12:09 p.m.[403] This direction was taken and accepted by some officers on each side of the hallway. Multiple sets of keys were tried on room 109 and apparently did not work. Officers tried breaching with a pocketknife, to no avail. Observing the unsuccessful attempts to breach room 109, at least one UCSO deputy suggested evacuating through the window for expediency, and that notion was rejected by Chief Arredondo. Notably, another option to access room 109 could have been through the adjoining door in room 110, which Chief Arredondo had cleared earlier on in the incident. This option was never explored. When the subject fired more shots at 12:21 p.m., Chief Arredondo directed that room 109 be evacuated through the window. Children were evacuated from room 109, including one child struck in the nose by shrapnel, along with a teacher who had suffered a gunshot wound from one of the subject's barrages of gunfire.

Responding officers spent 12 minutes (12:09 p.m.–12:21 p.m.) searching for and trying keys on room 109 in order to evacuate, an effort that was eventually abandoned for a more expedient evacuation approach through the window.

All of these efforts—to negotiate with the subject, to seek additional equipment or personnel, and to evacuate other classrooms—would arguably be appropriate for a lone barricaded subject. However, there were several factors that established that this remained an active shooter situation. The FOS responders heard gunfire inside the classrooms as they were arriving, and officers were injured by shrapnel. There was also confirmation of the likely presence of victims at 11:42 a.m. when officers on scene confirmed that classrooms 111/112 were in session. Soon after, a single shot was fired from inside classrooms 111/112 at approximately 11:44 a.m. Several officers were also made aware that there was an injured teacher inside the classroom at approximately 11:56 a.m. As law enforcement began evacuations of other classrooms around noon, there was a growing realization that many classrooms in the West Building were full of children. Then, at 12:12 p.m., dispatch broadcasted over the radio that a child called 911 and said they were in "a room full of victims." This communication was transmitted to law enforcement radios on both sides of the hallway. By this time, at 12:12 p.m., there were multiple stimuli occurring in the presence of multiple officers, indicating it was an active shooter incident, including shots fired from inside the classroom, an officer on scene indicating his wife is inside one of the classrooms and shot, and confirmation over the radio that class was in session. For more on the stimulus indicating an active shooter incident, please see "Appendix D. Leadership, Incident Command, and Coordination Supplemental Materials."

---

[402] Uvalde Police Department Body-Worn Camera Footage; Uvalde County Sheriff's Office Body-Worn Camera Footage; Uvalde Police Department Radio Traffic.

[403] Uvalde Police Department Body-Worn Camera Footage.

Stacks in the Hallway and Entry into Rooms 111/112

At 12:21 p.m. (49 minutes after the first officers arrived on scene), four shots were fired from inside the classroom. The events and information at that point—shots fired, casings in the hallway, classes being evacuated with children and teachers present, 911 calls from inside room 112—provided further confirmation that this was an active shooter incident. Although there was still communication over radio and through word of mouth among law enforcement responders on and off scene about the subject being barricaded, it was evident at this point that the officers in the hallway had stopped treating the incident like a barricade situation and were now actively seeking a way in, demonstrating, for the first time since the initial retreat, a sense of urgency to breach the doors to classrooms 111/112 and stop the shooter. Entry, however, did not occur for 29 more minutes.

More than one survivor recalled hearing someone state, "Say 'help' if you need help," and when a child tried to say "help," the subject reentered room 112 from room 111 and shot the victim.[404] The adult survivor from room 111 also provided a similar account and said that the subject also shot the victim in the back around this time.[405] Some survivors thought it was the subject, while others heard the statement from the hallway. The CIR team could not determine if the four shots at 12:21 p.m. were connected to the recounted events from the survivors. Whether the statement was made by law enforcement in the hallway or the subject, the recounted stories reinforce the need for an immediate entry into the classroom, as well as a caution about asking children and staff to speak up in the same space as a deadly threat.

Officers positioned at the T-intersection of the north side of the hallway responded to the four shots fired from inside the classroom at 12:21 p.m. (see figure 2-3 on page 102). The first four officers moved forward in what was initially a modified T-formation, followed by a long single file of seven additional officers down the hallway. Two shields were present in the large stack, while one was left behind.

As the stack of officers approached the door, they stopped near the janitor's closet, adjacent to classrooms 111/112.[406] They presumed the classroom doors were locked.[407] The U.S. Customs and Border Protection (CBP) BORTAC Commander on scene received a set of supposed master keys shortly after. After consulting with an officer in the hallway who had a map of the building (which was later found to be lacking sufficient detail), the BORTAC commander tested the keys on the janitor's closet door, next to room 112, and learned that they did not work. This set off a search for more keys, including by Chief Arredondo on the south side of the hallway.[408] After this, there was a period of about 10 minutes in which there appeared to be stagnation in the hallway. At 12:32 p.m., the BORTAC commander left the hallway to retrieve breaching tools as an alternative option to breach the presumed-to-be-locked door.

---

[404] CIR Fact Finding.

[405] CIR Fact Finding.

[406] Robb Elementary School CCTV Footage.

[407] CIR Fact Finding

[408] Uvalde Police Department Body-Worn Camera Footage.

The commander realized they were going to need a sledgehammer with a Halligan bar (see figure 2-4 for an example) and the game warden asked a UCSO deputy to go retrieve it from their (game warden's) truck, which they did. However, shortly after, TX Ranger 1 found the BORTAC commander and handed him a set of keys. They were tested on the janitor's closet and worked.

Figure 2-3. Personnel from Zavala County, CBP, and TXDPS advancing after shots fired

Source: Robb Elementary School CCTV Footage.

Figure 2-4. Example of a Halligan bar

Photo: Wikimedia Commons

Around this time, more BORTAC members arrived, including a sniper. There was a pause in making entry, so that they could see if the sniper could get a visual on and take out the subject. A drone operated by a TXDPS trooper was also used to try to see into the room. Due to lockdown protocols, which call for windows to be covered, neither the sniper nor the drone were successful.

At approximately 12:48 p.m., the BORTAC commander put the key inside the door to room 111, turned it, and pulled the door open toward him.[409] The entry team was composed of three BORTAC members, a Border Patrol Search, Trauma, and Rescue (BORSTAR) member, and deputies from two local sheriff's departments—Uvalde and Zavala counties. There was one shield in the stack, which had been provided by the U.S. Marshals Service (USMS) and was rifle-rated. As the entry team prepared to move in, the door began to swing back closed. One member attempted to move a chair against the door to prop it open, but the door was too heavy and eventually another member of the entry team simply held it open, as they made entry. According to officers who witnessed the entry, the entry team was in the doorway for at least one minute while they repositioned themselves and held the door open. Members of the entry team reported an eerie silence as they entered the darkened room.[410] Inside, they were surprised to learn the two rooms (111 and 112) were connected. A second entry team was initially stacked up on the opposite side, outside of the door to room 112. However, when the first stack entered and saw the adjoining door was open, realizing it was one big room, the second entry team was called off due to concerns over crossfire.[411] They began clearing corners inside the classroom, when suddenly the shooter emerged from inside a closet. Gunfire erupted at approximately 12:50 p.m. The shooter was killed. One BORTAC member suffered a gunshot wound and graze wound.

Within seconds, there were more officers and law enforcement medics entering the room, attempting to help triage and evacuate the room (see "Chapter 3. Leadership, Incident Command, and Coordination" for assessment of medical triage). Inside were 33 children and three teachers; among the shooter's carnage were traumatized, injured, and dead victims. The shooter, armed with an AR-15 style rifle and donning body armor, was killed and lying near the closet he emerged from.

Equipment Use and Deployments

Equipment for Active Shooter Response

There is no specific list of what tools and equipment an agency or officer should have to prepare for active shooter incidents. The CIR team focus our analysis on radios, shields, CS gas, and breaching tools, as each were part of the decision-making calculus in the law enforcement response to Robb Elementary.

---

[409] This is not an indication that the door was locked. The CIR team determined the status of the door's lock to be inconclusive but likely unlocked. The shooter gained entry unimpeded through the door and it was unlikely to have been locked afterwards.

[410] Some also acknowledged the phenomenon of tunnel vision and auditory exclusion.

[411] CIR Fact Finding.

It is important to note that the specific tools and equipment needed can vary based on agency policies, local regulations, and the nature of the response. Regular training, maintenance, and updates to equipment are crucial to ensure effectiveness and readiness during an active shooter incident. Additionally, depending on the agency's size and geographical jurisdiction, access to tactical gear and tools, if not assigned per capita, should be mobile available.

The subsections that follow provide additional detail on some of these key forms of equipment.

Radios

Radios serve a crucial role in facilitating communications among first responders during a crisis event, especially when there is a large convergence of multiple agencies on scene. Radios need to have not only the technological capability to perform, but also be operated appropriately by the end users. First responders must ensure that their communication is clear, succinct, and in commonly understood terminology. Situation updates should be provided routinely, as the nature of the incident evolves and those on scene and en route need to be aware of the changing conditions. At the same time, first responders must adopt a minimalist approach, to not overload the communication system, which can lead to the most important pieces of information being missed.

Shields

According to the FBI's 20-Year Review of Active Shooter Incidents (2000–2019), approximately 43 percent of the 333 identified active shooter incidents included the presence of a long gun/rifle by the subject. A tactical ballistic shield, capable of absorbing impact from rifle rounds, serves as an invaluable tool for law enforcement officers, providing an added layer of safety in high-risk situations. Given active shooter response protocols require immediate action, oftentimes from officers in a patrol function, in many law enforcement agencies throughout the U.S., it is unlikely that a responding officer will be able to respond with a shield. If a shield is available, they must be used in accordance with tactical training in order to be effective. However, an officer should *never* wait for the arrival of a shield before moving toward the threat to stop the shooter. Proper training on the use of a shield is essential for an officer to master the maneuvering, tactical positioning, proper handling, firearm position and accurate fire, and transitioning off the shield. Although many officers may receive some exposure to the use of a shield at academy training, it is typically with a non-ballistic rated shield, typically used for crowd control. Furthermore, they are often not retrained on their use unless they are for specialized training, such as SWAT. Without SWAT experience, most patrol officers will not have training on use of a shield in a tactical situation such as an active shooter.

CS Gas

The deployment of chemical agents, such as CS gas,[412] which is commonly known as tear gas, is a significant law enforcement action that must be carefully assessed before use. Some factors that must

---

[412] The scientific name for CS gas is 2-chlorobenzylidene malononitrile.

be considered include the severity of the situation and danger posed by the subject; the presence and impact on civilians, in particular elderly, children, and others with potentially aggravating health conditions; alternative options; the physical structure of the room, including size, dimensions, exits, and ventilation; the likelihood of successfully bringing the incident to a final resolution as a result of deploying the gas; availability of medical assets to treat anyone adversely affected; and weather conditions, which can cause the gas to disperse to areas outside of the intended target.

Equipment Used at Robb Elementary

Responders at Robb Elementary used or considered using several of the types of equipment described above, to varying degrees of success.

Radios

One particular challenge in the response was the fact that Chief Arredondo, the de facto on scene commander, had tossed his radios to the ground while running to the scene and during the incident neither requested nor was supplied another radio to facilitate communication.[413] In lieu of radios, he communicated with Constable Field on the other side of the hallway via cellphone. According to Chief Arredondo, he tossed his radios because he wanted his hands to be free—and that he knew the radios did not work inside the building.[414]

Throughout the incident response at Robb Elementary, first responders had intermittent challenges with radio transmission inside the building. The building was generally known to have such issues by UCISD PD officers and UCISD staff. UCISD PD officers would typically carry two radios—one specific for the school district and the other to communicate with outside agencies, mainly UPD. The school district radio was a two-way radio for communication with other UCISD PD officers while inside buildings or around campus. These radios worked relatively well inside the building. The other radios, for communicating with external law enforcement agencies, did not work well inside the building, as they were designed to be most effective in open spaces, the common terrain in the nine rural counties in south Texas.

In the CIR team's review of BWC and CCTV footage, the team observed radios failing to transmit or receive communications repeatedly inside the building. However, it was not a total failure, and for much of the incident, there were radio communications being transmitted to one or more officers who were inside the hallway, on both sides, and just outside the west and south doors, such as by UPD Acting Chief Mariano Pargas and others.

---

[413] CIR Fact Finding.

[414] CIR Fact Finding.

Shields

At Robb Elementary, officers on scene called out a need for shields early on. The first official callout over the radio for shields came at approximately 11:39 a.m., which coincides with the time at which officers in the hallway transitioned to a barricaded subject response and the initial callouts over the radio that the subject was contained or barricaded.

The first shield arrived at the T-intersection of the hallway at approximately 11:52 a.m. A second and third arrived at the T-intersection 12 minutes later at 12:04 p.m. None of the shields were rifle rated. See figure 2-5.

Figure 2-5. Positioning of three shields at T-intersection at 12:04 p.m.

Source: Robb Elementary School CCTV Footage.

At 12:11 p.m., the fire marshal took one of the three shields at the T-intersection to bring over to the south side of the hallway, which did not have any shields at that time. At 12:21 p.m., just before shots were fired from inside classrooms 111/112, the first rifle-rated shield arrived at the T-intersection, brought in by a USMS deputy. The 12:21 p.m. stack moved forward with one of the two ballistic shields and the USMS rifle-rated shield. See table 2-1 and figure 2-6 on page 107.

At approximately 12:30 p.m., an additional rifle-rated shield arrived on the south side of the hallway, also from USMS. Over the course of the response, five shields, two of which were rifle-rated, were brought into the West Building.

At the time they made entry into classrooms 111/112, the entry team used one of the ballistic-rated shields from USMS on the north side hallway (see table 2-2 on page 107). The shield was handled by an operator with BORTAC. This was entirely appropriate, given that the shield was available on scene at the time the stack was formed, and entry had been made. Throughout the incident response, officers in the hallway often referenced a need for shields, even at one point saying they were waiting for shields.

Others noted the inadequacy of the non-rifle rated shields in addressing the threat. The CIR team cannot say that these officers were representative of the overall response. Nor can the team say that the entry into rooms 111/112 was held up because officers were awaiting the arrival of shields. The CIR team's analysis indicates that the long pause in entry up until 12:21 p.m. was largely due to the evacuation of the building, and not waiting for shields.

Nevertheless, the CIR team concludes our analysis of the use of shields with the following: In an active shooter response, officers should never wait for the arrival of a shield or any other ancillary equipment before moving toward the threat to stop shooter.

Table 2-1. Shield locations at 12:21 p.m.

Northside Hallway/T-Intersection	Southside Hallway
2 ballistic shields (not rifle-rated) 1 rifle-rated shield	1 ballistic shield (not rifle-rated)

Table 2-2. Shield locations when classrooms 111/112 were entered around 12:47 p.m.

North Side Hallway/T-Intersection	South Side Hallway
2 ballistic shields (not rifle-rated) 1 rifle-rated shield	1 ballistic shield (not rifle-rated) 1 rifle-rated shield

Figure 2-6. Personnel from Zavala County, CBP, and TXDPS advancing after shots fired

Source: Robb Elementary School CCTV Footage.

CS Gas

At approximately 12:14 p.m., UPD Ofc. 4 brought CS gas cannisters near the T-intersection, with several gas masks arriving shortly after. Officers began to formulate a plan for using the gas, which was to drop the cannisters in through the classroom window. This plan persisted through the 12:21 p.m. shots fired, as they simultaneously were waiting for the master keys. It is not clear what time the use of gas was called off, but ultimately it was on account of children being in the classroom.[415]

Chemical agents are intended to be utilized primarily for a barricaded subject situation or for the execution of search warrant with the intent of overloading the subject's motor sensory skills, as well as to create an element of surprise that offers a tactically advantageous position. However, it is an unconventional risk to utilize chemical agents during an active shooter situation or in an environment with a significant number of victims, in particular a school setting. The dispersion of gas in this instance would have been a tactical flaw which would have further compromised the officer's response. The decision to ultimately call off the use of gas was no doubt a judicious one.

Breaching Tools

On both sides of the hallway, the primary mode of entering classrooms that were either known or presumed to be locked was with master keys. No breaching tools were used to enter any rooms in the West Building.

Although the doors to rooms 111/112 were presumed to be locked, our analysis of video and radio communications does not indicate any request for breaching tools until approximately 12:19 p.m. (43 minutes after first on scene), and that request was in reference to breaching the door to room 109, which officers on the south side of the hallway were attempting to evacuate. At that time, UPD Sgt. 1 asked the question of the hallway full of about 12 officers, from at least three different agencies, and none of them indicated they had breaching tools. Eventually, the room was evacuated via the window.

On the north side of the hallway, the BORTAC commander went to retrieve his breaching tools at 12:32 p.m., after one set of master keys did not work and while waiting for a new set. Eventually, the new set of keys arrived, were tested on the janitor's closet, and then eventually used to open the door to classrooms 111/112. As stated previously in this report, whether the door was in fact locked is unknown. However, the fact that the shooter had entered one of the classroom doors indicates that it was unlocked at that time and would have likely remained unlocked.

---

[415] CIR Fact Finding.

Observations and Recommendations

Observation 1: The first officers on scene immediately moved toward the sound of gunfire and into the West Building of Robb Elementary to stop the shooter, which was in adherence to active shooter response generally accepted practices. Once inside the building, five of the first officers on scene continued to press down the hallway and toward a barrage of gunfire erupting inside of rooms 111/112.

Observation 2: Officer movements down the hallway were uncoordinated and not tactically sound, creating potential crossfire between officers entering on the south side and north side of the hallway.

> **Recommendation 2.1:** Officers responding to an active shooter and other dynamic scenes should maintain cognizance of potential crossfire upon their initial approach and make tactical adjustments as soon as feasible.

> **Recommendation 2.2:** Law enforcement agencies should ensure officers are trained on one-, two-, three-, and four-person team formations that are taught in active shooter training courses. These formations are designed to allow the greatest opportunity for success for officers in locating and addressing the threat with whatever weapon system they have on their person.

Observation 3: After officers suffered graze wounds from shrapnel, the first officers on scene did not penetrate the doors to rooms 111/112 and repositioned to a barricaded subject situation. This mindset permeated throughout much of the incident response, even impacting many of the later responding officers. Despite their training and despite multiple events indicating the subject continued to pose an active threat to students and staff in the building, including the likelihood and then confirmation of victims inside the room, officers on scene did not attempt to enter the room and stop the shooter until for over an hour after they entered the building. The shooter was not killed until approximately 77 minutes after law enforcement first arrived.

> **Recommendation 3.1:** Officers responding to an active shooter incident must continually seek to eliminate the threat and enable victim response. The shooter's immediate past actions and likely future actions serve as "triggering points" that indicate the appropriate response should be in line with active shooter response protocols.[416] An active shooter with access to victims should *never* be considered and treated as a barricaded subject.

> **Recommendation 3.2:** Officers responding to an active shooter incident or dynamic scenes with evolving threats should continually assess their surroundings and stimuli and seek to obtain an accurate picture of the incident to inform their decision-making and tactical approach.

> **Recommendation 3.3:** Law enforcement training academies and providers should ensure that active shooter training modules include the factors in determining active shooter versus barricaded subject situations.

---

[416] IACP, *Model Policy on Active Shooter*.

Observation 4: A callout over the radio that the subject is "contained" and "barricaded" was repeated time and again, and spread rapidly throughout the collection of agencies and individual officers responding to the scene. Although it was also stated that the subject was still shooting in some instances, the abundance of radio communications made it inevitable that some first responders would hear one communication but not the other.

> **Recommendation 4.1:** Officers on the scene of an active shooter incident should be cognizant of their description of the situation and how it can influence other officers as they arrive. These status updates, known as L-CANs (Location, Conditions, Actions, Needs) are integral to an effective and informed law enforcement response, particularly with assets en route to an evolving situation.

> **Recommendation 4.2:** Law enforcement agencies and training providers should ensure L-CANs are routinely included in training scenarios where applicable, including active shooter training. Other options for improving officer L-CAN discipline may include incorporating into rollcall, running L-CAN drills, and including as part of an agency's formal after action review process for all critical incidents.

Observation 5: Officers on scene did not consistently mark rooms that were cleared and evacuated, leading to instances of rooms unnecessarily and unintentionally being cleared multiple times over the course of the response.

> **Recommendation 5.1:** Room clearings and evacuations must be conducted systematically. Officers should establish a standard approach that physically mark rooms that are cleared. The approach should be simple and achievable for any room. For many law enforcement agencies, a marker or chalk is used to mark an "X" on the door once its room is cleared. Doing so serves both an officer safety and resource management purpose. Law enforcement agencies and training providers should ensure this instruction is provided when training on clearing buildings.

Observation 6: The effort to clear and evacuate the entire West Building was intentional and directed by Chief Arredondo, to preserve and protect the lives of the children and teachers who remained in the hot zone, while the shooter remained an active threat with multiple victims in rooms 111/112. This was a major contributing factor in the delay to making entry into rooms 111/112. The time it took to evacuate the entire building was 43 minutes, beginning at around 11:38 a.m., when Chief Arredondo realized there were occupants in room 109 that he could not access, and ending at 12:21 p.m., when four shots were fired, and that same room was finally evacuated through the windows. During this time and prior to 12:21 p.m., there were multiple stimuli indicating that there was an active threat in classrooms 111/112—including: the barrage of gunfire during the initial response; the children and teachers observed when evacuating the classrooms; the single shot fired at 11:44 a.m.; the notification that class was in session; the notification from an officer on scene that his wife, a teacher, was inside classrooms 111/112 and shot; and multiple radio broadcasts of a 911 call from a student inside the classroom.

Recommendation 6.1: Officers responding to an active shooter incident must first and foremost drive toward the threat to eliminate it. In the event there are resources available and an opportunity to evacuate bystanders and victims from the hot zone, officers must balance the risk posed by evacuation versus the risk posed by remaining in lockdown and potentially in the crossfire. Evacuations in such circumstances must be conducted in the most expeditious manner, limited to those immediately in harm's way, and not at the expense of the priority to eliminate the threat. In the case of Robb Elementary, the CIR team concludes that the effort to evacuate was protracted and should not have caused such significant delay in the eventual entry into rooms 111/112.

Observation 7: Some officers on scene believed that they were waiting for more assets to arrive, such as shields and a specialized tactical team, to make entry.

Recommendation 7.1: Officers responding to an active shooter incident must be prepared to approach the threat and breach or enter a room using just the tools they have with them, which is often a standard-issue firearm/service weapon.

Recommendation 7.2: Law enforcement agencies should adopt active shooter training national standards. The adoption of such standards is critical in the support and development of effective response tactics. The training, by design, enables a de-facto team of similarly trained officers who could rapidly assemble, communicate, and act as a team to rapidly stop the killing and stop the dying.

Recommendation 7.3: Law enforcement leaders on scene must work with available resources and personnel on scene and when the situation becomes stagnant, create an operational inner perimeter with a tactical team, removing all other personnel to avoid overcompensating the situation with unnecessary personnel.

Observation 8: The entry team assumed the door to rooms 111/112 were locked, based on information they received from officers who were on scene for a longer period of time. However, throughout the entirety of the incident, this assumption was never tested and the doorknob was never checked. Our analysis indicates that eight interior doors in the West Building were unlocked and discovered to be unlocked by responding officers during evacuations.

Observation 9: With master keys in hand and confirmed to work, the BORTAC commander paused on the room entry so that a sniper and drone could attempt to get a visual on the classroom. If successful, the sniper could have mitigated a great deal of risk posed by a gun battle inside the classroom. The sniper or drone could have provided valuable intelligence on the layout of the room, location of victims, and the shooter that would create a great tactical advantage for the entry team. However, assessing these options added 10 minutes to the overall response time.

Recommendation 9.1: Leaders providing direction in an active shooter incident must balance the urgency to stop the shooter with capabilities and approaches that may be time-consuming. The amount of time that has passed and the probability of success or improved outcomes should be considered when making such decisions.

Recommendation 9.2: The assessment on the viability of using a sniper should have been conducted earlier in the incident, as soon as the location of the subject was known. There were multiple officers with SWAT training and experience that could have conducted such an assessment within the first 10 minutes of the law enforcement response.

Observation 10: Active shooter incidents are responded to by law enforcement officers with a variety of experience and training, but rarely is there a fully functioning specialized tactical team on scene to respond.

Observation 11: Active shooter response protocol does not require any equipment that is not standard to a patrol officer.[417] Officers on scene during the initial response in the West Building, even with only their standard issue service weapon, had sufficient equipment to formulate a plan and attempt to make entry into classrooms 111/112, by first checking the doorknob and, if necessary, making a forced entry through the classroom window, or using ballistic breaching methods.[418]

Recommendation 11.1: All equipment assigned by an agency requires specific training and may only be utilized by those officers assigned to that particular piece of equipment. Ideally, an agency may consider assigning specialized equipment to patrol officers to enhance the operational capacity of an emergency response. It should be noted that the equipment listed is not all required as collective response and is recommended to be utilized individually as available to further enhance the on-scene capabilities of an officer(s) responding to a critical emergency such as an active shooter situation. Each tool enhances its capacity and capability, but no single piece of ancillary equipment is required for a response to an active shooter.

Recommendation 11.2: Agencies should also consider ensuring equipment is available at critically vulnerable locations, such as schools and other soft targets. Depending on the capacity of the police department, "readily available" may be defined as having the equipment in the possession of a trained officer or within close proximity to acquire the equipment for an emergency response.

Observation 12: UPD radios did not work well inside of the West Building, causing communications challenges throughout the incident response. Despite the known challenges in radio communications, video evidence shows that there are radio communications being broadcasted on both sides of the hallway throughout the incident, sharing key facts and circumstances of the incident.

Recommendation 12.1: When experiencing radio voids or dead zones inside a building, officers on scene must be prepared to identify and utilize other modes of communicating—especially in large

---

[417] TCOLE, "Active Shooter Response for School-Based Law Enforcement."

[418] ALERRT, *Robb Elementary School Attack Response.*

Recommendation 12.1: When experiencing radio voids or dead zones inside a building, officers on scene must be prepared to identify and utilize other modes of communicating—especially in large complex incidents with multiple agencies operating in multiple locations. Some common practices in law enforcement for such circumstances is to assign "runners," who will relay information to key actors within an incident response.

Recommendation 12.2: Law enforcement agencies must maintain and upgrade all equipment, including radios, when vulnerabilities are presented. In Uvalde, police radios should perform not just in the wide-open spaces that are prevalent throughout the county, but also in high density environments, such as school buildings. Furthermore, agencies should establish and train on radio operability contingency plans, such as point-to-point communication, which does not require repeaters or internal transmitters.

Chapter 3. Leadership, Incident Command, and Coordination

Introduction

Leadership in law enforcement is absolutely critical, especially in moments of a dire challenge, such as the active shooting incident at Robb Elementary School. It requires courageous action and steadiness in a chaotic environment. Leadership can be displayed internally within an agency, and publicly when providing service to the community; it arises regardless of rank or title. Situations like the incident at Robb Elementary School require steady and commanding actions. Based on facts gathered for this report, this leadership was absent for too long at Robb Elementary School.

The active shooter incident at Robb Elementary should have been resolved in far fewer than the 77 minutes that it took to enter classrooms 111 and 112.[419] Accordingly, much of this chapter's discussion focuses not on the actions of leadership after the conclusion of the incident, but rather on leadership, incident command, and coordination in that critical period of time during the active shooter response. It addresses the need to establish an incident command post or unified command structure in the midst of an active shooter situation. And it discusses the importance of a coordinated and collaborative command and coordination strategy in responding to and resolving complicated incidents involving multiple agencies. The recommendations identified are critical to defining what occurred on May 24 for the Uvalde community and for law enforcement and other responding agencies to learn, practice, and prepare in order to prevent the next tragedy or lessen the harm it causes.

Scope

This chapter describes the law enforcement leadership actions and inactions; incident command and management; coordination with other law enforcement agencies, including mutual aid; self-deployment by other local, state, and federal law enforcement personnel; and emergency medical services/fire medical response.

As with any after-action assessment, the Critical Incident Review (CIR) team benefited from hindsight during this review. Review of video, body-worn camera (BWC) footage, and other post-incident data often provided clarity to the actions and inactions on that tragic day that was not available to the first

---

[419] Based on analysis from the U.S. Secret Service on active attacks from the period of 2016 to 2020, "over one-third of the attacks (n=65, 38 percent) ended quickly. . .one-quarter of the attacks (n=45, 26 percent) were longer in duration, lasting over 15 minutes." NTAC, *Mass Attacks in Public Spaces;* according to the FBI, "the average active-shooter incident lasts 12 minutes. Thirty-seven percent last less than five minutes." Schweit, "Addressing the Problem of the Active Shooter."

Critical Incident Review: Active Shooter at Robb Elementary School |
Chapter 3. Leadership, Incident Command, and Coordination

114

responders at Robb Elementary. The CIR team also benefited from the expertise of subject matter experts, who assisted in developing the observations and recommendations. Where not otherwise cited, the practices identified in this chapter derive from the experts' collective knowledge and experience.

This chapter is organized into two sections:[420]

- Leadership During an Active Shooter Response—This section describes leadership action and inaction over the course of the incident in responding to the active shooter threat, coordinating incoming resources, and establishing command and control.

- Coordination of Medical Response—This section describes the coordination of the emergency medical services response.

Each section discusses the generally accepted practices and standards related to leadership, incident command and coordination, and any relevant background before analyzing what occurred at Robb Elementary. The chapter concludes with observations and recommendations.

While "Chapter 1. Incident Timeline Reconstruction" provides a comprehensive account of pertinent facts leading up to, during, and immediately after the tragic mass shooting, this chapter incorporates those facts and includes an analysis from the perspective of leadership and incident command and coordination.

Only chief executives, government executives, and those elected to civic/government positions will be named. Other law enforcement personnel who were critical or played a key role in the areas of leadership and incident command and coordination will have a number assigned and be referenced by title and number. All other individuals are unnamed.

Additional background and resources are included in "Appendix D. Leadership, Incident Command, and Coordination Supplemental Materials."

Leadership During an Active Shooter Response

Prior to, during, and following a response to a critical incident, leadership plays a critical role in setting the stage for an effective response to the incident and the events that follow. A coordinated and collaborative command and coordination strategy is also critical to the response and resolution of complicated incidents involving multiple agencies.

During incident responses, leadership is invaluable for supporting coordination and communication. The significance of collaboration within the agency, with other law enforcement agencies, and across public safety disciplines cannot be overstated, as evidenced by the failures identified in this review.

---

[420] The displayed times may differ in the videos and images due to errors in synchronized systems. The team used actual, verified times. To read more about that analysis and a detailed explanation for the methodology for the report, see the "Report Methodology."

Critical Incident Review: Active Shooter at Robb Elementary School |
Chapter 3. Leadership, Incident Command, and Coordination

115

Leadership, Incident Command, and Active Shooter Principles

When law enforcement take the oath of office, they pledge to serve and protect their communities. Officers are trained to approach critical situations from a position of finding tactical solutions. They are frequently called upon to make split-second decisions, and these decisions have long-term, sometimes irreversible, consequences. This profession carries great responsibility and comes with deep costs physically, mentally, and emotionally to the officers and the communities they serve.

Ranked law enforcement leaders set the tone for law enforcement policy, procedures, and ethical behavior.[421] Ranked leaders have "a distinct responsibility requiring persistent efforts to proactively develop themselves and motivate, inspire, train, and develop others."[422] In one model, effective law enforcement leadership includes eight principles:

1. Service – The essence of law enforcement is to serve, and an "effective manager exemplifies service, self-giving, and selflessness."

2. Honesty – Leaders' communication and actions must be honest and forthright, and that honesty extends to leaders being honest with themselves.

3. Integrity – Effective leadership "[d]epends on consistently doing what is right, meaning that which is in the best interest of the organization and of others."

4. Humility – Leadership involves "looking for ways to learn from others and improve ourselves."

5. Purpose – A sense of shared purpose enables leaders to develop personnel who identify with the central purpose and nobility of law enforcement.

6. Mentoring – Leaders have a duty and responsibility to develop their personnel.

7. Positive/Constructive Attitude – Leaders should "[c]onsistently . . .portray the attitude of moving forward constructively, always looking for positive improvement and the willing cooperation of others."

8. Trust – Effective leaders need to trust their personnel.[423]

As part of effective leadership, ranked leaders need to be honest and tell their fellow leaders their opinions ". . . when they believe they have done or are about to do something not in the best interest of their position or that of the department."[424] Effective leaders should question a decision, action, or inaction. It requires moral courage, but research has shown that if one person shows that courage and acts, others are likely to follow.[425]

---

[421] Fortenbery, "Developing Ethical Law Enforcement Leaders."

[422] Willis, "Perspective: Principles of Effective Law Enforcement Leadership."

[423] Willis, "Perspective: Principles of Effective Law Enforcement Leadership."

[424] Willis, "Perspective: Principles of Effective Law Enforcement Leadership."

[425] *Psychology Today*, "Bystander Effect;" Staub, *Overcoming Evil*; Staub, *The Roots of Goodness*; Aronie and Lopez, "Keeping Each Other Safe."

Critical Incident Review: Active Shooter at Robb Elementary School |
Chapter 3. Leadership, Incident Command, and Coordination

116

The law enforcement code of ethics aids agencies and law enforcement in practicing these core values.[426] Leading by example sets the stage for an effective agency.

An organization's shortcomings are a direct reflection of its leadership. All sworn police officers at every rank have to hold each other accountable. No matter who is watching, doing the right thing is the only way to change law enforcement culture and build trust within the organization and the public (the community we all serve). We must always remember to embrace our organization's code of ethics, and it should be a constant reminder to lead by example. Also, effective communication is essential.[427]

During a critical incident, effective leadership is paramount, and leaders have a responsibility to act with forward momentum.

Those with formal positional authority—including executives, command staff, and all other supervisors—have a duty and responsibility to exercise command, control, management, and authority, irrespective of an acting designation. They have an obligation to protect innocent lives based on their oath of office (See "IACP Law Enforcement Oath of Honor" callout box for an example of one widely used oath).

IACP Law Enforcement Oath of Honor

The International Association of Chiefs of Police law enforcement oath of honor demonstrates ethical standards via a public affirmation. The oath of honor is:

> On my honor, I will never betray my integrity, my character, or the public trust. I will treat all individuals with dignity and respect and ensure that my actions are dedicated to ensuring the safety of my community and the preservation of human life. I will always have the courage to hold myself and others accountable for our actions. I will always maintain the highest ethical standards and uphold the values of my community, and the agency I serve.*

---

* IACP, *Law Enforcement Oath of Honor*.

---

[426] Morris, "The Importance of Leading by Example;" Fortenbery, "Developing Ethical Law Enforcement Leaders;" IACP, "Law Enforcement Code of Ethics."

[427] Morris, "The Importance of Leading by Example."

Critical Incident Review: Active Shooter at Robb Elementary School |
Chapter 3. Leadership, Incident Command, and Coordination

117

Active Shooter Response Principles

Given the lessons learned from Columbine, the standards promulgated by the International Association of Chiefs of Police,[428] and training developed by the Department of Justice[429] and Department of Homeland Security,[430] it should be widely understood that law enforcement response in active shooter situations requires immediate action by first responding officers, regardless of the availability of specialized units or equipment. In an ideal situation, four or five first responders arrive at the scene of an ongoing active shooter simultaneously, and quickly search and eliminate the threat. Recent developments in tactical response and training also emphasize solo officer response when the situation demands.[431] For further explanation of active shooter response principles, see "Chapter 2. Tactics and Equipment."

National Incident Management System

Where multiple agencies or entities are involved in responding to an incident, it is also critical for leaders to develop a coordinated and collaborative command and coordination strategy. Mass violence incidents, in particular, often draw the response of many law enforcement agencies, fire departments, medical transport agencies, and emergency medical facilities. A lack of a shared understanding among responders regarding roles can create confusion.

---

[428] IACP, *Model Policy on Active Shooter.*

[429] ALERRT, *Active Shooter Response Level 1 Version 7.2*; Elkins, "Prepare Today for What Can Happen Tomorrow."

[430] DHS, *Law Enforcement Active Shooter Emergency Response.*

[431] Martaindale and Blair, "The Evolution of Active Shooter Response."

Critical Incident Review: Active Shooter at Robb Elementary School |
Chapter 3. Leadership, Incident Command, and Coordination

118

Figure 3-1. Sample incident command structure with a single incident commander

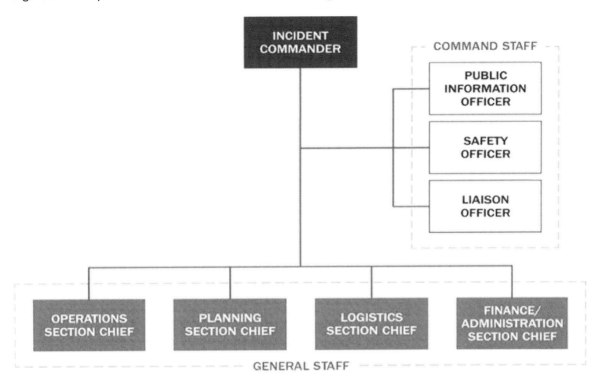

The National Incident Management System (NIMS) is a useful framework for coordinating responses among multiple agencies, including ". . .all levels of government, nongovernmental organizations, and the private sector to work together to prevent, protect against, mitigate, respond to, and recover from [all] incidents."[432] As Federal Emergency Management Agency (FEMA) states, "The command and coordination component of NIMS describes the systems, principles, and structures that provide a standard, national framework for incident management."[433] The ability to respond in a coordinated manner does not happen by accident but is a product of a regionwide commitment to NIMS and the requisite preparation and training. FEMA describes NIMS as a ". . .shared vocabulary, systems, and processes. . ." while defining key systems, ". . .including the Incident Command System (ICS), Emergency Operations Center (EOC) structures, and Multiagency Coordination Groups (MAC Groups) that guide how personnel work together during incidents."[434]

Emergency responders can use different components of NIMS to conduct operations so that responders at all levels can work together more effectively and efficiently. Because ICS is scalable, it can be used for small, planned events such as search warrants, event security, or department celebrations. The fire service can serve as a model of how routine use of ICS and NIMS improves performance during critical incidents.

---

[432] FEMA, *National Incident Management System.*

[433] FEMA, *National Incident Management System.*

[434] FEMA, *National Incident Management System.*

Critical Incident Review: Active Shooter at Robb Elementary School |
Chapter 3. Leadership, Incident Command, and Coordination

119

Figure 3-2. Sample unified command structure

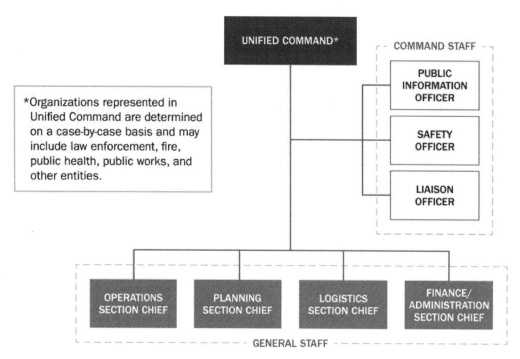

Furthermore, the National Qualification System (NQS) promotes interoperability by establishing a common language for defining job titles/responsibilities and by enabling jurisdictions and organizations to plan for, request, and have confidence in the capabilities of personnel not just in local incidents but in deployments to mutual aid events.[435]

The NQS uses an experience approach that builds on the NIMS framework by focusing on verifying the capabilities of personnel to perform as required in the various ICS positions. Experience includes the necessary education, training, and demonstrated capability that establishes proficiency in the required role or roles.[436] This practical application approach enhances response to critical incidents and reduces the potential for staff to be placed in roles for which they are not best suited.

---

[435] FEMA, *NIMS Guideline for the National Qualification System*.

[436] FEMA, *NIMS Guideline for the National Qualification System*.

Critical Incident Review: Active Shooter at Robb Elementary School |
Chapter 3. Leadership, Incident Command, and Coordination

120

NIMS establishes two generally accepted command structures: a single incident commander and unified command. In a command structure with a single incident commander (see figure 3-1 <u>on page 119</u>), the incident commander has overall incident management responsibility and relies on staff and section chiefs to assist in managing the incident. Effective incident management consists of four overarching areas of responsibility:

1. Direct tactical response to save lives, stabilize the incident, and protect property and the environment.

2. Incident support through resource acquisition, information gathering, and interagency coordination.

3. Policy guidance and senior-level decision-making.

4. Outreach and communication with the media and public to keep them informed about the incident.[437]

A commonly accepted way to organize multiple agencies is by establishing a unified command structure. The unified command generally includes the primary law enforcement responders, as well as the emergency medical liaison, victim services, and others as needed. Unified command improves unity of effort in a multiagency response to an incident. Unified command also facilitates the joint management of common incident objectives and strategies. However, under unified command, each agency maintains authority, responsibility, and accountability for its personnel and resources.[438] Figure 3-2 <u>on page 120</u> illustrates a sample unified command structure.[439]

To facilitate efforts of the unified command and coordinate efforts of multiple agencies, leaders can establish an incident command post (ICP). The ICP is usually located near the incident and is where on-scene command functions are performed.[440] When determining an ICP, leaders should consider space, security, accessibility, and facilities such as technological capabilities. An ICP can also serve as a base for the incident command if only one agency is involved. Under incident command structure principles for establishing a command post/presence, the command leader utilizes an elevated physical position so that arriving personnel have an immediate understanding of where to go for instructions. In best case situations, green strobe lights are used to attract attention to the command post's location.[441]

For more information on NIMS, see "<u>Chapter 8. Pre-Incident Planning and Preparation</u>."

---

[437] FEMA, "Command and Coordination."

[438] FEMA, *National Incident Management System.*

[439] FEMA, *National Incident Management System.*

[440] FEMA, *National Incident Management System.*

[441] Justice Technology Information Center, *Law Enforcement Vehicle Lighting.*

Critical Incident Review: Active Shooter at Robb Elementary School |
Chapter 3. Leadership, Incident Command, and Coordination

121

Relevant Policies and Roles in Uvalde

The following sub-sections introduce the relevant law enforcement policies and leadership roles that informed the response at Robb Elementary.

Active Shooter, Incident Command, and Coordination Policies

On the day of the tragedy, there were policies in place related to establishing incident command and responding to active shooters in several, but not all, of the agencies that are a part of the CIR review: UPD (Uvalde Police Department), UCISD PD (Uvalde Consolidated Independent School District Police Department), the Uvalde County Sheriff's Office (UCSO), Texas Department of Public Safety (TXDPS), U.S. Customs and Border Protection (CBP), and U.S. Marshals Service (USMS). The other agencies included in the CIR review were not present prior to the law enforcement entry into the classrooms.

UPD Policies

Per the UPD Policy 8.6 Active Shooter Response:

- The first officer to arrive should attempt to determine the situation and communicate information and direction to other responding officers and supervisors. Ideally, if time permits, the first two to five officers arriving should form a single team and enter the involved structure. A single officer entering a structure must understand the inherent risk assumed in taking such action.

- The first officers entering the structure should recognize that their primary objective is to stop further violence. Officers must move quickly and deliberately to the source of gunfire and stop the violence. Officers should attempt to identify and communicate locations of victims needing medical attention. If practical, and absent continued shooting, officers should treat any massive hemorrhaging that may result in the immediate loss of life.

- Upon arriving to the scene of an active shooter event and assessing the scene, the agency should implement their mutual aid agreements with other police agencies if necessary, and [with] fire and rescue agencies. Additionally, it may be necessary after the incident to collaborate with recovery agencies to assist with the scene and any victims.[442]

The policy also provides guidance on incident command:

- The first responding supervisor, if not needed as part of a Contact Team, will assume the role of Incident Commander and establish a Command Post in a safe area away from the structure. (If the first arriving supervisor is needed and becomes a part of a Contact Team, the second arriving supervisor will become Incident Commander.)

- This supervisor will begin coordinating other parts of the incident including the deployment of Rescue Teams, until relieved by a higher ranking or assigned Incident Commander.

---

[442] CIR Document and Data Request.

Critical Incident Review: Active Shooter at Robb Elementary School |
Chapter 3. Leadership, Incident Command, and Coordination

122

- The initial Incident Commander should focus their activities to:
  - Maintaining open communications with any Contact Teams deployed.
  - Assembling and sending in Rescue Teams as soon as possible.
  - Establishing an inner perimeter.
  - Establishing a[n] evacuee area.
- The department will provide training to all department supervisors on the Incident Command process and priorities for command.[443]

UCISD Policies

UCISD PD did not have an active shooter policy; however, UCISD did have an annex specifically related to incident command roles and responsibilities that states:

- Once an active shooter has been verified, the District police department Chief will become the person in control of the efforts of all law enforcement and first responders that arrive at the scene.
- If able, secure the administration office as a command post and retrieve the critical information and data about the school's emergency systems . . . If the incident is occurring at the administration office, designate an alternate command post.
- District police department has the functions / responsibilities: 'shall be responsible for the Incident Command Center and first on scene to prevent or stop an active shooter.'
- Line of succession:
  - UCISD PD Chief Pete Arredondo
  - UCISD PD Lt. [*removed by CIR team*]
  - Director of Student Services [*removed by CIR team*] [Note: Director of Student Services is a civilian position within UCISD.][444]

On the day of tragedy, there were some policies in place to govern coordination among agencies with overlapping jurisdiction. The UCISD policies, for example, contained an annex that identified the school district police chief as the incident commander for active shooters. At the same time, however, it stated that the Uvalde CISD police department, Uvalde County Sheriff's Office, Uvalde City Police Department, Local Border Patrol, game wardens, and the Uvalde County Emergency Management Team will "participate in the development, implementation, and evaluation in this annex."[445] (See "Chapter 7. School Safety and Security" and "Chapter 8. Pre-Incident Planning and Preparation.")

---

[443] CIR Document and Data Review.

[444] CIR Document and Data Review.

[445] CIR Document and Data Review.

Critical Incident Review: Active Shooter at Robb Elementary School |
Chapter 3. Leadership, Incident Command, and Coordination

123

The UCISD Multi-Hazard Emergency Basic Operations Plan (EOP) 2021-2022 states under the planning assumptions section:

> The District is not an emergency response organization and therefore depends upon local emergency first responders for life safety and protection, including the services of law enforcement, fire, emergency medical and public health.
>
> . . .
>
> Action is required immediately to save lives and protect school property. An incident (e.g., fire, gas main breakage) could occur at any time without warning and the employees of the school affected cannot, and should not, wait for direction from District administration or local response agencies.
>
> Outside assistance from local fire, law enforcement and emergency managers will be available in most incidents. Because it takes time to request and dispatch external assistance, it is essential for the school to be prepared to carry out the initial incident response until responders arrive at the incident scene.[446]

The plan further states that the expectations of the city and county in support of the school district are to "provide emergency response for life safety and protection."[447]

UCISD PD officers also taught a 2021 SBLE-Active Shooter Course just months before the attack at Robb Elementary School.[448] That course was based on the *Active Shooter Response for School-Based Law Enforcement* (SBLE) guide developed by the Texas Commission on Law Enforcement (TCOLE) in January 2020.[449] As described more fully in "Chapter 8. Pre-Incident Planning and Preparation," the guide include a number of statements and guidance that diverge from the generally accepted active shooter practices described above.

For example, the guide states "an event that starts as an active shooter event can easily morph into a hostage crisis and vice versa,"[450] which is particularly concerning language and not in accord with generally accepted practices and standards. As detailed in "Chapter 2. Tactics and Equipment," an active shooter rarely ceases to be an active shooter. Based on generally accepted practices and standards in active shooter response and based on national training materials,[451] the situation should be considered an active shooter, especially in a school setting, based on the high probability of the presence of victims and innocent civilians.

---

[446] CIR Document and Data Review.

[447] CIR Document and Data Review.

[448] CIR Fact Finding.

[449] TCOLE, *Active Shooter Response for School-Based Law Enforcement*.

[450] TCOLE, *Active Shooter Response for School-Based Law Enforcement*.

[451] ALERRT, *Active Shooter Response Level 1 Version 7.2*; DHS, *Law Enforcement Active Shooter Emergency Response*; CIR Document and Data Review.

Critical Incident Review: Active Shooter at Robb Elementary School |
Chapter 3. Leadership, Incident Command, and Coordination

124

The guide also states, "In the event of an active school attack, school-based law enforcement officers should do the best they can to fill the gap until other first responders can arrive."[452] The language counters the trainings of the National Association of School Resource Officers and the Texas Association of School Resource Officers, which instruct trainees to move toward the stimuli indicating an active shooter threat and seek to eliminate it in a tactically sound way, without waiting for additional resources.

It is also problematic that the guidebook states the three primary goals in responding to an active attack in schools are to:

- **ISOLATE** – Drive or segregate the attacker in an area where their capacity to harm students, staff, or visitors is minimized until more first responders arrive.

- **DISTRACT** – Engage the attacker so that they have a diminished capacity to hurt students, staff, or visitors. If they are engaged with the officer(s) they will be less capable of hurting innocents. It also buys time for students, staff, and visitors to implement their Avoid-Deny-Defend (ADD) strategies.

- **NEUTRALIZE** – Take away the attacker's capacity to harm other people. This may include the use of deadly force, disabling an attacker, or disarming an attacker and taking them into custody.[453]

In particular, UCISD's course guidance to "distract" the attacker is concerning and goes against the entire mindset of an active shooter, who has the goal of killing as many people as possible. There is no negotiation with an active shooter. The strategy should be consistent with generally accepted training, which focuses on stopping the killing and stopping the dying.

UCISD-UPD Agreements

In addition to the active shooter and incident command policies, there were some policies in place to govern coordination among agencies with overlapping jurisdiction. UCISD PD and UPD entered into a memorandum of understanding (MOU) dated August 5, 2019, per the requirement of Texas Education Code 37.081(g).[454] The agreement between UCISD and UPD, effective August 5, 2019, is intended to "outline reasonable communication and coordination efforts" when agencies have "overlapping jurisdiction."[455]

---

[452] TCOLE, *Active Shooter Response for School-Based Law Enforcement.*

[453] TCOLE, *Active Shooter Response for School-Based Law Enforcement.*

[454] Texas Education Code 37.081(g) requires school district police departments and local law enforcement agencies with overlapping jurisdictions to "enter into a memorandum of understanding that outlines reasonable communication and coordination efforts between the department and the agencies."

[455] CIR Document and Data Review.

Critical Incident Review: Active Shooter at Robb Elementary School |
Chapter 3. Leadership, Incident Command, and Coordination

125

The MOU states in part:

> Uvalde Consolidated Independent School District Department's primary duty is to respond to and investigate all crimes, including infractions, misdemeanors, and felonies, as set forth herein:
>
> A. Crimes committed by or against district students, employees, or the general public, on or near district property, during regular school hours or while attending school-sponsored events, or while traveling directly to and from school and/or school-sponsored events.
>
> B. Crimes committed against district property.[456]

It further states that "Uvalde CISD PD generally does not field units during evenings, weekends, and some holidays. Uvalde City Police Department will generally respond during those times."[457] The MOU does not directly address emergency situations or MOUs with multiagency responses to critical incidents.

Texas Education Code Related to School Safety

In 2001, the Texas Legislature authorized the establishment of the Texas School Safety Center (TxSSC), under Texas Education Code—Chapter 37.201.* The TxSSC serves as a research center and clearinghouse for safety and security information.† Under Section 37.2121 of the statute, the TxSSC has direction, guidance, and responsibilities related to MOUs and mutual aid agreements between school districts and other responders regarding school safety and security. The section reads:

Sec. 37.2121

Memoranda of Understanding and Mutual Aid Agreements

(a) The center shall identify and inform school districts of the types of entities, including local and regional authorities, other school districts, and emergency first responders, with whom school districts should customarily make efforts to enter into memoranda of understanding or mutual aid agreements addressing issues that affect school safety and security.

(b) The center shall develop guidelines regarding memoranda of understanding and mutual aid agreements between school districts and the entities identified in accordance with Subsection (a). The guidelines:

(1) must include descriptions of the provisions that should customarily be included in each memorandum or agreement with a particular type of entity.

(2) may include sample language for those provisions. *continues on page 127*

---

[456] CIR Document and Data Review.

[457] CIR Document and Data Review.

Critical Incident Review: Active Shooter at Robb Elementary School |
Chapter 3. Leadership, Incident Command, and Coordination

126

Texas Education Code Related to School Safety, cont'd.

(3) must be consistent with the Texas Statewide Mutual Aid System established under Subchapter E-1 (Creation of the Texas Statewide Mutual Aid System), Chapter 418 (Emergency Management), Government Code.

(c) The center shall encourage school districts to enter into memoranda of understanding and mutual aid agreements with entities identified in accordance with Subsection (a) that comply with the guidelines developed under Subsection (b).

(d) Each school district that enters into a memorandum of understanding or mutual aid agreement addressing issues that affect school safety and security shall, at the center's request, provide a copy of the memorandum or agreement to the center.

(1) A copy of a memorandum of understanding or mutual aid agreement provided to the center under Subsection (d) is confidential and not subject to disclosure under Chapter 552 (Public Information), Government Code.

(e) The center shall include information regarding the center's efforts under this section in the report required by Section 37.216 (Biennial Report).

Added by Acts 2009, 81st Leg., R.S., Ch. 1280 (H.B. 1831), Sec. 6.09, eff. September 1, 2009.[‡]

See "Chapter 7. School Safety and Security" for more on this topic.

———————————

* Tx. Ed. Code § 37.201.

† Texas School Safety Center, "About."

‡Tx. Ed. Code § 37.201.

While UCISD PD had a general communication and collaboration MOU with UPD, there were no MOUs with first responders related to the response to a critical incident such as an active assailant.

USMS Policy

The USMS Policy Directive *10.7 Active Shooter/Active Threat* (ASAT) establishes guidance that directs the development of an ASAT plan for each facility with USMS presence; annual training and drills; and a designated ASAT Coordinator.[458] The directive includes critical elements for a facility ASAT plan but does not provide details and guidance on what those elements should include. The CIR team was unable to ascertain what is included in the individual facility plans and whether those individual facility plans would be in line with the circumstances that occurred on May 24, 2022.

———————————

[458] CIR Document and Data Review.

Critical Incident Review: Active Shooter at Robb Elementary School |
Chapter 3. Leadership, Incident Command, and Coordination

127

Other Policies

UCSO does not have a specific, applicable policy on active shooter response.[459] CBP reports that it also does not have a relevant policy.[460] Based on public reporting, the CIR team's understanding is TXDPS also did not have a policy but instead relied on Advanced Law Enforcement Rapid Response Training (ALERRT) guidance/doctrine.

Leadership Roles in Uvalde

The following sub-sections are provided to introduce the Texas law enforcement roles, including the sheriff, constable, and the Texas Rangers, that had a leadership role during the incident. More universally applicable types like municipal and school are not included below.

The Role of the Sheriff

The role, authority, and responsibility of the sheriff include:

- Under the Texas Code of Criminal Procedure Article 2.17, "Each sheriff shall be a conservator of the peace in his county, and shall arrest all offenders against the laws of the State, in his view or hearing, and take them before the proper court for examination or trial. He shall quell and suppress all assaults and batteries, affrays, insurrections and unlawful assemblies. He shall apprehend and commit to jail all offenders, until an examination or trial can be had."[461]

- According to the *2021 Guide to Texas Laws for County Officials* prepared for the Texas Association of Counties, "Sheriff is a constitutionally created office with duties to be described by the legislature (Texas Constitution Article V, Section 23). The Sheriff is the Chief Law Enforcement officer for the county and is responsible for operating county jails, investigating crimes, enforcing judgments, and maintaining communications with other law enforcement organizations. The sheriff has countywide jurisdiction, but in practice, most sheriff departments concentrate their activities outside city limits where municipal officer[s] cannot operate."[462]

- A Texas Attorney General Opinion, JC-125, states, "The Sheriff is conservator of the peace in the county and has authority to perform law enforcement services throughout the county including the area within the boundaries of an incorporated city, absent an interlocal contract with the city. It is for the Sheriff, in the exercise of reasonable discretion, to determine how the law enforcement efforts of his office should be allocated to different areas of the county."[463]

---

[459] CIR Fact Finding; CIR Document and Data Review.

[460] CIR Fact Finding.

[461] TEX. CRIM. CODE § 2.17, General Duties of Officers: Conservator of the Peace.

[462] Brooks, *2021 Guide to Texas Laws for County Officials*.

[463] Cornyn, *Opinion No. JC-0125 Re: Authority of County*.

Critical Incident Review: Active Shooter at Robb Elementary School |
Chapter 3. Leadership, Incident Command, and Coordination

128

Further, the City of Uvalde is a home-rule municipality. Under the Texas Constitution, Article XI, Section 5, because its population is greater than 5,000, Uvalde can adopt a charter and have full control over its municipal affairs, including law enforcement duties. Uvalde has adopted a charter, and below is a section from the City of Uvalde Charter which says that the city's police chief "shall have like power with the sheriff of the county" and "shall have, possess and execute like power, authority and jurisdiction as the sheriff." The charter further states the following:

> 2.56.030 -Chief—Powers and duties.
>
> The chief of police shall, in person or by deputy, attend upon the municipal court while in session, and shall promptly and faithfully execute all writs and process issued from the court. The chief shall have like power with the sheriff of the county to execute warrants and the chief shall be active in quelling riots, disorder and disturbance of the peace within the city limits and shall take into custody all persons so offending against the peace of the city and shall have authority to take suitable and sufficient bail for the appearance before the municipal court of any person charged with an offense against the ordinances or laws of the city. It shall be the chief's duty to arrest, without warrant, all violators of the public peace, and all who obstruct or interfere with him or her in the execution of the duties of the office or who shall be guilty of any disorderly conduct or disturbance whatever to prevent a breach of the peace or preserve quiet and good order, the chief shall have authority to close any theater, ball room or other place or building of public resort. In the prevention and suppression of crime and arrest of offenders, the chief shall have, possess and execute like power, authority and jurisdiction as the sheriff. The chief shall perform such other duties and possess such other powers and authority as the city council may require and confer, not inconsistent with the constitution and laws of the state. (Prior code § 21-3)[464]

Based upon the Texas Code of Criminal Procedure, the Texas Constitution, and the Texas Attorney General Opinion, the sheriff is the chief law enforcement officer for the county and has the authority to perform law enforcement duties in the county and within the boundaries of incorporated cities, like Uvalde. The UPD chief has the same power and authority to perform those duties in Uvalde. However, how to allocate law enforcement resources to different areas in the county is within the sheriff's discretion.[465]

The Role of the Constable

In the state of Texas, the constable is constitutionally elected for 4 years and serves as "an authorized peace officer and is the chief process server of the justice court."[466] The constable has "statewide jurisdiction to execute any criminal process, and countywide jurisdiction to execute any civil process . . .

---

[464] Uvalde Municipal Code of Ordinances, Title 2, Chapter 2.56, Police Department.

[465] TEX. CRIM. CODE § 2.17, General Duties of Officers; John Cornyn, *Opinion No. JC-0125 Re: Authority of County*; Uvalde Municipal Code of Ordinances, Title 2, Chapter 2.56, Police Department.

[466] Brooks, *2021 Guide to Texas Laws for County Officials*.

Critical Incident Review: Active Shooter at Robb Elementary School |
Chapter 3. Leadership, Incident Command, and Coordination

129

[and] may also execute process issued by some state agencies."[467] The number of constables is determined by the population according to the most recent federal census, and in Uvalde County, they have five constables with one per precinct.[468]

The constable "may assist other law enforcement officers under interlocal agreements" (Secs. 362.001, 362.002, 362.003), is "made [an] associate member of [the Texas Department of Public Safety (TXDPS)]" (Sec. 411.009), and "cooperate[s] with director of public safety in crime prevention and public safety" (Sec. 411.009).[469]

The Role of the Rangers

In instances of multiple jurisdictions and per *The Texas Ranger Division Manual,* the Texas Rangers are the primary criminal investigative branch of TXDPS and the role, authority, and responsibility of the Rangers include the following (40.03.10.00):

> Officers of the Texas Ranger Division have the authority to make arrests, to execute process in criminal cases, and to execute process in civil cases when specifically directed by a judge of a court of record. They shall be governed by laws regulating and defining the authority and duties of sheriffs when discharging similar duties, except that they shall have the authorization to make arrests and to execute all processes of criminal cases in any county in the state. Texas Rangers have the authority to make arrests as directed by warrants and to make arrests without a warrant under conditions authorized by law.[470]

Further, Rangers should be "protecting life and property; and rendering assistance to local, state, and federal law enforcement officials in suppressing crime and violence."[471] In addition, "the Texas Ranger Division, through investigation and communication with federal, state, county, and municipal law enforcement agencies, shall be responsible for gathering and disseminating criminal intelligence pertaining to all facets of organized crime."[472] Furthermore, "under orders of the Director, the Texas Ranger Division shall suppress criminal activity in a given area when it is apparent that the local officials are unwilling or unable to maintain law and order."[473]

---

[467] Brooks, *2021 Guide to Texas Laws for County Officials*.

[468] Uvalde County, "Contact Us: Constables."

[469] Brooks, *2021 Guide to Texas Laws for County Officials*.

[470] CIR Document and Data Review.

[471] CIR Document and Data Review.

[472] CIR Document and Data Review.

[473] CIR Document and Data Review.

Critical Incident Review: Active Shooter at Robb Elementary School |
Chapter 3. Leadership, Incident Command, and Coordination

130

Rangers—and, to a certain extent, the broader TXDPS—are directed by policy to serve as a support asset and only take the lead position if asked by the requesting agency. However, in practice there is mixed feedback from local and county agencies about the role of TXDPS and specifically the Rangers when they arrive on a scene, with some saying they wait to be asked to lead and others saying it is standard practice that TXDPS takes over.[474]

Leadership and Command at Robb Elementary

From the time that law enforcement entered Robb Elementary, there were several stimuli that should have prompted leadership to direct a team to enter the classrooms and engage the subject. For the span of more than 1 hour, between 11:37 a.m. and 12:49 p.m., there were at least 10 stimulus events, including at least six separate instances of gunfire totaling approximately 45 rounds in law enforcement officer presence, as well as officer injuries and the presence of victims. Any one of these events should have driven the law enforcement response to take steps to immediately stop the killing per the active shooter protocols and guidance described above (see "Stimulus Throughout the Incident" in "Appendix D. Leadership, Incident Command, and Coordination Supplemental Materials").

During that period, no one assumed a leadership role to direct the response toward the active shooter, provide situational status to responding officers, establish some form of incident command, or clearly assume and communicate the role of incident commander. Interviews with responding officers confirmed that there was confusion about who, if anyone, was in charge, what to do, or the status of the incident.[475] Some officers were confused about why there was no attempt to confront the active shooter and rescue the children.[476] Without structure, agency leadership was unaware of the facts surrounding the incident and therefore unable to challenge the repeated decisions not to make entry into the classrooms.

The analysis in this section proceeds by examining leadership action and inaction at several critical points in the response, including: the initial response, the transition to a barricaded subject, the arrival of additional resources, the establishment of a command post, and post-incident.

Initial Response

Eleven law enforcement officers, including supervisors, were inside the hallway within a span of 21 seconds of each other and only 3 minutes after the subject made entry into the school (see figure 3-3 on page 132 for the arrival order). These 11 individuals are considered first on the scene (FOS).

---

[474] CIR Fact Finding.

[475] CIR Fact Finding.

[476] CIR Fact Finding.

Critical Incident Review: Active Shooter at Robb Elementary School |
Chapter 3. Leadership, Incident Command, and Coordination

131

Figure 3-3. First on the scene

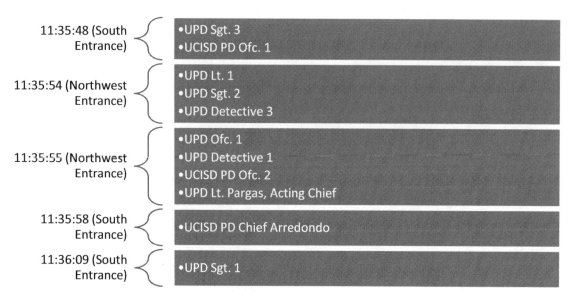

11:35:48 (South Entrance)	•UPD Sgt. 3 •UCISD PD Ofc. 1
11:35:54 (Northwest Entrance)	•UPD Lt. 1 •UPD Sgt. 2 •UPD Detective 3
11:35:55 (Northwest Entrance)	•UPD Ofc. 1 •UPD Detective 1 •UCISD PD Ofc. 2 •UPD Lt. Pargas, Acting Chief
11:35:58 (South Entrance)	•UCISD PD Chief Arredondo
11:36:09 (South Entrance)	•UPD Sgt. 1

Note: The Incident Timeline Reconstruction rounds to the nearest minute, while this chart shows the exact seconds.

The FOS were from two agencies: UPD and UCISD PD. UPD had direct jurisdictional authority, since the initial calls for service were about the crash by the funeral home and, therefore, inherently had command of this initial incident. UPD is also the main responding agency to incidents such as bailouts, which are high-speed law enforcement pursuits of undocumented immigrants who attempt to evade arrest by abandoning (or after crashing) their vehicles and running away on foot. UCISD PD also had concurrent jurisdiction. As a full-service campus law enforcement agency with on-site leadership, policy directives on responding to active shooter incidents, training, and certified law enforcement officers, it also shares ownership of the incident response responsibilities. However, UCISD PD also has limited tactical equipment and training, and a staffing schedule that is not 24/7, which requires them to be reliant on UPD for 911 and police dispatch services.

Leaders from either UPD or UCISD PD, including UPD Acting Chief Pargas[477] and UCISD PD Chief Arredondo, should have taken charge. In his position as UCISD PD Chief, Chief Arredondo—who responded in the capacity of an initial responder to an active shooter—should have observed the failure to establish an incident command structure. Arredondo had an obligation to recuse himself from the role of an officer and assume the role of a leader commensurate with his title, rank, experience, and training. He had direct knowledge of the school footprint and the knowledge that school was in session and students were still in class. A review of Chief Arredondo's training records also revealed that he had incident command structure, active shooter, school-based, and managing critical incident training—all of which provided him with the necessary exposure to assume initial command of the incident, as dictated by the UCISD policy described above. Given his years of experience, training, title, and direct knowledge of the school, Chief Arredondo should have either assumed incident command or conferred

[477] UPD Chief Daniel Rodriguez was out of the state on leave.

Critical Incident Review: Active Shooter at Robb Elementary School |
Chapter 3. Leadership, Incident Command, and Coordination

132

with UPD Acting Chief Pargas to have him assume and maintain command. Acting Chief Pargas, for his part, was a 21-year law enforcement veteran and the highest ranked officer of an agency with overlapping jurisdiction. A review of his training records, however, revealed that he had not received any incident command, active shooter, or tactical training.[478]

The FOS responded to the calls for service (see "Chapter 1. Incident Timeline Reconstruction") and made immediate entry into the hallway from the south and northwest entrances. Of the three senior ranking law enforcement officers who were FOS, UPD Lt. 1 and UCISD PD Chief Arredondo actively moved toward rooms 111 and 112 along with two UPD sergeants and a UCISD PD officer. These five FOS demonstrated forward momentum by focusing on the mission and bypassing unsecured classrooms in pursuit of the active shooter.

At the T-intersection (see figure 3-4 on page 134), the remaining FOS, including Acting Chief Pargas, did not advance down the hallway and instead maintained their initial positions in this area. At least two of the FOS at the T-intersection appeared to look to Acting Chief Pargas for direction;[479] however, Pargas did not maintain tactical communication with those officers. With the focus of UPD Lt. 1 and Chief Arredondo on the classrooms, UPD Acting Chief Pargas, in his role as the acting chief with concurrent authority, should have assumed a leadership role and taken control of the situation.

As shooting continued from inside the classrooms, and while FOS assessed the situation outside the classroom doors (see figure 3-5 on page 134), two officers were struck by shrapnel and debris. All FOS retreated to their respective sides of the hallway. During the FOS retreat due to the gunfire inside the classrooms, UCISD PD Ofc. 1 pointed in the direction of the gunfire and said, "that's my wife's classroom,"[480] providing the first indication captured on video that there were victims in classrooms 111 and 112. Shortly after, UPD Sgt. 2 asked over the radio whether room 112 (the wife's classroom) was in session,[481] and dispatch confirmed that "the class should be in session right now . . . the class should be in session right now . . .."[482] Around the same time, UCISD PD Chief Arredondo—who had "chucked" his radios while running to the building, since he was "fumbling with them"[483]—called dispatch (see "Chapter 1. Incident Timeline Reconstruction") and dispatch referenced a call that came in seconds before from a teacher who was in room 102, heard gunshots, and also heard that a teacher in another classroom was wounded.[484] Chief Arredondo confirmed this information.[485]

---

[478] CIR Training Analysis.

[479] Robb Elementary School CCTV Footage.

[480] Uvalde Police Department Body-Worn Camera Footage.

[481] Uvalde Police Department Radio Traffic.

[482] Uvalde Police Department Radio Traffic.

[483] CIR Fact Finding.

[484] Uvalde Police Department Dispatch Landline.

[485] Uvalde Police Department Dispatch Landline.

Critical Incident Review: Active Shooter at Robb Elementary School |
Chapter 3. Leadership, Incident Command, and Coordination

133

Figure 3-4. Hallway north of classrooms 111/112

Source: Robb Elementary School Hallway Footage.

From left to right: UPD Acting Chief Pargas (left foreground), UPD Det. 3 (middle background left), UPD Lt. 1 (far background left), UPD Sgt. 2 (far background right), UPD Ofc. 1 (center), UPD Det. 1 (right foreground), and UCISD PD Ofc. 1 (far right foreground).

Figure 3-5. FOS surrounding classrooms 111 and 112

Source: Uvalde Police Department Body-Worn Camera Footage.

From left to right: UPD Lt. 1, UPD Sgt. 3, UCISD PD Ofc. 2, and UCISD PD Chief Arredondo. Point of view is from UPD Sgt. 2.

Critical Incident Review: Active Shooter at Robb Elementary School |
Chapter 3. Leadership, Incident Command, and Coordination

134

In the subsequent three minutes, UPD Lt. 1 advanced three times toward the classrooms without any backup, and each time retreated back to the T-intersection.[486] Prior to advancing down the hallway each time, UPD leadership should have reconfigured the officers in a tactical formation to initiate entry into the classrooms (see "Chapter 2. Tactics and Equipment" for more on formations). This should have been under the responsibility of UPD Acting Chief Pargas as the highest ranked leader on this side of the hallway and as a 21-year law enforcement veteran. However, in the absence of that leadership direction, as the one advancing toward the room and a ranked officer, UPD Lt. 1 should have directed officers into formation, rather than advancing without directing backup personnel to follow.

At this point, 4 minutes since FOS made entry, both sides of the hallway had some knowledge that school was in session and there were teachers and children in the classrooms. As described in the active shooter response principles above and explained in more detail in "Chapter 2. Tactics and Equipment," the FOS also had sufficient training and equipment, as well as personnel, to engage the subject (see table 3-1 for available assets).

Table 3-1. Available assets from FOS

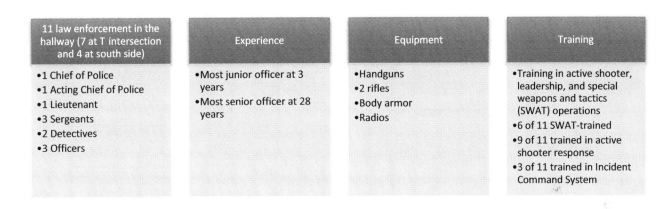

11 law enforcement in the hallway (7 at T intersection and 4 at south side)	Experience	Equipment	Training
•1 Chief of Police •1 Acting Chief of Police •1 Lieutenant •3 Sergeants •2 Detectives •3 Officers	•Most junior officer at 3 years •Most senior officer at 28 years	•Handguns •2 rifles •Body armor •Radios	•Training in active shooter, leadership, and special weapons and tactics (SWAT) operations •6 of 11 SWAT-trained •9 of 11 trained in active shooter response •3 of 11 trained in Incident Command System

No one entered the classrooms. Instead, the third retreat by UPD Lt. 1 ended all forward momentum by the FOS. Another 4 minutes later, UPD Acting Chief Pargas exited the hallway to obtain a radio from someone outside the doorway. This provided the ability to transmit and receive information to properly coordinate and align all responding resources via radio communication. On the south side, UCISD PD Chief Arredondo did not direct entry into the classrooms, and instead called dispatch. The resulting delay provided an opportunity for the active shooter to have additional time to reassess and reengage his deadly actions inside of the classroom. It also contributed to a delay in medical interventions with the potential to impact survivability.

With the lack of action by the FOS and UCISD PD Chief Arredondo's leadership decision to transition to a barricaded posture, all forward momentum stopped for the substantial number of officers in the hallway. This was the initial leadership mistake that created disengagement of the police resources in

---

[486] Robb Elementary School CCTV Footage.

Critical Incident Review: Active Shooter at Robb Elementary School |
Chapter 3. Leadership, Incident Command, and Coordination

135

the hallway, even though the resources were readily available, equipped, and physically and tactically trained to engage the active shooter directly. At this point, leadership should have seized the forward momentum of the officers and penetrated the classroom without hesitation. This tactical leadership decision at this critical point would have likely been avoided if law enforcement had opted to follow basic and generally accepted policing practices and training.

While the FOS were in the hallway, more law enforcement personnel were arriving on the scene, some of whom are important to highlight from a leadership perspective. In front of Robb Elementary School, an SUV pulled up with two constables and two Southwest Texas Junior College (SWTJC) instructors at the criminal justice academy who were also sworn law enforcement. A UPD officer who had been outside the school trying to determine what to do, approached one of the instructors and said ". . . where do you want us?"[487] As the team of constables and instructors advanced forward, the UPD officer followed and called over other officers, saying, ". . . we're behind you."[488]

This example highlights the confusion early on and throughout the incident around the role of leadership and how interconnected the law enforcement community was in Uvalde. From interviews and observations of body-worn camera footage, it is apparent that the Uvalde law enforcement community, though divided into different agencies, operated with a close familiarity with one another, irrespective of agency. For some officers, this familiarity extended to an ad hoc and inadequately executed cooperative response, as exemplified by officers seeking direction from leadership of other law enforcement entities. This highlights the importance of pre-incident planning and the value of multijurisdictional agreements and training, which did not occur prior to this incident (see "Chapter 8. Pre-Incident Planning and Preparation" for more on this topic).

Transition to Barricaded Subject

With the conclusion of the forward momentum among the FOS, some leadership and law enforcement began treating the incident as a barricaded subject as opposed to an active shooter situation. As explained in more detail in "Chapter 2. Tactics and Equipment," a barricaded subject situation generally involves a subject or suspect who is being sought by law enforcement, has placed themselves in a physical location that is not immediately accessible, and has refused orders to exit.[489] In such situations, time is on the side of law enforcement, who can marshal resources such as negotiators, SWAT teams, and specialized equipment and tools, and continually assess options to resolve the situation. By contrast, in an active shooter situation, as described in "Chapter 2. Tactics and Equipment," priority concerns of law enforcement are the neutralization of the threat, the prevention of more injuries and death, and beginning to triage and provide appropriate medical aid to the injured.

---

[487] Uvalde Police Department Body-Worn Camera Footage.

[488] Uvalde Police Department Body-Worn Camera Footage.

[489] *Model Policy on Response to Barricaded Individuals,* International Association of Chiefs of Police.

Critical Incident Review: Active Shooter at Robb Elementary School |
Chapter 3. Leadership, Incident Command, and Coordination

136

As the incident progressed, there was neither command presence nor direction to align personnel and equipment, especially as the numbers were increasing for both. Law enforcement personnel displayed a general lack of urgency and inaction toward penetrating classrooms 111 and 112, with some trying to evacuate the children and staff from other classrooms, others trying to find keys and access equipment, and still others on the phone with superiors or other law enforcement personnel not on the scene.[490] Some in law enforcement also referenced penetrating the classrooms as a "suicide mission" because of the "fatal funnel"[491] as reasons to delay their response.[492]

Within 8 minutes from when FOS entered the school, at least three calls for service had been made from inside the school from civilians in classrooms.[493]

Sixteen minutes later, at 11:57 a.m., UCISD PD Ofc. 1 received confirmation that his spouse was shot in one of the classrooms. While attempting to move toward the mouth of the T-intersection, several people called the officer by name to stop him, and Uvalde County Precinct 1 Constable Johnny Field held him back from moving forward.[494] Although UPD Acting Chief Pargas came from behind and redirected the officer out of the hallway,[495] Pargas did not obtain support for the officer or collect intelligence about the situation.

After the officer was removed from the hallway, Constable Field was on one of many phone calls with UCISD PD Chief Pete Arredondo. At one point Constable Field appeared to relay directions from a call with Arredondo, when he directed personnel to clear the other side of the hallway due to crossfire (see figure 3-6 on page 138).[496] This was an example of filling a leadership void with command presence. However, the lack of response from the officers illustrated the confusion on who was in charge of the incident.

---

[490] CIR Fact Finding.

[491] Jimmy Pearce and Scott Goldstein, "EMS Tactical Movement Techniques."

[492] CIR Fact Finding.

[493] Uvalde Police Department Radio Traffic.

[494] Uvalde Police Department Body-Worn Camera Footage.

[495] Uvalde Police Department Body-Worn Camera Footage.

[496] Uvalde Police Department Body-Worn Camera Footage.

Critical Incident Review: Active Shooter at Robb Elementary School |
Chapter 3. Leadership, Incident Command, and Coordination

137

Figure 3-6. Uvalde County Constable Field providing direction to law enforcement personnel

Source: Uvalde Police Department Body-Worn Camera Footage.

Around this time outside of the West Building, a Texas Parks and Wildlife game warden was on the phone providing a situational update. The game warden referenced that a CBP Border Patrol Tactical Unit (BORTAC) was on its way to make possible entry and that they "have everything covered, working on reunification right now."[497]

Around 12:08 p.m., UCISD PD Chief Arredondo and a UPD detective again attempted to begin a dialogue with the shooter in both English and Spanish. The attempts to negotiate were unsuccessful.

Around this time, law enforcement personnel began to express frustration with the inaction toward penetrating classrooms 111/112. For example, an unknown law enforcement officer asked UPD Acting Chief Pargas, "Are we just waiting for BORTAC or what's going on?" Acting Chief Pargas nodded and referenced that the "[TX]DPS Ranger called someone to come in as well."[498] However, there was a significant amount of personnel and firepower, and Acting Chief Pargas should have coordinated with other leaders to make entry.

At approximately 12:12, a law enforcement stack/entry team with a shield tried to enter the south side hallway and Chief Arredondo put up a hand as if to slow them down or stop them, saying "Guys, hold on, we are going to clear the building first . . . empty these classrooms first."[499]

---

[497] Texas Parks and Wildlife Body-Worn Camera Footage.

[498] Uvalde Police Department Body-Worn Camera Footage.

[499] Uvalde County Constables Body-Worn Camera Footage.

Critical Incident Review: Active Shooter at Robb Elementary School |
Chapter 3. Leadership, Incident Command, and Coordination

138

Around this same time, a call for service came across the police radios saying, "child on the line."[500] The dispatcher further stated, "He [subject] is in a room full of victims."[501] Outside the northwest entrance, an officer was stressing to UPD Acting Chief Pargas that "the room is full of victims."[502] Acting Chief Pargas grabbed the radio and walked away to make the phone call to dispatch to get clarity. Four minutes after the radio transmission, Acting Chief Pargas asked dispatch if there were enough emergency medical services (EMS) on standby, then asked about the call from the child.[503] He received confirmation that there were "8, 9 still alive" and that the dispatcher was "not too sure" about the number of wounded.[504]

At this point, it was shared broadly across the radio channel that there were students and teachers injured and dying in room 112, which should have made clear to all law enforcement personnel listening that this incident was and always had been an active shooter situation and that law enforcement should act to stop the dying per the active shooter principles described above.

By 12:13, the CBP BORTAC Commander arrived in the hallway. A UPD officer came into the hallway via the northwest entrance, walked past UPD Acting Chief Pargas, and said "Hey, who's in charge of tac?"[505] Everyone looked to BORTAC Commander,[506] who had just arrived in the hallway, suggesting that he was then in charge tactically. An unknown officer told the CBP BORTAC commander that there were victims in the room, to which the commander acknowledged verifying the information, and several officers in the hallway said that was correct.[507] The commander should have then coordinated with other leaders to urgently execute a plan to enter the classrooms and engage the subject.

Around 12:16, while Chief Arredondo and UPD Lt. 1 were trying the keys on the door of room 109, a group of officers advanced up the hallway to where they were, and Chief Arredondo told a TXDPS sergeant to "Tell them to f***ing wait."[508] TXDPS Sgt. conveyed this direction from Chief Arredondo to the BORTAC commander, who was perceived to be about to make entry.[509] While they were trying the keys, radios could be heard in the hallway, and the deference to Chief Arredondo was apparent. There were now at least nine officers within close proximity to the door with four rifles and one ballistic (not rifle-rated) shield readily available on the southside of the hallway (see "Chapter 2. Tactics and Equipment" for more on the number of shields present on each side of the hallway).

---

[500] Uvalde Police Department Body-Worn Camera Footage.

[501] Uvalde Police Department Body-Worn Camera Footage.

[502] Uvalde Police Department Body-Worn Camera Footage.

[503] Uvalde Police Department Dispatch Landline.

[504] Uvalde Police Department Dispatch Landline.

[505] Uvalde Police Department Body-Worn Camera Footage.

[506] Uvalde Police Department Body-Worn Camera Footage.

[507] Uvalde Police Department Body-Worn Camera Footage.

[508] Uvalde County Constables Body-Worn Camera Footage.

[509] CIR Fact Finding.

Critical Incident Review: Active Shooter at Robb Elementary School |
Chapter 3. Leadership, Incident Command, and Coordination

139

At 12:21, four shots were fired inside classrooms 111 and 112 (see "Chapter 1. Incident Timeline Reconstruction"). Some law enforcement, including the BORTAC commander in the T-intersection, immediately and wordlessly moved into formation (see figure 3-7). However, the forward momentum stopped steps away from classrooms 112 and 111 (see figures 3-8, 3-9, and 3-10 on pages 141 and 142) near the janitor's closet. Although there was confusion about why the team stopped without making entry, many believed it was because the door was thought to be locked.[510]

Figure 3-7. Personnel from Zavala County, CBP, and TXDPS advancing after shots fired

Source: Robb Elementary School CCTV Footage.

---

[510] CIR Fact Finding.

Critical Incident Review: Active Shooter at Robb Elementary School |
Chapter 3. Leadership, Incident Command, and Coordination

140

Figure 3-8. Personnel lined up feet away from the vestibule for rooms 111/112 (arrow) at 12:26

Source: Uvalde Police Department Body-Worn Camera Footage.

Figure 3-9. Personnel lined up feet away from rooms 111/112 at 12:29, with significant firepower and a shield

Source: Uvalde Police Department Body-Worn Camera Footage.

Critical Incident Review: Active Shooter at Robb Elementary School |
Chapter 3. Leadership, Incident Command, and Coordination

141

Figure 3-10. Personnel lined up feet away from rooms 111/112

Source: Uvalde Police Department Body-Worn Camera Footage.

At this point, the victims in rooms 111 and 112 would wait another 29 minutes before law enforcement entered the classroom. This was another critical point where the active shooter principles described above would have suggested that leadership should organize an entry team and penetrate the classroom.

Sixteen minutes before law enforcement made entry into the classrooms, an unknown TXDPS trooper asked Constable Zamora the name of the building so he could try to get more ambulances in the teacher parking lot at the west side of the building. The trooper asked, "Are they good on manpower?" Constable Zamora responded "Yes, they are good on manpower." With an absence of strong formal leadership, natural leaders stepped up to try to coordinate and ensure enough resources were available, as evidenced in this exchange.

Minutes before the entry by law enforcement, a FOS UPD sergeant asked Constable Zamora, "When he [subject] shot again . . . was he shooting toward the hallway?" Constable Zamora responded, "We didn't see no dust come in the hallway." Yet UCISD PD Chief Arredondo could be heard still shouting to negotiate with the shooter and taking no action to penetrate the classroom.

Arrival of Additional Resources

Over the course of the incident, extraordinary numbers of additional law enforcement personnel were arriving on the scene. In total, at least 380 personnel from 24 agencies across local, county, state, and federal agencies deployed to the school. Self-deployment (where law enforcement personnel respond to a scene without authorization) can be a common occurrence in critical incidents, but due to the shared connections in this community, the tragedy at an elementary school, and the number of local, state, and federal law enforcement agencies within close proximity, a remarkable number of personnel descended on Robb Elementary. Figure 3-11 on page 143 and table 3-2 on page 144 include all verified

Critical Incident Review: Active Shooter at Robb Elementary School |
Chapter 3. Leadership, Incident Command, and Coordination

142

and known law enforcement that arrived during the incident and/or soon after the entry by the law enforcement team and assisted with evacuations, perimeter, or room clearings. The map includes locations of personnel where known and is not meant to be an exhaustive list.

Figure 3-11. Responding agencies

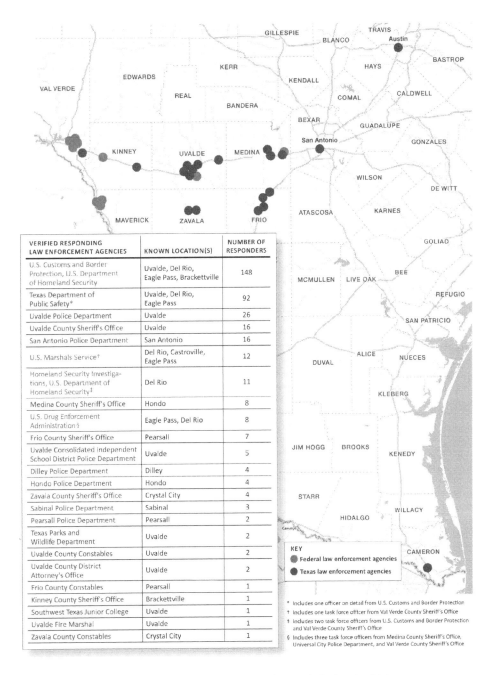

VERIFIED RESPONDING LAW ENFORCEMENT AGENCIES	KNOWN LOCATION(S)	NUMBER OF RESPONDERS
U.S. Customs and Border Protection, U.S. Department of Homeland Security	Uvalde, Del Rio, Eagle Pass, Brackettville	148
Texas Department of Public Safety*	Uvalde, Del Rio, Eagle Pass	92
Uvalde Police Department	Uvalde	26
Uvalde County Sheriff's Office	Uvalde	16
San Antonio Police Department	San Antonio	16
U.S. Marshals Service†	Del Rio, Castroville, Eagle Pass	12
Homeland Security Investigations, U.S. Department of Homeland Security‡	Del Rio	11
Medina County Sheriff's Office	Hondo	8
U.S. Drug Enforcement Administration§	Eagle Pass, Del Rio	8
Frio County Sheriff's Office	Pearsall	7
Uvalde Consolidated Independent School District Police Department	Uvalde	5
Dilley Police Department	Dilley	4
Hondo Police Department	Hondo	4
Zavala County Sheriff's Office	Crystal City	4
Sabinal Police Department	Sabinal	3
Pearsall Police Department	Pearsall	2
Texas Parks and Wildlife Department	Uvalde	2
Uvalde County Constables	Uvalde	2
Uvalde County District Attorney's Office	Uvalde	2
Frio County Constables	Pearsall	1
Kinney County Sheriff's Office	Brackettville	1
Southwest Texas Junior College	Uvalde	1
Uvalde Fire Marshal	Uvalde	1
Zavala County Constables	Crystal City	1

KEY
● Federal law enforcement agencies
● Texas law enforcement agencies

* Includes one officer on detail from U.S. Customs and Border Protection
† Includes one task force officer from Val Verde County Sheriff's Office
‡ Includes two task force officers from U.S. Customs and Border Protection and Val Verde County Sheriff's Office
§ Includes three task force officers from Medina County Sheriff's Office, Universal City Police Department, and Val Verde County Sheriff's Office

Map source: National Geographic MapMaker. Data source: CIR data analysis chart/multiple sources.

Critical Incident Review: Active Shooter at Robb Elementary School | Chapter 3. Leadership, Incident Command, and Coordination

143

Table 3-2. Responding agencies

Verified responding law enforcement agencies	Known location(s)	Number of responders
U.S. Customs and Border Protection, U.S. Department of Homeland Security	Uvalde, Del Rio, Eagle Pass, Brackettville	148
Texas Department of Public Safety*	Uvalde, Del Rio, Eagle Pass	92
Uvalde Police Department	Uvalde	26
Uvalde County Sheriff's Office	Uvalde	16
San Antonio Police Department	San Antonio	16
U.S. Marshals Service[†]	Del Rio, Castroville, Eagle Pass	12
Homeland Security Investigations, U.S. Department of Homeland Security[‡]	Del Rio	11
Medina County Sheriff's Office	Hondo	8
U.S. Drug Enforcement Administration[§]	Eagle Pass, Del Rio	8
Frio County Sheriff's Office	Pearsall	7
Uvalde Consolidated Independent School District Police Department	Uvalde	5
Dilley Police Department	Dilley	4
Hondo Police Department	Hondo	4
Zavala County Sheriff's Office	Crystal City	4
Sabinal Police Department	Sabinal	3
Pearsall Police Department	Pearsall	2
Texas Parks and Wildlife Department	Uvalde	2
Uvalde County Constable	Uvalde	2
Uvalde County District Attorney's Office	Uvalde	2
Frio County Constables	Pearsall	1
Kinney County Sheriff's Office	Brackettville	1
Southwest Texas Junior College	Uvalde	1
Uvalde Fire Marshal	Uvalde	1
Zavala County Constables	Crystal City	1

Federal agencies are underlined.

* Includes one officer on detail from U.S. Customs and Border Protection

† Includes one task force officer from Val Verde County Sheriff's Office

‡ Includes two task force officers from U.S. Customs and Border Protection and Val Verde County Sheriff's Office

§ Includes three task force officers from Medina County Sheriff's Office, Universal City Police Department, and Val Verde County Sheriff's Office

As agencies arrived, the incident command structure should have transitioned from a single incident commander to a unified command. Within the unified command should have been the primary law enforcement responders—i.e., UPD, UCISD PD, UCSO, TXDPS, and CBP—as well as the emergency medical liaison, UCISD/school liaison, victim services, and others as needed. There was, however, no

Critical Incident Review: Active Shooter at Robb Elementary School |
Chapter 3. Leadership, Incident Command, and Coordination

144

incident command and therefore no basic structure for establishing a unified command to provide the necessary awareness and direction. Nor was there a staging area, a structured perimeter around the hallway or the school, or a readily identifiable command post outside the hallway that could serve as a base for the coordination of agency leaders and the assignment of responsibilities to incoming resources. Without structure, agency leadership was unaware of the facts surrounding the incident and therefore unable to challenge the repeated decisions not to make entry into the classrooms.

The lack of clear command structures and coordination among personnel from different agencies left arriving resources to position themselves however they assumed to be the most appropriate, without direction or alignment. This, in turn, overwhelmed the hallway with excess police resources that created sensory overload for the FOS in the hallway and potentially dangerous crossfire situations, further stagnating the required immediate action to enter the classroom (see figures 3-12, 3-13, and 3-14 on pages 145 and 146 for depictions of the overabundance of personnel.) The lack of clear command presence also left arriving officers in limbo with a lack of urgency. The lack of urgency became confusing to later arriving officers, many of whom arrived from jurisdictions as far as an hour away and, when they saw the lack of urgency, sadly and incorrectly assumed that the threat had been eliminated. Once it became clear that the incident was still active, most were surprised. Post-incident interviews of FOS confirmed that the resources within the hallway were perceived to have been disorganized and without purpose.[511]

Figure 3-12. Personnel outside of the south entrance door

Source: Uvalde County Constables Body-Worn Camera Footage.

---

[511] CIR Fact Finding.

Critical Incident Review: Active Shooter at Robb Elementary School |
Chapter 3. Leadership, Incident Command, and Coordination

145

Figure 3-13. Personnel in the T-intersection

Source: Uvalde County Sheriff's Office Body-Worn Camera Footage.

Including the CBP commander (left, wearing camo and a helmet), BPAs, and UPD officers

Figure 3-14. Personnel in the T-intersection

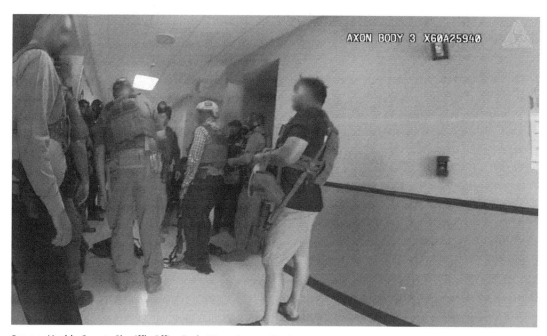

Source: Uvalde County Sheriff's Office Body-Worn Camera Footage.

Including UCSO chief deputy (far left), TX Ranger 1 (back view, in green), and game warden (far right in shorts)

Critical Incident Review: Active Shooter at Robb Elementary School |
Chapter 3. Leadership, Incident Command, and Coordination

146

The CIR team also heard from responders that they were not provided with a situational status and were given limited to no direction.[512] Without an incident command structure, responders were left with unofficial information that may not have been accurate.[513] Rumors were spread that UCISD PD Chief Arredondo was in the classroom with the subject.[514] Others heard that the subject had made his way into the ceiling or could be exiting to the roof.[515]

Leadership also did not establish a coordinated perimeter further away from the scene to coordinate parents, family, and community members that arrived on the scene. As discussed in more detail in "Chapter 6. Trauma and Support Services," upon learning about the incident, several parents and loved ones went immediately to Robb Elementary School, where they were met by law enforcement outside the school building. Most personnel self-deployed to the scene and, without much guidance, attempted to establish an outer perimeter. For example, the game warden was on the phone outside the West Building, asking for someone to reach out to the Emergency Operations Center (EOC) to help with setting up the perimeter security.[516] The game warden also talked with Uvalde County Precinct 6 Constable Emmanuel Zamora about getting the families away from the West Building, as well as the need to set up a perimeter.[517] Without proper command and control, a game warden and constable were taking on roles traditionally performed by an incident commander. Family and community members received little to no consistent information, misinformation (see "Chapter 5: Public Communications During and Following the Crisis"), and, in some instances, rough treatment that included use of force (see "Chapter 6. Trauma and Support Services").

The establishment of an inner and outer perimeter and a staging area would have allowed for the alignment of approaching resources and management of a coordinated and disciplined response. It also would have created a working platform designed for all responding resources to have a purpose and intended outcome. Leadership could have taken the basic action to direct an officer to control the perimeter and stop any additional personnel from entering the hallway; that simple step would have provided an opportunity for the FOS to adjust and provide a safer tactical platform. One of the FOS leaders other than Chief Arredondo, who was engaged with the immediate response in the building, could have positioned outside of the hallway to provide the most advantageous command position for observing, visualizing the broader scope of the incident, summoning all support agency leaders to his location to establish a coordinated response, and providing direction (e.g., to clear the roads and other egresses) for those officers inside the perimeter. This simple structure would have first attracted the responding resources and other leaders to Acting Chief Pargas or Sheriff Nolasco, who could then have structured and organized the plan of action and provided greater support for the FOS personnel directly addressing the active situation inside the hallway.

---

[512] CIR Fact Finding.

[513] CIR Fact Finding.

[514] CIR Fact Finding.

[515] CIR Fact Finding.

[516] Texas Parks and Wildlife Body-Worn Camera Footage.

[517] Texas Parks and Wildlife Body-Worn Camera Footage.

If leadership had established a clear command structure and presence, only those resources required in the hallway would have been allowed to enter the inner perimeter. It also would have allowed officers to shift individuals in plainclothes, in unidentifiable uniforms, or without (or properly fitted) body armor out of the hallway and away from the frontlines of the perimeter, including officers like UCISD PD Ofc. 1, who were emotionally involved due to a family member's presence in the classrooms or even one officer who was struggling to breathe "due to anxiety" and being told by several officers to "take deep breaths and relax."[518] These resources could have been taken to a command post to obtain any additional information to help with the response. UPD Acting Chief Pargas, as a FOS and the highest ranked leader of an agency with concurrent authority over the scene, was in the best position to perform a number of other tasks per UPD policies, including:

- Providing communication with situational status and request for resources.

- Setting up a command post and staging area to control and organize the anticipated flood of self-deployed personnel.

- Establishing inner and outer perimeters.

- Establishing a unified command with allied law enforcement agencies and emergency medical responders.

- Determining hot, warm, and cold zones.

As explained, however, despite his formal positional authority to assume command, Acting Chief Pargas lacked the requisite training to manage the incident. A review of Texas Commission for Law Enforcement (TCOLE) training records[519] revealed that UPD Acting Chief Pargas had not received any incident command, active shooter, or tactical training. This lack of training is not in accordance with UPD policy and suggests a failure of agency leadership to hold personnel accountable.

Chief Arredondo, who had the requisite training, experience, and knowledge of the school, attempted to lead at times by coordinating evacuations of and searching for keys to classrooms other than 111/112. His actions, however, were inconsistent with the generally accepted practices and standards for leadership active shooter response and incident command described above. Chief Arredondo continuously stated post-incident that he was not the incident commander "because [an] incident commander is at an incident command post."[520] However, Chief Arredondo did state that he was giving instructions on evacuating the children and securing the keys because "nobody else was giving direction."[521] He was in communication with the other side of the hallway via calls with Uvalde County

---

[518] Uvalde Police Department Body-Worn Camera Footage.

[519] CIR Training Analysis.

[520] CIR Fact Finding.

[521] CIR Fact Finding.

Critical Incident Review: Active Shooter at Robb Elementary School |
Chapter 3. Leadership, Incident Command, and Coordination

148

Precinct 1 Constable Johnny Field.[522] Chief Arredondo explained that "I was not going to walk out of that hallway and assume incident command, was not going to leave those children . . . every bullet was needed. . . . I didn't go in there with a title."[523]

Uvalde County Sheriff Ruben Nolasco, who arrived on school grounds 35 minutes after the FOS made entry into the school, should also have assisted with coordinating the law enforcement personnel present and establishing a command post and unified command. Although Sheriff Nolasco's training records revealed that he did not have any active shooter or ICS training and had minimal leadership/supervision training,[524] Sheriff Nolasco was the highest ranking officer for his agency; therefore, he had the authority to lead those resources from his agency in line with his positional authority. Sheriff Nolasco also had direct awareness of and intelligence about the subject's identity based on the information obtained from the grandparents' house, including the subject's name and background (see "Chapter 1. Incident Timeline Reconstruction"). Sheriff Nolasco did not seek out or establish a command post, establish unified command, share the intelligence he learned from both relatives, nor did he assign an intelligence officer to gather intelligence on the subject. At one point, Sheriff Nolasco and UPD Acting Chief Pargas were within 10–15 feet of each other outside the exterior door of the northwest hallway;[525] however, they were not coordinating with one another and continued to act independently.

At 12:11, Sheriff Nolasco, TX Ranger 1, UCISD PD Lt., UPD Ofc. 3, and a Texas Parks and Wildlife game warden were gathered outside the northwest door discussing coordination around evacuating the children from the classrooms (see figure 3-15 on page 150).[526] During the interaction, the various leaders looked to Sheriff Nolasco for guidance, and he appeared to be providing direction, although it is unclear, based on interviews and documentation review, to what end.[527] This was a critical leadership point, because leaders from three different agencies were within reach of the sheriff and accessible to coordinate resources and deconflict information. UPD Acting Chief Pargas had also just left the area to return to the hallway. At this point, the leaders should have coordinated resources and, most importantly, coordinated the rescue of the children and staff injured and dying in rooms 111 and 112.

---

[522] CIR Fact Finding.

[523] CIR Fact Finding.

[524] Since the time of the incident, UCSO personnel, including Sheriff Nolasco, have attended ALERRT Level 1 training and Sheriff Nolasco has been through some ICS classes. (CIR Fact Finding.)

[525] Uvalde County Sheriff's Office Body-Worn Camera Footage.

[526] Uvalde County Sheriff's Office Body-Worn Camera Footage.

[527] Uvalde County Sheriff's Office Body-Worn Camera Footage.

Critical Incident Review: Active Shooter at Robb Elementary School |
Chapter 3. Leadership, Incident Command, and Coordination

149

Figure 3-15. Leadership discussing evacuations

Source: Uvalde County Sheriff's Office Body-Worn Camera Footage.

From left to right: Uvalde County Sheriff Nolasco, unknown UPD officer, TX Ranger 1, the UCISD PD Lt., and (partially obscured) game warden. Point of view is UCSO deputy's body-worn camera.

Shortly after meeting with Sheriff Nolasco and others, TX Ranger 1 tried to coordinate efforts among different responders. The Ranger intercepted the CBP BORTAC commander and briefed the commander on the situation.[528] In that interaction, the Ranger told the BORTAC commander, "do whatever you need to do, you have my support."[529] Typically, CBP needs authorization from local law enforcement before responding, and the commander took this to mean he was authorized by an official authority to proceed with his actions and command.[530]

Within 40 minutes of the first attack on students and teachers inside classrooms, TX Ranger 1 requested that leadership from UPD and UCSO meet and coordinate.[531] Acting Chief Pargas referenced UPD Lt. 1 as someone who could coordinate.[532] The Texas Ranger appeared to be one of the few leaders on scene who attempted to coordinate with other agency personnel and ended up in different interactions with all the major responding agencies.[533]

---

[528] CIR Fact Finding.

[529] CIR Fact Finding.

[530] CIR Fact Finding.

[531] Uvalde County Sheriff's Office Body-Worn Camera Footage.

[532] Uvalde County Sheriff's Office Body-Worn Camera Footage.

[533] CIR Fact Finding; Uvalde County Sheriff's Office Body-Worn Camera Footage.

Critical Incident Review: Active Shooter at Robb Elementary School |
Chapter 3. Leadership, Incident Command, and Coordination

150

Based on their locations and titles, there were several other individuals that responders considered or perceived to be in charge at various points, including Uvalde County Precinct 6 Constable Emmanuel Zamora (perimeter), Constable Field (near T-intersection), and the CBP BORTAC Commander (near T-intersection/north side and mid-hallway). Although these individuals at times attempted to direct or coordinate with other law enforcement resources around them, none coordinated to develop a plan to enter classrooms 111 and 112 or establish an incident command structure.

In addition to the difficulties coordinating among law enforcement, the lack of a command structure also contributed to an absence of coordination with non-law enforcement entities and individuals, including emergency medical services (described more fully below), school personnel, and families and loved ones. At around 12:27, Constable Zamora was outside, directing the personnel outside the south entrance to get kids out of classroom 109 "because children are present."[534] The teacher in that classroom reported that she had been shot and required assistance to be evacuated through the window. Law enforcement walked her around the corner to the teacher parking lot, where she stood with an officer on either side of her without an ambulance nearby (see figure 3-16).

Figure 3-16. Law enforcement supporting a teacher from room 109 who has been shot

Source: Uvalde County Constables Body-Worn Camera Footage.

This also demonstrated the lack of coordination among law enforcement and the school. More than 40 minutes earlier, at 11:40, the injured teacher sent a message to a group text of school personnel saying, "Im shot bleeding help" (see figure 3-17 on page 152).[535] This message was relayed and shown to the principal, who "text[ed] the assistant principal to get help" and then messaged the injured

---

[534] Uvalde County Constables Body-Worn Camera Footage.

[535] CIR Fact Finding; CIR Document and Data Review.

Critical Incident Review: Active Shooter at Robb Elementary School |
Chapter 3. Leadership, Incident Command, and Coordination

151

teacher that "Someone's coming to help you."[536] In response, the assistant principal called 911 and asked if EMS was en route, which was confirmed; the assistant principal hung up without any further discussion.[537] The principal did not talk to any law enforcement, because she thought law enforcement was already aware.[538]

Figure 3-17. Message from injured teacher

Source: CIR Document and Data Review.

It is also important to note that, in spite of sources of information and indications to the contrary, law enforcement stated repeatedly during CIR interviews that they did not know students and staff were present, or that they thought school was out for the summer.[539] This language highlights the need for proactive communication between local agencies and school district police departments to ensure that there are clear lines of coordination. This could be easily addressed by providing the school district calendar to local law enforcement agencies and the communications/dispatch center.

---

[536] CIR Fact Finding.

[537] Uvalde Police Department Calls for Service.

[538] CIR Fact Finding.

[539] CIR Fact Finding.

Critical Incident Review: Active Shooter at Robb Elementary School |
Chapter 3. Leadership, Incident Command, and Coordination

152

Establishment of a Command Post

Statements from involved responders also describe a delay in the establishment of an obvious incident command post. Senior leaders from UPD, UCISD PD, UCSO, and TXDPS can be seen on video walking around without trying to establish a command and control structure or command post.

Several officers asked at various points whether an ICP had been established. At 12:06, UPD Patrol Lt. 2 asked over the radio if anyone had set up an ICP and if so, where it was located. An unknown officer said "negative."[540] Nine minutes later, at 12:17, TX Ranger 1 communicated with UPD Acting Chief Pargas about the need to establish an incident command structure and an ICP. At 12:19, UPD Acting Chief Pargas requested that UPD Lt. 2 start setting up the command post.[541] However, the UPD Chief—who was out of the state during the incident—requested Pargas set up ICS during a situational awareness briefing earlier.[542]

At one point, TXDPS gathered staff near the southwest corner of the school and referred to that as the command post.[543] While it may have been a gathering place for some, the leadership and decision makers for UPD, UCISD PD, UCSO, TXDPS, and CBP were seen on numerous videos walking around the exterior of the school, inside the hallways, or engaged in activities in the hallway near classrooms 111 and 112, making it impossible for the southwest corner to have functioned as an ICP. UPD Lt. 2 announced over the radio at 12:42 that the UPD command post was at the Hillcrest Funeral Home across the street from Robb Elementary School (see figure 3-18 on page 154).[544] The review team, however, determined that an identifiable ICP was not established until 1:00 p.m., when TXDPS command staff utilized a meeting room at the funeral home,[545] which also happened to be a crime scene and, unknown to the commanders, the location to which close to 100 Robb Elementary children and Robb Elementary staff had been evacuated at least 90 minutes earlier, including at least one victim in need of medical attention.

---

[540] Uvalde Police Department Radio Traffic.

[541] Uvalde Police Department Radio Traffic.

[542] CIR Fact Finding.

[543] CIR Fact Finding.

[544] Uvalde Police Department Radio Traffic.

[545] Hillcrest Memorial Funeral Home CCTV Footage.

Critical Incident Review: Active Shooter at Robb Elementary School |
Chapter 3. Leadership, Incident Command, and Coordination

153

Figure 3-18. UPD Acting Chief Pargas talking to Hillcrest Memorial Funeral Home staff

Source: Hillcrest Memorial Funeral Home Footage.

Post-Incident

Chaos unfolded once children and teachers were finally rescued from rooms 111 and 112. At this point, leadership should have established the outer perimeter in the hallway for the stability and preservation of the integrity of the crime scene. The TXDPS South Texas regional director, who arrived on the scene shortly before law enforcement entered the classrooms, could have filled this role, implementing ICS protocols, establishing unified command, and bringing order to the chaos in the hallway and perimeter, as the highest TXDPS official on the ground and for the South Texas region, under which Uvalde falls. The regional director did not, however, provide direction or coordinate with other leadership personnel in the hallway.

Instead, the TXDPS regional director, and some other officers, walked past the law enforcement officers bringing injured and deceased victims out of the classrooms and entered classrooms 111 and 112 with no identifiable purpose or action, therefore compromising the crime scene (see "Chapter 4. Post-Incident Response and Investigation" for more on the crime scene). However, minutes later, an unknown Texas Ranger took control and ordered all law enforcement out of the rooms.[546] See the "Emergency Medical Response at Robb Elementary" section below for more on the post-incident response in the hallway. Eventually a San Antonio special weapons and tactics (SWAT) team member stood in front of room 112 to preserve the crime scene.[547] While the TXDPS regional director was in the classrooms, UCISD PD Chief Arredondo remained in the hallway and did not take steps to provide leadership to those in the room.

---

[546] CIR Document and Data Review.; CIR Fact Finding.

[547] Texas Department of Public Safety Body-Worn Camera Footage.

Critical Incident Review: Active Shooter at Robb Elementary School |
Chapter 3. Leadership, Incident Command, and Coordination

154

Outside the building, cooperation among the agencies present began to improve following entry into classrooms 111 and 112. Constable Zamora attempted to move emotionally affected responders away from the scene. When Constable Zamora was outside the external northwest doors, an adult victim was being treated on the sidewalk by law enforcement and medics, with the FOS UCISD PD Ofc. 1 and husband of the victim watching.[548] Constable Zamora guided the officer away from the scene, giving him a couple of reassurances, and handed him off to another law enforcement officer away from the scene.[549] This was the type of handoff that should have occurred within minutes of the FOS officer describing his personal involvement with a victim.

Minutes after the entry by law enforcement, all the leaders from the major agencies met outside the south entrance, including a TXDPS captain, UCISD PD Chief Arredondo, the UCISD PD lieutenant, Uvalde County Sheriff Nolasco, UPD Sgt. 3, UPD Sgt. 1, and a recently arrived Texas Ranger who would lead the investigation (see figure 3-19 on page 156).[550] This was the first time that coordination was occurring among the on-site leaders for the four primary agencies (UPD, UCSO, UCISD PD, and TXDPS). The leaders were coordinating about a press conference and who would be handling the investigation.[551] This is an example of the type of coordination that should have occurred minutes into the incident and focused on the urgency of getting to the victims. Throughout this conversation, a victim's body was outside of the hallway door on the floor.[552] This victim should have been moved into the hallway or into designated rooms 131/132.

While this huddle was occurring, UPD Acting Chief Pargas was still moving around the school shooting scene and was not at the command post. Meanwhile, after leaving the crime scene classrooms, the TXDPS regional director deliberately coordinated with his personnel to take control of the outer perimeter and assign troopers to entry points to secure the area and the scene.[553]

---

[548] Uvalde County Constables Body-Worn Camera Footage.

[549] Uvalde County Constables Body-Worn Camera Footage.

[550] Texas Department of Public Safety Body-Worn Camera Footage.

[551] CIR Fact Finding.

[552] Texas Department of Public Safety Body-Worn Camera Footage.

[553] Texas Department of Public Safety Body-Worn Camera Footage.

Critical Incident Review: Active Shooter at Robb Elementary School | Chapter 3. Leadership, Incident Command, and Coordination

155

Figure 3-19. Agency leaders begin coordination

Source: Texas Department of Public Safety Body-Worn Camera Footage.

Additional personnel from multiple agencies were also gathering at the funeral home around the same time. By 1:11, law enforcement personnel from UPD, TXDPS, and USMS, along with Uvalde Mayor Don McLaughlin, were in the same space, though each entity still appeared to be operating independently (see figure 3-20 on page 157).[554]

---

[554] Hillcrest Memorial Funeral Home CCTV Footage.

Critical Incident Review: Active Shooter at Robb Elementary School |
Chapter 3. Leadership, Incident Command, and Coordination

156

Figure 3-20. Post-incident command post at 1:11

Source: Hillcrest Memorial Funeral Home CCTV Footage.

By 1:22, an unknown TXDPS official started incident command structure protocols (see figure 3-21 <u>on page 158</u>),[555] but the coordination still appeared disconnected. The coordination changed in the next couple of minutes, and by 1:31 there finally appeared to be the start of a unified command system where officers from different agencies began working together (see figure 3-22 <u>on page 158</u>).[556]

---

[555] Hillcrest Memorial Funeral Home CCTV Footage.

[556] Hillcrest Memorial Funeral Home CCTV Footage.

Critical Incident Review: Active Shooter at Robb Elementary School |
Chapter 3. Leadership, Incident Command, and Coordination

157

Figure 3-21. Disjointed activities in the post-incident command post

Source: Hillcrest Memorial Funeral Home CCTV Footage.

Figure 3-22. The start of a unified command system

Source: Hillcrest Memorial Funeral Home CCTV Footage.

Critical Incident Review: Active Shooter at Robb Elementary School |
Chapter 3. Leadership, Incident Command, and Coordination

158

After the incident, the Uvalde County EOC did activate to support the post-incident command post in the days and weeks following (see "Chapter 8. Pre-Incident Planning and Preparation" for further details on the Uvalde County EOC).[557]

Coordination of Medical Response

Another important feature of leadership in response to active shooters is the integration of fire and emergency medical response (EMS) into a unified command structure.

Emergency Medical Response Principles

Responses by fire and EMS has improved as awareness of field trauma care has developed from lessons learned in combat by the U.S. military.[558] In 2013, the U.S. Fire Administration published *Fire/Emergency Medical Services Department Operational Considerations and Guide for Active Shooter and Mass Casualty Incidents*.[559] The publication "takes into consideration the diverse local service levels across America," with their unique sizes and capabilities, and provides recommendations for increasing the survivability of victims through coordinated and integrated planning and response, such as:[560]

- Jointly developing local protocols for responding to active shooter (AS)/mass casualty incidents (MCIs). Fire/EMS and law enforcement (LE) should plan and train together.

- Planning for and practicing rapid treatment and evacuation, including who, what, when, where, and how it will be carried out.

- Using the National Incident Management System (NIMS) and the Incident Command System (ICS). Accordingly, fire/EMS and LE should establish a single Incident Command Post (ICP) and establish Unified Command (UC).

- Fire/EMS, LE, and all public safety partners planning and training together.

- Including AS/MCIs in tabletop and field exercises to improve familiarity with joint protocols. Regularly exercise the plan.

- Using common communications terminology. In addition to NIMS and ICS terminology, fire department personnel must learn common LE terms and vice versa. Share definition of terms to be used in AS/MCIs and establish a common language.

- Incorporating tactical emergency casualty care (TECC) into planning and training. Training must include hemorrhage control techniques, including use of tourniquets, pressure dressings, and hemostatic agents. Training must also include assessment, triage, and transport of victims with lethal internal hemorrhage and torso trauma to definitive trauma care.

---

[557] CIR Fact Finding.

[558] *Strategies to Enhance Survival.*

[559] U.S. Fire Administration, *Fire/Emergency Medical Services Department Operational Considerations.*

[560] U.S. Fire Administration, *Fire/Emergency Medical Services Department Operational Considerations.*

Critical Incident Review: Active Shooter at Robb Elementary School |
Chapter 3. Leadership, Incident Command, and Coordination

159

- Providing appropriate protective gear to personnel exposed to risks.

- Considering fire hazards secondary to the initial blast if improvised explosive devices (IEDs) are used.

- Considering secondary devices at main and secondary scenes.

- Determining how transportation to and communications with area hospitals/trauma centers will be accomplished.[561]

The basis for these recommendations comes from the Hartford Consensus for improving survival by early hemorrhage control.

The Hartford Consensus

The Hartford Consensus created a protocol for national policy to enhance survivability from active shooter and intentional mass casualty events. The committee behind the consensus, composed of medical experts and first responders, established a new algorithm for initial response to deadly injury: THREAT, which is built on the concept of Threat suppression, Hemorrhage control, Rapid Extrication to safety, Assessment by medical providers, and Transport to definitive care.[562]

The algorithm developed by the Hartford Consensus supports the need for speed in the expedited delivery of medical care during an active shooter event in order to increase the chance of survivability.[563] In an active shooter incident, time is not on the responder's side. When the initial momentum toward the active shooter was lost at Robb Elementary, the clock started on survivability for the victims inside classrooms 111 and 112. "Rapid first responder access to victims in an active shooter incident can make the difference between life and death, as the survival rate diminishes rapidly for seriously injured trauma victims the longer they must wait to receive definitive hospital care."[564] The CIR team reviewed documentation that suggests that at least one deceased victim was alive at 11:56 a.m., 20 minutes after the first officers entered the school.[565]

A generally accepted practice and standard EMS response for an active shooter incident is to stage resources in a secure location until law enforcement can mitigate the threat and secure the area. This can lead to a significant delay in providing medical care to the victims. Empirical evidence demonstrates that in an active shooter scenario, expeditious medical intervention, more than capability or capacity, is the key to preventing loss of life.[566] Emerging alternatives to the "standby" policy suggest a level of first responder collaboration that allows EMS (with appropriate protective equipment) to quickly enter the incident scene with law enforcement officers in order to stabilize patients and reduce fatalities from

---

[561] U.S. Fire Administration, *Fire/Emergency Medical Services Department Operational Considerations.*

[562] *Strategies to Enhance Survival in Active Shooter and Intentional Mass Casualty Events: A Compendium,* Supplement to the Bulletin of the American College of Surgeons.

[563] *Strategies to Enhance Survival.*

[564] Morrissey, "EMS Response to Active-Shooter Incidents."

[565] Uvalde Police Department Body-Worn Camera Footage; Uvalde Police Department 911 Call.

[566] *First Responder Guide for Improving Survivability.*

Critical Incident Review: Active Shooter at Robb Elementary School |
Chapter 3. Leadership, Incident Command, and Coordination

160

readily treatable injuries. Variability exists in the training and deployment of law enforcement officers to rescue and care for victims. Law enforcement planners should employ strategies that enable all law enforcement officers to provide lifesaving care until additional resources can be moved forward.[567]

Relevant Triage and EMS Protocols

For EMS, the *National Model EMS Clinical Guidelines* provide evidence-based or consensus-based guidelines, protocols, and operating procedures for field EMS professionals.[568] In the state of Texas there are no statewide protocols but instead delegated practice, i.e., "permission given by a physician licensed by the board, either in person or by treatment protocols or standing orders to a specific prehospital provider[,] to provide medical care."[569] Delegated practice means that each medical director decides the mandates and models that the ambulance services under their direction will follow.[570] This applies to whether an ambulance service operates in a warm zone,[571] whether EMS personnel train for rescue task forces, and the level of medical intervention they provide. EMS personnel operating in rural counties may be allowed to administer intravenous interventions or conduct airway management, while a state like Pennsylvania would not allow that under their current system, which has a mandatory statewide protocol.[572]

Medical care is a priority in a mass violence or mass casualty incident once law enforcement declares the scene a safe zone or a cold zone. Significant quantities of "stop the bleed" supplies (e.g., tourniquets, pressure dressings, and exam gloves) need to be stocked on all response vehicles and in "go bags" with roaming personnel, in addition to the supplies stored in the medical response vehicles. These supplies can also be housed at schools, businesses, and other vulnerable locations. If properly trained, EMS, rescue task forces, or similar groups composed of law enforcement, EMTs, and medically trained fire and law enforcement personnel should be allowed to quickly enter a safe zone by securing a "corridor" for accessing and evacuating the wounded—a critical component of active threat (shooter or blast event) responses.[573]

Emergency medical teams who are first to arrive conduct triage—checking for immediate life-threatening concerns, providing treatment (where possible), and transporting to a medical facility that can provide the needed services. There is currently no accepted measure to judge the appropriateness of any given system in mass casualty triage.[574] The simple triage and rapid treatment (START) model is a

---

[567] *First Responder Guide for Improving Survivability*.

[568] NASEMSO, *National Model EMS Clinical Guidelines*.

[569] Phelps, "Why Paramedics Are Qualified Emergency Care Providers."

[570] CIR Fact Finding.

[571] A warm zone is where tactical field care takes place. It's less dangerous than the hot zone (where active weapon use and shooting are present) but still not completely safe. See "Appendix D. Leadership, Incident Command, and Coordination Supplemental Material" for more on the zones.

[572] CIR Fact Finding.

[573] Administration for Strategic Preparedness and Response, *Mass Violence/Active Shooter Incidents*

[574] Lerner et al., "Mass Casualty Triage: An Evaluation."

Critical Incident Review: Active Shooter at Robb Elementary School |
Chapter 3. Leadership, Incident Command, and Coordination

161

triage method widely used by first responders in the U.S. to quickly classify victims during a mass casualty incident based on the severity of their injury. To utilize START or any triage method of emergency medical attention, the medics and other responders trained to provide medical care need access to the victims, as described above, where a path or corridor is created for them.[575]

In Texas, each regional advisory council has a triage plan.[576] Most triaging systems are moving into a risk-based tagging system such as green, yellow, red, and black (see figure 3-23). In some communities, the tagging system includes multiple barcode stickers to ensure belongings stay with the patient. Marking tape is another example.[577] There is also new software that allows patient tracking starting in the field and continuing all the way to the hospital and throughout care.[578]

Traditionally, EMS is responsible for establishing a triage area and determining the process for a casualty collection point (CCP). EMS professionals stress that the act of triage is critical, since there is the risk of under- or over-triaging if it is done by an untrained professional.[579] The decision needs to be made under a clinical determination.

Figure 3-23. Example of risk-based tagging

Source: Provided with permission from NASEMSO

---

[575] Lerner et al., "Mass Casualty Triage: An Evaluation."

[576] CIR Fact Finding.

[577] *Regional Field Triage Algorithm.*

[578] CIR Fact Finding.

[579] CIR Fact Finding.

Critical Incident Review: Active Shooter at Robb Elementary School |
Chapter 3. Leadership, Incident Command, and Coordination

162

Nationally, EMS professionals are taught to use the walk-wave triage system during mass casualty incidents: If you can hear me, walk this way; if you can hear me and can't walk, then wave; and if the person is still, that's the first priority of care.[580] In this format, EMS professionals can quickly triage numerous individuals to determine priority levels. If implemented uniformly during the incident at Robb Elementary School, this system could have contributed to a more orderly triage. For more on this topic, see *Mass Casualty Trauma Triage Paradigms and Pitfalls* released by the U.S. Department of Health and Human Services.[581]

Tactical Emergency Medical Training

Training those responders who are first to enter a hot zone also affords an opportunity for more rapid care.[582] At the 2013 International Association of Chiefs of Police (IACP) Conference, the Police Physicians Section recognized that early and rapid medical intervention during an active shooter event improves the chance for survival. A resolution was adopted by IACP recommending that:

Every law enforcement officer should receive tactical emergency medical training including critical core skills of early, life-threatening hemorrhage control and rapid evacuation of mass casualty victims to a casualty collection point. Tactical emergency medical skills are critical life-saving interventions in the officer-down situation, whether as officer-applied self-aid or aid given to a fellow officer, or to victims of a mass casualty situation such as an active shooter or bombing event. Specific elements of training are the purview of each agency depending on availability of resources and training programs.[583]

After-action reviews of numerous critical incidents have continually shown the benefits of regular, regional, multidisciplinary first responder planning, training, and exercises.[584] It is an accepted principle that training improves performance in a crisis response. Therefore, training should be regional and include all disciplines and levels of first responders—both sworn and civilian. Fire, EMS, and other potential first responders should be included in active shooter training.

Responders need to incorporate tactical emergency casualty care into planning and training. Training must include hemorrhage control techniques, including use of tourniquets, pressure dressings, and hemostatic agents. Training must also include assessment, triage, and transport of victims with lethal internal hemorrhage and torso trauma to definitive trauma care.[585]

---

[580] CIR Fact Finding; Chemical Hazards Emergency Medical Management, "SALT Mass Casualty Triage Algorithm;" "SALT Mass Casualty Triage: Concept Endorsed," *Disaster Medicine and Public Health Preparedness,* 245–246.

[581] Administration for Strategic Preparedness and Response; Technical Resources, Assistance Center, and Information Exchange, *Mass Casualty Trauma Triage: Paradigms and Pitfalls.*

[582] See "Appendix D. Leadership, Incident Command, and Coordination Supplemental Materials" for a description of the zones and rescue task forces.

[583] IACP, "Tactical Emergency Medical Training for Law Enforcement Personnel."

[584] The National Policing Institute established a collection of after-action reviews conducted by multiple sources, available online at https://www.policinginstitute.org/aarlibrary.

[585] U.S. Fire Administration, *Fire/Emergency Medical Services Department Operational Considerations.*

Critical Incident Review: Active Shooter at Robb Elementary School |
Chapter 3. Leadership, Incident Command, and Coordination

163

In addition, agencies must continually plan and evaluate ingress and egress routes during critical incidents. Medical assistance and transport should be given the highest priority, and all responding officers should be aware of this priority in how they respond, park, and manage traffic flow.

Three key themes emerged from work done around the Hartford Consensus: early, aggressive hemorrhage control; use of protective equipment; and greater first responder interoperability and incident management. The recommendations in these areas help to save lives by mitigating first responder risk and improving the emergent and immediate medical management of casualties encountered during active shooter and other mass casualty incidents.[586]

As discussed throughout this review, the CIR team noted failures in each of the areas identified in the Hartford Consensus. The team also noted lessons learned with collaboration between law enforcement and medical responses in other critical incidents in the United States.

Emergency Medical Response at Robb Elementary

When incident command at Robb Elementary School failed to be established, so did the natural progression to a unified command and, with it, the opportunity to have Fire/EMS in the command/decision-making structure. Instead, EMS providers were staged on the streets outside the school and not involved in the rescue and initial triage and treatment of the victims. While CBP EMTs and TXDPS personnel established a CCP in an adjoining hallway, a collaborative medical plan was not made that included EMS providers. See "Appendix D. Leadership, Incident Command, and Coordination Supplemental Materials" for information on rescue task forces and zones.

EMS Deployment

The first EMS can be seen on scene approaching Robb Elementary School around 11:41 a.m.[587] At 11:48, Uvalde EMS (UEMS) started staging a couple blocks away from the scene.[588] The EMS on-scene commander struggled to obtain information or identify who was in charge,[589] and dispatch was so overwhelmed with calls that EMS was not getting clear information and guidance.[590] Communications were lacking between the law enforcement responders at Robb Elementary and the EMS staff and transportation services that were available and ready to respond. The frustration of the EMS staff interviewed was evident, as several interviewees were visibly upset and even in tears several weeks later when relaying the difficulties they experienced in trying to help the victims and do their jobs, which they were ready on-site to perform.[591]

---

[586] Brinsfield and Mitchell, "The Department of Homeland Security's Role."

[587] Hillcrest Memorial Funeral Home CCTV Footage.

[588] Uvalde Police Department Radio Traffic.

[589] CIR Fact Finding.

[590] CIR Fact Finding.

[591] CIR Fact Finding.

Critical Incident Review: Active Shooter at Robb Elementary School |
Chapter 3. Leadership, Incident Command, and Coordination

164

At 11:53, UEMS activated its mutual aid partners, including the private ambulance service Alamo Ambulance EMT, surrounding agencies,[592] and Airlife. UEMS, however, faced difficulties coordinating its operations due to the lack of unified command. For example, during the incident, UEMS transported a victim who needed to be flown to San Antonio.[593] One ambulance company offered access to an Airlife stationed at the Uvalde Airport, and instead the UEMS ambulance drove past the usable helicopter, equipped with medical personnel, and traveled another 15–20 minutes to another city to access a helicopter.[594] This was an example of the lack of communication and coordination extending outside of law enforcement.

Responders to Robb Elementary School also reported that traffic congestion in and around the school made it difficult for critical personnel to deploy close to the scene and interfered with emergency medical access.[595] Ambulances driving to the scene encountered streets blocked by law enforcement vehicles.[596] Around the time the stack made entry into the classrooms, a call went out over the radio that vehicles needed to be moved from the roadways to clear a path.[597] Even so, law enforcement was too preoccupied with care for the victims and maintaining the perimeter. Many of the more than 380 law enforcement responders drove to Robb Elementary and left their cars haphazardly parked, many in the middle of the roads leading directly to the school.[598] Most of the vehicles were locked or, if accessible, did not have their keys inside, so when one of the responders began to attempt to move cars, they could not do so. Responders reported having to ask colleagues which cars were theirs, gather keys, go back to find the vehicles, and finally move them, an effort that was time consuming and never fully accomplished.[599] This is another failure due to no incident command structure or command presence from leadership within the perimeter.

Establishment of Triage

At 12:24, the location of triage was identified by CBP medics and CBP Border Patrol Search, Trauma, and Rescue (BORSTAR) personnel (see figure 3-24 on page 166).[600] The plan was for the triage to occur in the hallway by the restrooms (see figure 3-25 on page 167).

No coordination occurred with the EMS on-scene commander or any of the staged ambulances.[601]

---

[592] CIR Fact Finding.

[593] CIR Fact Finding.

[594] CIR Fact Finding.

[595] CIR Fact Finding.

[596] CIR Fact Finding.

[597] Uvalde Police Department Radio Traffic.

[598] CIR Fact Finding; Uvalde Police Department Radio Traffic.

[599] CIR Fact Finding; Uvalde Police Department Radio Traffic.

[600] Uvalde Police Department Body-Worn Camera Footage.

[601] CIR Fact Finding.

Critical Incident Review: Active Shooter at Robb Elementary School |
Chapter 3. Leadership, Incident Command, and Coordination

165

Figure 3-24. Medical triage near restrooms

Source: Texas Department of Public Safety Body-Worn Camera Footage.

TXDPS medic personnel soon joined the effort to unpack and prepare materials for injuries.[602] Identification and subsequent establishment of the triage was needed, and the emergency medical personnel should have also been coordinating with the EMS on-scene commander and the ambulance companies outside of the school. Prior to the entry into the classrooms, a CBP paramedic-emergency medical technician (PM-EMT) attempted several times to provide direction to the law enforcement personnel about the post-breach plan, including where to bring the injured (figure 3-26 on page 168 demonstrates one example).[603]

---

[602] CIR Fact Finding.

[603] Texas Department of Public Safety Body-Worn Camera Footage.

Critical Incident Review: Active Shooter at Robb Elementary School |
Chapter 3. Leadership, Incident Command, and Coordination

166

Figure 3-25. Map of West Building, star designates the location of triage

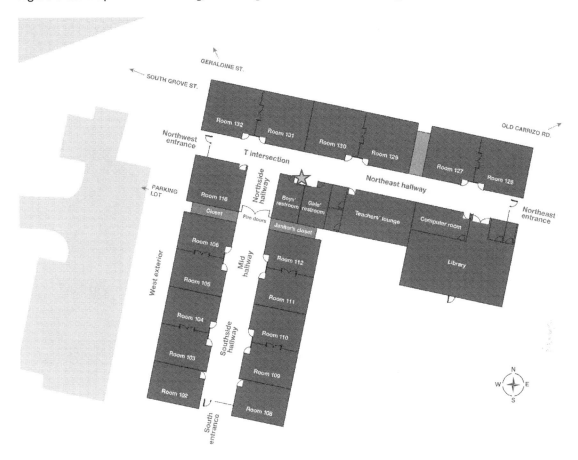

Triage and Patient Care

Chaos unfolded once children and teachers were finally rescued from rooms 111 and 112. There continued to be no leadership direction, negating any triage planning. Minutes after entry into the classrooms, an unknown Texas Ranger took control and ordered all law enforcement out of the rooms.[604] Constable Zamora also advanced toward the classrooms yelling "kids, kids, EMTs first."[605] At one point, a TXDPS trooper signaled and a UPD detective yelled for law enforcement to hold before rushing toward the rooms (see figure 3-27 on page 169). UCISD PD Chief Arredondo remained in the hallway but did not provide any direction to those exiting the classrooms.[606]

---

[604] CIR Document and Data Review.; CIR Fact Finding.

[605] Uvalde County Constables Body-Worn Camera Footage.

[606] Uvalde County Constables Body-Worn Camera Footage.

Critical Incident Review: Active Shooter at Robb Elementary School |
Chapter 3. Leadership, Incident Command, and Coordination

167

Figure 3-26. CBP PM-EMT providing triage direction at 12:42

Source: Texas Department of Public Safety Body-Worn Camera Footage.

Constable Zamora even pulled law enforcement back, insisting on medics first (see figure 3-28 on page 169).[607] As Constable Zamora continued down the hallway past the classrooms, he continued to provide direction to the overwhelming number of law enforcement, yelling "We need EMTs," telling officers to give him their weapons and "Go get bodies," and yelling "Clear the hallway."[608]

Despite these efforts, EMS staff were not the first to assess the situation in the classrooms and ensure the most appropriate use of critical resources. Deceased victims were moved out of the classrooms, left in or outside of the hallway, or transported to the hospital; at the same time, injured child victims were being tended to or put on school buses with injuries unknown to law enforcement.[609]

---

[607] Uvalde County Constables Body-Worn Camera Footage.

[608] Uvalde County Constables Body-Worn Camera Footage.

[609] CIR Fact Finding; multiple BWC; Robb Elementary School CCTV Footage.

Critical Incident Review: Active Shooter at Robb Elementary School |
Chapter 3. Leadership, Incident Command, and Coordination

168

Figure 3-27. A still image of TXDPS trooper and UPD detective signaling for law enforcement to hold instead of advancing toward the rooms

Source: Uvalde County Constables Body-Worn Camera Footage.

Figure 3-28. Uvalde County Constable Zamora (point of view) holding back a TXDPS trooper to allow medics to enter

Source: Uvalde County Constables Body-Worn Camera Footage.

Critical Incident Review: Active Shooter at Robb Elementary School |
Chapter 3. Leadership, Incident Command, and Coordination

169

As EMS personnel started working on patients, law enforcement in a rush to help other patients started pulling equipment and supplies from the ambulances and medical bags.[610] One ambulance rushed from the scene with two patients who were not secured on stretchers because they had been taken from their ambulance.[611] Another ambulance transported both a deceased victim and an injured survivor to the hospital.[612]

One of the responders reported observing "law enforcement moving injured kids in ways that were probably more harmful."[613] Still breathing, injured victims were moved out of the classrooms, but there were no stretchers inside the hallway readily available to move them.[614] For an unknown reason, responders placed one of the victims on the ground outside the door to administer care.[615] The victim, one of the teachers, died on the walkway and was covered before being moved into an ambulance.[616] Another deceased victim was placed outside of another exterior door and left unattended while law enforcement gathered only steps away.[617]

Some of the EMS reported being outside the West Building while shots were being fired, but most EMS personnel reported that they were not initially allowed into the hallway.[618] Some ambulance services reported that they were restricted from deploying to the school once entry was made, delaying valuable resources and access to whole blood (see callout box "Deployment of STRAC").[619] Reports indicated that one of the private EMS companies thoughtfully and rapidly accessed air ambulance services to bring blood supplies to the school site that went unused.[620] The private EMS staff noted the use of another air ambulance without such supplies that was located well beyond where the private air ambulance was on site waiting to respond.[621]

The chaos continued with EMS personnel bringing out a victim on a stretcher to find that their ambulance was missing after a crew from another agency had commandeered it.[622]

---

[610] CIR Fact Finding.

[611] CIR Fact Finding.

[612] CIR Fact Finding.

[613] CIR Fact Finding.

[614] CIR Fact Finding.

[615] CIR Fact Finding.

[616] CIR Fact Finding.

[617] CIR Fact Finding; Texas Department of Public Safety Body-Worn Camera Footage.

[618] CIR Fact Finding.

[619] CIR Fact Finding.

[620] CIR Fact Finding.

[621] CIR Fact Finding.

[622] CIR Fact Finding.

Critical Incident Review: Active Shooter at Robb Elementary School |
Chapter 3. Leadership, Incident Command, and Coordination

170

In addition, there were three life flights available to land at the school for assistance.[623] Medical air transport services were used to transport one of the seriously injured teachers, who received treatment at a San Antonio hospital.[624]

EMS was also not included in triaging or assessing any of the "walking" victims' potential medical needs.[625] Several students with bullet wounds, grazes, and other injuries were directed onto buses that went to the civic center without ever having been brought to the medics' attention.[626]

Deployment of STRAC

The Southwest Texas Regional Advisory Council (STRAC),* one of 22 regional advisory councils across Texas, is a regional emergency management and health care system that coordinates across the trauma system and responder community.† STRAC serves 26,000 square miles, approximately 3 million people, 56 hospitals, 70 EMS agencies, and 18 medical aircraft and possesses mobile medical units and fully functional mobile medical facilities.‡ STRAC also built and maintains MedCom, which is a technology platform to allow for the most efficient rapid trauma transfers possible based on the availability, capacity, and location of necessary assets for the type of trauma response that is needed.§ All of these resources are available and accessible to Uvalde.

On the day of the incident, UEMS reached out to STRAC to notify them of the situation, and STRAC deployed 15 units of whole blood and more units of O positive blood within 67 minutes.** This was in addition to the whole blood that was available on certain Airlife carriers in the Uvalde region.†† Whole blood is the "natural, unseparated blood collected from a donor" and contains all components of healthy blood.‡‡

The coordination of STRAC and the accessibility of whole blood proved to be beneficial on the day of the incident.

---

* Southwest Texas Regional Advisory Council, "About Us."

† CIR Fact Finding.

‡ CIR Fact Finding.

§ CIR Fact Finding.

** CIR Fact Finding.

†† CIR Fact Finding.

‡‡ Fisher et al., "Whole Blood in EMS May Save Lives." To read more about the use of prehospital blood products, see Pokorny et al., "The Use of Prehospital Blood Products."

---

[623] CIR Fact Finding.

[624] CIR Fact Finding.

[625] CIR Fact Finding.

[626] CIR Fact Finding.

Critical Incident Review: Active Shooter at Robb Elementary School |
Chapter 3. Leadership, Incident Command, and Coordination

171

Not only do EMS personnel have advanced life support, but also, in most cases, they have a higher level of training and experience than law enforcement-based medics.

Ultimately, EMS personnel had to force their way into the school to do vital checks on the remaining victims.[627]

Observations and Recommendations

Observation 1: All 11 FOS initially responded to Robb Elementary School as dictated by policy and practice for an active shooter response. However, only 5 of the 11 FOS ran toward the gunfire from rooms 111 and 112, but they retreated when UPD Lt. 1 and another FOS were grazed. After that initial response, only UPD Lt. 1 made further attempts to move toward the classrooms, and leadership did not direct entry into the classrooms.

> **Recommendation 1.1:** Agencies should develop and annually review policy that directs officers to make entry and engage the subject as quickly as possible during an active attacker incident.

> **Recommendation 1.2:** Agencies should provide training to direct officers to make entry and engage the subject as quickly as possible during an active attacker incident.

> **Recommendation 1.3:** Agencies should train supervisors and implement accountability measures to direct officers to make entry and engage the subject as quickly as possible during an active attacker incident.

Observation 2: The FOS included experienced law enforcement personnel with sufficient training and equipment to engage the subject in rooms 111 and 112. Relevant policies and training directed officers to drive toward the threat and engage the subject to stop the killing. This did not happen.

> **Recommendation 2.1:** The FOS should engage the subject regardless of whether they have additional officers on site.

Observation 3: The first information captured on video of possible victims in rooms 111 and 112 was heard on body-worn camera at 11:37 a.m. Within minutes there was confirmation that room 112 was in session. UCISD PD Chief Arredondo was told that there was an injured teacher. This information was not widely and immediately shared.

> **Recommendation 3.1:** Any intelligence should be shared immediately with all law enforcement present via police radio or any means possible.

---

[627] CIR Fact Finding.

Critical Incident Review: Active Shooter at Robb Elementary School |
Chapter 3. Leadership, Incident Command, and Coordination

172

Observation 4: Leadership from UPD, UCISD PD, UCSO, and TXDPS demonstrated no urgency for establishing a command and control structure, which led to challenges related to information sharing, lack of situational statuses, and limited-to-no direction for personnel in the hallway or on the perimeter.

> **Recommendation 4.1:** Agency leaders must immediately determine incident status and the appropriate command structure for the event. Leadership must continually assess and adjust as the threat and incident evolve.

> **Recommendation 4.2:** Leadership should ensure responders are appropriately provided with a situation status and decisions that affect their responsibilities and actions.

> **Recommendation 4.3:** As soon as leadership is aware of an emotionally involved responder, they should make every attempt to extricate that officer from the hot zone once sufficient personnel are present. Based on the involvement, that officer can be directed to the command post for sharing of any information relevant to the response and incident.

Observation 5: Failure to establish a unified command led to limited multiagency coordination.

> **Recommendation 5.1:** As soon as possible and practical, the lead agency should establish a unified command that includes a representative from each primary first responder agency to facilitate communication, situational awareness, operational coordination, and allocation and delivery of resources.

> **Recommendation 5.2:** As part of their pre-incident planning and preparation, regional agency leaders should determine a process for identifying a lead agency in a multi-jurisdiction response.

Observation 6: Local, county, state, and federal law enforcement personnel self-deployed, adding to the challenges at the scene. At least 380 law enforcement personnel were on the scene from 24 law enforcement agencies.

> **Recommendation 6.1:** A staging area manager should be designated to identify an appropriate area and direct additional personnel there for assignment of duties.

> **Recommendation 6.2:** Agencies should examine their policies and procedures to ensure they address self-deployment guidance and protocols, to include uniform, equipment, and resources.

> **Recommendation 6.3:** Officers should follow agency policies and procedures that address self-deployment.

Observation 7: Leadership failed to establish an ICP until after the incident and, once the ICP was established, it was in a location that was also a crime scene. Lack of strong leadership extended to the establishment and start of an ICP and include failing to sweep the facility (which would have revealed more than 90 children and staff in need of support); create control measures to limit access to other personnel; or, crucially, provide any clarity of purpose, continuity, or unity of effort. However, within 30 minutes, TXDPS took control of the ICP along with the scene.

Critical Incident Review: Active Shooter at Robb Elementary School |
Chapter 3. Leadership, Incident Command, and Coordination

173

Recommendation 7.1: The establishment of an ICP for all agency leaders to report to so that brief and decisive action can be directed out toward the front-line officers is critical to resolving inaction and poor/no decision-making.

Recommendation 7.2: Agencies should be prepared to provide critical services or supplement these services by establishing interagency agreements and plans for mutual aid.

Recommendation 7.3: Agencies should engage with the EOC for assistance in implementing operational stability and a continuity of operations plan.

Recommendation 7.4: The ICP should provide timely direction, control, and coordination to the agency leadership, other agencies, and other critical stakeholders before, during, and after an event or upon notification of a credible threat. The ICP must also serve as an intelligence collection and dissemination hub.

Recommendation 7.5: Agency leadership should provide uninterrupted communication within the internal organization of the agency (or agencies if there is a unified command structure), externally to other agencies, and to all identified stakeholders.

Recommendation 7.6: The ICP should establish and enact time-phased implementation procedures to activate various components of the plan to provide sufficient operational capabilities relative to the event or threat.

Observation 8: There was no uniformly recognized incident commander on the scene throughout the incident.

Observation 9: UCISD PD Chief Arredondo was the de facto incident commander on the day of the incident. Chief Arredondo had the necessary authority, training, and tools. He did not provide appropriate leadership, command, and control, including not establishing an incident command structure nor directing entry into classrooms 111 and 112.

Observation 10: UPD Acting Chief Pargas did not have incident command training and did not demonstrate adequate command leadership during the incident.

Observation 11: Uvalde County Sheriff Nolasco, despite being the chief law enforcement officer for the county, lacked leadership and incident command training and did not demonstrate adequate command leadership during the incident by not coordinating the resources from the Sheriff's Office or helping to establish a unified command.

Recommendation 8–11.1: Agencies should ensure that persons in positions of authority have the requisite training and qualifications to carry out the responsibilities and duties of the title, including those serving in an acting capacity.

Recommendation 8–11.2: Agencies should train, plan, and prepare for mass violence incidents, including the need for incident command structure.

Critical Incident Review: Active Shooter at Robb Elementary School |
Chapter 3. Leadership, Incident Command, and Coordination

174

Recommendation 8–11.3: Leaders should be trained and prepared to transition an incident or response to another leader within or outside of their agency when needed.

Observation 12: On the day of the incident, no leader effectively questioned the decisions and lack of urgency of UCISD PD Chief Arredondo and UPD Acting Chief Pargas toward entering classrooms 111/112, including within their respective agencies and agencies with concurrent/overlapping jurisdiction (e.g., Uvalde County Sheriff Nolasco, Constable Zamora, Constable Field, TX Ranger 1).

Recommendation 12.1: Agencies should create and train on a policy, and set an expectation that leaders will act in a manner consistent with that policy during critical incidents.

Recommendation 12.2: An MOU/memorandum of agreement (MOA) needs to be developed among agencies within a county or region that provides clarity on who is in command, taking into consideration an agency's training, experience, equipment, and capacity to take the lead during a multiagency response to a critical incident.

Recommendation 12.3: Agencies should train and practice together the areas covered in the MOU/MOA. The drills should include all first responders, elected officials, and critical infrastructure stakeholders.

Recommendation 12.4: Law enforcement policy and training should be informed by research on leadership and decision-making theories, behaviors, functions, and practices.[628]

Observation 13: No law enforcement leadership established incident command or unified command.

Recommendation 13.1: Agencies should use the Incident Command System (ICS) for more than large-scale tactical events. They should incorporate as many of the ICS principles as possible in response to varying levels of emergencies or planned events, so ICS becomes a regular component of the agency's culture.

Recommendation 13.2: Agencies should fully adopt NIMS throughout the region, even if not mandated as a FEMA Preparedness Grant recipient.

Recommendation 13.3: Agencies should consider using the NQS to improve response, command, and coordination.

Recommendation 13.4: Agencies should ensure training and retraining of all staff regarding NIMS and the importance of standardized ICS implementation.

Recommendation 13.5: Agencies should conduct drills, exercises, and tabletops on NIMS and include all first responders, elected officials, and other critical infrastructure stakeholders.

---

[628] See "Appendix D. Leadership, Incident Command, and Coordination Supplemental Materials" for more on this topic.

Observation 14: CBP- and TXDPS-trained medics provided leadership for establishing a CCP and triage area and developed a triage process. However, due to the overabundance of law enforcement personnel, the plan was not operationalized once the classrooms were entered by law enforcement.

> **Recommendation 14.1:** Law enforcement agencies should develop and train personnel in tactical emergency medicine and provide the appropriate equipment, as well as collaborate with local EMS to provide this capability.

> **Recommendation 14.2:** First responder agencies should train and equip personnel using a rescue task force model.

Observation 15: Due to the lack of leadership, incident command, and coordination, law enforcement medics failed to coordinate with medical responders, including EMS and hospitals.

> **Recommendation 15.1:** Agencies should work with emergency medical responders to develop a response, triage, and transport plan for mass casualty events. The protocols should be agreed upon, and member agencies should enter a formalized MOU.

> **Recommendation 15.2:** Agencies at the regional level should conduct executive-level, multiagency tabletop exercises through their EOC that include elected and appointed officials as well as department heads from other government agencies, relevant nongovernmental agencies, and hospitals and other responder agencies. This will not only prepare personnel, but also help define roles and responsibilities, identify available resources, and establish an agreed-upon unified command system.

> **Recommendation 15.3:** Agencies should consider adopting the recommendations from the U.S. Fire Administration (USFA) publication Fire/Emergency Medical Services Department Operational Considerations and Guide for Active Shooter and Mass Casualty Incidents.[629]

Observation 16: Local ambulances had difficulty accessing Robb Elementary School due to lack of coordination and law enforcement vehicles blocking the streets. This delayed critical medical services.

> **Recommendation 16.1:** An incident safety officer should be designated as quickly as possible during incident response and should pay special attention to the access or egress of emergency vehicles.

---

[629] U.S. Fire Administration, *Fire/Emergency Medical Services Department Operational Considerations.*

Critical Incident Review: Active Shooter at Robb Elementary School |
Chapter 3. Leadership, Incident Command, and Coordination

176

Chapter 4. Post-Incident Response and Investigation

Introduction

This chapter covers the post-incident response and investigation of the active shooter incident at Robb Elementary, including the criminal and administrative investigations and associated activities and processes, such as management of the crime scene, evidence collection, and interagency coordination in such efforts. Additionally, it includes critical incident reviews that are outside of the investigative processes intended for the purpose of broader organizational learning objectives.

In the wake of a critical incident involving a law enforcement response, it is most often the case that multiple investigations and reviews will occur as a result. It is also often the case that these investigations and reviews will be housed within a single agency. For large-scale incidents, where multiple agencies respond and play an integral role in the outcome, post-incident response requires careful coordination among the involved agencies. The public expects the subsequent investigations of such incidents to be comprehensive, transparent, and timely.

Investigators must take important steps to ensure the scene is safe and secure. They must identify and mitigate all risks and hazards that can result in potential injuries to those remaining on scene, as well as protect against anything that may compromise the integrity of the crime scene. Coordination between different respondents, such as investigators, forensic teams, and paramedics, is vital, as regular briefings and information sharing can promote teamwork and increase efficiency.

Scope

This chapter includes the establishment of investigative command, crime scene management, and the investigative activities of involved agencies. In preparing this chapter, the Critical Incident Review (CIR) team benefited from the expertise of subject matter experts, who assisted in developing the observations and recommendations for this chapter. Where not otherwise cited, the practices identified in this chapter derive from the experts' collective knowledge and experience.

As of the end of the review period, neither the Texas Department of Public Safety (TXDPS) nor the Uvalde County District Attorney have completed their criminal investigations. Administrative investigations also remain underway with TXDPS, Uvalde Police Department (UPD), and U.S. Customs and Border Protection (CBP). The only completed works are the Texas House of Representatives Investigative Committee report and the Advanced Law Enforcement Rapid Response Training (ALERRT) assessment report, each of which were published as an interim report and a "living document" respectively.

This chapter is organized by three aspects of post-incident response at Robb Elementary.

- Investigative Command—This section describes principles of establishing an investigative command and the actions taken by law enforcement in the wake of the tragedy at Robb Elementary.

- Crime Scene Management—This section describes the principles of crime scene management and how they were applied in the wake of the tragedy at Robb Elementary.

- Investigations and Incident Reviews—This section describes the nature and purpose of various investigative and review processes that take place in the wake of a critical incident, and how they were implemented after the tragedy at Robb Elementary.

Each section discusses the general principles and best practices related to the particular topic and any relevant background before analyzing what occurred on the ground at Robb Elementary. The chapter concludes with observations and recommendations.

Investigative Command

Investigative Command Principles

Establishing investigative command after a multi-agency response to a mass casualty incident is critical to ensure effective control and coordination of the scene and responsive resources, assignment of investigative assets, collection of information and intelligence, and external and internal communication.

Investigative Command at Robb Elementary

After the subject was killed and victims were being triaged and evacuated, the Texas Rangers took control of the crime scene at the request of the Uvalde County District Attorney. Typically, this would be done in conjunction with the local agency of jurisdiction, and often in support rather than as lead. In the immediate aftermath of the incident, Chief Pete Arredondo of the Uvalde Consolidated Independent School District Police Department (UCISD PD) was operating on this principle, requesting support assets from the Rangers and continuing to provide direction to close off the crime scene and establish an outer perimeter. However, given the involvement of UCISD PD, UPD, and the Uvalde County Sheriff's Office (UCSO) in the incident, the District Attorney and Texas Rangers reasoned that those agencies should not be involved in the investigation.[630] All five UCISD PD members were involved in the response, four of whom were in the hot zone. Similarly, a large number (at least 26) of UPD's officers responded to the scene. Additionally, more than a dozen UCSO members, including the Sheriff, responded. Ultimately, the District Attorney made the determination that Texas Rangers would lead the investigation without the involvement of local agencies. While TXDPS had the second-largest number of personnel on scene, they also have the depth and resources to ensure that involved personnel are not part of the investigative team.

---

[630] CIR Fact Finding.

Under ordinary circumstances, the Ranger assigned to the district in which the crime had occurred would be assigned lead investigator. However, that Ranger was also heavily involved in the incident response; therefore, it was decided by that Ranger's supervisor that they would not lead or participate in the investigation. Therefore, another Ranger was assigned lead investigator, and the involved Ranger was not part of the investigative team.[631]

The lead investigator with the Rangers assumed investigative command and control of the scene inside the building and began controlling access at the West Building's entry points and interior rooms to preserve the scene.

An investigative command post was established inside the funeral home where the TXDPS Regional Director assumed command upon arrival.[632] The exact time is unknown, but law enforcement eventually realized that the funeral home was one of six crime scenes designated by the Rangers' investigative team, as it was where children and UCISD staff were evacuated to during the incident. It was also the scene of the subject's gunfire toward funeral home employees. As a result, later that evening, the investigative command post was moved to a mobile command post.[633] The Rangers did not establish a log at the investigative command post at any time.[634]

Crime Scene Management

Crime Scene Management Principles

In the wake of an incident, the crime scene must be rapidly secured with the establishment of inner and outer perimeters, controlled access, and a log of all individuals who access the crime scene. Doing so will also allow investigators and crime scene analysts to complete their tasks without external distractions or security risks. In addition to coordinating assets and assessing the crime scene, investigators must begin locating witnesses, taking initial statements, tracking down leads, and conducting interviews to ascertain a complete understanding of what occurred. Investigators must conduct a neighborhood canvass to help identify potential witnesses, who may have video or audio evidence, and who may not come forward or be otherwise identified. In the case of many mass casualty events and most active shooter incidents, there is no suspect to search for or apprehend because the subject is killed. However, there is a need to take into account that threats such as secondary devices, improvised explosive devices (IEDs) that may have been left behind, accomplices, and copycats will need to be mitigated. Additionally, in the investigative process, other individuals may be uncovered as legally liable for some of the killer's actions.

The crime scene must be processed rigorously and systematically even if the subject is deceased. All artifacts should be treated as evidence and collected, documented, and preserved. Various aspects of the crime scene should also be captured through video and photography. Victims should be

---

[631] CIR Fact Finding.

[632] CIR Fact Finding.

[633] CIR Fact Finding.

[634] CIR Fact Finding.

photographed, processed, and removed from the scene as quickly as possible. Crime scene analysts, technicians, and investigators should work closely with the lead detectives or investigators responsible for the overarching investigation of the incident.

Crime Scene Management at Robb Elementary

The crime scene at Robb Elementary was managed by Texas Rangers and TXDPS. Due to the nature of the incident and how it unfolded, the crime scene was divided into six separate crime scenes:

- Subject's grandparents' house
- Location of the car wreck at the ditch near Robb Elementary
- Classroom 111
- Classroom 112
- West Building hallway and classrooms 131 and 132
- Funeral home

The interior building crime scenes—in classroom 111, classroom 112, and the hallway and classrooms 131 and 132—were especially challenging due to the nature of the incident, even for seasoned investigators. Another related factor complicating the scene was the sheer number of unnecessary officers who entered classrooms 111 and 112 after the shooter was neutralized. While triaging, officers moved deceased victims within the classrooms, into the hallway, into classrooms 131 and 132, and outside. Other items inside the room may have also been inadvertently moved during the chaotic scene.

The crime scene teams documented and processed an extremely challenging scene. Five teams worked tirelessly to document and process the entirety of the crime scene multiple times. However, the hellfire trigger system[635] was not initially catalogued as evidence, as the crime scene teams were not aware of what the device was or that it was integral to the investigation. Three days later, investigators learned that the device may have been on the scene after reviewing closed-circuit television (CCTV) footage from inside the hallway and hearing the rapidity of the gunfire during the subject's initial assault on classrooms 111 and 112. Because of the copious crime scene photography, the crime scene team was able to locate the hellfire in a trash receptacle in the classroom. Notably, the device was incidentally photographed on the floor in crime scene photos from days prior.[636]

Walk-throughs of the crime scene also hindered the work of the crime scene teams. Multiple interview participants who were present reported an excessive amount of crime scene walk-throughs by senior officials in the hours and days following the incident. For example, the TXDPS regional director walked past the law enforcement officers bringing injured and deceased victims out of the classrooms and

---

[635] The hellfire is a device that allows semi-automatic firearms to fire rounds at an increased rate.

[636] The crime scene team promptly conducted an internal after-action review to identify strengths and areas for improvement they learned as a result of their response to this incident.

entered classrooms 111 and 112 with no intended purpose or action identifiable. Eventually a San Antonio special weapons and tactics (SWAT) team member stood in front of room 112 to preserve the crime scene.[637]

When these walk-throughs occur, the processing of the crime scene must come to a halt, which is particularly disruptive given the methodical nature that the job requires. Additionally, they unnecessarily compromise the crime scene. Some officials walked through the scene multiple times, often not alone. Furthermore, none of the officials filed reports after their walk-throughs, as is reportedly required by TXDPS.[638]

The Federal Bureau of Investigation (FBI) deployed various support assets to their command center at the San Antonio Field Office and on the ground in Uvalde. In Uvalde, the Victim Services Response Team and Evidence Response Team (ERT) assisted with gathering non-evidentiary personal effects from Robb Elementary and returning them to UCISD staff, families, and survivors of the tragedy. FBI agents also ensured that soiled items were cleaned to the greatest extent possible and handled with care.

With a major storm forecasted for the area, there was an urgent need to process the car wreck crime scene. Despite an offer of assistance to process the vehicle and associated evidence by the FBI's ERT, TXDPS declined and the scene was not processed that day.[639] The storm brought heavy rainfall and winds that washed out the crime scene and compromised the evidence, which included one of the subject's two rifles, casings from shooting at the funeral home employees, and other personal items inside the vehicle.

Victim identification was conducted by TXDPS with the assistance of UCISD PD Chief Arredondo. Families provided photos and descriptions of their children to the Rangers for the purpose of identification. Identifications were made for all victims the night of the incident, and notifications were made at the hospital and Civic Center to families of the deceased (see "Chapter 6. Trauma and Support Services").

The crime scene was processed over a period of 10 days and on June 3, the command post shut down and the building was handed back to the school district.[640]

Investigations and Incident Reviews

Investigation and Incident Review Principles

In the wake of a critical incident that involves serious injury or the loss of life, there are usually two investigations that take place: a criminal investigation into the actions of the assailant, and an administrative investigation examining the adherence to policies and procedures and the response of

---

[637] Texas Department of Public Safety Body-Worn Camera Footage.

[638] CIR Fact Finding.

[639] CIR Fact Finding.

[640] CIR Fact Finding.

the responding law enforcement personnel. Additionally, in some circumstances, other special reviews (e.g., critical incident reviews, after action reports, use of force reviews) that are outside of the formal investigative processes but an integral part of organizational learning may occur.

A criminal investigation into a mass casualty incident still plays a crucial role in the criminal justice system, even though the subject is often deceased and the defendant will never stand trial for the crimes committed. The criminal investigation is essential in uncovering potential accomplices to the crime, understanding the offender's motives, providing an official record of the incident, and helping to provide resolution to the victims, survivors, families, and the community. These investigations can be complex and time-consuming, but nonetheless serve a vital purpose in our criminal justice system.

In addition to a criminal investigation, critical incidents often result in one or more administrative investigations of officer conduct during the incident. Depending on the agency and incident in question, it could include, but not necessarily be limited to: officers who used force; supervisors or other officers who made critical decisions that impacted public safety; officers who may have been engaged in or witnessed misconduct; and officers who have had complaints filed against them in connection to the incident, whether internal or external.

A third lane of review following a critical incident is generally known as critical incident reviews or after-action reviews (AARs). The form and function of these boards will vary and are often designed within the constraints of the agency's internal and external environments—including the size of the agency, resources available, and collective bargaining agreements that may be in place. Law enforcement agencies vary in their use of such reviews, with many larger agencies having standing boards and formalized processes for both small- and large-scale incidents. While such reviews are routinely conducted internally, agencies will also seek external assistance with such reviews, especially for high-profile incidents that challenge public trust and demand an independent, outside review. AARs play a crucial role in law enforcement, aiding in both personal career development and organizational growth. They provide a systematic approach for agencies to assess and analyze their actions after a particular incident. In essence, AARs in law enforcement contribute to continuous learning and improvement, fostering a culture of self-assessment and learning from both successes and failures. Importantly, the law enforcement profession has largely embraced the value in AARs as a learning tool to understand the lessons learned from other law enforcement agencies in responding to unique events.

Investigations and Incident Reviews in Uvalde

As of the end of the review period, there are currently ongoing criminal and administrative investigations. Two interim incident reviews have been published.

Ongoing Criminal Investigation

At the onset of the investigation, the Uvalde County District Attorney requested that the Texas Rangers take lead on the investigation and exclude the participation of the local agencies: UCISD PD, UPD, and UCSO.[641] The unusual arrangement was decided because of the involvement of the local agencies' officers in the response. Texas Rangers supported this decision.[642]

A criminal investigation of the incident is being conducted by the Texas Rangers. The scope of the investigation by the Texas Rangers includes not just the criminal case file regarding the deceased subject, but also any criminal wrongdoing by officers who responded. Both aspects of the investigation are ongoing as of the end of the review period. The district attorney has received a preliminary report from the Texas Rangers and expects to decide whether to decline or pursue charges once the investigation is complete.

While the FBI is not conducting an independent criminal investigation, the FBI assisted the Texas Rangers with witness interviews for a period of time early in the investigation. One area in which the FBI provided substantial assistance is regarding child witnesses. The FBI provided highly trained and experienced forensic child witness interviewers to assist with this especially sensitive aspect of the investigative process. These agents interviewed 31 child witnesses, including survivors from inside rooms 111/112.[643]

Administrative Investigations

The post-incident actions of all responding agencies are beyond the scope of this review. In this section, the CIR team brings five key agencies into focus:

- Uvalde Police Department (UPD)
- Uvalde Consolidated Independent School District Police Department (UCISD PD)
- Uvalde County Sheriff's Office (UCSO)
- Texas Department of Public Safety (TXDPS), to include the Texas Rangers
- U.S. Customs and Border Protection (CBP)

Each of these agencies played substantial roles in the overall response to the incident, including at the leadership level. Below, the CIR team offers a synopsis of the status of each agency's administrative investigation at the time of this report.

---

[641] CIR Fact Finding.

[642] CIR Fact Finding.

[643] During the incident, all children present in room 111 died. The survivors interviewed from room 111 were students that left after the awards ceremony and prior to the incident.

UPD. As a matter of practice, UPD utilizes external, independent investigators to conduct administrative investigations of serious uses of force or critical incidents. In the wake of the incident, TXDPS collected evidence, including body camera recordings, from Uvalde officers. TXDPS has not cooperated with requests by the City of Uvalde for data and documentation to support UPD's internal investigation. UPD's internal investigation is currently ongoing.

UCISD PD. The school district terminated all officers from employment and began to establish a new force. No internal investigations were completed.

UCSO. The Sheriff's Office has not initiated any internal investigations into their deputies, citing the ongoing criminal investigation. It is common practice for law enforcement agencies to wait for the completion of a criminal investigation prior to an administrative investigation. However, this practice is known to significantly hamper the timeliness of the administrative investigation. In the case of the Robb Elementary active shooter response, this has meant that over one year has passed before any administrative investigations have been conducted in the Sheriff's Office.

TXDPS and Texas Rangers. TXDPS Director Steve McCraw has publicly indicated that seven TXDPS members are under investigation for their actions that day and the cases are under review by the TXDPS Office of the Inspector General. To date, two TXDPS employees have been terminated from employment, including one Ranger. One TXDPS trooper was under investigation and voluntarily resigned.

CBP. CBP's Office of Professional Responsibility (CBP OPR) has broad scope and conducts both criminal and administrative investigations CBP-wide—including all agents—regarding corruption, misconduct, and mismanagement. As a matter of practice, when an agent is under criminal investigation for their conduct on duty, CBP waits to complete its administrative investigation until after the completion of the criminal investigation. CBP had delayed its administrative investigation, pending the Uvalde County District Attorney's decision, for 9 months before beginning its administrative investigation, despite the local criminal investigation not being completed.

ATF. Title 28 of the United States Code provides ATF the authority to investigate criminal and regulatory violations of federal firearms law at the direction of the Attorney General.[644] Under that authority, ATF examined, tested, and classified the hellfire device found at Robb Elementary School.[645] Based on the objective design features of the device, the marketing of the device, and instructions associated with the device, ATF made their classification.[646] The ATF Firearms and Ammunition Technology Division determined the device was a part designed and intended solely and exclusively for use in converting a weapon into a machinegun and therefore is a machinegun under Federal law, 18 U.S.C. 922(o).[647]

---

[644] CIR Document and Data Review.

[645] CIR Document and Data Review.

[646] CIR Fact Finding.

[647] CIR Fact Finding; CIR Document and Data Review.

Incident Reviews

Two incident reviews were conducted and released by July 2022, 2 months after the school shooting occurred, both acknowledging the limitations that were inherent in providing an assessment at such an early stage in the investigation.

The first review was commissioned by TXDPS to the ALERRT Center out of Texas State University. The focus of this review was primarily on active shooter response tactics. In the report, ALERRT acknowledges the limitations in the sources of information used to develop their assessment and notes that it is subject to change as new evidence becomes available. This report was released July 6, 2022.

Soon after the incident, the Texas House of Representatives established an investigative committee to review the incident, producing an interim report on July 17, 2022. In its report, the committee acknowledged that it did not have a complete record of the incident, as multiple investigations were still ongoing. At the same time, the committee was established in response to early calls for transparency and an understanding of what had unfolded at Robb Elementary, as early accounts were found to be at times inaccurate or misleading. In full transparency of its own work, the committee acknowledged that some aspects of its reports may be found to be disputed or disproved in the future.

CBP OPR also initiated a critical incident review focused on the response of CBP personnel on scene on May 24. CBP OPR began collecting data and documentation soon after the incident, constructing a comprehensive incident timeline focused on CBP personnel and assets deployed, and formulating the scope of its review. A large team of analysts were dedicated to the reconstruction of the incident and timeline, collecting body-worn camera footage, CCTV, interviews, radio logs, and more to piece together the incident. Interviews with involved agents were conducted in March 2023. CBP OPR brought together investigators from across the country and ensured they all received trauma-informed interview training. Additionally, during the interviews, they ensured that support counselors were on site and available throughout the day for both interview participants and the investigative team. The review remains underway.

Observations and Recommendations

Observation 1: The involvement of local agencies in the hallway during the incident led the district attorney, in consultation with TXDPS, to assign Texas Rangers to solely investigate the incident.

> **Recommendation 1.1:** Agencies should have a formal agreement or understanding on investigative command after a multiagency response.

Observation 2: An investigative command post was initially established at the funeral home, which was soon discovered to be one of six crime scenes. As a result, the command post was moved into a TXDPS mobile command post.

Recommendation 2.1: Agencies should carefully assess the location of any command post during and after a critical incident to ensure it is suitable for the operations of a command post. Some considerations include accessibility, size and capacity, availability of resources, and safety and security.

Observation 3: TXDPS did not maintain a log for the investigative command post. As a result of this oversight, there is no record of which agencies or individuals were present at various times throughout the crime scene investigation.

Recommendation 3.1: Law enforcement agencies investigating any crime scene—especially complex, multiagency responses—should ensure a log is kept not only at the crime scene, but at the command post as well. The log ensures accurate record keeping and accountability for actions taken by the investigative team. Access to the command post should be limited to those with a need to be there.

Observation 4: Body-worn camera (BWC) video captures officers walking into the crime scene without an investigative purpose or responsibility in the immediate aftermath of the incident. Furthermore, in the days that followed, crime scene preservation was compromised, and the crime scene team had to continually stop and start their important work when non-investigatory personnel entered the hallway and classrooms 111/112 for the purpose of viewing the scene.[648]

Recommendation 4.1: Leaders must respect the integrity of the crime scene and only access it with a declared and documented legitimate purpose. Crime scenes need to be held without contamination until completed. The crime scene team should be permitted to do their methodical work without continuous interruptions by VIPs who want to enter the crime scene but have no probative need to do so.

Recommendation 4.2: Investigative teams should ensure that inner and outer perimeters are established at all crime scenes. There was an outer security presence at the campus gate, but there was not a secured entrance to the building of the crime scene.[649]

Observation 5: The crime scene at the car wreck was washed out by rain prior to the collection of any evidence. The FBI offered to process the truck and warned of the rain coming, suggesting they move the truck to a secure and dry location. They also offered to cover the truck with a tarp. These offers were rebuffed by TXDPS leadership.

Recommendation 5.1: Investigative teams must properly assess weather conditions and the timing of investigative activities—particularly evidence collection—that must be conducted outside in the elements.

---

[648] CIR Fact Finding.

[649] CIR Fact Finding.

Observation 6: Texas Rangers conducted an exterior door test, documenting the operation and locking mechanisms of each exterior door in the West Building. The critical incident review (CIR) team was unable to ascertain whether the Texas Rangers conducted the same test on interior doors—specifically rooms 111 and 112—which witnesses have also indicated could have had faulty closing and locking mechanisms. The interior doors were removed from their frames by the Uvalde County District Attorney as evidence. The functionality of the doors should have been assessed prior to their removal from the crime scene.

> **Recommendation 6.1:** Law enforcement agencies investigating such incidents in which the form and functionality of physical evidence, such as doors, would benefit from testing should refrain from removing such items until they have been tested and such testing is formally documented via video recording and a written report.

Observation 7: The hellfire trigger system was not initially collected as evidence, as crime scene Rangers were not aware of its presence or that they should be looking for it. After reviewing crime scene photos, they uncovered an approximate location of the device at the crime scene and recovered the device.

> **Recommendation 7.1:** Agencies in regional proximity to each other should conduct multiagency tabletop exercises (TTX) for complex investigations that may necessitate mutual aid and support from each other. Doing so will build greater interagency coordination in activities like evidence collection as well as understanding of jurisdictional boundaries, capabilities, processes, and expectations among partner agencies. The TTX should include local, state, and federal agencies, as appropriate, and be designed to exploit weaknesses, uncover strengths, and develop solutions.

Observation 8: Given the influx of investigative support assets from out of town, often spending multiple days on site, there were logistical challenges with lodging and transportation. Many hotels were sold out. The team lead was able to secure housing on a hunter's ranch, which helped alleviate the lodging issue.

> **Recommendation 8.1:** Crime scene teams need to plan for logistical support, especially when traveling long distances to mass shootings. Identifying a dedicated coordinator for such efforts can help in the planning and ensure personnel arriving from out of town are able to find lodging nearby, including nontraditional options as needed, such as a private housing.

Observation 9: The Texas Rangers Crime Scene Team processed and exhaustively documented an incredibly challenging crime scene that put their training, policies, and procedures to the test. The team conducted an after-action review to examine their efforts and learn as an organization.

> **Recommendation 9.1:** Organizational subunits should conduct after action reviews, particularly in the wake of critical incidents that provide a real-world test to their training, policies, and procedures.

Observation 10: To account for the number of victims and personal items, the Crime Scene Team implemented an alphanumeric tracking system for items found so that they could be quickly, easily, and accurately aligned.

> **Recommendation 10.1:** Crime scene investigators responding to incidents of mass violence should be prepared with a predesignated system to collect and align personal belongings to victims.

Observation 11: Among the agencies with the most involved personnel, most have not completed administrative investigations into their officers' actions on May 24.

> **Recommendation 11.1:** Agencies should adopt parallel investigations policy for criminal and administrative investigations, including for major incidents, while taking diligent steps to ensure that information derived from compelled administrative interviews are completely walled off from any criminal investigation into the officer's or agent's actions.

Observation 12: CBP OPR stood up a comprehensive analytical operation, dedicating staff to the reconstruction of the incident, which provided high-value intelligence to investigators as they began conducting interviews with involved agents.

> **Recommendation 12.1:** Agencies that engage in after action/critical incident reviews should adequately resource the effort to ensure high-quality and timely reports of lessons learned and areas for organizational improvement.

Observation 13: CBP OPR trained all investigators in trauma-informed interview techniques in advance of interviewing their involved agents, some of which were deeply involved in the incident response.

> **Recommendation 13.1:** Agencies' personnel conducting interviews of individuals involved in a critical incident should be trained in trauma-informed interview techniques.

Observation 14: UPD officers involved in the incident did not maintain a record of their own incident reports. Rather, UPD records show a reference back to the Texas Rangers' records, which serve as the official statement of UPD officers.

> **Recommendation 14.1:** Agencies should maintain a duty to collect officer statements for their own administrative records and investigations even as an external agency is conducting an investigation into the same matter.

Observation 15: UPD's internal investigation has been hampered by a lack of access to evidence that TXDPS was in possession of and not willing to share.

> **Recommendation 15.1:** Memoranda of understanding on sharing investigative data should be established among partner agencies.

Observation 16: The FBI provided forensic interview specialists for conducting child witness interviews, filling a gap in available resources and expertise within the lead agency.

Recommendation 16.1: Agencies should ensure they have procedures in place to identify and utilize forensic child witness interviewers, whether in-house or through mutual aid agreements.

Observation 17: The FBI's child witness forensic interview specialists were not representative of the racial and gender makeup of the child witnesses.

Recommendation 17.1: When conducting investigations, law enforcement agencies should account for the racial, ethnic, gender, and cultural diversity of witnesses when making investigative assignments, including interviews.

Chapter 5. Public Communications During and Following the Crisis

Introduction

Well-executed and trauma-informed public communications during and after a disaster, emergency, or mass violence event can help victims and community members prepare and respond effectively to such events. Communications from trusted leaders who adopt a trauma-informed approach to providing information and demonstrate a sense of calm, competency, control, and compassion can also help impacted individuals and communities manage their stress and distress reactions to these events. Thus, communications—both internal to organizations or groups and external—are critically important in every disaster, emergency, and mass violence incident. Communications must be timely and accurate and provide as much information as appropriate at a given time. Doing so helps provide individuals and communities with a sense of trust and confidence in their leaders even when receiving what, in many cases, is some of the most devastating news that anyone can receive.

Inaccurate information combined with inconsistent messaging created confusion and added to the victims' suffering, both on the day of the Robb Elementary School tragedy and in the days, weeks, and months after the mass shooting. While it is understandable that public information officers (PIOs) in smaller jurisdictions like Uvalde would have little experience in crisis communication, it does not alleviate the need to prepare—even in the most basic sense—for a worst-case scenario. The unfortunate reality is that the significant increase in mass shootings in every size of jurisdiction means that all law enforcement agencies, fire/emergency medical services (EMS), local governments, officials and city leaders, and health and behavioral health agencies should create trauma-informed plans for such critical incidents.

Organizations must be prepared to swiftly develop proactive messages in an organized fashion to keep community members informed and establish confidence in leadership that can unite a community and assist with the healing process. This is also a critical opportunity to provide the community with safety information and reassurance of the efforts underway to both end the threat and begin the recovery process. Unfortunately, none of this happened in Uvalde, which led to an erosion of public trust in the involved organizations. Historically, Uvalde has been a community split into two tight-knit segments: one predominantly comprising ethnic Mexican residents, many of whom are third-generation Americans, and the other predominantly comprising white residents, who occupy the majority of positions of authority in the community. The failures during the response, compounded by the refusal to communicate openly and honestly about the law enforcement response, has weakened many bonds within and between each of these groups.[650]

---

[650] CIR Fact Finding.

Critical Incident Review: Active Shooter at Robb Elementary School |
Chapter 5. Public Communications During and Following the Crisis

190

Scope

This chapter describes generally accepted practices and protocols for keeping the public informed during a crisis, along with PIO duties and responsibilities in the initial response; media staging and relations; during- and post-incident public communications to family members, social media, and the general public, including proactive messaging, and rumor monitoring, control, and response; and initial family support, unification, and notification.

In preparing this chapter, the CIR team benefited from the expertise of subject matter experts, who assisted in developing the observations and recommendations for this chapter. Where not otherwise cited, the practices identified in this chapter derive from the experts' collective knowledge and experience.

The chapter is organized based on three aspects of public communications related to this tragedy.

- Public Communications During a Tragedy—This section covers the day of the tragedy and the subsequent three days.

- Public Communications in the Aftermath of a Mass Casualty Incident—This section covers communications since the initial tragedy.

- Communications with Victims and Families—This section covers communication with the victims and families in Uvalde.

Each section discusses the generally accepted practices and standards related to public communications during and following a crisis, and any relevant background before analyzing what occurred in Uvalde. The chapter concludes with observations and recommendations.

Additional background and resources are included in "Appendix E. Public Communications Supplemental Materials."

Public Communications During a Tragedy

Public Communications Principles

Several key principles can help to guide successful communications during a tragedy.

Role of Public Information Officers and Joint Information System

A critical component for coordinated communication during a tragedy is the identification of a public information officer (PIO) and the establishment of a Joint Information System (JIS). A JIS is the "processes, procedures, and tools that facilitate communication to the public, incident personnel, the media, and other stakeholders." JIS operations are housed in a Joint Information Center (JIC).[651]

---

[651] FEMA, NIMS Guidance for Public Information Officers.

Critical Incident Review: Active Shooter at Robb Elementary School |
Chapter 5. Public Communications During and Following the Crisis

191

FEMA guidance for PIOs provides a summary of the PIO function in an incident command structure (see figure 5-1 on page 193):

- Proactively develop accurate, accessible, and timely information for use in press/media briefings, written media releases, or web and social media posts.

- Monitor information from traditional media, the web, and social media that is relevant to incident planning and forward it as appropriate.

- Understand and advise incident command on any necessary limits on information release.

- Obtain the Incident Commander's approval of public materials.

- Conduct and prepare officials for media briefings.

- Arrange for tours, community outreach events, interviews, and briefings.

- Make information about the incident available to incident personnel.

- Participate in planning meetings.

- Identify and implement rumor control methods.

- In incidents involving multiple agencies, leadership may establish a JIC. The PIO participates in or leads the JIC.[652]

The command post addresses the operational aspect of a response, while the JIC becomes the focal point for feeding the public and media information and direction during a devastating, high-profile incident. The JIC and media staging area should typically be in line of sight of the command post. A JIC can be virtual via phone calls and text messages until there is time to set up a physical JIC location near the scene or in the command post.

While in a JIC, PIOs:

- identify key information to be communicated to the public

- craft clear messages in plain language that all can understand, including people with limited English proficiency (LEP), with disabilities, or with access and functional needs (AFN)

- prioritize messages to ensure timely delivery of information without overwhelming the audience

- verify information accuracy

- disseminate messages using the most effective means.[653]

Most importantly, each PIO contributes to a unified message that is accurate and consistent, and like the command post, the JIC will include PIOs from all relevant multidisciplinary stakeholders.

---

[652] FEMA, NIMS Guidance for Public Information Officers.

[653] FEMA, NIMS Guidance for Public Information Officers.

Critical Incident Review: Active Shooter at Robb Elementary School |
Chapter 5. Public Communications During and Following the Crisis

192

Figure 5-1. Sample incident command structure with a single incident commander

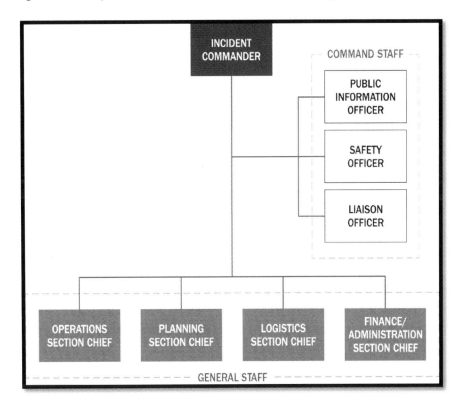

It is also critical to establish a lead agency for each phase of the response during an incident from a communication perspective. A social media tactic that has been successful for many agencies and has become recognized as a best practice is to establish the lead agency as the official source of information during a high-profile, large-scale incident by stating in a post or tweet that all information will be released from a specific agency's social media platform.[654] That agency should also instruct that it is shutting down other modes of communication (such as telephone calls and emails) so the public and media are aware that information will be released only through one official source.[655]

It is simply impossible to staff the onslaught of calls and emails that follow an event of this magnitude. This technique is useful for de-escalating the media because it informs the media that the agency is aware of the appetite for timely information. It also helps the agency impact the narrative forming on social media.

Content of Communications

During a tragedy, it is the responsibility of a government organization to verify information before it is released. It should be confirmed by at least two sources before it is shared, if at all possible. In the event that information shared is discovered to be false, it must be corrected as quickly as possible. The faster

---

[654] McElroy, Developing a Crisis Communication Plan.

[655] McElroy, Developing a Crisis Communication Plan.

inaccurate information is corrected, the better the chance of maintaining public trust. It is also important to inform the public that information is preliminary and will continue to evolve as the situation unfolds or as the investigation progresses.

Intentionally and thoughtfully considering how culture is influencing an impacted population after a mass violence event can also help to increase the possibility impacted individuals will understand and accept the messaging being communicated, access the support provided, and trust in those delivering it. Culture is a very complex concept that encompasses values, traditions and beliefs, spirituality, customs, ways of thinking, systems of language, and communication; behaviors and practices; and ways of living together that people share in common and that can be used to define them as a collective, or a group.[656] There are many different ways of being within different cultures and subcultures, and there are always those who act in countercultural ways.

During a crisis, providing information in the individuals' primary or preferred language is critical.[657] It is essential for law enforcement agencies, government entities, and other community organizations to provide information for limited-English-proficient individuals. Communications in communities for whom English is not their first language should be provided in the primary languages of those impacted.[658] Even when the majority of the population indicates that translation is not necessary, it may be prudent to continue to provide such translation to ensure that anyone needing the service is not feeling stigmatized or outcast as a result.

In all situations, those working with impacted communities other than their own require information about the cultures of the impacted groups. Responders and PIOs must ensure they are accurately pronouncing names and spelling them correctly, and using the syllabic emphasis as spoken by the locals. It is imperative to work closely and build relationships with formal and informal leaders. Ideally, an informed community member can act as a resource for cultural information, but more than one source should be sought. Census data can help identify little-known or unknown subgroups of people impacted and, as noted earlier, recognize that cultural expression varies even within identified groups. Those providing services to the community should research the demographics and any information that can be found on the impacted community. Providers should avoid making assumptions about a particular person, population, or community, but rather ask and learn. Everyone interacting with victims needs to refrain from stereotyping and relying on sources from outside the specific population they are working with to decrease the chances of noticing gossip, insinuation, myth, bias, and racism.

---

[656] World Health Organization, "Definition of Health."

[657] Fetcher, Oxner, and Garcia, "Authorities Ignore Spanish Speakers at Uvalde Press Conferences."

[658] For resources in this area, see "Overcoming Language Barriers in Policing and Building an Effective Language Access Program" in the COPS Training Portal.

Critical Incident Review: Active Shooter at Robb Elementary School |
Chapter 5. Public Communications During and Following the Crisis

194

Responders and PIOs should attempt to engage more than one resource for cultural information so that they verify and expand the understanding of who is impacted by and may need support following an incident. They should ensure all sources are credible, ideally from within the impacted community itself. Inquiries to be addressed should include the following.[659] Also, look for gaps in information and work with community leaders to identify:

- Who might be able to inform in those areas?

- How do people in the community understand health, mental health, and wellness?

- What does recovery look like?

- What is the context of the incident and the community within which it occurred?

- What is the history of the area?

- What is the community's previous experience with government?

- What are social issues within the community?

- Is there community unrest or discourse?

- Has the community experienced more than one disaster, emergency, or mass violence incident within the past five years?

- Is the community well-resourced or lacking in economic, health, and mental health services?

Conducting Briefings

Industry practice with a large-scale incident of this nature is for a law enforcement executive to speak first about the incident in a briefing.[660] The chief or sheriff may be standing next to an elected official or next to a law enforcement or community partner, but the best source of calm and security for the community is a high-ranking local law enforcement official.[661]

After the first news briefing, the lead agency should be working to release basic details in follow-up news conferences, such as an update on the number of victims and their conditions, information about the subject, the type of weapon(s) used, and the status of the investigation. Some activities take place at every crime scene and can be shared, such as meeting with victims' family members, identifying witnesses, conducting interviews with witnesses and the involved officers, and processing the crime

---

[659] *Communicating in a Crisis: Risk Communication Guidelines*; Inter-Agency Standing Committee, *IASC Guidelines on Mental Health*; War Trauma Foundation, *Psychological First Aid*; Naturale et al., "Lessons Learned from the Boston Marathon Bombing;" Flynn et al., "Curriculum Recommendations for Disaster Health Professionals;" Mental Health Technology Transfer Center, *After a School Tragedy*; Center for the Study of Traumatic Stress, *Leadership Communication*.

[660] Global Programme on Preventing and Countering Violent Extremism, *Crisis Communications Toolkit*; FEMA, *NIMS Guidance for Public Information Officers*.

[661] Global Programme on Preventing and Countering Violent Extremism, *Crisis Communications Toolkit*; FEMA, *NIMS Guidance for Public Information Officers*.

Critical Incident Review: Active Shooter at Robb Elementary School |
Chapter 5. Public Communications During and Following the Crisis

195

scene. In general, talking about these activities at the news conference does not compromise the investigation, and it shows the community that law enforcement is making progress. Releasing the victims' names or photographs once gathered is also a critical step for acknowledging the devastating loss of life and uniting the community in its grief.

When the situation is resolved, a law enforcement leader should work to establish a feeling of safety in the community with a news briefing that announces the resolution and includes details of how that was accomplished. If an incident is not quickly resolved, the leader should hold regular news briefings to keep the community informed. The leader should strive to show strength balanced with compassion and care for those suffering tragic injuries and losses.

During any briefings, the media will likely have many questions that cannot be fully answered so early in the investigation, but it is vital to establish transparency and accountability by responding to media questions, even if the response is, "We don't have that information yet, but we'll keep you advised." Answering the media's questions not only invokes a spirit of transparency, but also sometimes helps an agency recognize prominent issues it may have inadvertently overlooked. Ultimately, if an organization treats the media with suspicion and mistrust, the media may respond in kind.

Finally, consistency in messaging is critical in the hours following a mass casualty incident, and the community needs consistent leadership to avoid confusion. Thus, a consistent message should be shared by a single consistent leader in briefings. An agency should avoid one-on-one interviews during large-scale incidents while information is still evolving. This can lead to unintended inaccuracies when releasing information.

Uvalde Communications Day 1–4

The mass casualty incident at Robb Elementary School dominated local and national coverage with continual breaking news updates. Initially, the narrative started with the heroic actions of law enforcement, but by the 4th day it devolved to local law enforcement's failures. This section describes, in chronological order, the key communications events on each of the first 4 days of the tragedy. The section demonstrates the news, inaccuracies, and confusion that the initial narrative caused until the turning point on May 27 when the initial false narrative started to fall apart. The narrative continued to evolve.

May 24—Day 1

11:33 a.m. Subject enters the school. [662]

11:43 a.m. UPD Facebook Post: large police presence at the school, avoid the area.

Initially, it appeared that communication would be rapid. The Uvalde Police Department (UPD) sent out the first public message 10 minutes after the subject entered the school. The 11:43 a.m. Facebook post (see figure 5-2 on page 197) notified community members that there was a "large police presence" and asked

---

[662] Unless otherwise noted, all times are in Central Time.

Critical Incident Review: Active Shooter at Robb Elementary School |
Chapter 5. Public Communications During and Following the Crisis

196

"the public to avoid the area." The post was a strong start for public messaging, but that momentum almost immediately fell flat. Based on the Facebook post, it appeared that UPD would be the lead agency; however, neither UPD nor any other agency messaged that it would serve as the official source of information.

Figure 5-2. UPD Facebook post

ACTIVE POLICE SCENE
AVOID THE AREA

Large Police presence at Robb Elementary 715 Old Carrizo St. We ask the public to avoid the area.
Uvalde CISD
City of Uvalde

12:06 p.m. UCISD PD Facebook Post: school on lockdown, students and staff are safe.

At 12:06 p.m.,[663] the Uvalde Consolidated Independent School District (UCISD) Police Department created its first social media post about the incident (see figure 5-3 on page 198). The post reassured parents that "students and staff are safe in the buildings." This message came 33 minutes after the subject began shooting in the school. This reassurance was later determined to be inaccurate. The language was copied and pasted from a template that the UCISD Communications and Marketing Office created for posting about law enforcement pursuits of undocumented immigrants (also referred to as "bailouts," see callout box in "Chapter 7. School Safety and Security") that had increased significantly in previous months.[664] This false reassurance from UCISD was never corrected. The office was so accustomed to sharing the same messaging on a weekly and sometimes daily basis that it was done

---

[663] Time shown in image is in Eastern Time.

[664] CIR Fact Finding.

Critical Incident Review: Active Shooter at Robb Elementary School |
Chapter 5. Public Communications During and Following the Crisis

197

without much forethought.[665] The message had "always been true in the past."[666] The Communications Office, like the rest of the region, had become immune to the urgency of the emergency alerts (known as Raptor Alerts), school lockdowns, and crisis messaging.[667]

Figure 5-3. UCISD PD Facebook post

Uvalde CISD Police Department
May 24 at 1:06 PM · 🌎   ...

All campuses are under a Lockdown Status
Uvalde CIDS Parents:
Please know at this time all campuses are under a Lockdown Status
due to gun shots in the area. The students and staff are safe in the
buildings. The buildings are secure in a Lockdown Status. Your
cooperation is needed at this time by not visiting the campus. As soon
as the Lockdown Status is lifted you will be notified.
Thank you for your cooperation!
Anne Marie Espinoza
Executive Director of Communications and Marketing
Uvalde CISD

It is impossible to measure the damage done by the inaccurate messaging during this incident, but the actions of the first responding officers along with the false messaging about the response prompted outcry against the local law enforcement agencies. It appears to have a lingering impact on community trust, and relationships have remained strained more than a year after the incident. A flood of negative messages took over the UPD's social media sites starting two days after the shooting.

At the time of the incident, UCISD used a campus-wide notification system for all Uvalde schools known as Raptor.

Anyone on the campus could initiate a Raptor alert and therefore a lockdown of the campus if there was a crisis or emergency at the school. During the incident, the UCISD Communications and Marketing Office received the Raptor lockdown alert as part of the normal protocol at 11:32 a.m. (see figure 5-4 on page 199). In addition, the UCISD communications director also received a telephone call from UCISD PD

---

[665] CIR Fact Finding.

[666] CIR Fact Finding.

[667] CIR Fact Finding.

Critical Incident Review: Active Shooter at Robb Elementary School |
Chapter 5. Public Communications During and Following the Crisis

198

Chief Pete Arredondo while he was responding to Robb Elementary, reporting there was "a man with a gun in the area."[668] After that call at 11:35 a.m., the communications director notified the superintendent and the School Board trustees.[669]

Figure 5-4. Image of the Raptor text message notification sent at the start of the incident

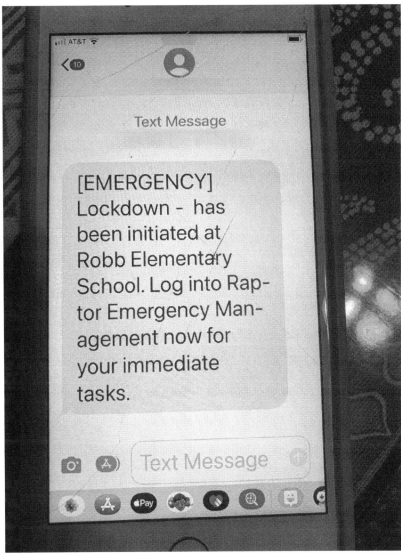

Source: CIR Document and Data Review.

---

[668] CIR Fact Finding.

[669] CIR Fact Finding.

Critical Incident Review: Active Shooter at Robb Elementary School |
Chapter 5. Public Communications During and Following the Crisis

199

The UCISD Communications Team used the following process:

- **Mass Notification Software Blackboard:** to distribute an email message to parents.

- **Recorded Phone Call:** email message was edited and recorded as a voice message for parents.

- **Text Message:** the same shortened message was also sent via text messages to parents.

- **Social Media:** the shortened version was then used for the first social media post at 12:06 p.m., incorrectly reassuring parents and the community that students and staff were safe.

All messaging was provided only in English.

12:17 p.m. UCISD Facebook Post and Tweet: "There is an active shooter at Robb Elementary. Law enforcement is on site. Your cooperation is needed at this time by not visiting the campus. As soon as more information is gathered it will be shared. The rest of the district is under a Secure Status."

The next communication from UCISD was 11 minutes later when both a Facebook post and tweet stated that there was an active shooting at Robb Elementary School (see figure 5-5). This came 44 minutes after the incident began. By then, students had been calling and texting parents and making calls to 911. Although the message asked parents and guardians not to visit the campus at this time, a crowd was growing on the perimeter. This type of delay allowed for rumors and misinformation to establish the narrative.

Figure 5-5. UCISD tweet regarding an active shooter at Robb Elementary

Critical Incident Review: Active Shooter at Robb Elementary School |
Chapter 5. Public Communications During and Following the Crisis

200

Figure 5-6. Two UCISD posts with information regarding reunification site

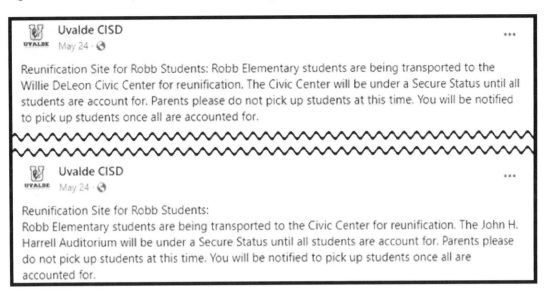

12:20 p.m. UCISD Post: Reunification Site for Robb Students: Robb Elementary students are being transported to the Willie DeLeon Civic Center for reunification. The Civic Center will be under Secure Status until all students are accounted for. Parents please do not pick up students at this time. You will be notified to pick up students once all are accounted for.

Three minutes after UCISD's active shooter post (see figure 5-6), it posted urging parents not to go to the reunification location looking for their children. Parents and guardians, nonetheless, went to the Civic Center in an attempt to reunite with their children.

12:23 p.m. UPD Updates FB post: active scene, pick up children at Civic Center.

12:30 p.m. UCISD Updates FB: reunification details, do not pick up children.

12:38 p.m. UPD Updates FB post: reunification details, pick up at Civic Center.

12:55 p.m. UCISD FB post: Do not pick up children.

UPD and UCISD sent out reunification messages to parents that contradicted each other (see figures 5-6 on page 201 and 5-7 on page 203).

This type of confusion is fairly common during a mass incident; however, it can be minimized if a plan is established before the incident so that the lead reunification agency creates the posts, and all other agencies and stakeholders share those posts.

Critical Incident Review: Active Shooter at Robb Elementary School |
Chapter 5. Public Communications During and Following the Crisis

201

Based on the metadata of UPD's first post, it was edited four times over the next 73 minutes. However, the Facebook algorithm did not recognize the edits as a new post, so it did not appear as fresh content on a user's timeline, which means it did not reach as many users as a new post would reach.

1:06 p.m. UPD Facebook post: shooter in custody.

At 1:06 p.m., UPD updated its original post again with the information that the shooter was in custody (see figure 5-8 on page 204). That misinformation was never corrected, which further undermined the public's trust. Understandably, misinformation is sometimes shared during a dynamic and chaotic event, but it must be corrected as quickly as possible. The person posting for UPD heard over the police radio that the subject was in custody and distributed the message on social media.[670] When the agency realized that was an error, it assumed the information would be corrected during a news conference.[671] The information should have been corrected on social media as well.

UCISD never posted that the threat to the community was over. At 12:20 p.m., it shared UPD's original post that said the scene remains active and to avoid the area, which was later updated with the incorrect message about the subject being in custody. After the UCISD shared UPD's original post, it then created five more posts of its own. Therefore, a user on the UCISD page would have to scroll back five posts to learn that the incident was over. UCISD never posted on social media or distributed a news release to announce the subject was deceased and community members were safe. This was unsettling to the entire community, as it was difficult for community members and family members to know when the situation was resolved without confirmation from the official source.[672] The UCISD police chief eventually announced the death of the subject at its news conference, but that was almost 5 hours after the incident began.

---

[670] CIR Fact Finding.

[671] CIR Fact Finding.

[672] CIR Fact Finding.

Critical Incident Review: Active Shooter at Robb Elementary School |
Chapter 5. Public Communications During and Following the Crisis

202

Figure 5-7. Conflicting UCISD and Uvalde Police Department posts regarding reunification site

Critical Incident Review: Active Shooter at Robb Elementary School |
Chapter 5. Public Communications During and Following the Crisis

203

Figure 5-8. Updated UPD post regarding the shooter

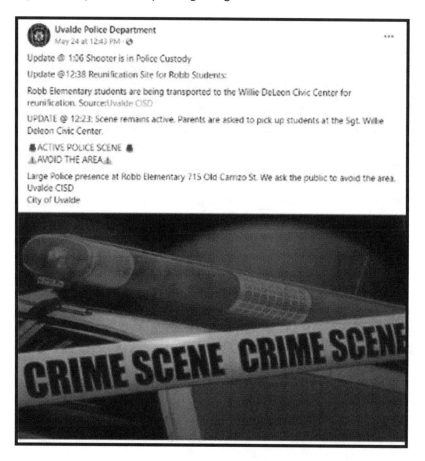

Uvalde Police Department
May 24 at 12:43 PM · 🌐

Update @ 1:06 Shooter is in Police Custody

Update @ 12:38 Reunification Site for Robb Students:

Robb Elementary students are being transported to the Willie DeLeon Civic Center for reunification. Source:Uvalde CISD

UPDATE @ 12:23: Scene remains active. Parents are asked to pick up students at the Sgt. Willie Deleon Civic Center.

🚨 ACTIVE POLICE SCENE 🚨
⚠️ AVOID THE AREA ⚠️

Large Police presence at Robb Elementary 715 Old Carrizo St. We ask the public to avoid the area.
Uvalde CISD
City of Uvalde

1:30 p.m. Uvalde Memorial Hospital social media post.

UMH also launched its emergency preparedness plan, which included an internal communication section but lacked an external one. The hospital's chief executive officer, who took on the role of public information officer during the incident, did not respond to the flood of media calls that took over the phone line set up in the ad hoc Emergency Command Center.[673] The hospital did release patient information on social media starting at 1:30 p.m. (see figure 5-9 on page 205), which was 24 minutes after the first patients arrived at the hospital. If a JIC had been established, UMH could have posted a message on social media directing the media to the JIC for timely information.

---

[673] CIR Fact Finding.

Critical Incident Review: Active Shooter at Robb Elementary School |
Chapter 5. Public Communications During and Following the Crisis

204

Figure 5-9. UMH Facebook post regarding medical treatment of Robb Elementary students

Uvalde Memorial Hospital
May 24 at 2:30 PM · 🌐 ・・・

‼️ Information at this time is that the active shooter at Robb Elementary is in custody. UMH is currently caring for several students in the ER. Immediate family of those students are to report to the cafeteria on the second floor. UMH staff will be in constant communication with the family members. If you are not an immediate family member, we are asking you to refrain from coming to the hospital at this time.

In an example of inconsistent messaging, the UMH message stated where parents and loved ones could check in at the hospital to check on their children (cafeteria on the second floor) and that hospital staff would be in constant contact with families. However, many families described being held up for significant periods of time by law enforcement and security as they tried to get into the parking lot and the hospital.[674] Once the families were admitted, they were not given information for significant periods of time.[675] The hospital's guidance to victims' families was either misinformation, was not accurately communicated to law enforcement, or was not accurately followed by law enforcement tasked with securing entry to the hospital. Whatever the circumstance, the result was more confusion and pain for the families.

The hospital should have coordinated its posts with the lead law enforcement agency. Victim information should be released via the lead agency at a news briefing and through social media. The hospital should then release condition updates. This requires relationship building, planning, and preparing before a large-scale incident. If the lead agency had instituted incident command and established a JIC, then there would have been coordination of the release of all public information, including victim information from Uvalde Memorial Hospital and other medical facilities. The lead agency could then have invited an Emergency Department doctor to discuss the treatment of victims and share current patient conditions at one of the news briefings.

---

[674] CIR Fact Finding.

[675] CIR Fact Finding.

Critical Incident Review: Active Shooter at Robb Elementary School |
Chapter 5. Public Communications During and Following the Crisis

205

1:44 p.m. University Health San Antonio Twitter: University Health tweeted about patients' conditions.

Some of the victims were also transported to University Hospital in San Antonio. University Health San Antonio began releasing patient information on its Twitter and continued to do so over the next four days. One post requested blood donations, while another addressed the myriad emotions that may impact the victims' families and Uvalde community members in the days after the incident. This swift release of information can help minimize the flood of media calls after a high-profile incident. However, if it is done in a silo, it can lead to contradictory news reports. It is vitally important for hospital information about victims to be coordinated with the JIC. Often, there are several hospitals treating patients. If, for example, one hospital releases information about a patient dying, it can cause even more confusion about the total the number of victims. These types of details should come from the Incident Commander via the JIC.

3:23 p.m. Texas Governor Greg Abbott provided the first media briefing.

The first official to speak publicly about the tragic incident was Governor Greg Abbott at 3:23 p.m. (see figure 5-10).[676] He was providing an update on wildfires in Abilene, Texas, when he gave the first briefing on the Robb Elementary School shooting. The Governor released specific details that would typically come from a police chief or sheriff. He announced an inaccurate number of those killed, stating that 14 students and one teacher were killed.[677] The Governor also gave the wrong last name of the subject.[678] He stated that the UCISD Police Department (PD) was the investigating agency.[679] Several other details were preliminary and evolved throughout the day.

Figure 5-10. Texas Governor Abbott speaking during the first media briefing

Source: Used with permission from KTXS-TV, Abilene, TX.

---

[676] "Texas Gov. Greg Abbott's Statement about Robb Elementary School Shooting."

[677] Transcript of Texas governor's news conference, May 24, 2022, in Abilene, TX.

[678] Transcript of Texas governor's news conference, May 24, 2022, in Abilene, TX.

[679] Transcript of Texas governor's news conference, May 24, 2022, in Abilene, TX.

Critical Incident Review: Active Shooter at Robb Elementary School |
Chapter 5. Public Communications During and Following the Crisis

206

4:16 p.m. UCISD news conference, streamed live by UCISD and UPD.

Only UCISD PD Chief Arredondo spoke at the first local news conference. He released the following details and did not answer any media questions:

- Confirmation of the incident: "At approximately 11:32 a.m., this morning, there was a mass casualty incident at Robb Elementary School in Uvalde, Texas."

- Confirmation of "several injuries, adults and students, and some deaths," but the total number of victims was not released.

- The subject was deceased and acted alone.

- Texas Department of Public Safety (TXDPS) was assisting UCISD PD with the investigation.

- UCISD safely released all students from other campuses.

- Asked for prayers for the families.

This news conference lacked the specificity necessary after a tragedy of this magnitude. The current number of victims should have been released. The lead agency should have released the names of the victims within 24 hours of notification of next of kin. Name releases are the first step in honoring the victims. No local, state, or federal agency, including UCISD, ever released the victims' names or photographs.

The UCISD's first news conference took place four hours and 46 minutes after the incident began, which created a window for misinformation to spread and left the community without leadership. At the news conference, the public was directly told that UCISD PD was the lead agency for the investigation. A TXDPS sergeant, UPD acting chief, city and county leadership, and the UPD PIO attended the news conference, but they did not speak on behalf of their agencies.[680] Neither the UCISD Communications Office nor the TXDPS Media and Communications Office reached out to coordinate messaging for the news conference.[681] A TXDPS spokesperson was en route to the scene when this first local news conference took place but UCISD, the UPD PIO, and the acting UPD chief were not aware of that.[682]

The news conference was held at the civic center, away from the scene. However, holding the news conference at the scene would have helped demonstrate that law enforcement was managing the critical incident with urgency. That setting could have restored calm and projected strength. It should have established a joint information approach by either setting up a physical JIC at the scene or a virtual one so the news conference would have coordinated messaging by the responding agencies.

The UCISD news conference began with an announcement that there would be "no questions." This is often perceived as withholding information.

---

[680] CIR Fact Finding.

[681] CIR Fact Finding.

[682] CIR Fact Finding.

4:25 p.m. Brooke Army Medical Center in San Antonio Twitter and Facebook.

The San Antonio Medical Center began using Twitter and Facebook to keep the public informed about the patients they were treating, but again, there was no coordination with any agencies or organizations in Uvalde. By this point, the TXDPS regional director had arrived on the scene and had started establishing a command post to organize the operational side of the incident. The public information component of the incident should have followed this same format. However, the director was not familiar with the JIC concept.[683]

5:00 p.m. to 6:00 p.m. TXDPS spokesperson conducts interviews.

The TXDPS spokesperson arrived at the scene later, between 5:00 p.m. and 6:00 p.m., and began conducting live national and local media interviews. There was no announcement that TXDPS was taking over as the lead agency for the investigation or the public messaging. The TXDPS spokesperson was not aware of the local news conferences, nor were the local agencies aware of the media interviewing the TXDPS spokesperson.[684] TXDPS did not announce interview availability on social media or through a news release. It was more happenstance, with outlets calling the spokesperson directly or flagging them down on a first-come, first-served basis.[685] Instead, a schedule of briefings should have been created, and the local and federal agencies should have been invited to send PIOs to work with the TXDPS spokesperson to coordinate the release of information and host joint news conferences.

Does FERPA Protect the Identities of Deceased Students?

UCISD explained that they never released the names of the adult and child victims due to privacy concerns and the Family Educational Rights and Privacy Act (FERPA).* Our analysis reveals that FERPA alone may not prevent a school from releasing all information. FERPA applies to the education records of students of any K-12 schools that receive funding from the U.S. Department of Education.†

FERPA states that education information, including personally identifiable information (PII) such as name, Social Security number, or date of birth cannot be shared without written parental consent for youth under the age of 18.‡ A child's FERPA rights are vested or held by the parents.§ Notably, both biological parents have rights under FERPA, regardless of physical custody unless there is a specific court order.**

Once a student turns 18 or attends an institution of postsecondary education at any age, the student becomes an "eligible student," and all rights under FERPA transfer from the parent to the student.†† *continues on page 209*

---

[683] CIR Fact Finding.

[684] CIR Fact Finding.

[685] CIR Fact Finding.

Critical Incident Review: Active Shooter at Robb Elementary School |
Chapter 5. Public Communications During and Following the Crisis

208

Does FERPA Protect the Identities of Deceased Students?, cont'd.

In terms of deceased students, FERPA rights differ based upon the age of the child. Specifically, the Student Privacy and Policy Office website states,

> Consistent with our analysis of FERPA and common law principles, we interpret the FERPA rights of eligible students to lapse or expire upon the death of the student. Therefore, FERPA would not protect the education records of a deceased eligible student (a student 18 or older or in college at any age) and an educational institution may disclose such records at its discretion or consistent with State law. However, at the elementary/secondary level, FERPA rights do not lapse or expire upon the death of a non-eligible student because FERPA provides specifically that the rights it affords rest with the parents of students until that student reaches 18 years of age or attends an institution of postsecondary education. Once the parents are deceased, the records are no longer protected by FERPA.[‡‡]

It is important to note that even with parent permission, a school is not required to release sought information since all FERPA exceptions are permissive.[§§] Schools also have the option of releasing de-identified information regarding victims and status.[***]

Regarding referencing FERPA as a basis for not releasing the names of the non-student adult victims in this incident, FERPA is not relevant to that decision.[†††]

For more resources on FERPA, see the following links:

- A Parent Guide to the Family Educational Rights and Privacy Act (FERPA) | Protecting Student Privacy https://studentprivacy.ed.gov/resources/parent-guide-family-educational-rights-and-privacy-act-ferpa

- https://studentprivacy.ed.gov

---

* CIR Fact Finding.

† CIR Fact Finding.

‡ CIR Fact Finding.

§ CIR Fact Finding.

** CIR Fact Finding.

†† U.S. Department of Education, "An Eligible Student Guide."

‡‡ U.S. Department of Education, "Does FERPA Protect the Education Records."

§§ CIR Fact Finding.

*** CIR Fact Finding.

†††CIR Fact Finding.

The TXDPS spokesperson served as a supervisor of the PIOs in the TXDPS southern region.[686] TXDPS has a total of seven regional PIO supervisors throughout the state who all report to the director in their region, but they also report to the assistant chief of the Media and Communications Office. The spokesperson supervised a total of four PIOs and drove one to the scene who was proficient in Spanish and conducted interviews with Telemundo and Univision. Also under the spokesperson's supervision was the PIO assigned to the Del Rio District where Uvalde is located. The spokesperson attended the UCISD news conferences but did not publicly speak.

The TXDPS spokesperson spoke regularly with the agency's media chief, but they did not establish any specific talking points.[687] The TXDPS live interviews still became the only source of detailed information. The spokesperson provided the number of victims and facts of the incident, including the events leading up to the subject entering the school and their actions once inside. The spokesperson's interviews were also a source of appropriate compassion and empathy for the victims. But a sizable portion of the interviews was spent "praising the brave actions of law enforcement, first responders who arrived on scene . . ." The spokesperson focused on law enforcement's "heroic actions" and their willingness to put themselves in harm's way to save the lives of students and teachers in addition to their evacuation efforts. This could be perceived as strategic talking points. Ultimately, this storyline was proved to be inaccurate, and many victims shared that it added to their pain during a challenging time.

Consistency in messaging is critical in the hours following a mass casualty incident. Some media outlets challenged the TXDPS spokesperson for inadvertently using different wording in different interviews. They questioned whether the word choices meant the meaning was being changed. A news conference prevents this confusion. The media chief referred to the hallway where officers were waiting to confront the shooter as, "the sphere of misinformation."[688]

Figure 5-11. UCISD spokesperson opening up the first press conference

Source: Used with permission from KSAT 12.

---

[686] CIR Fact Finding.

[687] CIR Fact Finding.

[688] CIR Fact Finding.

Critical Incident Review: Active Shooter at Robb Elementary School |
Chapter 5. Public Communications During and Following the Crisis

210

The TXDPS spokesperson communicated with the TXDPS media chief while en route to the scene who said to, "get on scene and tell me what you see, and we'll go from there."[689] They spoke countless times over the next few days as the spokesperson conducted the live interviews.[690]

6:45 p.m. UCISD second news conference, streamed live on Facebook by UPD and UCISD.

UCISD's second news conference provided even less information than the first news conference (see figure 5-11 on page 210). Some perceived the conference to lack the strength and compassion necessary to lead a community after a devastating incident.[691] There was no update on the number of victims or their names. The UCISD PD chief's comments lasted only 45 seconds and included the following details:

- We will update you when we can.
- The intruder is deceased.
- Please keep the families in your prayers.

The UCISD PD chief's brief comments did not provide the community with a true update, which then left it up to the public to find details from another source—such as social media—that may be less accurate. UCISD Superintendent Hal Harrell spoke briefly as well, but he also refused to answer media questions. It is worth noting again that the Governor had previously released more details at his 3:23 p.m. news briefing.[692]

Figure 5-12. UMH prescheduled post

---

[689] CIR Fact Finding.

[690] CIR Fact Finding.

[691] CIR Fact Finding.

[692] Transcript of Texas governor's news conference, May 24, 2022, in Abilene, TX.

Critical Incident Review: Active Shooter at Robb Elementary School |
Chapter 5. Public Communications During and Following the Crisis

211

Only the local San Antonio and Uvalde media were present at the second UCISD news conference, even though the national media were in town and broadcasting live from Robb Elementary School. While UCISD held a second news conference off-site, the TXDPS spokesperson was conducting live national interviews at the scene. Again, the school district was not aware of the TXDPS interviews, and the TXDPS spokesperson was not aware of the UCISD news conference.[693] Neither knew what the other was doing or what information they were sharing about a critical incident that both agencies were playing a significant role in handling.

Prescheduled posts that were off topic from the Robb School shooting appeared on UPD's and the Uvalde Memorial Hospital's Facebook pages while the incident was still fresh (see figure 5-12 on page 211) for an example).

8:42 p.m. Final Day 1 UPD FB post: street closures, pray for Uvalde.

9:04 p.m. Final Day 1 UCISD FB post: letter to parents and faculty.

The final UPD post was at 8:42 p.m. (see figure 5-13). It asked for prayers for the people of Uvalde.

Figure 5-13. Last UPD post of the day

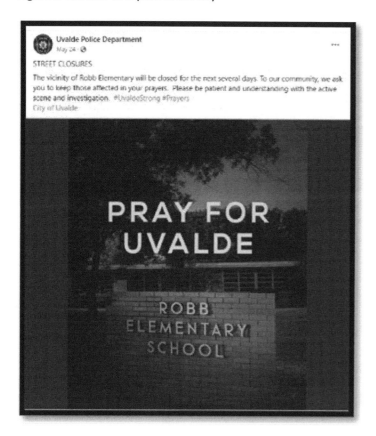

---

[693] CIR Fact Finding.

Critical Incident Review: Active Shooter at Robb Elementary School |
Chapter 5. Public Communications During and Following the Crisis

212

UCISD made its final post at 9:04 p.m. with a letter to parents and faculty reminding the community to console one another and pray for the victims' families. It also announced that school was canceled for the rest of the year, instructed staff to report to school the next day, and informed the community of counseling services available. UCISD sent out its last communication on this tragic day without ever announcing when reunification was complete, or the number of victims lost and injured.

8:41 p.m. ET. President Joe Biden addresses the nation about the school shooting in Uvalde.

The President of the United States addresses the nation, saying,

> I had hoped when I became President, I would not have to do this again. Another massacre. Uvalde, Texas. An elementary school. Beautiful, innocent second, third, fourth graders. And how many scores of little children who witnessed what happened see their friends die as if they're on a battlefield, for God's sake. . . .
>
> So, tonight, I ask the nation to pray for them, to give the parents and siblings the strength in the darkness they feel right now. . . .
>
> May God bless the loss of innocent life on this sad day. And may the Lord be near the brokenhearted and save those crushed in spirit, because they're going to need a lot of help and a lot of our prayers. . . .[694]

The president also made a proclamation on May 24, 2022, honoring the victims of the tragedy in Uvalde, Texas. He stated that the flag of the United States would be flown at half-staff at the White House and upon all public buildings and grounds, at all military posts and naval stations of the Federal Government in the District of Columbia, and throughout the United States and its Territories and possessions until sunset May 28, 2022, and that the flag should be flown at half-staff for the same length of time at all United States embassies, legations, consular offices, and other facilities abroad, including all military facilities and naval vessels and stations.[695]

11:04 p.m. U.S. Border Patrol chief Twitter.

Three tweets from the U.S. Border Patrol chief became the final communication from the responding agencies on the first day (see figure 5-14 on page 214). The tweets focused on efforts of law enforcement to protect students by placing themselves in harm's way and were not coordinated through a JIC.

---

[694] The White House, "Remarks by President Biden on the School Shooting in Uvalde, Texas."

[695] The White House, "A Proclamation Honoring the Victims of the Tragedy in Uvalde, Texas."

Critical Incident Review: Active Shooter at Robb Elementary School |
Chapter 5. Public Communications During and Following the Crisis

213

Figure 5-14. U.S. Border Patrol chief Twitter

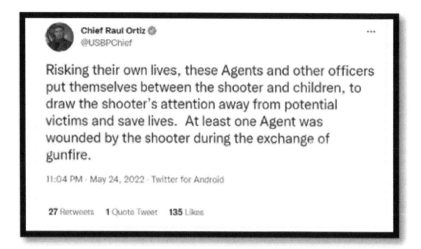

Chief Raul Ortiz ✓
@USBPChief

Risking their own lives, these Agents and other officers put themselves between the shooter and children, to draw the shooter's attention away from potential victims and save lives. At least one Agent was wounded by the shooter during the exchange of gunfire.

11:04 PM · May 24, 2022 · Twitter for Android

27 Retweets   1 Quote Tweet   135 Likes

May 25—Day 2

The next day, the TXDPS spokesperson continued conducting live interviews on national media morning shows. The agency still did not officially announce its role or that it was now leading the investigation. The TXDPS spokesperson relied on media relationships that they previously built with the national media during Operation Lone Star[696] along the Texas-Mexican border. The spokesperson called those contacts, and vice versa, to schedule live interviews.[697] These interviews continued to focus on "heroic" law enforcement actions at Robb Elementary School.

When TXDPS assumed control of the investigation, it should have made an official announcement to the community. This level of transparency ensures accountability to the public when people are seeking reassurance, order, and answers.

---

[696] Operation Lone Star is a border security initiative launched by the Texas governor In March 2021. It is run by TXDPS and Texas Military Department. For more information, read Hernandez, "What is Operation Lone Star?;" Texas Department of Public Safety, "Operation Lone Star: In the News."

[697] CIR Fact Finding.

Critical Incident Review: Active Shooter at Robb Elementary School |
Chapter 5. Public Communications During and Following the Crisis

214

Figure 5-15. Tweet announcing Texas Governor Abbott in Uvalde

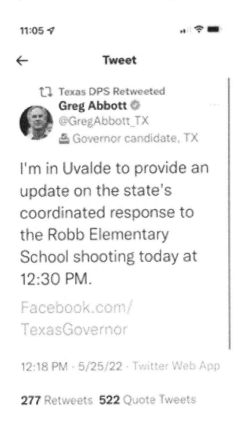

11:05

← **Tweet**

↺ Texas DPS Retweeted
Greg Abbott ✓
@GregAbbott_TX
🏛 Governor candidate, TX

I'm in Uvalde to provide an update on the state's coordinated response to the Robb Elementary School shooting today at 12:30 PM.

Facebook.com/
TexasGovernor

12:18 PM · 5/25/22 · Twitter Web App

277 Retweets **522** Quote Tweets

Source: CIR Document and Data Review.

12:30 p.m. Texas Governor Abbott's news conference with local and state officials.

The Governor's Office and UPD live-streamed a news conference with the Governor and the TXDPS Director Steve McCraw and other state and local officials in Uvalde (see figure 5-15 for the announcement).[698] It was during this news conference that the community learned for the first time that the TXDPS Rangers would lead the investigation.

Unfortunately, several of the speakers at the press conference shared what turned out to be inaccurate information. Both the Governor and TXDPS Director McCraw suggested that a UCISD officer had engaged with the shooter outside the school. That turned out to be false.

Director McCraw also described UPD and UCISD officers rushing toward the subject when they first arrived, stating the school was "immediately breached [because] we know as officers every second is a life, they breached it and engaged the active shooter and continued to keep him pinned down in that

---

[698] C-SPAN, "Governor Abbot News Conference on School Shooting in Uvalde, Texas."

Critical Incident Review: Active Shooter at Robb Elementary School |
Chapter 5. Public Communications During and Following the Crisis

215

location, afterwards until the tactical team could be put together. . ." This detailed description led people to believe law enforcement immediately made entry into the classroom and engaged with the subject. It was later learned that law enforcement waited 77 minutes to confront the subject.

The spokesperson should be briefed by those most knowledgeable of the facts, and while several first responders were present with the Governor prior to his press conference in Uvalde, none provided any information. UPD Acting Chief Mariano Pargas was designated to speak during the briefing; however, during the briefing he had to leave unexpectedly.[699] UCISD PD Chief Arredondo, a UPD lieutenant, and others were in the green room and on the stage with the Governor, and they report that they were not asked about what happened (nor did they offer any information).[700]

Two days later, the TXDPS director amended his description of events and his characterization of it when he said at his final news conference, ". . . of course, it was not the right decision. It was the wrong decision. There's no excuse for it. . ." The actions of the responding officers, combined with the "heroic" storyline that started with the TXDPS spokesperson and continued the next day during the Governor's and director's news conference, dealt a serious blow to public confidence in local and state law enforcement.

When an organization makes a mistake, it must admit that error publicly as quickly as possible. Human errors are not an indictment of the entire organization but an admission of bad decision-making at that moment. In Uvalde, not only did it take 4 days for the real story to emerge, but the perpetuation of a different storyline appeared to feed a perception held by some that law enforcement will "circle the wagons" to protect its own versus doing the right thing by the community members they serve. It is critical to establish community relationships built on mutual trust, respect, and accountability.

2:50 p.m. TXDPS Twitter: TXDPS tweeted for the first time about the incident, more than 24 hours after it took over the investigation. The agency asked people to share information or tips about the Uvalde shooting.

The agency did not use social media to announce that it was leading the investigation, nor did it ever name victims, both of which were conspicuously absent from the local release of information on the first day.

TXDPS should have used social media sooner to provide the community with clarity and confidence that this devastating loss of life would be investigated quickly and appropriately. This accountability serves as reassurance and is necessary for any critical incident that significantly impacts a community.

May 25–28 FBI San Antonio Field Office Twitter

The San Antonio FBI Field Office became the first agency to tweet in both Spanish and English on the second day, when it tweeted about the Family Assistance Center (see figure 5-16 on page 217).

---

[699] CIR Fact Finding.

[700] CIR Fact Finding.

Critical Incident Review: Active Shooter at Robb Elementary School |
Chapter 5. Public Communications During and Following the Crisis

216

Figure 5-16. Spanish-language FBI tweet

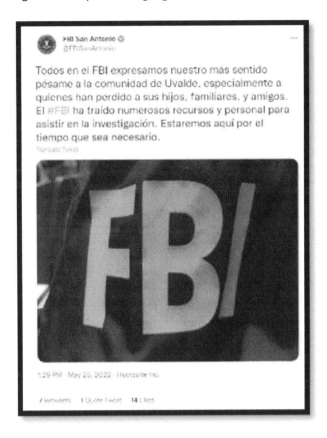

May 26—Day 3

On day 3, the TXDPS Regional Director became the fifth leader to speak on the tragedy, which contributed to the growing confusion (see figure 5-17 on page 218 for the announcement). To review, the Governor held the first news conference, followed by the UCISD police chief, the TXDPS spokesperson, and then the TXDPS director. A consistent message should be shared by a single consistent leader. After a devastating event, the community needs consistent leadership to avoid confusion.

Critical Incident Review: Active Shooter at Robb Elementary School |
Chapter 5. Public Communications During and Following the Crisis

217

Figure 5-17. TXDPS Facebook post announcing regional director's press conference

Source: CIR Document and Data Review.

As media questions about the timeline persisted, the TXDPS regional director held the news conference with the goal of "clearing up the encounter" with the UCISD PD officer outside the school (which never actually happened) and to provide a basic timeline. However, the media frustration grew over the refusal to answer questions about the delayed response, which was reflected in the media questions that became more suspicious and aggressive. The media questions were an extension of the pressing questions from the victims' family members and others.

It is also worth noting that at the end of the news conference, viewers could hear two media requests for a statement to be made in Spanish, but they were not acknowledged. Notably, 81.8 percent of the population in Uvalde is Hispanic or Latino.[701] However, the news conferences and all the posts from UCISD, UPD, and TXDPS were in English. None were translated into Spanish.

[701] U.S. Census Bureau, "QuickFacts: Uvalde city, Texas."

Critical Incident Review: Active Shooter at Robb Elementary School |
Chapter 5. Public Communications During and Following the Crisis

218

The TXDPS spokesperson conducted the last one-on-one interview on the evening of May 26 after the TXDPS regional director's news conference, which focused on why officers delayed their entry into the classroom. The "heroes" storyline soured community members and the national audience while the significant delay dominated news coverage. That was a turning point in the coverage, which began to focus heavily on law enforcement mistakes.

May 26 UPD Facebook

Also on the third day, the UPD chief posted a letter on Facebook (see figure 5-18) that was intended to express sympathy and condolences, but ultimately fueled more criticism of UPD. The chief's letter stated, ". . . responding UPD Officers sustained gunshot wounds from the subject. Our entire department is thankful that the officers did not sustain life-threatening injuries." While the relief was valid, it appeared insensitive to the grieving families of those who were not so fortunate and lost loved ones in the shooting.

Figure 5-18. UPD letter

PRESS RELEASE

For Immediate Release

My department and I will never be able to express in words the deepest sympathy and condolences to the individual families and the entire community of Uvalde. We extend our most sincere gratitude for the enormous outpour of support from all Law Enforcement Agencies, our community members and the nation. I want to thank all the personnel of my department for their dedicated and tireless efforts to continue to provide service to our community during this difficult time. Our personnel have displayed the utmost commitment to our community during this difficult time as we all are suffering as members of the community, that is the family of Uvalde.

It is important for our community to know that our Officers responded within minutes alongside Uvalde CISD Officers. Responding UPD Officers sustained gun-shot wounds from the suspect. Our entire department is thankful that the officers did not sustain any life threating injuries. This is an ongoing investigation that is led by the Texas Rangers. I understand questions are surfacing regarding the details of what occurred. I know answers will not come fast enough during this trying time, but rest assured that with the completion of the full investigation, I will be able to answer all the questions that we can. I know words will never ease the pain that we are all suffering, but I hope you will join me in taking some solace in knowing that the pain comes from the fact that we all have such deep love for all the victims who have been taken from us, those who are recovering, and those who only time and love will continue to heal. As the close-knit community that we are, I know we will come together and help each other heal as the family that is #UvaldeStrong.

Daniel Rodriguez,
Chief of Police

Critical Incident Review: Active Shooter at Robb Elementary School |
Chapter 5. Public Communications During and Following the Crisis

219

May 27—Day 4

On the 4th day, TXDPS Director McCraw held the final TXDPS news conference in Uvalde (see figure 5-19 for announcement). This news conference provided a detailed timeline of the events. It was disturbing to local and national audiences to hear specifics of students calling 911 desperate for help while they could hear officers outside in the hallway. It was also the first time the community learned the incident was treated as a barricaded subject rather than an active shooter.

Figure 5-19. TXDPS announcing Director McCraw's press conference

11:04 ✈

Texas DPS ⦿
@TxDPS

Happening Today: Friday,
5/27 at 11:00 a.m.
(Near Robb Elementary; Int.
of Old Carrizo Rd. &
Geraldine St.)

DPS will hold a press
conference to provide an
update on the deadly
shooting that occurred at
Robb Elementary School.
DPS Director Steven
McCraw will brief the
media.

7:40 AM · 5/27/22 · TweetDeck Web

Source: CIR Document and Data Review.

The director initially released details of the incident timeline, the timeline of 911 calls, and a rundown of the subject's social media activity. Director McCraw also incorrectly said that the "gunman entered the school through a back door that minutes before had been propped open by a teacher."[702]

During questions, almost every single answer focused on the incident commander treating it as a barricaded subject. It appeared that the director intended to share this information since it was repeated multiple times, but it was not part of his initial comments. It is also worth noting that this was the first news conference to offer interviews in Spanish.

---

[702] Fetcher and Oxner, "'The Wrong Decision': Texas DPS."

Critical Incident Review: Active Shooter at Robb Elementary School |
Chapter 5. Public Communications During and Following the Crisis

220

3:30 p.m. Texas Governor Abbott's second news conference

Later that day, the Governor held a final news conference on free mental health services. Unfortunately, although that was vital information for the victims' families, the media was only interested in pursuing details about the law enforcement delay that TXDPS revealed earlier in the day. The Governor provided the following details:

- OneStar Foundation Fund for family expenses
- School Board's Victim Services Center
- Victim Assistance Center—Open until June

Public Communications in the Aftermath of a Mass Casualty Incident

Throughout the days, weeks, and months following the shooting, there continued to be significant failings in public communications. The CIR team reviewed and analyzed daily media reports up to June 8, 2023.

Post-Tragedy Communications Principles

Impact of Misinformation and Leaks

One of the responsibilities of public communications dissemination in the immediate aftermath of a mass violence incident is to respect the experience of those who remain after victims have been killed; to control for leaks of information that has not yet been shared with family members and other victims; and to ensure that when information is shared, it is done so with permission, where appropriate, and in a trauma-sensitive way. Another responsibility is to track and monitor the information being shared; identify and correct misinformation; support and promote accurate narratives, especially the voices of victims and family members; and correct those narratives that do not represent the truth.

Leaks, misinformation, and incorrect narratives in these incidents further harm the surviving victims and family members as they suffer the traumatic effects of the incident, cope with memories of the horror, and struggle with their grief. They should not have to bear misinformation or misleading narratives, and certainly not exposure to leaked information that causes more harm and pain without the respect of a conversation, an expression of concern for their feelings, a request for their input, or at minimum, a warning.

Law Enforcement and the Media

Local and national journalists may be considered frontline responders, playing a critical role in the hours and weeks following an incident in calibrating the community response, highlighting the need for specific resources or actions, and laying out facts, commentary, and discussion points for the public. Given the key role journalists and news media play following an incident, it is important for law enforcement officers to understand how to effectively interact and communicate with them.

Critical Incident Review: Active Shooter at Robb Elementary School |
Chapter 5. Public Communications During and Following the Crisis

221

As previously stated, when journalists, reporters, and others in the media do not receive information and answers, they will often become more assertive to find the details. For example, during the incident, the dispatchers started receiving calls from the media searching for the UPD PIO.[703] Understandably, the dispatchers notified the media that they were unable to pass along the message due to being tied up with the emergency.[704] The media asked to talk to the PIO repeatedly and were told that they could not give out the PIO's information and that the PIO did not have a cellphone.[705] When the media asked about a press conference, no details were provided.[706]

In situations where law enforcement has clearly communicated legitimate restraints on releasing information, journalists have understood and reported on those restraints to keep the public informed of the process. However, when it is not clearly communicated, the news outlets are not sympathetic.[707] For context, many of the national journalists had just finished reporting on the mass casualty incident in Buffalo, New York, less than 10 days earlier, when they responded to Uvalde. The contrast of openness in Buffalo compared to the limited release of information in Uvalde contributed to the more investigative reporting approach that was adopted early on during this incident.[708]

Communications in the Aftermath of the Tragedy at Robb Elementary

In the weeks and months following the tragedy at Robb Elementary, inaccurate information, weak communication, and conflicting messages lead to misinformation, rumors, and a lack of trust and confidence in the relevant authorities.

Some of that misinformation caused further harm to victims of the tragedy. For example, one Robb Elementary staff member falsely accused by Texas Department of Public Safety (TXDPS) Director Steve McCraw in a press conference of propping the door open through which the subject entered, was vilified and suffered significant emotional distress as a result of this misinformation.[709] In fact, UCISD Staff 1 was among the first to alert staff, students, and 911 of the subject and did not prop open the door.

There also continued to be inconsistencies in messaging.

Furthermore, journalists continued to serve as an important source of information for the communities. In an interview prior to the one-year mark, Uvalde Mayor Don McLaughlin stated "most of the information we get, I'm sad to say, I'm glad it's coming out, but it's coming from people like yourself [CNN's Senior Crime and Justice Correspondent Shimon Prokupecz] or another agency. We got more from that than we did anything." Prokupecz clarified "Journalists?" and the mayor responded "Yeah, it's

---

[703] Uvalde Police Department Dispatch Landline.

[704] Uvalde Police Department Dispatch Landline.

[705] Uvalde Police Department Dispatch Landline.

[706] Uvalde Police Department Dispatch Landline.

[707] CIR Fact Finding.

[708] CIR Fact Finding.

[709] Jacobo and El-Bawab, "Timeline: How the Shooting at a Texas Elementary School Unfolded;" CIR Fact Finding.

Critical Incident Review: Active Shooter at Robb Elementary School |
Chapter 5. Public Communications During and Following the Crisis

222

ridiculous, isn't it? It's pretty sad, it's pretty sad."[710] This sentiment was shared by victims, families, and the community.[711] When asked if they are receiving information about the incident, one family member of a victim responded, "We aren't getting it from nobody."[712]

Moreover, there were claims of the media invading the privacy of the victims, families, and the community. During the funerals and in the interest of protecting the families, the city used tactics such as placing fire trucks to block funerals.[713] There appeared to be a lack of understanding of how to manage the media during a high-profile incident, which is understandable in a community the size of Uvalde. However, these incidents continue to happen in small towns, so establishing best practices in this area could be useful to other jurisdictions.

Additionally, some news outlets released explicit and gratuitous images.

Communications with Victims and Families

While the previous sections of this chapter described the communications about the tragedy to the general public, this section focuses specifically on communications with victims and families.

Principles for Communicating with Victims and Families

Communications at the time of an emergency with the family members and other loved ones that are timely and accurate and that come from a trusted source in the community, can help control the level of anxiety that will naturally occur. Law enforcement should provide family members and other loved ones with status reports, even when there is no new information about the situation. This means that stating the known facts in a trauma sensitive manner and where appropriate, even if there are few, helps establish trust with the audience. To be clear, bringing disturbing details or detailed descriptions of pain and suffering is neither appropriate nor necessary. Facts discussed in group settings should be limited to helpful information about where to go to find a loved one, what hospitals people are being taken to, when more information is expected, etc. Importantly, even when there are no confirmed facts, that information, in itself, can still be helpful.

Thus, the PIO, and others designated as in charge of communications, can help people remain calm by informing them of the situation, reinforcing who is in charge and the efforts to address the problem. Those agencies designated to provide victim advocacy and support should also be coordinated with public communications messaging. In addition to supporting victims and family members through the event, community leaders and advocates can provide messaging about the availability of continued support services to help them navigate the complexity of available resources, application requirements, registration processes, and more.

---

[710] CNN, "Mayor of Uvalde Sits Down with CNN One Year after School Shooting."

[711] CIR Fact Finding.

[712] CNN, "Surviving Uvalde."

[713] CIR Fact Finding.

Critical Incident Review: Active Shooter at Robb Elementary School |
Chapter 5. Public Communications During and Following the Crisis

223

Timely communications mean that the PIO or liaison or other designated leadership should meet with those awaiting news and who need to be updated at frequent intervals, wherever possible. For example, in reunification or resiliency centers, leadership will often schedule an hourly communications update in the early post-incident time frame, and maybe twice daily as time moves further away from the event. Again, even if there is no new information to share, showing up and saying so, allowing for questions, and showing concern for those awaiting notification can help reduce anxiety and traumatic stress responses. See "Chapter 6. Trauma and Support Services" for an in-depth discussion and robust observations and recommendations related to resiliency centers.

Crisis and emergency risk communications (CERC) best practices have come from the Centers for Disease Control and Prevention (CDC) and the U.S. Health and Human Services Office of Substance Abuse and Mental Health Services Administration (SAMHSA) since 2002 when the first guide to effective communications during crises was published.[714] Since then, guidelines and best practices have been revised and updated to address emerging challenges and to incorporate lessons learned from various incidents.

Of primary importance is that deceased and injured victims' family members receive information before the general public and especially prior to any public media announcements. Media communications should not be the way family members are receiving information about their loved one nor the details of the incident. Trauma-informed practice tells us that timeliness, privacy, and compassionate messaging are best practices when communicating to families and other victims about what happened to them/their loved ones in a mass violence incident or other criminal act. Using compassionate practices that help mitigate retraumatizing people is a responder/provider responsibility that shows respect and basic, human concern for those impacted.

Informing family members and other victims in a trauma-informed, victim-centered, and culturally sensitive manner means doing so without providing detailed descriptions of pain, fear, torture, bodily injuries, bodily fluids (e.g., blood), or other graphic, disturbing materials, and especially eliminating any imagery (e.g., pictures, video, audio recordings). Certainly, there will be situations in which sharing disturbing details or imagery is necessary to specific, defined audiences, but that requires careful consideration as to what the reasoning is and notification to the victims and family members who are likely to be negatively emotionally impacted beforehand. Exposing anyone to traumatic material, even those not directly impacted, through media images and videos can have as strong an impact as if they witnessed the event. It can be particularly harmful to children who may not be at a developmental level where they can understand what they see or others who are negatively activated due to a prior traumatic experience.[715]

---

[714] CDC, "CERC Manual;" CDC, "Training;" *Communicating in a Crisis*.

[715] Draper et al., "Mental Health Services Support;" Marshall, "Learning from 9/11;" Schlenger et al., "Psychological Reactions to Terrorist Attacks."

Critical Incident Review: Active Shooter at Robb Elementary School |
Chapter 5. Public Communications During and Following the Crisis

224

There is sufficient, informative instruction and training for responders and other community leaders on delivering proper communications to family members and to the public in the aftermath of mass violence and other emergencies. Every responder should be trained and follow best practices regarding designated spokespersons, timely and verified (accurate) information, trauma-informed approaches, and establishment of trusted leaders in time of such disasters.

Impacted community members need accurate information delivered in a timely, trauma-informed, victim-centered, and culturally sensitive manner. This means that the speaker needs to understand their audience, the environment, and the tenor of the situation and choose their words accordingly, anticipating their impacts. Communicating effectively means the speaker identifies the goals and creates the key messages to support that goal, speaking directly in a way the community can understand, and incorporates repetition in an effort to ensure the message is heard.

Public information is often delivered as part of a press conference in the immediate aftermath of a mass violence event. Additionally, more formal public communications for the families, victims, and other impacted community members should be planned (in a media-free setting where appropriate) where family members and victims can receive updates with privacy. These might be in the form of a family forum/meeting where leadership speaks to family members and other victims alone or in a town hall, or community meetings where leadership has the opportunity to speak to the public at large.

Victim and family forums provide information as to what to expect in the weeks, months, and even years to come post-incident. Information from other survivors who have shared their lessons in terms of what they would have liked to have known earlier is brought forward. Psychoeducational materials about common, expected reactions should be a focus in the forum, and opportunities to discuss different reactions to different situations should be provided. Good coping tools and resources are shared and best practices for these should be introduced. Referrals for when and where to access best-practice mental health treatment should be available. Ideally, a victim and family forum will have providers available to share resource and referral information and even dedicated staff such as victim advocates to assist with victim compensation applications.

It is important to note that victim forums are not a debriefing where victims are asked to share their traumatic experiences. Such activity is more appropriate for a victim support group, one-on-one crisis intervention meeting, or therapy session. Additionally, these forums are not appropriate for young children, as they may be exposed to too much information beyond what their development level can tolerate.

It is expected that some trauma material may come up for victim survivors and family members in a forum environment. This means they may re-experience some of the same disturbing reactions and feelings that occurred at the time of the event. This is quite common, and victim survivors and family members should be forewarned and given the message that this is expected and ok. Facilitators should address this at the start of a forum, and it is recommended that behavioral health staff be present to monitor and support any victims or family members who may be in need.

Critical Incident Review: Active Shooter at Robb Elementary School |
Chapter 5. Public Communications During and Following the Crisis

225

Communications with Victims and Families in Uvalde

In the mass casualty incident at Robb Elementary School, the families have not received transparent, trauma-informed, or compassionate communications. The lack of accurate, proper, and compassionate communications in Uvalde after the Robb Elementary School incident, both in the immediate aftermath as well as over a year later, resulted in further harm to victims and family members most directly impacted and more distrust in the community.

The TXDPS regional director and the Uvalde County district attorney held a family briefing the evening of Friday, May 27. The briefing's description of the subject's activity timeline resulted in significant emotional distress for the families. The families were asking what happened to their loved ones, and after a lot of back and forth with no direct answers, a TXDPS official stood up and re-enacted the incident including taking steps and holding their finger like a gun.[716] This information was of no real use to the families, did not answer the questions they did have about what happened to their children, and was not delivered in a trauma-sensitive manner. One witness indicated that, describing the family briefing as "inflict[ing] secondary traumatic stress is putting it mildly."[717] It was described as "awful,"[718] and it was reported that "families walked out."[719] The authorities providing the information in this family briefing did not have a goal or a plan of which information to deliver, how to deliver it, or the purpose of the meeting. This only served to frustrate and anger those present and did not help build trust in the responders in this community or provide a sense of compassion that might help families with their recovery.

The Uvalde school administrators and School Board held several School Board meetings which could have integrated some of the principles of a family forum. Instead, they were used as a venue for victims and family members to express their concerns about how the shooting was handled in a limited manner and with little to no feedback or helpful information from leadership. In the first School Board meeting held on July 25, 2022, victims and family members were limited to a five-minute time frame to speak. In this circumstance, when families were actively grieving and none of their questions had yet to be answered, five minutes was regarded as an insult and resulted in anger and frustration on the part of family members.

There were several subsequent school board meetings where family members were given either unlimited or more time to ask questions and make statements. It was evident in an August 2022 school board meeting that school board members were instructed to or agreed to remain silent in the face of these family members' questions and comments. The school board members were not communicative; they did not acknowledge comments, nod or shake their heads, and provided little or no information in response to directed questions. These meetings were, to many families, the only platform to voice their concerns publicly, and yet, as a communication tool, they proved ineffective and injurious.

---

[716] CIR Fact Finding.

[717] CIR Fact Finding.

[718] CIR Fact Finding.

[719] CIR Fact Finding.

Critical Incident Review: Active Shooter at Robb Elementary School |
Chapter 5. Public Communications During and Following the Crisis

226

At one such meeting, the UCISD superintendent stated that he intended to "honor our families at this time with support, love, and the commitment to move forward as a district for our students."[720] Around the same time, however, UCISD hired as an employee for the UCISD PD a former TXDPS trooper who was at Robb Elementary during the shooting and had made an offensive remark, captured on body-worn camera footage, about the delayed law enforcement response.[721] This action enraged the Uvalde community, especially the families of the victims. As a result of the outcry, the UCISD, who knew the background of the former trooper, dismissed the officer, and eventually suspended the entire UCISD PD. The fact that the decision to hire the former trooper was made in a vacuum without communication to the public further enraged an already skeptical community.

The Uvalde law enforcement community and other leaders did not continue to attempt to provide communications to the families and victims of this event. There was no follow up and no continued communications regarding any aspect of this event from leadership to family members.[722] Shortly before the one-year mark on May 24, 2023, several family members expressed that they still do not know what happened to their child, that they still do not have an autopsy report, and that their trust in the leadership of Uvalde is gone.[723]

Federal and state leaders engaged in outreach to the families and victims. President Biden and First Lady Jill Biden came to Uvalde and stayed for hours, meeting with the families who lost a loved one in the Robb Elementary Shooting. This meeting became a de facto family forum. A total of 200 family members attended and relayed their appreciation for being "heard" by the President and Dr. Biden. In late summer 2022, Governor Abbott met privately with families of victims, inviting every family who requested a meeting.[724]

When the Department of Justice COPS Office CIR team held a formal family and victim forum on the evening of August 15, 2022, for those impacted by the mass casualty incident at Robb Elementary School, it was planned as a supportive, informational listening opportunity for the CIR team to share the work scope and activity, and to hear from family members and victims as to what they needed. There was no limit on the closing time of the event. Family members spoke, asked questions, and expressed their hope that the report would give them answers about their family members' last hour. The victim advocate in attendance reported that this family meeting was the first one where she had seen family members without tears at the close and planning to spend additional time together that evening with smiles on their faces.[725]

The CIR team held a second family and victim forum on April 26, 2023, which was led by the Associate Attorney General (ASG) of the United States Vanita Gupta, who appeared in person with key team

---

[720] Allen, "Uvalde School District Officials Hold Press Conference 6/09/22 Transcript."

[721] CIR Fact Finding.

[722] CIR Fact Finding.

[723] CIR Fact Finding

[724] Estrada et al., "Abbott Meeting with Uvalde Victims, Families Under Scrutiny."

[725] CIR Fact Finding.

Critical Incident Review: Active Shooter at Robb Elementary School |
Chapter 5. Public Communications During and Following the Crisis

227

members to stress that she, as well as the Attorney General of the United States and other senior leadership at the Justice Department, were paying attention and concerned about what was happening in Uvalde almost one year later. Again, there was no time limit to the meeting. Family members and victims asked questions and talked about the need to remember and memorialize their loved ones who were killed. ASG Gupta answered questions directly and assigned a team member to provide details of the team's review process.

Victim forums are often a place for those impacted to learn of their eligibility for available resources. Nearly one year after the shooting at Robb Elementary School, there were family members and victims who reported that they were not receiving victim advocate services or support.[726] Many were unsure as to whether they were eligible or where to go to access services.[727] Others reported being overwhelmed and confused by the excessive paperwork to file for victim compensation and did not have an assigned victim advocate to help them.[728] To address this information gap, victim and family forums can also be tied into a larger public media campaign to bring awareness to the services available (See "Appendix E. Public Communications Supplemental Materials").

Understandably, many victims and survivors are in shock and may have experienced expected trauma reactions of cognitive/memory issues in the early days after the disaster; thus, it is possible that a victim advocate may have contacted them, but they do not remember. This underscores the necessity for victim advocates and other victim/family support responders to link back around with every victim and survivor at many different points after an incident to ensure they have the information and help they need to complete applications and access the support they require. See "Chapter 6. Trauma and Support Services" for an in-depth discussion on services.

The Uvalde community has yet to hear adequate information of the tragic events that transpired. Victims, family members, and other members of the Uvalde community have attended public meetings with the Governor of Texas, law enforcement representatives, numerous school board members, as well as had individual meetings with the school superintendent and other local leaders asking to know what happened to their children in the last 77 minutes of their lives. They have requested details from investigative reports, from the district attorney's office, from law enforcement, from school board members, from autopsy reports and any other resource that could possibly provide them answers. Several family members indicate they cannot move forward with their lives and do the things they normally need to do until they know what happened to their children.[729] Some have asked if their child was alone or near friends.[730] Others want to know if their child would have lived had law enforcement entered the classroom earlier.[731] Many victims and family members have reported that no one has taken accountability for what happened, no one has apologized, nor even acknowledged that the

---

[726] CIR Fact Finding.

[727] CIR Fact Finding.

[728] CIR Fact Finding.

[729] CIR Fact Finding.

[730] CIR Fact Finding.

[731] CIR Fact Finding.

Critical Incident Review: Active Shooter at Robb Elementary School |
Chapter 5. Public Communications During and Following the Crisis

228

families deserve this information.[732] This void of information about the circumstances of the death of their loved ones has contributed to their trauma. Families report they cannot heal without the information they need about what happened to their family members on May 24, 2022, and they are unable to even begin to recover until those in charge are held accountable. See "Appendix E. Public Communications Supplemental Materials" for more on this topic.

Observations and Recommendations

Observation 1: Inaccurate information combined with inconsistent messaging created confusion and added to the victims' suffering, both on the day of the incident and in the days after the mass shooting.

> **Recommendation 1.1:** Due to the possible occurrence of mass shootings regardless of jurisdiction size, all law enforcement agencies and local governments should plan for such critical incidents from a public messaging and crisis communication perspective. This requires relationship building, planning, training, and preparing before a large-scale incident.

> **Recommendation 1.2:** Organizations must be prepared to swiftly develop proactive messages in an organized fashion to keep community members informed and establish a source of strength and leadership that can unite a community and assist with the healing process.

Observation 2: UPD posted the first public message 10 minutes after the subject entered Robb Elementary School, a strong start for public messaging. However, the post was edited four times over the next 73 minutes. Since the Facebook algorithm does not recognize the edits as a new post, it did not reach as many users.

> **Recommendation 2.1:** As quickly as possible, an agency should inform the public regarding the nature of the critical incident and how it will release information regarding it.

> **Recommendation 2.2:** An agency should create a new social media post or message each time it has new information to release. This will help reach a larger audience instead of updating the initial post.

Observation 3: At no time was a specific agency designated as the official source of information, nor was a lead agency identified.

> **Recommendation 3.1:** The first or second post from an agency should establish the agency as the official source of information, which reduces confusion about how information will be released.

> **Recommendation 3.2:** Agencies should instruct the public that other modes of incoming communication, with the exception of emergency calls, will be shut down to allow staff to focus on the accuracy and timeliness of information via the official platform.

---

[732] CIR Fact Finding.

Critical Incident Review: Active Shooter at Robb Elementary School |
Chapter 5. Public Communications During and Following the Crisis

229

Recommendation 3.3: Messaging to the public should include identification of the lead agency or a transition to another agency as the lead. This level of transparency ensures accountability to the public when people are seeking reassurance, order, and answers.

Observation 4: UCISD PD posted their first public message 33 minutes after the subject entered Robb Elementary School. The message references that the students and staff are safe. This reassurance was false and never corrected.

Recommendation 4.1: Information should be confirmed by two sources if at all possible before it is shared publicly. If false information is shared, it must be corrected as soon as possible on social media, and if the content is highly newsworthy, it should be addressed in the next news conference as well. The agency should explain how the false information ended up being released. Delays will erode public trust in the organization.

Recommendation 4.2: Agencies should monitor social media and media coverage to understand the totality of the circumstances, which includes community sentiment. This may guide the incident commander to share information that initially was being withheld in order to refute a false narrative. The role of monitoring social media and media coverage should be assigned to a specific individual as stipulated by the communication plan and can even involve a neighboring agency.

Recommendation 4.3: To establish leadership and a sense of order, the lead agency must be swift, proactive, accurate, and transparent in its messaging. Relevant information that is not law enforcement-sensitive should typically be released as soon as it is confirmed. However, speed must be balanced with the need for accuracy. It is critical that information is verified before it is released even when there is tremendous pressure to release information quickly.

Observation 5: Family members encountered many obstacles to locating their loved ones, getting access to the hospital, and getting information from leadership, law enforcement, and hospital staff in a timely manner. This includes initial information posted by UCISD on the reunification site followed by a series of contradictory posts between UPD and UCISD on reunification. This added to the confusion, pain, and frustration.

Recommendation 5.1: As part of a community-wide comprehensive emergency response protocol, school districts should have a safety plan for each school which includes a reunification and communication section on how they will direct parents/family members when a crisis occurs. Selected district personnel should be designated in advance to assist emergency personnel as family members rush to the school or reunification location.

Recommendation 5.2: School district leadership needs to develop a system for documenting which children are present and which parent or guardian has retrieved them using a sign in/out, checkoff, and/or smartphone picture system to document for safety, notification, and reunification purposes.

Recommendation 5.3: Information about locations for notification, family assistance, and property return should be as specific as possible, including the location address. These posts should be

Critical Incident Review: Active Shooter at Robb Elementary School |
Chapter 5. Public Communications During and Following the Crisis

230

prepared in advance when possible and pre-tested during exercises testing the crisis communications plan.

Recommendation 5.4: As soon as any type of mass casualty or active assailant incident occurs, law enforcement should serve as the lead on public safety messaging and updates on status of the incident and the criminal investigation. Once the situation has been rendered safe, the affected entity should take the lead with providing information to the public about operations and issues affecting the facility. Each agency (e.g., school district and law enforcement agency) should share or link to the others' content on social media. This will help them avoid contradicting each other.

Observation 6: UPD and UCISD never posted when the threat to the community was over. UPD did post a message at 1:06 p.m., however, the post incorrectly stated that the subject was in custody and that information was never corrected.

Recommendation 6.1: When a community suffers a traumatic incident, a law enforcement leader should work to establish a feeling of safety in the community with a news briefing as soon as possible. The news briefing should announce the status of the situation and when the situation is resolved, and include details of how that was accomplished. If an incident is not quickly resolved, the leader should hold regular news briefings to keep the community informed. The leader should strive to show strength balanced with compassion and care for those suffering tragic injuries and losses.

Recommendation 6.2: When reunification is complete and the victims' families have been notified, the lead agency should release that information to the community. This is a crucial step in unifying the community to start the healing process.

Observation 7: Uvalde Memorial Hospital and University Health San Antonio swiftly released information regarding patients arriving at the hospitals.

Recommendation 7.1: The lead agency should institute incident command and establish a JIC for coordinating the release of all public information, including victim information from all medical facilities that can be incorporated into coordinated news briefings.

Recommendation 7.2: Once the agency leading the JIC learns that patients are being transported to hospitals outside the region, a PIO should be assigned to call the hospitals to coordinate the release of information. This duty can be filled by an outside PIO who has arrived to assist, which should be outlined in the crisis communication plan.

Observation 8: Texas Governor Greg Abbott was the first official to publicly speak about the incident, during an unrelated press conference, and shared preliminary information that turned out to be incorrect. All officials who speak to an incident that is still unfolding should ensure that they have timely, accurate information.

Observation 9: At 4:16 p.m., UCISD held the first news conference at the Civic Center. Basic information was provided and did not include details such as the current number of victims. This information was never released. The media were not allowed to ask any questions.

> **Recommendation 9.1:** A news conference with a law enforcement executive from the lead agency, who was not intrinsically involved in the response and so would not risk jeopardizing a criminal case or consciously or unconsciously provide unreliable facts, should take place on scene as soon as the scene is rendered safe. If the incident is elongated, a briefing should take place while the event is still in progress and should be held nearby the scene to reassure the community.

> **Recommendation 9.2:** An on-scene location for the press conference helps instill confidence that law enforcement is effectively handling the situation and that the people watching the news conference are safe.

> **Recommendation 9.3:** The law enforcement leader conducting news conferences should attempt to be responsive to all media questions. While it may not be possible to answer questions related to the ongoing investigation, it is possible to be responsive by explaining the process or announcing when more specific information may be released.

> **Recommendation 9.4:** An agency should release the number of deceased and injured victims as soon as the information is confirmed. There is no benefit to gain from a delay.

> **Recommendation 9.5:** Consistent leadership needs to unite the community through a projection of strength and empathy. This is also vital for the community's healing process.

Observation 10: TXDPS as the lead agency post-incident did not establish a JIC or media staging area and did not schedule a series of briefings and interviews with media. Instead, the TXDPS spokesperson conducted ad hoc interviews as they were flagged down.

> **Recommendation 10.1:** The designated lead spokesperson and agency should establish a JIC and a media staging area in line of sight of the command post.

> **Recommendation 10.2:** A schedule of briefings should be created, and other agencies should be invited to send PIOs to work with the lead spokesperson to coordinate the release of information. If possible, joint news conferences of local, state, and federal agencies should take place at this location, based on that schedule.

> **Recommendation 10.3:** All media should be given the opportunity to receive the same information at the same time via news conferences or previously identified social media or other releases. This prevents inadvertent contradictory news stories that can be caused by using a different selection of words in each interview. It also avoids the appearance of an agency favoring a specific media outlet or outlets, which can cause other reporters to become more assertive.

Critical Incident Review: Active Shooter at Robb Elementary School |
Chapter 5. Public Communications During and Following the Crisis

232

Observation 11: Spokespersons for UCISD and TXDPS, the only agencies speaking publicly, did not coordinate their messaging the afternoon of the incident. Some conflicting information was shared by the two agencies.

> **Recommendation 11.1:** The lead agency should be working to release basic details in follow-up news conferences, such as an update on the number of victims and their conditions, information about the subject, the type of weapon(s) used, and the status of the investigation. Some activities take place at every crime scene and can be shared, such as meeting with victims' family members, identifying witnesses, conducting interviews with witnesses and the involved officers, or processing the crime scene. Talking about these activities at the news conference does not compromise the investigation, and it shows the community that law enforcement is making progress.

Observation 12: Off-topic prescheduled posts appeared on the UPD's and Uvalde Memorial Hospital's Facebook pages while the incident was still immediately recent.

> **Recommendation 12.1:** An agency should disable scheduled posts during a critical incident as part of its crisis communication plan.

Observation 13: During the May 25 news conference, Texas Governor Abbott and TXDPS Director McCraw provided inaccurate information. This further perpetuated the misinformation and rumors.

> **Recommendation 13.1:** When an organization recognizes that an error has occurred, it should admit the mistake and share what actions it is taking to rectify the problem and prevent it from happening again. Even when the mistake is egregious, an agency can maintain or seek to regain public trust by being open and holding itself accountable to the community. In these moments, a law enforcement agency can build community trust by holding itself to the highest possible standard.

> **Recommendation 13.2:** Agencies should use social media and the local media to reassure the community with clarity and confidence that any loss of life would be investigated quickly and appropriately. This accountability is necessary for any critical incident that significantly impacts a community.

> **Recommendation 13.3:** Agency spokespersons should be briefed by those most knowledgeable on the facts of the incident prior to public comments.

Observation 14: The involved law enforcement agencies were unresponsive to the growing concerns in the community. Many of the media's questions were an extension of the pressing questions from the victims' family members and others.

> **Recommendation 14.1:** Effective communication requires law enforcement agencies to listen to their communities' concerns and be responsive to them.

Critical Incident Review: Active Shooter at Robb Elementary School |
Chapter 5. Public Communications During and Following the Crisis

233

Observation 15: All social media public messaging was posted in English. The one exception to this was the FBI San Antonio Field Office's messaging starting on May 25.

> **Recommendation 15.1:** In a community with a large population with limited English proficiency, officials should post emergency information in English and in other predominant languages. This inclusive approach will help ensure that critical public safety messages reach a larger audience and will help boost trust.

> **Recommendation 15.2:** In a community with a large population with limited English proficiency, officials should enlist the assistance of a local television, radio, or social media channel that caters to the non-English predominant culture and language of the community.

Observation 16: On day 4, the TXDPS director changed the narrative from a heroic local law enforcement response to a failed response, but only during the question-and-answer section of the news conference. This approach prompted even more questioning from the media and caused anguish among family members of the victims.

> **Recommendation 16.1:** An agency should be as direct as possible when it is revealing law enforcement mistakes in responses and actions. An indirect approach can undermine faith and trust in law enforcement.

Observation 17: Attending to the cultural needs of different community members is of the utmost importance and requires extensive effort to understand the community, familial, and individual impacts of cultural influences on victims. Local law enforcement and other responders in Uvalde rarely ensured that those impacted were given information in their primary language (Spanish). Behavioral health supports that were offered did not take into account cultural considerations that may have helped those impacted to accept behavioral health supports and seek help for other case management-type needs.

> **Recommendation 17.1:** Formal and informal leaders and other community members can help responders to better understand the community's cultural beliefs around health, mental health, and help-seeking. Demographic information should be integrated into tailoring services to make them less stigmatized and more acceptable to those in need. Services should be culturally appropriate for the community they serve.

> **Recommendation 17.2:** Agencies should incorporate culturally sensitive communications into early communications during a crisis.

Critical Incident Review: Active Shooter at Robb Elementary School |
Chapter 5. Public Communications During and Following the Crisis

234

Observation 18: The extent of misinformation, misguided and misleading narratives, leaks, and lack of communication about what happened on May 24 is unprecedented and has had an extensive, negative impact on the mental health and recovery of the family members and other victims, as well as the entire community of Uvalde.

Recommendation 18.1: All persons involved in delivering information during and after a mass violence incident should be trained in best practices that are victim-centered, trauma-informed, and culturally appropriate. Typically, a trained PIO or designated representative should be the person speaking to the press and family members or advising the designated representative as to the best-practices approach.

Observation 19: Investigative journalists and reporters became the main source of information, and their reporting served as the accountability measure for the victims, families, and the community due to a lack of open and transparent information from government officials.

Recommendation 19.1: Law enforcement and other government officials within the affected community should develop a comprehensive plan for media engagement to centralize information sharing, maintain consistency in messaging, and build trust within the community as a legitimate source of information.

Observation 20: There was extensive media exposure on mainstream and social media that included

- images of law enforcement entering Robb Elementary School;

- law enforcement officers restricting, yelling at, and falsely reassuring parents outside the school that they were taking care of the incident inside the school;

- audio recordings of young children calling 911 asking for help and reporting they were afraid to die; and

- a continuous flow of body camera footage showing a significant number of law enforcement officers not taking actions to save the children trapped in classrooms 111 and 112.

Recommendation 20.1: Images and reports of the details of violent crimes, especially those involving the injury and death of children, are traumatic to anyone exposed to them. Those who conduct investigations, legal representatives, and government officials, as well as family members who request such details, should be prepared and supported before and after such exposure.

Observation 21: Throughout the days, weeks, and months following the incident, there continued to be significant failings in public communications.

Critical Incident Review: Active Shooter at Robb Elementary School |
Chapter 5. Public Communications During and Following the Crisis

235

Observation 22: While notifying victims and families of an impending release of traumatic, violent, or graphic materials (e.g., body camera footage, crime scene images) is traditionally the role of government, in many instances, the media obtained a copy from a leak. Family members should be advised well ahead of the planned release of such materials. Not doing so was harmful.

> **Recommendation 22.1:** Any details shared publicly by government officials should have a purpose and not be gratuitous.

Observation 23: Family members and victims who attended school board meetings felt their concerns and requests for information and accountability were ignored, experiencing a lack of communication and empathy from authorities.

> **Recommendation 23.1:** Local leaders and law enforcement representatives providing information to victims and family members need to be trained or, at a minimum, knowledgeable about how and when it is appropriate to hold a family and victim forum, the purpose of such an informational forum, and how to conduct it in a victim-centered, trauma-sensitive manner. Giving voice to victims and family members (active and deep listening), allowing them the time they need to express themselves, validating their concerns, identifying actions that can be taken, providing resources, and ensuring follow up to outstanding questions are all best practices that should be followed by anyone engaging with victims and family members.

Observation 24: Families asking what happened to their loved ones were traumatized by a re-enactment by a law enforcement official during the first family and victims' forum.

> **Recommendation 24.1:** Intentional transparency is needed for the victims, survivors, and loved ones who are seeking answers about what happened; however, authorities need to provide information in a trauma-informed, victim-centered, and culturally sensitive manner.

Observation 25: Family members in Uvalde have struggled for more than a year to be heard, to get a full accounting of what transpired during this incident, and to be able to fully grieve and begin to adapt to the losses in their lives as a result of the horrific circumstances of the deaths of their loved ones and the failed response. Their recovery is delayed and more complex than it needed to be due to the lack of attention to their needs.

> **Recommendation 25.1:** Law enforcement, local leaders, and other responders can support the recovery of victims and families by giving them opportunities to be fully heard, have their concerns validated, and receive information through a transparent lens.

Observation 26: The misinformation, lack of timely and accurate information, and the poor manner in which many families and other loved ones were treated at Robb Elementary at the time of the shooting can contribute to poorer mental health outcomes for the impacted individuals. The ongoing unresolved questions about the law enforcement response to the shooting can inhibit recovery for the entire community, individual victims, and family members.

Critical Incident Review: Active Shooter at Robb Elementary School |
Chapter 5. Public Communications During and Following the Crisis

236

Chapter 6. Trauma and Support Services

Introduction

Preparation and prevention discussions often intensify after incidents of mass violence and active shooter events, especially following those tragedies that garner significant media attention. Additionally, a wealth of resources is now widely available, including reports, toolkits, articles, and studies on active shooter events and how to prepare and respond to them with education, training, and preparedness measures such as target hardening, equipment, and models of response. Notably, however, discussions and resources regarding the emotional aftermath that include immediate and long-term care are often not on the forefront of planning, preparation, or response.

It is essential, however, to focus also on support services for individuals who are exposed to tragedies like a mass casualty incident. Helping those affected understand that they can access crisis counseling, learn good coping skills, reach out to social supports, and access their innate strengths to build their resilience may decrease the number of people who go on to develop a mental illness as a result of their exposure to the traumatic event and its aftermath. In disaster studies, the size, vitality, and closeness of a survivor's social network are also strongly and consistently related to positive mental health outcomes. Adequate support, services, and resources all contribute to recovery and healing.

The goal is to return affected individuals and communities to their pre-disaster level of functioning, or achieve a sufficient level of adaptation to resume their lives by doing the things they would normally do, working, participating in family and community events, and having moments of joy again.[733] This is why attention to behavioral health (mental health and substance abuse) service delivery matters. It matters to people directly impacted and their families; it matters to those indirectly affected, such as responders and their families; and it matters to the community at large. Crisis intervention and other mental health supports can help mitigate severe emotional distress or the development of a mental illness and allow people to remain productive members of their communities, preventing them from entering our public health and mental health systems for a significant segment of their lives as a direct result of a traumatic event.

Effects of Traumatic Events on Victims, Families, and Community

On May 24, the children and staff in Robb Elementary School went through unspeakable horrors. Of significant impact was that many students heard the police outside their classroom doors, and at least two children called 911, engaging for substantial periods with dispatchers, reporting that they were in the room with classmates who were seriously injured or dead, and begging for help. The survivors waited 77 minutes for law enforcement to make entry. The survivors were huddled near or next to

---

[733] Hobfoll et al., "Five Essential Elements;" Norris et al., "Toward Understanding and Creating Systems of Postdisaster Care."

classmates and teachers who were injured and dying from bullet wounds and shrapnel from a high-powered weapon shot at close range. Some of those survivors had their own physical injuries from the shooting. Whether they had physical injuries or not, they all left those classrooms injured. Their trauma, in the form of the sheer terror they experienced in those 77 minutes from the threat of death, serious injury, and witnessing the deaths of their friends and, in some cases, family members, is a mental and emotional anguish that is immeasurable.

The trauma suffered by an individual who experiences a traumatic event goes beyond the horrific minutes of the tragedy itself. The memory, as well as the emotional distress, can last a lifetime. Notably, incidents of mass violence with intent to harm, such as the school shooting at Robb Elementary, have a longer recovery trajectory overall than the mass loss of lives caused by natural disasters. Humans need to make meaning of tragedies. And sadly, in these types of events, meaning just cannot be found. After natural disasters, the risk of developing post-traumatic stress disorder (PTSD) can increase by 10 percent for those exposed to that event from the general population.[734] However, for those exposed to mass violence, that risk doubles to 20 percent or more, along with increased risk of major depressive disorder, other anxiety-related disorders, and varying health problems and social concerns.[735] From a well-being perspective, research shows that 4 weeks after a mass shooting, there is a 27 percent decline in the likelihood of having excellent community well-being and a 13 percent decline in the likelihood of having excellent emotional health.[736] Focusing on youth, research released in May 2022 analyzed data from students exposed to school shootings in Texas and found an increase in absenteeism and grade repetition; a decrease in high school graduation, college enrollment, and college completion; and a decrease in employment and earnings into their mid-20s.[737]

Moreover, it has been documented that trauma can be passed down through generations. Although the study/field of intergenerational trauma is relatively new,[738] recent studies reveal how survivors' initial reactions to an event may affect future generations.[739] The repercussions of what happened in Uvalde will reverberate not only within the immediate survivors, victims' families, and those directly impacted, but also with the participating responders and the community at large. Fear, distrust, anger, and similar natural reactions and emotions may be felt, discussed, and passed on to other generations by many of those impacted.

---

[734] Norris, Friedman, and Watson, "60,000 Disaster Victims Speak: Part II. ;" Norris et al., "Early Physical and Health Consequences."

[735] Norris, Friedman, and Watson, "60,000 Disaster Victims Speak: Part II;" Norris et al., "Early Physical and Health Consequences."

[736] *Uvalde Region Mental Health Needs Assessment.*

[737] *Uvalde Region Mental Health Needs Assessment*; Cabral et al., *Trauma at School.*

[738] DeAngelis, "The Legacy of Trauma."

[739] O'Callaghan, ed., "What is Generational Trauma and How Long Can it Last?"

In Uvalde, it is overwhelmingly evident that the victims, their families, and the community as a whole have a complexity of thoughts, emotions, and feelings, and although they are all valid, they are not all the same. It is also evident that there are those who are upset not only about the police response but also about the lack of communication, transparency, accountability, and speed of the investigations.

The subject initiated this trauma with his acts of violence. Unfortunately, the failed response by those charged with keeping the children and staff safe compounded the trauma of the victims and their families. The failure of law enforcement to stop the killing of the teachers and students—the failure to respond to their calls for help in a timely manner—may decrease these children's future trust in adults to take care of them, decrease their sense of the safety of their world, and interrupt their developmental growth and psychological health. This is coupled with the anxiety, grief, and depression imposed by the subject's actions, these children may have some adverse mental health impacts.[740] Uvalde-area law enforcement will need to rebuild trust with the children, school personnel, parents/caregivers, and the entire community impacted on that tragic day. Meaningful activities and genuine efforts at repairing their relationships will need to be intentional for the community to move toward recovery.

In the end, the community will never be the same. The victims and their families may stay or leave the area, but the emotions and trauma will continue in their lives. Once the media cameras are gone, the temporary memorials are dismantled, and the investigations are completed, the pain of that day will not be displaced or packed away. The pain will go on and potentially affect those hurt not only emotionally but also physically.

Effects of Traumatic Events on Responders

Alongside the impact of this horrific crime on victims and families, there is an increased recognition of the risk that responders face because of their work in emergencies.

Occupational stress in responders is associated with increased risk of mental health issues, including hopelessness, anxiety, depression, and PTSD, as well as suicidal behaviors such as suicidal ideation (thinking about or planning suicide) and suicide attempts.[741] Mass violence incidents, as seen in Uvalde, increase the negative emotional effects on responders, which may manifest as PTSD. Although current understanding of the impact of mass shootings on the psychological well-being of responders is limited, studies have demonstrated that the prevalence of probable PTSD increases over several years after a mass casualty incident.[742] Responders may also experience secondary traumatization, also known as compassion fatigue, which refers to the psychological distress caused by exposure to the traumatic experiences of others. It is important to note that everyone's experience of trauma is unique and can vary depending on factors such as their role in the incident, level of exposure, and personal coping

---

[740] National Child Traumatic Stress Network, "Mass Violence Resources."

[741] Tiesman et al., "Suicides among First Responders: A Call to Action."

[742] Wilson, "A Systematic Review of Probable Posttraumatic Stress Disorder in First Responders Following Man-Made Mass Violence."

strategies.[743] A comprehensive approach to psychological support services for responders to a mass casualty incident should include immediate and ongoing interventions, along with education and training to promote mental health and wellness.

When discussing services for responders, it is important also to consider those who may not be labeled "first responders" in the traditional sense, including civilians, technicians, and other support personnel who may be exposed to traumatic aftermath or material, as well as those responsible for cleaning up crime scenes, journalists on site, and funeral home workers. In Uvalde, some people in nontraditional responder roles essentially took on positions akin to traditional emergency responders. For example, school bus drivers ended up taking injured victims to the hospital. In another example, hospital human resources staff assisted with victim identification. While bus drivers and human resources personnel may not be considered responders in the traditional sense, given their actions on May 24, it is critical to include them in the support services provided to responders.

Given the significant effects of traumatic events on victims, families, responders, and the community, it is essential to have trauma-informed, victim-centered, culturally sensitive services, approaches, and practitioners following a mass casualty incident (see the "A Shift in Disaster Mental Health Response" section in "Appendix F. Trauma and Support Services Supplemental Materials" for a discussion on the evolution of post-incident mental health services). We need to prioritize the trauma support and wellness of law enforcement professional staff, including dispatch and communications personnel, ambulance drivers, records management staff, evidence technicians, and other support staff who are involved in major incidents as seen in Uvalde.

To use an iceberg analogy, the tip of the iceberg is the operational and tactical preparedness and response to the active shooter incident; this is the area that receives the most significant attention and resources. However, the trauma component that lies beneath the waterline should be given the same recognition, education, follow up, support, and resources, as the psychological impacts are second only to injury and death.

Scope

To mitigate the trauma impact and help communities prepare in the future, this Critical Incident Review (CIR) includes an assessment of the support and resources provided to survivors, victims, responders, and other stakeholders. This chapter describes the immediate, ongoing, and long-term support for and communication with survivors and victim families; support services for law enforcement and other responders; and management of emotional/trauma support for the broader Uvalde community following the tragic incident at Robb Elementary School.

---

[743] SAMHSA, "Mass Violence and Behavioral Health."

In preparing this chapter, the CIR team benefited from the expertise of subject matter experts, who assisted in developing the observations and recommendations for this chapter. Where not otherwise cited, the practices identified in this chapter derive from the experts' collective knowledge and experience.

Despite the comprehensive nature of the CIR, it was not without limitations. First, due to the sensitivities of the traumatic experience of victims who are minors, the team did not interview any youth directly, but did gather information through interviews with their families, review of media accounts, and review of other interviews and data. Further, due to privacy concerns regarding child victims, the CIR team did not have access to a full list of victim survivors, so was not able to make outreach to all victims and/or their families. The team utilized a "snowball approach"[744] to make outreach to as many survivors and their families, victim families, and other impacted individuals as possible using interviewee referral.

Throughout this chapter the CIR team refers to victims and survivors interchangeably to respect that some people prefer to be referenced as survivors and others as victims. In addition, the CIR team is cognizant of and has attempted to avoid terminology like "triggered," "targeted," and other gun-related language as well as time frame references which typically convey celebrations such as "anniversaries," out of respect that these terms are often activating for some victims, survivors, responders, and family members.

The timeline of movement from one disaster phase to another is not exact but is generally divided into acute, immediate/intermediate, and long-term phases. The chapter is organized into sections based on the phases in which support services were delivered:

- Acute Support Services—this section covers the first 24-72 hours post-incident.

- Immediate or Intermediate Support Services—this section covers the first year post-incident.

- Long-Term Support—this section covers support that can continue for years beyond an incident.

Each section discusses the generally accepted practices and standards related to trauma and support services, and any relevant background, before analyzing what occurred in Uvalde. The chapter concludes with observations and recommendations.

Additional background and resources are included in "Appendix F. Trauma and Support Services Supplemental Materials."

---

[744] This refers to a nonprobability sampling technique in which each person contacted by the CIR team is asked to identify other individuals. This method is often used when there may be difficulty in identifying or reaching all individuals.

Acute Support Services

During any emergency at a school, it is the responsibility of the adults overseeing the care and safety of their students to remain calm and reassure the children that the teachers, school staff, and law enforcement are the ones in charge and will take care of them. Children look to the adults around them for guidance—not only on what to do, but also on how to respond, since children have a "felt sense" that helps them detect adults' fear and anxiety. In younger children, their emotional responses tend to mirror those of their adult caregivers regardless of the reality of the situation. Thus, it is essential that caregivers and all adults understand the importance of regulating their own emotions, reassuring the children under their care that the adults are in charge, and providing calming messaging. At times, adults need to provide clear, firm, and direct instruction and direction, but it can still be provided in a trauma-sensitive manner.

Throughout an incident, the adults can reassure the students that they will be ok, that they are cared about, and that they can help each other to feel better by being supportive and caring. While no one can guarantee that everyone will be safe, it is more psychologically damaging to take hope away from anyone in a traumatic event. It is especially problematic to instill fear in children. Even if the children perceive danger, their fear can be mitigated with the trust and hope that the adults will take care of everything and keep them safe.[745]

The developmental age of the children will contribute to their understanding of the situation. Still, even the most practical individuals—especially optimists—can use denial, in the short term, as a coping mechanism to help keep calm, have hope, and believe they will survive, regardless of the reality of the situation. Optimism is a characteristic of resilience that can guard against development of mental illness. Optimism can even move victims toward post-traumatic growth, which is the ability to see how traumatic experiences can bring some positive aspects or positive change to our lives, including the realization that we have personal strength; an appreciation for what we have, especially our relationships; spiritual growth, including a sense of meaning and purpose; and hope for the future.[746]

Beyond these general principles, the sections below key in on specific processes or activities in the acute phase—the first 24-72 hours following an incident—that require discussion from a trauma perspective. In the acute time frame, individuals moving from the "threat to life/serious injury" to "a sense of safety" can dramatically decrease their fear and anxiety reactions. See "Chapter 1. Incident Timeline Reconstruction" for a detailed analysis of the incident.

---

[745] La Greca et al., *Helping Children Cope with Disasters and Terrorism*; Silverman and La Greca, "Children Experiencing Disasters: Definitions, Reactions, and Predictors of Outcomes."

[746] Tedeschi et al., "Developmental Research on Posttraumatic Growth."

Evacuations and Perimeter

Key to reducing trauma on the day of a tragedy like the one that occurred at Robb Elementary are the evacuation process and the interactions with family and community members around perimeters.

Trauma-Informed Evacuation and Perimeter Principles

The tactics and operations of coordinating evacuations are described in greater detail in "Chapter 2. Tactics and Equipment." From a trauma perspective, however, it is important to note that evacuation planning should involve designating safe evacuation routes and safe spaces, or cold zones, where the evacuees can be guided. Once in a safe zone, evacuees should receive medical triage and screening, and emotional support. Evacuees should also receive mental health screening.

Where possible, responders should also establish an on-site system to identify those evacuated, along with the guardians or next of kin who will be notified of the victims' location or destination.

Those in charge of the incident scene are also responsible for establishing perimeters that can keep all nonessential individuals away from the hot zone or crime scene, especially on roadways that need to remain clear for emergency vehicles to get through quickly and easily. Perimeters, however, can increase fear and anxiety in those awaiting news about their loved ones, because individuals outside the perimeter may feel helpless—especially if the area of impact is kept out of sight. A feeling of helplessness is one of the indicators of a poor mental health response, while information can help decrease anxiety.[747] Thus, in establishing perimeters around the scene, law enforcement should balance public safety and security with compassion and empathy for family members. Law enforcement should also endeavor to provide timely and accurate updates to families awaiting news of their loved ones. For more details on communications to victims and families, see "Chapter 5. Public Communications During and Following the Crisis."

Finally, responders, family members, school employees, and any staff without a role or a job related to the care of the deceased victims' bodies or the crime scene should refrain or be restricted from such exposure. Everyone in the affected community should also be protected from exposure to a crime scene that the assigned staff has not cleared and cleaned. The sights, sounds, and smells become wrapped up in the emotional response, and some people cannot separate the exposure from their emotional reaction, even well after the event. This inability to separate the distressing emotional response from the memory of the incident is what can develop into PTSD.

Evacuation and Perimeters at Robb Elementary

During the evacuation process at Robb Elementary, it is unclear from the CIR team's analysis who identified the hot, warm, and cold zones in the areas surrounding the school, or even if there was such identification. A lack of safe evacuation routes meant that some evacuees were hurt, others had their

---

[747] Hamblen et al., "Cognitive Behavioral Therapy for Postdisaster Distress: A Community Based Treatment Program for Survivors of Hurricane Katrina."

physical and psychological injuries exacerbated, and still others could have been lost. For example, one of the responders[748] decided to start breaking windows to evacuate students and teachers in classrooms where it was known the shooter was not present. One student in room 109 moved a desk under the window so everyone could get out.[749] Glass remained on the windowsills, and while some responders picked students up and out, other students propped themselves forward, pressing and injuring their hands on the glass shattered on the windowsills.

Responders helping students out of the windows did not follow the students to a designated cold zone. Body-worn camera video shows law enforcement responders yelling at the students to "go, go, go" and pointing them away from the school.[750] There are images of other law enforcement responders directing students toward the funeral home, but it is unclear what the path was or who was receiving students at the other end of their escape journey.

Once evacuated, children were moved onto school buses to be sent to the Reunification Center (described in more detail below). This process, however, meant that some children were not triaged or screened for medical care. One child who was shot in the leg walked on their own to evacuate;[751] another with a bullet injury was walked onto a bus without any medical clearance; one child reported that their friend got hurt on the leg from climbing out of the window.[752] One suffered hand injuries from the broken window glass during the evacuation, and yet they were released to their parent without any medical assessment or care. Additionally, the child experienced the trauma of "feeling like I was going to die."[753]

Two other victims who were evacuated after the shooter was neutralized experienced ear pain and continuous ringing in the ear, likely due to their proximity to the shooter. Sadly, even months later, one of these injured children's parents reported not knowing that victim compensation may be able to pay for the required hearing aid.[754] One family member treated their child's injuries, and another took their child to a physician days after the incident. Another parent "discovered hundreds of shards of glass embedded under [victim]'s arms, in his stomach and his legs" on the night of May 24, requiring the parent to spend "hours pulling the glass out."[755] Only those victims who were brought to the hospital were fully assessed.

---

[748] CIR Fact Finding.

[749] CIR Fact Finding.

[750] Footage from Multiple Body-Worn Cameras.

[751] CIR Fact Finding.

[752] CIR Fact Finding.

[753] CIR Fact Finding.

[754] CIR Fact Finding.

[755] Kantor, "14 Months After Uvalde School Shooting, Survivors' Mom Shares His Mental Health Battle: 'Lives with His Scars Daily.'"

The next day, when the Federal Bureau of Investigation (FBI) victim specialists were staffing the Reunification Center, they asked those who showed up for services if they had been checked out medically or had a mental health assessment and tried to triage the victims' needs.[756] There is still a gap of significant concern for those victims who were not seen in the hospital or who did not show up to the Reunification Center and did not receive any outreach or follow up care.

All the children at Robb Elementary at the time of the shooting were involved in the lockdown due to the presence of a shooter, experiencing the threat of injury or death. Most heard gunshots, and many heard their classmates screaming. Others witnessed not only their deaths but the horrific violence of their teachers, friends, and classmates being murdered. Those who survived in the classrooms with the subject underwent an explicitly traumatizing situation for 77 minutes of imminent threat to their lives, in addition to witnessing what happened to their friends, classmates, and teachers. Many were not immediately guided to a secure area or reunited with their families for many hours. These factors dictate that all victims should have undergone a mental health screening to determine if they were experiencing symptoms predictive of depression, anxiety, or post-traumatic stress.[757]

Responding law enforcement also experienced response challenges along the perimeters. Upon learning about the incident, several parents and loved ones went immediately to Robb Elementary School, where they were met by law enforcement outside the school building. Some family members saw their children being evacuated from their classrooms via broken windows to school buses but were not allowed to join their children.[758] However, many of these same family members witnessed law enforcement staff pulling their own children out of the line and reuniting with them directly.[759] This inequity caused even more distress to parents and caregivers.

Family members also did not receive accurate and timely updates. The only thing the perimeter law enforcement officers could do for long periods was to ask the family members to step back from blocking emergency vehicles and law enforcement access to the scene.[760] All information provided at the perimeter, moreover, was available only in English.

In some instances, outside the school and near the funeral home across the street, officers also used force to keep concerned parents from approaching the school or funeral home, where some of the evacuated students had been taken. One mother was handcuffed by the U.S. Marshals, who accused her of being uncooperative regarding where to park her car and remaining outside the law enforcement

---

[756] CIR Fact Finding.

[757] Neria, Galea, and Norris, eds., *Mental Health and Disasters.*

[758] CIR Fact Finding.

[759] CIR Fact Finding.

[760] Ray Sanchez, "'We're in Trouble.' 80 minutes of Horror at Robb Elementary School;" CIR Fact Finding.

perimeter.[761] As soon as she was released from the handcuffs, she ran and got her two children out of the school and to safety. She indicated that law enforcement "was more aggressive with keeping us parents out than going in to get the shooter."[762]

In another instance, one family member who was very upset on the scene, trying to get information on the whereabouts of their child, was thrown to the ground by law enforcement and threatened with a Taser when they tried to go to their child.[763] The officer told the CIR team that they had to "put a parent on the ground" because the parent would not stay behind the roped area when the evacuated children were being put on buses.[764] Accusing the parent of being noncompliant, a second officer then put their hand on the parent's shoulder while the officer did a "leg sweep" and tossed the parent to the ground.[765] While the parent was on the ground, the officer did not place them in handcuffs but stayed on top of them until they became compliant.[766] In this situation, the parents had just witnessed their child coming out of the building covered in blood with their head leaning back like they were going to pass out.[767] The parent was running to get to their child and instead, due to this interaction, the bus with their injured child left the grounds.[768]

In another exchange, a parent told law enforcement, "You need to f***ing get in there;" the law enforcement officer told the parent to calm down and said, "We got this, we got this, no one is going to get hurt."[769] Later at the Reunification Center, this parent, who lost their child, went up to the law enforcement officer from earlier, said, "I f***ing told you," and received the following response back: "I know, I'm sorry."[770]

Another parent who lost their child recalled that while they were outside the school, they heard gunshots. The families started pushing forward, and an officer said, "Do you hear the shooting? We could be in there stopping this, but instead we have to be outside corralling you all."[771]

---

[761] Cowen, "Mother Who Was Cuffed by Marshals Amid Response to Uvalde School Shooting Speaks Out as New Details Emerge."

[762] Cowen, "Mother Who Was Cuffed by Marshals Amid Response to Uvalde School Shooting Speaks Out as New Details Emerge."

[763] CIR Fact Finding.

[764] CIR Fact Finding.

[765] CIR Fact Finding.

[766] CIR Fact Finding.

[767] CIR Fact Finding.

[768] CIR Fact Finding.

[769] CIR Fact Finding.

[770] CIR Fact Finding.

[771] CIR Fact Finding.

Another parent had to be physically restrained by officers when they saw their child, a gunshot victim, lying on a stretcher on the ground just outside the school building.[772] The victim was then placed in an ambulance and transported to the hospital.[773]

None of the officers filed written reports that day, or anytime thereafter, describing the details of their use of force against parents or other onlookers.[774]

According to one parent, "Police were very aggressive in moving parents away from the school. There was a lot of confusion and no clear direction."[775] Police told some families that children were evacuated from the other side of the school, near the front and opposite the funeral home.[776] Other families were told their children might be at the Civic Center.[777] One family desperately searched for their child in three places—an area hospital, Uvalde High School, and the Civic Center.[778]

There were also instances where individuals on the perimeter received care and compassion from law enforcement personnel. For example, one parent (who later learned of their child's death) was trembling and looked like they were going into shock.[779] A law enforcement officer took note, helped the parent sit down in the shade (the temperature was in the 80s and humid), and got them water that had been brought from the funeral home for law enforcement.[780]

There also was unnecessary exposure to the deceased at the scene. Many law enforcement officers entered the classrooms at Robb Elementary before being told to clear out if they were not medics.[781] One officer became sick at the site of the carnage due to the murder of the children. This is a human reaction, and other responders likely had strong emotions when they left their shift that day or on subsequent days. Likewise, late in the evening of May 24, the San Antonio medical examiner arranged for the deceased to be moved out of the school into mass casualty buses behind curtains constructed for privacy.[782] Unfortunately, there was a family member/student who witnessed some of the medical examiner's activities before the privacy curtain went up.[783]

---

[772] CIR Fact Finding.

[773] CIR Fact Finding.

[774] CIR Fact Finding; Cowen, "Mother Who Was Cuffed by Marshals Amid Response to Uvalde School Shooting Speaks Out as New Details Emerge;" Chute, "Police Boasted of Heroism after Uvalde Parents Begged for Rescue of Their Children Amid School Shooting."

[775] CIR Fact Finding.

[776] CIR Fact Finding.

[777] CIR Fact Finding.

[778] CIR Fact Finding.

[779] CIR Fact Finding.

[780] CIR Fact Finding.

[781] CIR Fact Finding.

[782] CIR Fact Finding.

[783] CIR Fact Finding.

Reunifications and Notifications

Another central aspect of reducing trauma on the day of a tragedy involves the process of coordinating reunifications and notifications.

Principles for Reunification, Notification, and Reception

Traditionally, disaster responders have identified a "reunification center" as a place where family members can go to find out the status of victims and, hopefully, be reunited with victims who survived and have not required hospitalization. Because "reunification" implies that people will be brought together, more recent recommendations are to create a "Notification Center" or a "Family and Friends Reception Area" so that anyone looking for a victim does not enter with the assumption that their loved one is alive. Care should be taken not to build false hope that everyone will be reunified with their loved ones. The Notification/Reception Center should be staffed with a team that is trained in working with victims and families in emergencies and that will coordinate with school personnel, emergency management, medical examiners and coroners, law enforcement, and faith leaders in providing information on fatalities, injuries, recovery, temporary identification, missing persons, and the release and disposition of personal effects.[784] During disaster preparedness planning, the emergency manager and a planning committee should determine the entity that will run the Notification/Reception Center.

While identifying potential locations for the Notification/Reception Center should be part of disaster preparedness planning, drills, tabletops, and other exercises, it is not always possible to do so, as an incident's location is unpredictable. Still, in many communities, there may be one or more buildings—community centers, recreation areas, or even hotels—that could be considered appropriate to serve as a Notification/Reception Center. Ideally, such sites will be easy to locate but not so close to the area of the incident that any sights, sounds, or smells (e.g., care and removal of the deceased, site clean-up, lingering odors of destruction, blood) will traumatize surviving victims and family members. The key to a Notification/Reception Center is that information distribution about its location is timely and accurate. Such a location should be determined as soon as possible (if not before the incident), and family members/loved ones should be provided with location information as quickly as possible using multiple pathways and modalities (telephone, email, text, social media, radio, print and other digital media outlets). It is also important to include the address for the location. Based on language access needs and the prominent languages spoken in the community, information should be shared in multiple languages as appropriate. A Notification /Reception Center should also have security to keep out media and unaffiliated onlookers.

All those with access to the Notification/Reception Center should be encouraged to refrain from social media posting to protect everyone's privacy and to allow for confirmation of any information that has not been through a validation or vetting process. Since many members of the general public use social media as a modality for communicating with friends and loved ones, asking them to refrain from posting would likely be impractical. But creating gentle messaging requesting that they refrain from posting,

---

[784] FBI, "In the Aftermath."

reposting, or sharing any information that they do not know to be accurate and refrain from posting disturbing images and harsh or cruel messaging would likely help remind people to be responsible in their use of social media channels that are open to the general public.

Death/Trauma Notifications

A death notification process is also essential for those individuals who tragically lose a loved one. Death or trauma notifications are a challenging experience for loved ones and those assigned to deliver the information. Trauma notifications should only be made by a responder who is well-trained specifically in how to properly deliver them. Training can be accessed online at government sites such as the Office for Victims of Crime (OVC)[785] and the FBI.[786] Best practice dictates that trauma notifications should be made in person by a team of two trained law enforcement/victim service provider staff (even when the next of kin lives outside the jurisdiction of the response agency).[787] It is not recommended to have more than two team members, as family members can become easily overwhelmed.

Trauma notifications should be culturally as well as trauma informed. Having a trauma notification team member who is familiar with the recipients' cultural understanding of death and the spiritual meaning, rituals, and customs of the loved ones is important. It is also important to incorporate cultural values, beliefs, and practices, as well as race, ethnicity, and faith/religion. This information can be gathered from local leaders or other community members if it is unknown to those delivering the messaging. For example, in working with an observant Jewish family, the trauma notification team should anticipate the family's request to have the body released immediately and be prepared for to address it in circumstances where law enforcement officials are required to hold the body until investigative staff clears it for release.

Teams of staff providing trauma notifications are often made up of a law enforcement individual and a victim advocate or behavioral health staff member, each of whom should be trained in trauma notification. Even trained staff can have a difficult time after delivering these notifications, and assignments should be limited, especially when there is a short amount of time to address numerous deaths. Ideally, staff who provide trauma notifications should not conduct more than one notification per shift and should have an opportunity to debrief with supervisors and/or peers before engaging in another notification.[788] Care should be taken to ensure that the person assigned to the trauma notification is not someone related to, in a close relationship with, or otherwise familiar with the victim and their family (e.g., a school counselor).

---

[785] OVC, "Mass Violence: Death Notifications: Best Practices;" OVC, "Mass Violence and Terrorism Death Notification."

[786] FBI, "We Regret to Inform You. . . Impact Video."

[787] FBI, "We Regret to Inform You. . . Impact Video."

[788] FBI, "We Regret to Inform You. . . Impact Video."

When delivering notifications regarding the death of a child, the team needs to be well grounded and prepared to absorb the intensity of emotion that is often expressed by parents. The death of a child can also be difficult for any adult to hear about, thus notification teams who are specialized in working on cases where there is the death of a child are most appropriate wherever possible. It is recommended that teams who deliver trauma notifications not be assigned to more than one in a mass casualty incident. This is, of course, best-case scenario, and not always possible in situations where there are many deaths, but this is where an agency can reach out to teams from different agencies or in other jurisdictions that are working on the response or authorized to support the process. Debriefings and/or peer support should be offered to all involved in the trauma notification process, along with assigned downtime after completing a trauma notification.

Trauma notifications need to be delivered with compassion, without judgment as to the circumstances of the incident, and preferably with more than one family member present. If a notification needs to be made to a lone individual, it is good practice to ask them to contact a nearby family member, friend, or even a caring neighbor to stay with them for a while after notification instead of leaving them alone. This is so that isolation is reduced, and support is there when the person processes the news and may have difficulty functioning due to the shock and grief. There is no way to predict how anyone will respond to the news of the death of a loved one, especially when that loved one is a victim of crime. Those providing the notification should be aware and anticipate many emotional responses, such as crying, screaming, silence, shock resulting in rigidity or collapse, anger, denial, and more. For this reason, it is ideal that the notification is made in an indoor area where a next of kin can sit down and access water, tissues, a bathroom, and social support.

A critical part of the notification process is also to help family members decide which of the immediate family will identify the deceased, limiting their exposure to the severely injured body of a loved one. Families whose loved one is unidentifiable due to the severity of their injuries should also be provided a dedicated crisis counselor or victim advocate (i.e., one staff person dedicated to one family). It does not usually help for a family member to see a loved one severely injured, so the victim/family advocate might help them reframe their thoughts to remembering their loved one as they were before the incident and focusing on that image rather than having a lasting memory of a troubling picture. If a victim advocate or crisis counselor is not available, then the responder may be able to assign another professional who is skilled in working with grief, such as a hospice nurse.

Reunification and Notification in Uvalde

Establishing the Reunification/Notification Center in Uvalde

The response to the incident was chaotic in many ways. The lack of an incident command process impacted all aspects of the response, including the designation of a Notification/Reception Center.

No one identified or established the Reunification Center[789] at the start of the response. While the delay was partly because of the difficult and time-consuming process of identifying the children, it was exacerbated because there was no structure. Many family members were at the school for hours without status updates, becoming more fearful and anxious than needed. Some family members were sent to the high school, others to the Civic Center, others to the hospital, and back around again, eventually winding up at the Civic Center.[790] All the while, at least 91 children were right across the street from the school in the funeral home, the front of which was being used as a Command Center at some point.[791] None of the leadership was aware of the children in the funeral home's chapel being secured by a funeral home staff and parents who were too frightened and protective to let anyone in to locate their children.[792] One responder ended up calling 911 to report the need for medics in the chapel at 12:05 p.m., when the first group of children evacuated from Robb Elementary entered the funeral home and a crew arrived minutes later.[793] However, the crew left shortly after (12:16:54 p.m.).[794] One member of the private ambulance crew arrived later and went in and out of the back rooms of the funeral home.[795] The children waited at least another hour for the beginning of their evacuation from the funeral home to the Reunification Center.[796]

The Reunification Center was originally set up at the Civic Center by the City of Uvalde assistant city manager and other city staff in coordination with Uvalde Consolidated Independent School District (UCISD) Superintendent Hal Harrell.[797] By the time the first bus had arrived at the Reunification Center, law enforcement and family members were already present outside.[798] Law enforcement created a

---

[789] For this incident, the Reunification Center was designated as such and will be referenced accordingly.

[790] CIR Fact Finding.

[791] CIR Fact Finding; Hillcrest Memorial Funeral Home CCTV Footage.

[792] CIR Fact Finding.

[793] Uvalde Police Department 911 Calls.

[794] Hillcrest Memorial Funeral Home CCTV Footage.

[795] Hillcrest Memorial Funeral Home CCTV Footage.

[796] CIR Fact Finding.

[797] CIR Fact Finding.

[798] CIR Fact Finding.

corridor for the children and staff to exit the bus and enter the building.[799] All the while, parents were calling for their children.[800] After the first bus was emptied, school administrators arrived and took control of the process at the Reunification Center.[801]

Inside the Reunification Center, children, teachers, and school staff filed into rows where teachers took roll call of each class.[802] Once the school administrators had a count, they started releasing children to their parents.[803] They set up a dry erase board with a list of all the classrooms as they arrived from the school and started calling parents by each classroom.[804] Those parents were let inside the center.[805] Sadly, the four teachers who were shot (two fatally) were not present to receive their students. See "Reunifications and Notifications at the Hospital" section for the reunifications that occurred at the hospital and the "Death Notifications in Uvalde" section for those who lost a loved one.

Reunifications and Notifications at the Hospital

The Uvalde Memorial Hospital (UMH) building had just been opened in March 2022, and many of the responders were not familiar with the building. This created challenges. For instance, the first two child victims were brought in through the public entrance to the emergency room (ER).[806] One victim was dead on arrival, while the other child was injured and bleeding.[807] Coming in through these doors exposed these victims to the public and, in one case, a family member looking for that child.[808] Some families that were arriving were directed to the UMH chapel, which is connected to the ER and thus provided a view onto the victims on hospital beds throughout the ER floor.[809]

Families encountered issues entering the parking lot and front doors of UMH, adding to the frustration, emotions, and chaos of the incident. In fact, some families reported that they only gained access to the entrance of the hospital when law enforcement personnel left to attend to an urgent potential threat at another location. See "Chapter 5. Public Communications During and Following the Crisis" for more on the communications challenges.

---

[799] CIR Fact Finding.

[800] CIR Fact Finding.

[801] CIR Fact Finding.

[802] CIR Fact Finding.

[803] CIR Fact Finding.

[804] CIR Fact Finding.

[805] CIR Fact Finding.

[806] CIR Fact Finding.

[807] CIR Fact Finding.

[808] CIR Fact Finding.

[809] CIR Fact Finding.

One family who had an injured child in the ER was told that they could not see their child because they were too emotional: "as soon as you calm down, we'll let you in."[810] Their wait was worsened when they saw their child, covered in blood and crying in a wheelchair go past the doorway.[811] The parents were eventually taken back to see their child and ended up helping to clean up the blood.[812] Hours later, they were released.[813]

Another family was frantically looking for their child at the Reunification Center when they received a call from UMH asking if they would provide permission to admit their child into the hospital.[814] When the family asked what had happened, they were told that those details could not be released but that they should head to UMH.[815] However, there was no process to receive the family when they arrived at UMH as directed. In fact, the family waited about 20 minutes to get through security at both the parking lot and the front entrance of the hospital. Eventually the family was allowed to see their child briefly after first being incorrectly told the injury was a flesh wound; they later learned that the child needed to be airlifted to San Antonio for surgery.[816] While the parent and the child waited for the airlift, the child—who earlier that day was wearing a new shirt and shoes for the awards ceremony—said that they had ruined their new shoes and shirt and could not find their eyeglasses.[817]

UMH After-Action

UMH conducted their own after-action assessment soon after the incident and started their own process to address their recommendations soon after. Some of those included changing the door between the chapel and the ER, relocating families from the chapel after a mass violence or critical incident, and creating an emergency management process for the identification of victims and survivors.*

---

* CIR Fact Finding.

---

[810] CIR Fact Finding.

[811] CIR Fact Finding.

[812] CIR Fact Finding.

[813] CIR Fact Finding.

[814] CIR Fact Finding.

[815] CIR Fact Finding.

[816] CIR Fact Finding.

[817] CIR Fact Finding.

Two families received notifications of their deceased children while at the hospital.[818] At the time of the incident, UMH did not have a location to put deceased victims nor a local coroner, so they put the two children in an operating room and had staff from human resources search the bodies for birthmarks and other identifying markers to help identify them.[819] In some cases, these same human resources staff assisted with the notifications, even though they were not properly trained in death notification.[820] They brought in family members one-by-one to identify bodies, some of which were very difficult to identify. This was a traumatic experience for those hospital staff. One such individual said, "I'm HR and I was telling families the status of their child. I had no training, no support."[821] And it was not helpful to family members who were then left on their own to wonder where their loved one was or what next steps needed to be taken to attend to their deceased loved one. Leaving family members on their own to worry, grieve, and wonder what had happened to their 9- or 10-year-old child prolonged their emotional distress, delaying their ability to process the information and impeding them from being able to begin to stabilize their traumatic stress responses. In this situation, UMH could have reached out to staff at the hospice facility next door for assistance in this task.

One family member reported that they had been told their child was seen being brought into the hospital.[822] They went from one hospital staff member to another describing their child and being told the child was not there.[823] It was hours before a hospital staff member, who found out through a family member of another deceased child (who was shown the other family members' child), that their child had, in fact, been there at the hospital, deceased and unidentified, for hours.[824] Another family reported that their child had been washed before they were asked to go in and identify them, and they were disturbed by this. While it may be routine to wash a body before having loved ones view it for identification, it may have helped the family to be informed at the point they went to view the body. Preparing family members about what to expect when they view a body is trauma-informed practice.

Death Notifications in Uvalde

In Uvalde, the death notification process outside of the hospital was similarly disorganized, chaotic, and at times perceived by victims' family members as cruel. Once all reunifications occurred, families that were still at the Reunification Center were brought inside; this was around 4 p.m., several hours after the shooting had begun.[825] Several law enforcement agencies were represented, including the Texas Department of Public Safety (TXDPS), U.S. Customs and Border Protection (CBP), the FBI, and Uvalde Police Department (UPD), along with school personnel and city and county officials. Families were not provided any information and mainly received information from social media, friends and family who

---

[818] CIR Fact Finding.

[819] CIR Fact Finding.

[820] CIR Fact Finding.

[821] CIR Fact Finding.

[822] CIR Fact Finding.

[823] CIR Fact Finding.

[824] CIR Fact Finding.

[825] CIR Fact Finding.

were texting, or word of mouth.[826] At one point, an official incorrectly reported that an additional bus was coming to the Reunification Center, creating hope that more kids were alive.[827] At another point, the family of a deceased victim was told that their child was still at the school, giving them hope that they would be reunified with their child.[828] Families were asked to provide descriptions of their children, but due to the condition of the victims' bodies, families were also asked for descriptions of their children's clothing, or for photos in lieu of verbal descriptions.[829] Since Robb Elementary School hosted their awards ceremony just that morning, most of the parents had recent photos that they were able to share with the Texas Rangers who were collecting the information.[830] The photos and, in particular, the clothing descriptions aided in the identification of the children.[831]

The notification process was so chaotic that the Uvalde County district attorney started talking to family members about the need to wait for autopsy results before death notifications were made.[832] Family members were highly distressed and yelled, "what, our kids are dead? No, no!"[833] DNA swabs were also taken from some family members, who were then told it would take a couple of days for the DNA match results to come back and allow for the identification of their children; this sent the family members into even more severe distress and created an angry backlash that eventually resulted in that information being rescinded.[834] Eventually, officials moved forward with the notifications without DNA results.[835]

Family members also received inaccurate information. Several people reported that responders told them their family member was being treated at the hospital.[836] At the same time, it was already known that none of the children who were present during the incident in room 111 had survived. One person reported asking the community leaders in the Reunification Center if those remaining in the room were the families of the dead, since everyone else had been notified.[837] The leaders told them that this was not the case, when in fact it was. This was another misleading communication that added to family members' decreasing trust in the government leaders and law enforcement representatives to provide truthful and timely information about the victims and the response itself. Additionally, in an unrelated press conference on the day of the incident, before any families were told that children were deceased, the Texas governor announced inaccurately that 14 students and one teacher had been killed.[838]

---

[826] CIR Fact Finding.

[827] CIR Fact Finding.

[828] CIR Fact Finding.

[829] CIR Fact Finding.

[830] CIR Fact Finding.

[831] CIR Fact Finding.

[832] CIR Fact Finding.

[833] CIR Fact Finding.

[834] CIR Fact Finding.

[835] CIR Fact Finding.

[836] CIR Fact Finding.

[837] CIR Fact Finding.

[838] Transcript of Texas governor's news conference, May 24, 2022, in Abilene, TX.

Death notifications also were not provided by trained personnel, consistent with best practices. Initially, the death notification teams included school counselors, who were not trained to provide these notifications and were themselves victims.[839] The counselors received anger and frustration from the families about why the school could not keep their kids safe.[840] The structure of the teams changed after that notification, with each team consisting of a Texas Ranger and a TXDPS victim service professional.[841] FBI victim specialists, who are all trained in death notification, were present in Uvalde to support the death notification process but were denied the ability to participate.[842] They were told "we got this" by TXDPS, even though the TXDPS staff was untrained in this process.[843] In other cases, family members found out about a death on social media or from the Uvalde County district attorney announcing they were going to conduct autopsies.[844] Additionally, staff who conducted the notifications were assigned numerous family members to work with for several hours, and many reported experiencing compassion fatigue as a result.[845] The CIR team was informed of at least one TXDPS member who became overwhelmed in delivering the death notices.[846]

While some families were given notice of their loved one's death by approximately 8 p.m., the final notifications were not completed until midnight.[847] Although family members described the process as chaotic, painful, and infuriating, families also said that the actual notification by the Rangers was as compassionate as it was possible to be when sharing this type of news.[848] Families were not rushed and were escorted out the back entrance of the Reunification Center, where they were led away from media and other onlookers.[849]

Acute Services for Responders

Trauma services are also crucial to the well-being and resilience of responders during a critical incident. It is known that responders who have been involved in mass casualty incidents (MCI) may experience various forms of psychological trauma.

---

[839] CIR Fact Finding.

[840] CIR Fact Finding.

[841] CIR Fact Finding.

[842] CIR Fact Finding.

[843] CIR Fact Finding.

[844] CIR Fact Finding.

[845] CIR Fact Finding.

[846] CIR Fact Finding.

[847] CIR Fact Finding.

[848] CIR Fact Finding.

[849] CIR Fact Finding.

Acute Services for Responders Principles

During an MCI, the incident commander should appoint a command officer to coordinate the trauma support services for the law enforcement and other relevant responder agencies. This role monitors the levels of traumatic exposure, acute stress, and distress in the responder population; it is like an incident commander's role, but specifically for attending to the wellness of law enforcement personnel.[850] Other non-law enforcement responders can use this model as well. Additionally, this command officer may be responsible for:

- managing all mental health-related tasks during an MCI;

- coordinating with the officer wellness work group;

- developing relationships between the agency and mental health service providers;

- reviewing policies and procedures for providing psychological services to officers after a critical incident;

- providing training and consultation for supervisors;

- providing education and support for officers' family members.[851]

Responder agencies should have trained disaster behavioral health professionals available on the scene or nearby to provide immediate psychological support, such as Psychological First Aid (PFA) or Stress First Aid (SFA), to personnel during an MCI. This support can include debriefing sessions, counseling, and other supportive interventions. Support provided during the response is usually most welcomed at the end of each shift or after responders have had time to settle themselves and come together to support each other or access peer support. It is important to note that some responders need to access support as soon as possible, while others may take some time to process. Thus, it is recommended that psychological support services should be available immediately for those who require onsite, acute support, and as part of 24- to 72-hour post-incident support for others who might need the first 24 hours to rest, settle their emotions, or process before joining a debriefing or counseling session.

This support also needs to be on site during the crime scene processing for the technicians and investigators who are spending hours sifting through the tragic aftermath of an MCI to piece together the investigation, return personal effects, and answer the questions of what happened.

Responder agencies should develop a system for monitoring personnel stress during an MCI and in the months afterward. This can include regular check-ins with personnel and using assessment tools to identify individuals who may be struggling.

---

[850] Usher et al., *Preparing for the Unimaginable*.

[851] Usher et al., *Preparing for the Unimaginable*.

Counseling and Support Services

Counseling and other support services are critical for promoting the mental health and well-being of law enforcement and other responders. Here are some examples of counseling and support services that can be provided:

- PFA is an evidence-informed practice recommended for those who have been exposed to a mass violence incident, community violence, a natural disaster, or another emergency situation.*

- SFA is a variation on PFA that is focused on responders. SFA prepares fire, emergency medical services (EMS), and rescue personnel to use this technique, which includes actions responders can take to manage stress for themselves and their teams.†

- Employee Assistance Programs (EAPs) are employer-sponsored programs that provide confidential counseling, referral services, and other resources to support employees' mental health and well-being. EAPs can be an effective way to provide ongoing support to law enforcement and other responders.‡

- Peer support programs involve trained peers who provide emotional and psychological support to other responders. Peer support can be a powerful tool for building resilience and promoting the well-being of law enforcement and other responders.§

- Mental health professionals such as psychologists and social workers can provide counseling and other mental health services to law enforcement and other responders. These professionals can help responders cope with trauma exposure, manage stress, and develop healthy coping strategies.**

- Chaplaincy programs provide spiritual and emotional support to law enforcement and other responders. These programs can benefit responders dealing with existential or spiritual issues related to their work.††

Importantly, effective counseling and support services for law enforcement and other responders require a comprehensive and integrated approach. This includes providing a range of services that address the unique needs of different responders, ensuring that services are confidential and stigma-free, and promoting a culture of support within law enforcement agencies and the community.

---

* SAMHSA, "Stress First Aid for Fire and EMS Personnel;" National Center for PTSD, "Stress First Aid: Manuals and Resources for Health Care Workers."
† National Center for PTSD, "Stress First Aid: Manuals and Resources for Health Care Workers."
‡ Milliard, "Utilization and Impact of Peer-Support Programs."
§ SAMHSA, "Provide Support."
** Usher et al., *Preparing for the Unimaginable.*
†† Usher et al., *Preparing for the Unimaginable.*

Acute Services for Responders at Robb Elementary

On May 24, first responders were dispatched to Robb Elementary School, and upon arrival, they were exposed to traumatic experiences that placed them at an elevated risk for emotional distress and mental health concerns. The agencies that responded to the scene can be categorized as initial tactical response, crowd/perimeter control, medical treatment/evacuation, criminal/forensic investigators, and support services. Although not physically present at the scene, 911 dispatch and communications operators were also affected by the trauma of this incident. Indeed, while not all responders were on site, they may all have experienced traumatic exposures during this incident. It is critical for law enforcement executives to provide services to all involved—meaning, in some agencies, the entire agency.

After the MCI on May 24, there was a lack of coordination among the vast influx of counseling services from agencies and nonprofits. There were, at the same time, both overlap and voids in counseling services for law enforcement and other responders.

Uvalde first responders (law enforcement, EMS, and fire) were not provided timely, immediate access to trauma services. Initially, there was no on-site critical incident stress management (CISM) team to provide emotional and psychological support to the responders. After several hours, several agencies responded with their support services teams, such as the FBI Victim Services Division (VS) and FBI EAP, the TXDPS Victim and Employee Support Services' (VESS) Critical Incident Response Services (CIRS), and a Texas Health and Human Services Commission (HHSC) CISM team. The teams were composed of trained mental health professionals and peer contacts. Finally, the Law Enforcement Management Institute of Texas in Sam Houston State University's College of Criminal Justice sent mental health professionals to Uvalde to assist with one-on-one support services.[852]

Several counselors and support services personnel noted that during the first few days after the incident, resources should have been more organized, and there should have been precise coordination of support services. Instead, each agency appeared to operate independently.[853]

The initial trauma services and support were limited in scope and effectiveness. Initially, the HHSC CISM, TXDPS CIRS VESS, and FBI VS teams focused primarily on individual interventions, such as debriefings and crisis counseling. They did not address the broader organizational and systemic factors contributing to trauma exposure and psychological distress among responders. Furthermore, the trauma services and survivor support provided to the responders lacked consistent follow-up and ongoing support. While the initial response was key, many responders reported feeling abandoned and unsupported in the weeks and months following the critical incident.

In reference to the responding federal agencies, there is mixed information regarding whether or not support services were readily available and how those resources were being communicated. It was mentioned that by May 27, 2022, chaplains, EAP personnel, support canines, and counselors

---

[852] Atkins, "Program Deploys to Uvalde to Provide Support."

[853] CIR Fact Finding.

were walking around the scene at Robb Elementary School to offer assistance.[854] It was also reported that support services were not readily available for some victim specialists (see "Victim Services Specialists" section).[855]

Immediate or Intermediate Support Services

The immediate or intermediate phase covers the first year following an incident. In this phase, there are many supportive actions and interventions that can help those impacted to mitigate the development of a diagnosable mental health concern, including PTSD, other anxiety-related disorders, and major depression. The intermediate phase is still considered a viable time frame in which victims can actively address any disturbing symptoms through positive coping; reaching out to social supports; engaging in remembering, memorializing, creating narratives, storytelling, and other expressive activities; as well as following evidence-based treatments such as cognitive behavioral therapy for post-disaster distress. All of these are known to help mitigate the development of a diagnosable mental illness after a traumatic event. For many victims, engaging in these types of recovery efforts sooner rather than later can increase their effectiveness.

Helping families, victims, and responders to avoid developing mental health concerns can allow them to move onto a recovery path. This strengthens their ability to adapt and support each other, rather than having a significant percentage wind up with health issues (e.g., cardiac-related illnesses, autoimmune deficiencies) and mental health needs that stop them from functioning—from going to work, caring for their families, and having joy in their lives again. Research has shown that when there are outstanding issues concerning a violent, traumatic incident such as a criminal trial, lack of accountability, or continued political infighting regarding an incident, recovery for family members, victims, and other community members is slower and may even be stalled.[856]

The following sub-sections discuss generally accepted practices and standards for post-incident support services, and the response in Uvalde.

---

[854] CIR Fact Finding.

[855] CIR Fact Finding.

[856] *Unexpected Challenges for Communities in the Recovery Phase of a Mass Violence Incident*; Carlson, "Why Prosecutors Need to Understand the Impact of Trauma;" Goldman, "Restorative Justice as a Trauma-Informed Approach;" Parsons and Bergin, "The Impact of Criminal Justice Involvement on Victims' Mental Health."

Identifying the Affected Communities

A critical step in providing post-incident support services is to identify the communities affected by the incident and to analyze their specific needs.

Principles for Identifying Affected Communities

Following an MCI, it is a best practice to conduct a needs assessment of the community. The needs assessment is intended to identify the number of deceased and injured victims directly impacted multiplied by the average number of immediate family members, the number of present but not injured persons exposed to the traumatic stress of the event, the number of responders in general and those responders who were injured, and an estimation of high-risk populations from within the exposed community who may develop mental or physical health concerns. The needs assessment should gather demographic, geographic, economic, social, cultural, and infrastructure capacity information, as well as any other information that can help determine if the incident can be managed by the community or if outside assistance in the form of grant funding, staffing, training, and technical assistance may be needed. The needs assessment should clearly identify any gaps that currently exist in the community that could negatively affect their ability to support those impacted toward recovery. A comprehensive needs assessment can also include an estimated budget of the amount of funds needed for victims and family members, responder organizations, and other provider agencies to be able to support the community in its recovery.

Incidents of violence are traumatic, and although each person will respond differently based on their level of exposure, previous history with trauma, and other risk factors, as well as their coping and adaptation skills, there is sufficient research on terrorism, school shootings, and other such incidents that describes the most common reactions and distress symptoms to expect in specific populations.

The "spheres of influence" model[857] (see figure 6-1 on page 262) categorizes survivors into groups defined by their exposure level to the incident. Exposure is the critical indicator for potential negative impacts. This model illustrates that the risk for developing severe mental disorders is based on individuals' proximity, both emotionally (relationship-wise) and geographically, to the incident/disaster. The combination of the information gathered in the needs assessment, follow-up survivor and family forums, provider reports, community activities related to the disaster, direct case studies, and anecdotal information can suggest the type of services to be provided to whom, where, how, and when. The model should be used to inform the program's overall outreach strategy. Updated needs assessments should be conducted at reasonable intervals (every 6 months, for example) to note any changes in the identified target populations. New findings should be integrated into a revised needs assessment and distributed to the victim services staff, behavioral health staff, and provider programs responsible for support, resource distribution, and outreach/follow on. The outreach staff should then revise their strategies and adjust their efforts to reach newly identified populations or those in continuing need.

---

[857] DeWolfe, *Training Manual for Mental Health and Human Service Workers in Major Disasters*.

Figure 6-1. The spheres of influence model

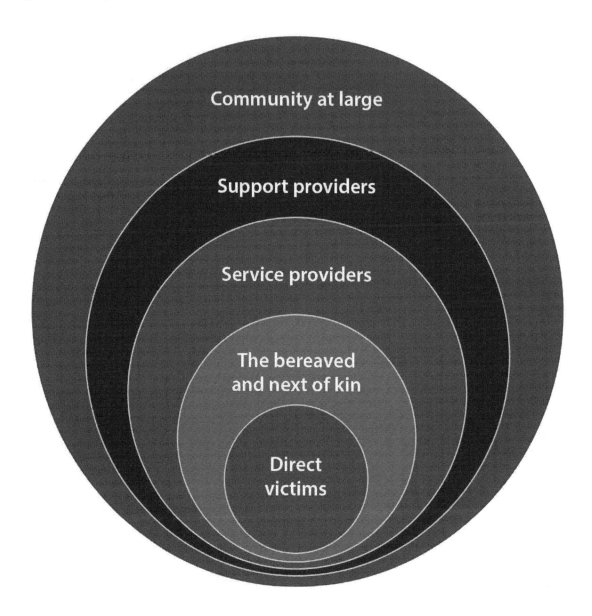

As shown in figure 6-1, the smallest circle is of those most highly impacted and, thus, at the highest risk for developing a mental illness. These direct victims/survivors have been injured and have suffered the most losses. The next sphere of those most at-risk includes the family members of victims who were killed or seriously injured in the event. The third sphere encompasses "service providers," which generally refers to rescue and responder staff who were on the event scene in the first minutes and hours post-event. The next sphere includes support providers, who are typically defined as all other responders who arrived to assist once the location had been declared safe enough—that is, no longer a hot zone. Examples of support providers are staff who served as support to the family or worked at family reunification or assistance centers, faith-based representatives, communications officials, and volunteers who acted as responders. The last sphere includes the community at large, which may have some broader connection to the event or personal concern that influences their responses to the event, and those in the general public who may have been exposed to the event via radio, television, or word of mouth.

In this figure, it is essential to note that while the numbers of survivors increase as the sphere of influence moves to lesser degrees of direct exposure to the event, the intensity of exposure decreases. Less exposure to the event usually means a lower risk of developing more serious mental health concerns. This lower risk, though, is only in relation to exposure and does not include other risk variables that may influence the development of a mental illness, such as age, prior traumatic experiences, prior mental health or substance use problems, immigrant and socioeconomic status, and function and access needs.

See "Appendix F. Trauma and Support Services Supplemental Materials" for more on high-risk populations.

Affected Communities and Needs Assessment in Uvalde

In the shooting at Robb Elementary School, there were 587 children present in the school on that day and many other teachers and staff members.[858]

Many of the children and adults present that day needed treatment for physical injuries. There were at least 17 survivors who were physically injured. Fifteen victims were treated at UMH on May 24, 2022: 11 children and four adults. Four of the children and one adult were transferred to hospitals in San Antonio the next day. The other patients were treated in Uvalde before being discharged home.[859]

Three hospitals in the San Antonio area reported receiving patients from the shooting: Brooke Army Medical Center, University Hospital, and Methodist Children's Hospital. Brooke Army Medical Center, in Fort Sam Houston, treated two adult patients in critical condition with injuries from the shooting. Four victims were treated at University Hospital, an adult and three child victims; one of the children was in critical condition upon admission, another was in good condition, and the third was in fair condition. Another child victim was treated at Methodist Children's Hospital.[860]

By July 29, 2022, over 2 months after the shooting, the last of the injured victims was discharged from University Hospital in San Antonio.[861] It is expected that some victims will require continued medical care because of the injuries they received in the shooting. Additionally, some victims were injured but were not brought to hospital. One family reported taking care of their child's significant injury themselves, and another reported bringing their child to their primary care physician.[862] Since not all the

---

[858] CIR Fact Finding.

[859] Schonfeld, "What We Know about the Uvalde Victims Who Were Hospitalized."

[860] Schonfeld, "What We Know about the Uvalde Victims Who Were Hospitalized."

[861] Prieb, "Last Uvalde Victim Injured in School Shooting Discharged from San Antonio Hospital."

[862] CIR Fact Finding.

children and staff present at Robb Elementary at the time of the shooting were brought to a hospital or otherwise assessed for any medical concerns, it is unknown how many in total sustained physical injuries as a result of this incident.

The victims of the shooting are also likely to have mental health needs going forward. Some of the victims lost all of their friends that day, amplifying the lasting impacts of the trauma. For other families, multiple family members were inside the school; in one case, a victim had 23 cousins present there.[863] As noted in this and other sections of this report, because of the negative emotional impact of both the mass violence and the poor response to it, all of those exposed are expected to have approximately a 20 percent risk of developing a mental health concern over the long term.

In addition to the negative mental health impacts from direct exposure to this MCI, Uvalde residents have several other layers of social and psychological complexity that are known to influence recovery. One of the characteristics of Uvalde is that the community is intricately intertwined by relationships and associations that leave almost no one in the town without the experience of shared trauma. Not only does most everyone in Uvalde know everyone else, but there are formal and informal relationships (e.g., marriages, cohabitation, co-parenting, alternative families, multiple-family dwelling) that make even distant relations seem closer. Many people regularly interact with each other in caregiving; accessing schools, stores, healthcare, and practical services; and leisure activities (see figure 6-2 on page 265 for a selection of shared connections in Uvalde). In addition, based on the school system structure, the vast majority of Uvalde's second through fourth graders in public school were enrolled at Robb Elementary School. This, alongside the size and scope of this event, makes the experience of shared trauma in this incident nearly unavoidable. Shared trauma describes the extraordinary circumstances in which those responding to an event are experiencing the same community trauma as those they are serving, and it can result in unique stressors.[864]

---

[863] Kantor, "14 Months After Uvalde School Shooting, Survivors' Mom Shares His Mental Health Battle: 'Lives with His Scars Daily.'"

[864] Tosone, Nuttman-Shwartz, and Stephens, "Shared Trauma: When the Professional is Personal;" Tosone et al., "Shared Traumatic Stress and the Long-Term Impact of September 11th on Manhattan Clinicians."

Figure 6-2. Examples of shared connections among the victims, first responders, families, and the community

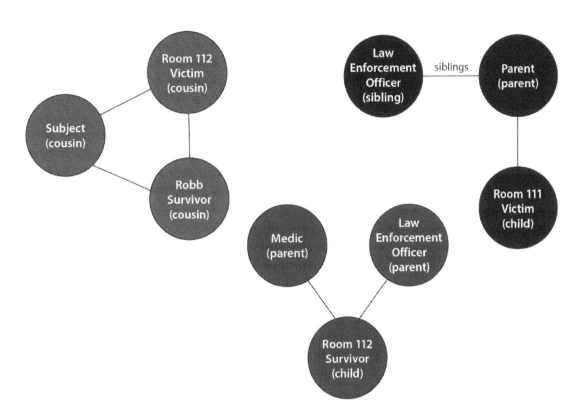

The Robb Elementary victims are considered to be at the highest risk of developing a mental illness because of their exposure to this shooting and its aftermath, based on the spheres of influence model. School-aged children make up a high-risk group in and of themselves due to their young age and intellectual development levels, all of which influence their perceptions and understanding of—and thus their response to—the event. The responses of very young children (generally age 5 and under) mirror those of their caretakers. A certain percentage of all children have a history of trauma.[865] People of color, those of limited economic means, those living in the United States for whom English is not their first language, those of Mexican decent in Uvalde, the LGBTQ+ community, and those in other minority groups all have a higher risk of developing a serious mental health condition in the aftermath of a traumatic event.[866]

Each of these risk factors alone can potentially increase the actual number of people impacted by the event who go on to develop a mental illness. The potential consequences of multiple, intersecting risk factors create sufficient concern that current disaster behavioral health recommendations include screening all school-aged children involved in a traumatic event, such as a school shooting, for mental

---

[865] CDC, "Adverse Childhood Experiences (ACEs)."

[866] Norris et al., "60,000 Disaster Victims Speak: Part I."

health concerns. Screening allows for a fairly rapid and efficient process of determining who may need a full clinical assessment for mental health treatment, and it reserves limited clinical treatment resources for those most in need. This is especially important in rural areas throughout the United States, where mental health clinicians are scarce and child mental health specialists even more so.[867]

In order to assess the needs of these populations and Uvalde's capacity to address those needs, the Texas Department of Health and Human Services (HHS) contracted with the Hill Country Mental Health and Development Disabilities Center, the local mental health authority that services Uvalde County, to prepare a needs assessment.[868] In turn, Hill Country engaged with the Meadows Mental Health Policy Institute (MMHPI) to conduct a needs assessment, which MMHPI indicated is not a traditional needs assessment in that it focuses on the existing need for mental health services in Uvalde and the surrounding 32 counties.[869] This does not meet the definition of a needs assessment as outlined at the beginning of this section. Because of this specific, limited scope, MMHPI maintains that they relied on local leadership and available statistical data to gather the information they used to make their determinations.[870] The needs assessment, as described by MMHPI, "accomplishes what was requested of them,"[871] makes useful recommendations regarding the need for formal mental health services in this area of the state, addresses workforce issues, and points to evidence-based services and related resources available from the field.[872]

The scope and focus of the report inhibited MMHPI from gathering information from those within the community who were most heavily impacted, with the exception of formal leaders. Thus, the experiences of the victims, family members and other loved ones, service providers, law enforcement and other responders not in leadership positions, and informal community leaders (who often have more accurate perceptions than formal leaders of what the community is experiencing) are missing from the needs assessment. In addition to missing the voices, input, and feedback from those most highly impacted by the event, MMHPI's needs assessment does not actually define any behavioral health needs related to the Robb Elementary School shooting event specifically (including the needs for public communications, social supports, and memorializing those who died). Thus, the needs assessment does not detail information about who (to protect confidentiality, a population group and numbers are usually identified) has received services, who has been identified as potentially in need of services, nor who is currently receiving services from OVC, the State Attorney General's Office, responder support agencies, or any other providers.

---

[867] Ramirez et al., "Listen Protect Connect for Traumatized Schoolchildren;" Steinberg et al., "Psychometric Properties of the UCLA PTSD Reaction Index: Part I."

[868] CIR Fact Finding.

[869] CIR Fact Finding.

[870] CIR Fact Finding.

[871] CIR Fact Finding.

[872] CIR Fact Finding; CDC, "Adverse Childhood Experiences (ACEs)."

The MMHPI needs assessment accurately describes the tier system being utilized to identify which populations will likely need which levels of mental health services in generalities. It recommends evidence-based treatments, though it does not quantify the amount of treatment needed nor identify who will provide which services, how will they be trained, or who will be deployed to train them (other than identifying their Trauma and Grief Center as a provider). The needs assessment contains a general recommendation that schools should screening for mental health concerns, but it does not specify the need to assess all the children who were present in Robb Elementary on May 24, 2022. There is no reference of the need for outreach to those who could benefit from crisis counseling, or of check-ins or referrals for formal mental health services.

The report says that the community of Uvalde will likely require long-term services, but other than describing details about some of the most restrictive services for those with a diagnosable mental illness, it contains no discussion of building capacity to address the ongoing acute state of crisis, the lack of helpful public communications, nor incident details for family members. There is no reference to any discussion of training providers to be able to provide all tiers of services in the long term in order to sustain the supports that will continue to be needed in Uvalde. There is no reference to guiding the community to build more social support and to gather for discussion of key activities that might help them begin to unite and move onto a recovery path, such as how to mark significant time frames (holidays, birthdays, and the yearly marker) and to begin planning for a permanent memorial.

Identifying and Coordinating Providers of Support Services

Following a tragedy like Robb Elementary, the most informed, trauma-focused services need to be operationalized to minimize the potential for imposing any further traumatic stressors and to increase the ability of those impacted to recover in a reasonable time frame with the support they need. Models of intervention—such as crisis counseling, PFA, grief counseling, group support, peer support, and other services like case management that assist with practical needs—can help to mitigate the development of mental illnesses. In the intermediate phase, trauma-focused therapy can help when individuals are diagnosed by a skilled professional in situations where a victim's experience or history have raised the risk of illness and more formal care is indicated.

Principles for Identifying and Coordinating Services Providers

The responsibility for providing support and services following a tragedy falls on the designated response agencies that become involved in these activities as part of federal, state, and local emergency, disaster, and mass violence response policies. The capacity of local agencies to meet the needs of those most highly impacted during the event may determine which of them becomes part of the response. For example, victim advocates need to be provided to every victim of an MCI, which often requires a larger workforce than most agencies normally employ. Funds made available through the victim compensation programs described below can be utilized to hire these staff for temporary jobs. Memoranda of understanding (MOU) or mutual aid agreements can facilitate the sharing of victim advocates for a period, as needed.

The lead agency responsible for coordinating support providers may also differ in each locality and state depending on their regulations. For example, disaster response funding and services may flow through public health, emergency management, victim assistance, law enforcement, or behavioral health offices. These offices are encouraged to include appropriate local providers in their response efforts. Guidance may be provided by experienced consultant representatives, such as those available from the OVC TTAC.[873] As with all aspects of emergency response, providing timely and appropriate crisis intervention and mental health services requires extensive coordination and collaboration.

Legislative Programs

OVC's Victim Compensation Program provides direct reimbursement to or on behalf of a crime victim for various crime-related expenses, such as medical costs, mental health counseling, lost wages, and funeral and burial costs. OVC administers federal funds to support compensation programs in all U.S. states and territories, including Washington, D.C., the U.S. Virgin Islands, Puerto Rico, and Guam. Crime Victim Compensation (CVC) is a state-based reimbursement program for victims of crime, found in every U.S. state and territory, but with eligibility criteria and benefits unique to each state.* The Crime Victims Fund is financed by fines and penalties paid by those convicted of federal offenses, not from tax dollars. Federal revenues deposited into the fund also come from gifts, donations, and bequests by private parties. Eligibility for crime victim compensation for costs incurred due to a crime varies by state and territory.

The Victims of Crime Act (VOCA) Fix to Sustain the Crime Victims Fund Act of 2021† instructed OVC not to deduct restitution payments recovered by state victim compensation funds when calculating victim compensation awards. CVC is the last source of payment by law. All other available resources must pay before any payment by the program. A collateral source is any other readily available resource that can be used to cover crime-related costs. Examples of these other resources are:

- Medical insurance

- Dental insurance

- Medicare/Medicaid

- Vehicle insurance

- Homeowner's/renter's insurance

- Workers' compensation

- Settlements

continues on page 269

---

[873] Office for Victims of Crime Training and Technical Assistance Center, "About Us."

Legislative Programs, cont'd.

Total compensation is limited to $50,000 per victim and may vary based on laws in effect at the time of the crime.[‡]

In addition to the statewide victim compensation programs, OVC oversees the Antiterrorism Emergency Assistance Program, authorized by the Victims of Crime Act of 1984 (VOCA), 42 USC §§ 10601(d)(5), 10603b(a) (international) and 10603b(b) (domestic). This assistance is available in situations where a criminal act is of sufficient magnitude that the jurisdiction cannot provide needed services to victims of the incidents with existing resources.[§] OVC is committed to promoting justice and healing for all victims of mass violent crimes and terrorist attacks, recognizing that these incidents leave victims with physical and emotional wounds.[**]

The Stafford Act of 1974, as amended in 1988, allows for the provision of mental health and substance abuse services through the Federal Emergency Management Agency's (FEMA) Crisis Counseling Assistance and Training Program in the aftermath of federally declared disasters that also authorize individual assistance.[††] The Substance Abuse and Mental Health Services Administration administers the program. It provides the mechanism by which states can apply for funding to support communities in need. In the case of the shooting at Robb Elementary, the president declared a federal disaster, thus enabling Texas to apply for one of these short-term disaster grants if they desired to do so.

These critical pieces of legislation essentially acknowledge the need for, and provide, funding sources to address the adverse mental health effects, both acute and long-term, of traumatic events on victims and on the family members of those killed and injured. For those injured, eligibility for compensation varies by state, but most states have adopted a definition of reimbursable medical expenses that includes a hospital stay by the individual.

---

* IACP, *Law Enforcement-Based Victim Services – Template Package IV: Pamphlets.*

† OVC, "The VOCA Fix."

‡ Office of the Texas Attorney General, "Costs Covered by the Crime Victims' Compensation Program."

§ OVC, "Types of Assistance Available Through AEAP."

** OVC, "Antiterrorism and Emergency Assistance Program (AEAP)."

†† 42 U.S.C. § 5121.

There are federal and state programs specifically designed to ensure that local communities can support victims and their families as well as responders and the community at large. The guidance provided by these programs stresses the importance of the local providers having as much control of the implementation of the response activities as possible to empower the affected community to care for its own. This guidance recognizes that the local community knows its own needs and customs best, ensuring that when federal and state assistance ends, the local providers will have the capacity to sustain the needed supports for the long term.[874]

In communities with existing disaster response teams trained and poised to respond in the immediate aftermath of an event, crisis counseling and victim advocacy can begin as soon as these teams are made aware and can deploy to the designated meeting site. The availability and type of victim services vary by state but are generally somewhat similar. Each state may define the categories of "victim" and "survivor" slightly differently.

The Texas Crime Victim's Assistance Program is run out of the governor's office and is aimed at helping victims navigate the justice system. The program provides funds via subgrants to local community-based organizations that can provide direct services to crime victims and reimbursement for crime-related out-of-pocket expenses.

The Texas Crime Victims' Compensation (CVC) program is managed by the Texas Office of the Attorney General and helps crime victims and their immediate families with the financial costs of crime. CVC covers crime-related expenses such as counseling, medical treatment, funerals, and loss of income not paid by other sources. The Texas CVC program's definitions of eligibility for compensation include: "1) A victim who was injured or died because of the crime; 2) Someone who came to the aid of a crime victim and was injured or died; and 3) First responders who were injured or died while responding to a crime. An injury can include physical or mental harm."[875]

Additionally, victims may experience distress from crimes through their participation in the justice system process. Participating in depositions, awaiting subject arrests, and witnessing trials are all emotional stressors. Another example of this is the collection and management of victims' property. Most state statutes indicate that victims have the right to the prompt return of property as soon as it is no longer needed for investigations or prosecutions. OVC provides resources that can help law enforcement efforts to provide victim-centered, trauma-informed support to all crime victims and law enforcement personnel.[876]

---

[874] SAMHSA, "Crisis Counseling Assistance and Training Program (CCP)."

[875] Texas Department of Criminal Justice, "Definitions and Acronyms."

[876] IACP, "Law Enforcement-Based Victim Services (LEV) Webinar Series."

Texas Disaster Behavioral Health Services

The Disaster Behavioral Health Services (DBHS) program is responsible for managing disaster behavioral health preparedness, response, and recovery efforts for Texas before, during, and after local, state, or federally declared disasters, public health emergencies, and incidents of mass violence as defined by OVC. Depending on the size and scope of the incident, the DBHS program may:

- Coordinate the inclusion of disaster behavioral health best practices and resources in federal, state, and local emergency management planning efforts.

- Coordinate the deployment of available disaster behavioral health resources in response to State of Texas Assistance Requests.

- Provide technical assistance and guidance to incident command, committees, local providers, contractors, disaster survivors, and first responders in affected communities.

- Coordinate the long-term behavioral health recovery efforts for communities impacted by disasters, public health emergencies, and criminal events.

Following incidents of mass violence, DBHS provides coordination, support, and technical assistance to Texas nonprofits, city and county governmental entities, and the statewide network of 39 local mental health authorities and local behavioral health authorities throughout the comprehensive spectrum of the criminal incident cycle. Following an incident, DBHS assists in a myriad of tasks geared toward fostering resiliency and recovery within the affected community. Key components include:

- Developing a comprehensive community needs assessment to inform local leaders and community members of the behavioral health providers available for immediate response and long-term recovery.

- Providing technical assistance and training, and assisting with recovery phase-specific strategic planning.*

---

* As provided by Texas Disaster Behavioral Health Services in place of an interview.

Family Assistance Center/Family Resiliency Center

In the aftermath of a tragedy, a Family Assistance Center (FAC) or Family Resiliency Center (FRC) can serve as a base for the provision of coordinated support services. Since the early days of disaster response, the American Red Cross (ARC) has been the leader in setting up FACs in the aftermath of events. The ARC continues to be the legislatively designated response agency in many states and for all aviation-related disasters nationwide.[877] More recently, an FAC has been referred to as a Family and

---

[877] Office of Transportation Disaster Assistance, *Federal Family Assistance Framework for Aviation Disasters.*

Friends Assistance Center (FFAC) to be more inclusive. An FFAC should be located in a convenient and easy place for family members to get to with available parking, or by public transportation if that is the standard mode of transportation in the affected area, especially if those impacted are less likely to have private transportation or the economic means for travel. Those determining the location of the FFAC also need to pay attention to trauma activators. For example, the FFAC should be far enough away from the incident site so that people will not have to pass it when coming or going or see it easily from the FFAC itself. The FFAC should have basic comforts such as places to sit together, meals or snacks, water, toilets, and physical and emotional warmth.

An FFAC is designed to be a safe place for victims, family members, and responders to come together for information, resources, and support. It is meant to be available in the short term, often in the acute post-disaster phase while family members access information , immediate crisis intervention and disaster behavioral health support, and practical resources (e.g., living accommodations, clothing, food/water, safety, emergency funds).

Once all victims, survivors, and family members are identified and receive initial direct support, the FFAC will quickly transition into an FRC or to be more inclusive, a Resiliency Center. The FFAC may transition to an FRC within 1 week or 3 or more months after the event, depending on the nature and scope of the event.[878] The FRC will typically continue to provide ongoing services and assistance to victims, family members, responders, and community members.

These types of centers are an emerging best practice meant to provide initial and continuing support and resources to victims, family members, and sometimes even responders, acting as a gathering space for those impacted as they make their way through the recovery process. They are often referred to as the "one-stop shop" where various agencies have a presence with representatives to assist in providing services to the disaster-impacted community. Many FRCs will invite multiple agencies to assist victims and family members with the crime victim compensation application process, healthcare, mental health supports, childcare, legal matters, travel, creditors, work-related issues, financial planning, insurance benefits, tax policies, and social security/disability. The FRC may also have representatives from many organizations, including FEMA and serve as an access point for other support such as food, clothing, and toys. At the FRC, impacted individuals can gain information, engage in healing activities, and connect with other survivors and family members. These activities can help people build resilience while still acknowledging their grief and their need to connect with each other and the available support services. In the past decade, it has become more common for FFACs to have not only a physical location but also a website for online access.

---

[878] OVC, *Helping Victims of Mass Violence and Terrorism.*

Providers of Support Services in Uvalde

In the immediate aftermath of the tragedy at Robb Elementary, service providers, mental health clinicians, and therapists from across the country descended on Uvalde to provide assistance. Most of the service providers responded to Uvalde on the day of the incident or shortly thereafter and remained for a minimum of 2 weeks, with some staying for 30 days.

Establishment of a Family Assistance Center/Family Resiliency Center in Uvalde

The FBI and TXDPS, in partnership with the ARC, quickly established an FAC[879] to coordinate the provision of services. The FAC was set up initially at the Reunification Center in the Civic Center (see figure 6-3) to focus on a gathering space. By the third day, it was moved outside of the City of Uvalde to the Uvalde County Fairplex (see figure 6-3, bottom left of the map).[880]

Figure 6-3. Map of Uvalde showing location of Uvalde County Fairplex, Robb Elementary School, and Willie DeLeon Civic Center

Image source: National Geographic MapMaker.

---

[879] FAC is the term used for the incident in Uvalde.

[880] CIR Fact Finding.

At the beginning, the FAC was run by the law enforcement victim personnel from the FBI and TXDPS. TXDPS invited the FBI Victim Services Response Team (VSRT) to help set up the FAC and gather necessary information and resources. The FBI VSRT is a multidisciplinary, rapid deployment team that responds upon request with an incident response manager and a victim services coordinator as part of its response structure, which allows the team to focus primarily on victims. In Uvalde, the VSRT agents were embedded within the command post, where they were involved in meetings twice a day with the whole team to ensure good communications and planning. The team would normally participate in death/trauma notifications, as they are highly trained, but while at the FAC in Uvalde they were not utilized for this. Instead, they shared best practices from other events and put the county staff in touch with other localities that had managed mass violence events previously. They attended to victims' families, many of whom came with over a dozen extended family members. They also helped with immediate needs, assisted family members in completing applications, and brought their facility dog, a specialist in supporting disaster victims and bringing a sense of calm to child victims.[881]

While the FBI VSRT personnel were on scene, they were also responsible for working with TXDPS to return personal effects as requested.[882] If a family member wanted an item returned and it was not deemed evidentiary, the FBI would search for and collect the item.[883] They would then send the item out to be cleaned and individually packaged in a white box.[884] The FBI personnel would then deliver the item in person.[885] For the FBI, "presentation is important. It is one thing to receive your loved ones' items in an evidence bag or folder, and another to receive [the personal item] in a respectful manner. It shows that someone cares to present it in a compassionate manner."[886]

As families came into the FAC, they were met in a welcoming space where they would sign in and receive a wristband, as a way to prevent media and other onlookers from entering the premises. This process helped ensure that the space was safe and secure. For example, several people claimed that they had children at Robb Elementary, but it was later discovered that they did not have children, but were trying to gain access to the services or wanted to see what was going on inside.[887] Law enforcement also created a barrier to prevent media from getting too close to the entrance.

Families started the initial intake process with a law enforcement victim service provider from the FBI, TXDPS, or the National Organization of Victim Assistance (NOVA) Victim Navigator.[888] The intake was a one-page form that covered the family's basic contact information and relationship to the incident, as

---

[881] CIR Fact Finding.

[882] CIR Fact Finding.

[883] CIR Fact Finding.

[884] CIR Fact Finding.

[885] CIR Fact Finding.

[886] CIR Fact Finding.

[887] CIR Fact Finding.

[888] CIR Fact Finding.

well as checkboxes for the resources available at the FAC. The Victim Navigator or victim service provider would help the family identify the assistance they needed and then help route the family to the appropriate services.[889]

Approximately 18 organizations[890] were available to provide services, including the following, with an asterisk (*) marking the organizations that were continuing to provide assistance as of June 8, 2023:

- American Red Cross

- Bluebonnet Children's Advocacy Center—provides trauma-informed care, particularly for child victims and their families*[891]

- Children's Disaster Services—provided childcare services (see the callout box "Childcare Services at the FAC")

- Ecumenical Center—activated 32 counselors to provide services including long-term mental health counseling with a trauma and grief specialist for all ages; music, art, and play therapy; support groups; and no-cost support for families and the community*[892]

- Health insurance companies such as Blue Cross Blue Shield

- Hill Country—the local mental health authority that provides mental health services and counseling*[893]

- Legal Aid—provided legal advice and other legal services

- Mexican Consulate—assisted with immigration services, including for family members who needed to travel for funerals

- Nueva Vida Counseling—provides long-term mental health counseling services and child and adult psychiatry*[894]

- Salvation Army

- Texas Health and Human Services—assisted with enrollment in Medicaid/Food Stamps

- Texas Office of the Attorney General—assisted with completing the CVC applications

- Uvalde County District Attorney Victim Service Advocate

- Workforce Development—helped to identify open positions

---

[889] CIR Fact Finding.

[890] CIR Fact Finding.

[891] Uvalde Together Resiliency Center, "Participating Organizations."

[892] Uvalde Together Resiliency Center, "Participating Organizations."

[893] Uvalde Together Resiliency Center, "Participating Organizations."

[894] Uvalde Together Resiliency Center, "Participating Organizations."

Families and their navigator worked through the free services, sometimes spread out over several days. For those who required formal mental health treatment, short-term evidence-based services were often available, including through a referral process from Hill Country. FBI VSRT personnel also eventually took FAC resources to injured victims in San Antonio hospitals.[895]

On June 4, 2022, the FAC transitioned to an FRC,[896] and by mid-June it had changed its name to the Uvalde Together Resiliency Center (UTRC) (see figures 6-4 to 6-12 on pages 276–281).

Figure 6-4. Entrance to the Uvalde Resiliency Center

One of the initial barriers to the process of accessing services was the size of the physical space, which restricted the number of representative agencies and staff that could be present at the site. Another challenge that the leadership team faced was outreach and marketing, which typically take a significant amount of funding, planning, and skilled staff to accomplish successfully.[897] (See the "Public Media Campaign Examples" section in "Appendix E. Public Communications Supplemental Materials" for more on public marketing campaigns.) Relatedly, the FAC never received a complete list of all victims, so

---

[895] CIR Fact Finding.

[896] CIR Fact Finding.

[897] CIR Fact Finding.

although the FAC believed that all families had received outreach, they could not confirm it.[898] This may have been the result of several obstacles, including the failure to identify all victims, a lack of information sharing or policies that allow such information, and the ongoing investigation.[899]

There were gaps in some services, and needed support for children and youth was not as accessible in the days immediately following the tragedy. Some survivors and first responders expressed concern about confidentiality (a need amplified by the growing negative sentiment toward first responders after the shooting), which kept them from seeking help until they felt more certain their privacy would be protected.[900] In some cases, surviving families expressed frustration with the cumbersome bureaucracy of the state government's victim compensation process, citing the excessive amount of paperwork that was required and redundancy among the various forms.[901] One of the more challenging issues for the FRC was addressing the housing insecurities some families experienced in the weeks following the tragedy, due in large part to lost wages.[902]

Figure 6-5. Counseling space at the family resiliency center

[898] CIR Fact Finding.

[899] CIR Fact Finding.

[900] CIR Fact Finding.

[901] CIR Fact Finding.

[902] CIR Fact Finding.

Figure 6-6. Counseling space at the family resiliency center

Another challenge was the volume of service providers that descended on Uvalde. While the overwhelming support was appreciated, the FAC/FRC and the community could not handle the substantial number of people who self-deployed.[903] Concerns arose around the credentials and licensure of the unknown volunteers, coordination of services, and lack of adequate experience in responding to MCIs.[904] In one case, a large service provider deployed to the community and after a couple of days had to leave due to the trauma their own staff faced by not being prepared for the grief and emotions in the community.[905]

In another case, a team trained their responders before deploying on what to expect, how to help to identify signs of vicarious stress/trauma, and how to take care of themselves and their colleagues.[906] They found that the training helped to reinforce resiliency in their team and also helped them to understand their role of bearing witness in the immediate aftermath.[907] Based on the success of this training, the organization will continue to use it for future disaster responses.[908]

---

[903] CIR Fact Finding.

[904] CIR Fact Finding.

[905] CIR Fact Finding.

[906] CIR Fact Finding.

[907] CIR Fact Finding.

[908] CIR Fact Finding.

Figure 6-7. Outside view of the Uvalde Resiliency Center

Figure 6-8. Inside the Uvalde Resiliency Center

Figure 6-9. Inside the Uvalde Resiliency Center

Figure 6-10. Inside an FRC therapy room

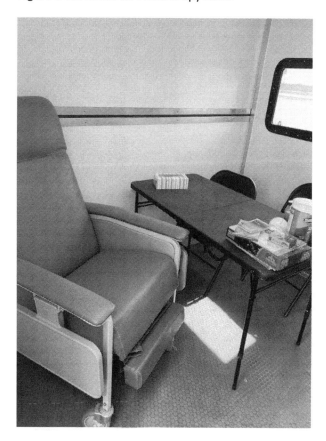

Figure 6-11. Inside an FRC therapy room

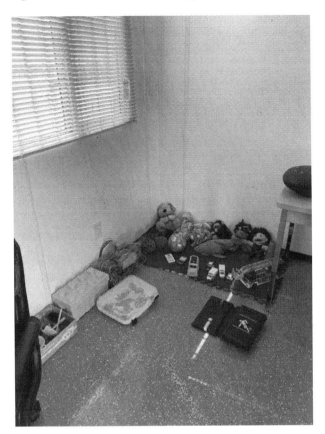

Figure 6-12. Inside an FRC therapy room

Housing Challenges

Due to the size of Uvalde and the limited number of available hotels and lodgings, lodging space became scarce. Reporters, journalists, and TXDPS personnel who were deployed to the border security initiative known as Operation Lonestar had booked the majority of rooms early on. TXDPS worked with local ranchers to shift their personnel and open up space for family members coming into town. But it still was not enough. When the governor came to Uvalde, he met with the leadership running the FAC and asked what gaps they had at the FAC. When informed of the housing challenges for family members, he committed to getting that gap filled. The Uvalde County Fairplex hosts rodeos year-round and has 75 hookups for water and electricity. By that afternoon, the governor had four RVs brought in from the Texas Department of Emergency Management, with an additional 25 arriving the next day.* Families of victims explained how meaningful this space was for their family members as they came in from out of town, especially during the funerals. Deployment of RVs became a recommendation for future disaster response planning.†

Limited space also impacted the numerous victim service providers. Some had to stay in San Antonio, over 80 miles away, and travel back and forth each day. The FBI VSRT personnel, however, were able to stay locally in the dorms at Southwest Texas Junior College.‡ While these lodgings were far from ideal, many VSRT personnel reported that they felt the dorm housing helped them prepare at the beginning of the day and decompress as a team each evening in a safe and secure space without an arduous commute.§

---

* CIR Fact Finding.

† CIR Fact Finding.

‡ CIR Fact Finding.

§ CIR Fact Finding.

Some services and organizations like Endeavors provided a range of free services (see figure 6-13 on page 285), including individual and family counseling off site. These services were also made available to law enforcement and other emergency response personnel. In Uvalde, there was such intense anger at the law enforcement responders that it was determined that the FRC would not be made accessible to law enforcement staff and their families.[909] Given the circumstances, it was the best decision to keep law enforcement away from the FRC as much as possible, so not to activate or increase any emotional distress in the victims and family members accessing services at the FRC. At the same time, planning efforts should have ensured that support services to responders are immediately available as needed, especially when those responders are also family members of the victims as was the case in this incident.

---

[909] CIR Fact Finding.

VIPs and Other Dignitaries Visiting the FAC/FRC

Politicians, government representatives, celebrities, and other dignitaries arrived in Uvalde to meet with the community, listen to concerns, make statements, and/or provide services or donations. In particular, it is important that an FAC/FRC remain free of media and continue to be a space of support, counseling, and assistance. As part of the pre-planning, agencies, organizations, and communities should make a plan for these high-level visits, including the security needed.

In one such visit, President Joe Biden and First Lady Dr. Jill Biden visited Uvalde to meet with the families of the victims and the community. This meeting happened to occur on the day after the first family forum hosted by TXDPS and the Uvalde County district attorney, from which families walked out angry and hurt (See "Principles for Communicating with Victims and Families" for more on this forum). It was decided that the FBI victim services personnel assigned to each family would be present for the presidential meeting and introduce the families to the president and first lady.* The president and first lady's compassion, and the time they spent with the families, elicited positive feedback from those who attended.† While this meeting was happening, the FAC leadership and U.S. Secret Service worked together to keep the FAC open in a limited capacity,‡ highlighting the need for pre-planning to include security needs.

_____

* CIR Fact Finding.

† CIR Fact Finding.

‡ CIR Fact Finding.

In addition to off-site services, various organizations, such as the H-E-B chain of grocery stores and the National Compassion Fund (see callout box "National Compassion Fund" on page 288), set up funds or financial assistance. Distribution of the financial assistance became complicated when it came to eligibility, allowable costs, and familial relationship. Some individuals were deemed ineligible because they were not a student in the West Building or at Robb Elementary School;[910] however, it is important not to forget the spheres of influence and the broad set of victims in this incident, including not only everyone present at Robb Elementary, but also funeral home employees and all families with a connection to the shooting. Familial dynamics also complicated the financial assistance process for some parents and family members, including unmarried parents and stepparents. The length of time to complete the applications, the redundancy, and the proof needed added to the burden on victims, survivors, family members, and the community. Finally, the lengthy processing time for the various funds added to the problems.

_____

[910] CIR Fact Finding.

Childcare Services at the FAC

The Children's Disaster Services (CDS), part of the Church of the Brethren, has been providing disaster response programs since the early 1970s and began focusing on the needs of children starting in 1980. When asked to come into a community after a mass shooting, they provide services to victims and families in the form of a safe space for the children to play while the adults interact with FAC staff. The adult providers do not ask questions but play with the children and listen if the children wish to express themselves. For example, in Uvalde two children who had been in classroom 112 of Robb Elementary were playing with some dolls and began reenacting what they had experienced, including rendering first aid to a doll and making funeral arrangements for the fatalities.*

The children who take part in the CDS programming do not have to be directly involved in the disaster; however, as family members, children may nonetheless be traumatized by the direct impact of an incident on another family member.

In Uvalde, CDS deployed 15 volunteers for approximately 30 days. CDS received overwhelmingly positive feedback from the families and other service providers in the FAC, with children leaving more at ease and some not even wanting to leave the FAC. Some parents said that they had not seen their children smile so much since the tragedy. The only challenge the team faced was the small space in the FAC/FRC, which meant that they had only a small corner set aside for play. However, the volunteers said this limitation actually work to their advantage, since parents were able to keep an eye on their children as they were in such a visible location.†

For every CDS deployment, a clinician is assigned to the team to ensure that the volunteers have necessary support. Volunteers receive 24 hours of training in child development, the history of child victims of disaster, and other related topics. Team leaders go through an additional 2- to 3-day seminar on understanding critical response protocols.‡

---

* CIR Fact Finding.

† CIR Fact Finding.

‡ CIR Fact Finding.

As a layer on top of all of these challenges, victims and family members also experienced additional victimization from scammers. Several family members expressed outrage and pain at scammers and criminals setting up GoFundMe pages or other fundraisers ostensibly on their child's behalf without authorization from the families.[911] Ultimately, those families never saw any of the funds raised from those criminal actions. When this issue was brought to the Uvalde County District Attorney's Office, they

---

[911] CIR Fact Finding.

reached out to TXDPS.[912] A TXDPS special agent with experience in this area investigated the claims and worked directly with GoFundMe to successfully shut down the fraudulent accounts without the need for protracted court interventions.[913] Generally, TXDPS sees fraudulent accounts surface over the course of 48 hours after an incident and then taper off.[914]

Figure 6-13. Sign marketing services for victims, first responders, and families

---

[912] CIR Fact Finding.

[913] CIR Fact Finding.

[914] CIR Fact Finding.

The Use of Canines

"Animal-assisted crisis response (AACR) is an intervention that harnesses the human-animal bond for therapeutic benefit through specially trained animal-handler teams deployed to provide comfort following a mass traumatic event."* AACR teams are specially trained, evaluated, and credentialed dog teams who have at least 12 visits providing animal-assisted therapy in various settings.[†] There is scientific research that shows the positive influence of emotional supporting dogs with victims of traumatic events, such as an MCI.[‡]

Moreover, just the act of petting a dog can help calm a survivor of an MCI and offer physical comfort at an extremely uncomfortable time. Studies involving animal-assisted interventions have found that the physical benefits of this interaction include decreased heart rate, blood pressure, and stress hormones. Since physiological arousal has been linked to the development of PTSD, AACR as an early intervention modality may prevent more serious, long-term effects.[§]

At the time of the shooting, the FBI Victim Services Division (VSD) deployed two crisis response canines that were instrumental during the FBI interviews of the children who survived the shooting. The canines were specially trained for children and seniors.** These facility canines are different than therapy canines in that:

> A therapy dog is typically someone's pet and lives with that family. Therapy dogs are usually trained to provide comfort and affection to people in hospitals, retirement homes, and other settings.[††] Certifying a dog as a therapy dog requires passing obedience and temperament tests. An owner must also become certified as a volunteer handler, which typically requires a background check.[‡‡]

The FBI only has facility dogs (not therapy dogs) for crisis response deployment.[§§] Their two facility canines are trained dogs with a temperament for hospital and criminal settings. Their presence in courtrooms, for example, has helped ease stress in children giving testimony.*** Crisis response canine handlers and other canine handlers who respond to MCIs can get fatigued and should be included in any post-incident trauma counseling.

---

* Robino et al., "Sustained Effects of Animal-Assisted Crisis Response."

† Eaton-Stull, "Mental Health Monitor: Animal-Assisted Crisis Response."

‡ Hennemann et al., "Therapy Dogs as a Crisis Intervention."

§ Hennemann et al., "Therapy Dogs as a Crisis Intervention."

** CIR Fact Finding.

†† Alliance of Therapy Dogs, "Therapy Dog Certification."

‡‡ American Humane, *Definition of a Service Dog.*

§§ CIR Fact Finding.

*** FBI, "Finding Solace."

Figure 6-14. Two English-language flyers for Uvalde Strong mental health assistance services and the Robb School Memorial Fund

In the end, organizations in the community and across the country stepped up to assist the victims and families (see figures 6-14 and 6-15 on pages 287and 288). Gas cards were provided to the family members, especially since several family members had to drive back and forth to San Antonio (typically a 1.5 hour trip one way) for medical and mental health care for their injured or hospitalized children.[915] The City of Uvalde covered water/garbage and natural gas services, and two electricity companies waived overdue payment fees.[916] The Ministerial Alliance created the Hope for Uvalde campaign in conjunction with the local bank and gave $5,500 checks to each family of a deceased or physically injured victim.[917]

---

[915] CIR Fact Finding.

[916] CIR Fact Finding.

[917] CIR Fact Finding.

Figure 6-15. English and Spanish contact information flyer for Uvalde Strong services

National Compassion Fund

The National Compassion Fund (NCF) is an arm of the National Center for Victims of Crime that helps communities impacted by mass violence gather and distribute donated funds to those impacted. The NCF works with the community by forming a steering committee made up of local leaders, providers, and victim representatives. The committee develops an application process and the protocols for fund distribution, ensuring that 100 percent of donated funds are distributed to victims or designated beneficiaries via this process.

Supporting School Personnel and Students in School Settings

In addition to the FAC/FRC, Texas HHS also contracted with MMHPI to train school personnel to support those under their care. MMHPI established the Trauma and Grief (TAG) Center, which focuses on the behavioral and mental health needs of educators, school-based clinicians, and community clinicians who have interactions with the children from Robb Elementary School.[918]

The TAG team trained the UCISD school-based clinicians[919] on a standard battery for risk screening and assessment, which is the only validated scale for kids experiencing trauma and grief.[920] Clinicians are able to complete the online screening and receive an immediate score and explanation of what the score means.[921] Based on the assessment, they can tailor necessary interventions for the child, which can include the use of Trauma and Grief Component Therapy (TGCT),[922] another intervention implemented by the TAG team.[923] TGCT is an evidence-based program for kids aged 11 and up that is geared toward children who have experienced trauma, loss, or complex grief and can be used in a school setting for groups or one-on-one interventions.[924] TGCT includes four modules (Basic Coping Skills, Trauma Processing, Grief Processing, and Future Trajectories), and based on the risk assessment results, a child can receive a customized intervention.[925] For younger children, a program called Bounce Back is being implemented,[926] which is a form of Cognitive Behavioral Intervention for Trauma in Schools.[927] The program is rated as a "promising practice"[928] by the Administration for Children and Families within the U.S. Department of Health and Human Services.[929]

---

[918] CIR Fact Finding.

[919] Of note, the UCISD school-based clinician model is unique, with only a couple of other school districts in the state of Texas implementing it. This model allows UCISD to provide direct counseling support. Under the director of recovery services, a position that was renamed after the incident, three tiers of support are provided by support counselors and school psychologists. (Source: CIR Fact Finding.)

[920] CIR Fact Finding.

[921] CIR Fact Finding.

[922] National Child Traumatic Stress Network, "Trauma and Grief Component Therapy for Adolescents."

[923] CIR Fact Finding.

[924] CIR Fact Finding.

[925] CIR Fact Finding.

[926] CIR Fact Finding.

[927] HHS, "Bounce Back."

[928] HHS, "Bounce Back." According to the U.S. Department of Health and Human Services, "A program or service is designated as a promising practice if it has at least one contrast in a study that achieves a rating of moderate or high on study design and execution and demonstrates a favorable effect on a target outcome." See HHS, "Program and Service Ratings."

[929] HHS, "Welcome."

Only children who are referred by teachers in Uvalde are being assessed through the battery.[930] The children at Robb Elementary School were referred to interventions outside of the school, which has presented challenges for coordination with school-based clinicians.[931]

In addition to the support for the children in the schools, the TAG Center and Hill Country have been providing targeted counseling support to school personnel.[932] Through support from the University of Texas San Antonio via a Substance Abuse and Mental Health Services grant, the TAG Center is providing *Parenting Matters* workshops for parents and family members.[933] This 4-week virtual workshop, offered in both English and Spanish, provides psychoeducational training to families on how trauma and grief manifest in children, how best to support the child, and how families can take care of themselves.[934] Since these workshops launched in October 2022, four have been completed with approximately 40 families.[935] The trainers are "hearing that the families are grateful that it is in Spanish, since not a lot of psychoeducation is provided in Spanish."[936]

Providing Post-Incident Support Services for Responders

Post-incident support is also essential for responders involved in an MCI. The most common traumatic stress responses of sleeplessness, headaches/stomachaches, jumpiness, irritability, poor judgment and decision-making, anxiety, and depression-like symptoms are prevalent. Responders often do not associate these symptoms with the incident when they could be directly related, even if they occur days, weeks, and months after the incident.

An increased recognition of the risk that responders face because of their work in emergencies has created more urgency around addressing the mental health of the responder population. Responder organizations are providing pre- and post-response behavioral health supports to help mitigate and address the development of compassion fatigue, secondary traumatic stress, and vicarious trauma. However, these services are not universal across responder organizations, and at times they are not comprehensive enough for the extent of the exposure.

---

[930] CIR Fact Finding.

[931] CIR Fact Finding.

[932] CIR Fact Finding.

[933] CIR Fact Finding.

[934] CIR Fact Finding.

[935] CIR Fact Finding.

[936] CIR Fact Finding.

Responder Support Services Principles

Evidence-based practice dictates that any responders, from law enforcement to medics, dispatchers, and others, be provided support services as soon after the incident as possible.[937] Several models of intervention are used by the responder community in the aftermath of a disaster response deployment. Most of these are evidence informed or emerging best practices, as gold standard research is not available. The most popular model among the first responder community is debriefings, discussed more fully in the "Debriefings" section below. Additionally, the term "debriefing" has come to be used in reference to a number of different interventions, from formal CISM debriefings (CISD) to psychoeducational/informational sessions, general group support, or peer supports. More recently, the peer support model is emerging as a best practice, as it is more acceptable to many different responder populations (in addition to victims and family members) and, with training, can ensure there is no harm done. Thus, debriefings, peer support, psychoeducational sessions, and group supports are commonly applied to help mitigate secondary traumatic stress and compassion fatigue.

There are many different paths for responders to access support services. Some agencies use their EAP; others contract with agencies who specialize in debriefings, such as the Critical Incident Stress Foundation. Other responder agencies have developed their own peer support programs, such as the Police Organization Providing Peer Assistance available to New York law enforcement officers.[938] TXDPS VESS offers CIRS, which supports TXDPS employees and their families who experience work-related or personal stress due to a critical incident.[939] And the Texas HHSC offers the CISM Network, which assists emergency response personnel who witness or survive a critical incident, such as a line-of-duty death, death of a child, multiple casualties, or a fatality scene. The CISM Network also provides responsive, supportive crisis intervention services and stress management education to any Texas emergency responder agency or organization.[940]

However these services are accessed, it is the responsibility of agencies to offer pre- and post-incident support services to their staff as an occupational health intervention. It may also be helpful to streamline the type and availability of support to responders, so they all have the same information to make informed choices as to how to access stress management, peer support, and mental health services. In Uvalde, there should be a separate place exclusively for responders to go (like the Resiliency Center) where they can receive a list of all the available responder-specific resources, potentially helping hundreds of responders find appropriate, needed support.

---

[937] National Center for PTSD, *Stress First Aid (SFA) for Law Enforcement*.

[938] Police Organization Providing Peer Assistance, "Mission."

[939] CIR Document and Data Review.

[940] Texas Health and Human Services Network, "Texas Critical Incident Stress Management Network."

Debriefings

Historically, one popular way to help law enforcement and other responders de-stress after a critical incident has been through CISD. This method has become well integrated into many disciplines within emergency response and law enforcement. The debriefing involves mandatory attendance, but voluntary participation, in homogeneous groups (responders with similar exposure) to receive psychoeducational information about what to expect in terms of physical, cognitive, emotional, behavioral, and spiritual symptoms related to the exposure; recommendations for simple, effective, and safe coping activities; as well as connection to peer supports and other resources. Caution regarding negative coping (e.g., alcohol and substance use, isolation, extensive avoidance) is also recommended.

Several studies have revealed, however, that not only is there "no evidence that single session individual psychological debriefing is a useful treatment for the prevention of post-traumatic stress disorder after traumatic incidents," but that several aspects of CISD could actually cause harm.[941] These aspects include making the debriefing process mandatory. While it is helpful for attendance at debriefing to be mandatory so that everyone hears the same information, requiring participation could be retraumatizing for a small percentage of the participants and add to their risk of developing PTSD. Additionally, retelling every aspect of what one remembers of the event is not recommended; thus, participants should not be prompted to go over details of what they saw, heard, smelled, etc. Another aspect of CISD that could be harmful is to have heterogenous groups debrief together. This is related to the exposure of different participants. If there are certain members that did not hear, see, or experience the same elements of the trauma, they should not be exposed to the traumatic material of other participants. Operational debriefings to capture and report specific response activities undertaken by those responders directly involved should be held separately.

A modified version of CISD has been adopted by many of the CISD teams that provide support after emergencies.[942]

More recently, the National Center for Post-Traumatic Stress at the U.S. Department of Veterans Affairs has developed PFA and SFA as "do no harm" interventions that have less stigma associated with them and have been more easily accepted in the law enforcement and fire communities. SFA is a framework to improve recovery from stress reactions, both in oneself and in coworkers. The model aims to support and validate good friendship, mentorship, and leadership through core actions that help to identify and address early signs of stress reactions in an ongoing way (not just after critical incidents). The goal of SFA is to identify stress reactions in oneself and others along a continuum and to help reduce the likelihood that stress outcomes develop into more severe or long-term problems. The core actions of SFA are appropriate for many occupational settings during critical events as well as for ongoing care.[943]

---

[941] Rose et al., *Psychological Debriefing for Preventing Post Traumatic Stress Disorder (PTSD)*; National Center for PTSD, "Types of Debriefing Following Disasters;" Pomerantz, "Can Posttraumatic Stress Disorder Be Prevented?"

[942] Rose et al., *Psychological Debriefing for Preventing Post Traumatic Stress Disorder (PTSD)*.

[943] Watson et al., *Stress First Aid for Firefighters and Emergency Medical Services Personnel;* National Center for PTSD, "Stress First Aid: Manuals and Resources for Health Care Workers."

Another intervention could involve a "screen and treat" model."[944] For populations at considerable risk of PTSD, such as MCI responders, consideration should be given to using a validated, brief screening tool for PTSD (such as the Harvard Trauma Questionnaire or the Post-Traumatic Diagnostic Scale) 1 month after the disaster. This practice is recommended in the United Kingdom's National Institute for Clinical Excellence Guidelines for PTSD.[945]

Peer Support

Peer support programs can also provide valuable emotional and psychological support to first responders during and following an MCI. Responder agencies should have a comprehensive support services plan (see the "Establishing and Maintaining a Responder Support Services Program" section in "Appendix F. Trauma and Support Services Supplemental Materials"), which should include an agency's peer support team. If the agency does not have one, they should establish a peer support program.

In the case of law enforcement, officers seem to be more comfortable talking to fellow officers than with mental health professionals about stressful or traumatic situations. Law enforcement officers are also often wary of using mental health services that might appear on their employment or medical records. Well-trained peer support volunteers can offer confidential support and education, providing officers with easy access to help they can trust. Some peer support programs also offer help lines to provide support for day-to-day stresses and mobile crisis teams that can be deployed to the scene of a critical incident.[946]

The Texas State Association of Fire Fighters has a peer support team that provides emotional and mental health support to firefighters in Texas.[947] The Texas EMS Alliance has an EMS peer referral program provided by the Texas HHSC.[948]

TXDPS,[949] the FBI,[950] CBP,[951] and the Bureau of Alcohol, Tobacco, Firearms and Explosives[952] all have employee support services and counseling programs for their employees. The local Uvalde agencies do not have formal programs of assistance outside of their EAPs.

---

[944] Rose et al., *Psychological Debriefing for Preventing Post Traumatic Stress Disorder (PTSD)*.

[945] DeAngelis, "The Legacy of Trauma;" National Institute for Health and Care Excellence, "Post-Traumatic Stress Disorder."

[946] Usher et al., *Preparing for the Unimaginable*.

[947] Texas State Association of Firefighters, "TSAFF Peer Support."

[948] Texas EMS Alliance, "Peer Assistance."

[949] Texas Department of Public Safety, "Human Resource Operations."

[950] FBI, *Employee Assistance Program Policy Guide*.

[951] CBP, "Employee Assistance Program (EAP)."

[952] ATF, "Benefits for Federal Employees."

Texas Law Enforcement Peer Network

Texas Senate Bill 64 established a peer support network for law enforcement officers. The bill was passed and signed into law by the governor in June 2021.[953] Before the legislature created the program, more than 70 percent of the state's law enforcement agencies had no peer counseling.[954] This bill created the Texas Law Enforcement Peer Network (TLEPN), which is a statewide program designed to give every Texas law enforcement officer access to specially trained peers to address stressors, trauma, fatigue, and other needs in order to combat workforce burnout and end police suicide and self-harm. The network, supported by MMHPI, trains and mentors police officer volunteers to assist their fellow officers on how to manage stressors both on and off the job. Each volunteer for TLEPN receives training designed by subject matter experts and approved by the Texas Commission on Law Enforcement (TCOLE) to assist their peers in handling the day-to-day stress and trauma associated with life as a police officer. The officers are provided with a safe and anonymous environment for sharing their experiences, needs, and concerns without fear of negative consequences. Anonymity and confidentiality are assured. The legislation prohibits any information from being shared or used as action against a licensee.[955]

If an officer is interested in connecting with a trained peer supporter, they use the QR code on flyers, emails, or the MyTCOLE or TLEPN websites. The officer obtains an access code from their MyTCOLE account, which ensures that the person is a certified Texas officer.

TLEPN uses the GreenLight Balance app, which can be confidentially used by law enforcement officers in need of mental health assistance.[956] The app has been in use since April 2022.[957] In the app, an officer is able to set parameters on region and then can select a peer.[958] The app allows peer supporters to stay anonymous until they are ready to share information.[959] The connection is always virtual first and then can expand to text, phone, email, or in-person meetings once the officers identify themselves.[960]

---

[953] SB 64, Relating to a peer support network for certain law enforcement personnel, Texas State Legislature.

[954] Rabb, "Texas Launches First-of-Its-Kind Mental and Emotional Support Group for Law Enforcement."

[955] University of North Texas at Dallas, "Texas Law Enforcement Peer Network."

[956] Smith, "Hundreds of Police Officers Have Signed up for Texas Mental-Health Program, Officials Say."

[957] Rabb, "Texas Launches First-of-Its-Kind Mental and Emotional Support Group for Law Enforcement."

[958] CIR Fact Finding.

[959] CIR Fact Finding.

[960] CIR Fact Finding.

Post-Incident Support for Responders in Uvalde

Post-Incident Support for Law Enforcement

At the time of the incident in Uvalde, TLEPN had 1,000 peers across the state.[961] As a result of the MCI at Robb Elementary School, TLEPN was deployed with the goal to have resources for an immediate response and then a post-180-day response.[962]

TLEPN ramped up its services in collaboration with CopLine partners by 8 p.m. on May 25, 2022.[963] CopLine is a national crisis intervention hotline for law enforcement officers and their families. It offers a confidential, 24-hour hotline answered by retired law enforcement officers who have gone through a strenuous vetting and training process to become an active listener. The retired officer–listeners help callers manage various psychosocial stressors that impact a considerable number of law enforcement officers and their families. When any officer called CopLine and referenced Uvalde or Robb Elementary School, the call takers ensured that the caller was aware of TLEPN's resources.[964]

In addition, TLEPN sent out a briefing to all TLEPN-trained peers, prepared a list of vetted and culturally competent clinical providers for the local agencies and CBP, and prepared an informational handout with information to connect affected officers with TLEPN.[965] TLEPN also directly reached out to the law enforcement executives for UPD, UCISD PD, TXDPS, and CBP.[966]

In addition to the CopLine partnership, TLEPN partnered with Endeavors, a nongovernmental agency that provides urgent clinical services for responding personnel, establishing a direct hotline and email for UPD, UCISD PD, TXDPS, and CBP and setting up space at the Endeavors clinic in San Antonio.[967] The Texas Municipal Police Association and Fraternal Order of Police also sent out an email blast encouraging their members to do a buddy check on May 25; in that email, they encouraged the use of the TLEPN network and app.[968]

TLEPN is a promising practice, since it offers services to all agencies regardless of their size or resources. For a small, rural community like Uvalde, confidentiality when seeking services is also a strong consideration. These services should continue to be marketed to all responder agencies in the Uvalde region.

---

[961] CIR Fact Finding.

[962] CIR Fact Finding.

[963] CIR Document and Data Review.

[964] CIR Fact Finding.

[965] CIR Document and Data Review.

[966] CIR Document and Data Review.

[967] CIR Document and Data Review.

[968] CIR Document and Data Review.

In addition to deployment of peer support networks, debriefings were also conducted with some responders; these debriefings received mixed responses, with some considered harmful by their participants. The TXDPS CIRS team utilized CISD for TXDPS responders.[969] Several EMS personnel participated in a CISD session and were asked questions such as, "What smell do you remember?" Many personnel left the session early because they were disturbed by the exercises and discussion.[970]

Post-Incident Support for Others in Uvalde

In addition to law enforcement responders, it is also important to consider the post-incident support provided to individuals in nontraditional first responder roles, such as victim services personnel and dispatchers. It is also critical to consider services for the family members of responders.

Victim Services Specialists

Several different victim services teams deployed to Uvalde. The FBI VSRT, for example, spent 11 days on the ground. Because there was a housing issue in Uvalde due to the media taking up so many hotel rooms, the team stayed at the dorms in the local college. This allowed them to be away from the crowds and to decompress together every evening, which they reported was immensely helpful to their sense of social and mental health support.[971] TXDPS VESS was called to the scene by the TXDPS highway patrol chief, and the team arrived in the late afternoon on May 24.[972] The team originally deployed to the school to monitor the officers and troopers, but then shifted to the FAC to assist with the death notifications.[973] TXDPS VESS was deployed for about 6 weeks and left when the FRC was established.[974]

Those victim specialists reported receiving varying degrees of support after they concluded their work in Uvalde. For example, some victim specialists were offered the opportunity to take time off, but indicated that they found it a challenge to take any time off and were restricted in when they could do so.[975] Taking the allotted time off was also difficult for personnel because many of the victim specialists had no coverage for their regularly assigned duties; when they returned to their home offices, they had a backlog of work waiting.[976] One victim specialist recommended that if someone is going to be deployed to an incident, leadership should assign someone else to cover their office,

---

[969] CIR Fact Finding.

[970] CIR Fact Finding.

[971] CIR Fact Finding.

[972] CIR Fact Finding.

[973] CIR Fact Finding.

[974] CIR Fact Finding.

[975] CIR Fact Finding.

[976] CIR Fact Finding.

without that deployed person worrying about the office work or having to take calls while on the deployment.[977] This would have helped the victim specialists feel more comfortable taking trauma leave after leaving Uvalde.[978]

There were also opportunities to debrief about the experience. Some victim specialists debriefed among themselves about what went well and what could have been improved upon,[979] and they created an action plan to ensure that they were tracking the best practices. One victim specialist noted that they were contacted by EAP personnel but felt that the outreach was inappropriate because the EAP staff were peers—either support persons or agents who had also deployed to the same situation (not trauma trained or licensed). Furthermore "[s]ome of the EAP calls turned into us [victim specialists] doing crisis interventions for the peers … They didn't do a good job of taking care of us."[980] And some victim specialists observed that the debriefs were, in some cases, contentious and took too long to schedule, given the level of trauma the victim services specialists experienced.[981] Some victim specialists did not come forward and say they were traumatized because they were afraid they would not be called out to go next time.[982]

Some victim specialists criticized the lack of mental health support or wellness services offered to their teams following their deployment. One victim specialist indicated that it was "unacceptable that we were not provided mental health assistance or anything immediately afterwards."[983] Another victim specialist stated that in August or September 2022, some victim specialists attended a critical incident seminar—Vital Hearts—that was very helpful in terms of coping and support services.[984]

Dispatch/Communications Personnel

There was no coordinated effort to reach out to the dispatch/communications personnel who responded to the Robb Elementary School shooting to provide services and support. The dispatchers took calls, including from children trapped with the shooter, and dispatched and coordinated efforts via the police radio and cellphones. There should have been follow-up on their health and wellness. The responsibilities of dispatch/communications personnel are critical to the successful conclusion of an incident, as seen at Robb Elementary. Dispatchers who listened to and tried to comfort children who were afraid or dying experienced severe stress and are at an elevated risk of developing a mental health concern as a result.

---

[977] CIR Fact Finding.

[978] CIR Fact Finding.

[979] CIR Fact Finding.

[980] CIR Fact Finding.

[981] CIR Fact Finding.

[982] CIR Fact Finding.

[983] CIR Fact Finding.

[984] CIR Fact Finding.

Although rarely exposed to direct danger, dispatchers are exposed to several intense stressors, such as: dealing with multiple, sometimes simultaneous, calls; having to make time-pressured, life-and-death decisions; having little information about, and little control over, the emergency situation; intense, confusing, and frequently hostile contact with frantic or outraged callers; and exclusion from the status and camaraderie typically shared by on-scene personnel who "get the credit" for responding to the situation.[985]

Although dispatchers are not at the scene of the incident, they still may show "many of the classic post-traumatic reactions and symptoms, but they are often overlooked by police supervisors and consulting mental health clinicians alike."[986]

Families of Law Enforcement

One group often forgotten after an MCI is the family members of the law enforcement and other responders, who can also be impacted by what is known as trauma by association.[987] Lori Kehoe, a registered nurse and the wife of the retired police chief who oversaw the law enforcement response to the 2012 Sandy Hook school shooting in Newtown, Connecticut, has spoken about the personal impact that the shooting had on her.[988] She eventually sought help for her mental health at a law enforcement spouse treatment program. She stated that part of her treatment was using eye movement desensitization and reprocessing, an approach designed to reduce the emotion that goes with the thoughts about a traumatic experience. She stated that it was highly effective.[989]

Numerous interviews with Uvalde responders revealed that their family members and those closest to them were their support network during a time when they were afraid to reach out for professional help, be in public, or interact with certain friends and family members due to the divide in the community.[990] While social support is important for a healthy trajectory, several Uvalde responders also said that their spouses and family members were seeking help of their own due to the trauma by association.[991] For some, this trauma came not only from being the family member of a responder, but also being the family member of a victim or survivor, complicating their emotions.

TXDPS and the federal law enforcement agencies all have policies and resources for the well-being of their personnel and families. This support was lacking, however, within the local law enforcement agencies that responded to Robb Elementary.

---

[985] Miller, "Law Enforcement Traumatic Stress"

[986] Miller, "Law Enforcement Traumatic Stress."

[987] Ryser, "Trauma by Association."

[988] Usher et al., *Preparing for the Unimaginable.*

[989] Usher et al., *Preparing for the Unimaginable.*

[990] CIR Fact Finding.

[991] CIR Fact Finding.

Long-Term Support

National attention to traumatic incidents like the shooting at Robb Elementary is usually short-lived—a few weeks, if that long—and such attention is often cut short as soon as another incident is reported via national news. As mentioned in the opening of this chapter, we know that the negative behavioral health impacts on the victims, families, and impacted communities do not disappear with the media. Those who experience human-caused traumatic events with intent to harm have a much longer recovery trajectory than those who experience natural disasters or human-caused accidents. Many people experiencing various types of trauma may not recognize the negative mental health impacts or identify themselves as victims for years. Some family members and victims in Uvalde shared that culturally, seeking help from mental health professionals is not something that is commonly acceptable to them.

Stigma, cost, and difficulty finding a professional with the knowledge and skills to address their traumatic responses also influence whether someone seeks professional help. Some tend to seek informal care and social support as a way of helping themselves and those close to them heal. This will help most people to adapt and recover, but those who require more formal mental health services may not seek them for a long period of time. Each person has their own timeline for adaptation and recovery. The experience of trauma will remain with them. Depending on the severity of their distress symptoms, the avoidance and denial that are common throughout the United States mean that many will not seek behavioral health care for months and even years. Even after finally acknowledging their continuing distress, emotional difficulties, depression, or anxiety-like symptoms, it may still take time for some individuals to accept the need to seek help and allow themselves to focus on their own physical and mental health self-care.

It is thus critical in responding to a tragedy like that at Robb Elementary to provide long-term care for the community, including by establishing structures to transition victim service providers, building resiliency of law enforcement and the community, facilitating the memorializing of victims, and improving communications and rebuilding trust.

Transitioning Victim Service Providers and Providing Long-term Support

Principles for Transitioning Services

As nongovernmental agencies, government law enforcement victim personnel, and other entities end their deployments following a mass violence incident, transitioning of victim services are important. This is especially important when an assigned victim service provider or victim navigator who was working with a family needs to end that involvement. When victim navigators transition out, they should make sure to provide training on victim navigation to those remaining behind before they leave. One way to achieve that goal is to plan for overlap between the team leaving and the team remaining to help with the transition.[992] Another idea is to create a checklist or benchmarking plans to help with the transition.[993]

Transitions in Uvalde

The level and success of transitions between victim service providers varied in Uvalde. When the FBI's victim service personnel left Uvalde after almost two weeks on the ground, they formally met with TXDPS Victim Services and the district attorney and her victim service coordinator.[994] This meeting was important because FBI personnel had worked much more closely with the families than TXDPS had, since the FBI had close to 20 counselors on site compared to the two to three staff from TXDPS.[995] During this meeting, the FBI team gave a briefing on every victim and family they were working with and provided folders of all the information they had learned over the course of their deployment.[996] One area of concern from the FBI was the lack of a plan for victim navigation when they left, a concern which was also shared by TXDPS Victim Service personnel.[997] At the same time, the FBI team worked with the Ecumenical Center (which was leading the FRC efforts) and the OVC TTAC team (see "Office for Victims of Crime Training and Technical Assistance Center" callout box on page 301) to transition the FRC operations.[998] When the FBI ended their deployment, they also returned all of the personal effects recovered from Robb Elementary to TXDPS to continue the process of returning personal effects as requested.[999] Even after the FBI deployment, FBI victim service personnel were still being contacted by the Uvalde County district attorney for assistance with cleaning personal effects.[1000]

Other organizations shared that they wished there had been more overlap between the team leaving and the team remaining to help with the transition[1001] or that they had been given a checklist or plan to help.

---

[992] CIR Fact Finding.

[993] CIR Fact Finding.

[994] CIR Fact Finding.

[995] CIR Fact Finding.

[996] CIR Fact Finding.

[997] CIR Fact Finding.

[998] CIR Fact Finding.

[999] CIR Fact Finding.

[1000] CIR Fact Finding.

[1001] CIR Fact Finding.

Office for Victims of Crime Training and Technical Assistance Center

The U.S. Department of Justice's Office for Victims of Crime (OVC) Training and Technical Assistance Center (TTAC) provides training and technical assistance for victim service providers and allied professionals who serve crime victims.* Under their Mass Violence and Terrorism focus area, they provide assistance for developing comprehensive plans to respond to the immediate, short-term, and long-term needs of victims of mass violence incidents.†

OVC TTAC deployed to Uvalde a week after the incident and worked to help with the FAC and planning for a permanent FRC in the future.‡ The two-person team arrived Tuesday, May 31, with a third team member participating remotely, and assisted with "guidance on just about everything with the planning for the resiliency center being a big topic."§ While on site, they explored the new space for the resiliency center; attended meetings with TXDPS, Ecumenical Center, the district attorney, and HHS; and provided resources as needed. The team left that Friday.** Since then, the team has provided assistance as needed, and they returned to Uvalde at the beginning of May 2023 to focus on long-term healing.††

---

* OVC Training and Technical Assistance Center, "About Us."

† OVC Training and Technical Assistance Center, "About Us."

‡ CIR Fact Finding.

§ CIR Fact Finding.

** CIR Fact Finding.

†† CIR Fact Finding.

The UTRC continues to have a presence in the Uvalde community. In May 2023, the UTRC moved into a permanent facility on the other side of town. With more space, the UTRC has plans for yoga classes, a community multipurpose space, and playrooms.[1002] It will be important for the center to focus on outreach for all victims and responders, including emergency medical technicians,[1003] hospital staff,[1004] and law enforcement agencies outside the City of Uvalde.[1005] Part of this work is determining the full list of victims and their families, as well as responding agencies and their personnel, since the UTRC still does not have this information.[1006] The UTRC could benefit from assistance from other FRCs, as well as connecting with the National Mass Violence Victimization Resource Center Monthly Resiliency Center Forums, which are funded by OVC.[1007]

[1002] CIR Fact Finding.

[1003] CIR Fact Finding.

[1004] CIR Fact Finding.

[1005] CIR Fact Finding.

[1006] CIR Fact Finding.

[1007] CIR Fact Finding.

Despite these efforts, victims and family members have overwhelmingly expressed that they do not have a current victim service provider or victim navigator assigned to them to help with resource and support services.[1008] Many said that the last time they had a victim service provider assigned to them was in the days immediately following the incident, and that these providers had been mainly FBI personnel.[1009] During meetings with family members, the CIR team continuously had to provide awareness and education about the UTRC, crime victim compensation, mental health resources, and other financial and support services.[1010] Family members expressed concerns with lost wages and access to reliable mental health services.[1011] This theme was also repeated with law enforcement and other responders, who were not aware of the services and support being provided by the UTRC.[1012] Finally, the two injured teachers who continue to recover from their injuries have had lapses in their support, since worker's compensation only applies during working hours. This means that during school vacations and holidays, they cannot access their therapy and other services.[1013] This is especially concerning with major breaks, such as summer break.

Memorializing the Victims

Spontaneous, temporary, and permanent memorials have become common throughout the United States and are often very public responses to large-scale disasters, including school shootings. Memorials transform private grief into public loss, allowing the larger community to take on the burden of grief together and often creating intimacy among them.[1014] When a death is sudden, violent, and untimely, it can create very intense and persistent grief, with intrusive thoughts and distressing ideas that can inhibit the healing process for many years. This may be especially true if circumstances create the sense that the death is unfair. Memorializing via public ceremonies such as moments of silence, reading of names, and storytelling is beneficial to those impacted; by remembering the victims and the event, they are appeasing their trauma and allowing reconstruction of the community. Memorial structures or objects take on meaning and agency, such as hope. Memorials remind us to take some comfort in positive memories and establish a permanent sense of connection to the person who died, which helps to navigate loss. Sharing memories also allows the emergence of lessons learned, which are necessary for any community to address disaster risk reduction in the future.

[1008] CIR Fact Finding.

[1009] CIR Fact Finding.

[1010] CIR Fact Finding.

[1011] CIR Fact Finding.

[1012] CIR Fact Finding.

[1013] CIR Fact Finding.

[1014] Pike, "Memorializing in the Aftermath of Disaster."

Funerals

Once all the victim identifications in Uvalde were completed, the medical examiner was able to start releasing bodies to the funeral homes. This process began on May 26, when nine bodies were released from the county morgue by 6 p.m.; the next day, the rest were released.[1015] Five bodies went to the Hillcrest Funeral Home and the rest stayed with the Rush Funeral Home.[1016] Professionals came from San Antonio to prepare the victims' bodies.[1017]

The subject's body was not held in the same funeral homes as the victims, but rather was sent to a funeral home outside San Antonio and held there until all the victims' bodies were released.[1018]

The two funeral homes offered to pay for the funerals, but in the end, government officials covered the financial expenses for the funerals.[1019] A gentleman from outside the community offered to make the caskets in whatever shape the families chose.[1020] By June 16, 2022, all of the victims were buried except one, who was being returned to their hometown for burial.

During the first funeral, someone from the media was able to access the services and was ultimately escorted out.[1021] After that, the fire department brought fire trucks to function as a barrier, allowing for privacy during the funerals and services.[1022]

Finally, the Uvalde County district attorney, the Mexican Consulate, and the FBI assisted family members with travel and immigration needs to ensure that the services included those not living in the United States who had close ties to the victims.[1023]

Informal Memorials

Since the day of the MCI at Robb Elementary School, informal memorials expressing the grief and sorrow of the entire Uvalde community have been set up at the site of the former school campus (see figures 6-16 on page 304 and 6-17 on page 305), at the town square (see figures 6-18, 6-19, and 6-20 on pages 305–307), and at the community welcome sign.

[1015] CIR Fact Finding.

[1016] CIR Fact Finding.

[1017] CIR Fact Finding.

[1018] CIR Fact Finding.

[1019] CIR Fact Finding.

[1020] CIR Fact Finding.

[1021] CIR Fact Finding.

[1022] CIR Fact Finding.

[1023] CIR Fact Finding.

Figure 6-16. Memorial outside of Robb Elementary School

Additionally, heeding the call to action, a local professor and artist produced the idea for the Healing Uvalde Mural Project and partnered with MAS Cultura.[1024] Together they organized and brought to life giant portrait murals of the 21 victims fatally wounded on May 24, which have been painted by over 22 artists from across the world and appear on buildings at various locations in Uvalde's downtown area.[1025] The Smithsonian National Museum of the American Latino is currently featuring an online virtual exhibit on the Healing Uvalde Mural Project, which allows anyone around the world to view these beautiful and impactful murals.[1026] These and other memorials (see figure 6-21 on page 308) have been placed in public spaces with the hope of helping the community heal. Along with providing some measure of healing, the memorials let the families know the victims matter and they will not be forgotten.[1027]

[1024] National Museum of the American Latino, "Healing Uvalde: Community Healing and Resistance."

[1025] National Museum of the American Latino, "Healing Uvalde: Community Healing and Resistance."

[1026] National Museum of the American Latino, "Healing Uvalde: Community Healing and Resistance."

[1027] Morgan, "Texas Artists Honor the Uvalde Victims with 21 Murals They Hope Will Help Healing;" Moreno-Lozano, "Color del dolor: 21 Uvalde Murals of Robb Elementary Victims Use Paint to Heal Pain."

Figure 6-17. Memorial outside of Robb Elementary School

Figure 6-18. Memorial at Uvalde Town Square

Figure 6-19. Memorial at Uvalde Town Square

Figure 6-20. Memorial at Uvalde Town Square

The temporary memorials at the plaza were reduced to just the crosses and small bunches of flowers surrounding them.[1028] Most of the toys, wilted flowers, and other gifts that people left to honor the victims were removed and are being held until a decision about how to store or otherwise use them is made.[1029] This was a difficult issue for families and community members, as would be expected, since people need to be able to come together to memorialize the victims. Just after the one-year mark of the shooting, family members were notified that some of the murals would be taken down or covered as building ownership had changed.[1030] Family members have expressed their desire for these murals to be saved and possibly become part of a permanent memorial.[1031] A permanent memorial will take an extensive amount of energy, both emotionally and in the planning and implementation process. This could be a significant activity in joining community members together toward recovery, as long as the families, victims, and others most impacted have a voice in planning where the memorial will be placed and what it will look like.

[1028] CIR Fact Finding.

[1029] CIR Fact Finding.

[1030] CIR Fact Finding.

[1031] CIR Fact Finding.

Figure 6-21. Uvalde Strong mural painted on the side of a building

El Progreso Memorial Library

Several local artists created portraits of the victims, including shadow boxes of them engaged in favorite activities and other creative arts pieces, along with compassionate notes that have been displayed at the Uvalde Memorial Library (see figures 6-22 to 6-28 on pages 309–313). The librarian reports learning how to archive trauma response materials from staff who managed to do so after the bombing of the Alfred P. Murrah federal building in Oklahoma City in 1995, and the Uvalde library has preserved thousands of items received in the aftermath of the shooting.[1032]

[1032] CIR Fact Finding.

Figure 6-22. A handmade memorial banner posted inside the Uvalde library

Figure 6-23. Display case of mementos inside the Uvalde library

Figure 6-24. Additional view of the display case of mementos inside the Uvalde library

Figure 6-25. Blanket donated to the library

Figure 6-26. Message board inside library

Communications and Rebuilding Trust

During the aftermath of an MCI, it is often comforting to the victims, families, and the community for leaders of government and law enforcement to reach out to those affected. These statements may seem reasonable and appropriate at the time. However, those statements may circle back and affect the credibility and validity of the individual leader and their respective agency/entity.

One avenue for sharing information in a consistent manner is survivor and family forums, which are discussed in "Chapter 5. Public Communications During and Following the Crisis." However, these forums are also an opportunity to cause further distress or even harm to the survivors, victims, and families when they are not conducted correctly and with compassion. For example, in the first forum on the Friday after the incident, families asked what had happened to their loved ones.[1033] After a lot of back and forth with no straight answers, a TXDPS official stood up and reenacted the incident, at one point holding their finger like a gun.[1034] The entire situation created further trauma for those present.[1035] The families ultimately left the forum early feeling angry, frustrated, and hurt.[1036]

Figure 6-27. Blanket donated to the library

[1033] CIR Fact Finding.

[1034] CIR Fact Finding.

[1035] CIR Fact Finding.

[1036] CIR Fact Finding

Figure 6-28. Painting sent to the UCISD headquarters

Local authorities made other missteps that impacted community trust. For example, the UCISD hired a former TXDPS trooper to join UCISD PD. The trooper had been at Robb Elementary on the day of the shooting and had made an offensive remark about the delayed law enforcement response. This action, captured on body-worn camera footage, enraged the Uvalde community, especially the families of the victims. As a result of this outcry, the UCISD—which had known of the former trooper's background before hiring them—dismissed the officer and eventually suspended the entire UCISD PD. The fact that the decision to hire the former trooper was made without considering their connection to the Robb Elementary response further enraged an already skeptical community.[1037] The UCISD superintendent had stated in a public board meeting that he intended to "honor our families at this time with support, love, and the commitment to move forward as a district for our students."[1038] Hiring a former TXDPS trooper who had responded to the shooting was not seen by the victims' families and the community as supportive.

Victims, family members, and other members of the Uvalde community have attended public meetings with the governor of Texas, law enforcement representatives, and numerous school board members. They have also had individual meetings with the school superintendent and other local leaders, asking to

---

[1037] CIR Fact Finding

[1038] Allen, "Uvalde School District Officials Hold Press Conference 6/09/22 Transcript."

know what happened to their children in the last 77 minutes of their lives.[1039] They have requested details from investigative reports, the district attorney's office, law enforcement, school board members, autopsy reports, and any other resource that could possibly provide them answers.[1040] Several family members indicate they cannot move forward with their lives until they know what happened to their children. Some have asked if their child was alone or near friends.[1041] Others want to know if their child would have lived, had law enforcement entered the classroom earlier.[1042] Many victims and family members have reported that no one has taken accountability for what happened, apologized, or even acknowledged that the families deserve this information.[1043] This void of information about the circumstances of their loved ones' deaths is unacceptable and has exacerbated their trauma.

"Chapter 5. Public Communications During and Following the Crisis" makes extensive recommendations regarding communications with victims and family members. Overall, those responsible for response efforts need to be trained in proper public and risk communications for a mass violence incident. Communications are a key element that will influence recovery, and any leader or responder who engages in public communications needs to know the most appropriate, trauma-informed timing, approach, language, and messaging that can help convey a sense of competence, confidence, support, and compassion from leadership to establish trust and legitimacy with the affected community members.

One-Year Commemoration

As communities approach the one-year mark after a mass violence incident or other traumatic event, mental health distress symptoms tend to rise in the weeks just prior. Research after the terrorist attacks on 9/11/2001 informs us that those impacted by the event can experience the same intensity of distressing emotions at the one-year mark as they experienced at the time of the actual event.[1044] We also know that commemorations, rituals, memorials, and community events honoring the memories of those lost and injured can help with the healing process, and that getting through what many survivors call "the year of firsts" usually results in a significant drop in distress symptoms to below the levels experienced at the time of the incident.

Family members and other loved ones often note that they do not relate to the term "closure," as it implies their memories and their pain will be gone. But we know from human behavior and history that we do not forget those whom we have loved when they die. We remember them until the day we die. What we need to do is learn to adapt, changing our lives so that we can go on living without them.

[1039] CIR Fact Finding

[1040] CIR Fact Finding

[1041] CIR Fact Finding

[1042] CIR Fact Finding

[1043] CIR Fact Finding

[1044] Draper, McCleery, and Schaedle, "Mental Health Services Support in Response to September 11th: The Central Role of the Mental Health Association of New York City."

Leadership can initiate or support those who take the reins in planning the first year commemorative events (and further commemorations thereafter). Many family members and victims choose to do something privately first, and then later with supportive others. Humans tend to function well with repetition and routine. Our bodies tend to relax when we are doing things that we are familiar with; thus, engaging in known rituals can help decrease the distress symptoms that may arise around commemorations and other significant times. Victims may engage—individually, with family members, in groups who have had similar experiences, and as a whole community—in various rituals, including vigils, prayer or meditation services, candle lightings, reading of names, and creating art.

DOJ Assistance for the One-Year Commemoration

In advance of the one-year commemoration, the DOJ Office of Community Oriented Policing Services (COPS Office) offered additional technical assistance and support to the Uvalde community. With a multidisciplinary working group from across the city and county of Uvalde, the COPS Office and a separate team of experts worked to assist in the planning and preparation of the one-year mark. The assistance included appropriate, victim-centered, trauma-informed crisis communications and assistance with operations and planning for large gatherings. The leaders worked together, endeavored to honor the families' individual choices, and created a safe space for the families to mourn on the one-year commemoration. The families and community were still hurting because they were still awaiting answers to the questions they had had for a year.

Observations and Recommendations

Observation 1: Once the children and adults were rescued from their classrooms during the evacuation process, they received limited instruction and direction on where to proceed. Due to the chaotic nature of the evacuation, children and school personnel were not adequately evaluated medically prior to being transported to the Reunification Center. As such, injured victims had delayed medical care and were at risk of further injury.

> **Recommendation 1.1:** The responsibility of responders is to rely on training and preparation to remain calm when interacting with children so as not to increase the children's fear or lessen their sense of safety.

> **Recommendation 1.2:** Evacuation planning should involve designating dynamic evacuation routes and safe spaces where the evacuees will be guided for safety, medical triage, and emotional support.

> **Recommendation 1.3:** Evacuees should be provided clear instructions and directions on where to proceed. Where resources are available, a corridor of law enforcement personnel should be set up to ensure the evacuees are unimpeded and directed in a safe manner.

Recommendation 1.4: Evacuees should be triaged and medically assessed once evacuated and prior to reunification with next of kin to ensure that all injuries are immediately identified and that victims receive necessary care.

Recommendation 1.5: As part of evacuation planning, school officials should develop an identification system for tracking students who leave with their parents or guardians, to include on site where possible.

Observation 2: Not all victims of the incident at Robb Elementary School received medical and mental health screenings following the incident.

Recommendation 2.1: Officials should ensure all victims of a mass violence incident are screened medically and assessed for mental health concerns soon after evacuation and no later than 24-48 hours post-incident.

Recommendation 2.2: In the weeks and months following an incident, victims and family members should receive follow-up or continued monitoring to ensure they are receiving the necessary mental health care and other services.

Observation 3: At least 91 children were evacuated from the school and hid in the back chapel of the funeral home (which was an active crime scene) with funeral home staff, teachers, and some parents. They were held there for hours. At the same time, law enforcement personnel, many of whom were aware of the children and staff present, moved in and out of the front of the funeral home and throughout the perimeter. At least one child in the back chapel was bleeding and required medical attention. Parents and guardians were outside of the funeral home demanding access to their children.

Recommendation 3.1: School officials should create a process that allows reunification outside of the Notification/Reception Center, whenever necessary and collect victims' names, photos of their guardians, and location of reunification.

Recommendation 3.2: As part of establishing a command post, law enforcement and other officials should secure the entire facility around the post and, if possible, evacuate civilians. In all cases, family members, community members, media, and other onlookers need to be kept out of the hot zone for their safety.

Observation 4: At the scene of Robb Elementary, some families and loved ones on the perimeter seeking information and questioning the law enforcement delay were treated with physical and verbal aggression, were shown no compassion or empathy, and received limited information.

Recommendation 4.1: The incident commander should assign a communications officer or liaison officer to provide timely and accurate information on the status of the response to family members and the community, help provide a sense of calm and trust, and maintain order.

Recommendation 4.2: Agencies should incorporate de-escalation tactics and trauma-informed, victim-centered, culturally sensitive approaches into their training on crowd control, emergency management, mass casualty response, and emergency/crisis communications.

Observation 5: Those without a formal role in the response at Robb Elementary, such as community members, school personnel, and certain responder personnel, were unnecessarily exposed to the deceased victims' bodies or the crime scene.

Recommendation 5.1: Law enforcement and other responder agencies have a responsibility to limit exposure to traumatic crime scenes—including deceased victims' bodies—to those with a formal role. Leaders should consider using tents or vehicles to shield the crime scene from view, or widening the perimeter to keep it out of sight.

Recommendation 5.2: Responding agencies should also limit the exposure of community members, school staff, and their own agency staff to traumatic materials.

Observation 6: The establishment of a Reunification Center was delayed and chaotic. Families and next of kin received conflicting instructions on the location of the center.

Recommendation 6.1: As part of disaster preparedness, communities should plan to establish a Notification/Reception Center. Planning should include determining where the center will be, who will be in charge, what security measures it will have, how the reunification process will be conducted, what screening of victims and families will take place, and how public communications and media will be handled. Establishing and managing a Notification/Reception Center should also be part of the community's critical incident drills.

Recommendation 6.2: All evacuees and their next of kin should receive information about where to receive services and resources once they leave the Notification/Reception Center. Victim advocates should contact all identified victims for follow up at various points after the incident to ensure they are aware of services and engaging in help seeking.

Observation 7: The public, including family members, witnessed child victims being brought to Uvalde Memorial Hospital (UMH) via the visitors' front door. The UMH chapel door also inadvertently provided a view of the victims in the ER.

Recommendation 7.1: Pre-incident planning and preparation should include determining where to have families wait for their loved one during a mass violence incident.

Observation 8: Family members had unreasonable challenges accessing the hospital and their injured loved ones.

Recommendation 8.1: Pre-planning should include developing a plan that removes barriers for families and loved ones to enter the hospital, receive updates, and see their loved ones.

Observation 9: The death notification process was disorganized, chaotic, and at times not conducted in a trauma-informed manner.

> **Recommendation 9.1:** Clear, accurate, and frequent communication needs to be provided to the families and loved ones at the Notification/Reception Center.

> **Recommendation 9.2:** Any information about the number of deaths or the process of identification should be communicated by a single trained and trusted leader who has verified the information and invites each family to a private space to discuss the situation involving their loved one.

> **Recommendation 9.3:** Law enforcement agencies should assign compassionate and trauma-trained personnel to collect identifying information and descriptions of victims, including clothing and photos. These individuals can also be a constant presence with the families, monitoring them for any medical or security needs, answering any questions, and ensuring they have necessities such as water, tissues, and medication.

> **Recommendation 9.4:** Victim advocates should be assigned to communicate with and assist families. Each family member of a deceased person and each injured victim should be assigned a victim advocate who works with that family/victim consistently throughout the treatment and recovery period, having frequent communications to ensure the family/victim is aware of and able to access needed services and supports.

Observation 10: The TXDPS personnel, including the civilians who conducted the death notifications, varied in training and experience. Some did not have any experience in this type of communication. However, family members described the Rangers providing the notifications as compassionate and said that the Rangers gave them the time they needed before being escorted to their car.

> **Recommendation 10.1:** Officers or other representatives tasked with death notification should be trained in accordance with agency policies and procedures. This is a highly sensitive function that should not be performed by those who have not received specialized training in how to conduct victim-centered, trauma-informed, and culturally appropriate death notifications.

Observation 11: An FBI notification team that was trained and experienced in trauma and death notifications was excluded from performing this task by staff from TXDPS who did not have the training or experience to provide this care.

> **Recommendation 11.1:** Local officials engaging in trauma and death notifications should consult national resources and ensure best practices are followed when providing these notifications. Preparedness and planning can help a locality identify areas where they have fewer trained or experienced staff, thus the areas where they need mutual aid supports.

Observation 12: The number of people in the room during the death notifications varied. Some were made by the primary team only, while others—including the first death notification—were made in the presence of other law enforcement or school staff.

Recommendation 12.1: A trauma notification team should comprise two people: one law enforcement officer and one victim advocate or behavioral health provider.

Recommendation 12.2: The number of trauma notifications that an individual makes should be closely monitored, and trauma services should be made available to those providing notifications.

Observation 13: Each agency and organization providing support services for responders operated independently. The lack of coordination among the providers complicated the process for personnel interested in obtaining support, leading to overlaps and gaps in services.

Recommendation 13.1: The post-incident command post should assign a central coordinating entity to track law enforcement and responder agencies at the incident and others who may have been involved (e.g., dispatchers, technicians, and other support services personnel). This tracking should continue after the incident to ensure that appropriate trauma-related services are offered in a coordinated effort with appropriate follow-ups.

Observation 14: Responders were not provided timely, immediate access to trauma and support services, and many reported feeling abandoned and unsupported in the weeks and months following the critical incident. Others reported being aware of the services but electing not to use them.

Recommendation 14.1: A comprehensive approach to psychological support services for responder personnel during an MCI should include immediate and ongoing interventions, education, and training to promote mental health and wellness.

Recommendation 14.2: Support services for responder personnel should be provided on site for the duration of the incident, including while law enforcement and other personnel are on site processing the scene, collecting evidence, and conducting their investigation.

Recommendation 14.3: Responder agencies should have a system for monitoring personnel stress during and in the months after an MCI. This can include regular check-ins with personnel and using assessment tools to identify individuals who may be struggling.

Recommendation 14.4: Responder agencies should develop a comprehensive and integrated trauma support plan that includes outreach, follow-up, and ongoing support for responders.

Recommendation 14.5: Leaders from responder agencies need to provide services to all personnel involved in an MCI, which for some agencies means everyone on their staff. These services should include resources on post-disaster behavioral health and secondary traumatic stress, referrals to health care providers, and peer support.

Recommendation 14.6: Responder agencies should consider memoranda of understanding (MOUs) and memoranda of agreement (MOAs) with regional agencies for trauma support services if none exist in the local area.

Observation 15: In the MCI at Robb Elementary School, 587 children and many other teachers and staff members were present. At least 17 survivors were physically injured. Due to the lack of medical and mental screening of survivors/victims and lack of information sharing among agencies and providers, the exact number of survivors/victims both directly and indirectly impacted remains unknown. Based on interviews, there are both physical and emotional needs that have been unidentified and unattended.

> **Recommendation 15.1:** Multiagency cooperation, collaboration, and communication are necessary to help identify all those impacted by an incident and ensure outreach and follow on to all victims. MOUs/MOAs between agencies, as part of a comprehensive incident response plan, should be considered.

Observation 16: Shared trauma is a concern for the Uvalde community due to compounding factors, including the size of the community and its interrelatedness. For the hundreds of law enforcement, medical, behavioral health, and government personnel who responded to this incident, shared trauma can make what happened even more overwhelming. Law enforcement's trauma is also exacerbated by the backlash from the community—as the community's trauma is exacerbated by the lack of an adequate response from law enforcement.

> **Recommendation 16.1:** Preparation for an MCI should include a plan for multiagency deployment when an incident impacts a large segment of the community. The plan should include a written agreement (e.g., MOUs, mutual aid agreements, interagency agreements, jurisdictional agreements) that can be operationalized at the time of an event and allow for rapid identification and deployment of responders. If possible, leaders should shift resources to avoid those who will not have the risk of a shared trauma experience.

> **Recommendation 16.2:** A multiagency response can also assist in the transfer of services to other victim advocates when personal relationships impede generally accepted practices and when the scope of the trauma overwhelms the local community responders.

> **Recommendation 16.3:** As part of disaster preparedness planning, communities—including law enforcement—need to plan for the aftermath of a critical incident. This planning should include generally accepted practice processes, education and training, support, and resources. A trauma-informed, culturally sensitive approach should be applied to the victims, survivors, and impacted community members, as well as responders and their families.

Observation 17: The mental health needs assessment conducted in Uvalde by MMHPI was not focused on the MCI that occurred at Robb Elementary School and did not identify all of those in the spheres of influence who may be direct and indirect victims. Based on CIR interviews, there are victims who remain unidentified and do not have the information, resources, and referrals they need to access support services.

> **Recommendation 17.1:** Following an MCI, local and government officials should conduct a needs assessment within a specific time frame and in collaboration with the county or state health services authority to capture the needs of the community. In Uvalde, the Texas Office for Victims of Crime or

another entity should complete a new, comprehensive mental health needs assessment that addresses the families, victims, responders, and community members of the impacted Uvalde community specifically. The agency performing this needs assessment should conduct extensive outreach efforts to find and attend to the victims and families in Uvalde who require guidance, referrals, and concrete assistance with obtaining funds, medical care, and behavioral health services.

Recommendation 17.2: The needs assessment should inform an outreach plan to identify impacted persons who may have been left out of the original assessment.

Recommendation 17.3: Post-incident care should ensure that all people in the spheres of influence receive outreach, support, and services either directly or through broad public communications outreach.

Recommendation 17.4: A lead community agency should be designated to take on this important activity and coordinate services with other response organizations in Uvalde and across Texas.

Observation 18: The FAC was established the day after the MCI by the FBI and TXDPS, with assistance from the American Red Cross. The FAC provided access to a robust number and type of services. A process was established to keep the space safe and secure.

Recommendation 18.1: An FAC should be established within 24 hours of an incident with a security plan that includes external law enforcement presence and a process for internal vetting of providers and those seeking services.

Recommendation 18.2: The FAC should be staffed with a robust number and type of organizations that meet the needs of the community.

Observation 19: As victims and families arrived to the FAC, they were met by a victim navigator or law enforcement victim service staff member who accompanied them throughout the process. That initial person became the point of contact for the family as long as that individual was assigned to the FAC.

Recommendation 19.1: Victims, families, and community members should be met at the FAC by a professional and be aided throughout the process by a victim navigator or victim service personnel.

Observation 20: FAC/FRC leadership never received a complete list of all victims.

Recommendation 20.1: An MOU or MOA should be signed between key organizations (such as state law enforcement organizations and the FBI) to allow for the sharing of vital victim information, ensuring that outreach is made to all victims, families, and those affected.

Observation 21: Some victims' families reported that they would not use the FAC/FRC created for the Robb Elementary incident due to concerns about the location and confidentiality.

Recommendation 21.1: The location for an FAC/FRC needs to be decided based on space, convenience, public transportation accessibility, and privacy, if possible.

Observation 22: There was limited housing available to family members, victim service personnel, and other authorities arriving from out of town. In Uvalde, authorities took creative approaches to meet the housing challenges, such as bringing in RVs, using dorms at the local college, and partnering with local ranches.

> **Recommendation 22.1:** As part of the pre-planning for an MCI, FAC leadership officials need to consider housing implications. It may be useful to model housing needs based on Uvalde or use local partnerships to reserve room blocks with the goal of having space for families, service providers, and law enforcement coming into the area.

Observation 23: Spontaneous, unaffiliated volunteers descended on Uvalde to help. Their presence was overwhelming, unmanageable, and disruptive.

> **Recommendation 23.1:** Unaffiliated, unknown, and spontaneous volunteers need to be managed by an agency with experience in identifying needs in the community, managing volunteers, and verifying the credentials or experience of those who come to help but are not affiliated with any known response agency. There is training available to learn how to address this phenomenon.[1045]

Observation 24: The FBI facility dogs were reported to be a help, especially when working with young victims as they were being interviewed.

> **Recommendation 24.1:** Therapy dogs or crisis response dogs that have completed their certification and handler training may be of help in mass violence events, especially when victims include children. Organizations can deploy certified, trained teams of dogs and handlers to support victims.[1046]

Observation 25: Victims and families experienced a number of challenges with receiving and accessing financial assistance, including redundant forms, eligibility criteria, and fraudulent accounts.

> **Recommendation 25.1:** When establishing eligibility for support programs, the "spheres of influence" or other similar models should be factors for eligibility. Eligibility criteria for state compensation programs should be in line with those established by state law and federal rules.

> **Recommendation 25.2:** A single form should be used to capture basic contact information, as well as information needed about the victim and the incident. This form should be usable for all applications for financial and other support services, to avoid adding to the burden of the victims and families.

> **Recommendation 25.3:** Law enforcement agencies need to be prepared for scammers to establish fraudulent accounts and other criminals to use a tragedy for their personal gain. The FAC should have law enforcement representation to assist families with navigating these situations.

[1045] OVC Training and Technical Assistance Center, "About Us."

[1046] Such as the FBI but also non-governmental agencies such as such as HOPE Assisted Therapy and K-9 Disaster Relief.

Recommendation 25.4: The FAC/FRC, including victim service providers, law enforcement, and other authorities, should proactively work with the families of victims and survivors to set up alerts, freeze credit reports, and quickly identify other criminal and fraudulent activity.

Recommendation 25.5: In preparing for long-term needs, the FRC should provide financial literacy and security education and awareness to victims and family members.

Observation 26: The FBI VSRT effectively handled the initial cleaning and returning of personal effects to family members. This trauma-informed, victim-centered approach demonstrated compassion and respect during a difficult task.

Recommendation 26.1: Law enforcement agencies should develop a trauma-informed, victim-centered process for returning personal effects.

Observation 27: The CISD method was used by at least two responding agencies, even though studies have revealed no evidence that one CISD session is useful treatment for the prevention of PTSD after traumatic incidents and have also shown that several aspects of CISD could cause harm.

Recommendation 27.1: Responder agencies should use a modified version of CISD, such as SFA, as part of their trauma and support services following an incident.

Observation 28: TLEPN was deployed on the day of the shooting for law enforcement officers and their families. TLEPN partnered with CopLine and Endeavors to provide urgent clinical services for responding personnel.

Recommendation 28.1: Agencies should include peer support services and resources in their comprehensive support services plan, which may include regional or statewide networks.

Observation 29: FBI VSD rapidly deployed a team that took the lead for victim services in the first two weeks. The team received praise from victims, family members, and other service providers. Victim service personnel from TXDPS and the FBI reported that they did not receive enough support from their agencies when the deployment ended.

Recommendation 29.1: Agency leadership needs to support the supporters and ensure that adequate trauma leave is provided to help deployed personnel decompress and return from a traumatic event.

Recommendation 29.2: Responder agencies should provide in-depth trauma and counseling services to staff who provide victim services at an MCI.

Recommendation 29.3: Agency leadership should consider offering or expanding the window for trauma leave to ensure that a deployed member can take the necessary leave and will not be perceived as incapable of future deployments simply because they utilized available resources.

Observation 30: Law enforcement victim services personnel were deployed without coverage of their normal victim service duties.

Recommendation 30.1: Agency leaders should ensure there is coverage for the normal duties of deployed personnel so that the deployed individuals can focus on their deployment and take the necessary leave.

Observation 31: The mental health needs of the dispatchers exposed to the stress in this incident were unidentified and untreated.

Recommendation 31.1: Dispatchers should be recognized as first responders to a critical incident and screened for services. They should be included in efforts to provide mental health screenings and care as well as peer and other supports post-incident. All agencies should have policies and resources for the well-being of their personnel and families.

Recommendation 31.2: The definition of responders should be expanded, consistent with generally accepted practices, to include disciplines other than law enforcement, fire, and rescue staff, such as dispatchers, EMTs, health care providers, ambulance drivers, behavioral health providers, and faith-based leaders. This should be reflected in all support services provided by resiliency centers, nongovernmental and governmental entities, and other support service providers.

Observation 32: Family members of law enforcement and other responders became the support system for the responders and may not be receiving assistance themselves.

Recommendation 32.1: When developing or reviewing trauma support and counseling services, agencies should include spouses, partners, and family members of responders.

Observation 33: Responder agencies are not prepared for the long-term impact of the incident.

Recommendation 33.1: Responder agencies should organize and implement a formalized plan that outlines the roles and responsibilities of each stakeholder for the effective management of emotional and trauma support.

Recommendation 33.2: Responder agencies should provide initial support services within hours of a critical incident and within 24 hours should provide access to services such as PFA/SFA, crisis counseling, debriefing, and peer support.

Recommendation 33.3: Responder leaders can reduce the stigma associated with seeking help for emotional and psychological distress and can promote the importance of self-care through training, education, and effective messaging and modeling.

Recommendation 33.4: After a critical incident, responder agencies should evaluate the effectiveness of their emotional and trauma support services. This can be achieved through gathering feedback from responders and their family members and using this information to improve future services and support.

Observation 34: FBI victim services personnel transitioned services for victims and families to TXDPS and the Uvalde County District Attorney's Office prior to their departure. However, TXDPS and the District Attorney's Office did not have enough personnel to provide the needed level of care.

> **Recommendation 34.1:** A transition plan and a warm, organized handoff should occur whenever law enforcement victim services personnel, or other victim navigators, transition away from the FAC/FRC.

> **Recommendation 34.2:** A checklist should be used by the FAC/FRC to ensure that all transitions are conducted in a deliberate and compassionate manner.

> **Recommendation 34.3:** Agencies should consider MOUs/MOAs with neighboring or state agencies for assistance providing victim services.

Observation 35: Victims require multiple efforts by victim advocates to contact them and to share information about available resources. Months after the shooting at Robb Elementary, victims and family members reportedly did not have active victim compensation applications on file and had little to no information about what medical, mental health, lost wages, or other resources they may be eligible for.

> **Recommendation 35.1:** Research on trauma-informed care teaches that some victims will have memory deficits and other cognitive impacts as a result of the brain's response to the trauma. This means that advocates and other support staff need to provide continuous support, follow on, and monitoring to ensure that applications for services and referrals are completed.

Observation 36: The City of Uvalde eventually identified another building that was renovated to meet the longer-term needs of the UTRC. This permanent site in town is an inviting and comfortable space to meet with victims, family members, and other community members.

> **Recommendation 36.1:** The UTRC should offer more community-based activities with opportunities for victims, family members, and the community to come together, receive services, and share space to help them on their recovery path.

> **Recommendation 36.2:** The UTRC should engage with the OVC-funded National Mass Violence Victimization Resource Center Resiliency Center Director Forum network. Connecting with other FRCs can help the UTRC ensure it is meeting the Uvalde community's needs in a trauma-informed, victim-centered approach and appropriate cultural adaptations.[1047]

> **Recommendation 36.3:** The UTRC must develop a plan to ensure all victims, family members, and responders receive outreach and education on its services, crime victim compensation, and resources.

[1047] OVC Training and Technical Assistance Center, *"Helping Victims of Mass Violence and Terrorism: How to Design and Implement a Community Resiliency Center."*

Observation 37: Some family members and victims in Uvalde shared that seeking help from mental health professionals is not something that is commonly acceptable to them culturally. They tend to seek informal care and social support as a way of helping themselves and those they care about. This may help some people to adapt and recover, but those who require formal mental health services for a diagnosable mental health concern may not seek services for a long period of time.

> **Recommendation 37.1:** The UTRC should plan to sustain this space and its offerings, especially since support services need to be made available for an extended period of time in this community.

> **Recommendation 37.2:** Behavioral health services offered in various modalities, such as individual, group, and family therapies, may help people feel more comfortable, as they will be able to choose which modality they prefer.

> **Recommendation 37.3:** Evidence-based mental health care is necessary so that victims and family members do not become discouraged by continuing symptoms and a lack of effective treatment.

> **Recommendation 37.4:** Training on evidence-based behavioral health supports—including resilience-building activities, cognitive behavioral therapy for disaster distress, peer support for victims of mass violence, writing for recovery, and other supports—should begin as soon as possible so that providers in the community have the knowledge and skills to provide effective mental health treatment.

> **Recommendation 37.5:** Efforts to attract professionals who are interested and able to live and work in the Uvalde community also need to begin as soon as possible.

> **Recommendation 37.6:** Advocating for the broader use of teletherapy could increase access to competent providers who could serve this highly impacted population.

Observation 38: Due to the nature of the deaths, and the young age and the number of victims, funeral arrangements took longer than they normally would. Families had to navigate the process with limited emotional and mental support.

> **Recommendation 38.1:** Victim advocates and grief specialists can support victims' families through the funeral arrangement process and help the community determine where to hold activities like candlelight vigils.

Observation 39: Media and other onlookers attempted to access the funerals and services for some of the victims.

> **Recommendation 39.1:** Law enforcement and other governmental officials need to create a security plan to protect the safety, security, and privacy of those mourning their loved ones during funerals for an MCI.

Recommendation 39.2: As part of the planning for a disaster, authorities should assign a public information officer or communications representative who will work with the media in advance of funerals. This role should include setting up a media staging area as well as consulting with families to determine if relatives or friends would like to speak on their behalf.

Observation 40: Since the day of the incident, informal memorials expressing the grief and sorrow of the entire Uvalde community have been set up at the site of the former school campus and across town. The Healing Uvalde Mural Project, the result of a partnership between a local artist and a nonprofit, organized a creative collaborative memorial across downtown. Artists from across the world came to Uvalde to paint giant portrait murals of the 21 victims fatally wounded on May 24. The Smithsonian National Museum of the American Latino is currently featuring an online virtual exhibit, which allows anyone around the world to view these beautiful and impactful murals.

Observation 41: Items left at informal memorials in Uvalde have been moved, removed, or cleared out without proper discussion and planning with the victims and family members.

Recommendation 41.1: Victims and family members need to be involved in the movement of any informal memorials prior to action being taken.

Observation 42: As of the end of the review period, there is no known plan for gathering representative community members together to plan a permanent memorial to those killed, injured, and impacted on May 24, 2022.

Recommendation 42.1: The planning for a permanent memorial should include a broad community coalition of advisers, including survivors, family members of victims, school personnel, victim service providers, and other relevant stakeholders.

Recommendation 42.2: The memorial should honor those lost, those injured, and all those directly impacted by the incident.

Observation 43: The Uvalde community continues to need support and guidance as it struggles with the negative impacts of the failed response, a lack of accountability for those implicated in this failure, and remaining gaps in the information about what happened to their loved ones.

Recommendation 43.1: The Uvalde community could benefit from long-term support from grief and loss specialists who can help guide the community in rituals, memorial planning, spiritual activities, and social supports as they move through the next few years.

Recommendation 43.2: Community organizers, disaster behavioral health specialists, victim support staff, and those skilled in helping communities repair societal damage and build resilience may be able to help Uvalde get onto a recovery path. This will require strong, compassionate, collaborative, and honest efforts by community leadership.

Chapter 7. School Safety and Security

Introduction

Active shooter incidents in U.S. schools have been a tragic reality for decades. The Columbine High School shooting in 1999 is widely recognized as a watershed moment when schools across the country began reassessing their security posture; increasing training and preparedness for teachers and students; enhancing physical security, planning, and policy development in attempts to both prevent and better respond to such crises; and building stronger ties with local law enforcement agencies. Since that time, school shootings have continued to claim innocent lives, devastate families and communities nationwide, and shock the national conscience.

Between 2000 and 2022, the Federal Bureau of Investigation (FBI) estimated that there were 68 active shooter incidents in educational settings[1048] (e.g., schools, institutions of higher education) nationwide. During this time frame, there were 206 lives lost, 279 injuries (see figure 7-1), and countless survivors, family members, communities, and, at times, the entire nation impacted by the trauma, grief, and devastation wrought by such tragedies.[1049] The dates, locations, and circumstances of these incidents have often been etched inside a collective consciousness, only to be evoked yet again when another such a tragedy strikes.

Figure 7-1. School-based active shooter casualties 2000–2022

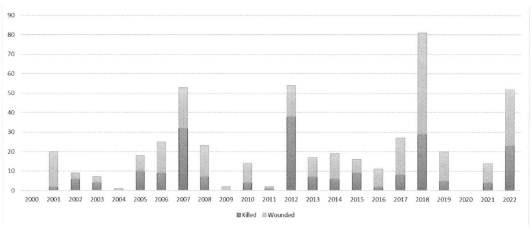

Source Data: FBI

[1048] These numbers include all educational settings, including colleges and universities.

[1049] FBI, *Active Shooter Incidents: 20-Year Review, 2000–2019*.

While the primary goal of school districts across the United States is to educate, they must also prepare for myriad threats to school safety and security, ranging widely in scale and seriousness, including incidents of mass violence. In addition to certain safety functions maintained at the school district administration level—such as threat assessment teams, school safety committees, student counseling services, and physical security maintenance and upgrades—many school districts throughout the nation partner with local law enforcement agencies to establish school resource officer programs, and some create their own police departments. Among Texas' 1,207 independent school districts,[1050] 309 (~26 percent) have their own police department, including the Uvalde Consolidated Independent School District (UCISD).[1051]

About the School District

UCISD is a public school district serving the educational needs of pre-K through 12th grade students in Uvalde County. In the 2021–2022 school year, UCISD's student population was 4,103 students.[1052] UCISD's eight school buildings range in age. The oldest is over 100 years old and the newest is Uvalde High School, which is approximately 40 years old.[1053] Robb Elementary was built in 1955 (68 years ago), and newer buildings were constructed on campus approximately 23 years ago.[1054]

The overarching governance structure for UCISD is common in communities throughout the United States. The school district is governed by an elected Board of Trustees. The board consists of 7 members who are elected to 2-year terms. Three trustees are at-large representatives, and there are two representatives from each zone (East and West) within the school district.[1055] The board establishes policies, procedures, and strategic direction for the school district.

The superintendent is hired by the board to serve as the chief executive of the school district and take leadership in the implementation of the board's policies, procedures, and strategic direction. The superintendent is the overarching authority for all school district functions, including curriculum development, human resources, budgeting, finance, and, as of 2018, the school district's established police department. The superintendent informs and advises the Board of Trustees, while representing campus, parent, and community concerns and interests. Like many school districts, the central office is supported by various assistant superintendents and directors who are tasked with the implementation of districtwide and specialized functions.

[1050] Texas Education Agency, "Texas Schools."

[1051] María Méndez, "Almost 100 Texas School Districts."

[1052] *Texas Tribune*, "Uvalde CISD."

[1053] Investigative Committee, *Robb Elementary Shooting Interim Report*.

[1054] Investigative Committee, *Robb Elementary Shooting Interim Report*.

[1055] UCISD, "U.C.I.S.D. School Board."

UCISD is among the growing number of school districts that have established its own police department. The UCISD Police Department (UCISD PD) was established in 2018 with a sworn force of five officers, plus one security officer, who is not a sworn law enforcement officer. The sworn force included three full-time police officers, in addition to a chief and lieutenant. Notably, UCISD terminated the employment of its entire police department in October 2022 and began hiring new officers, starting with a new chief. UCISD also added two nonsworn safety monitor positions to the police department. The chief of police is hired by and reports directly to the UCISD superintendent.

Scope

The scope of this review encompasses the fundamental safety and security apparatus of UCISD on May 24, 2022. The Critical Incident Review (CIR) Team conducted interviews with dozens of UCISD personnel, including administrators, principals, teachers, school police officers, and staff from across the school district, with special focus on individuals connected to Robb Elementary. The team also reviewed UCISD policies, procedures, and other data and documentation related to key safety and security functions of the school district, including threat assessment, emergency operations planning, teacher and staff training, safety drills, maintenance records, audits, and other UCISD reports and records. Interviews conducted as part of the Texas Rangers' criminal investigation into the incident were also reviewed, as appropriate.

From this review, the CIR team derived a baseline understanding of UCISD's safety and security posture on May 24, 2022, and compared it to industry standards and best practices. In preparing this chapter, the CIR team benefited from the expertise of subject matter experts, who assisted in developing the observations and recommendations for this chapter. Where not otherwise cited, the practices identified in this chapter derive from the experts' collective knowledge and experience.

The remainder of this chapter is organized by the following subtopics:

- Active Shooter Response—This section describes UCISD policies and procedures on active shooter response and incident command.

- Safety and Security Planning—This section describes district-wide and campus planning processes around school safety.

- UCISD Police Department (UCISD PD) —This section describes the establishment of the school district's police department.

- Doors, Locks, Maintenance, and Magnets—This section describes UCISD policy and compliance regarding locked doors on campus.

- Emergency Alerts—This section describes the school districts' use of electronic emergency alert systems.

- Drills and Exercises—This section describes the school districts drill and exercise requirements and history.

Under each subtopic, the CIR team provides a summary of UCISD functions and conclude with a series of observations and recommendations. While prevention of mass shooter threats in schools is undoubtedly a critically important topic, a comprehensive discussion of prevention policies and practices, including student behavioral health and support services, is beyond the scope of this review. For resources on those topics, please visit www.schoolsafety.gov.

Active Shooter Response at UCISD—Who's in Charge?

Texas law requires that each school district adopt and implement a multihazard emergency operations plan to address prevention, mitigation, preparedness, response, and recovery.[1056] The state requirements are comprehensive and include training, communication capabilities, drills and exercises, coordination with other agencies, audits, providing trauma-informed care, chain of command, and active shooter response.[1057] UCISD's Emergency Operations Plan (EOP) is reviewed and updated by UCISD's Safety and Security Committee annually and submitted to the Texas Education Agency (TEA). The UCISD active shooter policy was one of the few school district policies in Texas deemed to be viable.[1058]

Policy and MOU in Place on May 24

The school district's EOP in place on May 24 made clear that the district was not an emergency response organization and depended on local emergency first responders for life safety and protection, including the services of local law enforcement, fire, and emergency medical and health personnel. An updated plan for the 2022–2023 school year also addresses this issue clearly.

The EOP expresses a commitment to the National Incident Management System (NIMS) and the Incident Command System (ICS) principles and acknowledges some fundamental concepts, such as the first responder on scene being designated incident commander until relieved by a more qualified individual and that the convergence of multiple agencies on scene will necessitate the establishment of a unified command structure. At the same time, the district's plan makes specific designations regarding the incident commander role.

[1056] TEX. ED. CODE § 37.108(g); Safety and Security Audit.

[1057] TEX. ED. CODE § 37.108(g); Safety and Security Audit; Texas School Safety Center, "School Safety Law Toolkit: 86th Session Updates (2019)."

[1058] CIR Fact Finding; Investigative Committee, *Robb Elementary Shooting Interim Report.*

UCISD PD did not have an active shooter policy; however, the school district's active shooter response protocol in place on May 24 was established in 2020 and is included as an annex to the EOP. It was authored by UCISD PD Chief Pete Arredondo and signed off on by the UCISD public safety director. The protocol designates the school district police chief as the incident commander, with the responsibility of implementing the ICS and establishing an incident command post (ICP). Specifically, the plan states—

> Once an active shooter has been verified, the District police department Chief will become the person in control of the efforts of all law enforcement and first responders that arrive at the scene. [1059]

The protocol further states that other responding law enforcement agencies are under the command of the school police chief as incident commander. [1060] The plan states that local law enforcement and first responders will "follow direction of the ICS leader to ensure proper procedures are followed. Accept assigned roles of ICS leader." [1061]

The school district's active EOP on May 24 included a memorandum of understanding (MOU) with only one of the 23 law enforcement agencies that responded: the Uvalde Police Department (UPD). The MOU delineates UCISD PD as having broad jurisdiction to respond to all crimes on or near district property during regular school hours, while attending school-sponsored events, or while traveling directly to and from the school or school-sponsored events. [1062] According to the MOU, UPD will respond during evenings, weekends, and holidays when UCISD generally does not have field units in operation. The MOU also establishes the expectation that both agencies will make general efforts to openly coordinate and communicate, in addition to each assigning a liaison officer. The MOU does not address incident command or any instances in which UPD would be operating alongside UCISD PD on or off school property.

Based on UCISD's EOP on May 24, the appropriate incident command would be as follows: the first responder on scene assumes the position of incident commander until a more experienced and qualified individual arrives on scene and relieves them of that duty; when the UCISD PD chief arrives on scene, they assume ultimate incident command; and as more agencies arrive on scene, a unified command should be established, of which UCISD PD is a part (see "Chapter 3. Leadership, Incident Command, and Coordination" for an in-depth analysis of incident command on May 24).

On May 24, UCISD PD officers, including the chief of police, were on scene at or around the same time that UPD officers, including UPD Acting Chief Mariano Pargas, arrived on scene. The collection of first officers on scene were made up entirely of UCISD PD and UPD officers. All of the first responding officers were aware of the active shooter incident (i.e., "verified," as per UCISD's EOP), and according to UCISD PD's MOU with UPD, this put UCISD PD Chief Arredondo in command of the law enforcement response

---

[1059] CIR Document and Data Request.

[1060] CIR Document and Data Request.

[1061] CIR Document and Data Request.

[1062] CIR Document and Data Request.

at that time. (For a full discussion on this and the MOU, see "Chapter 3. Leadership, Incident Command, and Coordination" and "Chapter 8. Pre-Incident Planning and Preparation.") As more agencies arrived on scene, UCISD's EOP stipulates that a unified command should be set up. The number of agencies and complexity of the scene that would necessitate a unified command are not explicitly stated.

Post–May 24 Updates

In August 2022, the school district's EOP was updated to reflect that Texas Department of Public Safety (TXDPS) troopers were assigned to temporary duties at UCISD, while the school district sought termination of Chief Arredondo and was actively seeking new officers. UCISD's Active Shooter Annex no longer designates any specific individual or title responsible for incident command in such an incident. However, the EOP designates a TXDPS officer as the authoritative decisionmaker and incident commander for all incidents, reflecting the fact that UCISD PD did not have an active police chief at the time of the EOP revision:[1063]

> During the 2022–2023 school year Uvalde CISD will have DPS officers located on each campus. During this time, if there is an event requiring an Incident Commander, the DPS will take on the role of Incident Commander.[1064]

An updated MOU, dated August 23, 2022, clearly establishes UCISD PD as the default jurisdictional authority and implies incident command will remain with UCISD unless explicitly relinquished.

> In the event that the Uvalde Police Department responds to assist the U.C.I.S.D. Police Department on district property, protocols followed will be those of U.C.I.S.D. Police Department unless otherwise communicated by an Incident Commander, at which time the Uvalde Police Department will follow all UPD protocols, policies and procedures. UPD's response will be limited to assisting the U.C.I.S.D. Police Department Incident Commander unless and until the U.C.I.S.D. Police Department commander directly communicates otherwise.[1065]

The current, updated EOP does not include any specific provision regarding the role of local law enforcement and first responders who respond to an emergency incident on school property. However, UCISD PD's jurisdictional boundary and explicit role in incident command is stronger in the recently developed MOU and clearly establishes UCISD PD as the agency in charge if UPD responds to an incident within UCISD's jurisdiction, unless that command is relinquished. The MOU did not specify, as the EOP did, that TXDPS officers would be located at UCISD school districts for the 2022–2023 school year and that a TXDPS officer would be the incident commander.

[1063] This reflects the latest EOP provided to DOJ by UCISD for the purpose of this review.

[1064] CIR Document and Data Request.

[1065] CIR Document and Data Request.

Recognizing the lack of standard procedures and the need to rebuild an effectively defunct school police department, after the entire force was terminated, UCISD requested a management study from the Texas Police Chiefs Association, which completed a draft of their study in October 2022. In addressing incident command during an emergency, the report recommends the police chief be designated as incident commander for all district emergency operations.[1066]

Safety and Security Planning and Organization within UCISD

There are generally two safety and security administrative bodies within the UCISD—a district-level Safety and Security Committee, which is required by state law; and Campus Safety Teams, which are required by UCISD's EOP. These components of UCISD's bureaucracy are intended to serve distinct and complementary safety and security needs within the district.

School Safety and Security Committee

Texas state law requires school districts to have a School Safety and Security Committee, which must include, "to the greatest extent practicable," the following representatives:[1067]

- One or more representatives of an office of emergency management of a county or city in which the district is located

- One or more representatives of the local police department or sheriff's office

- One or more representatives of the district's police department, if applicable

- President of the district's board of trustees

- Member of the district's board of trustees other than the president

- District's superintendent

- One or more designees of the district's superintendent, one of whom must be a classroom teacher in the district

- If the district partners with an open-enrollment charter school to provide instruction to students, a member of the open-enrollment charter school's governing body or a designee of the governing body

- Two parents or guardians of students enrolled in the district

The purpose of the committee is to participate in the emergency operations planning process, provide recommendations to the board of trustees and district administrators on updates, respond to data and information requests pursuant to school safety and security audits, and consult with local law enforcement on public safety issues around school district campuses.[1068]

[1066] CIR Document and Data Request.

[1067] TEX. EDUC. CODE § 37.109.

[1068] TEX. EDUC. CODE § 37.109.

UCISD's School Safety and Security Committee was established in May 2020[1069] and, in compliance with the Texas Education Code, convened 7 times in the 2 years preceding the incident at Robb Elementary, covering a range of topics including cyberbullying, the school's safety audit, an all hazards analysis, COVID-19 concerns, and on more than one occasion, "bailouts"—that is, instances in which suspected undocumented migrants flee from law enforcement, initiating a high-speed vehicular pursuit.

This committee is charged with reviewing the EOP and UCISD published notice of agendas stating the committee would meet to do that review. However CIR review of the minutes from those meetings do not note the committee as having received or approved the EOP.

The composition of UCISD's committee has been generally reflective of the guidance offered in state law. Representatives are selected by the heads of the respective agencies being represented. Teacher and parent representatives are selected by the UCISD superintendent. UPD has representation on the committee, but UCSO does not, and committee members recognized this as a weakness in its composition.

Campus Safety Planning and Teams

In addition to the district-level committee described above, each campus is required to have its own Campus Safety Team, developed by the principal to meet the needs of that campus.[1070] These teams are required to meet at least twice annually and support the district's overarching safety and security apparatus, including participating in audit processes and supporting the planning and execution of training, drills, and exercises on their campus. According to the EOP, Campus Safety Team procedures are supposed to be described in greater detail in each Campus Safety Plan. However, none of the Campus Safety Plans provided to the CIR team included such information. Many of the UCISD staff interviewed were unaware of Campus Safety Teams or plans on their campuses.

Although the plans are intended to be tailored to the unique needs of each campus, they include largely template information, including the following:

- A list of UCISD preventive security measures/assets

- Instructions for submitting maintenance work orders

- Forms for documenting school safety drills

- Fact sheets on standard response protocols: lockout, lockdown, evacuate, and shelter in place

- Standard reunification method instructions[1071]

[1069] CIR Document and Data Review.

[1070] CIR Document and Data Review.

[1071] Handout produced and distributed by the I Love You Guys Foundation.

Below, the CIR team provides an overview specifically of the Robb Elementary Campus Safety Plan that was in place on May 24, 2022, focusing on areas that played a role in the incident and overall response.

Preventative Security Measures. The plan includes a list of 11 security measures, some of which were available or present at Robb Elementary and some of which were not. Police officers are listed first; however, UCISD PD, with its five sworn-member force, is such a small police department that it did not have enough officers to maintain a constant presence at each campus. Reportedly, UCISD PD officers would visit each of the eight campuses at least once a day, primarily for door checks.[1072] The plan also lists security staff and threat assessment teams. While UCISD had both at the district level, neither were campus-specific functions at Robb Elementary.

Campus Mitigation Checklist. The checklist includes a classroom-specific list, as well as exterior campus issues that are intended to be managed/mitigated, mostly through upkeep and maintenance. The plan indicates that three areas of fencing were in need of repair.[1073] Another item on the classroom list is that "doors can be locked." The Robb plan does not indicate any concerns with this item on its Campus Safety Plan. However, some interviewees from UCISD indicated that doors not closing or locking properly were a continual issue on campus.

Instructions for Submitting Work Orders. Includes clear guidance on submitting a work order via UCISD's online system.

Drill Documentation Forms. Standard templates provided by the Texas School Safety Center and Texas Department of Insurance.

Standard Response Protocols. An infographic highlighting lockout, lockdown, evacuation, and shelter protocols.

Since May 24, 2022, UCISD has developed a more consistent framework for emergency operations plans. As noted by one school administrator, "where the content is the same, but the context is unique," relative to the size and grade level of the schools, "the district is supportive of unique development of safety planning for each campus, but with a consistent foundation and framework."[1074]

[1072] CIR Fact Finding.

[1073] The fencing issues described indicate that they had been pulled up from the bottom or "kicked in." These issues did not impact the shooting subject's access to the school on May 24 because he climbed over the fence, which is approximately 5 feet tall.

[1074] CIR Fact Finding.

UCISD Police Department

UCISD established its police department during the 2018 school year. Pursuant to Chapter 37 of the Education Code, the UCISD board set forth a policy authorizing commissioned peace officers to enforce rules adopted by the board and focused on the protection of school district students, staff, buildings, and grounds. The UCISD PD is directed to enforce appropriate rules for the orderly conduct of the district in carrying out its purposes and objectives as a separate jurisdiction relating to the conduct of its students and personnel.[1075]

In a peace officer's jurisdiction, a peace officer commissioned by the board

- has the powers, privileges, and immunities of peace officers;

- may enforce all laws, including municipal ordinances, county ordinances, and state laws;

- may take a child into custody in accordance with Family Code Chapter 52 or Code of Criminal Procedure 45.058;

- may dispose of cases in accordance with Family Code 52.03 or 52.031.

The UCISD board determines the scope of the on-duty and off-duty law enforcement activities of UCISD PD officers. The district must authorize, in writing, any off-duty law enforcement activities performed by a UCISD PD officer.

A UCISD PD officer may provide assistance to another law enforcement agency. The school district may contract with a political subdivision for the jurisdiction of a UCISD PD officer to include all territory in the jurisdiction of the political subdivision.[1076]

UCISD PD was established with a chief, one assistant chief, and three commissioned officers. Under state law and in accordance with requirements set forth by the Texas Commission on Law Enforcement (TCOLE), certified school-based peace officers must successfully complete the School-Based Law Enforcement (SBLE) Training Program within 180 days of employment.[1077]

School district leadership created its own police department with the rationale that students and staff should be policed by their own officers as opposed to an outside law enforcement agency. At the time, some city government leaders and segments of the Uvalde community were opposed to the idea of UCISD PD.[1078] At the time, throughout the state of Texas, there was a significant spike in the number of new school district police departments, as reported by the *Texas Tribune* (see figure 7-2 on page 338).[1079]

[1075] Tex. Ed. Code § 37.103.

[1076] CIR Document and Data Review.

[1077] TCOLE, "School Based Law Enforcement Training."

[1078] CIR Fact Finding.

[1079] Méndez, "Almost 100 Texas School Districts Have Added Their Own Police Departments since 2017, but Not Everyone Feels Safer."

Figure 7-2. Newly established school police departments in Texas, 2010–2022

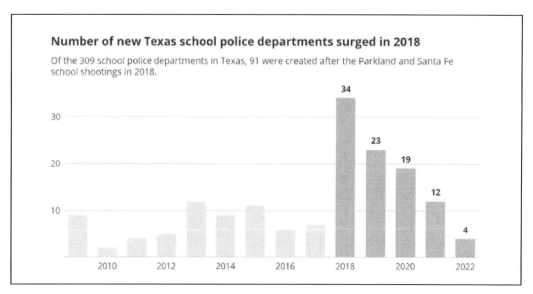

Source: Méndez, "Almost 100 Texas School Districts Have Added Their Own Police Departments since 2017, but Not Everyone Feels Safer."

Policies and Procedures

The first UCISD PD chief was hired by a former school superintendent but subsequently removed from the position by their successor. The new chief, Pete Arredondo, was hired in 2020, but without the professional assistance of anyone experienced in the hiring of police executives,[1080] particularly for school safety and security. Moreover, policing, school safety, and the development of policies and procedures were the sole responsibility of the new school police chief. According to the then-superintendent, it was most important that district leadership focus on teaching and learning, and he was not involved in safety planning or school police training. Instead, that role was assigned to a school public safety director, who was liaison to the superintendent on such issues. The public safety director was not a sworn member of UCISD PD; this was a UCISD administrator position.

Nearly 4 years into its existence, UCISD PD did not have any standard operating procedures, which, consistent with generally accepted professional practices, are a foundational and fundamental requirement. At the time this CIR began, there were still no policies and procedures. None of the officers interviewed as part of this review had ever seen a policy or procedure manual for the police department. In October 2022, the Texas Police Chiefs Association completed a management study at the request of UCISD and found that UCISD PD still did not have a policy manual; the association listed creating a policy manual as one of its most critical recommendations.[1081]

[1080] For example, professional law enforcement association staff, current or former law enforcement executives, or other parties who could provide insight into the executive hiring process and selection for law enforcement.

[1081] CIR Document and Data Review.

Training

The Texas Legislature controls the number of training hours a peace officer in the state of Texas must successfully complete to maintain peace officer status—40 hours every 2 years.[1082] Additionally, the Texas Legislature has the authority to mandate a portion of those 40 hours for specific training courses for all peace officers across the state or for certain segments of peace officers (e.g., SBLE training for school resource officers and school district police officers).

On May 24, UCISD PD had in its employ five experienced officers (see table 7-1). All of them had received a TCOLE-accredited active shooter training in December 2021, just 6 months prior to the incident. Just two had received incident command training, one of whom was Chief Arredondo (see "Chapter 3. Leadership, Incident Command, and Coordination" for a full treatment of this issue as it unfolded on May 24).

Table 7-1. UCISD PD officer training as of May 24, 2022

	UCISD Lt.	UCISD Ofc. 1*	UCISD PD Chief Arredondo*	UCISD Ofc. 2*	UCISD Ofc. 3
Total Policing (Years/Months)	32y 7m	14y 7m	28y 9m	11y 10m	5y 10m
Active Shooter Training (SBLE and Other)	Yes	Yes	Yes	Yes	Yes
ICS	Yes	No	Yes	No	No
Patrol/Advanced Tactical Training (Special Weapons and Tactics, Rifle, etc.)	Yes	Yes	Yes	Yes	No
Leadership/Command Training	Yes	Yes	Yes	Yes	No
SBLE Training (Non-Active Shooter)	Yes	Yes	Yes	Yes	Yes
Crisis Intervention Training (Negotiator, Hostage, Communications, etc.)	Yes	Yes	Yes	Yes	Yes

* Represents one of the 11 officers first on scene at Robb Elementary School on May 24, 2022

Source: CIR Document and Data Review; CIR Training Analysis

Threat Assessment Team and Process

School threat assessment is a comprehensive process that educators, law enforcement, and mental health professionals undertake to identify, assess, and manage potential threats in a school environment. It aims to prevent acts of violence and harmful behaviors while enhancing school safety. The process involves identifying individuals who exhibit behaviors indicating a potential for harm to themselves or others; analyzing the credibility, nature, and seriousness of the threat; and devising intervention strategies. These strategies can include mental health support or disciplinary action,

---

[1082] TCOLE, "Training Requirements."

mentoring of those involved, adjustments to individual educational plans, addressing and reducing issues resulting from an adverse school climate (e.g., bullying, bias, discrimination, etc.) The ultimate goal is creating a safe and secure school environment that is conducive to learning.

School districts in Texas are required to have threat assessment teams at each campus, which are to be consistent with model policies and procedures from the Texas School Safety Center (TxSSC). The policies and procedures adopted under Education Code 37.115 must

- be consistent with the model policies and procedures developed by TxSSC (see Education Code 37.220);

- require each team to complete training provided by the TxSSC or a regional education service center regarding evidence-based threat assessment programs;

- require each team established under this section to report the required information regarding the team's activities to TEA.

The statute also includes provisions for Threat Assessment Team membership, stating "to the greatest extent possible" each team should have expertise in counseling, behavior management, mental health and substance use, classroom instruction, special education, school administration, school safety and security, emergency management, and law enforcement.

In 2019, at the direction of the Board of Trustees, UCISD established a threat assessment program and team at the district level. The team is responsible for developing and implementing the safe and supportive school program in compliance with TEA rules at the district campus served by the team. At least some team members attended training provided by TxSSC, a one-day content-based training with no exercises to practice applying the concepts taught. Those team members noted that the training was "not super informative" and "left more questions than answers."

Ideally, the team schedules meetings on a monthly basis to discuss assessment requests, which can come from campus administrators or designated staff members. An assessment is conducted when there is a threat made by a student. The Threat Assessment Team will determine whether it is transient and if a specific intervention or support needs to be developed for the student. The team discusses what led up to the incident, the history of the student, and whether there are any patterns of risk behaviors. The threat levels are placed in categories of transient, substantive, serious, and very serious. The team makes recommendations regarding any support or interventions that are needed and submits them to the director of student services. However, in practice, the team does not meet regularly and is not operationalized as a formal threat assessment team.

School staff are required to document and report immediately to administrators any student whose behavior poses an obvious threat or safety risk. However, UCISD staff reported that there is no training for teachers and staff on developmentally appropriate responses to students with behavior problems, which makes determining reportable behavior particularly challenging. Members of the school counseling staff reported minimal knowledge of the Threat Assessment Team or involvement in threat cases. In fact, they identified a couple of instances in which they had been asked by law enforcement to sit with students who had engaged in threatening behaviors without being told that a threat existed.

The Threat Assessment Team does not analyze campus or school district trends in behavior or threats. They also do not make recommendations for discipline, leaving that decision with the school administrator, who is provided a copy of the team's assessment of the incident.

In its updated EOP for the 2022–2023 school year, UCISD includes an Active Threat Annex, which describes the function of the Threat Assessment Team and references a district School Behavioral Threat Assessment (SBTA) policy for more detail. The school district has not produced such a policy for review, though it did acknowledge that it did not have any policy as of May 24, 2022.

There is recognition within UCISD that its Threat Assessment Team lacked formalized policies and procedures and was not fully functional at the time of the May 24 shooting, despite having existed on paper for approximately 2½ years prior. UCISD staff conveyed renewed efforts to improve their Threat Assessment Team and process. At the beginning of the 2022–2023 school year, the UCISD Threat Assessment Team went through revised training provided by Texas State University. The training is based on a new model that includes updated language and emphasizes utilizing screeners as well as campus-level threat assessment teams.[1083]

Although required for each campus, at the time of this report, Uvalde High School is the only campus that has its own Threat Assessment Team. UCISD is in the process of establishing campus-level Threat Assessment Teams for all other campuses. The vision for the existing district-level team is to serve as coordinator of campus-level teams and receive only "serious" and "very serious" threat assessment referrals.

Doors, Locks, Magnets, and Maintenance

UCISD policy requires exterior and interior doors throughout campus to be locked when class is in session. According to former Robb Elementary Principal, the locked-door policy is discussed from the beginning of the school year and continues all year long. One enforcement mechanism for the policy is door-lock auditing conducted by UCISD PD, whereby officers would check doors throughout the day at UCISD campuses and, if found unlocked, let the teacher or UCISD staff person in the room know that the door needs to be locked.[1084] According to UCISD, a second offense of leaving the door unlocked results in a written reprimand.[1085]

The classroom doors in the West Building were exterior-locking doors, meaning they can only be locked with a key from outside of the classroom into the hallway. These doors are very common in school buildings throughout the country and were designed to prevent students from accidentally or

---

[1083] CIR Fact Finding; CIR Document and Data Review.

[1084] CIR Fact Finding.

[1085] CIR Fact Finding.

intentionally locking the door from the inside and causing a disruption in classroom activities. The exterior locking mechanism, however, poses a risk if a student or instructor does not know whether the door is locked (or knows it to be unlocked) and there is an intruder or active shooter in the building. The design of these doors means that someone must open the door and at least partially expose themselves to the threat to ensure it is locked or to lock it.

The doors and keying system both were a topic of controversy at Robb Elementary, even prior to the tragedy that unfolded. It was widely acknowledged in our interviews that both exterior and interior doors were often left unlocked while classes were in session. Additionally, exterior doors would be held open, sometimes with a rock, when staff needed to use the door for something (e.g., bringing in materials, stepping outside for a moment, etc.) There is also a lack of systematic tracking and documentation of policy violations regarding locked doors, as UCISD was unable to produce any documentation on this topic.

The keying system for the doors at Robb Elementary was a complicating factor in the district's locked-door policy. The West Building was in the process of being rekeyed because the building key cut for locks on the doors was "retired," which meant if a key went missing or was broken, UCISD would have to replace the entire lock because a new key could no longer be made.[1086] In the West Building, there were two master keys. Some locks were rekeyed for the newer master key, and some remained keyed to the old one. There was not a single master key that opened all interior doors in the West Building.

Not all UCISD PD officers possessed master keys to all of the campuses and buildings. Only UCISD PD Lt. 1 has said that they believed they possessed a set of master keys that opened all of the doors in the West Building.[1087] During the response on May 24, UCISD Lt. 1 provided all of their keys to officers on the south side of the hallway with Chief Arredondo, first to open the door to room 109 and evacuate it, then to test them to see if they would work on rooms 111/112. After trying all keys on doors other than rooms 111/112, Chief Arredondo determined none of them would work on rooms 111/112.

Additionally, custodial staff and some other UCISD staff were believed to have master keys, but there was no system of tracking this information at UCISD.

Because of the shortage of keys, some UCISD teachers used magnetic strips that are designed to keep doors unlocked (see figure 7-3 on page 343). These magnetic strips are often advertised as "lockdown magnets," with the intended purpose of enabling the user to keep a door in locked status mechanically and only have to open the door slightly, remove the strip, and close the door to lock. This magnet is especially attractive for doors that can only be locked and unlocked from the outside because the user can keep the door "locked" and only need to pull the magnetic strip out from the doorway, rather than leave the door unlocked and need to then fully open and lock the door from the outside in the event of a lockdown.

[1086] CIR Fact Finding.

[1087] Investigative Committee, *Robb Elementary Shooting Interim Report*; CIR Fact Finding.

These magnetic strips were used for convenience and in cases where teachers, particularly substitute teachers, did not have keys to the classroom.[1088] UCISD leadership approved the use of magnets as a lower-cost solution than rekeying doors.[1089]

Figure 7-3. Example of a lockdown magnetic strip (not an actual strip used at Robb Elementary)

Photo: GINFH

Some interview participants referenced both exterior and interior doors not closing and locking properly, attributing it variously to the buildup of paint, the door latch malfunctioning, or the door and jamb expanding or contracting with extreme heat or cold.[1090] UCISD staff who believed any interior or exterior door to be malfunctioning were to submit maintenance requests through a software program, allowing for the tracking and prioritization of such requests. In practice, maintenance requests were often submitted via front office staff; interview participants reported that front office staff were very diligent in doing so.

[1088] CIR Fact Finding.

[1089] CIR Fact Finding.

[1090] CIR Fact Finding.

From 2021–2022, there were 244 maintenance requests at Robb Elementary, 13 of which were related to interior or exterior doors not closing or locking properly. Of the 13, 2 work orders were for the West Building, where the west and south exterior doors were each said to not close properly. Both work orders were initiated in 2022. Notably, the work orders were completed and closed out prior to May 24. The system showed no work orders for interior doors in the West Building in the 2021 and 2022 calendar years.

Texas Rangers tested and documented the door-locking mechanisms for the south, west, east, and library exterior doors to the West Building.[1091] None of the doors failed to operate. Each door closed and latched on its own without any additional effort. It was demonstrated that each door can only be locked and unlocked with a key from the outside. From the inside of the doors, they could be opened with the push bar (see figure 7-4), whether the door was locked or unlocked from the outside.

Figure 7-4. Example image of door with push bar—interior view (not image of door at Robb Elementary)

Photo: iStock/Vuchikul Ocharoen

On May 24, the subject entered the West Building through the west door unimpeded. Video footage shows that the door is fully closed, though the CIR team can deduce that it was unlocked at that time as well. Law enforcement arriving on scene entered through the west, south, and east doors, all unimpeded, as *all* doors were, contrary to policy, apparently unlocked.

On May 24, teachers and students initiated lockdown procedures, largely in compliance with UCISD policy and the Campus Safety Plan with one critical exception. Teachers and students remained inside classrooms, out of sight in a darkened room, and maintained silence. However, some doors were not locked during the lockdown procedure, as required and stated in the Campus Safety Plan.[1092] There were

---

[1091] CIR Document and Data Review.

[1092] CIR Document and Data Review.

19 rooms (17 classrooms, one library, and one teacher lounge) in the West Building that should have been locked once lockdown was initiated. Our analysis indicates that at least eight doors were confirmed to be unlocked on that day.

Emergency Alerts

In October 2021, UCISD purchased an emergency alert software system from Raptor Technologies, with the intent of modernizing emergency alerts and making them available on UCISD staff's phones. The previous emergency alert method was through the traditional public announcement (PA) system at each campus. Raptor Technologies software was already in use at UCISD for digital check-in of visitors.[1093] The Raptor system was not intended to replace but rather to supplement the traditional PA announcements.

UCISD began using the system around February 2022, when the first Raptor alert went out. The rollout of the new system was not smooth. Some UCISD staff indicated that the training was not informative enough and they did not have a full comprehension of how the new system was to be used. For example, there was some miscommunication among UCISD staff about whether the PA system should or should not continue to be used. That information was later clarified—that the PA system could still be used, in conjunction with the Raptor alerts.

In interviews, some UCISD staff indicated that they had trouble receiving alerts on their phones—some did not know why, some apparently were not in the alert notification system and had to be added to receive alerts, and others stated that it was due to poor reception inside the building (see figure 7-5 on page 346 for an example of the alert that went out on May 24.[1094] The data output from Raptor shows several transmitted alerts on May 24 (see table 7-2 on page 346), the first issued by the school principal shortly before the subject entered the West Building (one minute or less). Multiple interview participants stated that they never received an alert on May 24, while others did.[1095]

[1093] Investigative Committee on the Robb Elementary Shooting, House Investigative Committee on the Robb Elementary Shooting Interim Report 2022.

[1094] The Texas House Committee report states that the committee received evidence demonstrating UCISD employees not consistently receiving Raptor alerts.

[1095] CIR Fact Finding.

Figure 7-5. Raptor alert received by UCISD employees on May 24, 2022

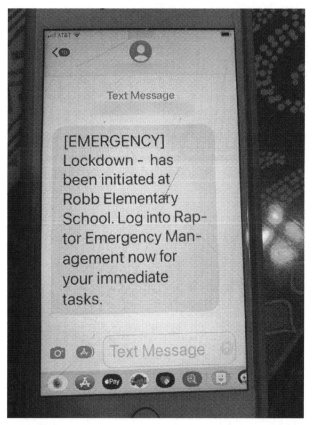

Source: CIR Document and Data Review.

Table 7-12. Raptor Alerts—May 24, 2022

Campus	Incident Type	Emergency Type	Start Time
Uvalde Elementary School	Emergency	Lockdown	11:32 AM
Flores Elementary School	Emergency	Lockdown	11:34 AM
Uvalde High School	Emergency	Lockdown	11:47 AM
Batesville Elementary School	Emergency	Lockdown	11:50 AM
Morales Junior High School	Emergency	Secure	11:53 AM
Flores Elementary School	Emergency	Secure	11:58 AM
Uvalde Dual Language Academy	Emergency	Secure	11:59 AM
Crossroads Academy	Emergency	Secure	12:00 PM
Dalton Early Childhood Center	Emergency	Secure	12:01 PM
Flores Elementary School	Emergency	Lockdown	2:11 PM
Uvalde Dual Language Academy	Emergency	Lockdown	2:30 PM

Source: Data export provided by UCISD.

Many interview participants, especially law enforcement and school district staff, expressed an ongoing concern over "bailouts" in Uvalde and their effect on school safety and security.

The CIR team examined UCISD's Raptor alert data, focusing on all emergency incidents (i.e., not drills) that resulted in evacuations, lockdowns, secure status, or shelter-in-place.[1096] The data show that there were a total of 106 Raptor alerts fitting these criteria from the system's inception in February 2022 through May 2023.[1097] With the exception of July 2022, there was at least one alert per month—with many months showing more than one emergency. Leading up to May 24, there were 28 Raptor alerts that were not drills. However, it is important to note that some UCISD staff acknowledged that during the early rollout of Raptor, the assignment of the incident type (i.e., "emergency" vs. "drill") was not reliable, as UCISD staff were still getting used to the system. The Raptor system allows for a subtype of emergency, which enables the user to provide more detail as to what the cause of the emergency was; however, this feature is rarely used. Therefore, it is not possible to count the number of emergencies resulting from bailouts, given UCISD's use of the Raptor system.

What Is a Bailout?

The term is used to describe instances in which suspected undocumented migrants flee from law enforcement, initiating a high-speed vehicular pursuit. The "bailout" refers to the fleeing suspects exiting their vehicle (i.e., "bailing out") and running. However, the term is now used colloquially to refer to these pursuits, whether the subject exits the vehicle and flees on foot or not.

In testimony to the Texas House Investigative Committee, former UCISD Director of Student Services, testified that high-speed chases have been a daily event in the Uvalde area, causing 47 "secure" or "lockdown" events in the school district between February and June 2022, and estimated that 90 percent were from bailouts.*

---

* Investigative Committee, *Robb Elementary Shooting Interim Report.*

[1096] Texas Education Agency definitions. "Secure": A response action schools take to secure the perimeter of school buildings and grounds during incidents that pose a threat or hazard outside of the school building. Secure uses the security of the physical facility to act as protection to deny entry. "Lockdown": A response action schools take to secure interior portions of school buildings and grounds during incidents that pose an immediate threat of violence inside the school. The primary objective is to quickly ensure all school students, staff, and visitors are secured away from immediate danger. "Evacuate": A response action schools take to quickly move students and staff from one place to another. The primary objective of an evacuation is to ensure that all staff, students, and visitors can quickly move away from the threat. Evacuation examples include a bomb threat or internal gas leak. "Shelter-in-place": A response action schools take to quickly move students, staff, and visitors indoors, perhaps for an extended period of time, because it is safer inside the building than outside.

[1097] Each campus alert is counted as a separate alert, meaning a single event that affects multiple campuses results in more than one alert.

Nonetheless, many UCISD staff indicated that bailouts were frequently occurring and initiating Raptor alerts, and that the volume of such alerts may have desensitized them. Some interview participants stated that they initially thought the alert they received on May 24 was a bailout.[1098]

The UCISD EOP in place on May 24 required the district and campus administrators to "Establish a redundant notification system to alert employees regarding emergency situations and expectations that includes emergency tasking and details of operational closings or delays."[1099] On that day, the Raptor alert did not reach all employees. In some instances, the PA system was used, though not consistently and not in all rooms at Robb Elementary.[1100] In one instance, the school principal attempted to communicate with classroom 103, at the request of first responders on the scene, to let them know that the windows were about to be broken for evacuation. That announcement was not heard, as the teacher had turned off the sonic board in that room in order not to alert the subject to her and her students' presence.[1101] The classroom was not evacuated (through the window) until approximately 12:03 p.m.

Drills and Exercises

Like most school systems in the United States, UCISD holds drills to help prepare staff and students to take appropriate action in the event of an emergency. TEA requires that Texas school districts conduct the following types of drills each school year, as a minimum:[1102]

- Secure (one per school year)
- Lockdown (two per school year/one per semester)
- Evacuate (one per school year)
- Shelter in place for hazmat (one per school year)
- Shelter for severe weather (one per school year)
- Fire evacuation drill (four per school year/two per semester)

School districts may choose to conduct more drills but are limited to a maximum of 8 per semester or 16 per school year in total.

At Robb Elementary, drills were typically practiced inside the classroom. Some teachers reported they never practiced these drills when they had a class at recess, at lunch, or elsewhere on the campus, as was the case on May 24, when children and teachers were outside of the building on campus at recess and in the cafeteria for lunch.

[1098] CIR Fact Finding.

[1099] CIR Document and Data Review.

[1100] CIR Fact Finding.

[1101] CIR Fact Finding.

[1102] Texas School Safety Center, "Drill Frequently Asked Questions;" TEX. EDUC. CODE § 37.114, Best Practices for Emergency School Drills and Exercises; Mandatory School Drills.

On May 24, teachers and students largely followed lockdown procedures as trained, except for doors being left unlocked. In the West Building, all occupied classrooms had turned the lights off and moved to a corner of the room away from the door. In classrooms where the doors were locked, teachers and students did not open the door, not even when asked to do so by law enforcement. Students and teachers who were outside when they realized there was a shooter on or near campus ran *into* the building to initiate lockdown.

Observations and Recommendations

Observation 1: UCISD PD had jurisdictional authority at the onset of the incident on May 24 as per governing doctrine (i.e., UCISD's EOP and MOU) between UCISD PD and UPD. This MOU, however, is silent on other agencies. Each agency, UPD and UCISD PD, is not only a signatory to the MOU but serves on UCISD's School Safety and Security Committee, which manages updates to the EOP. These documents signal an expectation to both agencies that UCISD PD would take command in an active shooter incident and UPD would respond to requests for assistance and follow the direction of the ICS leader. This comports with the prevailing perception among many officers on the scene that Chief Arredondo was in charge that day.[1103]

Observation 2: UCISD PD has an MOU establishing jurisdictional responsibilities in place with just one neighboring law enforcement agency, UPD. The majority of agencies on scene on May 24—at the local, state, and federal level—did not have any mutual aid agreements with UCISD PD. This includes agencies which, like UPD, have concurrent jurisdiction with UCISD PD, such as the Uvalde County Sheriff's Office (UCSO), Zavala County Sheriff's Office (ZCSO), and TXDPS.

> **Recommendation 2.1:** School district police departments should enter into MOUs that establish mutually agreed upon clear jurisdictional responsibilities with other neighboring agencies that are likely to respond to a critical incident on school property. The MOUs should account for not only routine criminal activity, but also critical incidents. The MOU should address the issue of unified command, in addition to incident command, and account for the capacity and capabilities of the respective agencies.

Observation 3: UCISD's EOP and Active Shooter Policy were considered viable by the Texas School Safety Center and satisfied requirements set forth by TEA. However, the response on May 24 demonstrated that agencies responding to such an incident within UCISD's jurisdiction were not prepared for the large-scale multiagency response resulting from the incident.

[1103] CIR Fact Finding.

Recommendation 3.1: Law enforcement, first responders, emergency management, and other municipal government agencies should coordinate with school districts to conduct multiagency preparedness exercises on at least an annual basis. Exercises should operate in accordance with the state and local regulations regarding active threat exercises.[1104] The exercises should be incorporated into the EOPs and Campus Safety Plans.

Observation 4: The UCISD School Safety and Security Committee has not had any participation from the UCSO, which is the largest law enforcement agency in the county and had more than a dozen members respond to the active shooter incident at Robb Elementary. Additionally, ZCSO—which had four members respond—does not participate in the committee, despite being the local law enforcement agency for one of UCISD's eight campuses.

Recommendation 4.1: All law enforcement agencies within school districts should participate in safety and security planning. Law enforcement agencies with jurisdiction should assign leaders from within their agencies (either the sheriff or chief deputy sheriff) to participate on the committee. That individual can serve as a liaison between the school district and the sheriffs' offices and help both entities maintain awareness of safety and security concerns that may intersect the two.

Recommendation 4.2: Communities should adopt a multidisciplinary approach to school safety that includes school police, law enforcement, school officials, mental health professionals, and other community stakeholders. It is especially important that all voices in the school community be heard, including faculty, staff, administrators, counselors, nurses, resource officers, parents, and students. Every stakeholder must feel empowered to play a role in reducing fear and raising the level of safety in and around schools. Each campus should establish and train school safety committees that will meet at least monthly for this purpose.

Observation 5: UCISD's campus safety teams met infrequently, and annual safety plans were based largely on templated information that was, at times, inaccurate.

Recommendation 5.1: School district campus safety teams must be intentional and deliberative in the development of their campus-specific plans and ensure they are reviewed and updated regularly. UCISD should work with campus administrators across the district to institutionalize a set of expectations for these plans that reflects the specific physical and social environments and safety and security needs of each campus.

Observation 6: The district Threat Assessment Team has been complacent and in need of strong oversight of its implementation. The new district leadership, including the school police chief, has expressed a stronger commitment to ensure they become fully operational as soon as possible. As of June 8, 2023, the UCISD threat assessment team does not have standard operating procedures and has been noncompliant with Texas Education Code.

[1104] Tex. Ed. Code § 37.115.

Recommendation 6.1: School district threat assessment teams must establish a systematic procedure for identifying, assessing, and managing threat assessments under their review.

Recommendation 6.2: Threat assessment teams must develop an operations manual that governs and documents their activities, outputs, roles and responsibilities, and coordination across the school district. At minimum, the manual should adhere to standards set forth by oversight bodies. In the case of UCISD, this would be the Texas School Safety Center, as required in the Texas Education Code.

Observation 7: Teachers and school staff at UCISD received no training on developmentally appropriate responses to students with behavioral problems, although they were required to document and report immediately to administrators any student whose behavior posed an obvious threat or safety risk.

Recommendation 7.1: All school district staff and school district police personnel should receive training on the district's threat assessment processes, including the role of all staff in appropriately identifying and reporting concerning behavior. The training should be interactive and include scenarios and discussion to help trainees practice applying the course content.

Observation 8: UCISD had a culture of complacency regarding locked-door policies. Both exterior and interior doors were routinely left unlocked, and there was no enforced system of accountability for these policies. Door audits were conducted, but not done systematically, nor were they documented. On May 24, all of the exterior doors and at least eight interior doors of the West Building, where the incident took place, were unlocked.

Recommendation 8.1: School districts should implement a system of door audits that are conducted routinely and systematically, and they should be documented. At UCISD, this responsibility can be assigned to the new safety monitor positions it has recently created. Door audits should be incorporated into school district campus safety plans. All school district staff and school district police personnel should have a shared responsibility to ensure doors are locked, as per policy.

Observation 9: The exterior and interior doors require a UCISD staff member or student to expose themselves to a threat to check that a door is locked or to lock a door in the event of a school lockdown.

Recommendation 9.1: School districts should invest in upgrading or replacing all doors (or locks) throughout its campuses to remedy this issue, so that doors can be locked from the inside.

Observation 10: Law enforcement arriving on scene searched for keys to open interior doors for more than 40 minutes. This was partly the cause of the significant delay in entering to eliminate the threat and stop the killing and dying inside classrooms 111 and 112.

Recommendation 10.1: School districts should implement universal access boxes. A universal access box refers to a locked box that contains master keys, located near the entry points of school buildings, that can be accessed by authorized emergency first responders and school district staff.

Observation 11: The rollout of the Raptor system caused some confusion in emergency alert procedures and some UCISD staff did not find the training helpful. Some teachers were under the belief that the Raptor system was supplanting the traditional PA system.

> **Recommendation 11.1:** School districts should ensure that emergency alert systems are well-understood by all staff. In the case of UCISD, district leadership should issue a district-wide clarification on the use of PA systems in conjunction with Raptor emergency alerts.

> **Recommendation 11.2:** School districts should offer both standard training and refresher training, as needed, on the use of their emergency alert system, available to all district employees.

Observation 12: UCISD Raptor alerts indicate the type of response, but not the type of emergency (e.g., bailout, suspicious person on campus, hail storm). The Raptor emergency alert system enables users to offer more detail, though this feature is rarely used by UCISD staff.

> **Recommendation 12.1:** School districts should implement a policy that requires the type of emergency event to be formally documented in their emergency alert system, so that school administrators can better identify and report trends and the most frequent causes of lockdowns and other emergency response protocols.

Observation 13: The poor reception (Wi-Fi and cell) issues at Robb Elementary are well documented. While the Raptor alert was promptly initiated through the system, it was not received by all teachers and staff.

> **Recommendation 13.1:** School districts must ensure that all campus buildings where there is student activity are retrofitted for Wi-Fi communication to ensure that emergency alerts are received in a timely manner.

Observation 14: UCISD drills are typically conducted inside classrooms. On May 24, there were several classes outside of their classrooms at the time the incident began.

> **Recommendation 14.1:** Active threat training for students and staff should be expanded to include all areas of the school campus. UCISD should ensure that drills take place in the many settings that teachers and students find themselves in throughout the school year, not just inside the classroom. While the classroom is the most likely location of students in a real-life emergency, they should be prepared to engage in standard response protocols from other locations on campus.

> **Recommendation 14.2:** UCISD should invite other law enforcement agencies to attend, observe, and participate in drills.

Observation 15: According to documents provided and reviewed by the CIR team, Robb Elementary School was in compliance with Texas Education Code 37.114 regarding drills during the 2019–2020 school year but not in the 2020–2021 school year. No documents were provided by UCISD for the 2021–2022 school year.

Recommendation 15.1: Drills should be conducted in accordance with the Texas Education Code 37.114, and proper documentation should be submitted to appropriate UCISD leadership for record-keeping.

Observation 16: Lockdown procedures are predicated on a locked door, impenetrable doors and walls, and other physical security that did not exist at Robb Elementary. One teacher at Robb was shot through several walls and many other teachers and students were at risk of the same fate, given the high-powered rifle used in the attack.

Recommendation 16.1: UCISD must reconsider the preeminence of the lockdown procedure in a dynamic, evolving situation, where the risk of remaining in place may outweigh the risk of finding a way to exit the area, which in the incident at Robb Elementary led to UCISD staff and students running *into* the building to lock down. Teachers, staff, and students must be provided with options for protecting themselves and helping to protect others.

Observation 17: At the time the UCISD PD was established, there was no coordination of safety plans with any other city agency, nor was there any citywide coordination of school safety planning. The superintendent did not meet regularly with the school police chief (reportedly they met "from time to time"). Despite reporting directly to the superintendent, the UCISD PD chief was not a member of the district senior leadership team and would only attend the weekly leadership team meetings "as needed," e.g., planning for special events like football games and other activities that would draw large crowds to school facilities. The chief did attend quarterly school safety meetings that were convened by the superintendent.

Observation 18: Four years into its existence, the UCISD PD was functioning without any standard operating procedures. A range of UCISD employees, including administrators, faculty, support staff, and police officers, told the CIR team they had no knowledge of, nor had they been informed about, their school police department's policies and procedures. The UCISD PD has recently drafted standard operating procedures.

Recommendation 18.1: School districts should meticulously consider, plan, and execute if they decide to establish their own police department. Budgeting, hiring practices, training, development of standard operating procedures, and student/community engagement should all be built into the design and execution of a school district police department.

Observation 19: The existing UCISD policies and procedures do not include information or guidelines around crisis management, MOUs, threat assessment or emergency response and multi-hazard planning. These topics are instead covered in the UCISD Revised EOP and EOP annexes for Active Shooter and Active Threat, which should not serve as the UCISD PD's standard operating procedures on these issues.

Recommendation 19.1: The draft version of the UCISD PD policies, procedures, and operational plans should be evaluated to ensure alignment with the highest industry standards, starting with high-risk operations such as response to an active attack and other potential crises that threaten school climate and safety. Professional organizations, including the International Association of Chiefs of Police and National Association of School Resource Officers, offer a range of model policies, toolkits, technical assistance, training, and other resources to inform the policy and operational planning evaluation process.

Recommendation 19.2: UCISD PD should undergo an accreditation process that measures compliance against generally accepted standards and practices. Accreditation is a voluntary process administered by state police associations as well as national organizations like the Commission on Accreditation for Law Enforcement Agencies. Many standards require the development of written directives or activities that reflect the agency's policies, procedures, and general orders. The accreditation process enables the review and revision of policies to ensure practices meet current professional criteria for excellence in service, strengthen agency operations, and increase public trust.

Observation 20: Some staff reported being unfamiliar with the school police department due to UCISD PD officers' sporadic presence on elementary school campuses. Reportedly, the UCISD PD chief would come at the beginning of the school year to deliver informal training in the event of an active shooter, reminding teachers to lock doors, turn off lights, and hide away from windows. Essentially, the chief would give a briefing to the teachers.

Recommendation 20.1: A school police department has the responsibilities of both a law enforcement agency and a member of the school environment, necessitating a heavy burden on the agency and officers to serve in these dual roles. The reconstituted UCISD PD must make intentional efforts to routinely engage with UCISD staff and students at all campuses. Regular engagement can help contribute to a safer learning environment by promoting safety, fostering positive relationships, discouraging misconduct, and improving the perception of law enforcement throughout the school district. The UCISD PD chief and all officers should be evaluated on these efforts.

Chapter 8. Pre-Incident Planning and Preparation

Introduction

Pre-incident planning is crucial in preparing for and responding to mass violence incidents, as it enables agencies and organizations to develop strategies and procedures to respond quickly and effectively to such incidents. The planning process involves identifying potential risks and hazards, assessing the likelihood and potential impact of incidents, and creating plans and procedures to respond to them. It also includes anticipating multiple phases and transitions that may occur over the course of an event and subsequent investigation. An after-action review (AAR) of the response to the San Bernardino terrorist attacks at the Inland Regional Center notes that, "Agencies should anticipate and plan a timely transition from the somewhat chaotic active shooter response to a more methodical search for possible suspects, triage victims, and victim and witness extraction."[1105]

When a mass violence incident occurs, it is never the response of one agency, but rather multidisciplinary stakeholders, including law enforcement, fire, emergency medical services, hospitals, victim service providers, prosecutors, emergency management, government and civic leaders, media, businesses, and the community as a whole. Through the planning process, coordinating routinely among all relevant stakeholders; developing agreements; and conducting multidisciplinary training, exercises, and drills are foundational to the process, as well as relationship- and trust-building.

Most failures in response can be traced back to failures in pre-incident planning and preparation, and this is true in the mass casualty incident at Robb Elementary School. As evidenced by the information in this chapter, the planning and preparation varied by agency and organization; however, one of the biggest failures from a pre-incident perspective was the lack of multijurisdictional and multidisciplinary coordination, exercises, drills, and communication. The lack of pre-planning hampered even well-prepared agencies from functioning at their best.

Even with the advantage of the best pre-incident planning, responding to mass violence incidents can be complex and challenging since it requires quick thinking, clear communication, and effective coordination among all responding agencies to minimize the harm caused by such incidents. Setting up a solid foundation in the pre-incident phase better ensures that agencies and organizations have the organizational capacity, structure, and relationships to focus on the mission while providing continuity and unity of purpose.

[1105] Braziel et al., *Bringing Calm to Chaos.*

Scope

This chapter describes the training, agreements, and procedures for law enforcement agencies, other responding organizations, and other relevant stakeholders in the areas of active shooter response, incident command, emergency management, and other significant areas. This discussion is about preparation and planning and not prevention; while preparation and pre-planning may mitigate an attack, it should not be confused with prevention. It is critical for all law enforcement agencies, government entities, and communities to plan and prepare for active attacker incidents and mass violence events. Communities cannot think they are immune from these attacks or allow for complacency. These incidents can happen in any community—big or small; urban, suburban, or rural— and in any location.

For purposes of this chapter, the following law enforcement agencies are included:

- Uvalde Police Department (UPD)

- Uvalde County Sheriff's Office (UCSO)

- Texas Department of Public Safety (TXDPS)

- Customs and Border Protection (CBP), U.S. Department of Homeland Security (DHS)

- U.S. Marshals Service (USMS), U.S. Department of Justice (DOJ)

- Federal Bureau of Investigation (FBI), U.S. DOJ

- Bureau of Alcohol, Tobacco, Firearms, and Explosives (ATF), U.S. DOJ

However, based on their role in the incident, each agency may not be included in individual subsection analysis and background. The Uvalde Consolidated Independent School District Police Department (UCISD PD) is discussed in "Chapter 7. School Safety and Security" since the agency is housed under the UCISD and under that chapter's scope.

In addition, other agencies or organizations are included in the discussion as appropriate, including Uvalde County Office of Emergency Management, emergency medical services (EMS), Uvalde Memorial Hospital (UMH), and the City and County of Uvalde.

Finally, this chapter compares the pre-incident processes in Uvalde (policies and procedures, training, and mutual aid agreements and other formal coordination efforts) to generally accepted practices and standards. The Critical Incident Review (CIR) team focuses on the processes prior to the incident on May 24 and does not account for changes that agencies have made post-incident.

In preparing this chapter, the CIR team benefited from the expertise of subject matter experts, who assisted in developing the observations and recommendations for this chapter. Where not otherwise cited, the practices identified in this chapter derive from the experts' collective knowledge and experience.

The chapter is organized into five key aspects of preparation and planning.

- Policies and Procedures—this section covers policies and procedures for active shooter response and other relevant topics.

- Coordination Among Agencies—this section covers multi-agency coordination training, drills, plans, and agreements.

- Training—this section covers training for incident command, leadership, active shooters, and resiliency.

- Preparation and Planning in Schools to Mitigate the Extent of Trauma—this section covers pre-planning to reduce trauma in school settings.

- Planning and Preparing for Public Messaging—this section covers pre-planning for public information officers and other communication personnel.

Additional background and resources are included in "Appendix G. Pre-Incident Planning and Preparation."

Policies and Procedures

Policies and procedures are the anchors for agencies. The contents of the policies and procedures are just as important as how they are implemented, trained, and overseen. An agency can have a strong policy and lack in training and oversight, and vice versa, which highlights the need not only for a comprehensive approach to policy writing, but also implementation.

Policies should be clear, concise, and strike the balance between providing sufficient guidance and structure and offering discretion to all who fall under their purview. Policies and procedures should detail roles and responsibilities, and be tailored for the agency and their processes, organized, and properly sourced and legally defensible.[1106]

Principles for Developing Active Shooter Policies

Policies and protocols on active shooter responses should include the following guidance:

- Rapid response: Upon receiving reports of an active shooter, law enforcement agencies aim to respond quickly to the scene. The first officers on the scene must first stop the killing and then stop the dying.

- Forming a response team: Additional officers and specialized units may be called in to assist. They should work together to secure the area, evacuate people to safety, and search for the shooter.

[1106] For more on creating strong policies and procedures, see Orrick, *Best Practices Guide*; Carpenter, "Put It in Writing;" and Power DMS, "Writing Effective Policies and Procedures in Law Enforcement."

- Establishing a command center: Law enforcement should establish a command center near the incident site to coordinate the response. This helps with communication, decision-making, and resource allocation.

- Containment and isolation: Law enforcement should aim to contain the shooter and prevent them from causing further harm. They may establish a perimeter around the area to prevent the shooter from escaping and to keep civilians and other responders safe.

- Engaging the shooter: Law enforcement personnel must enter the area to confront the shooter and stop the threat. Their approach may depend on several factors, such as the location of the shooter and the number of potential victims. The primary goal is to neutralize the shooter as quickly as possible and minimize harm to innocent individuals.

- Evacuation and triage: Once the immediate threat is eliminated, law enforcement should work with other emergency responders, such as emergency medical technicians and firefighters, to evacuate injured individuals and provide medical assistance. They may also set up triage areas to prioritize medical treatment based on the severity of injuries.

- Investigation and follow-up: After the situation is under control, law enforcement should initiate an investigation into the incident. This includes gathering evidence, interviewing witnesses, and working with forensic experts. The investigation aims to determine the motive, gather intelligence, and prevent future incidents.

Although this report references an active shooter incident, when developing a policy and associated procedures and training, consider broadening the policy to apply to "active attackers."

Principles for Mutual Aid Policies

Mutual aid agreements established by local governments generally follow the guidelines set forth by state law and include the use of established pre-incident agreements by the primary requester ("donor") and requesting jurisdictions. Protocols for documenting and inventorying disaster response resources by category, a deployment inventory, or catalog of preidentified resources and an automated resource management system to access and search the inventory to locate, request, order, and track resources requested by incident management personnel are key components that form the basis for establishing regional mutual aid agreements.[1107] Additionally, the mutual aid agreement should include an operational plan and schedule of training and exercises prior to implementation of the agreement. Mutual aid training and exercises are a best practice that provide responders the opportunity to practice their procedures and responsibilities and help build a solid foundation for implementing mutual aid.[1108]

[1107] IACP, *Model Policy on Mutual Aid.*

[1108] FEMA, National Incident Management System Guideline for Mutual Aid, 11.

Principles for Incident Command Policies

Policies and protocols on incident command should detail the below.

The incident command system (ICS) requires the chief executive or their designee to be the incident commander (IC) and exercise command and control over all law enforcement resources committed to an incident or event that is citywide or multijurisdictional in nature. Various components of the ICS should be activated depending on the size and complexity of the incident or event. Operational need is the primary factor in determining which components or functions are activated. In addition to establishing a command post and function, the IC, utilizing the standardized ICS structure, shall activate those components necessary for the incident. These components include operations, planning, logistics, finance/administration, and intelligence, if necessary. The IC shall establish an Incident Command and will determine the incident command post (ICP) location. This location should be carefully chosen based on such factors as incident size, need for security, proximity to the incident, and support issues such as communications and shelter from the elements. The IC will inform communications of the establishment of command and the ICP's specific location.

When the incident has been resolved or stabilized to such a point that command is no longer necessary, the IC shall notify communications that the incident is being terminated. The IC shall submit an after action report which should include, but may not be limited to, a brief description and outcome of the incident; a statement of personnel and equipment utilized; a cost analysis to include salaries, equipment, food, and incidentals; a copy of incident/event logs and all submitted reports; any maps, forms, or related documentation; a summary of deaths and injuries to citizens and responders; an assessment of damage to private and public property; any information relating to the status of criminal investigations and subsequent prosecutions; a final evaluation and any subsequent conclusions relating to the agency's overall response to the critical incident or event, to include any problems encountered regarding personnel, equipment, resources, or multiagency response; suggestions to revise policy or improve training and equipment; and any other consideration that would improve the agency's response to critical incidents or events in the future.[1109]

Principles for Emergency Management Policies

According to the Federal Emergency Management Agency (FEMA), a successful emergency management operations plan should include the following components:

- Risk identification and analysis: Identify and analyze the risks that could affect your organization or community.

- Operational assumptions and resource demands: Identify the resources required to respond to an emergency and the assumptions that underlie the plan.

[1109] IACP, *Incident Command Model Policy.*

- Prioritization of plans and planning efforts: Prioritize plans and planning efforts to support the transition from development to execution for any threat or hazard.

- Integration and coordination: Integrate and coordinate efforts across all levels of government, the private sector, and nonprofit organizations.

- Community-based planning: Conduct community-based planning to engage the whole community through a planning process that represents the actual population in the community and involves community leaders and the private sector.[1110]

Additionally, effective emergency plans convey the goals and objectives of the intended operation and the actions needed to achieve them. Successful operations occur when organizations know their roles, understand how they fit into the larger response effort, and are able to work together to achieve common goals. There are ten steps for developing the emergency response plan:

1. Review performance objectives for the program.

2. Review hazard or threat scenarios identified during the risk assessment (https://www.ready.gov/business/risk-assessment).

3. Assess the availability and capabilities of resources for incident stabilization including people, systems, and equipment available within your business and from external sources (https://www.ready.gov/business/resource-management).

4. Talk with public emergency services (e.g., fire, police, and emergency medical services) to determine their response time to your facility, knowledge of your facility and its hazards, and capabilities to stabilize an emergency at your facility.

5. Determine if there are any regulations pertaining to emergency planning at your facility; address applicable regulations in the plan.

6. Develop protective actions for life safety (evacuation, shelter, shelter-in-place, lockdown).

7. Develop hazard and threat-specific emergency procedures using the Emergency Response Plan for Businesses (https://www.ready.gov/sites/default/files/2020-09/business_emergency-response-plans.pdf).

8. Coordinate emergency planning with public emergency services to stabilize incidents involving the hazards at your facility.

9. Train personnel so they can fulfill their roles and responsibilities (https://www.ready.gov/business/training).

10. Facilitate exercises to practice your plan (https://www.ready.gov/business/exercises).[1111]

[1110] FEMA, *Developing and Maintaining Emergency Operations Plans.*

[1111] Ready.gov, "Emergency Response Plan."

Principles for Post-Incident Responses Policies

Law enforcement agencies must be prepared to respond in the days and weeks following a mass casualty incident in their jurisdictions. Agency policy and emergency management plans should reflect procedures to prepare for and effectively manage the aftermath of a mass casualty incident. Several important takeaways from recent incidents include:

- preparation for the massive media turnout that will shape the perception of how a major disaster is being managed;

- identifying and deploying resources for trauma support services available to families of victims;

- coordination of logistics for handling casualties;

- recognizing and preparing for the physical and emotional needs of responders;

- including medical facilities in planning, preparation, and exercises in anticipation of a surge in the aftermath of a mass casualty incident;

- following social media for awareness of vigils and public gatherings that might require police coverage;

- defining a clear trauma notification process and ensuring the availability of mental health professionals to support families that are acutely grief-stricken.

Important lessons learned remind law enforcement that, in addition to planning and training for the immediate response to a critical incident scene, local agency leaders, healthcare systems, and elected officials should have a comprehensive understanding of the many challenges they could face during and after a mass casualty incident, if it happens in their jurisdiction. Studying after action reports and hearing directly from emergency response leaders who have handled these incidents is the first step in being prepared for post-incident management.[1112]

Policies in Uvalde

As outlined in previous chapters (see "Chapter 2. Tactics and Equipment," "Chapter 3. Leadership, Incident Command, and Coordination," and "Chapter 7. School Safety and Security"), the policies and procedures for the responding agencies at Robb Elementary School ranged in quality, if policies were present at all. A summary for each agency is provided below in table 8-1 on page 362.[1113]

[1112] Hulsman, "When the Guns Go Silent"

[1113] UCISD PD is covered in "Chapter 7. School Safety and Security." ATF and FBI were only reviewed for post-incident responses due to their role during the incident.

Table 8-1. Summary of policy review for each responding agency

Agency	Policies
UPD	Policy manual included active shooter and mutual aid policies. Policies lacked details on active shooter priorities, as well as incident command / emergency management.
UCSO	Lacked policies for active shooter, incident command, and emergency management.
TXDPS	Lacked policy on active shooter. Otherwise, policies align with generally accepted standards and practices.
CBP	Lacked policy on active shooter. Unknown on other policies since not provided to CIR team.
ATF	Policies align with generally accepted standards and practices for post incident responses.
USMS	Policy on active shooter / active threat. Policy lacked details on agency wide expectations in areas such as active shooter priorities and command and control. Unable to ascertain individual USMS facility specific policy and whether it meets generally accepted standards and practices. Otherwise, policies for post incident responses align with generally accepted standards and practices.
FBI	Policies align with generally accepted standards and practices for post incident responses.

Coordination Among Agencies

Emergency planning needs to include all relevant stakeholders, to include all responder agencies, government and civic leaders, businesses, non-governmental agencies that provide victim assistance, media, and other community groups. For each of the agencies and organizations, leaders need to consider planning, training, and awareness for a robust group of individuals. For example, in law enforcement agencies, dispatchers and other professional staff need to be included in emergency planning. Regarding schools, bus drivers and administrative staff need to be included.

One group that is often left out of pre-planning is private sector and industry partners, who play a key role before, during, and after disasters. Businesses are involved in emergencies because substantial portions of infrastructure are privately owned. In addition, copious amounts of the hazardous materials are handled by private industry. Business and industry partners should observe standards for the protection of critical infrastructure and develop individual continuity of operations plans. During disasters, many businesses may also work with the state and with Voluntary Organizations Active in Disaster (VOAD) to provide resources during incident response and recovery.[1114]

As the AAR of the shooting at Marjory Stoneman Douglas High School described, "Involving all relevant stakeholders in a unified incident command, as well as planning and exercising roles and responsibilities prior to an event, can help build familiarity with the emergency response and recovery system and aid its implementation during critical incidents."[1115] Participation must include civilian staff, including communications and dispatch personnel.

NFPA 3000: Standard on Active Shooter and Hostile Event Response Program

In 2018, the National Fire Protection Association (NFPA), working with more than 100 expert stakeholders across law enforcement, Fire/EMS, emergency management, hospitals, education, victim services, and facility management, published NFPA 3000: Standard on Active Shooter and Hostile Event Response Program. This is the first and only multidisciplinary consensus standard that provides information on how to prepare for, respond to, and recover from an active shooter event. Revised in 2021 to reflect the constantly changing landscape of events and lessons learned from more recent incidents, NFPA 3000 reinforces the importance of consistent training, preparation, and planned coordination across first responders, facilities that may become targets, and other local leaders.*

----

* FireRescue1 Academy, "NFPA 3000: Preparing and Training Firefighters for Active Shooter Incidents."

Multi-Agency Coordination Principles

There are several ways that agencies and entities can use the emergency planning process to facilitate collaboration and coordination during a mass violence incident.

National Incident Management System

Emergency planning can include laying the groundwork for the consistent use of the National Incident Management System (NIMS) to ensure that responders at all levels can work together more effectively and efficiently. NIMS is derived from the authority of the Homeland Security Presidential Directive (HSPD)-5, which focuses on "enhanc[ing] the ability of the United States to manage domestic incidents by establishing a single, comprehensive national incident management system."[1116]

[1114] FEMA, *Local and Elected Appointed Officials Guide.*

[1115] Straub et al., *Recovering and Moving Forward.*

[1116] DHS, Homeland Security Presidential Directive 5.

14 NIMS Implementation Objectives

The 14 NIMS Implementation Objectives are to:*[1117]

1. Adopt NIMS throughout the jurisdiction.

2. Designate a point of contact/principal coordinator for implementation of NIMS.

3. Ensure incident personnel receive training aligned with the NIMS Training Program.

4. Identify and inventory deployable incident resources consistent with national NIMS resource typing definitions and job titles/position qualifications.

5. Adopt NIMS terminology for the qualification, certification, and credentialing of incident personnel.[1118]

6. Use the NIMS Resource Management Process during incidents.

7. At the jurisdictional level, develop, maintain, and implement mutual aid agreements (including agreements with the private sector and nongovernmental organizations).

8. Apply ICS as the standard approach to the on-scene command, control, and coordination of incidents.

9. Implement Joint Information System (JIS) for the dissemination of incident information to the public, incident personnel, traditional and social media, and other stakeholders.

10. Use MAC/Policy Groups during incidents to enable decision-making among elected and appointed officials and support resource prioritization and allocation.

11. Organize and manage EOCs and EOC teams consistent with pertinent NIMS guidance.

12. Apply plain language and clear text communications standards.

13. Enable interoperable and secure communications within and across jurisdictions and organizations.

14. Develop, maintain, and implement procedures for data collection, analysis, and dissemination to meet organizational needs for situational awareness.

_____

* FEMA, *NIMS Implementation Objectives*.

As discussed in "Chapter 3. Leadership, Incident Command, and Coordination," NIMS "provides stakeholders across the whole community with the shared vocabulary, systems, and processes to successfully deliver the capabilities described in the National Preparedness System."[1119] NIMS does so by

_____

[1117] FEMA, *NIMS Implementation Objectives*.

[1118] Developing or participating in a qualification, certification, and credentialing program that aligns with the National Qualification System (NQS) is recommended but not required.

[1119] FEMA, *National Incident Management System: Third Edition*.

defining operational systems, including the Incident Command System (ICS), Emergency Operations Center (EOC) structures, and Multiagency Coordination Groups (MAC Groups) that guide how personnel work together during incidents.

In critical incidents, particularly events involving multiple jurisdictions and disciplines, the understanding and use of NIMS and ICS are essential to the successful sharing of information and coordination of resources, tactics, and investigations. FEMA requires local, state, tribal, and territorial jurisdictions to adopt NIMS to receive federal preparedness grants.[1120] While the NIMS mandate is a requirement for receiving preparedness funding, this tragedy demonstrates the need for mandated NIMS implementation for all jurisdictions across the country regardless of funding requirements (see "14 NIMS Implementation Objectives" callout box).

Multiagency Training and Drills

In regions where agency size and resources limit response capabilities, interagency and regional training is a valuable preparation for major incident responses, enabling personnel—both sworn and civilian—from various agencies to develop relationships and become familiar with each other's resources, limitations, processes, and protocols. Tabletops and other similar training exercises can be valuable tools to collaborate with stakeholders from other organizations, including public safety organizations.[1121]

Multiagency training allows for cost- and resource-sharing and, more importantly, allows law enforcement to train with other agencies that are typically going to respond jointly to a major incident. Building relationships through training and in advance of a major incident are critical in the successful response to, management of, and resolution of a major incident when one happens.

As part of the multijurisdictional training, it is also important to conduct multidisciplinary training. Government leaders told the CIR team they had never been trained to deal with this type of critical incident, largely because mass shootings are viewed as "anomalies."[1122] Trainings should aim to include all relevant disciplines, when possible, including other responder agencies (fire, EMS, hospitals), government and elected officials (mayors, city managers, judges), prosecutors, school personnel, media, victim advocate organizations, and other relevant stakeholders. A part of multijurisdictional trainings should be annual exercises and drills through the EOC to ensure that all challenges are addressed.

Training with other agencies enables those involved to identify issues such as communication interoperability ahead of time, which can save valuable time during a major incident response. As an AAR of the impact of communications systems and processes on the response to the

---

[1120] FEMA, "National Incident Management System."

[1121] Straub et al., *Advancing Charlotte.*

[1122] CIR Fact Finding.

shooting at Marjory Stoneman Douglas High School found, holding joint training and regular practical exercises can help to identify and resolve communication and coordination issues under a variety of strenuous circumstances.[1123]

Mutual Aid and Formal Agreements

Mutual aid is a system where law enforcement agencies from different jurisdictions work together to respond to a major incident. Agencies and organizations that decide on the need for an agreement should ensure that the agreement is customized to the capability or resource for which the agreement is developed. It should also include, where appropriate, training expectations across the interdisciplinary functions necessary to create familiarity and coordination of resources. The agencies should also train and exercise the agreement responsibilities and duties. These exercises help build preparedness for threats and hazards by providing a low-risk, cost-effective environment. The exercises also help to test and validate the plans, policies, procedures, and capabilities. Finally, this process provides space to identify resource requirements, capability gaps, strengths, areas for improvement, and potential best practices.

Building familiarity, coordination, and relationships will help to improve the response, especially to a critical incident. The FEMA National Exercise Program (NEP) is a strong preparedness tool to help communities with these functions.[1124]

Emergency Plans, Agreements, and Multiagency Training in Uvalde

Prior to the tragedy at Robb Elementary School, there were plans and agreements in place aimed at promoting coordination among agencies in response to a tragedy. These efforts, however, failed to operationalize on the day of the incident, underscoring the need for full participation by all stakeholders in the development of such plans and in further interagency training and exercises.

Uvalde County Emergency Management Plan

The State of Texas Emergency Management Basic Plan provides guidance to senior officials regarding planning and preparation before a critical incident or disaster occurs. It offers concepts and principles that should be reviewed and implemented well ahead of incidents. Senior officials should coordinate with emergency managers, leverage local government operations, and engage with a diverse range of community stakeholders, including business and non-government organizations, and the whole community to be well-prepared for success during and after incidents.[1125]

According to the State of Texas Emergency Management Basic Plan, in Texas, mayors and county judges serve as emergency management directors and bear the responsibility for maintaining an emergency management program within their jurisdictions.[1126] A mayor or county judge may appoint an emergency

---

[1123] Straub et al., *Recovering and Moving Forward.*

[1124] FEMA, "Homeland Security Exercise and Evaluation Program."

[1125] FEMA, *Local and Elected Appointed Officials Guide.*

[1126] TEX. GOV. CODE § 418.1015, Emergency Management Directors.

management coordinator (EMC) to help discharge these duties.[1127] In Uvalde County, the County Judge, Mayor of Uvalde, and Mayor of Sabinal (a neighboring city within Uvalde County), along with the EMC, are responsible for the duties in the *Uvalde County Basic Emergency Management Plan* ("the Plan").[1128] The following section discusses the Uvalde County Plan, which as outlined is consistent with generally accepted practices and standards. The Plan requires full participation by all stakeholders, but the failure of the Plan to operationalize on the day of the incident demonstrates that further training and exercises are needed.

The Plan sets forth the approach to emergency operations and provides general guidance for emergency management activities and an overview of methods of mitigation, preparedness, response, and recovery in Uvalde County. The Plan describes the emergency response organization and assigns responsibilities for various emergency tasks. The plan applies to all local officials, departments, and agencies in Uvalde County and the Cities of Uvalde and Sabinal.[1129]

The Plan adopts the NIMS in accordance with the Homeland Security Presidential Directive 5 (HSPD-5).[1130] It provides a consistent approach to the effective management of situations involving natural or human-made disasters, or terrorism. Further, NIMS allows Uvalde County to integrate their response activities using a set of standardized organizational structures designed to improve interoperability between all levels of government, private sector, and nongovernmental organizations.

One of the key components of NIMS is ICS, and the Plan directs "the first local emergency responder to arrive at the scene of an emergency to implement the incident command system and serve as the incident commander until relieved by a more senior or more qualified individual."[1131] The incident commander will "establish an incident command post (ICP) and provide an assessment of the situation to local officials, identify response resources required, and direct the on-scene response from the ICP."[1132] (For more on incident command, see "Chapter 3. Leadership, Incident Command, and Coordination.")

The Plan further states:

> In emergency situations where other jurisdictions or the state or federal government are providing significant response resources or technical assistance, it is generally desirable to transition from the normal ICS structure to a Unified Command structure. This arrangement helps to ensure that all participating agencies are involved in developing objectives and strategies to deal with the emergency.[1133]

[1127] Texas Division of Emergency Management, *State of Texas Emergency Management Plan: Basic Plan*, 11.

[1128] *Basic Emergency Management Plan for Uvalde County.*

[1129] *Basic Emergency Management Plan for Uvalde County.*

[1130] For more on HSPD-5, see DHS, *Homeland Security Presidential Directive 5.*

[1131] *Basic Emergency Management Plan for Uvalde County.*

[1132] *Basic Emergency Management Plan for Uvalde County.*

[1133] *Basic Emergency Management Plan for Uvalde County.*

The County Judge, Mayors, City Managers, and the EMC make up the Executive Group, which provides guidance and direction for emergency management programs and for emergency response and recovery operations, all in compliance with NIMS.[1134] During disasters, they may carry out those responsibilities from the Uvalde County EOC, which should be activated during major emergencies and disasters.[1135] In these situations, a clear division of responsibilities between the incident command post and the EOC is established.[1136] The EMC will manage the EOC. The incident commander will manage the emergency response at the incident site. In incidents where local resources are insufficient, the cities should approach the county prior to requesting assistance from the state.[1137]

During emergency operations in Uvalde, department heads retain administrative and policy control over their employees and equipment. However, personnel and equipment will carry out mission assignments directed by the incident commander. Each department or agency is responsible for having its own operating procedures to be followed during response operations, but interagency procedures, such as common communications protocol, may be adopted to facilitate coordinated effort.[1138]

During major emergencies in Uvalde County, it may be necessary to transition from the normal ICS structure to a multiagency coordination system. The EOC is central to this, and functions as a conduit for coordinating information and resources. The incident commander will manage and direct the on-scene response from the ICP. The Uvalde County EOC will mobilize and deploy resources for use by the incident commander, coordinate external resource and technical support, research problems, provide information to senior managers, disseminate emergency public information, and perform other tasks to support on-scene operations.[1139]

The Plan includes a separate document, *Annex G (Law Enforcement)*, which is assigned to the Sheriff's Office/Police Chief. *Annex G* does not contain specific language regarding violent attacks on schools but does direct law enforcement to take the lead in pre- and post-crisis management activities such as investigation, evidence gathering, and pursuit of suspects.[1140]

The local law enforcement agencies identified in *Annex G* include UCSO, UPD, Sabinal Police Department, and Southwest Texas Junior College (SWTJC) Police Department.[1141] Upon request, the Uvalde County Constables will augment the Sheriff's Office, and the School District police, when requested by the police chief, will augment the police department during major emergencies.[1142]

[1134] *Basic Emergency Management Plan for Uvalde County.*

[1135] *Basic Emergency Management Plan for Uvalde County.*

[1136] *Basic Emergency Management Plan for Uvalde County.*

[1137] *Basic Emergency Management Plan for Uvalde County.*

[1138] *Basic Emergency Management Plan for Uvalde County.*

[1139] *Basic Emergency Management Plan for Uvalde County.*

[1140] CIR Document and Data Review.

[1141] CIR Document and Data Review.

[1142] CIR Document and Data Review.

Law enforcement referenced in *Annex G* are required to take the lead in crisis management activities, and several functions outlined in the preparedness protocol in *Annex G* include: regular review and updating of emergency plans and procedures; identifying pre-planned evacuation routes and preparation of traffic control plans; development of communication systems that provide for connectivity of all law enforcement agencies and external agencies that may respond pursuant to inter-local agreements; training primary and auxiliary law enforcement personnel to conduct emergency operations; identifying and training law enforcement personnel to staff the EOC and ICP; and conducting drills and exercises to test plans, procedures, and training. [1143]

Each agency director has a responsibility to ensure their agency personnel have the necessary training and "in accordance with the NIMS, possess the level of training, experience, credentialing, currency, physical and medical fitness, or capability for any positions they are tasked to fill."[1144]

The Plan authorizes the following individuals to activate the EOC: County Judge, Sheriff, Police Chief, Mayors, and EMC, with the following line of succession for the County Judge and Mayors: Sheriff, Police Chief, and EMC.[1145] Line of succession for the Sheriff/Police Chief are left blank.[1146]

At a basic level of readiness (normal conditions), Uvalde County law enforcement agencies are required to review and update emergency operations plans and procedures; maintain a list of law enforcement resources; maintain and periodically test equipment; conduct appropriate training, drills, and exercises; identify potential evacuation, traffic control, and security issues and estimate law enforcement requirements; develop tentative task assignments; and identify potential resource shortfalls. [1147]

After a large-scale event, the executive leadership group is to organize and conduct a review of emergency operations following guidance outlined in the plan.

[1143] CIR Document and Data Review.

[1144] *Basic Emergency Management Plan for Uvalde County.*

[1145] *Basic Emergency Management Plan for Uvalde County.*

[1146] CIR Document and Data Review.

[1147] CIR Document and Data Review.

December 2021 Tabletop Exercise

As part of the Plan, the Uvalde EOC coordinates a drill on an annual basis for all participants.[1148] These exercises are generally designed to improve strategic planning and increase readiness for a worst-case scenario.[1149] On December 2, 2021, the EOC held a Sand Table-Tabletop Exercise titled "Concan Wildfire."[1150] In the scenario, a barbeque fire pit was knocked over near a popular state park that brings in thousands of summer visitors. The wildfire scenario was designed to focus on "Incident Command, communication issues . . . how to establish an Incident Communications Plan, Staging area issues . . . as well as managing public information and warning . . ."[1151]

Thirty-one agencies from the public and private sectors attended the exercise, including one media outlet. The attendees at the Uvalde County EOC included the UCSO, UPD, two local volunteer fire departments, the Uvalde Fire Marshal Office, the local newspaper *Uvalde Leader News*, along with Uvalde Memorial Hospital and others.[1152] TXDPS was not in attendance, nor were several other agencies which are in close proximity to the city of Uvalde, that responded to the shooting at Robb Elementary School, including UCISD PD, U.S. Border Patrol, ATF, and the FBI.

After the exercise, the Uvalde County EOC drafted an *After-Action Improvement Plan on December 10, 2021* ("the Report"), and rated the performance of capabilities as observed during the exercise:

- Develop Awareness of Public Information and Warning was performed with "some challenges."[1153]

- Awareness of Incident/Operational Communications was performed with "major challenges."[1154]

- Develop Operational Coordination, Mass Care Issues, Develop Situational Awareness, and Develop Fatality Management Issues was performed with "some challenges."[1155]

[1148] CIR Document and Data Review.

[1149] CIR Document and Data Review.

[1150] CIR Document and Data Review.

[1151] CIR Document and Data Review.

[1152] CIR Document and Data Review.

[1153] Performed with Some Challenges (S): The targets and critical tasks associated with the core capability were completed in a manner that achieved the objective(s) and did not negatively impact the performance of other activities. Performance of this activity did not contribute to additional health and/or safety risks for the public or for emergency workers, and it was conducted in accordance with applicable plans, policies, procedures, regulations, and laws. However, opportunities to enhance effectiveness and/or efficiency were identified.

[1154] Performed with Major Challenges (M): The targets and critical tasks associated with the core capability were completed in a manner that achieved the objective(s), but some or all of the following were observed: demonstrated performance had a negative impact on the performance of other activities; contributed to additional health and/or safety risks for the public or for emergency workers; and/or was not conducted in accordance with applicable plans, policies, procedures, regulations, and laws.

[1155] CIR Document and Data Review.

The Report also acknowledged that the executive levels understand ICS, but not lower-level ranked staff.[1156] There was an acknowledgement of the difficulties of finding money and time for trainings, and there is a reference about bringing in future courses on ICS. The Report did include the following reference as part of the analysis of operational conditions/mass case:

> Uvalde County does not have the resources to respond and manage a large scale MCI. Situational Awareness is critical to foresee the need and establish mutual aid and resources to deal with all aspects of [an] MCI, medical, EMS, LEO, shelter, food, health, security, and transportation are critical issues to manage and be cognizant of.[1157]

It further continues with the following from the analysis of situational awareness:

> Leadership at the response area is cognizant of the issues in managing events on a daily basis. However, volunteer levels and lower rank personnel need continued updated training in ICS to learn situational awareness factors, life safety, mutual aid issues, operational period management, equipment, assets, and tools available to respond to, manage, [and] recover from [an] MCI on a larger scale. Continued training and practice is the key to improving this capability. This was discussed during the exercise.[1158]

Finally, the areas for improvement under public information and warning included:

> Rumors and Social Media can create panic and misinformation. PIO Development to use one message, and the one outlet for managing communications is critical. While other Major Casualty Incidents have been handled through the Texas Department of Public Safety, and Texas Parks and Wildlife, due to the size and nature of past events, we are working towards and have both the City of Uvalde PIO and the County of Uvalde PIO for Social Media efforts. Getting on top of messaging from the outset is critical to managing an event of this type to reduce panic, provide timely information to the affected populations, and to advise the public in general.[1159]

The Report, drafted five months before the shooting at Robb Elementary School, included the following corrective actions:

- Establish PIO and messaging early, train for this type of event (start May 2022)
- Bring in specific training for MCI (start April 2022)
- Bring in ICS 300-400 classroom level instruction (Start May 2022)
- Train Leadership with ICS Command Level courses (start September 2022)
- Bring in ICS level specific courses for MCI management (start September 2022)[1160]

[1156] CIR Document and Data Review.

[1157] CIR Document and Data Review.

[1158] CIR Document and Data Review.

[1159] CIR Document and Data Review.

[1160] CIR Document and Data Review.

As is now known, the local agencies never completed these actions.

The Plan as outlined meets generally accepted practices and standards; however, the CIR team's review revealed that key stakeholders were not engaged in the EOC planning, drills, and training.[1161] The approach to emergency operation planning was lackadaisical at times and relied more on individual relationships to stay informed when a critical incident occurs[1162] instead of a formal coordination and response process.

This lack of coordinated pre-planning contributed to the failure in the response on May 24, 2022, at Robb Elementary School. Law enforcement who responded were mostly siloed within their own agency's protocols, procedures, and training and did not effectively operate in a multiagency environment, other than on a personal basis. Personnel stated that although they do not cross-train together, they "often have officers attend the same training."[1163]

For example, at least two Uvalde constables were at the scene of the shooting at Robb Elementary School as part of the overall law enforcement response. Despite performing a law enforcement function, these constables did not participate in any formalized planning, preparation, or active shooter training and tabletop exercises with their counterparts in the city police department or county sheriff's office.[1164] The fragmentation and siloed agency operations, training, drills, and coordination contributed to a lack of clarity and a failed response. Based on interviews, an after action review of the tragedy at Robb Elementary School has not been completed per the plan.[1165]

From a pre-incident planning and preparation perspective, there must be greater emphasis on collaborative leadership and emergency management training with local, state, and federal law enforcement agencies,[1166] as well as all relevant stakeholders. It is essential that all relevant agencies and organizations actively engage in emergency operation plans, drills, exercises, and training. This tragedy also highlights the need for robust emergency response planning that covers a range of critical incidents and not just natural disaster preparation.[1167]

[1161] CIR Fact Finding.

[1162] CIR Fact Finding.

[1163] CIR Fact Finding.

[1164] CIR Fact Finding; CIR Training Analysis.

[1165] CIR Fact Finding.

[1166] CIR Fact Finding.

[1167] CIR Fact Finding.

Operation Coyote Overwatch

After the shooting at Robb Elementary, on May 31, 2022, a Mutual Aid Agreement known as "Operation Coyote Overwatch" was established by and between the City of Uvalde, Texas and a combination of certified Texas law enforcement and telecommunications officer volunteers.* Pursuant to an executive order issued by the City of Uvalde, Mayor Don McLaughlin delegated authority to the Operation Coyote Overwatch incident commander, Dilley, TX Chief Homer Delgado. In this role, Chief Delgado was charged to manage the on-scene operations related to the City's response and recovery from the May 24, 2022, mass shooting event that impacted the City of Uvalde, including direction of all City employees and resources to meet several objectives set forth in the agreement and under the authority of the mayor and in conjunction with the chief of the Uvalde Police Department.[†]

Essentially, the agreement was reached after a request from the City of Uvalde mayor to the Texas Police Chiefs Association and surrounding agencies in the form of law enforcement services and public emergency response resources and equipment.[‡] The activities and response of Operation Coyote Overwatch came under the direct control of the City of Uvalde, while the direct supervision of the personnel, equipment, resources, and accountability of personnel remained the responsibility of the designated supervisory personnel of Operation Coyote Overwatch.[§]

Through Operation Coyote Overwatch, 497 officers from 41 different agencies from across the state of Texas came to Uvalde over a 3-week period.[**] The officers provided security for families, officers, and employees, as well as escorts for the funerals.[††]

This type of interagency response is an example of how a well-coordinated and managed effort marshalling resources toward a specific goal can alleviate the resource restrictions of any single responding agency. Those agencies and law enforcement personnel who responded are to be commended for their contributions to this coordinated, officially sponsored effort.

---

* CIR Document and Data Request.

† CIR Document and Data Request.

‡ CIR Fact Finding.

§ CIR Document and Data Request.

** CIR Fact Finding.

†† CIR Fact Finding.

Mutual Aid Agreements and Memoranda of Understanding

In addition to the Plan, other agreements are discussed in this section. The UPD Policy 1.5. *Mutual Aid* was issued in 2015 to establish procedures, duties, and responsibilities for helping or requesting assistance from another law-enforcement agency and to provide for the use of statewide law-enforcement support systems. The UPD is to assist neighboring law enforcement agencies, UCSO, or TXDPS in handling emergency calls, and at times when they are unable to respond immediately, or when they need assistance in safely completing a task or assignment.[1168]

There was also a memorandum of understanding (MOU)[1169] between the UPD and UCISD PD, which was signed on August 5, 2019, about 1 year after the UCISD PD was established. The two-page MOU dictates that UCISD PD will respond to and be responsible for investigating all crimes, infractions, misdemeanors, and felonies committed by or against district students, employees, or the general public; on or near District property; during regular school hours or while attending school-sponsored events; or while traveling to and from school and/or school-sponsored events. The UCISD PD will also investigate crimes committed against school district property. The MOU requires both police departments to openly communicate with each other, and mandates that each department identify a "liaison" who reports directly to the respective police chief as a means to formalize this communication process. Both departments are required to make reasonable efforts to coordinate activities that impact the other department.[1170] (See "Chapter 7. School Safety and Security" and "Chapter 3. Leadership, Incident Command, and Coordination" for more on this MOU.) However, the MOU did not specify how law enforcement should respond to an active shooter situation. This lack of clarity contributed to the delayed response by law enforcement during the Robb Elementary School shooting on May 24, 2022.

Training

A component of planning and preparation is supporting personnel with the necessary skills and equipment to manage their roles and responsibilities effectively.

[1168] CIR Document and Data Review.

[1169] According to Texas Administrative Code, a memorandum of understanding (MOU) is defined as, "A written document evidencing the understanding or agreement of two or more parties regarding the subject matter of the agreement. Because the underlying agreement may or may not be legally binding and enforceable in and of itself, a memorandum of understanding may or may not constitute a contract. It is generally considered a less formal way of evidencing an agreement and is ordinarily used in state government only between or among state agencies or other government entities. The term is used interchangeably with 'memorandum of agreement'." TEX. ADMIN. CODE § 392.303(14), Texas Health and Human Services Commission: Definitions—Memorandum of Understanding (MOU).

[1170] CIR Document and Data Request.

Peace Officer Standards and Training

State legislatures and state Peace Officer Standards and Training (POST) entities play a significant role in mandating the types and frequencies of training for peace officers within each state that guide and ensure officers are trained and in compliance with necessary training regulations. In the state of Texas, the regulatory state agency is the Texas Commission on Law Enforcement (TCOLE), which has the following mission:

> To establish and enforce standards to ensure that the people of Texas are served by highly trained and ethical law enforcement, corrections, and telecommunications personnel.[1171]

The 9 commissioners, along with the 46 employees, handle TCOLE's statutory charges and "as of August 1, 2019, these employees oversee 2,595 law enforcement agencies with 110,452 active licenses, 299 training providers, and 97,276 licensees."[1172]

The current training cycle, which started on September 1, 2021, and goes until August 31, 2025, is divided into two training units with August 31, 2023, the transition point.[1173] All licensed peace officers, including county sheriffs and deputy constables, have the following requirements:

- First 2-year Training Unit (9/1/21—8/31/23)
  - 40 hours to include Legislative Update course
- Second 2-year Training Unit (9/1/23—8/31/25)
  - 40 hours to include Legislative Update course
- 4-Year Training Cycle (9/1/21—8/31/25)
  - For licensed peace officers without intermediate (or higher) proficiency certification.[1174] Must complete: Cultural Diversity, Crisis Intervention, Special Investigative Topics, De-escalation[1175]

There are also other requirements based on new roles or the year of the licensing.[1176] For example, school-based law enforcement officers must obtain a "TCOLE School-Based Law Enforcement Proficiency Certificate."[1177]

[1171] TCOLE, "TCOLE Mission."

[1172] TCOLE, "TCOLE History."

[1173] TCOLE, "Legislatively Mandated Training."

[1174] For more on proficiency certificates, see TCOLE, "Proficiency Certificates."

[1175] TCOLE, "Legislatively Mandated Training."

[1176] TCOLE, "Legislatively Mandated Training."

[1177] Tex. Admin. Code § 221.1; Tex. Admin. Code § 221.43.

Twelve Tenets of Training Concepts

The 12 tenets of training are meant to help leaders and training personnel identify training that has been vetted and proven to be effective, and is taught by qualified, certified, and continually evaluated instructors. The CIR team developed these tenets based on robust discussions, experience, and expertise of the CIR team.*

The 12 Tenets of Training

1. What is the problem you are trying to solve through training?

2. What is the curriculum and how is the course taught (in person, virtually, lecture, scenarios, etc.)?

3. How long is the course and is the length appropriate for the learning objectives to be effectively taught, and are they learned by the students?

4. How frequently should the training be taken (aka refresher), and should the entire course be taken or is a shorter refresher option viable?

5. Who is providing the training?

6. What are the training entity's bona fides?

7. How does the training entity train and certify their instructors?

8. How does the training entity evaluate their instructors?

9. How often does the training entity evaluate their instructors for consistency in deliverance of the training curriculum?

10. How often is the training curriculum evaluated, reviewed, and updated to ensure the learning objectives are being taught with the most relevant data?

11. Can the training be taught to multiple agencies at the same time or is it agency-specific (e.g., Internal Policies and Procedures of a particular law enforcement agency)?

12. Does the training effectively solve the learning problem?

---

* These CIR-developed tenets were also used by the CIR team during their review and analysis of the responding agencies' training materials as well as the observations by the CIR team. To see a full list of the trainings that the CIR team observed, please see "Appendix B. Report Methodology."

Mandatory training time/requirements spent on duties a peace officer performs daily (e.g., traffic stops, etc.) may be better shifted to training options focused on unique, complex tactical events, such as an active attacker. Such low-frequency/high-impact events are usually the ones that come with the steepest costs—in lives lost, injuries sustained, community fractures, litigation, ensuing mental health issues (victims/community/officers), and subsequent media scrutiny. Yet, training for these events may not be required. Notably, the current TCOLE training cycle does not have active shooter as a required course or topic. TCOLE and other state POSTs should work to conduct coordinated routine reviews of mandatory training programs for officers within their state to determine what is the appropriate balance of training topics and courses.

Outside of the TCOLE mandates, agencies set their own requirements, as well as offer trainings in topics of their choosing. However, budgetary and staffing shortages are rampant among law enforcement agencies at all levels across the country, including the local agencies under this review. Information provided by peace officers as a part of this review highlighted these challenges and indicated training opportunities are typically the first things that get cut in times of fiscal constraints. Many law enforcement agencies do not have sufficient funding to pay the costs associated with training, including officers' overtime, adequate training facilities, or necessary equipment, and resources to provide reality-based training offerings. Multijurisdictional training can help with these budgetary constraints, while also improving coordination during an emergency, as explained above.

Another solution is to send officers to "Train-The-Trainer" courses, where agency trainers learn the curriculum and, where possible, are certified to go back to their agencies to teach the curriculum, which potentially serves a greater long-term benefit to the agency and surrounding departments. That trained peace officer then becomes an asset to provide the training more frequently and locally so that cost and resources are less impacted. However, it is important that the trainers continue to follow the certified training curriculum rather than deviating from the materials.

The next three sections discuss in detail incident command/leadership, active shooter, and resiliency training, including analysis of the available records of personnel present at Robb Elementary.[1178]

Incident Command and Leadership Training

Proper training includes training on ICS and leadership to help individuals who will take on—or who may be expected to act in—leadership positions during a response to a major incident to understand and fulfill their roles and responsibilities. Supervisors play key roles in managing critical incidents, from assuming roles in the incident command structure to assisting in discouraging the unnecessary self-deployment of their officers.[1179] Training can help to practice these roles prior to a critical incident response.

[1178] See "Appendix B. Report Methodology" for more on the training analysis.

[1179] Braziel et al., *Bringing Calm to Chaos.*

Figure 8-1. ICS training progression

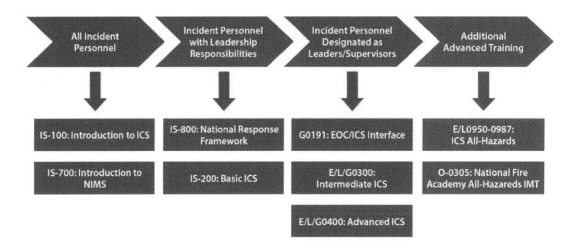

Incident Command and Leadership Training Principles

The NIMS Training Program has set the standard for ICS training, which is outlined in the *National Incident Management System Training Program*.[1180]

To accomplish the NIMS objectives, FEMA has issued training guidelines based on three basic levels of responsibility for responders:[1181]

- *All Incident Personnel:* Associated courses provide the foundational knowledge to help nonsupervisory incident personnel understand where they fit in the overall incident structure. Many incident personnel never advance beyond these baseline courses.

- *Incident Personnel with Leadership Responsibilities:* Associated courses provide additional background on external incident management systems for mid-level incident personnel responsible for establishing the initial incident command or for those preparing for a future supervisory role.

- *Incident Personnel Designated as Leaders/Supervisors:* Courses provide enhanced knowledge and increased comfort in using NIMS structures and processes for senior level incident personnel. Trainees are typically those designated as ICS or EOC leaders/supervisors for large or complex incidents that extend beyond a single operational period and generate an incident action plan.

[1180] FEMA, *National Incident Management System Training Program*.

[1181] FEMA, *National Incident Management System Training Program*.

The training requirements and progression of courses for field personnel who will operate within ICS are illustrated in figure 8-1 on page 378.

IS-700 NIMS, an Introduction and *ICS-100 Introduction to the Incident Command System* are considered the baseline courses.[1182] Even if the agency has not fully committed to NIMS, it is still recommended that agency leaders have this awareness through the baseline courses.

The *International Association of Chiefs of Police Incident Command Model Policy* likewise emphasizes the importance of NIMS/ICS trainings, recommending:

- An annual NIMS/ICS training should be conducted through a tabletop exercise or actual field exercises.

- Training should be multijurisdictional.

- Awareness-level NIMS courses are required for all sworn members.

- NIMS is required for all supervisors.

- An after action review should be prepared after each training exercise.[1183]

Incident Command and Leadership Training in Uvalde

Reviewing the training records for 135 responding personnel from 9 agencies, 61 personnel took at least one distinct ICS/NIMS course, with only 7 officers receiving ICS-100 and 6 officers receiving IS-700 (considered the baseline courses as stated in the previous paragraph).[1184] The most frequent ICS/NIMS courses are *PER-200 FEMA Field Force Operations* (n = 29), *ICS-300 Intermediate ICS for Expanding Incidents* (n = 29), and *ICS-400 Advanced ICS* (n = 23), which all tend to be offshoots of the baseline courses focusing on particular topics.

Although all officers should be exposed to NIMS and ICS for familiarity, it is critical for the top leadership of the responding agencies. Based on the CIR analysis and CIR-conducted interviews, of the leaders from the main responding agencies, only UCISD PD Chief Arredondo and the TXDPS Regional Director[1185] attended ICS/NIMS training prior to the incident (see table 8-2 on page 380).[1186]

[1182] FEMA, "Emergency Management Institute | ICS Resource Center."

[1183] IACP, *Incident Command Model Policy.*

[1184] CIR Training Analysis. Note: Some officers took multiple trainings, so the number of personnel for each course will total more than 61.

[1185] Although the TXDPS Regional Director was the highest TXDPS staff member to respond to the incident, he is not the highest official at TXDPS. The CIR team is not including the names of anyone other than chief executives and governmental/elected officials, so the name of the Regional Director is intentionally blank.

[1186] CIR Training Analysis.

Table 8-2. Distinct NIMS, ICS, and emergency management training for leaders from main responding agencies

Agency	Leader and training
UPD	Acting Chief Pargas
	• 0 hrs.
UCISD PD	Chief Arredondo
	• 32 hrs.
	• ICS-300 (2008), ICS-400 (2008)
UCSO	Sheriff Nolasco
	• 0 hrs.
TXDPS	Regional Director
	• 88 hrs.
	• ICS-300 (2010), ICS-400 (2010), Incident Command Simulation Training (2016), Campus Based Emergency Training (2016)

The incident and associated analysis demonstrates that agencies need to prioritize ICS/NIMS training for all ranked personnel, especially for the rank of commanders and above, since they may be in a position to implement ICS.

Why Do All Levels Need Incident Command Training?

When a call for service comes into the dispatch center, dispatchers become the first incident commander of a problem until they assign it to a patrol officer for a response. There is a requirement to successfully transition the call for service to relinquish their function as the incident commander and to pass the torch to the patrol officer who then serves as incident commander until the problem is resolved, or a more senior law enforcement officer is called to the incident to assist. The process continues until the Chief is involved or the incident is resolved at a lower leadership level. All law enforcement officers should receive Incident Command Training to be able to assume the role as incident commander, whether it be on a routine daily call for service or an active attacker incident. Training on incident command should include all levels of law enforcement within an agency, external law enforcement partners, dispatchers, fire/EMS, Community leaders, and Office of Emergency Management personnel.

From a leadership perspective, at least 86 personnel on site took a distinct leadership training in advance of the incident. For the leaders of the four main responding agencies (see table 8-3), the majority of leadership training was focused on supervision and management. However, all but Uvalde County Sheriff Nolasco have attended a more focused leadership series or institute.

With strains on training budgets, leadership courses may be de-prioritized; however, providing leadership skills to manage day-to-day activities and to manage critical incidents is vital.

Table 8-3. Distinct leadership training for leaders from main responding agencies

Agency	Leader and training
UPD	Acting Chief Pargas • 188 hrs. • 2005–2021, management/supervision, leadership styles, FBI LEEDA Command Institute, and Command Staff Leadership Series
UCISD PD	Chief Arredondo • 315 hrs. • 2002–2021, management/supervision, chief's course, and Command Staff Leadership Series
UCSO	Sheriff Nolasco • 49 hrs. • 1998–2014, management/supervision
TXDPS	Regional Director • 833 hrs. • 2010–2018, supervisor's course, effective leadership/leadership training, management/supervision, DPS Command College

Active Shooter Training

Active shooter training is also a key component of planning for a mass violence incident like the tragedy at Robb Elementary.

Complacency in Training

Complacency in the training environment does not build positive muscle-memory which results in an ineffective real-world response. Training must be physically challenging and psychologically demanding in order for your body to take over your mind's doubts in a real-world incident.* Training must recognize and prepare law enforcement personnel to make decisions in overwhelming, novel, complex, and rapidly evolving environments.

_____

* CIR Fact Finding; ALERRT, *Active Shooter Response Level 1 Version 7.2*; DHS, *Law Enforcement Active Shooter Emergency Response Version 3.1: Instructor Guide*; CIR Document and Data Review.

Active Shooter Training Principles

To evaluate best practices and identify available active shooter training options, the CIR team observed multiple national active shooter trainings taught by different entities. In every instance the desire and want by the instructors to best prepare their students for an efficient and effective response to an active attacker threat was impressive. While a majority of the curricula was consistent between the training courses, there were some stark differences worth noting:

- In one course, the trainers had the flexibility to modify the curriculum to suit the needs of the host agency. While on the surface this may seem like a promising idea, it goes against the mindset of standardized training for all officers in order to execute a quick and decisive resolution to an active attacker incident. A standardized foundational curriculum and a common language must first be taught and understood before modifications and enhancements are made to the curriculum.

- While all courses discussed the importance of a solo-officer response to an active attacker incident, some only briefly drilled on the concept. Others allotted time for drills and scenarios based upon this type of necessary response.

- While all courses discussed the importance of gaining access to a location where an active attacker is present utilizing any means necessary, only one course provided an in-depth presentation of the topic of mechanical breaching through a classroom-based presentation, hands-on drills, and scenarios utilizing the three key breaching tools (Halligan, sledgehammer, and bolt cutters).

Across all the trainings, the value of scenario-based training cannot be overstated. Based on these observations, analysis of the incident, data, interviews with personnel on the ground, and consultations with subject matter experts in the field, the CIR team recommends 8 hours of scenario-based stress-induced active shooter training annually for front-line officers with all levels of rank-and-file in the training. However, with budgetary and staffing shortages, the CIR team encourages agencies to explore creative solutions to training on active shooter situations. For example, scenarios can be incorporated into firearm qualifications, reinforcement of concepts during in-service, and mini exercises during roll call. Wherever possible, baseline foundational training content must be consistent across training providers. Agencies' training, as well as policies and procedures, should clearly articulate the differences between an active shooter situation and barricade situation, as well as the priorities in a response, to stop the killing and stop the dying.

Training must also cover lockdown protocols, so that law enforcement understands how critically vulnerable locations teach their occupants how to respond to an active threat. On the day of the incident, an overwhelming majority of responding officers who arrived later in the incident indicated that they did not hear sounds of distress coming from any of the classrooms (e.g., screams, calls for help, etc.), so they assumed the rooms were not occupied by students or school staff. Additionally, classroom lights were out, exterior-facing window shades/blinds were drawn, classroom door windows covered, and no signs of human presence in the classrooms was observed, adding to the perception of an empty school building, other than the subject. Had the officers understood the school's lockdown protocols during an active threat, and what actions were mandated to be taken during a lockdown by students and school staff, the response may have been different.

In line with this education, officers should help instruct options-based civilian response to an active attacker training (Run, Hide, Fight / Avoid, Deny, Defend, etc.) so that they are aware of the usual or typical operations or "normal environment" and the occupants' response plan during an active attacker incident. The environment is ever-changing, and so should the options available to those who find themselves in an active shooter incident.[1187] Active shooter incidents across America last, on average, about 12.5 minutes in duration.[1188] Every movement by the shooter, every response action by those innocents involved, the closing response of law enforcement, and structures and open spaces in the area are aspects of the environment that are ever-changing throughout an active shooter incident. Those involved must be trained to transition from one aspect of an options-based response to another until the threat is neutralized to enhance their chances of survival. For example, the after action review of the Columbine tragedy in 1999, where 12 people were killed and 24 injured, discussed the Run, Hide, and Fight concept.[1189] Many students who ran were uninjured or were injured but able to survive.[1190] Those who took the lockdown approach were left with no options and many were killed or severely wounded.[1191] This mass shooting changed the entirety of law enforcement and medical response to an active attack.

Moreover, research should be conducted to determine whether or not changing the "normal environment" of a space in response to an active attacker threat provides any additional protections from being targeted by the active attacker. For example, consideration is warranted to assess if the protocol requiring staff and students to turn off classroom lights in an otherwise normally lit environment draws attention or diverts attention away. Inherent in this needed analysis is also the

---

[1187] CIR Fact Finding.

[1188] FBI, *Active Shooter Incidents in the United States in 2021*.

[1189] *Report of Governor Bill Owens' Columbine Review Commission*.

[1190] *Report of Governor Bill Owens' Columbine Review Commission*.

[1191] *Report of Governor Bill Owens' Columbine Review Commission*.

challenge that creating an artificial environment of lights out, window coverings drawn, and no signs of human presence presents to responding peace officers. In many instances, it places the officer at greater risk and limits the environmental clues that help them locate, isolate, and neutralize the threat. An active attacker has no rules to follow when they fire their weapon. The environment matters much less to them than to a responding officer who must account for every round that they fire from their weapon and rely heavily on sight, sound, touch, and smell to identify stimulus to determine an appropriate response.

What Should a Successful Active Shooter Course Have?

The CIR team developed this list of topics/activities to help law enforcement leaders and trainers determine whether an active shooter training fits their needs:

- Standardization of instruction across instructors and over time

- History of key active shooter incidents that led to the changing tactics and medical response. There are lessons to be learned from past active shooter incidents, such as good/bad command and control, good/bad communications, good/bad tactical response, good/bad leadership, etc. Many things that failed in Uvalde were in previous significant active shooter after-action reviews

- Breaching and hands-on drills utilizing mechanical breaching tools (e.g., bolt cutter, sledgehammer, Halligan)

- Solo officer and two-, three-, and four-officer response, drills, and scenario

- Superiority of firepower

- Equipment necessary to combat an active attacker

- Ensure only efficient classroom time (e.g., convert some classroom time to pre-class required reading)

- Realistic scenarios with doors closed and locked in some instances, requiring the law enforcement officer to find alternate entrances to the threat area

- Incorporating simunitions in training scenarios to most effectively simulate real-world conditions of an officer being confronted and shot by a subject

- A module on safety during the training course *continues on page 385*

What Should a Successful Active Shooter Course Have?, cont'd.

- Stop the killing, stop the dying, and evacuate the wounded to a higher level of trauma care, including

    - tactical: Decision-making beyond shoot/don't shoot scenarios. Articulate the "why" behind any decision, and the ability to support by law and policy. Gather information/intelligence en route, upon arrival, and throughout the incident. Parking at scene. Bound and Overwatch to breach point. Use all senses to identify stimulus and determine appropriate response. Drive toward sound of last known gunfire and search for, locate, and neutralize the shooter. Tactical reloads, checking for injuries to self, room entries. Speed, surprise, violence of action;

    - medical: Tourniquets, pressure application to control blood loss, when to use chest seals, when to pack a wound with gauze, recovery position. Casualty collection points, link up with EMS. Law enforcement evacuation of wounded. Establishing a safe corridor for evacuation.

- Mental/Psychological Training to include

    - move only as fast as you can see, think/process information, and shoot;

    - drills on controlling breathing and stress reduction so tunnel vision and auditory exclusion is lessened;

    - the will to go into a situation knowing you may be shot and/or killed but doing it anyway because it is your job. Many law enforcement officers interviewed stated that May 24 was a "suicide mission" and the will to solve the problem was not there after the initial assault failed and was never regained again until the final assault into the room and killing of the subject;

    - the mindset of an active shooter to indiscriminately kill as many people as possible before being killed/captured by law enforcement. This is not a person who wants to negotiate for freedom of victims or him/herself. This should be reinforced in all law enforcement trainings so responding officers can take appropriate action;

    - the mindset of "it can't or won't happen here" sets all involved up for failure. The mindset of law enforcement should be, "it will happen here, so how do we prepare and ready ourselves for when it happens;"

    - priority of life: community members, officers, subject. Ensure the officers know the most important task is to save the lives of innocent citizens involved in the attack.

Finally, active shooter training should include instruction and scenarios on gaining entry to the threat environment, such as breaching, KNOX boxes (emergency key boxes), and secured equipment located on site. A stronger breaching model should be taught. Training should discuss all aspects of gaining entry to the threat environment (e.g., windows, alternate doors, Keys, Key Cards, Breaching, etc.) and also how to "read" a door to know what type of locking mechanisms it has, how it opens, what keeps it shut (lock, magnet, etc.), and how to defeat most types of commercial doors utilizing a Halligan, sledge, and/or bolt cutters.

Active Shooter Training in Uvalde

The CIR team analyzed the *Active Shooter Response for School-Based Law Enforcement* (SBLE) guide developed by TCOLE in January 2020.[1192] This is the foundation for the 2021 SBLE-Active Shooter Course taught by UCISD PD officers just months before the attack at Robb Elementary School.[1193] The team found that the 29-page document is merely a guide for a law enforcement agency to develop their own training, which leaves far too much latitude for interpretation and deviation from accepted curricula.

The guide includes a number of statements and guidance that diverge from generally accepted practices, including the definition of an active shooter, which differs from the definition used by the federal government, by including the term "unrelated":

- An individual actively engaged in killing or attempting to kill people in a populated area. (FBI definition)[1194]

- An active shooter event involves one or more persons engaged in killing or attempting to kill people in an area occupied by multiple unrelated individuals (TCOLE definition)[1195]

The addition of the term, "unrelated," can be confusing to officers in terms of trying to determine the relation, but also does not comport with the traditional understanding of an active shooter situation.

Further into the training, it states, "an event that starts as an active shooter event can easily morph into a hostage crisis and vice versa,"[1196] which is particularly concerning language and not in accord with generally accepted practices and standards. As detailed in "Chapter 2. Tactics and Equipment," an active shooter rarely ceases to be an active shooter. Based on generally accepted practices and standards in active shooter response and based on national training materials,[1197] the situation should be considered an active shooter especially in a school setting based on the high probability of the presence of victims and innocent civilians.

[1192] CIR Document and Data Review; Texas Commission on Law Enforcement, "*School Based Law Enforcement Training.*"

[1193] CIR Fact Finding.

[1194] FBI, *Active Shooter Incidents in the United States in 2021*.

[1195] CIR Document and Data Review.

[1196] CIR Document and Data Review.

[1197] ALERRT, *Active Shooter Response Level 1 Version 7.2*; DHS, *Law Enforcement Active Shooter Emergency Response Version 3.1: Instructor Guide*; CIR Document and Data Review.

The guide also states, "In the event of an active school attack, school-based law enforcement officers should do the best they can to fill the gap until other first responders can arrive."[1198] The language counters what the National Association of School Resource Officers and the Texas Association of School Resource Officers teach,[1199] which is consistent with the DOJ *Guiding Principles for School Resource Officer Programs guidance* that discusses school resource officers and school-based law enforcement, who have "the authority of a front-line police officers – to solve problems, respond to calls for service, make arrests, and document incidents that occur in their jurisdiction – and additional responsibilities specific to their job working with K-12 students in a school setting."[1200] As such, generally accepted training principles in active shooter training should be consistently taught for all law enforcement, including SROs and school-based law enforcement, including that the officer must drive toward the threat, even if it means a solo response until other law enforcement can arrive and provide assistance. See "Chapter 2. Tactics and Equipment" for further discussion.

It is also problematic that the guidebook states the three primary goals in responding to an active attack in schools are to

- **ISOLATE**—Drive or segregate the attacker in an area where their capacity to harm students, staff, or visitors is minimized until more first responders arrive.

- **DISTRACT**—Engage the attacker so that they have a diminished capacity to hurt students, staff, or visitors. If they are engaged with the officer(s) they will be less capable of hurting innocents. It also buys time for students, staff, and visitors to implement their Avoid-Deny-Defend (ADD) strategies.

- **NEUTRALIZE**—Take away the attacker's capacity to harm other people. This may include the use of deadly force, disabling an attacker, or disarming an attacker and taking them into custody.[1201]

In particular, UCISD's course guidance to "distract" the attacker is concerning and goes against the entire mindset of an active shooter, who has the goal of killing as many people. There is no negotiation with an active shooter. The strategy should be consistent with generally accepted training, which focuses on stopping the killing and stopping the dying. Finally, the first scenario outlined in the guidebook is not an active shooter situation but rather a domestic violence scenario and goes against the definition of an active shooter according to the training as it focuses on a "scorned lover."[1202]

Irrespective of the problematic points in this training guide, according to the training, the incident at Robb Elementary School was never a hostage situation. It was, at all times, an active shooter situation.

This training guide should be re-assessed to correct and strengthen the language for school-based law enforcement agencies to be consistent with generally accepted training.

[1198] CIR Document and Data Review.

[1199] CIR Fact Finding.

[1200] COPS Office, *Guiding Principles for School Resource Officer Programs*.

[1201] CIR Document and Data Review.

[1202] CIR Document and Data Review.

The CIR team also reviewed the training records of the local, county, and state personnel who responded on May 24, 2022 (see table 8-4 <u>on page 389</u>). Eighty percent of training records reviewed[1203] include at least one distinct active shooter course (n=108). However, the courses range in number of hours, format, and type (see table 8-4). For example, personnel who completed the *Active Shooter Response* training ranged in training hours from 2 to 40 hours, which falls in line with the TCOLE range of hours granted for each class (1–40).

The training data also highlight the need for more frequent deliveries of active shooter training. For example, of the 11 officers first on the scene (see "<u>Chapter 3. Leadership, Incident Command, and Coordination</u>"), nine had received active shooter training. Of those, five officers received training within a year of the incident, with the others last receiving training in active shooter as far back as 11 years earlier (in 2011). From a content perspective, five of the officers received at least one ALERRT training and four received the *School-Based Law Enforcement Active Shooter Training Mandate* in December 2021.

For the leaders of the main responding agencies,[1204] only UCISD PD Chief Arredondo had active shooter training (48 hours total, between 2019–2021).[1205]

Interviews of law enforcement at all levels by the CIR team revealed that while all had some level of training, disparities in the amount, frequency, and quality of training existed as highlighted above. Federal and state law enforcement agencies commented that they had access to quality training and were afforded the opportunities to take training. UCSO, UPD, and UCISD PD commented that funding and limited resources prohibited them from being able to receive sufficient and quality training. Across the board, all levels of law enforcement commented that active shooter training had not adequately prepared them for what they witnessed at Robb Elementary School. Additionally, while federal and state police indicated opportunities to train in a multiagency environment, there were limited opportunities, if any, to train with other agencies at the local level.

[1203] See "Appendix B. Report Methodology" for more on the analysis, including the number of training records analyzed.

[1204] Since the TXDPS regional director did not arrive until right before the entry into the classrooms, he is not included in this portion of the analysis.

[1205] CIR Training Analysis.

Table 8-4. Active shooter classes by frequency

Course Title	Hours	Frequency
ALERRT Terrorism Response Tactics—Active Shooter	16–24 hrs.	52
ALERRT Level 1	16–32 hrs.	37
Active Shooter Response	2–40hrs.	36
ALERRT Update	4–10 hrs.	20
School-Based Law Enforcement Active Shooter Training Mandate	8 hrs.	15
Active Shooter—Response Network	4 hrs.	6
ALERRT Exterior Response to Active Shooter Events	24 hrs.	5
PoliceOne—Active Shooter 1	1 hr.	5
PoliceOne—Active Shooter 2	1 hr.	5
PoliceOne—Active Shooter 3	1 hr.	5
PoliceOne—Active Shooter 4	1 hr.	5
ALERRT First Responder Operations in Rural Terrain	24 hrs.	4
ALERRT—Level 1 Train the Trainer	40 hrs.	3
PoliceOne—Active Shooter Prep and Response for School	1 hr.	3
PoliceOne—Active Shooter: Phases and Prevention	1 hr.	3
PoliceOne—Active Shooter: Recognition and Response	1 hr.	3
Texas A&M Engineering Extension Service (TEEX) Active Attack Event Response Leadership	4 hrs.	3
ALERRT Active Attack Integrated Response (AAIR)	16 hrs.	2
PoliceOne—Law Enforcement Response to Active Shooter	2 hrs.	2
ALERRT Exterior Response to Active Shooter Events (ERASE) Train the Trainer	40 hrs.	1
First Responder to Active Shooter	10 hrs.	1
OSS Academy—Active Shooter Response	1 hr.	1
PoliceOne—Active Shooter: Active Shooter Phases & Prevention	1 hr.	1
PoliceOne—Dispatch: Active Shooter	2 hrs.	1
TEEX Active Attack Emergency Communications	3 hrs.	1

Resiliency Training

Comprehensive education and training will aid in building long-term resiliency in responder personnel. Pre-incident preparedness involves several different training paradigms, including models that help participants build a level of confidence and competence in their work. Other models involve preparing responders for what they might encounter in traumatic incidents so they are not completely shocked by exposure (which can still happen with some responders, especially in severe situations), especially now that so many have body-worn cameras that allow them to repeatedly watch video footage of traumatic events. They also include emotion regulation, such as cognitive behavioral work or cognitive strengthening to help responders control their autonomic stress response.[1206] These pre-incident training modules are not in widespread use, as budget constraints tend to lead agencies to focus only on competency skills and those training modules required by law or funding agencies.

As part of the TCOLE basic training requirements, all Texas-certified officers must complete 16 hours of Fitness, Wellness, and Stress Management training. The course focuses on total well-being that goes beyond performance and involves positive lifestyle and healthy behaviors for balanced physical, mental, spiritual, and socio-emotional well-being. It emphasizes that critical incident stress can occur from events such as working on a gruesome accident, involvement in a use-of-force incident or shooting, or body recovery of a child.[1207] Additionally, TCOLE mandates Stress, Health, and Awareness training for telecommunicators dispatchers in their basic training curriculum.[1208]

TXDPS, in collaboration with the FBI National Academy's Officer Safety and Wellness Committee, incorporates resilience training into all aspects of training with a goal of increased employee well-being and retention, improved communication, and an understanding of physical, mental, social, and spiritual resilience.[1209] TXDPS offers several standalone resilience training courses including a 32-hour train-the-trainer course.[1210] In addition, TXDPS offers wellness classes such as Coping with Grief, The TXDPS Resiliency Program, Incident Response: The After-Effects, Suicide Awareness for TXDPS Staff, Suicide Awareness for Supervisors, Stress Management, and Critical Incident Stress.[1211]

Reviewing the TCOLE records of involved nonfederal personnel reveals only minimal officer safety and wellness trainings.[1212] Out of the training records for 140 state and local responding officers, only 46 reported a health, physical fitness, and stress course or the TXDPS *Health, Safety, Physical, and Mental*

[1206] Bloom, Reddy, and Kleinman, "Trauma Debrief Prior to Release of Body-Worn Camera Footage."

[1207] TCOLE, "Basic Peace Officer Course 720;" CIR Document and Data Review.

[1208] TCOLE, "Basic Telecommunicator Licensing Course (2022)."

[1209] Texas Department of Public Safety, "Resilience Training."

[1210] Texas Department of Public Safety, "Resilience Training."

[1211] CIR Document and Data Review.

[1212] CIR analysis of the training records for 140 state and local responding officers.

Fitness course.[1213] The bulk of the safety and wellness courses include *Below 100* (27 officers), Officer Safety/Survival (27 officers), Suicide Prevention (20 officers), Stress Management (7 officers), and Bulletproof Mind and Mental Preparation for Combat (6 officers).[1214]

Outside of TXDPS, there is no indication that any other nonfederal agencies that responded to Robb Elementary provide specific training on wellness, stress management, or resiliency outside of the TCOLE mandates.

To learn more about establishing and maintaining a law enforcement support program, see "Establishing and Maintaining a Responder Support Services Program" in "Appendix F. Trauma and Support Services Supplemental Materials."

Preparation and Planning in Schools to Mitigate the Extent of Trauma

Everyone needs a sense of safety and a secure environment starting from childhood. When these needs are absent or unaddressed, it can cause children to react with fear and anxiety.[1215] For children to learn, a school needs to be a safe environment. An essential component of creating a safe environment is preparedness. Moreover, preparedness activities are one of the most helpful ways to mitigate the development of traumatic stress reactions. A sense of helplessness or confusion in emergencies can increase traumatic stress responses, increasing the risk of someone developing a diagnosable mental health problem. Involving the students and school staff, along with family members in emergency drills and exercises, can help prepare everyone involved with information on what to expect in specific emergencies and equip them with some tools to manage their stress as well as the emergency itself.

Preparedness includes the development of policies and exercises based on best and emerging practices related to planning, organizing, equipping, and training on possible emergency scenarios. An evaluation of the exercises should be conducted, after which corrective actions should be implemented (based on the findings). Corrective actions might involve changing a policy, identifying or clarifying roles and responsibilities, or including multiple response options as practical examples.[1216] Before an incident occurs, students, staff, and family members can learn what actions to take, such as following instructions to evacuate an area where a dangerous situation is located. Preparedness for families and schools may include teaching children to react to an alarm, getting out of a building, or identifying a safe place to meet away from danger. It also involves learning how to initiate coping mechanisms that will help keep emotions (the fear response) under control or manageable, so one can use good judgment and make good decisions during the response phase.

[1213] CIR analysis of the training records for 140 state and local responding officers.

[1214] CIR analysis of the training records for 140 state and local responding officers. (An officer may take more than one course.)

[1215] Salston and Figley, "Secondary Traumatic Stress Effects of Working with Survivors of Criminal Victimization."

[1216] DHS, "Plan and Prepare for Disasters."

Lockdown drills can be conducted for a variety of reasons, such as online threats, local police activity, weather, and other situations. However, in some circumstances, lockdowns may produce anxiety, stress, and traumatic symptoms in some students or staff, as well as loss of instructional time. Proper planning before lockdowns should be part of the emergency operations or preparedness plan. To mitigate possible negative reactions to a lockdown, "planning should include considerations for age and developmental levels, disabilities that might impede mobility and access to instructions, sensory disabilities such as autism that might heighten a distress reaction and/or impede response to instruction, and intellectual disabilities that might impede understanding a situation or instructions. Additionally, second language considerations for students and families must also be addressed."[1217] See "Chapter 5. Public Communications During and Following the Crisis" for more on the lack of public messaging in Spanish.

In 2021, the National Association of School Resource Officers released *Best Practice Considerations for Armed Assailant Drills in Schools*, which recommends "nonsensorial drills (i.e., drill done by calmly walking and talking through the procedures, with no simulation of a real-life event)" be conducted with age-appropriate students since over stimulation of the senses during a drill can cause trauma.[1218] More recently in 2023, a study conducted by Everytown Research and Policy along with Georgia Tech University concluded that "active shooter drills in schools are associated with increases in depression (39 percent), stress and anxiety (42 percent), and physiological health problems (23 percent) overall, including children from as young as 5 years old up to high schoolers, their parents, and teachers."[1219] It is important for school districts to keep trauma-informed practices in mind as part of the planning and implementation of drills, especially post-incident in Uvalde.

As detailed in "Chapter 7. School Safety and Security," the Uvalde community did not sufficiently prepare and engage in disaster, emergency, or mass violence incident planning within their own staff, with law enforcement and other responders, nor with the students, family members, and other caregivers.

Similarly problematic, materials, instructions, and communication generally were only provided in English and did not consider the needs of individuals with limited English proficiency (LEP). In 2013, the population of Uvalde County was 11.69 percent LEP individuals according to the DOJ Civil Rights Division LEP Data Map.[1220] Forty-six percent of individuals speak only English at home, with 52.5 percent speaking Spanish at home per the American Community Survey of 2015 (see figure 8-2 on page 393).[1221]

[1217] National Association of School Psychologists, *Mitigating Psychological Effects of Lockdowns.*

[1218] National Association of School Psychologists, *Best Practice Consideration for Armed Assailant Drills in Schools.*

[1219] Everytown for Gun Safety Support Fund, "The Impact of Active Shooter Drills in Schools." Other articles and stories about this topic: Schonfeld et al., "Participation of Children and Adolescents in Live Crisis Drills and Exercises;" Shalchi, "Psychological Effects of Active Shooter Drills in Schools;" Garcia-Navarro, "Experts Worry Active Shooter Drills in Schools Could Be Traumatic for Students;" Schildkraut and Nickerson, "Should We Or Shouldn't We? Arguments for and Against Lockdown Drills."

[1220] DOJ, "2015 Language Map App."

[1221] U.S. Census Bureau, "Language Spoken at Home by Ability to Speak English for the Population 5 Years and Over: Uvalde County, Texas."

Figure 8-2. Language spoken at home by ability to speak English for the population of individuals ages 5 years and older in Uvalde County, Texas

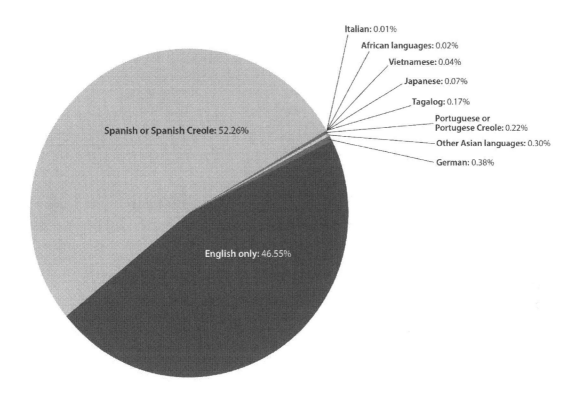

Source: U.S. Census Bureau, "Language Spoken at Home by Ability to Speak English for the Population 5 Years and Over: Uvalde County, Texas."

Effective communications are crucial to responding to an emergency. Many schools use commercial apps for structured alert systems, such as the Raptor, which was used at Robb Elementary. Preparedness exercises that test communication systems are imperative. Internal communications with staff and students on campus that can provide a warning that danger is imminent and specific actions to take (e.g., go to your rooms, lock the doors, stay where you are, etc.) are critical in training exercises that can help reduce anxiety in general as well as worry about "what to do" and creates a familiarity with the process that can increase the odds of carrying out the instructions correctly in a time of need.

Preparedness exercises that address external communications with various audiences are crucial for many reasons. Again, knowing what to do, where to go, who to call, and under which circumstances these actions apply can decrease the anxiety which often accompanies emergencies. In school shooting drills, children and staff practice keeping quiet and not using their phones once the alert has been sent out. Families need to be included in exercises and/or instructions that inform them as to where to call when, whether or not they should approach the school, whether or not their child may be in a hospital, and where a reunification/notification center may be located and how to obtain all of this information. Parents, caregivers, and school staff's families need to be provided information that helps them to understand that all these details may not be known in a preparedness drill; thus, following a prescribed set of instructions/procedures will be critical to respond efficiently as well as to help people remain calm. For most people, knowing what to expect can help decrease anxiety.

A good example is to explain in exercises/drills to parents, caregivers, and staff's families that they will likely be directed away from the site of the school in an emergency as it is critical for response vehicles, such as fire trucks and ambulances, to get through to the buildings without obstruction. Some schools may determine a meeting site (e.g., a nearby store parking lot) before an emergency occurs that is agreed upon with the site owner and the families in advance. Again, this type of preparedness planning can decrease some anxiety and chaos at the scene and increase the efficiency of the response overall.

Preparedness planning involves many aspects such as role determination (e.g., who is the primary caregiver with legal authority over school-aged children), decision trees (e.g., which caregiver is responsible on any given day for the well-being/whereabouts and communication with their child), up-to-date emergency contact information (with the school, within families, with the school-aged child who has memorized their own emergency contact information), and again, back-up information and plans in case the primary plan does not work for whatever reason. Involving parents, caretakers, school staff, and their families in preparedness exercises and drills can help them complete these plans for the school and their own families and identify gaps that need to be covered. All key players in the communications plans must know and utilize these systems from law enforcement radios to dispatch, 911, and 988 services for interoperability success.

Pre-incident preparedness regarding students' emotional and mental status while at school is generally the responsibility of school staff, including teachers, school counselors, social workers, and other staff whose role involves direct interactions with students. While a student's mental wellness is not often viewed from a pre-incident preparedness perspective, it can be a predictor of behavior and, with the proper attention, may help identify the need, which, if acted upon appropriately, has the potential to decrease the risk of a violent assault such as a school shooting. Specifics regarding best practices in assessing students' risk factors are found in "Chapter 7. School Safety and Security." But it is worth noting here that everyone can pay attention to engage with or refer a child in emotional distress or other serious need to appropriate caregivers, professionals, and other resources. Since we know that most mass violence in schools in recent decades has been committed by current and former students,[1222] then it is incumbent upon all who engage within the school setting to pay attention and to "say something," to those whose role it is to act upon a high-risk situation. And again, while a threat assessment needs to be conducted by trained professionals, these professionals need to be alerted to situations or people they may not encounter directly.

[1222] National Threat Assessment Center, U.S. Secret Service, *Averting Targeted School Violence: A U.S. Secret Service Analysis of Plots Against Schools*; Everly and Bienvenu, "'Profiling' School Shooters: Can we tell who will be the next to kill?"

Additionally, just as we can teach anyone to be a gatekeeper for suicide prevention by focusing on critical indicators, anyone can be trained to identify some of the signs of concern or red flags for the risk of school violence. These may include recent violent episodes or threats of violence, obsession with weapons, torture of animals, and clear threats to conduct violence advertised on social media posts or reported to family/friends or acquaintances. Coupled with a recent emotional loss, such as a breakup with a love interest, death of or serious conflict with an immediate family member, or incidents of public humiliation such as bullying (past or recent), these signs can indicate that someone needs some emotional/mental health support.[1223] While not all who require attention to emotional and mental health care will perpetrate incidents of violence, these signs do mean they should at least be referred for a proper, professional assessment.

Planning and Preparation for Public Messaging

As described in "Chapter 5. Public Communications During and Following the Crisis," the communication during and after the tragic event in Uvalde was disjointed, contradictory, and at times inaccurate. While a certain amount of confusion is common with incidents of this magnitude, some of it may have been prevented with better planning and preparation for a large-scale incident.

Communications Planning Principles

A crisis communications plan must exist prior to the onset of a critical incident. Each agency should create a crisis communication plan to achieve a rapid, organized, and open approach to communication during a crisis, and practice it at least once a quarter with smaller events. This will help identify problem areas and solutions and ensure everyone is familiar with the plan and knows their role instead of trying to figure that out during a critical incident.

All Public Information Officers (PIOs) in various fields of industry (e.g., police, government, schools) should obtain FEMA basic and advanced public information officer certifications as a baseline of training.[1224] Those courses teach the Joint Information System, which is a critical part of the Incident Command System. They also instruct on the use of a Joint Information Center (JIC) at a major incident to coordinate messaging and plan news briefings and other external communications.

The PIOs should also participate in regional training exercises to develop a system for sharing information and working together during unplanned major events, such as a mass casualty incident. This should take the form of a JIC that is tied to the operational aspect of training. All the partnering agencies should review their crisis communication plans together to ensure they complement each other. It is critically important that the idea of coordinating messaging is practiced with smaller events, so it is not a foreign concept when a large-scale incident takes place. Practice ensures the PIOs in the region have a

---

[1223] CIR Fact Finding.

[1224] FEMA, "Public Information Awareness and Basics;" FEMA, "Public Information Officer Advanced Level."

history of working together, establishing the lead agency, and coordinating messages before a mass incident. This planning should include agencies communicating with local journalists as a way of developing trust and good working relationships pre-incident.[1225]

PIOs can reference the U.S. Justice Department COPS Office publication, *Strategic Communications for Law Enforcement*, for insight and templates for developing a crisis communication plan.[1226]

In addition, school districts should also have a safety plan for each school which includes a reunification and communication section on how they will direct parents when a crisis occurs. District personnel should arrive to assist parents who are going to rush to the school or to redirect parents to the reunification location. Information about meeting locations should be as specific as possible, including the location address. This post can include pre-written phrases created during exercises testing the crisis communications plan.

Communications Planning in Uvalde

Unfortunately, the concept of the JIS or the physical creation of a JIC did not occur during the Robb Elementary School shooting. Almost none of the PIOs involved in the response had ever heard of these concepts, let alone been trained to master them.

The CIR team learned through interviews with PIOs involved in the response that the region never held PIO meetings or trainings. Nearly 1 month before the mass casualty incident, on April 21, 2022, the school district hosted a mock drunk-driving car accident at Uvalde High School.[1227] While the "Think Twice" exercise was designed to send a safety message to students about the dangers of drinking and driving before prom, it also created an opportunity for the UCISD Communications Director and the UPD PIO to connect with a planned event. This would have been an excellent opportunity to coordinate messaging and practice elements of a crisis communication plan or a virtual JIC. The Uvalde community is small, and many of the PIOs knew each other. That was useful on the day of the shooting; however, the lack of planning and training was a detriment to producing swift, organized, and accurate public messaging. Poor communications erode public trust.

The following sections focus on the training and preparation of PIOs from the various agencies involved in the response. See "Chapter 5. Public Communications During and Following the Crisis" for more details on the precise communications during the tragedy.

UPD

The UPD PIO took swift, proactive action when it came across over the radio that "shots were fired" at Robb Elementary School. The PIO confirmed with their first-line supervisor that there was a critical incident at the school. At 11:43 a.m., UPD was the first agency to post information about the incident.

[1225] CIR Fact Finding.

[1226] Pal et al., *Strategic Communications for Law Enforcement Executives*.

[1227] CIR Fact Finding.

The PIO was at Uvalde Memorial Hospital when the radio transmission occurred and quickly alerted the supervisor of the Emergency Department and the security supervisor so they could prepare for a possible influx of victims. Unfortunately, the hospital did not have anyone serving in a communications role on the date of the incident, so the chief executive officer (CEO) became the de facto PIO.[1228] Under a Joint Information System, a PIO from the lead agency would have contacted the people performing PIO roles at any local hospitals expected to receive victims. This is a vital step for coordinating the release of victim information. Hospital updates should be made public through the JIC and by the hospital simultaneously, in an organized and preplanned manner.

Another situation that could have benefited from pre-incident planning arose at the school. The UPD PIO responded to the scene and used the public announcement system in a sheriff deputy's car to guide parents to the Reunification Center.[1229] A brief time after arriving, the UPD PIO called the UCISD Communications Director to sort out confusion over the Reunification Center for parents and to suggest a news conference.[1230] The two never discussed coordinating messages and the UPD PIO assumed they would each post their own content.[1231] The PIO took the appropriate step of reaching out to a fellow PIO dealing with the incident; however, no one took the necessary step of establishing a JIC at the scene where media was arriving as a national tragedy was unfolding.

When the UPD PIO assumed the role of PIO in 2017, they were "thrown into the role, sink or swim."[1232] Unfortunately, this is quite common for law enforcement PIOs. On their own initiative, the UPD PIO completed PIO training through the Law Enforcement Management Institute of Texas in 2019.[1233] The UPD PIO also participated in the December 2021 tabletop exercise at the Uvalde EOC. The PIO had previously attended meetings at the EOC, but this was the first and only exercise that was offered during the 5 years that the PIO served.[1234]

Of course, not all PIOs take such steps, although that training could improve the likelihood that better communications will occur during multiagency incidents.

The PIO also proactively networked with the TXDPS PIO assigned to Uvalde, the UCSO employee who handles social media, and the UCISD Communication Director, who were helpful when the tragedy struck.[1235] And before the Robb Elementary School incident, the PIO worked with the TXDPS PIO on a reactive basis when there was an incident involving both agencies.[1236]

[1228] CIR Fact Finding.

[1229] CIR Fact Finding.

[1230] CIR Fact Finding.

[1231] CIR Fact Finding.

[1232] CIR Fact Finding.

[1233] CIR Fact Finding.

[1234] CIR Fact Finding.

[1235] CIR Fact Finding.

[1236] CIR Fact Finding.

The UPD PIO reported that they "rarely" had contact with the media before May 24, 2022. In the role as PIO, they managed the department's social media platforms and spent a significant percentage of time planning and executing community engagement activities. The PIO was proud of the community relationships they worked to build. In the months following the incident, the agency was left out of many events in which they typically played a significant role. The Department also stopped posting on social media due to the negative response that it would generate. Over time, the agency has slowly reconnected with the community. Its social media is now limited to a source of information versus an engagement tool with the community.[1237]

UCISD

In the two years leading up to May 24, 2022, Uvalde experienced an increase in the number of critical incidents that impacted school campuses. A school going to secure status became commonplace rather than an anomaly due to occurrences of undocumented immigrants fleeing from law enforcement in high-speed chases that often resulted in a crash and bailout with people running to escape capture.

The UCISD responded to the uptick in critical incidents by putting the Raptor Technologies system in place on all school campuses. This system allowed any faculty or staff member to send out a message calling for a lockdown of a campus. UCISD also established a protocol for informing parents and the community in an efficient manner that a school campus was locked down.

The UCISD Executive Director of Communications and Marketing would typically receive a message from the school police chief about why the campus was in lockdown.[1238] Then the director would notify the parents and community. The first step was drafting an email to parents, followed by modifying that message for a recorded voice message sent via telephone. Next, a message shortened to a 144-character text would go out on the mass notification system called Blackboard. The last step would be copying and pasting the shortened message onto the district's social media sites.[1239]

These messages always used the same verbiage. Initially, they stated only that the campus was on lockdown, but parents would then rush to the campus, so the director adjusted the message to include why the school was in secure status and asked the parents not to go to the campus. The director eventually added that everyone was safe and secure inside. This same message was used for each episode, which explains how the community was told "students and staff are safe in the buildings" on the fateful day (see figure 8-3 on page 399).[1240]

[1237] CIR Fact Finding.

[1238] CIR Fact Finding.

[1239] CIR Fact Finding.

[1240] CIR Fact Finding.

Figure 8-3. Initial UCISD post on May 24, 2022

Uvalde CISD Police Department •••
May 24 at 1:06 PM · 🌐

All campuses are under a Lockdown Status
Uvalde CIDS Parents:
Please know at this time all campuses are under a Lockdown Status
due to gun shots in the area. The students and staff are safe in the
buildings. The buildings are secure in a Lockdown Status. Your
cooperation is needed at this time by not visiting the campus. As soon
as the Lockdown Status is lifted you will be notified.
Thank you for your cooperation!
Anne Marie Espinoza
Executive Director of Communications and Marketing
Uvalde CISD

The TXDPS, Border Patrol, and the UCSO were often involved in the high-speed pursuits and crashes, but the UCISD Communications Director never contacted those agencies before distributing a news release.[1241]

At the time of the incident, the director was in their 20th year as communications director for a Texas school district, with nine years spent in Uvalde. Despite those years of experience, they had little to no experience dealing with crisis communications. The director interacted with the local media, which consisted of an Uvalde newspaper and two radio stations, on a weekly basis. Most of the communication shared positive news or informational content for parents. The exception was the messaging to parents on the high-speed pursuits, which had become rote due to their high frequency.[1242]

Through the Texas School Public Relations Association, the director attended crisis communication tabletop exercises during professional development meetings or conferences.[1243] The next step, which has not taken place, would be crafting a crisis communication plan, and practicing it with school district personnel. The increased frequency of these tragic events makes crisis communication planning and training more critical than ever. These skills are versatile and once developed can be used during any major incident in a community.

[1241] CIR Fact Finding.

[1242] CIR Fact Finding.

[1243] CIR Fact Finding.

Uvalde Memorial Hospital

Uvalde Memorial Hospital (UMH) learned of the incident within minutes of the first shots fired because the UPD PIO was coincidentally in the emergency department with a family member for an unrelated matter. At the time of the incident, the UMH CEO was handling the communications duties.[1244] Based on a news release posted on May 25, 2022, the hospital relied on an emergency operations plan to handle the influx of victims and public communications. The release stated, "UMH set up an emergency command center yesterday when we were made aware of the situation by law enforcement. We utilized our hospital emergency preparedness system to place on standby for additional support . . . Our staff consoled and comforted those while they waited to identify and reunite them with their children or provide information as it became available."

UMH posted its first social media content at 1:30 p.m. (see figure 8-4), less than an hour after the suspect was killed. This indicates the hospital's emergency preparedness system included a communication element that allowed them to keep community members informed. However, under FEMA's JIS, the information should have been released in coordination with the lead agency. Information about the victims should have been released in a holistic, planned, and coordinated fashion. That requires the hospital to plan and train with local law enforcement agencies and other responders, including EMTs. UMH did participate in the EOC tabletop exercise in December 2021; however, the public information component did not evolve from the training room to reality. Knowing fellow PIOs at partnering organizations is just the first step. Organizations must have a written plan that is practiced and improved before it is executed during a major event.

Figure 8-4. UMH post

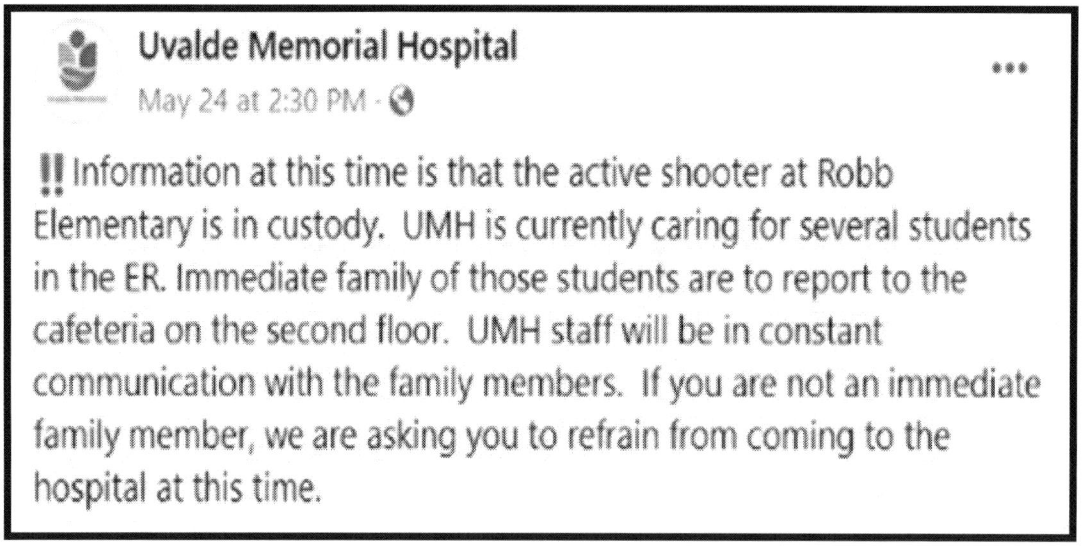

> **Uvalde Memorial Hospital**
> May 24 at 2:30 PM · 🌐
>
> ‼️ Information at this time is that the active shooter at Robb Elementary is in custody. UMH is currently caring for several students in the ER. Immediate family of those students are to report to the cafeteria on the second floor. UMH staff will be in constant communication with the family members. If you are not an immediate family member, we are asking you to refrain from coming to the hospital at this time.

[1244] CIR Fact Finding.

Texas Department of Public Safety

The TXDPS had a significant presence in Uvalde before the incident because it played a role in managing issues at the U.S.–Mexico border. The local PIOs worked regularly with the TXDPS PIO, but only on a reactive basis as incidents emerged. This interaction had increased in the 2 years prior to the incident, as ongoing border issues led to an increase in high-speed pursuits with crashes. Local agencies would discuss active scenes that involved TXDPS and sometimes mentioned TXDPS in news releases, but they did not draft joint news releases, nor did they plan, prepare, or train together for these incidents or a potential larger-scale incident.

On the day of the shooting, the regional supervisor of the TXDPS PIOs arrived between 5:00 p.m.–6:00 p.m.[1245] The TXDPS Regional Supervisor immediately took over messaging related to the incident. The Supervisor had served as the regional PIO supervisor for 2½ years, but was not certified through FEMA PIO classes, nor do their state records indicate that they took formal PIO courses.[1246] Training was limited to an internal class offered by TXDPS.[1247] That may explain why on May 24, 2022, the Regional Supervisor never spoke with any local agency PIOs or with UCISD. Instead, the Supervisor began conducting live national interviews based on the information they obtained from TXDPS operational supervisors. The Supervisor was not familiar with the concept of a JIC, nor was the TXDPS regional director, who served as the supervisor for the Regional Supervisor of the PIOs.[1248]

UCSO

While the UCSO was one of the agencies to respond to the scene and played a significant role throughout the incident, it never messaged anything to the public about its deputies' actions. There was no coordination with the UPD PIO who was leading the initial public messaging for local law enforcement.[1249] UCSO did not share UPD's social media posts or create content of its own. As a primary responding agency, it should help keep the public informed of its actions during a high-profile incident. While the agency is small, someone is assigned to create social media content.[1250] It is clear that the agency's social media policy[1251] does not address using social media to communicate with the community during regular policing activities or during a large-scale critical incident. It primarily prohibits deputies from posting about police work on their personal social media platforms from agency devices and guides deputies' use of social media when off duty.

[1245] CIR Fact Finding.

[1246] CIR Fact Finding; CIR Training Analysis.

[1247] CIR Fact Finding; CIR Training Analysis.

[1248] CIR Fact Finding.

[1249] CIR Fact Finding.

[1250] CIR Fact Finding.

[1251] CIR Document and Data Review.

Inevitably, even with careful pre-planning, mistakes will happen during dynamic large-scale incidents. However, if PIOs, public and private officials, and law enforcement agencies can learn from this incident and other high-profile incidents, they can translate those lessons into practical steps for planning and preparing best practice communications for a high-profile event. Thoughtful pre-planning; good training; and consistent, accurate messaging can minimize the number of errors, creating a more positive outcome for the agencies while providing the victims with vital information and support, which is a necessary step in the healing process.

Observations and Recommendations

Observation 1: Responding agencies lacked adequate related policies and, in most cases, any policy on responding to active attackers.

> **Recommendation 1.1:** Every agency must have a clear and concise policy on responding to active attacker situations.

> **Recommendation 1.2:** Agencies should regularly review AARs with other regional agencies to plan as a region for a coordinated and collaborative response to possible similar events.

> **Recommendation 1.3:** Agencies should consider obtaining state- or national-level accreditation to adopt and maintain standardized policies and procedures. This process also ensures accountability and transparency that can enhance confidence and trust in law enforcement among the communities they serve.[1252]

Observation 2: The Uvalde EOC developed an adequate emergency management plan. However, not all the relevant agencies and organizations actively participated in the process, drills, and exercises which ultimately contribute to a failed emergency response on May 24, 2022.

> **Recommendation 2.1**: Appointing authorities and senior officials of local government should develop a resilient emergency management system in which the emergency response plans of their respective units of government and operating departments, e.g., fire, police, sheriff, EMS, public health, public works, school system, planning, and social services, are understood and shared.[1253]

> **Recommendation 2.2**: Appointing authorities should direct the professional emergency manager at the highest level of local government to coordinate this system that would also include private sector stakeholders representing public utilities, healthcare providers and leaders responsible for critical infrastructure.[1254]

[1252] COPS Office, "Law Enforcement Agency (LEA) Accreditation."

[1253] FEMA, *Local and Elected Appointed Officials Guide*.

[1254] FEMA, *Local and Elected Appointed Officials Guide*.

Recommendation 2.3: Government leaders should consider adopting a resolution that demonstrates their commitment to NIMS.[1255]

Recommendation 2.4: Senior officials should guide all government, business, and organization leaders (including faith-based and secular nonprofit groups) to coordinate and collaborate with the emergency manager so they can act decisively before, during, and after disasters.[1256]

Recommendation 2.5: Senior officials should personally participate in and provide direction for conducting exercises and evaluation programs that enhance familiarity and coordination among the whole community.

Recommendation 2.6: Local governments should conduct outreach to state emergency management agencies and federal entities such as the Homeland Security Exercise and Evaluation Program and the NEP for assistance with exercise resources and training.[1257]

Recommendation 2.7: The Office of Emergency Management should identify volunteer groups and local businesses who will consistently play a role in emergency planning and preparedness before, during, and after disasters. Business and industry partners should work through voluntary organizations to support local government in planning, preparing, and providing resources when responding to emergency situations.[1258]

Recommendation 2.8: Senior officials should develop a pre-disaster recovery plan that enables them to anticipate what will be needed to restore the community as quickly as possible after an emergency. FEMA offers the Community Recovery Management Toolkit, which provides a three-step process of organizing, planning, and managing recovery.[1259]

Recommendation 2.9: Regional public safety partners should plan, train, and exercise unified command for complex incidents. This includes federal, state, and local law enforcement, fire, EMS, and emergency management as well as other governmental and non-governmental agencies that would respond to a critical incident.

Recommendation 2.10: Agencies should hold regular regional interdepartmental interoperability communication drills.[1260]

Recommendation 2.11: Elected officials should establish a Multi-Agency Coordination (MAC) Group to provide policy guidance to incident personnel and support resource prioritization and allocation. Typically, these groups are made up of government agency or private sector executives and

---

[1255] "Sample Municipal Resolution Adopting NIMS," Pennsylvania Emergency Management Agency.

[1256] FEMA, *Local and Elected Appointed Officials Guide.*

[1257] FEMA, *Local and Elected Appointed Officials Guide*; FEMA, "Homeland Security Exercise and Evaluation Program;" FEMA, "About the National Exercise Program."

[1258] *State of Texas Emergency Management Plan*, 12.

[1259] FEMA, "Community Recovery Management Toolkit."

[1260] Cybersecurity and Infrastructure Security Agency, *National Emergency Communications Plan.*

administrators whose organizations are either impacted by, or provide resources to, an incident. MAC Groups enable decision-making among senior officials and executives, and delegate command authority to the incident commander to cooperatively define the response and recovery mission and strategic direction. Additionally, MAC Groups identify operational priorities and communicate those objectives to the Emergency Operations Center and the pertinent functions of the Incident command system and the joint information center.[1261]

Recommendation 2.12: Elected and senior officials should receive training made available through the FEMA Emergency Management Institute (EMI) that provides a menu of courses designed specifically for senior officials. In addition to independent online study courses in the NIMS, ICS, Unified Command, and other basic emergency management training, EMI offers specialized in-person training for senior officials. The portfolio of courses includes Emergency Management for Senior Officials, NIMS Overview for Senior Officials, and Recovery from Disaster: Local Community Roles. Senior officials should work with their professional emergency manager for specific course recommendations. States may also have specific training programs and offerings.[1262]

Observation 3: The MOU between UPD and UCISD PD that was active the day of the incident failed to adequately outline the expectations and authorities for a response to a mass violence event. The agencies failed to exercise the MOU, nor cross-train in preparation for a critical incident.

Recommendation 3.1: Senior officials should establish mutual aid agreements that set forth terms and conditions under which the parties will agree to provide resources, personnel, facilities, equipment, and supplies to support responses to critical incidents that create an extreme risk to public safety.

Observation 4: The Texas Legislature plays a significant role in mandating the types and frequencies of training for peace officers in the state of Texas through TCOLE.

Recommendation 4.1: State POSTs and other training entities should work with state legislatures and law enforcement leaders within their state to conduct coordinated routine reviews of mandatory training programs for peace officers within their state to determine what is the appropriate balance of training topics and courses. Mandatory training time/requirements should include training options focused on unique, complex tactical events, such as an active attacker.

Observation 5: UPD and UCSO appear to show budgetary and staffing shortages, which prevent training opportunities.

Recommendation 5.1: Whenever possible, multiagency training should be offered to lessen the load of any one law enforcement agency. Multiagency training allows for cost- and resource-sharing and, more importantly, allows peace officers to train with other agencies that are typically going to

---

[1261] Cybersecurity and Infrastructure Security Agency, *National Emergency Communications Plan.*

[1262] Cybersecurity and Infrastructure Security Agency, *National Emergency Communications Plan*; FEMA, "Emergency Management Institute | EMI Courses & Schedules."

respond jointly to a major incident. Building relationships through training and in advance of a major incident are critical in the successful response to, management of, and resolution of a major incident when one happens.

Observation 6: Responding agencies had minimal exposure to ICS/NIMS. Of those serving in top leadership positions within the primary responding agencies, only UCISD PD Chief Arredondo and the TXDPS regional director had taken training in ICS/NIMS.

Recommendation 6.1: All law enforcement should be required to take awareness-level NIMS courses, such as ICS-100 and IS-700.

Recommendation 6.2: All ranked individuals should be required to take courses and refresher training on ICS/NIMS. These skills should be exercised through an annual multijurisdictional, multidisciplinary tabletop.

Observation 7: Responding officers had levels of active shooter training that varied in terms of their length of time and quality, leading to failures in operationalizing the training.

Recommendation 7.1: Law enforcement agencies should provide a total of 8 hours of scenario-based, stress-induced active shooter training annually for officers at all levels of ranks in the training.

Recommendation 7.2: Law enforcement agencies should work closely with schools and other vulnerable places to understand how occupants are taught to respond to an active attacker threat (e.g., kids were taught to be quiet in a dark room, while some officers reported they were listening for voices and believed the dark classrooms meant they were unoccupied).

Recommendation 7.3: Research should be conducted to determine if the response to an active attacker threat should include changing the "normal environment" (e.g., lights off).

Recommendation 7.4: TCOLE should consider revising the SBLE training guidebook based on the recommendations in the CIR.

Recommendation 7.5: Agencies must include in pre-incident planning timely access to building diagrams and universal building/room access, particularly critical infrastructure, schools, and buildings where large numbers of persons gather on a regular basis.

Observation 8: Personnel from responding agencies rarely trained and exercised in a multiagency environment.

Recommendation 8.1: Interagency training, drills, and exercises help to build relationships at the front-line officer level and, if attended by law enforcement supervisors, can further strengthen relationships and the efficacy of a multiagency response to a mass casualty incident. Though policies may differ slightly among agencies, overarching commonalities are the same in an active attacker incident.

Observation 9: Responder agencies lacked sufficient training in trauma, resiliency, and mental health and wellness.

> **Recommendation 9.1:** Agencies should provide preparedness education and training on trauma and stress management to all personnel, including coping strategies for managing stress and trauma during and after a mass casualty incident.

> **Recommendation 9.2:** Agencies should develop and maintain a comprehensive crisis response plan to address the mental health needs of their personnel during a mass casualty incident.

> **Recommendation 9.3:** Responder organizations should provide pre- and post-response behavioral health support to help mitigate and address the development of compassion fatigue, secondary traumatic stress, and vicarious trauma. This support can include education and training, policies and procedures, and services.

> **Recommendation 9.4:** The stigma of seeking mental health and trauma support in the law enforcement community needs to be counteracted by education, training, policies, protocols, and leadership, which create an environment that acknowledges and respects the mental wellness of law enforcement to the same extent as the physical aspects of policing.

> **Recommendation 9.5:** It is necessary to tailor the application of services for the diverse types of responders (fire/EMS, law enforcement, victim services, dispatchers, etc.) so that the language used and the examples of the types of symptoms they may experience are more applicable to their unique experiences and roles.

Observation 10: The Uvalde school community did not sufficiently prepare and engage in victim-centered disaster, emergency, or mass violence incident planning within their own staff, with law enforcement and other responders, nor with the students, family members, and other caregivers.

> **Recommendation 10.1:** Preparedness exercises should include regularly scheduled age-appropriate, trauma-informed drills; prescribed instructions/procedures; and clear communication. All stakeholders (school personnel, law enforcement, parents and guardians, students, and other relevant stakeholders) should be involved in the process and informed to help decrease anxiety and chaos.

> **Recommendation 10.2:** Preparedness planning should include considerations for language access for those with English as a second language. Materials, instructions, and communication should be provided in the languages prevalent in the community.

Observation 11: Regional PIOs and their managers did not have necessary training for mass casualty incidents from a communications perspective, to include how to establish JIC or coordinate a Joint Information System.

Recommendation 11.1: Law enforcement, fire, and any other relevant stakeholder PIOs should obtain FEMA basic and advanced public information officer certifications as a baseline of training.

Recommendation 11.2: The FEMA PIO courses should be only a first step in communications training. Agencies should research regional and national training opportunities for building upon the FEMA classes.

Recommendation 11.3: Law enforcement PIOs should network at the state and national level (e.g., attend national police conferences that have a PIO section) to learn common practices for managing the public messaging of major incidents and to network with peers in the field.

Recommendation 11.4: Concepts learned in basic crisis communication classes must then be adopted into a crisis communication plan that is drilled and practiced with all involved personnel.

Recommendation 11.5: Partnering agencies should review their crisis communication plans together to ensure they complement each other. It is critically important that the commitment to coordinating messaging is practiced with smaller events, so it is not a foreign concept when a large-scale incident takes place.

Recommendation 11.6: The social media policies of law enforcement agencies should clearly state how social media should be used to communicate with the community during critical incident situations.

Observation 12: Regional PIOs did not formally coordinate, cross-train, or practice multiagency communications.

Recommendation 12.1: When an agency is hosting operational exercises, it should establish a JIC and engage all participating agencies to ensure coordinated public messaging is practiced and incorporated into planning for a large-scale incident.

Recommendation 12.2: Each PIO should draft a crisis communication plan and practice it at least four times a year with smaller events. This will help identify problem areas and solutions and ensure everyone is familiar with the plan and knows their role instead of trying to figure that out during a crisis.

Recommendation 12.3: The EOC should host regional PIO meetings every quarter. The meetings should include law enforcement, fire, city and county government, hospitals, public and private schools, universities, airports, military bases, universities, and other large organizations in the area. This creates an opportunity for relationship building, planning for joint operations and large-scale incidents that cross jurisdictional lines, and devising plans to support each other during major events.

Recommendation 12.4: After a comprehensive discussion, regional PIO meetings should be opened to the local media. This builds productive working relationships and allows the media and communication professionals to work out issues that arise.

Observation 13: On the day of the school shooting at Robb Elementary School, each PIO acted independently and failed to coordinate the public messaging aspect of the response.

Recommendation 13.1: When incidents involve multiple agencies, it is critical for the lead organization sending out the public messaging to have previously established a process by planning with the other agencies. On the day of an incident, the lead organization should coordinate with the others to ensure the accurate messaging that the public expects and deserves.

Recommendation 13.2: When a mass casualty incident occurs, the lead agency should organize news conferences through the JIC. All supporting agencies should have an opportunity to contribute information about the incident. This ensures a comprehensive release of consistent information.

Conclusion

In summary, the response to the May 24, 2022, mass casualty incident at Robb Elementary School was a failure. The painful lessons detailed in this report are not meant to exacerbate an already tragic situation or further the pain and trauma to those directly impacted by the events on May 24 and the subsequent days, weeks, and months. This report provides an independent accounting of that tragic day and the events and activities leading up to June 8, 2023, when the Critical Incident Review (CIR) period ended. The CIR team kept accuracy in the forefront, while balancing transparency and trauma-informed approaches. The goal is that this report provides answers to those directly impacted, while also conveying recommendations and lessons learned to the nation. The CIR team included many recommendations for strengthening preparation and planning, improving tactical and strategic responses, increasing communications, and enhancing post-incident recovery, support, and investigations with the goal to help other communities in the preparation, response, and aftermath. We honor the victims, survivors, and all those impacted with this report. The bravery of the survivors and the lost voices of those murdered on May 24 should be a call to action for our nation's communities.

The Federal Government provides free training and technical assistance including the DOJ COPS Office Collaborative Reform Initiative program,[1263] DOJ Bureau of Justice Assistance National Training and Technical Assistance Center,[1264] and the Department of Education Readiness and Emergency Management for School Technical Assistance Center.[1265] The COPS Office can assist in identifying government resources related to this report.

[1263] COPS Office, "Collaborative Reform Initiative Technical Assistance Center."

[1264] BJA, "Bureau of Justice Assistance National Training and Technical Assistance Center."

[1265] Readiness and Emergency Management for Schools, "Readiness and Emergency Management for Schools Technical Assistance Center."

Appendix A. Remembrance Profiles

The language in the profiles reflects our respectful attempt to capture the spirit of each victim. These profiles can also be viewed online at https://cops.usdoj.gov/uvalde.

Nevaeh Alyssa Bravo

Nevaeh Alyssa Bravo, 10, is remembered as a little girl who always put a smile on everyone's face. Her name is Heaven spelled backwards. As part of the Healing Uvalde Mural Project, Artist Brittany "Britt" Johnson painted Nevaeh's mural, which includes a heart, two birds, a rose, and a handwritten note that reads "I love you." It also incorporates some of her favorite things, like purple and pink, butterflies, softball, and the TikTok symbol. The mural reflects cascading curls flowing over Nevaeh's shoulder, the way she loved to wear her hair.[1266]

[1266] CNN, "May 26 Texas Shooting News;" Briones, "Nevaeh Alyssa Bravo, an Uvalde Student Who Loved Her Family, Dies at 10;" Maldonado, "Nevaeh Alyssa Bravo."

Jacklyn "Jackie" Cazares

Jacklyn "Jackie" Cazares, 9, was very proud of her new white dress as she showed it off in front of her family when celebrating her First Communion a week before she passed. She was a social butterfly who loved to be the center of attention. Her family remembers her as peaceful, loving, affectionate, and compassionate. She would go out of her way to help anyone and make anyone laugh, no matter how bad they felt. She is also remembered as someone who "didn't like bullies; she didn't like kids being picked on." She loved to sing, make TikTok videos, and interact with friends on Snapchat. Her four dogs were her world. When artist Kimie Flores painted her mural as part of the Healing Uvalde Mural Project, she incorporated Jackie's photo in her First Communion dress. Additionally, the mural reflects Jackie's love of the Eiffel Tower; her bedroom was filled with images of the iconic monument, and she dreamed of traveling to Paris to visit it and experience French culture. Jackie had started a piggy bank to collect loose change for her trip to Paris one day. Her favorite color was sage green. Jackie dreamed of becoming a veterinarian.[1267]

[1267] Montgomery et al., "'She Was My Sweet Girl;'" "As Uvalde Starts School, One Family Stops;" Andreano et al., "Remembering the Victims of the Uvalde School Shooting;" "Uvalde School Mass Shooting: What We Know;" Chappell et al., "What We Know about the Victims;" Maldonado, "Jackie Jaylen Cazares;" "Remembering Jacklyn Cazares as a Free Spirit."

Makenna Lee Elrod

Makenna Lee Elrod, 10, was beautiful, funny, intelligent, and amazing. She had a big heart and loved her family and friends. It was often said that her smile would light up the room. Makenna loved to play softball and gymnastics, dance and sing, play with fidgets, and spend time with her family. She was a member of the 4-H club and loved animals, including Bailey the dog, Porkchop the pig, Twitty the steer, and Dude the horse; all the animals lived on the family's estate and were a big part of Makenna's life. She looked forward to going to the ranch with her dad to feed animals and ride on the range. The Texas 4-H Youth Development Foundation has set up a memorial scholarship honoring Makenna. She loved butterflies so much that they were released at her funeral. Makenna enjoyed writing notes to her family and leaving them in hidden places to be found later. She was a natural leader and loved school. Makenna's favorite color was purple. She had recently started reading the Bible and often sang her favorite song, "The Lion and the Lamb."[1268]

[1268] "Uvalde School Mass Shooting: What We Know;" Maldonado, "Makenna Lee Elrod;" "Makenna Lee Elrod Obituary;" Sturdevant, "Texas 4-H Scholarship;" Alfonseca and Estrada, "Mother of Uvalde Victim Speaks Out;" Briones, "Makenna Lee Elrod, a Bright and Caring;" Herron, "Exclusive: Father of Makenna Elrod-Seiler."

Jose Flores Jr.

Jose Flores Jr., 10, was fondly known as Josecito and Baby Jose; he loved cars and sports, especially baseball. Jose was a Houston Astros fan and wore number 6 on the Uvalde Little League team. He was often described as always energetic, and he enjoyed video games. Family and friends say they will always remember his big heart, and that he was in a perpetual good mood and always said hello to everybody. His favorite foods included Takis Chips and Cheetos Flamin' Hot. His favorite color was dark blue. When he grew up, Jose wanted to be a police officer to protect others. On the day of the shooting, he had just been honored for his academic work, earning a place on the honor roll.[1269]

[1269] Montgomery et al., "'She Was My Sweet Girl;'" Kantor, "Boy Killed in Texas Shooting;" "Uvalde School Mass Shooting: What We Know;" Hampton, "Texas School Shooting: What We Know;" Sandoval, "A Son Was Lost;" Briones, "Jose Manuel Flores, Jr.;" Uria, "Mourners Gather for Funerals of Student, Teacher."

Eliahna "Ellie" Amyah Garcia

Eliahna "Ellie" Amyah Garcia, 9, was very happy and outgoing; she loved dancing and playing sports. She had just won the basketball championship the previous Saturday. Artist Abel Ortiz, who painted her mural as part of the Healing Uvalde Mural Project, reflected Ellie's love of basketball by showing her in her jersey—number 21, which she chose because it was her mother's birthday—with the title "All Star." Ortiz's painting also incorporates her spirit, love of life, and love for Jesus. Eliahna wanted to be a cheerleader. She loved hot sauce, ramen noodles, dancing, and the Disney movie *Encanto*. Ellie was buried in a custom-made *Encanto* dress that the Walt Disney costume design team gifted to her family. The dress was in her favorite color, purple, covered with lilac flowers and cascading ruffles. Eliahna would light up everyone's world with big smiles and big hugs. She came from a large family, the second oldest of five girls, and loved to spend time with her little sisters. She loved making videos and was already practicing a choreography with her older sister for her quinceañera party, even though it was still 5 years away. Her dream was to be a teacher.[1270]

[1270] "Uvalde School Mass Shooting: What We Know;" "Texas Artists Honor Uvalde Victims with Murals;" Ortiz, "Eliahna 'Ellie' Amyah Garcia;" Medina, "Tejano Community Attend Funeral of Eliahna 'Ellie' Garcia;" "Disney Sends Family of Ellie Garcia a Gift;" Briones, "Eliahna Amyah Garcia;" Gomez Licon, "Uvalde: Visitations, Funerals and Burials;" Yan et al., "Remembering the Victims of the Uvalde, Texas Massacre."

Irma Linda Garcia

Irma Linda Garcia, 48, was a dedicated mother, wife, and educator known for her love of family and pride for her children and students. Mrs. Garcia was married to her high school sweetheart, Jose Garcia. She loved menudo and joining her husband in barbequing and listening to music. Fishing from the pier with her husband and children was another of her favorite pastimes. She started teaching a year after she married and was nearing 23 years of teaching at Robb Elementary School, 5 of which she co-taught with Ms. Eva Mireles. She received numerous professional honors, including Teacher of the Year in 2019. Mrs. Garcia was known for inspiring her students to go to college, and she celebrated her students returning for the "senior walk" ahead of their graduations. Her spirit is embodied in a post she wrote on social media at the time: "Seeing them return to their elementary schools wearing their cap and gown . . . is the reason every teacher in this district does what they do," Garcia wrote. "That moment makes all the struggles, long hours, and endless paperwork so worth it." Her husband, Jose Garcia, died 2 days after the shooting; they both are survived by 4 children, ranging from 12 to 23 years old.[1271]

[1271] Ura, "Irma and Joe Garcia;" "Irma Linda Garcia Obituary;" Sottile, "Their Mom Was Killed in Uvalde;" Anderson et al., "For Five Years, They Were Co-Teachers;" Wertheimer, "Texas Shooting: The Teachers Who Sacrificed."

Uziyah Sergio Garcia

Uziyah Sergio Garcia, 10, known to most as Uzi, was a loving, smart, sweet, and energetic child. Uzi loved his entire family and anything active such as running, gorilla tag, football, and swimming. He was known for being competitive but also fair and kind. Uzi had a deep love for Jesus, and whenever his family said, "I love you and Jesus loves you," he would reply, "and Jesus loves you too!" He loved a Nutella sandwich with blue Takis, which he wanted to get others to try. He was silly, had a contagious laugh, and was known for his shaggy hair—but outside of his silliness, Uzi is remembered for his beautiful soul.[1272]

[1272] "Uziyah Sergio Garcia Obituary;" King, "'It's Been 4 Months and Nothing's Changed;" Fraire, "Uvalde Victim Uziyah Garcia;" Maldonado, "Uziyah Sergio Garcia;" "'Loving' Boy Last Texas School Shooting Victim."

Amerie Jo Garza

Amerie Jo Garza turned 10 years old 2 weeks before the Robb Elementary shooting. She had spent her morning celebrating her appointment to the honor roll on that last day of school and went back to her classroom to finish out the day before anticipating her mother picking her up to start the summer vacation. Amerie is remembered as an outgoing child and a student who enjoyed excelling in class, hoping one day to combine teaching with one of her favorite subjects, art. She loved colored pencils and paint (especially the color purple), playing with clay, and wanting people to have fun. Amerie is described as having been the light in the room with the brightest attitude. She was confident and not afraid to be different, doing things that she liked regardless of others' opinions. A "daddy's girl," she also loved making things for her parents and brothers.[1273]

[1273] "Texas School Shooting Victims: Third and Fourth Graders, Beloved Teachers;" "Amerie Jo Garza Obituary."

Xavier James Lopez

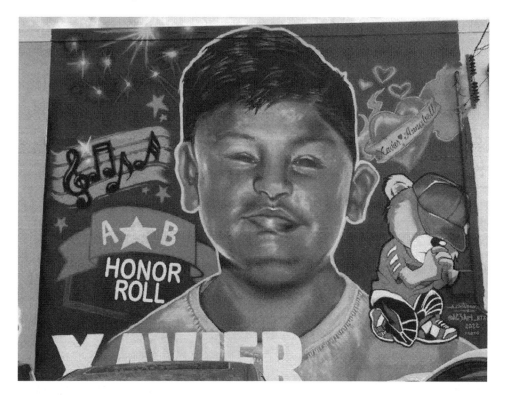

Xavier James Lopez, 10, was known as a fun-loving young man who, whether in school or at home, was always wearing a bright smile. And as a 4th grader, he never took things too seriously, often finding time to cheer up anyone who needed it. Still, he was excited about his recent academic achievement, proudly accepting his honor roll certificate. According to his family, "he really couldn't wait to go to middle school." Xavier enjoyed having fun with his friends, especially his classmate Annabell Guadalupe Rodriguez, and summertime activities like swimming and playing little league baseball. He learned at the age of 7 to make his father's favorite food, hot salsa. Xavier would sell his salsa to family and friends and use the money to buy toys for his little brothers. His outgoing and fun-loving nature was on display as he carried out pranks and joined in the South Texan partner dance, cumbia. He is fondly remembered as a boy with "lots of energy."[1274]

[1274] Cohen, "'I'm Not Ready:' 2 Uvalde Victims."

Jayce Carmelo Luevanos

Jayce Carmelo Luevanos, a 10-year-old 4th grader, loved attending school as much as he loved his family. He lived with his mother and grandparents, for whom it was Jayce's custom to get up in the morning and make a pot of coffee before heading to school. He regularly expressed his strong ties to family and community through the special love notes he wrote to his family and the open invitation he extended to the neighborhood friends and classmates who were welcomed frequently at his family's home. With an endearing personality and the ability to communicate effectively, Jayce was always surrounded by friends with whom he enjoyed playing outdoor games and simply doing fun things. And there were always plenty of refreshments for everyone! His smile was infectious, and he always enjoyed making others laugh. Jayce loved his dog, Fifi, and his favorite hobbies included dinosaurs, ninjas, and coloring pictures.[1275]

[1275] Ball, "'They're So Young:' A Grandfather in Uvalde;" Esquivel, "Artist's Statement;" "Jayce Carmelo Luevanos."

Tess Marie Mata

Tess Marie Mata loved her family dearly, as well as her cat, Oliver. Like many 10-year-olds, she wanted to follow in the footsteps of her older sibling. She even started saving for college because she wanted to attend the same school as her big sister, Texas State University, where she is now an honorary Bobcat.

To honor her life, the Tess Marie Mata Scholarship will be established to help students follow the fifth grader's dream to study the health sciences. Tess also saved money for a family vacation to Disney World. She loved the Nickelodeon show *Victorious,* and as an avid softball player, she enjoyed following her favorite baseball team, the Houston Astros. She played the same position as the Astros' Jose Altuve and cheered loudly for him whenever he came up to bat. Tess, known to others as "Tessy," had a love for TikTok videos and dreamed of one day going viral on the social media platform. Her TikTok dance video "My Sweet Baby Girl" has more than 200,000 views. Tess was athletic and loved sports. She also loved fancy dresses and pretty jewelry and will always be remembered for her beautiful smile and signature peace gesture.[1276]

[1276] Garcia, "Family of 10-Year-Old Uvalde Shooting Victim;" Craig and Waldman, "Scholarship Honors the Life;" Briones, "Tess Marie Mata;" Ronen, "Artist Statement."

Maranda Mathis

Maranda Mathis, who turned 11 years old about 2 weeks before the Robb Elementary shooting, had a huge, loving heart. She was a sweet, smart, and shy young lady who enjoyed being in nature and spending time outdoors, where she collected things like rocks, shells, and feathers. Those who knew Maranda remember her great imagination and her expressed love for unicorns and mermaids, especially if they were her favorite color, purple. Maranda was fun, spunky, and very smart. Her family describes her as "sweet, smart, and a shy tomboy who enjoyed being in nature and the outdoors." She made a similar impact on her peers: one of her schoolmates added that "she had manners and was a bright girl." Maranda was known for her sweet personality, cute smile, and kind eyes; beyond these, it was her loving heart that endeared her to friends and classmates. She enjoyed spending time with her younger brother, playing Roblox on her tablet, and eating her favorite foods: pizza, tacos, and boneless wings. She had a special love for animals, too. Although at times she was shy and quiet, she did not hesitate to demonstrate her love for family and friends through heartfelt expressions and acts of kindness, for which she will always be remembered. To all of her family and friends, Maranda was loving, kind, bright, and a genuine sweetheart.[1277]

[1277] Jimenez, "From Her 'Love of Animals and Pizza;'" Briones, "Maranda Gail Mathis;" "What We Know about the Victims;" "Maranda Gail Mathis."

Eva Mireles

Eva Mireles, 44, was a committed mother, wife, and educator known for her cheerful and active nature. Ms. Mireles had a love for CrossFit, hiking, and spending time with her family. She was known for combining her two passions by getting up before the sunrise to go for hikes during family gatherings. She lived her life to the fullest, with her daughter recalling memories of singing karaoke and re-enacting TikToks together. She was an educator for 17 years, specializing in special education; just a couple of years ago, she helped integrate children with developmental disabilities into regular classrooms in the Uvalde area. As one parent fondly remembered, Ms. Mireles "was a beautiful person and dedicated teacher [who] went above and beyond." Ms. Mireles co-taught 4th grade at Robb Elementary with Mrs. Garcia for 5 years. Ms. Mireles is survived by her husband and her daughter, who recently graduated college.[1278]

[1278] Wertheimer, "Texas Shooting: The Teachers who Sacrifice;" Anderson et al., "For Five Years, They Were Co-Teachers;" "Eva Mireles Obituary;" Dey et al., "21 Lives Lost."

Alithia Haven Ramirez

Alithia Haven Ramirez, 10, was a bright, talented, reliable, and extremely loving young lady who dreamed of attending art school in Paris. Her family and friends remember her as trustworthy, always wanting to care for everyone, and serving as a role model to her siblings. She also loved to play soccer. Alithia loved the color purple, eating pizza, and playing with her two younger siblings, for whom she would create unique characters, often modeled on their favorite Nintendo games or anime. She wanted to go to Paris because that's where famous artists are known to go. In January 2023, an exhibit of Alithia's art was displayed in her dream destination by L'AiR Arts at Atelier 11. When Alithia was 8, her best friend who shared a love of soccer and drawing sketches was struck and killed by a car. It was devastating, but little Alithia became a surprising source of strength and comfort for her best friend's family. A drawing Alithia sent to console her best friend's parents showed him sketching her portrait in heaven while she drew him on earth, revealing a kindness far beyond her years. Actor and Uvalde native Matthew McConaughey displayed this drawing when he was speaking at the White House. "I want the world to see my art and show the world what I can do; I want people to be happy when they see my passion in art," Alithia wrote when she submitted her artwork for a Google Doodle contest. Google honored Alithia by spotlighting her work on the Google Doodle. The Beeville Art Museum (https://www.bamtexas.org/) (BAM) hosted an exhibition of select pieces by Alithia in 2022 entitled "Eyes on the World," which included 48 pieces highlighting her signature style of incorporating large inquiring eyes.[1279]

[1279] "Alithia Haven Ramirez Obituary;" "Young Uvalde Victim's Art Displayed in Texas and Paris;" Miles, "Uvalde Victim Alithia Ramirez;" "Texas Artists Honor Uvalde Victims with Murals;" "In Memoriam: 2022 Doodle;" Alfonseca and Rothenberg, "Uvalde Shooting Victim Alithia Haven Ramirez;" "Uvalde Victim's Dream of Sharing Art."

Annabell Guadalupe Rodriguez

Known for her quiet demeanor, 10-year-old **Annabell Guadalupe Rodriguez** came from a close-knit family whom she loved dearly, always enjoying the many exciting and fun-filled experiences they shared. Annabell was a sweet young girl who loved the color blue, especially blue butterflies. She also enjoyed watching TikTok and spending quality time with her sisters and family. She was especially close to her cousin, Jackie Cazares, and her dear friend and 4th grade classmate, Xavier James Lopez. Their families arranged frequent cookouts together so the children could spend more time together, often playing tag. Annabell proudly wore a picture of Xavier around her neck at school and when attending his little league baseball games. She was also entrepreneurial, running a snow cone machine along with her family, who sold hot dogs. Annabell was conscientious and worked hard in school, earning a place on the honor roll. She rose each morning to first thank God for another day and would spend her evenings painting her grandmother's nails and braiding her hair. These acts of humility, kindness, and compassion reflected Annabell's strong values and underscored her remarkable character.[1280]

[1280] Martinez, "Two Best Friends;" Shakhnazarova, "Texas School Massacre Victims;" Helling, "10-Year-Old Uvalde Victims;" "'That Smile I Will Never Forget.'"

Maite Yuleana Rodriguez

Maite Yuleana Rodriguez was just 10 years old when she was killed at Robb Elementary School on May 24, 2022. Maite's mother said she wanted everyone to know that Maite was "sweet, charismatic, loving, caring, loyal, free, ambitious, funny, silly, goal driven," and her best friend. "She was determined, focused and competitive. She was smart, bright, beautiful, and happy." Maite was an AB honor student who had high aspirations of doing good in the world, with plans to attend Texas A&M University to become a marine biologist. Maite loved anime, especially Attack on Titan, and all kinds of animals, like dogs, but mostly marine animals like dolphins. She enjoyed Whataburger burgers with jalapeños. Maite was known to be giving, intelligent, and charismatic, as well as courageous. Her bravery was clear: classmates reported that, faced with danger, Maite lost her life telling her classmates where to hide. She will be remembered by her green Converse sneakers, which she decorated with a heart, and by a scholarship named in her honor at Texas A&M in Corpus Christi. Maite is now officially an Islander.[1281]

[1281] "Texas School Shooting Victims: Third and Fourth Graders, Beloved Teachers;" "Maite Yuleana Rodriguez Obituary."

Alexandria "Lexi" Aniyah Rubio

Alexandria "Lexi" Aniyah Rubio, 10, was an athlete who loved her family and school. Lexi was a fierce, intelligent girl who had dreams of earning a softball scholarship, majoring in math, and eventually becoming a lawyer. Lexi enjoyed practicing softball and basketball with her father and would practice on her own while he was at work. She was an impassioned debater who loved fishing with her dad, reciting jokes with her mom to see who would laugh first, baking with her great-grandmother, and hanging out with her five siblings. Her siblings fondly remember her love of the "Lexi burger"—a plain and dry McDonald's cheeseburger topped with fries and chicken nuggets, which McDonald's released as a special remembrance on her birthday. She had a love of bright colors, which reflected her bright personality inside and out.[1282]

[1282] Dey et al., "21 Lives Lost;" "Alexandria 'Lexi' Aniyah Rubio Obituary."

Layla Marie Salazar

Layla Marie Salazar, 11, grew to love singing so much that she sang every day on the way to and from school with her parents. Layla also enjoyed dancing and adored koala bears. She was smart, quick-witted, and full of an energy evidenced by all of the activities she engaged in, including swimming. Running track, though, was her favorite—her passion. At 11 years old, Layla had never lost a race, taking home 6 first-place ribbons on Field Day. Layla also made TikToks and other videos singing along to her favorite songs. She was a big fan of the Dallas Cowboys. Her family describes Layla as a super special child who was social and welcoming, and who was always respectful and helpful to family and friends. She enjoyed time with her many close family members, including her brothers, parents, grandparents, great-grandparents, aunts, uncles, and cousins. She had the gift of a loving family both nearby and in Illinois, where she was born. Her grandparents would pick Layla up from school and treat her to tacos, so she was known to ask her grandparents to pick her up often. Her family moved to Uvalde to be in a safer community, but now they have buried their loving 11-year-old child there.[1283]

[1283] "Texas School Shooting Victims: Third and Fourth Graders, Beloved Teachers;" "Layla Marie Salazar Obituary."

Jailah Nicole Silguero

Jailah Nicole Silguero, 10, was described as a big ray of sunshine with a big heart, especially with children younger than her. Jailah was a lovely little girl who enjoyed the outdoors, dancing, and making TikTok videos. Jailah was also a basketball player. She was very energetic and loved skateboarding, cycling, and playing with her cousins. Jailah and her cousin, Jayce Carmelo Luevanos, were both just 10 years old when they were killed on May 24, 2022, at Robb Elementary, lying next to each other.[1284]

[1284] "Texas School Shooting Victims: Third and Fourth Graders, Beloved Teachers;" "Jailah Nicole Silguero Obituary;" "Jailah Nicole Silguero."

Eliahna Cruz Torres

Eliahna Cruz Torres, 10, was known to those closest to her as Elijah. Eliahna was described as a loving, nurturing, and compassionate child who always put others before herself. Family referred to her as "enfermerita," the little nurse. Her grandfather recalls how she accompanied him on his prescribed walks after he had heart surgery, and Eliahna routinely made sure both her grandparents took their medications. She liked to be silly and loved making people laugh. She also loved TikTok videos. She was said to have the most beautiful smile. Eliahna was also an avid baseball player who loved the game and played on a local little league whose final game of the season was scheduled for the afternoon of the shooting. She was very excited for the game and hoped to make the All Stars. Eliahna's father was only a week away from a visit with her at the time of her death. Eliahna was said to have made a big impact during her short life, and her family note that she "fulfilled her purpose."[1285]

[1285] "Texas School Shooting Victims: Third and Fourth Graders, Beloved Teachers;" "Eliahna Torres Obituary;" "Eliahna Torres."

Rojelio Fernandez Torres

Rojelio Fernandez Torres, 10, was described by everyone who knew him as an intelligent, hardworking, and helpful person. Rojelio loved everybody and told his family he wanted to make a difference in the world. His teachers referred to him as a difference maker. Rojelio was very outgoing and loved life, showing this by always having a smile on his face and being willing to help wherever needed. He would help his mother with tasks and help his aunts, his teachers, and others. Rojelio was always wanting to do something and had many hobbies like playing Pokémon and video games. He was also very active and loved being outside with his brother and sisters, especially playing football.[1286]

[1286] "Rojelio Fernandez Torres Obituary;" "Texas School Shooting Victims: Third and Fourth Graders, Beloved Teachers;" "Rojelio Fernandez Torres;" Alvarado, "10-Year-Old Shooting Victim Rojelio Torres;" "Victims of the Texas School Shooting."

Appendix B. Report Methodology

On May 29, 2022, the U.S. Department of Justice (DOJ) agreed to conduct a Critical Incident Review (CIR) of the tragedy that occurred at Robb Elementary School on May 24. The team, led by the Office of Community Oriented Policing Services (COPS Office), comprised subject matter experts in the areas of leadership, school safety, tactics, trauma services, communications, critical incident response, and public safety. The COPS Office developed and operationalized a comprehensive methodology to thoroughly review and assess the public safety response to the mass casualty incident at Robb Elementary School, and to improve the preparedness of law enforcement and other stakeholders across the nation.

Areas of Examination

The CIR team was assigned to eight subteams based on the following areas of focus:

- Timeline and incident reconstruction
- Leadership, incident command, and coordination
- Tactics and equipment
- Public communications
- Post-incident response and investigation
- Trauma services and survivor support
- School safety and security
- Pre-incident planning and preparation

The scope for each area of examination is included in the respective chapter.

This process allowed the team members to leverage their areas of expertise, while focusing on the specific areas of examination in detail. Subteams regularly coordinated to allow for cross-pollination of ideas as well as team deliberations on the themes, observations, and recommendations across the report.

Responding Agencies

The assessment primarily focused on the responding law enforcement agencies, including:

- Uvalde Police Department (UPD)
- Uvalde Consolidated Independent School District Police Department (UCISD PD)
- Uvalde County Sheriff's Office (UCSO)
- Texas Department of Public Safety (TXDPS)

- U.S. Customs and Border Protection (CBP)

- U.S. Marshals Service (USMS)

- Bureau of Alcohol, Tobacco, Firearms and Explosives (ATF)

- Federal Bureau of Investigation (FBI)

The planning, preparation, and response of the Uvalde Consolidated Independent School District (UCISD) were also part of this assessment.

Due to the scope and areas of examination, other responder agencies, government entities, victim services providers, and other key stakeholders were also included in this assessment.

Period of Review

Based on the scope, the COPS Office determined that the period of review would extend for 1 year from the launch of the CIR work on June 8, 2022. Examining that tragic day and the subsequent events afterward up to June 8, 2023, allowed the team to assess the support services, public communications, and post-incident responses, including the 1-year mark (May 24, 2023). The team also examined pre-incident processes and planning in the days, weeks, and years prior to the incident.

Assessment Approach

The assessment approach involved four primary means of information gathering and collection: open source media review, document and data review, on-site data collection, and research and data analysis. Each method is described in more detail in the sections that follow.

Open Source Media Review

From the tragic day to the end of the review period (June 8, 2023), COPS Office staff collected and collated open source media on a daily basis. The CIR team read and analyzed news media articles, watched or listened to multimedia, reviewed social media posts, and more. This information, where probative, is incorporated throughout the report to provide context to interviews and other data points, as well as integrated heavily in "Chapter 5. Public Communications During and Following the Crisis," as well as "Appendix E: Public Communications Supplemental Materials."

Document and Data Review

The team collected and reviewed policies, procedures, training curricula, reports, data, body-worn camera (BWC) footage, radio and other audio files, and other documents and data as provided by responding agencies (see the subsections below for broad lists of documents and data). The team collected more than 14,100 pieces of data and documents, including thousands of images, 68 hours of footage from BWCs and other sources, and more than 4,500 hours of audio. The team spent hundreds of hours reviewing the evidence, crime scene images, records—including 911 calls, BWC videos, and closed-circuit television (CCTV) videos—and open source media articles, video footage, and social media articles. The team analyzed relevant videos and audio recordings regarding the incident in detail, second by second.

The CIR team made outreach to all responding agencies and organizations to request documents, data, and access to responding personnel. It takes courage to voluntarily undergo an assessment and the team acknowledges all agencies and organizations that provided documents and data, and in particular UPD, TXDPS, ATF, FBI, and CBP for their responsiveness and cooperation. Due to the multiple sources of verification, the CIR team was fully able to close any major gaps during the analysis, unless otherwise detailed in the text of the report.

Document Request List

At the outset of the CIR, the COPS Office submitted a formal document request list that was tailored to the primary responding entities. The full list was:

- Mission, vision, and values statements

- Organizational chart

- Annual reports (three years)

- Duty manual and general orders manual

- Collective bargaining agreement

- Policies, procedures, and special orders related to the scope of the review, including:

  - Active shooter/threat

  - Body armor/personal protective equipment

  - Code of conduct/courtesy and demeanor

  - Communications and dispatch

  - Complaint procedures

  - Crime investigation

  - Critical incident response, including public messaging

  - Crisis intervention

  - Critical incident stress management

  - Crowd control/management, including process for developing a coordinated message

  - Deployment of police-issued equipment

  - Disaster behavioral health services

  - Emergency management

- Employee mental health services
- Family assistance center
- Hostage/barricaded subjects
- Hostage situations
- Incident command processes/procedures, including Joint Information Center
- Interagency communications processes/procedures
- Internal affairs/professional responsibility
- Mutual aid
- Officer deployment/self-deployment
- Officer safety, wellness, and resilience
- Public information/interaction and information sharing with the public, including media relations
- School safety, including family support, unification, and notification
- Social media
- Special Weapons and Tactics (SWAT)/tactical operations and deployment
- Threat assessment
- Use of force, officer-involved shootings—investigation, practices, review, and oversight
- Violence prevention
- Victims of crime and resources

- Training records of all responding personnel and supervisors
- Any mutual agreements or memoranda of understanding with surrounding agencies or the UCISD and UCISD PD
- Documents, memos, reports, records, witness statements (including written, audio, or video), audio or video recordings (including in-car cameras, BWCs, and CCTV), transcripts, crime scene photos, distributed news releases, social media posts, emails or other communication regarding the planning and coordinating of news conferences and the development of public messaging, and any other documents related to the police response to the school shooting at Robb Elementary
- Any incident command procedures and any incident action plans
- Communication (911) codes and transcripts

- Annual or ad hoc training logs, or reports documenting training for law enforcement personnel for the last three years, including active shooter, barricaded subjects, hostage situations, critical incident response, crowd control, investigations, and incident command

- Training materials and lesson plans for the following topics: active shooter, incident command, school safety, use of force, internal affairs, de-escalation techniques, SWAT, Leadership, and/or management training, communications/public information officer, trauma care/tactical medical care, and any other topics relevant to the goal and scope of the review

- Inventories of equipment, including protective equipment and firearms

- Documents related to school safety, including physical building security, agreements, and threat assessment

- All reports generated by the city or governmental entities over the last three years that address the scope, including use of force, investigations, complaints, crowd control, school safety, community engagement, release of public information, and other appropriate documents

Data Requests

At the outset of the CIR, the COPS Office submitted a formal data request list that was tailored to the primary responding entities. The full list was:

- Agency and community data, including sworn force, number of civilians, population served, and accreditation status

- Fiscal expenses, including resources, equipment, staffing, and overtime

- Training data, including number of hours (academy and in-service) and format (in-person vs. online, scenario vs. other), broken out by topic and type

On-Site Data Collection

The team conducted nine site visits across 11 months:

- June 26–30, 2022

- July 17–21, 2022

- August 13–18, 2022

- August 22–24, 2022

- September 11–16, 2022

- November 13–18, 2022

- December 11–16, 2022

- April 4, 2023

- April 23–27, 2023

During these site visits, the team conducted and observed interviews[1287] with the following stakeholders:

- Local, state, and federal law enforcement personnel, including command staff; responding officers, deputies, troopers, and agents; SWAT/tactical teams; investigators; communication specialists; civilian staff; and others

- Other responding agencies, including federal, state, and local agencies that may have been involved in the pre-planning, response, post-incident response, and investigation

- Responding fire organizations

- Emergency medical services (EMS) and other medical responders

- Public information officers and media spokespersons

- Disaster coordinators

- Peer support members

- Victim services providers

- Businesses

- Other public safety responders

- State- and federal-level organizations responsible for training, leadership, union support, and mental health, as well as other relevant groups

- Victims, survivors, family members, and other community groups, to ensure their voices and experiences were reflected in our work

Due to the sensitivities and privacy considerations of its work, the team directly interviewed only adults and worked with appropriate officials and advocates to gather experiences from youth victims and witnesses, as well as gathered information from interviews with their families, review of media accounts, and review of other interviews and data. Additionally, due to privacy concerns regarding child victims, the CIR team did not have access to a full list of victim survivors, so was not able to make outreach to all victims or their families. The team utilized a "snowball approach"[1288] to make outreach to as many survivors and their families, victims' families, and other impacted individuals as possible using interviewee referrals.

The team also hosted two family and victim forums during the August 2022 and April 2023 site visits to provide updates to families and loved ones on the CIR and an opportunity for the team to hear, collectively, from those most directly impacted by the tragedy and answer questions as applicable.

[1287] Each interview conducted by the CIR team was voluntary. Participants were told that they had the option to answer or not answer, in whole or in part, any questions posed.

[1288] This refers to a nonprobability sampling technique in which each person contacted by the CIR team is asked to identify other individuals. This method is often used when there may be difficulty in identifying or reaching all individuals.

When appropriate, the team included a counselor or therapist on site during interviews and meetings to provide any assistance as needed. All team members were provided resources to assist with trauma-informed interviewing (see the section "Trauma-Informed Approach" below). The team also provided a Spanish interpreter during interviews and family forums.

Table B-1. Interviews conducted by CIR team, broken out by stakeholder type

Stakeholder	Number of interviews
Community/Faith-Based/Businesses	5
Federal/Agency (Non-Law Enforcement)	6
Federal/Law Enforcement Agency	31
Hospital/Medical	9
Local/Campus Agency	4
Local/Emergency Management	2
Local/Government Agency	12
Local/Nongovernmental Organization	3
Local/Police Department	37
Local/School District	35
Local/School Law Enforcement Agency	5
Local/Sheriff's Office	6
National/Nongovernmental Organization	21
Paramedics/Regional transportation	19
State/Association	3
State/Law Enforcement Agency	39
State/Nongovernmental Organization	7
Training Provider	8
Victim/Family/Witness	15
Grand Total	267

The team conducted multiple walkthroughs of Robb Elementary School and other critical locations, such as the Family Resiliency Center, the hospital, and the Reunification Center. More than 260 people were interviewed during these site visits and subsequent virtual meetings (see table B-1 for a complete tally).

In addition, the team participated in training observations of national-level active shooter trainings to inform its understanding of generally accepted practices and the available options. The following entities provided those trainings:

- Texas A&M Engineering Extension Service (online), January 24, 2023

- Texas State University Advanced Law Enforcement Rapid Response Training (ALERRT), February 20–22, 2023

- Louisiana State University (LSU) Academy of Counter-Terrorist Education, March 28–31, 2023

- National Tactical Officers Association, April 17–19, 2023

- ALERRT, April 24–27, 2023

- LSU, June 4–7, 2023

Trauma-Informed Approach

CIR team members used a trauma-informed approach for all interviews and interactions with victims, survivors, family members, first responders, and all other individuals affected by the incident. The team was trained with the following objectives:

- Understand the impact of traumatic stress on victims' ability to accurately access available memories of the traumatic incident

- Avoid retraumatizing or over-activating traumatic stress responses

- Understand the common emotional distress reactions to expect in some victims, family members, responders, and other witnesses that are likely to occur in anticipation of, during, and after an interviewing process in which they are asked to recall and provide a narrative—their account—of the activities they observed and participated in related to the traumatic event

- Understand when to slow, delay, or end an interview process to help stabilize, ground, and mitigate negative emotional distress responses in interviewee

- Understand when to refer an interviewee for mental health supports

- Learn key, basic emotional regulation, cognitive structuring/boundaries, and coping skills to mitigate and address the team members' own secondary traumatic stress responses to their exposure to disturbing and graphic information, pictures, videos, sounds, and stories of the incident both pre- and post-deployment/engagement

- Create team-based structural supports to implement, model, and encourage actions that can mitigate the development of serious emotional distress, secondary traumatic stress, and post-traumatic stress (e.g., briefings, debriefings including psychoeducation, buddy system/peer support, and self-care activities)

As needed, victims, family members, responders, and other witnesses were connected to local disaster mental health supports, resources, and more formal mental health care. The CIR team facilitated these connections through Texas professionals trained, skilled, and available to support those at risk and in need of emotional and mental health care (e.g., state and local offices for victim services, disaster behavioral health crisis counselors, and state voluntary organizations active in disasters). The CIR team also connected people to national supports (e.g., National Disaster Distress Helpline, National Suicide Prevention Lifeline, Veterans Crisis Line), if needed.

Research and Data Analysis

Throughout the duration of the project, the team researched open-source media; national standards, best practices, and generally accepted practices and standards in relevant areas of policing policy and practice; research literature; and any other relevant issues identified in the review to provide a foundation from which to conduct gap analysis. The team conducted a multidisciplinary literature review of promising and best practices, research, and other relevant standards and practices in the areas of active shooter, school safety, critical incident reviews, leadership, incident command, trauma, communications, and more.

Based on the information provided in the document and data requests, analysis was conducted to serve as the foundation for recommendations contained in the final report. The team analyzed hundreds of training records and certificates to develop a database of all relevant trainings. This analysis is included in "Chapter 8. Pre-Incident Planning and Preparation," "Chapter 3. Leadership, Incident Command, and Coordination," and "Chapter 7. School Safety and Security."

Moreover, the CIR team carefully analyzed daily media reports to determine major events, information sharing, inaccuracies, and misinformation. This analysis is included in "Chapter 5. Public Communications During and Following the Crisis."

In addition, the team analyzed in meticulous detail the movements, actions, and inactions of the responders. This involved second-by-second analysis over hundreds of hours. This analysis is included in "Chapter 3. Leadership, Incident Command, and Coordination."

The team recreated an incident timeline which is further detailed in the next section. Finally, the team analyzed available training data, which is discussed at the end of this chapter.

Incident Timeline Reconstruction

A critical component in assessing the public safety response to the shooting at Robb Elementary was an incident timeline reconstruction. Constructing an accurate, detailed timeline was essential, as it provided a chronological framework of the incident and facilitated a comprehensive understanding of the sequence of events that led up to the law enforcement response, occurred during the response, and followed in the immediate aftermath. The detailed account provided transparency in the factual occurrences throughout.

The timeline presented in the CIR report is based on the independent analysis, validation, and corroboration of documented information that can be aligned to a specific point in time through various sources. The CIR team analyzed the times down to the second and, in instances where possible, the fraction of a second.

In reconstructing the timeline, it was important to balance the need for comprehensive facts, while at the same time detecting and transmitting the signal of the events. This was especially important given the voluminous body-worn camera, CCTV, and audio recordings of the incident.

Data Sources

The CIR team reviewed and assessed voluminous primary and secondary data sources, including BWC footage, CCTV, radio communications, and 911 call logs, in addition to analytic products provided by CBP's Office of Professional Responsibility (OPR).

Primary sources of data included video, audio, and interviews from:

- Body-worn cameras
- CCTV
- Radio communications
- 911 calls
- CIR interviews and fact-finding activities

Secondary sources of data included the CBP OPR timeline data.

Analysis

Key to the timeline reconstruction were the following analytical tasks: time synchronization, identification of locations, and identification of phases, events, and actions.

Time synchronization

The various recording systems—such as officers' body-worn cameras, the nearby funeral home's CCTV, and radio communications—that were recording during this incident were not synchronized and, therefore, had different timestamps and inadvertently recorded the same event or action as occurring at different times. To resolve this issue, the CIR team conducted a careful analysis to align all actions in this Incident Timeline Reconstruction with one "true," synchronized time.[1289] The CIR team leveraged analytical work by the FBI and CBP OPR, which had aligned the time in the school hallway CCTV to the funeral home CCTV. This serves as the basis for "true time." All other times featured on body-worn cameras are aligned to this "true time," in order to synchronize across the data sources for this report.

[1289] All times, unless otherwise noted, are in Central Time.

Phases

The Incident Timeline Reconstruction is organized in five phases. Within each phase, every minute of key actions and events is detailed and specified per location. Where relevant, associated events and actions are also included. Each phase represents a span of time that conceptually captures a series of de facto related events and actions. Notably, the phases *are not intended to represent* predetermined response operations by any of the law enforcement agencies on scene.

Phase I (11:21 a.m.–11:39 a.m.) comprises the time period from when the subject shoots his grandmother through the end of the first responding officers' initial approach toward the classroom doors.

Phase II (11:40 a.m.–12:21 p.m.) comprises the time period following the officers' initial approach through a series of four shots fired at 12:21 p.m., which is a catalyst event within the broader response timeline.

Phase III (12:22 p.m.–12:49 p.m.) comprises the time period following the 12:21 p.m. shots fired through the breach and entry into rooms 111 and 112.

Phase IV (12:50 p.m.–1:15 p.m.) comprises the time period following the entry though the completion of medical triage and evacuation inside rooms 111 and 112.

Phase V (1:16 p.m.–3:15 p.m.) comprises the time period from the beginning activities of the investigation and establishment of investigative command of the scene, through a secondary threat at the high school.

Times

The timeline is largely a minute-by-minute narrative. For each minute of the incident, all data sources were reviewed for content that conveyed pertinent activities by officers, first responders, the subject, and victims—including movements inside and outside the hallway, key communication and direction being provided, and the request and arrival of various assets.

Locations

The incident and response unfolded across various locations inside and outside of the Robb Elementary campus. Each entry in the timeline is coded with the location. Additionally, "radio traffic" and "911 communications" are coded as locations. When these communications occur *from* a specific location that is known and the location is pertinent to understanding its context, both pieces of information are provided. Location is the overarching organization of data within each phase of the timeline. Over the course of the incident response and timeline, there are a total of 18 locations:

- Communications: 911

- Communications: Radio Traffic

- Communications: UCISD Raptor Alert

- Funeral Home

- Grandparents' Residence

- Robb Elementary: Northeast Hallway

- Robb Elementary: Perimeter

- Robb Elementary: West Building

- Robb Elementary: West Building Exterior, Parking Lot

- Robb Elementary: West Building Northeast Hallway

- Robb Elementary: West Building North Side Hallway

- Robb Elementary: West Building Northwest Entrance

- Robb Elementary: West Building South Entrance

- Robb Elementary: West Building South Side Hallway

- Robb Elementary: West Building T-Intersection

- Robb Elementary: West Building West Exterior

- Robb Elementary: West Building, Inside Classrooms 111 and 112

- Robb Elementary: West Building, Outside Classrooms 111 and 112

Events

The CIR team identified 33 events within the incident response, representing key thematic activities that recurred over the course of the incident and response. Notably, themes were often overlapping within the same time frame, and in some instances, a key activity was reflective of multiple events (for example, a communication by a first responder that referenced one or more of the events listed below).

The Key Events are:

- Air Support
- Callout of Containment and Barricade
- Closing off the Crime Scene
- Crowd Control
- Discussion of Classrooms 111/112 Layout
- EMS Arrivals and Actions
- Entry into Classrooms 111/112
- Establishing Incident Command Post
- Investigative Activity
- Medical Triage and Evacuation
- Negotiations
- Officer Arrivals
- Officers' Initial Approach to Classrooms 111 and 112
- Presence of Victims: Acknowledgment and Discussion
- Request for Shields
- Reunification
- Robb Elementary Lockdown
- Room Clearings and Evacuations
- Search for Keys
- Shooting at Grandparents' Residence
- Shots Fired
- Stack Formation
- Subject Enters School Grounds and Approaches West Building
- Subject Enters West Building and Classrooms 111 and 112
- Subject Identification
- Subject Killed
- Subject's Backpack: Observation and Recovery
- SWAT Callout

- Tactics: Sniper

- Tools and Equipment: Breaching

- Tools and Equipment: CS Gas

- UCISD: Other Campus Lockdowns

- Vehicle Crash Next to Robb Elementary

Training Analysis

The CIR team analyzed the training provided to local, county, and state personnel who responded on May 24, 2022 (see table B-2 for the breakdown of agency and personnel).[1290] No training data was provided for the federal agency personnel, as such the focus of the analysis is on the local and state personnel. This data reflects training data provided to the CIR team.

Data after May 24, 2022, was excluded from this analysis. Although the data does not reflect all law enforcement personnel present, there is a breakdown proportionate to the agencies and associated personnel present.

Table B-2. Agencies and associated personnel

State and local agencies	Number of personnel
Texas Department of Public Safety	89
Uvalde Police Department	27
Uvalde County Sheriff's Office	7
Uvalde Consolidated Independent School District Police Department	5
Southwest Texas Junior College	2
Hondo Police Department	1
Texas Parks and Wildlife Department	1
Uvalde County Constables	2
Zavala County Sheriff's Office	1
Grand Total	135

[1290] The numbers in table B-2 reflect the training data provided directly to the CIR team from local and state agencies. These numbers will not match the number of personnel on the scene.

The data was collected from the Texas Commission on Law Enforcement (TCOLE) records and/or training certificates for personnel on site during the incident. The CIR team reviewed the records and created a database of relevant trainings, dates, and training providers, and then categorized the trainings into the following buckets:

- Active Shooter
- Leadership
- Emergency Management, including ICS/NIMS
- School Based
- Crowd Control
- Special Weapons and Tactics (SWAT)
- Breaching Specific
- Hostage Negotiations
- Other Tactical, such as courses on patrol/tactical, tactical firearms training, armorer/gunsmith, patrol rifle, etc.
- Tactical Medical
- Basic Medical
- Officer Safety and Wellness
- Communications
- Other Relevant Trainings, such as post critical incident training, telecommunications, crime victims, risk assessment, etc.

As with all analysis, there are some limitations. The CIR team analyzed the training records for all known responding officers using the best available data and information provided. Furthermore, in-service trainings are notated on TCOLE as "in service" without any further details or description. As such, one caveat to the analysis is that trainings relevant to this review may have been provided during in service training. Wherever the CIR team validated or verified training deliveries through interviews, it has been noted.

Personnel that responded to Robb Elementary School ranged in law enforcement experience from 10 months to 43 years on the job, and on average had 4,229 hours of career/professional and TCOLE hours (range 1,018 to 16,238).[1291]

Overall, many of the officers, of all ranks, who responded to Robb Elementary School on May 24, 2022, had extensive and impressive training records which included thousands of hours of specialized tactical response and active shooter response training.

[1291] CIR Training Analysis.

Treatment of Names

Names are important. The team deliberated on the treatment of names and used the following:

- The subject's name is not used to avoid glorification.

- Only elected officials and chief executives of agencies are named where appropriate. All other individuals are left unnamed.

On a final note, this report refers to "victims" and "survivors" interchangeably to respect that some people prefer to be referenced as survivors and others as victims. In addition, the CIR team was cognizant of and attempted to avoid terminology like "triggered," "targeted," and other gun-related language as well as time frame references (which typically convey celebrations, such as "anniversaries"), out of respect for the fact that these terms are often activating for some victims, survivors, responders, and family members.

Appendix C. Observations and Recommendations

Chapter 2. Tactics and Equipment

Observation 1: The first officers on scene immediately moved toward the sound of gunfire and into the West Building of Robb Elementary to stop the shooter, which was in adherence to active shooter response generally accepted practices. Once inside the building, five of the first officers on scene continued to press down the hallway and toward a barrage of gunfire erupting inside of rooms 111/112.

Observation 2: Officer movements down the hallway were uncoordinated and not tactically sound, creating potential crossfire between officers entering on the south side and north side of the hallway.

> **Recommendation 2.1:** Officers responding to an active shooter and other dynamic scenes should maintain cognizance of potential crossfire upon their initial approach and make tactical adjustments as soon as feasible.

> **Recommendation 2.2:** Law enforcement agencies should ensure officers are trained on one-, two-, three-, and four-person team formations that are taught in active shooter training courses. These formations are designed to allow the greatest opportunity for success for officers in locating and addressing the threat with whatever weapon system they have on their person.

Observation 3: After officers suffered graze wounds from shrapnel, the first officers on scene did not penetrate the doors to rooms 111/112 and repositioned to a barricaded subject situation. This mindset permeated throughout much of the incident response, even impacting many of the later responding officers. Despite their training and despite multiple events indicating the subject continued to pose an active threat to students and staff in the building, including the likelihood and then confirmation of victims inside the room, officers on scene did not attempt to enter the room and stop the shooter until for over an hour after they entered the building. The shooter was not killed until approximately 77 minutes after law enforcement first arrived.

> **Recommendation 3.1:** Officers responding to an active shooter incident must continually seek to eliminate the threat and enable victim response. The shooter's immediate past actions and likely future actions serve as "triggering points" that indicate the appropriate response should be in line with active shooter response protocols. An active shooter with access to victims should *never* be considered and treated as a barricaded subject.

> **Recommendation 3.2:** Officers responding to an active shooter incident or dynamic scenes with evolving threats should continually assess their surroundings and stimuli and seek to obtain an accurate picture of the incident to inform their decision-making and tactical approach.

> **Recommendation 3.3:** Law enforcement training academies and providers should ensure that active shooter training modules include the factors in determining active shooter versus barricaded subject situations.

Observation 4: A callout over the radio that the subject is "contained" and "barricaded" was repeated time and again, and spread rapidly throughout the collection of agencies and individual officers responding to the scene. Although it was also stated that the subject was still shooting in some instances, the abundance of radio communications made it inevitable that some first responders would hear one communication but not the other.

> **Recommendation 4.1:** Officers on the scene of an active shooter incident should be cognizant of their description of the situation and how it can influence other officers as they arrive. These status updates, known as L-CANs (Location, Conditions, Actions, Needs) are integral to an effective and informed law enforcement response, particularly with assets en route to an evolving situation.

> **Recommendation 4.2:** Law enforcement agencies and training providers should ensure L-CANs are routinely included in training scenarios where applicable, including active shooter training. Other options for improving officer L-CAN discipline may include incorporating into rollcall, running L-CAN drills, and including as part of an agency's formal after action review process for all critical incidents.

Observation 5: Officers on scene did not consistently mark rooms that were cleared and evacuated, leading to instances of rooms unnecessarily and unintentionally being cleared multiple times over the course of the response.

> **Recommendation 5.1:** Room clearings and evacuations must be conducted systematically. Officers should establish a standard approach that physically mark rooms that are cleared. The approach should be simple and achievable for any room. For many law enforcement agencies, a marker or chalk is used to mark an "X" on the door once its room is cleared. Doing so serves both an officer safety and resource management purpose. Law enforcement agencies and training providers should ensure this instruction is provided when training on clearing buildings.

Observation 6: The effort to clear and evacuate the entire West Building was intentional and directed by Chief Arredondo, to preserve and protect the lives of the children and teachers who remained in the hot zone, while the shooter remained an active threat with multiple victims in rooms 111/112. This was a major contributing factor in the delay to making entry into rooms 111/112. The time it took to evacuate the entire building was 43 minutes, beginning at around 11:38 a.m., when Chief Arredondo realized there were occupants in room 109 that he could not access, and ending at 12:21 p.m., when four shots were fired, and that same room was finally evacuated through the windows. During this time and prior to 12:21 p.m., there were multiple stimuli indicating that there was an active threat in classrooms 111/112—including: the barrage of gunfire during the initial response; the children and teachers observed when evacuating the classrooms; the single shot fired at 11:44 a.m.; the notification that class was in session; the notification from an officer on scene that his wife, a teacher, was inside classrooms 111/112 and shot; and multiple radio broadcasts of a 911 call from a student inside the classroom.

> **Recommendation 6.1:** Officers responding to an active shooter incident must first and foremost drive toward the threat to eliminate it. In the event there are resources available and an opportunity to evacuate bystanders and victims from the hot zone, officers must balance the risk posed by evacuation versus the risk posed by remaining in lockdown and potentially in the crossfire. Evacuations in such circumstances must be conducted in the most expeditious manner, limited to

those immediately in harm's way, and not at the expense of the priority to eliminate the threat. In the case of Robb Elementary, the CIR team concludes that the effort to evacuate was protracted and should not have caused such significant delay in the eventual entry into rooms 111/112.

Observation 7: Some officers on scene believed that they were waiting for more assets to arrive, such as shields and a specialized tactical team, to make entry.

Recommendation 7.1: Officers responding to an active shooter incident must be prepared to approach the threat and breach or enter a room using just the tools they have with them, which is often a standard-issue firearm/service weapon.

Recommendation 7.2: Law enforcement agencies should adopt active shooter training national standards. The adoption of such standards is critical in the support and development of effective response tactics. The training, by design, enables a de-facto team of similarly trained officers who could rapidly assemble, communicate, and act as a team to rapidly stop the killing and stop the dying.

Recommendation 7.3: Law enforcement leaders on scene must work with available resources and personnel on scene and when the situation becomes stagnant, create an operational inner perimeter with a tactical team, removing all other personnel to avoid overcompensating the situation with unnecessary personnel.

Observation 8: The entry team assumed the door to rooms 111/112 were locked, based on information they received from officers who were on scene for a longer period of time. However, throughout the entirety of the incident, this assumption was never tested and the doorknob was never checked. Our analysis indicates that eight interior doors in the West Building were unlocked and discovered to be unlocked by responding officers during evacuations.

Observation 9: With master keys in hand and confirmed to work, the BORTAC commander paused on the room entry so that a sniper and drone could attempt to get a visual on the classroom. If successful, the sniper could have mitigated a great deal of risk posed by a gun battle inside the classroom. The sniper or drone could have provided valuable intelligence on the layout of the room, location of victims, and the shooter that would create a great tactical advantage for the entry team. However, assessing these options added 10 minutes to the overall response time.

Recommendation 9.1: Leaders providing direction in an active shooter incident must balance the urgency to stop the shooter with capabilities and approaches that may be time-consuming. The amount of time that has passed and the probability of success or improved outcomes should be considered when making such decisions.

Recommendation 9.2: The assessment on the viability of using a sniper should have been conducted earlier in the incident, as soon as the location of the subject was known. There were multiple officers with SWAT training and experience that could have conducted such an assessment within the first 10 minutes of the law enforcement response.

Observation 10: Active shooter incidents are responded to by law enforcement officers with a variety of experience and training, but rarely is there a fully functioning specialized tactical team on scene to respond.

Observation 11: Active shooter response protocol does not require any equipment that is not standard to a patrol officer. Officers on scene during the initial response in the West Building, even with only their standard issue service weapon, had sufficient equipment to formulate a plan and attempt to make entry into classrooms 111/112, by first checking the doorknob and, if necessary, making a forced entry through the classroom window, or using ballistic breaching methods.

> **Recommendation 11.1:** All equipment assigned by an agency requires specific training and may only be utilized by those officers assigned to that particular piece of equipment. Ideally, an agency may consider assigning specialized equipment to patrol officers to enhance the operational capacity of an emergency response. It should be noted that the equipment listed is not all required as collective response and is recommended to be utilized individually as available to further enhance the on-scene capabilities of an officer(s) responding to a critical emergency such as an active shooter situation. Each tool enhances its capacity and capability, but no single piece of ancillary equipment is required for a response to an active shooter.

> **Recommendation 11.2:** Agencies should also consider ensuring equipment is available at critically vulnerable locations, such as schools and other soft targets. Depending on the capacity of the police department, "readily available" may be defined as having the equipment in the possession of a trained officer or within close proximity to acquire the equipment for an emergency response.

Observation 12: UPD radios did not work well inside of the West Building, causing communications challenges throughout the incident response. Despite the known challenges in radio communications, video evidence shows that there are radio communications being broadcasted on both sides of the hallway throughout the incident, sharing key facts and circumstances of the incident.

> **Recommendation 12.1:** When experiencing radio voids or dead zones inside a building, officers on scene must be prepared to identify and utilize other modes of communicating—especially in large complex incidents with multiple agencies operating in multiple locations. Some common practices in law enforcement for such circumstances is to assign "runners," who will relay information to key actors within an incident response.

> **Recommendation 12.2:** Law enforcement agencies must maintain and upgrade all equipment, including radios, when vulnerabilities are presented. In Uvalde, police radios should perform not just in the wide-open spaces that are prevalent throughout the county, but also in high density environments, such as school buildings. Furthermore, agencies should establish and train on radio operability contingency plans, such as point-to-point communication, which does not require repeaters or internal transmitters.

Chapter 3. Leadership, Incident Command, and Coordination

Observation 1: All 11 FOS initially responded to Robb Elementary School as dictated by policy and practice for an active shooter response. However, only 5 of the 11 FOS ran toward the gunfire from rooms 111 and 112, but they retreated when UPD Lt. 1 and another FOS were grazed. After that initial response, only UPD Lt. 1 made further attempts to move toward the classrooms, and leadership did not direct entry into the classrooms.

Recommendation 1.1: Agencies should develop and annually review policy that directs officers to make entry and engage the subject as quickly as possible during an active attacker incident.

Recommendation 1.2: Agencies should provide training to direct officers to make entry and engage the subject as quickly as possible during an active attacker incident.

Recommendation 1.3: Agencies should train supervisors and implement accountability measures to direct officers to make entry and engage the subject as quickly as possible during an active attacker incident.

Observation 2: The FOS included experienced law enforcement personnel with sufficient training and equipment to engage the subject in rooms 111 and 112. Relevant policies and training directed officers to drive toward the threat and engage the subject to stop the killing. This did not happen.

Recommendation 2.1: The FOS should engage the subject regardless of whether they have additional officers on site.

Observation 3: The first information captured on video of possible victims in rooms 111 and 112 was heard on body-worn camera at 11:37 a.m. Within minutes there was confirmation that room 112 was in session. UCISD PD Chief Arredondo was told that there was an injured teacher. This information was not widely and immediately shared.

Recommendation 3.1: Any intelligence should be shared immediately with all law enforcement present via police radio or any means possible.

Observation 4: Leadership from UPD, UCISD PD, UCSO, and TXDPS demonstrated no urgency for establishing a command and control structure, which led to challenges related to information sharing, lack of situational statuses, and limited-to-no direction for personnel in the hallway or on the perimeter.

Recommendation 4.1: Agency leaders must immediately determine incident status and the appropriate command structure for the event. Leadership must continually assess and adjust as the threat and incident evolve.

Recommendation 4.2: Leadership should ensure responders are appropriately provided with a situation status and decisions that affect their responsibilities and actions.

Recommendation 4.3: As soon as leadership is aware of an emotionally involved responder, they should make every attempt to extricate that officer from the hot zone once sufficient personnel are present. Based on the involvement, that officer can be directed to the command post for sharing of any information relevant to the response and incident.

Observation 5: Failure to establish a unified command led to limited multiagency coordination.

Recommendation 5.1: As soon as possible and practical, the lead agency should establish a unified command that includes a representative from each primary first responder agency to facilitate communication, situational awareness, operational coordination, and allocation and delivery of resources.

Recommendation 5.2: As part of their pre-incident planning and preparation, regional agency leaders should determine a process for identifying a lead agency in a multi-jurisdiction response.

Observation 6: Local, county, state, and federal law enforcement personnel self-deployed, adding to the challenges at the scene. At least 380 law enforcement personnel were on the scene from 24 law enforcement agencies.

> **Recommendation 6.1:** A staging area manager should be designated to identify an appropriate area and direct additional personnel there for assignment of duties.

> **Recommendation 6.2:** Agencies should examine their policies and procedures to ensure they address self-deployment guidance and protocols, to include uniform, equipment, and resources.

> **Recommendation 6.3:** Officers should follow agency policies and procedures that address self-deployment.

Observation 7: Leadership failed to establish an ICP until after the incident and, once the ICP was established, it was in a location that was also a crime scene. Lack of strong leadership extended to the establishment and start of an ICP and include failing to sweep the facility (which would have revealed more than 90 children and staff in need of support); create control measures to limit access to other personnel; or, crucially, provide any clarity of purpose, continuity, or unity of effort. However, within 30 minutes, TXDPS took control of the ICP along with the scene.

> **Recommendation 7.1:** The establishment of an ICP for all agency leaders to report to so that brief and decisive action can be directed out toward the front-line officers is critical to resolving inaction and poor/no decision-making.

> **Recommendation 7.2:** Agencies should be prepared to provide critical services or supplement these services by establishing interagency agreements and plans for mutual aid.

> **Recommendation 7.3:** Agencies should engage with the EOC for assistance in implementing operational stability and a continuity of operations plan.

> **Recommendation 7.4:** The ICP should provide timely direction, control, and coordination to the agency leadership, other agencies, and other critical stakeholders before, during, and after an event or upon notification of a credible threat. The ICP must also serve as an intelligence collection and dissemination hub.

> **Recommendation 7.5:** Agency leadership should provide uninterrupted communication within the internal organization of the agency (or agencies if there is a unified command structure), externally to other agencies, and to all identified stakeholders.

> **Recommendation 7.6:** The ICP should establish and enact time-phased implementation procedures to activate various components of the plan to provide sufficient operational capabilities relative to the event or threat.

Observation 8: There was no uniformly recognized incident commander on the scene throughout the incident.

Observation 9: UCISD PD Chief Arredondo was the de facto incident commander on the day of the incident. Chief Arredondo had the necessary authority, training, and tools. He did not provide appropriate leadership, command, and control, including not establishing an incident command structure nor directing entry into classrooms 111 and 112.

Observation 10: UPD Acting Chief Pargas did not have incident command training and did not demonstrate adequate command leadership during the incident.

Observation 11: Uvalde County Sheriff Nolasco, despite being the chief law enforcement officer for the county, lacked leadership and incident command training and did not demonstrate adequate command leadership during the incident by not coordinating the resources from the Sheriff's Office or helping to establish a unified command.

> **Recommendation 8–11.1**: Agencies should ensure that persons in positions of authority have the requisite training and qualifications to carry out the responsibilities and duties of the title, including those serving in an acting capacity.

> **Recommendation 8–11.2**: Agencies should train, plan, and prepare for mass violence incidents, including the need for incident command structure.

> **Recommendation 8–11.3**: Leaders should be trained and prepared to transition an incident or response to another leader within or outside of their agency when needed.

Observation 12: On the day of the incident, no leader effectively questioned the decisions and lack of urgency of UCISD PD Chief Arredondo and UPD Acting Chief Pargas toward entering classrooms 111/112, including within their respective agencies and agencies with concurrent/overlapping jurisdiction (e.g., Uvalde County Sheriff Nolasco, Constable Zamora, Constable Field, TX Ranger 1).

> **Recommendation 12.1:** Agencies should create and train on a policy, and set an expectation that leaders will act in a manner consistent with that policy during critical incidents.

> **Recommendation 12.2:** An MOU/memorandum of agreement (MOA) needs to be developed among agencies within a county or region that provides clarity on who is in command, taking into consideration an agency's training, experience, equipment, and capacity to take the lead during a multiagency response to a critical incident.

> **Recommendation 12.3:** Agencies should train and practice together the areas covered in the MOU/MOA. The drills should include all first responders, elected officials, and critical infrastructure stakeholders.

> **Recommendation 12.4:** Law enforcement policy and training should be informed by research on leadership and decision-making theories, behaviors, functions, and practices.

Observation 13: No law enforcement leadership established incident command or unified command.

> **Recommendation 13.1:** Agencies should use the Incident Command System (ICS) for more than large-scale tactical events. They should incorporate as many of the ICS principles as possible in response to varying levels of emergencies or planned events, so ICS becomes a regular component of the agency's culture.

> **Recommendation 13.2:** Agencies should fully adopt NIMS throughout the region, even if not mandated as a FEMA Preparedness Grant recipient.

> **Recommendation 13.3:** Agencies should consider using the NQS to improve response, command, and coordination.

Recommendation 13.4: Agencies should ensure training and retraining of all staff regarding NIMS and the importance of standardized ICS implementation.

Recommendation 13.5: Agencies should conduct drills, exercises, and tabletops on NIMS and include all first responders, elected officials, and other critical infrastructure stakeholders.

Observation 14: CBP- and TXDPS-trained medics provided leadership for establishing a CCP and triage area and developed a triage process. However, due to the overabundance of law enforcement personnel, the plan was not operationalized once the classrooms were entered by law enforcement.

Recommendation 14.1: Law enforcement agencies should develop and train personnel in tactical emergency medicine and provide the appropriate equipment, as well as collaborate with local EMS to provide this capability.

Recommendation 14.2: First responder agencies should train and equip personnel using a rescue task force model.

Observation 15: Due to the lack of leadership, incident command, and coordination, law enforcement medics failed to coordinate with medical responders, including EMS and hospitals.

Recommendation 15.1: Agencies should work with emergency medical responders to develop a response, triage, and transport plan for mass casualty events. The protocols should be agreed upon, and member agencies should enter a formalized MOU.

Recommendation 15.2: Agencies at the regional level should conduct executive-level, multiagency tabletop exercises through their EOC that include elected and appointed officials as well as department heads from other government agencies, relevant nongovernmental agencies, and hospitals and other responder agencies. This will not only prepare personnel, but also help define roles and responsibilities, identify available resources, and establish an agreed-upon unified command system.

Recommendation 15.3: Agencies should consider adopting the recommendations from the U.S. Fire Administration (USFA) publication Fire/Emergency Medical Services Department Operational Considerations and Guide for Active Shooter and Mass Casualty Incidents.

Observation 16: Local ambulances had difficulty accessing Robb Elementary School due to lack of coordination and law enforcement vehicles blocking the streets. This delayed critical medical services.

Recommendation 16.1: An incident safety officer should be designated as quickly as possible during incident response and should pay special attention to the access or egress of emergency vehicles.

Chapter 4. Post-Incident Response and Investigation

Observation 1: The involvement of local agencies in the hallway during the incident led the district attorney, in consultation with TXDPS, to assign Texas Rangers to solely investigate the incident.

Recommendation 1.1: Agencies should have a formal agreement or understanding on investigative command after a multiagency response.

Observation 2: An investigative command post was initially established at the funeral home, which was soon discovered to be one of six crime scenes. As a result, the command post was moved into a TXDPS mobile command post.

> **Recommendation 2.1:** Agencies should carefully assess the location of any command post during and after a critical incident to ensure it is suitable for the operations of a command post. Some considerations include accessibility, size and capacity, availability of resources, and safety and security.

Observation 3: TXDPS did not maintain a log for the investigative command post. As a result of this oversight, there is no record of which agencies or individuals were present at various times throughout the crime scene investigation.

> **Recommendation 3.1:** Law enforcement agencies investigating any crime scene—especially complex, multiagency responses—should ensure a log is kept not only at the crime scene, but at the command post as well. The log ensures accurate record keeping and accountability for actions taken by the investigative team. Access to the command post should be limited to those with a need to be there.

Observation 4: Body-worn camera (BWC) video captures officers walking into the crime scene without an investigative purpose or responsibility in the immediate aftermath of the incident. Furthermore, in the days that followed, crime scene preservation was compromised, and the crime scene team had to continually stop and start their important work when non-investigatory personnel entered the hallway and classrooms 111/112 for the purpose of viewing the scene.

> **Recommendation 4.1:** Leaders must respect the integrity of the crime scene and only access it with a declared and documented legitimate purpose. Crime scenes need to be held without contamination until completed. The crime scene team should be permitted to do their methodical work without continuous interruptions by VIPs who want to enter the crime scene but have no probative need to do so.

> **Recommendation 4.2:** Investigative teams should ensure that inner and outer perimeters are established at all crime scenes. There was an outer security presence at the campus gate, but there was not a secured entrance to the building of the crime scene.

Observation 5: The crime scene at the car wreck was washed out by rain prior to the collection of any evidence. The FBI offered to process the truck and warned of the rain coming, suggesting they move the truck to a secure and dry location. They also offered to cover the truck with a tarp. These offers were rebuffed by TXDPS leadership.

> **Recommendation 5.1:** Investigative teams must properly assess weather conditions and the timing of investigative activities—particularly evidence collection—that must be conducted outside in the elements.

Observation 6: Texas Rangers conducted an exterior door test, documenting the operation and locking mechanisms of each exterior door in the West Building. The critical incident review (CIR) team was unable to ascertain whether the Texas Rangers conducted the same test on interior doors—specifically rooms 111 and 112—which witnesses have also indicated could have had faulty closing and locking mechanisms. The interior doors were removed from their frames by the Uvalde County District Attorney as evidence. The functionality of the doors should have been assessed prior to their removal from the crime scene.

> **Recommendation 6.1:** Law enforcement agencies investigating such incidents in which the form and functionality of physical evidence, such as doors, would benefit from testing should refrain from removing such items until they have been tested and such testing is formally documented via video recording and a written report.

Observation 7: The hellfire trigger system was not initially collected as evidence, as crime scene Rangers were not aware of its presence or that they should be looking for it. After reviewing crime scene photos, they uncovered an approximate location of the device at the crime scene and recovered the device.

> **Recommendation 7.1:** Agencies in regional proximity to each other should conduct multiagency tabletop exercises (TTX) for complex investigations that may necessitate mutual aid and support from each other. Doing so will build greater interagency coordination in activities like evidence collection as well as understanding of jurisdictional boundaries, capabilities, processes, and expectations among partner agencies. The TTX should include local, state, and federal agencies, as appropriate, and be designed to exploit weaknesses, uncover strengths, and develop solutions.

Observation 8: Given the influx of investigative support assets from out of town, often spending multiple days on site, there were logistical challenges with lodging and transportation. Many hotels were sold out. The team lead was able to secure housing on a hunter's ranch, which helped alleviate the lodging issue.

> **Recommendation 8.1:** Crime scene teams need to plan for logistical support, especially when traveling long distances to mass shootings. Identifying a dedicated coordinator for such efforts can help in the planning and ensure personnel arriving from out of town are able to find lodging nearby, including nontraditional options as needed, such as a private housing.

Observation 9: The Texas Rangers Crime Scene Team processed and exhaustively documented an incredibly challenging crime scene that put their training, policies, and procedures to the test. The team conducted an after-action review to examine their efforts and learn as an organization.

> **Recommendation 9.1:** Organizational subunits should conduct after action reviews, particularly in the wake of critical incidents that provide a real-world test to their training, policies, and procedures.

Observation 10: To account for the number of victims and personal items, the Crime Scene Team implemented an alphanumeric tracking system for items found so that they could be quickly, easily, and accurately aligned.

> **Recommendation 10.1:** Crime scene investigators responding to incidents of mass violence should be prepared with a predesignated system to collect and align personal belongings to victims.

Observation 11: Among the agencies with the most involved personnel, most have not completed administrative investigations into their officers' actions on May 24.

Recommendation 11.1: Agencies should adopt parallel investigations policy for criminal and administrative investigations, including for major incidents, while taking diligent steps to ensure that information derived from compelled administrative interviews are completely walled off from any criminal investigation into the officer's or agent's actions.

Observation 12: CBP OPR stood up a comprehensive analytical operation, dedicating staff to the reconstruction of the incident, which provided high-value intelligence to investigators as they began conducting interviews with involved agents.

Recommendation 12.1: Agencies that engage in after action/critical incident reviews should adequately resource the effort to ensure high-quality and timely reports of lessons learned and areas for organizational improvement.

Observation 13: CBP OPR trained all investigators in trauma-informed interview techniques in advance of interviewing their involved agents, some of which were deeply involved in the incident response.

Recommendation 13.1: Agencies' personnel conducting interviews of individuals involved in a critical incident should be trained in trauma-informed interview techniques.

Observation 14: UPD officers involved in the incident did not maintain a record of their own incident reports. Rather, UPD records show a reference back to the Texas Rangers' records, which serve as the official statement of UPD officers.

Recommendation 14.1: Agencies should maintain a duty to collect officer statements for their own administrative records and investigations even as an external agency is conducting an investigation into the same matter.

Observation 15: UPD's internal investigation has been hampered by a lack of access to evidence that TXDPS was in possession of and not willing to share.

Recommendation 15.1: Memoranda of understanding on sharing investigative data should be established among partner agencies.

Observation 16: The FBI provided forensic interview specialists for conducting child witness interviews, filling a gap in available resources and expertise within the lead agency.

Recommendation 16.1: Agencies should ensure they have procedures in place to identify and utilize forensic child witness interviewers, whether in-house or through mutual aid agreements.

Observation 17: The FBI's child witness forensic interview specialists were not representative of the racial and gender makeup of the child witnesses.

Recommendation 17.1: When conducting investigations, law enforcement agencies should account for the racial, ethnic, gender, and cultural diversity of witnesses when making investigative assignments, including interviews.

Chapter 5. Public Communications During and Following the Crisis

Observation 1: Inaccurate information combined with inconsistent messaging created confusion and added to the victims' suffering, both on the day of the incident and in the days after the mass shooting.

Recommendation 1.1: Due to the possible occurrence of mass shootings regardless of jurisdiction size, all law enforcement agencies and local governments should plan for such critical incidents from a public messaging and crisis communication perspective. This requires relationship building, planning, training, and preparing before a large-scale incident.

Recommendation 1.2: Organizations must be prepared to swiftly develop proactive messages in an organized fashion to keep community members informed and establish a source of strength and leadership that can unite a community and assist with the healing process.

Observation 2: UPD posted the first public message 10 minutes after the subject entered Robb Elementary School, a strong start for public messaging. However, the post was edited four times over the next 73 minutes. Since the Facebook algorithm does not recognize the edits as a new post, it did not reach as many users.

Recommendation 2.1: As quickly as possible, an agency should inform the public regarding the nature of the critical incident and how it will release information regarding it.

Recommendation 2.2: An agency should create a new social media post or message each time it has new information to release. This will help reach a larger audience instead of updating the initial post.

Observation 3: At no time was a specific agency designated as the official source of information, nor was a lead agency identified.

Recommendation 3.1: The first or second post from an agency should establish the agency as the official source of information, which reduces confusion about how information will be released.

Recommendation 3.2: Agencies should instruct the public that other modes of incoming communication, with the exception of emergency calls, will be shut down to allow staff to focus on the accuracy and timeliness of information via the official platform.

Recommendation 3.3: Messaging to the public should include identification of the lead agency or a transition to another agency as the lead. This level of transparency ensures accountability to the public when people are seeking reassurance, order, and answers.

Observation 4: UCISD PD posted their first public message 33 minutes after the subject entered Robb Elementary School. The message references that the students and staff are safe. This reassurance was false and never corrected.

Recommendation 4.1: Information should be confirmed by two sources if at all possible before it is shared publicly. If false information is shared, it must be corrected as soon as possible on social media, and if the content is highly newsworthy, it should be addressed in the next news conference as well. The agency should explain how the false information ended up being released. Delays will erode public trust in the organization.

Recommendation 4.2: Agencies should monitor social media and media coverage to understand the totality of the circumstances, which includes community sentiment. This may guide the incident commander to share information that initially was being withheld in order to refute a false narrative. The role of monitoring social media and media coverage should be assigned to a specific individual as stipulated by the communication plan and can even involve a neighboring agency.

Recommendation 4.3: To establish leadership and a sense of order, the lead agency must be swift, proactive, accurate, and transparent in its messaging. Relevant information that is not law enforcement-sensitive should typically be released as soon as it is confirmed. However, speed must be balanced with the need for accuracy. It is critical that information is verified before it is released even when there is tremendous pressure to release information quickly.

Observation 5: Family members encountered many obstacles to locating their loved ones, getting access to the hospital, and getting information from leadership, law enforcement, and hospital staff in a timely manner. This includes initial information posted by UCISD on the reunification site followed by a series of contradictory posts between UPD and UCISD on reunification. This added to the confusion, pain, and frustration.

Recommendation 5.1: As part of a community-wide comprehensive emergency response protocol, school districts should have a safety plan for each school which includes a reunification and communication section on how they will direct parents/family members when a crisis occurs. Selected district personnel should be designated in advance to assist emergency personnel as family members rush to the school or reunification location.

Recommendation 5.2: School district leadership needs to develop a system for documenting which children are present and which parent or guardian has retrieved them using a sign in/out, checkoff, and/or smartphone picture system to document for safety, notification, and reunification purposes.

Recommendation 5.3: Information about locations for notification, family assistance, and property return should be as specific as possible, including the location address. These posts should be prepared in advance when possible and pre-tested during exercises testing the crisis communications plan.

Recommendation 5.4: As soon as any type of mass casualty or active assailant incident occurs, law enforcement should serve as the lead on public safety messaging and updates on status of the incident and the criminal investigation. Once the situation has been rendered safe, the affected entity should take the lead with providing information to the public about operations and issues affecting the facility. Each agency (e.g., school district and law enforcement agency) should share or link to the others' content on social media. This will help them avoid contradicting each other.

Observation 6: UPD and UCISD never posted when the threat to the community was over. UPD did post a message at 1:06 p.m., however, the post incorrectly stated that the subject was in custody and that information was never corrected.

Recommendation 6.1: When a community suffers a traumatic incident, a law enforcement leader should work to establish a feeling of safety in the community with a news briefing as soon as possible. The news briefing should announce the status of the situation and when the situation is resolved, and include details of how that was accomplished. If an incident is not quickly resolved, the leader should hold regular news briefings to keep the community informed. The leader should strive to show strength balanced with compassion and care for those suffering tragic injuries and losses.

Recommendation 6.2: When reunification is complete and the victims' families have been notified, the lead agency should release that information to the community. This is a crucial step in unifying the community to start the healing process.

Observation 7: Uvalde Memorial Hospital and University Health San Antonio swiftly released information regarding patients arriving at the hospitals.

> **Recommendation 7.1:** The lead agency should institute incident command and establish a JIC for coordinating the release of all public information, including victim information from all medical facilities that can be incorporated into coordinated news briefings.

> **Recommendation 7.2:** Once the agency leading the JIC learns that patients are being transported to hospitals outside the region, a PIO should be assigned to call the hospitals to coordinate the release of information. This duty can be filled by an outside PIO who has arrived to assist, which should be outlined in the crisis communication plan.

Observation 8: Texas Governor Greg Abbott was the first official to publicly speak about the incident, during an unrelated press conference, and shared preliminary information that turned out to be incorrect. All officials who speak to an incident that is still unfolding should ensure that they have timely, accurate information.

Observation 9: At 4:16 p.m., UCISD held the first news conference at the Civic Center. Basic information was provided and did not include details such as the current number of victims. This information was never released. The media were not allowed to ask any questions.

> **Recommendation 9.1:** A news conference with a law enforcement executive from the lead agency, who was not intrinsically involved in the response and so would not risk jeopardizing a criminal case or consciously or unconsciously provide unreliable facts, should take place on scene as soon as the scene is rendered safe. If the incident is elongated, a briefing should take place while the event is still in progress and should be held nearby the scene to reassure the community.

> **Recommendation 9.2:** An on-scene location for the press conference helps instill confidence that law enforcement is effectively handling the situation and that the people watching the news conference are safe.

> **Recommendation 9.3:** The law enforcement leader conducting news conferences should attempt to be responsive to all media questions. While it may not be possible to answer questions related to the ongoing investigation, it is possible to be responsive by explaining the process or announcing when more specific information may be released.

> **Recommendation 9.4:** An agency should release the number of deceased and injured victims as soon as the information is confirmed. There is no benefit to gain from a delay.

> **Recommendation 9.5:** Consistent leadership needs to unite the community through a projection of strength and empathy. This is also vital for the community's healing process.

Observation 10: TXDPS as the lead agency post-incident did not establish a JIC or media staging area and did not schedule a series of briefings and interviews with media. Instead, the TXDPS spokesperson conducted ad hoc interviews as they were flagged down.

> **Recommendation 10.1:** The designated lead spokesperson and agency should establish a JIC and a media staging area in line of sight of the command post.

Recommendation 10.2: A schedule of briefings should be created, and other agencies should be invited to send PIOs to work with the lead spokesperson to coordinate the release of information. If possible, joint news conferences of local, state, and federal agencies should take place at this location, based on that schedule.

Recommendation 10.3: All media should be given the opportunity to receive the same information at the same time via news conferences or previously identified social media or other releases. This prevents inadvertent contradictory news stories that can be caused by using a different selection of words in each interview. It also avoids the appearance of an agency favoring a specific media outlet or outlets, which can cause other reporters to become more assertive.

Observation 11: Spokespersons for UCISD and TXDPS, the only agencies speaking publicly, did not coordinate their messaging the afternoon of the incident. Some conflicting information was shared by the two agencies.

Recommendation 11.1: The lead agency should be working to release basic details in follow-up news conferences, such as an update on the number of victims and their conditions, information about the subject, the type of weapon(s) used, and the status of the investigation. Some activities take place at every crime scene and can be shared, such as meeting with victims' family members, identifying witnesses, conducting interviews with witnesses and the involved officers, or processing the crime scene. Talking about these activities at the news conference does not compromise the investigation, and it shows the community that law enforcement is making progress.

Observation 12: Off-topic prescheduled posts appeared on the UPD's and Uvalde Memorial Hospital's Facebook pages while the incident was still immediately recent.

Recommendation 12.1: An agency should disable scheduled posts during a critical incident as part of its crisis communication plan.

Observation 13: During the May 25 news conference, Texas Governor Abbott and TXDPS Director McCraw provided inaccurate information. This further perpetuated the misinformation and rumors.

Recommendation 13.1: When an organization recognizes that an error has occurred, it should admit the mistake and share what actions it is taking to rectify the problem and prevent it from happening again. Even when the mistake is egregious, an agency can maintain or seek to regain public trust by being open and holding itself accountable to the community. In these moments, a law enforcement agency can build community trust by holding itself to the highest possible standard.

Recommendation 13.2: Agencies should use social media and the local media to reassure the community with clarity and confidence that any loss of life would be investigated quickly and appropriately. This accountability is necessary for any critical incident that significantly impacts a community.

Recommendation 13.3: Agency spokespersons should be briefed by those most knowledgeable on the facts of the incident prior to public comments.

Observation 14: The involved law enforcement agencies were unresponsive to the growing concerns in the community. Many of the media's questions were an extension of the pressing questions from the victims' family members and others.

Recommendation 14.1: Effective communication requires law enforcement agencies to listen to their communities' concerns and be responsive to them.

Observation 15: All social media public messaging was posted in English. The one exception to this was the FBI San Antonio Field Office's messaging starting on May 25.

Recommendation 15.1: In a community with a large population with limited English proficiency, officials should post emergency information in English and in other predominant languages. This inclusive approach will help ensure that critical public safety messages reach a larger audience and will help boost trust.

Recommendation 15.2: In a community with a large population with limited English proficiency, officials should enlist the assistance of a local television, radio, or social media channel that caters to the non-English predominant culture and language of the community.

Observation 16: On day 4, the TXDPS director changed the narrative from a heroic local law enforcement response to a failed response, but only during the question-and-answer section of the news conference. This approach prompted even more questioning from the media and caused anguish among family members of the victims.

Recommendation 16.1: An agency should be as direct as possible when it is revealing law enforcement mistakes in responses and actions. An indirect approach can undermine faith and trust in law enforcement.

Observation 17: Attending to the cultural needs of different community members is of the utmost importance and requires extensive effort to understand the community, familial, and individual impacts of cultural influences on victims. Local law enforcement and other responders in Uvalde rarely ensured that those impacted were given information in their primary language (Spanish). Behavioral health supports that were offered did not take into account cultural considerations that may have helped those impacted to accept behavioral health supports and seek help for other case management-type needs.

Recommendation 17.1: Formal and informal leaders and other community members can help responders to better understand the community's cultural beliefs around health, mental health, and help-seeking. Demographic information should be integrated into tailoring services to make them less stigmatized and more acceptable to those in need. Services should be culturally appropriate for the community they serve.

Recommendation 17.2: Agencies should incorporate culturally sensitive communications into early communications during a crisis.

Observation 18: The extent of misinformation, misguided and misleading narratives, leaks, and lack of communication about what happened on May 24 is unprecedented and has had an extensive, negative impact on the mental health and recovery of the family members and other victims, as well as the entire community of Uvalde.

Recommendation 18.1: All persons involved in delivering information during and after a mass violence incident should be trained in best practices that are victim-centered, trauma-informed, and culturally appropriate. Typically, a trained PIO or designated representative should be the person speaking to the press and family members or advising the designated representative as to the best-practices approach.

Observation 19: Investigative journalists and reporters became the main source of information, and their reporting served as the accountability measure for the victims, families, and the community due to a lack of open and transparent information from government officials.

Recommendation 19.1: Law enforcement and other government officials within the affected community should develop a comprehensive plan for media engagement to centralize information sharing, maintain consistency in messaging, and build trust within the community as a legitimate source of information.

Observation 20: There was extensive media exposure on mainstream and social media that included

- images of law enforcement entering Robb Elementary School;

- law enforcement officers restricting, yelling at, and falsely reassuring parents outside the school that they were taking care of the incident inside the school;

- audio recordings of young children calling 911 asking for help and reporting they were afraid to die; and

- a continuous flow of body camera footage showing a significant number of law enforcement officers not taking actions to save the children trapped in classrooms 111 and 112.

Recommendation 20.1: Images and reports of the details of violent crimes, especially those involving the injury and death of children, are traumatic to anyone exposed to them. Those who conduct investigations, legal representatives, and government officials, as well as family members who request such details, should be prepared and supported before and after such exposure.

Observation 21: Throughout the days, weeks, and months following the incident, there continued to be significant failings in public communications.

Observation 22: While notifying victims and families of an impending release of traumatic, violent, or graphic materials (e.g., body camera footage, crime scene images) is traditionally the role of government, in many instances, the media obtained a copy from a leak. Family members should be advised well ahead of the planned release of such materials. Not doing so was harmful.

Recommendation 22.1: Any details shared publicly by government officials should have a purpose and not be gratuitous.

Observation 23: Family members and victims who attended school board meetings felt their concerns and requests for information and accountability were ignored, experiencing a lack of communication and empathy from authorities.

Recommendation 23.1: Local leaders and law enforcement representatives providing information to victims and family members need to be trained or, at a minimum, knowledgeable about how and when it is appropriate to hold a family and victim forum, the purpose of such an informational forum, and how to conduct it in a victim-centered, trauma-sensitive manner. Giving voice to victims and family members (active and deep listening), allowing them the time they need to express themselves, validating their concerns, identifying actions that can be taken, providing resources, and ensuring follow up to outstanding questions are all best practices that should be followed by anyone engaging with victims and family members.

Observation 24: Families asking what happened to their loved ones were traumatized by a re-enactment by a law enforcement official during the first family and victims' forum.

> **Recommendation 24.1:** Intentional transparency is needed for the victims, survivors, and loved ones who are seeking answers about what happened; however, authorities need to provide information in a trauma-informed, victim-centered, and culturally sensitive manner.

Observation 25: Family members in Uvalde have struggled for more than a year to be heard, to get a full accounting of what transpired during this incident, and to be able to fully grieve and begin to adapt to the losses in their lives as a result of the horrific circumstances of the deaths of their loved ones and the failed response. Their recovery is delayed and more complex than it needed to be due to the lack of attention to their needs.

> **Recommendation 25.1:** Law enforcement, local leaders, and other responders can support the recovery of victims and families by giving them opportunities to be fully heard, have their concerns validated, and receive information through a transparent lens.

Observation 26: The misinformation, lack of timely and accurate information, and the poor manner in which many families and other loved ones were treated at Robb Elementary at the time of the shooting can contribute to poorer mental health outcomes for the impacted individuals. The ongoing unresolved questions about the law enforcement response to the shooting can inhibit recovery for the entire community, individual victims, and family members.

Chapter 6. Trauma and Support Services

Observation 1: Once the children and adults were rescued from their classrooms during the evacuation process, they received limited instruction and direction on where to proceed. Due to the chaotic nature of the evacuation, children and school personnel were not adequately evaluated medically prior to being transported to the Reunification Center. As such, injured victims had delayed medical care and were at risk of further injury.

> **Recommendation 1.1:** The responsibility of responders is to rely on training and preparation to remain calm when interacting with children so as not to increase the children's fear or lessen their sense of safety.

> **Recommendation 1.2:** Evacuation planning should involve designating dynamic evacuation routes and safe spaces where the evacuees will be guided for safety, medical triage, and emotional support.

> **Recommendation 1.3:** Evacuees should be provided clear instructions and directions on where to proceed. Where resources are available, a corridor of law enforcement personnel should be set up to ensure the evacuees are unimpeded and directed in a safe manner.

Recommendation 1.4: Evacuees should be triaged and medically assessed once evacuated and prior to reunification with next of kin to ensure that all injuries are immediately identified and that victims receive necessary care.

Recommendation 1.5: As part of evacuation planning, school officials should develop an identification system for tracking students who leave with their parents or guardians, to include on site where possible.

Observation 2: Not all victims of the incident at Robb Elementary School received medical and mental health screenings following the incident.

Recommendation 2.1: Officials should ensure all victims of a mass violence incident are screened medically and assessed for mental health concerns soon after evacuation and no later than 24-48 hours post-incident.

Recommendation 2.2: In the weeks and months following an incident, victims and family members should receive follow-up or continued monitoring to ensure they are receiving the necessary mental health care and other services.

Observation 3: At least 91 children were evacuated from the school and hid in the back chapel of the funeral home (which was an active crime scene) with funeral home staff, teachers, and some parents. They were held there for hours. At the same time, law enforcement personnel, many of whom were aware of the children and staff present, moved in and out of the front of the funeral home and throughout the perimeter. At least one child in the back chapel was bleeding and required medical attention. Parents and guardians were outside of the funeral home demanding access to their children.

Recommendation 3.1: School officials should create a process that allows reunification outside of the Notification/Reception Center, whenever necessary and collect victims' names, photos of their guardians, and location of reunification.

Recommendation 3.2: As part of establishing a command post, law enforcement and other officials should secure the entire facility around the post and, if possible, evacuate civilians. In all cases, family members, community members, media, and other onlookers need to be kept out of the hot zone for their safety.

Observation 4: At the scene of Robb Elementary, some families and loved ones on the perimeter seeking information and questioning the law enforcement delay were treated with physical and verbal aggression, were shown no compassion or empathy, and received limited information.

Recommendation 4.1: The incident commander should assign a communications officer or liaison officer to provide timely and accurate information on the status of the response to family members and the community, help provide a sense of calm and trust, and maintain order.

Recommendation 4.2: Agencies should incorporate de-escalation tactics and trauma-informed, victim-centered, culturally sensitive approaches into their training on crowd control, emergency management, mass casualty response, and emergency/crisis communications.

Observation 5: Those without a formal role in the response at Robb Elementary, such as community members, school personnel, and certain responder personnel, were unnecessarily exposed to the deceased victims' bodies or the crime scene.

Recommendation 5.1: Law enforcement and other responder agencies have a responsibility to limit exposure to traumatic crime scenes—including deceased victims' bodies—to those with a formal role. Leaders should consider using tents or vehicles to shield the crime scene from view, or widening the perimeter to keep it out of sight.

Recommendation 5.2: Responding agencies should also limit the exposure of community members, school staff, and their own agency staff to traumatic materials.

Observation 6: The establishment of a Reunification Center was delayed and chaotic. Families and next of kin received conflicting instructions on the location of the center.

Recommendation 6.1: As part of disaster preparedness, communities should plan to establish a Notification/Reception Center. Planning should include determining where the center will be, who will be in charge, what security measures it will have, how the reunification process will be conducted, what screening of victims and families will take place, and how public communications and media will be handled. Establishing and managing a Notification/Reception Center should also be part of the community's critical incident drills.

Recommendation 6.2: All evacuees and their next of kin should receive information about where to receive services and resources once they leave the Notification/Reception Center. Victim advocates should contact all identified victims for follow up at various points after the incident to ensure they are aware of services and engaging in help seeking.

Observation 7: The public, including family members, witnessed child victims being brought to Uvalde Memorial Hospital (UMH) via the visitors' front door. The UMH chapel door also inadvertently provided a view of the victims in the ER.

Recommendation 7.1: Pre-incident planning and preparation should include determining where to have families wait for their loved one during a mass violence incident.

Observation 8: Family members had unreasonable challenges accessing the hospital and their injured loved ones.

Recommendation 8.1: Pre-planning should include developing a plan that removes barriers for families and loved ones to enter the hospital, receive updates, and see their loved ones.

Observation 9: The death notification process was disorganized, chaotic, and at times not conducted in a trauma-informed manner.

Recommendation 9.1: Clear, accurate, and frequent communication needs to be provided to the families and loved ones at the Notification/Reception Center.

Recommendation 9.2: Any information about the number of deaths or the process of identification should be communicated by a single trained and trusted leader who has verified the information and invites each family to a private space to discuss the situation involving their loved one.

Recommendation 9.3: Law enforcement agencies should assign compassionate and trauma-trained personnel to collect identifying information and descriptions of victims, including clothing and photos. These individuals can also be a constant presence with the families, monitoring them for any medical or security needs, answering any questions, and ensuring they have necessities such as water, tissues, and medication.

Recommendation 9.4: Victim advocates should be assigned to communicate with and assist families. Each family member of a deceased person and each injured victim should be assigned a victim advocate who works with that family/victim consistently throughout the treatment and recovery period, having frequent communications to ensure the family/victim is aware of and able to access needed services and supports.

Observation 10: The TXDPS personnel, including the civilians who conducted the death notifications, varied in training and experience. Some did not have any experience in this type of communication. However, family members described the Rangers providing the notifications as compassionate and said that the Rangers gave them the time they needed before being escorted to their car.

Recommendation 10.1: Officers or other representatives tasked with death notification should be trained in accordance with agency policies and procedures. This is a highly sensitive function that should not be performed by those who have not received specialized training in how to conduct victim-centered, trauma-informed, and culturally appropriate death notifications.

Observation 11: An FBI notification team that was trained and experienced in trauma and death notifications was excluded from performing this task by staff from TXDPS who did not have the training or experience to provide this care.

Recommendation 11.1: Local officials engaging in trauma and death notifications should consult national resources and ensure best practices are followed when providing these notifications. Preparedness and planning can help a locality identify areas where they have fewer trained or experienced staff, thus the areas where they need mutual aid supports.

Observation 12: The number of people in the room during the death notifications varied. Some were made by the primary team only, while others—including the first death notification—were made in the presence of other law enforcement or school staff.

Recommendation 12.1: A trauma notification team should comprise two people: one law enforcement officer and one victim advocate or behavioral health provider.

Recommendation 12.2: The number of trauma notifications that an individual makes should be closely monitored, and trauma services should be made available to those providing notifications.

Observation 13: Each agency and organization providing support services for responders operated independently. The lack of coordination among the providers complicated the process for personnel interested in obtaining support, leading to overlaps and gaps in services.

Recommendation 13.1: The post-incident command post should assign a central coordinating entity to track law enforcement and responder agencies at the incident and others who may have been involved (e.g., dispatchers, technicians, and other support services personnel). This tracking should continue after the incident to ensure that appropriate trauma-related services are offered in a coordinated effort with appropriate follow-ups.

Observation 14: Responders were not provided timely, immediate access to trauma and support services, and many reported feeling abandoned and unsupported in the weeks and months following the critical incident. Others reported being aware of the services but electing not to use them.

Recommendation 14.1: A comprehensive approach to psychological support services for responder personnel during an MCI should include immediate and ongoing interventions, education, and training to promote mental health and wellness.

Recommendation 14.2: Support services for responder personnel should be provided on site for the duration of the incident, including while law enforcement and other personnel are on site processing the scene, collecting evidence, and conducting their investigation.

Recommendation 14.3: Responder agencies should have a system for monitoring personnel stress during and in the months after an MCI. This can include regular check-ins with personnel and using assessment tools to identify individuals who may be struggling.

Recommendation 14.4: Responder agencies should develop a comprehensive and integrated trauma support plan that includes outreach, follow-up, and ongoing support for responders.

Recommendation 14.5: Leaders from responder agencies need to provide services to all personnel involved in an MCI, which for some agencies means everyone on their staff. These services should include resources on post-disaster behavioral health and secondary traumatic stress, referrals to health care providers, and peer support.

Recommendation 14.6: Responder agencies should consider memoranda of understanding (MOUs) and memoranda of agreement (MOAs) with regional agencies for trauma support services if none exist in the local area.

Observation 15: In the MCI at Robb Elementary School, 587 children and many other teachers and staff members were present. At least 17 survivors were physically injured. Due to the lack of medical and mental screening of survivors/victims and lack of information sharing among agencies and providers, the exact number of survivors/victims both directly and indirectly impacted remains unknown. Based on interviews, there are both physical and emotional needs that have been unidentified and unattended.

Recommendation 15.1: Multiagency cooperation, collaboration, and communication are necessary to help identify all those impacted by an incident and ensure outreach and follow on to all victims. MOUs/MOAs between agencies, as part of a comprehensive incident response plan, should be considered.

Observation 16: Shared trauma is a concern for the Uvalde community due to compounding factors, including the size of the community and its interrelatedness. For the hundreds of law enforcement, medical, behavioral health, and government personnel who responded to this incident, shared trauma can make what happened even more overwhelming. Law enforcement's trauma is also exacerbated by the backlash from the community–as the community's trauma is exacerbated by the lack of an adequate response from law enforcement.

Recommendation 16.1: Preparation for an MCI should include a plan for multiagency deployment when an incident impacts a large segment of the community. The plan should include a written agreement (e.g., MOUs, mutual aid agreements, interagency agreements, jurisdictional agreements) that can be operationalized at the time of an event and allow for rapid identification and deployment of responders. If possible, leaders should shift resources to avoid those who will not have the risk of a shared trauma experience.

Recommendation 16.2: A multiagency response can also assist in the transfer of services to other victim advocates when personal relationships impede generally accepted practices and when the scope of the trauma overwhelms the local community responders.

Recommendation 16.3: As part of disaster preparedness planning, communities—including law enforcement—need to plan for the aftermath of a critical incident. This planning should include generally accepted practice processes, education and training, support, and resources. A trauma-informed, culturally sensitive approach should be applied to the victims, survivors, and impacted community members, as well as responders and their families.

Observation 17: The mental health needs assessment conducted in Uvalde by MMHPI was not focused on the MCI that occurred at Robb Elementary School and did not identify all of those in the spheres of influence who may be direct and indirect victims. Based on CIR interviews, there are victims who remain unidentified and do not have the information, resources, and referrals they need to access support services.

Recommendation 17.1: Following an MCI, local and government officials should conduct a needs assessment within a specific time frame and in collaboration with the county or state health services authority to capture the needs of the community. In Uvalde, the Texas Office for Victims of Crime or another entity should complete a new, comprehensive mental health needs assessment that addresses the families, victims, responders, and community members of the impacted Uvalde community specifically. The agency performing this needs assessment should conduct extensive outreach efforts to find and attend to the victims and families in Uvalde who require guidance, referrals, and concrete assistance with obtaining funds, medical care, and behavioral health services.

Recommendation 17.2: The needs assessment should inform an outreach plan to identify impacted persons who may have been left out of the original assessment.

Recommendation 17.3: Post-incident care should ensure that all people in the spheres of influence receive outreach, support, and services either directly or through broad public communications outreach.

Recommendation 17.4: A lead community agency should be designated to take on this important activity and coordinate services with other response organizations in Uvalde and across Texas.

Observation 18: The FAC was established the day after the MCI by the FBI and TXDPS, with assistance from the American Red Cross. The FAC provided access to a robust number and type of services. A process was established to keep the space safe and secure.

> **Recommendation 18.1:** An FAC should be established within 24 hours of an incident with a security plan that includes external law enforcement presence and a process for internal vetting of providers and those seeking services.

> **Recommendation 18.2:** The FAC should be staffed with a robust number and type of organizations that meet the needs of the community.

Observation 19: As victims and families arrived to the FAC, they were met by a victim navigator or law enforcement victim service staff member who accompanied them throughout the process. That initial person became the point of contact for the family as long as that individual was assigned to the FAC.

> **Recommendation 19.1:** Victims, families, and community members should be met at the FAC by a professional and be aided throughout the process by a victim navigator or victim service personnel.

Observation 20: FAC/FRC leadership never received a complete list of all victims.

> **Recommendation 20.1:** An MOU or MOA should be signed between key organizations (such as state law enforcement organizations and the FBI) to allow for the sharing of vital victim information, ensuring that outreach is made to all victims, families, and those affected.

Observation 21: Some victims' families reported that they would not use the FAC/FRC created for the Robb Elementary incident due to concerns about the location and confidentiality.

> **Recommendation 21.1:** The location for an FAC/FRC needs to be decided based on space, convenience, public transportation accessibility, and privacy, if possible.

Observation 22: There was limited housing available to family members, victim service personnel, and other authorities arriving from out of town. In Uvalde, authorities took creative approaches to meet the housing challenges, such as bringing in RVs, using dorms at the local college, and partnering with local ranches.

> **Recommendation 22.1:** As part of the pre-planning for an MCI, FAC leadership officials need to consider housing implications. It may be useful to model housing needs based on Uvalde or use local partnerships to reserve room blocks with the goal of having space for families, service providers, and law enforcement coming into the area.

Observation 23: Spontaneous, unaffiliated volunteers descended on Uvalde to help. Their presence was overwhelming, unmanageable, and disruptive.

> **Recommendation 23.1:** Unaffiliated, unknown, and spontaneous volunteers need to be managed by an agency with experience in identifying needs in the community, managing volunteers, and verifying the credentials or experience of those who come to help but are not affiliated with any known response agency. There is training available to learn how to address this phenomenon.

Observation 24: The FBI facility dogs were reported to be a help, especially when working with young victims as they were being interviewed.

Recommendation 24.1: Therapy dogs or crisis response dogs that have completed their certification and handler training may be of help in mass violence events, especially when victims include children. Organizations can deploy certified, trained teams of dogs and handlers to support victims.

Observation 25: Victims and families experienced a number of challenges with receiving and accessing financial assistance, including redundant forms, eligibility criteria, and fraudulent accounts.

Recommendation 25.1: When establishing eligibility for support programs, the "spheres of influence" or other similar models should be factors for eligibility. Eligibility criteria for state compensation programs should be in line with those established by state law and federal rules.

Recommendation 25.2: A single form should be used to capture basic contact information, as well as information needed about the victim and the incident. This form should be usable for all applications for financial and other support services, to avoid adding to the burden of the victims and families.

Recommendation 25.3: Law enforcement agencies need to be prepared for scammers to establish fraudulent accounts and other criminals to use a tragedy for their personal gain. The FAC should have law enforcement representation to assist families with navigating these situations.

Recommendation 25.4: The FAC/FRC, including victim service providers, law enforcement, and other authorities, should proactively work with the families of victims and survivors to set up alerts, freeze credit reports, and quickly identify other criminal and fraudulent activity.

Recommendation 25.5: In preparing for long-term needs, the FRC should provide financial literacy and security education and awareness to victims and family members.

Observation 26: The FBI VSRT effectively handled the initial cleaning and returning of personal effects to family members. This trauma-informed, victim-centered approach demonstrated compassion and respect during a difficult task.

Recommendation 26.1: Law enforcement agencies should develop a trauma-informed, victim-centered process for returning personal effects.

Observation 27: The CISD method was used by at least two responding agencies, even though studies have revealed no evidence that one CISD session is useful treatment for the prevention of PTSD after traumatic incidents and have also shown that several aspects of CISD could cause harm.

Recommendation 27.1: Responder agencies should use a modified version of CISD, such as SFA, as part of their trauma and support services following an incident.

Observation 28: TLEPN was deployed on the day of the shooting for law enforcement officers and their families. TLEPN partnered with CopLine and Endeavors to provide urgent clinical services for responding personnel.

Recommendation 28.1: Agencies should include peer support services and resources in their comprehensive support services plan, which may include regional or statewide networks.

Observation 29: FBI VSD rapidly deployed a team that took the lead for victim services in the first two weeks. The team received praise from victims, family members, and other service providers. Victim service personnel from TXDPS and the FBI reported that they did not receive enough support from their agencies when the deployment ended.

> **Recommendation 29.1:** Agency leadership needs to support the supporters and ensure that adequate trauma leave is provided to help deployed personnel decompress and return from a traumatic event.

> **Recommendation 29.2:** Responder agencies should provide in-depth trauma and counseling services to staff who provide victim services at an MCI.

> **Recommendation 29.3:** Agency leadership should consider offering or expanding the window for trauma leave to ensure that a deployed member can take the necessary leave and will not be perceived as incapable of future deployments simply because they utilized available resources.

Observation 30: Law enforcement victim services personnel were deployed without coverage of their normal victim service duties.

> **Recommendation 30.1:** Agency leaders should ensure there is coverage for the normal duties of deployed personnel so that the deployed individuals can focus on their deployment and take the necessary leave.

Observation 31: The mental health needs of the dispatchers exposed to the stress in this incident were unidentified and untreated.

> **Recommendation 31.1:** Dispatchers should be recognized as first responders to a critical incident and screened for services. They should be included in efforts to provide mental health screenings and care as well as peer and other supports post-incident. All agencies should have policies and resources for the well-being of their personnel and families.

> **Recommendation 31.2:** The definition of responders should be expanded, consistent with generally accepted practices, to include disciplines other than law enforcement, fire, and rescue staff, such as dispatchers, EMTs, health care providers, ambulance drivers, behavioral health providers, and faith-based leaders. This should be reflected in all support services provided by resiliency centers, nongovernmental and governmental entities, and other support service providers.

Observation 32: Family members of law enforcement and other responders became the support system for the responders and may not be receiving assistance themselves.

> **Recommendation 32.1:** When developing or reviewing trauma support and counseling services, agencies should include spouses, partners, and family members of responders.

Observation 33: Responder agencies are not prepared for the long-term impact of the incident.

> **Recommendation 33.1:** Responder agencies should organize and implement a formalized plan that outlines the roles and responsibilities of each stakeholder for the effective management of emotional and trauma support.

Recommendation 33.2: Responder agencies should provide initial support services within hours of a critical incident and within 24 hours should provide access to services such as PFA/SFA, crisis counseling, debriefing, and peer support.

Recommendation 33.3: Responder leaders can reduce the stigma associated with seeking help for emotional and psychological distress and can promote the importance of self-care through training, education, and effective messaging and modeling.

Recommendation 33.4: After a critical incident, responder agencies should evaluate the effectiveness of their emotional and trauma support services. This can be achieved through gathering feedback from responders and their family members and using this information to improve future services and support.

Observation 34: FBI victim services personnel transitioned services for victims and families to TXDPS and the Uvalde County District Attorney's Office prior to their departure. However, TXDPS and the District Attorney's Office did not have enough personnel to provide the needed level of care.

Recommendation 34.1: A transition plan and a warm, organized handoff should occur whenever law enforcement victim services personnel, or other victim navigators, transition away from the FAC/FRC.

Recommendation 34.2: A checklist should be used by the FAC/FRC to ensure that all transitions are conducted in a deliberate and compassionate manner.

Recommendation 34.3: Agencies should consider MOUs/MOAs with neighboring or state agencies for assistance providing victim services.

Observation 35: Victims require multiple efforts by victim advocates to contact them and to share information about available resources. Months after the shooting at Robb Elementary, victims and family members reportedly did not have active victim compensation applications on file and had little to no information about what medical, mental health, lost wages, or other resources they may be eligible for.

Recommendation 35.1: Research on trauma-informed care teaches that some victims will have memory deficits and other cognitive impacts as a result of the brain's response to the trauma. This means that advocates and other support staff need to provide continuous support, follow on, and monitoring to ensure that applications for services and referrals are completed.

Observation 36: The City of Uvalde eventually identified another building that was renovated to meet the longer-term needs of the UTRC. This permanent site in town is an inviting and comfortable space to meet with victims, family members, and other community members.

Recommendation 36.1: The UTRC should offer more community-based activities with opportunities for victims, family members, and the community to come together, receive services, and share space to help them on their recovery path.

Recommendation 36.2: The UTRC should engage with the OVC-funded National Mass Violence Victimization Resource Center Resiliency Center Director Forum network. Connecting with other FRCs can help the UTRC ensure it is meeting the Uvalde community's needs in a trauma-informed, victim-centered approach and appropriate cultural adaptations.

Recommendation 36.3: The UTRC must develop a plan to ensure all victims, family members, and responders receive outreach and education on its services, crime victim compensation, and resources.

Observation 37: Some family members and victims in Uvalde shared that seeking help from mental health professionals is not something that is commonly acceptable to them culturally. They tend to seek informal care and social support as a way of helping themselves and those they care about. This may help some people to adapt and recover, but those who require formal mental health services for a diagnosable mental health concern may not seek services for a long period of time.

Recommendation 37.1: The UTRC should plan to sustain this space and its offerings, especially since support services need to be made available for an extended period of time in this community.

Recommendation 37.2: Behavioral health services offered in various modalities, such as individual, group, and family therapies, may help people feel more comfortable, as they will be able to choose which modality they prefer.

Recommendation 37.3: Evidence-based mental health care is necessary so that victims and family members do not become discouraged by continuing symptoms and a lack of effective treatment.

Recommendation 37.4: Training on evidence-based behavioral health supports—including resilience-building activities, cognitive behavioral therapy for disaster distress, peer support for victims of mass violence, writing for recovery, and other supports—should begin as soon as possible so that providers in the community have the knowledge and skills to provide effective mental health treatment.

Recommendation 37.5: Efforts to attract professionals who are interested and able to live and work in the Uvalde community also need to begin as soon as possible.

Recommendation 37.6: Advocating for the broader use of teletherapy could increase access to competent providers who could serve this highly impacted population.

Observation 38: Due to the nature of the deaths, and the young age and the number of victims, funeral arrangements took longer than they normally would. Families had to navigate the process with limited emotional and mental support.

Recommendation 38.1: Victim advocates and grief specialists can support victims' families through the funeral arrangement process and help the community determine where to hold activities like candlelight vigils.

Observation 39: Media and other onlookers attempted to access the funerals and services for some of the victims.

Recommendation 39.1: Law enforcement and other governmental officials need to create a security plan to protect the safety, security, and privacy of those mourning their loved ones during funerals for an MCI.

Recommendation 39.2: As part of the planning for a disaster, authorities should assign a public information officer or communications representative who will work with the media in advance of funerals. This role should include setting up a media staging area as well as consulting with families to determine if relatives or friends would like to speak on their behalf.

Observation 40: Since the day of the incident, informal memorials expressing the grief and sorrow of the entire Uvalde community have been set up at the site of the former school campus and across town. The Healing Uvalde Mural Project, the result of a partnership between a local artist and a nonprofit, organized a creative collaborative memorial across downtown. Artists from across the world came to Uvalde to paint giant portrait murals of the 21 victims fatally wounded on May 24. The Smithsonian National Museum of the American Latino is currently featuring an online virtual exhibit, which allows anyone around the world to view these beautiful and impactful murals.

Observation 41: Items left at informal memorials in Uvalde have been moved, removed, or cleared out without proper discussion and planning with the victims and family members.

> **Recommendation 41.1**: Victims and family members need to be involved in the movement of any informal memorials prior to action being taken.

Observation 42: As of the end of the review period, there is no known plan for gathering representative community members together to plan a permanent memorial to those killed, injured, and impacted on May 24, 2022.

> **Recommendation 42.1**: The planning for a permanent memorial should include a broad community coalition of advisers, including survivors, family members of victims, school personnel, victim service providers, and other relevant stakeholders.

> **Recommendation 42.2**: The memorial should honor those lost, those injured, and all those directly impacted by the incident.

Observation 43: The Uvalde community continues to need support and guidance as it struggles with the negative impacts of the failed response, a lack of accountability for those implicated in this failure, and remaining gaps in the information about what happened to their loved ones.

> **Recommendation 43.1**: The Uvalde community could benefit from long-term support from grief and loss specialists who can help guide the community in rituals, memorial planning, spiritual activities, and social supports as they move through the next few years.

> **Recommendation 43.2**: Community organizers, disaster behavioral health specialists, victim support staff, and those skilled in helping communities repair societal damage and build resilience may be able to help Uvalde get onto a recovery path. This will require strong, compassionate, collaborative, and honest efforts by community leadership.

Chapter 7. School Safety and Security

Observation 1: UCISD PD had jurisdictional authority at the onset of the incident on May 24 as per governing doctrine (i.e., UCISD's EOP and MOU) between UCISD PD and UPD. This MOU, however, is silent on other agencies. Each agency, UPD and UCISD PD, is not only a signatory to the MOU but serves on UCISD's School Safety and Security Committee, which manages updates to the EOP. These documents signal an expectation to both agencies that UCISD PD would take command in an active shooter incident and UPD would respond to requests for assistance and follow the direction of the ICS leader. This comports with the prevailing perception among many officers on the scene that Chief Arredondo was in charge that day.

Observation 2: UCISD PD has an MOU establishing jurisdictional responsibilities in place with just one neighboring law enforcement agency, UPD. The majority of agencies on scene on May 24—at the local, state, and federal level—did not have any mutual aid agreements with UCISD PD. This includes agencies which, like UPD, have concurrent jurisdiction with UCISD PD, such as the Uvalde County Sheriff's Office (UCSO), Zavala County Sheriff's Office (ZCSO), and TXDPS.

> **Recommendation 2.1:** School district police departments should enter into MOUs that establish mutually agreed upon clear jurisdictional responsibilities with other neighboring agencies that are likely to respond to a critical incident on school property. The MOUs should account for not only routine criminal activity, but also critical incidents. The MOU should address the issue of unified command, in addition to incident command, and account for the capacity and capabilities of the respective agencies.

Observation 3: UCISD's EOP and Active Shooter Policy were considered viable by the Texas School Safety Center and satisfied requirements set forth by TEA. However, the response on May 24 demonstrated that agencies responding to such an incident within UCISD's jurisdiction were not prepared for the large-scale multiagency response resulting from the incident.

> **Recommendation 3.1:** Law enforcement, first responders, emergency management, and other municipal government agencies should coordinate with school districts to conduct multiagency preparedness exercises on at least an annual basis. Exercises should operate in accordance with the state and local regulations regarding active threat exercises. The exercises should be incorporated into the EOPs and Campus Safety Plans.

Observation 4: The UCISD School Safety and Security Committee has not had any participation from the UCSO, which is the largest law enforcement agency in the county and had more than a dozen members respond to the active shooter incident at Robb Elementary. Additionally, ZCSO—which had four members respond—does not participate in the committee, despite being the local law enforcement agency for one of UCISD's eight campuses.

> **Recommendation 4.1:** All law enforcement agencies within school districts should participate in safety and security planning. Law enforcement agencies with jurisdiction should assign leaders from within their agencies (either the sheriff or chief deputy sheriff) to participate on the committee. That individual can serve as a liaison between the school district and the sheriffs' offices and help both entities maintain awareness of safety and security concerns that may intersect the two.

> **Recommendation 4.2:** Communities should adopt a multidisciplinary approach to school safety that includes school police, law enforcement, school officials, mental health professionals, and other community stakeholders. It is especially important that all voices in the school community be heard, including faculty, staff, administrators, counselors, nurses, resource officers, parents, and students. Every stakeholder must feel empowered to play a role in reducing fear and raising the level of safety in and around schools. Each campus should establish and train school safety committees that will meet at least monthly for this purpose.

Observation 5: UCISD's campus safety teams met infrequently, and annual safety plans were based largely on templated information that was, at times, inaccurate.

Recommendation 5.1: School district campus safety teams must be intentional and deliberative in the development of their campus-specific plans and ensure they are reviewed and updated regularly. UCISD should work with campus administrators across the district to institutionalize a set of expectations for these plans that reflects the specific physical and social environments and safety and security needs of each campus.

Observation 6: The district Threat Assessment Team has been complacent and in need of strong oversight of its implementation. The new district leadership, including the school police chief, has expressed a stronger commitment to ensure they become fully operational as soon as possible. As of June 8, 2023, the UCISD threat assessment team does not have standard operating procedures and has been noncompliant with Texas Education Code.

Recommendation 6.1: School district threat assessment teams must establish a systematic procedure for identifying, assessing, and managing threat assessments under their review.

Recommendation 6.2: Threat assessment teams must develop an operations manual that governs and documents their activities, outputs, roles and responsibilities, and coordination across the school district. At minimum, the manual should adhere to standards set forth by oversight bodies. In the case of UCISD, this would be the Texas School Safety Center, as required in the Texas Education Code.

Observation 7: Teachers and school staff at UCISD received no training on developmentally appropriate responses to students with behavioral problems, although they were required to document and report immediately to administrators any student whose behavior posed an obvious threat or safety risk.

Recommendation 7.1: All school district staff and school district police personnel should receive training on the district's threat assessment processes, including the role of all staff in appropriately identifying and reporting concerning behavior. The training should be interactive and include scenarios and discussion to help trainees practice applying the course content.

Observation 8: UCISD had a culture of complacency regarding locked-door policies. Both exterior and interior doors were routinely left unlocked, and there was no enforced system of accountability for these policies. Door audits were conducted, but not done systematically, nor were they documented. On May 24, all of the exterior doors and at least eight interior doors of the West Building, where the incident took place, were unlocked.

Recommendation 8.1: School districts should implement a system of door audits that are conducted routinely and systematically, and they should be documented. At UCISD, this responsibility can be assigned to the new safety monitor positions it has recently created. Door audits should be incorporated into school district campus safety plans. All school district staff and school district police personnel should have a shared responsibility to ensure doors are locked, as per policy.

Observation 9: The exterior and interior doors require a UCISD staff member or student to expose themselves to a threat to check that a door is locked or to lock a door in the event of a school lockdown.

Recommendation 9.1: School districts should invest in upgrading or replacing all doors (or locks) throughout its campuses to remedy this issue, so that doors can be locked from the inside.

Observation 10: Law enforcement arriving on scene searched for keys to open interior doors for more than 40 minutes. This was partly the cause of the significant delay in entering to eliminate the threat and stop the killing and dying inside classrooms 111 and 112.

> **Recommendation 10.1:** School districts should implement universal access boxes. A universal access box refers to a locked box that contains master keys, located near the entry points of school buildings, that can be accessed by authorized emergency first responders and school district staff.

Observation 11: The rollout of the Raptor system caused some confusion in emergency alert procedures and some UCISD staff did not find the training helpful. Some teachers were under the belief that the Raptor system was supplanting the traditional PA system.

> **Recommendation 11.1:** School districts should ensure that emergency alert systems are well-understood by all staff. In the case of UCISD, district leadership should issue a district-wide clarification on the use of PA systems in conjunction with Raptor emergency alerts.

> **Recommendation 11.2:** School districts should offer both standard training and refresher training, as needed, on the use of their emergency alert system, available to all district employees.

Observation 12: UCISD Raptor alerts indicate the type of response, but not the type of emergency (e.g., bailout, suspicious person on campus, hail storm). The Raptor emergency alert system enables users to offer more detail, though this feature is rarely used by UCISD staff.

> **Recommendation 12.1:** School districts should implement a policy that requires the type of emergency event to be formally documented in their emergency alert system, so that school administrators can better identify and report trends and the most frequent causes of lockdowns and other emergency response protocols.

Observation 13: The poor reception (Wi-Fi and cell) issues at Robb Elementary are well documented. While the Raptor alert was promptly initiated through the system, it was not received by all teachers and staff.

> **Recommendation 13.1:** School districts must ensure that all campus buildings where there is student activity are retrofitted for Wi-Fi communication to ensure that emergency alerts are received in a timely manner.

Observation 14: UCISD drills are typically conducted inside classrooms. On May 24, there were several classes outside of their classrooms at the time the incident began.

> **Recommendation 14.1:** Active threat training for students and staff should be expanded to include all areas of the school campus. UCISD should ensure that drills take place in the many settings that teachers and students find themselves in throughout the school year, not just inside the classroom. While the classroom is the most likely location of students in a real-life emergency, they should be prepared to engage in standard response protocols from other locations on campus.

> **Recommendation 14.2:** UCISD should invite other law enforcement agencies to attend, observe, and participate in drills.

Observation 15: According to documents provided and reviewed by the CIR team, Robb Elementary School was in compliance with Texas Education Code 37.114 regarding drills during the 2019–2020 school year but not in the 2020–2021 school year. No documents were provided by UCISD for the 2021–2022 school year.

> **Recommendation 15.1:** Drills should be conducted in accordance with the Texas Education Code 37.114, and proper documentation should be submitted to appropriate UCISD leadership for record-keeping.

Observation 16: Lockdown procedures are predicated on a locked door, impenetrable doors and walls, and other physical security that did not exist at Robb Elementary. One teacher at Robb was shot through several walls and many other teachers and students were at risk of the same fate, given the high-powered rifle used in the attack.

> **Recommendation 16.1:** UCISD must reconsider the preeminence of the lockdown procedure in a dynamic, evolving situation, where the risk of remaining in place may outweigh the risk of finding a way to exit the area, which in the incident at Robb Elementary led to UCISD staff and students running *into* the building to lock down. Teachers, staff, and students must be provided with options for protecting themselves and helping to protect others.

Observation 17: At the time the UCISD PD was established, there was no coordination of safety plans with any other city agency, nor was there any citywide coordination of school safety planning. The superintendent did not meet regularly with the school police chief (reportedly they met "from time to time"). Despite reporting directly to the superintendent, the UCISD PD chief was not a member of the district senior leadership team and would only attend the weekly leadership team meetings "as needed," e.g., planning for special events like football games and other activities that would draw large crowds to school facilities. The chief did attend quarterly school safety meetings that were convened by the superintendent.

Observation 18: Four years into its existence, the UCISD PD was functioning without any standard operating procedures. A range of UCISD employees, including administrators, faculty, support staff, and police officers, told the CIR team they had no knowledge of, nor had they been informed about, their school police department's policies and procedures. The UCISD PD has recently drafted standard operating procedures.

> **Recommendation 18.1:** School districts should meticulously consider, plan, and execute if they decide to establish their own police department. Budgeting, hiring practices, training, development of standard operating procedures, and student/community engagement should all be built into the design and execution of a school district police department.

Observation 19: The existing UCISD policies and procedures do not include information or guidelines around crisis management, MOUs, threat assessment or emergency response and multi-hazard planning. These topics are instead covered in the UCISD Revised EOP and EOP annexes for Active Shooter and Active Threat, which should not serve as the UCISD PD's standard operating procedures on these issues.

Recommendation 19.1: The draft version of the UCISD PD policies, procedures, and operational plans should be evaluated to ensure alignment with the highest industry standards, starting with high-risk operations such as response to an active attack and other potential crises that threaten school climate and safety. Professional organizations, including the International Association of Chiefs of Police and National Association of School Resource Officers, offer a range of model policies, toolkits, technical assistance, training, and other resources to inform the policy and operational planning evaluation process.

Recommendation 19.2: UCISD PD should undergo an accreditation process that measures compliance against generally accepted standards and practices. Accreditation is a voluntary process administered by state police associations as well as national organizations like the Commission on Accreditation for Law Enforcement Agencies. Many standards require the development of written directives or activities that reflect the agency's policies, procedures, and general orders. The accreditation process enables the review and revision of policies to ensure practices meet current professional criteria for excellence in service, strengthen agency operations, and increase public trust.

Observation 20: Some staff reported being unfamiliar with the school police department due to UCISD PD officers' sporadic presence on elementary school campuses. Reportedly, the UCISD PD chief would come at the beginning of the school year to deliver informal training in the event of an active shooter, reminding teachers to lock doors, turn off lights, and hide away from windows. Essentially, the chief would give a briefing to the teachers.

Recommendation 20.1: A school police department has the responsibilities of both a law enforcement agency and a member of the school environment, necessitating a heavy burden on the agency and officers to serve in these dual roles. The reconstituted UCISD PD must make intentional efforts to routinely engage with UCISD staff and students at all campuses. Regular engagement can help contribute to a safer learning environment by promoting safety, fostering positive relationships, discouraging misconduct, and improving the perception of law enforcement throughout the school district. The UCISD PD chief and all officers should be evaluated on these efforts.

Chapter 8. Pre-Incident Planning and Preparation

Observation 1: Responding agencies lacked adequate related policies and, in most cases, any policy on responding to active attackers.

Recommendation 1.1: Every agency must have a clear and concise policy on responding to active attacker situations.

Recommendation 1.2: Agencies should regularly review AARs with other regional agencies to plan as a region for a coordinated and collaborative response to possible similar events.

Recommendation 1.3: Agencies should consider obtaining state- or national-level accreditation to adopt and maintain standardized policies and procedures. This process also ensures accountability and transparency that can enhance confidence and trust in law enforcement among the communities they serve.

Observation 2: The Uvalde EOC developed an adequate emergency management plan. However, not all the relevant agencies and organizations actively participated in the process, drills, and exercises which ultimately contribute to a failed emergency response on May 24, 2022.

Recommendation 2.1: Appointing authorities and senior officials of local government should develop a resilient emergency management system in which the emergency response plans of their respective units of government and operating departments, e.g., fire, police, sheriff, EMS, public health, public works, school system, planning, and social services, are understood and shared.

Recommendation 2.2: Appointing authorities should direct the professional emergency manager at the highest level of local government to coordinate this system that would also include private sector stakeholders representing public utilities, healthcare providers and leaders responsible for critical infrastructure.

Recommendation 2.3: Government leaders should consider adopting a resolution that demonstrates their commitment to NIMS.

Recommendation 2.4: Senior officials should guide all government, business, and organization leaders (including faith-based and secular nonprofit groups) to coordinate and collaborate with the emergency manager so they can act decisively before, during, and after disasters.

Recommendation 2.5: Senior officials should personally participate in and provide direction for conducting exercises and evaluation programs that enhance familiarity and coordination among the whole community.

Recommendation 2.6: Local governments should conduct outreach to state emergency management agencies and federal entities such as the Homeland Security Exercise and Evaluation Program and the NEP for assistance with exercise resources and training.

Recommendation 2.7: The Office of Emergency Management should identify volunteer groups and local businesses who will consistently play a role in emergency planning and preparedness before, during, and after disasters. Business and industry partners should work through voluntary organizations to support local government in planning, preparing, and providing resources when responding to emergency situations.

Recommendation 2.8: Senior officials should develop a pre-disaster recovery plan that enables them to anticipate what will be needed to restore the community as quickly as possible after an emergency. FEMA offers the Community Recovery Management Toolkit, which provides a three-step process of organizing, planning, and managing recovery.

Recommendation 2.9: Regional public safety partners should plan, train, and exercise unified command for complex incidents. This includes federal, state, and local law enforcement, fire, EMS, and emergency management as well as other governmental and non-governmental agencies that would respond to a critical incident.

Recommendation 2.10: Agencies should hold regular regional interdepartmental interoperability communication drills.

Recommendation 2.11: Elected officials should establish a Multi-Agency Coordination (MAC) Group to provide policy guidance to incident personnel and support resource prioritization and allocation. Typically, these groups are made up of government agency or private sector executives and administrators whose organizations are either impacted by, or provide resources to, an incident. MAC Groups enable decision-making among senior officials and executives, and delegate command authority to the incident commander to cooperatively define the response and recovery mission and strategic direction. Additionally, MAC Groups identify operational priorities and communicate those objectives to the Emergency Operations Center and the pertinent functions of the Incident command system and the joint information center.

Recommendation 2.12: Elected and senior officials should receive training made available through the FEMA Emergency Management Institute (EMI) that provides a menu of courses designed specifically for senior officials. In addition to independent online study courses in the NIMS, ICS, Unified Command, and other basic emergency management training, EMI offers specialized in-person training for senior officials. The portfolio of courses includes Emergency Management for Senior Officials, NIMS Overview for Senior Officials, and Recovery from Disaster: Local Community Roles. Senior officials should work with their professional emergency manager for specific course recommendations. States may also have specific training programs and offerings.

Observation 3: The MOU between UPD and UCISD PD that was active the day of the incident failed to adequately outline the expectations and authorities for a response to a mass violence event. The agencies failed to exercise the MOU, nor cross-train in preparation for a critical incident.

Recommendation 3.1: Senior officials should establish mutual aid agreements that set forth terms and conditions under which the parties will agree to provide resources, personnel, facilities, equipment, and supplies to support responses to critical incidents that create an extreme risk to public safety.

Observation 4: The Texas Legislature plays a significant role in mandating the types and frequencies of training for peace officers in the state of Texas through TCOLE.

Recommendation 4.1: State POSTs and other training entities should work with state legislatures and law enforcement leaders within their state to conduct coordinated routine reviews of mandatory training programs for peace officers within their state to determine what is the appropriate balance of training topics and courses. Mandatory training time/requirements should include training options focused on unique, complex tactical events, such as an active attacker.

Observation 5: UPD and UCSO appear to show budgetary and staffing shortages, which prevent training opportunities.

Recommendation 5.1: Whenever possible, multiagency training should be offered to lessen the load of any one law enforcement agency. Multiagency training allows for cost- and resource-sharing and, more importantly, allows peace officers to train with other agencies that are typically going to respond jointly to a major incident. Building relationships through training and in advance of a major incident are critical in the successful response to, management of, and resolution of a major incident when one happens.

Observation 6: Responding agencies had minimal exposure to ICS/NIMS. Of those serving in top leadership positions within the primary responding agencies, only UCISD PD Chief Arredondo and the TXDPS regional director had taken training in ICS/NIMS.

> **Recommendation 6.1:** All law enforcement should be required to take awareness-level NIMS courses, such as ICS-100 and IS-700.

> **Recommendation 6.2:** All ranked individuals should be required to take courses and refresher training on ICS/NIMS. These skills should be exercised through an annual multijurisdictional, multidisciplinary tabletop.

Observation 7: Responding officers had levels of active shooter training that varied in terms of their length of time and quality, leading to failures in operationalizing the training.

> **Recommendation 7.1:** Law enforcement agencies should provide a total of 8 hours of scenario-based, stress-induced active shooter training annually for officers at all levels of ranks in the training.

> **Recommendation 7.2:** Law enforcement agencies should work closely with schools and other vulnerable places to understand how occupants are taught to respond to an active attacker threat (e.g., kids were taught to be quiet in a dark room, while some officers reported they were listening for voices and believed the dark classrooms meant they were unoccupied).

> **Recommendation 7.3:** Research should be conducted to determine if the response to an active attacker threat should include changing the "normal environment" (e.g., lights off).

> **Recommendation 7.4:** TCOLE should consider revising the SBLE training guidebook based on the recommendations in the CIR.

> **Recommendation 7.5:** Agencies must include in pre-incident planning timely access to building diagrams and universal building/room access, particularly critical infrastructure, schools, and buildings where large numbers of persons gather on a regular basis.

Observation 8: Personnel from responding agencies rarely trained and exercised in a multiagency environment.

> **Recommendation 8.1:** Interagency training, drills, and exercises help to build relationships at the front-line officer level and, if attended by law enforcement supervisors, can further strengthen relationships and the efficacy of a multiagency response to a mass casualty incident. Though policies may differ slightly among agencies, overarching commonalities are the same in an active attacker incident.

Observation 9: Responder agencies lacked sufficient training in trauma, resiliency, and mental health and wellness.

> **Recommendation 9.1:** Agencies should provide preparedness education and training on trauma and stress management to all personnel, including coping strategies for managing stress and trauma during and after a mass casualty incident.

> **Recommendation 9.2:** Agencies should develop and maintain a comprehensive crisis response plan to address the mental health needs of their personnel during a mass casualty incident.

Recommendation 9.3: Responder organizations should provide pre- and post-response behavioral health support to help mitigate and address the development of compassion fatigue, secondary traumatic stress, and vicarious trauma. This support can include education and training, policies and procedures, and services.

Recommendation 9.4: The stigma of seeking mental health and trauma support in the law enforcement community needs to be counteracted by education, training, policies, protocols, and leadership, which create an environment that acknowledges and respects the mental wellness of law enforcement to the same extent as the physical aspects of policing.

Recommendation 9.5: It is necessary to tailor the application of services for the diverse types of responders (fire/EMS, law enforcement, victim services, dispatchers, etc.) so that the language used and the examples of the types of symptoms they may experience are more applicable to their unique experiences and roles.

Observation 10: The Uvalde school community did not sufficiently prepare and engage in victim-centered disaster, emergency, or mass violence incident planning within their own staff, with law enforcement and other responders, nor with the students, family members, and other caregivers.

Recommendation 10.1: Preparedness exercises should include regularly scheduled age- appropriate, trauma-informed drills; prescribed instructions/procedures; and clear communication. All stakeholders (school personnel, law enforcement, parents and guardians, students, and other relevant stakeholders) should be involved in the process and informed to help decrease anxiety and chaos.

Recommendation 10.2: Preparedness planning should include considerations for language access for those with English as a second language. Materials, instructions, and communication should be provided in the languages prevalent in the community.

Observation 11: Regional PIOs and their managers did not have necessary training for mass casualty incidents from a communications perspective, to include how to establish JIC or coordinate a Joint Information System.

Recommendation 11.1: Law enforcement, fire, and any other relevant stakeholder PIOs should obtain FEMA basic and advanced public information officer certifications as a baseline of training.

Recommendation 11.2: The FEMA PIO courses should be only a first step in communications training. Agencies should research regional and national training opportunities for building upon the FEMA classes.

Recommendation 11.3: Law enforcement PIOs should network at the state and national level (e.g., attend national police conferences that have a PIO section) to learn common practices for managing the public messaging of major incidents and to network with peers in the field.

Recommendation 11.4: Concepts learned in basic crisis communication classes must then be adopted into a crisis communication plan that is drilled and practiced with all involved personnel.

Recommendation 11.5: Partnering agencies should review their crisis communication plans together to ensure they complement each other. It is critically important that the commitment to coordinating messaging is practiced with smaller events, so it is not a foreign concept when a large-scale incident takes place.

Recommendation 11.6: The social media policies of law enforcement agencies should clearly state how social media should be used to communicate with the community during critical incident situations.

Observation 12: Regional PIOs did not formally coordinate, cross-train, or practice multiagency communications.

Recommendation 12.1: When an agency is hosting operational exercises, it should establish a JIC and engage all participating agencies to ensure coordinated public messaging is practiced and incorporated into planning for a large-scale incident.

Recommendation 12.2: Each PIO should draft a crisis communication plan and practice it at least four times a year with smaller events. This will help identify problem areas and solutions and ensure everyone is familiar with the plan and knows their role instead of trying to figure that out during a crisis.

Recommendation 12.3: The EOC should host regional PIO meetings every quarter. The meetings should include law enforcement, fire, city and county government, hospitals, public and private schools, universities, airports, military bases, universities, and other large organizations in the area. This creates an opportunity for relationship building, planning for joint operations and large-scale incidents that cross jurisdictional lines, and devising plans to support each other during major events.

Recommendation 12.4: After a comprehensive discussion, regional PIO meetings should be opened to the local media. This builds productive working relationships and allows the media and communication professionals to work out issues that arise.

Observation 13: On the day of the school shooting at Robb Elementary School, each PIO acted independently and failed to coordinate the public messaging aspect of the response.

Recommendation 13.1: When incidents involve multiple agencies, it is critical for the lead organization sending out the public messaging to have previously established a process by planning with the other agencies. On the day of an incident, the lead organization should coordinate with the others to ensure the accurate messaging that the public expects and deserves.

Recommendation 13.2: When a mass casualty incident occurs, the lead agency should organize news conferences through the JIC. All supporting agencies should have an opportunity to contribute information about the incident. This ensures a comprehensive release of consistent information.

Appendix D. Leadership, Incident Command, and Coordination Supplemental Materials

The following sections provide further context and information related to "Chapter 3. Leadership, Incident Command, and Coordination."

Stimuli Throughout the Incident

Table D-1 provides a high-level timeline of the incident, indicating stimulus events, which should have driven the law enforcement response to take steps to immediately stop the killing per active shooter protocols and guidance. The stimulus count starts once law enforcement are on the scene.

Table D-1. Stimulus events throughout the incident

Stimulus Once Law Enforcement Are Present	True Time	Time from Building Entry by Subject	Time to Entry by Law Enforcement into Rooms 111 and 112	Event	Source
	11:33:02	0:00:00	1:16:55	Subject enters the school's west door.	Robb Elementary School CCTV Footage.
	11:33:25	0:00:23	1:16:32	Subject fires into room 112, enters the alcove, and backs into the hallway.	Robb Elementary School CCTV Footage.
	11:33:48	0:00:46	1:16:09	Subject appears to enter room 111.	Robb Elementary School CCTV Footage.
	11:33:56	0:00:54	1:16:01	Firing continues inside the classrooms.	Robb Elementary School CCTV Footage.
	11:33:57	0:00:55	1:16:00	Sounds of gunfire go from rapid fire to single action. Shooting continues sporadically until 11:34:31.	Robb Elementary School CCTV Footage.

Critical Incident Review: Active Shooter at Robb Elementary School |
Appendix D. Leadership, Incident Command, and Coordination Supplemental Materials

486

Stimulus Once Law Enforcement Are Present	True Time	Time from Building Entry by Subject	Time to Entry by Law Enforcement into Rooms 111 and 112	Event	Source
	11:34:31	0:01:29	1:15:26	Shooting temporarily stops.	Robb Elementary School CCTV Footage.
	11:34:43	0:01:41	1:15:14	One shot fired.	Robb Elementary School CCTV Footage.
	11:35:07	0:02:05	1:14:50	Shooting resumes until 11:35:27.	Robb Elementary School CCTV Footage.
	11:35:18	0:02:16	1:14:39	Unknown person runs from light-colored truck parked by the funeral home toward school and disappears near the west door (LEO #1).	Hillcrest Memorial Funeral Home Footage.
	11:35:27	0:02:25	1:14:30	Firing stops. Approx. 30 rounds fired since 11:35:07.	Robb Elementary School CCTV Footage.
	11:35:27	0:02:25	1:14:30	UPD Lt. 1 runs toward school and disappears by west door (LEO #2).	Hillcrest Memorial Funeral Home Footage.
	11:35:33	0:02:31	1:14:24	LEO runs toward school and disappears outside west door (LEO #3).	Hillcrest Memorial Funeral Home Footage.
1	11:35:39	0:02:37	1:14:18	Subject resumes shooting; continues until 11:35:47.	Robb Elementary School CCTV Footage; Uvalde Police Department Body-Worn Camera Footage.
	11:35:40	0:02:38	1:14:17	LEOs (#4 and #5) run toward school and disappear near west door.	Hillcrest Memorial Funeral Home Footage.

Stimulus Once Law Enforcement Are Present	True Time	Time from Building Entry by Subject	Time to Entry by Law Enforcement into Rooms 111 and 112	Event	Source
	11:35:42	0:02:40	1:14:15	"Shots fired! Get inside! Go, go, go!" UPD Sgt. 1 hears the shots from outside. He directs UPD Sgt. 3 and UCISD PD Ofc. 2 to enter the building. They are outside the south door and enter during subject's active shooting.	Uvalde Police Department Body-Worn Camera Footage.
	11:35:45	0:02:43	1:14:12	LEO #6 runs toward school and west door.	Hillcrest Memorial Funeral Home Footage.
	11:35:47	0:02:45	1:14:10	Shooting stops temporarily. Approx. eleven rounds fired between 11:35:39 and 11:35:47.	Robb Elementary School CCTV Footage.
	11:35:48	0:02:46	1:14:09	UPD Sgt. 3 and UCISD PD Ofc. 2 enter the south hallway door.	Robb Elementary School CCTV Footage; Uvalde Police Department Body-Worn Camera Footage.
	11:35:51	0:02:49	1:14:06	LEO #7 runs toward school's west door.	Robb Elementary School CCTV Footage.
2	11:35:54	0:02:52	1:14:03	Shooting resumes with last round heard at 11:36:08.	Robb Elementary School CCTV Footage.
	11:35:54	0:02:52	1:14:03	Three officers race down the hallway from the north toward the active shooting in classrooms 111 and 112. Smoke from gun powder is in the air.	Robb Elementary School CCTV Footage.

Critical Incident Review: Active Shooter at Robb Elementary School |
Appendix D. Leadership, Incident Command, and Coordination Supplemental Materials

488

Stimulus Once Law Enforcement Are Present	True Time	Time from Building Entry by Subject	Time to Entry by Law Enforcement into Rooms 111 and 112	Event	Source
	11:35:58	0:02:56	1:13:59	UCISD PD Chief Arredondo enters the south hallway.	Robb Elementary School CCTV Footage; Uvalde Police Department Body Worn Camera Footage.
	11:36:08	0:03:06	1:13:49	Shooting stops. Approx. 17 rounds fired between 11:35:54 and 11:36:08.	Robb Elementary School CCTV Footage.
	11:36:09	0:03:07	1:13:48	UPD Sgt. 1 enters south hallway with Chief Arredondo in front of him approaching rooms 111 and 112.	Uvalde Police Department Body-Worn Camera Footage.
3	11:36:58	0:03:56	1:12:59	UPD Lt. 1 and UPD Sgt. grazed as four shots fired by the subject. Shooting continues for several seconds.	Robb Elementary School CCTV Footage; Uvalde Police Department Body-Worn Camera Footage.
4	11:37:09	0:04:07	1:12:48	Four shots end at 11:37:17.	Uvalde Police Department Body-Worn Camera Footage.
5	11:37:50	0:04:48	1:12:07	Three rounds fired. UPD Lt. 1 composes himself and goes back down the hallway.	Robb Elementary School CCTV Footage.
6	11:38:37	0:05:35	1:11:20	Subject fires possibly one round. UPD Lt. 1 is at the fire doors at this time.	Robb Elementary School CCTV Footage.

Stimulus Once Law Enforcement Are Present	True Time	Time from Building Entry by Subject	Time to Entry by Law Enforcement into Rooms 111 and 112	Event	Source
7	11:44:02	0:11:00	1:05:55	Single shot fired.	Uvalde Police Department Body-Worn Camera Footage; Uvalde County Sheriff's Office Body-Worn Camera Footage; Uvalde County Sheriff's Office Body-Worn Camera Footage.
8	11:56:54	0:23:52	0:53:03	UCISD Ofc. 1 remarks to Constable Field that his wife has been shot.	Uvalde Police Department Body-Worn Camera Footage.
9	12:13:48	0:40:46	0:36:09	UPD Acting Chief Pargas says "A child just called. They have victims in there. Called 911."	Uvalde Police Department Body-Worn Camera Footage.
10	12:21:07	0:48:05	0:28:50	Shots fired four times.	Numerous BWC, Uvalde Police Department Radio Traffic; Uvalde Police Department 911 calls.
	12:49:57	1:16:55	0:00:00	Law enforcement enters classrooms 111/112.	

Rescue Task Force

A rescue task force (RTF) is designed to expedite access to medical care of victims in active shooter or human-made mass casualty incidents. The RTF is made up of emergency medical services (EMS) trained personnel supported by law enforcement officers who serve as protection. The RTF is generally deployed into a warm zone. The roles of the team members are extremely specific, with medical team

Critical Incident Review: Active Shooter at Robb Elementary School |
Appendix D. Leadership, Incident Command, and Coordination Supplemental Materials

490

members quickly evaluating, treating, stabilizing, and removing injured victims to either a casualty collection point (CCP) or triage area. Law enforcement personnel within an RTF are tasked with protecting the medical providers and victims.

A CCP is generally located within a warm zone and is under force protection by law enforcement personnel. Based on the physical layout of the scene and preparation time, a CCP may not be the best system for rapid treatment and transportation of victims. In certain situations, victims should be moved directly from the initial location to either triage and treatment or an ambulance for transportation.

The assessment team noted that while emergency medical technicians from U.S. Customs and Border Protection set up a CCP near the classrooms, the extensive delay in rescue and treatment allowed time for a more comprehensive medical plan. This plan should have included an RTF that followed the entry team into the classroom and then established and coordinated a triage treatment area for immediate evacuation of victims. The triage area should have been staffed by advanced life support personnel, with mobile and air ambulances staged immediately adjacent. What the critical incident review team observed from video and learned through interviews, however, was an entry that did not take into consideration the assessment and treatment of victims. Dozens of law enforcement personnel—without purpose, need, or a plan—rushed into the classrooms behind the entry team and began removing victims to the hallway or outside the building.

The RTF model provides a planned, organized, and rapid response to treating the casualties resulting from an active shooter or similar mass casualty incident. The agencies in the region should adopt the model, training as a multiagency/multidisciplinary group to better respond to a critical incident. Equipment should include ballistic vests and helmets.

Zones

Hot Zone

The most dangerous zone of care within the tactical medicine environment, where active weapon use and shooting are present, is known as the "hot" or "red zone." This zone poses the highest risk to life, and limited care should be provided in this environment. An environment with active weapons use is not safe for anyone, regardless of firepower, protection, or training. In an area of active shooting, further injury or death is possible. Only the quickest and most necessary life-saving treatments should be employed to limit caregiver and patient risk.[1292] The emphasis in this zone is on threat suppression, preventing further casualties, extracting casualties from the high-threat area, and implementing control of life-threatening extremity hemorrhage.[1293]

[1292] Goldstein et al., *EMS Zones of Care*.

[1293] Pennardt and Schwartz, "Hot, Warm, and Cold Zones."

Warm Zone

The "warm zone" is where tactical field care takes place. This zone is less dangerous than the hot zone but still not completely safe. This zone is dynamic in nature and depends on the location of the threat, the mobility of the threat, and the mobility of the patient. In tactical medicine, the warm zone is where most of the care for injured patients is accomplished. Care can vary depending on the equipment available, the location of local hospitals, and the expertise of personnel.[1294] Warm zone care includes the other life-saving interventions associated with applying the MARCH algorithm (massive hemorrhage, airway, respiration, circulation, and hypothermia) in the tactical environment. CCPs and RTFs are typically employed within the warm zone.[1295]

Cold Zone

Finally, the "cold zone" is the area where no significant threat is reasonably anticipated and additional medical/transport resources may be staged.[1296] Basic emergency management services can be performed in this location. The zone is outside of the immediate danger area, and transportation is generally available.[1297]

Redefined Zones

The Hartford Consensus identified that the traditional hot, warm, and cold zones in an active shooter or intentional mass casualty event need to be compressed, following the military model to allow for a more rapid response from law enforcement and fire/EMS[1298] (see figure D-1 on page 493).

[1294] Goldstein et al., *EMS Zones of Care*.

[1295] Pennardt and Schwartz, "Hot, Warm, and Cold Zones."

[1296] Pennardt and Schwartz, "Hot, Warm, and Cold Zones."

[1297] Goldstein et al., *EMS Zones of Care*.

[1298] *Strategies to Enhance Survival*.

Figure D-1. Improving survival from an active shooter*

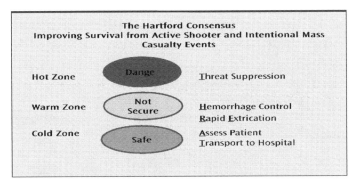

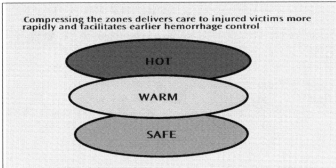

Goldstein et al., *EMS Zones of Care.*

Critical Incident Review: Active Shooter at Robb Elementary School |
Appendix D. Leadership, Incident Command, and Coordination Supplemental Materials

493

Appendix E. Public Communications Supplemental Materials

The following sections provide further context and information related to "Chapter 5. Public Communications During and Following the Crisis."

Public Media Campaign Examples

The development of a public awareness campaign is an excellent approach to ensuring that outreach extends to all individuals who are impacted by an event. Although these two examples are from larger cities, these campaigns can be developed with a lower budget and designed for use on a smartphone, via social media.

Figure E-1. Examples of commercials addressing the general public, youth, responders, older adults, and parents

Critical Incident Review: Active Shooter at Robb Elementary School |
Appendix E. Public Communications Supplemental Materials

494

New York 9/11 Project Liberty Media Campaign

To this day, one of the most successful post-disaster public media campaigns was launched in the aftermath of 9/11 by the New York state mental health response program, Project Liberty. The state's Office of Mental Health launched a $5 million public education campaign using television commercials (see figures E-1 on page 494 and E-2 on page 496), ads in train stations and bus shelters, billboards, radio, print and other traditional as well as electronic media. Social media did not exist in the formats or the extent to which it does today. But the lessons learned from this and later mass violence and terrorist incidents still apply:[1299]

- "Responding effectively requires an expansion of focus to the entire population. . . . The first step in doing so, was to use a broad Public Health approach to education in our media campaign."

- Outreach plans must focus on the general population, not just those individuals who present themselves for formal treatment.

- Public education materials need to incorporate normal psychological reactions to trauma and effective strategies for processing trauma.

- Public media creators should receive broad-based training in mental health interventions that are community-based, preventive, and restorative.

- Public media should foster the view that mental health is primary rather than secondary to mental illness, encouraging a wellness model that emphasizes personal and community resilience.

- A greater public health focus brings many other potential opportunities beyond disaster mental health preparedness, such as advancing an overall prevention agenda and further normalizing and reducing the stigma of mental health service.

The Boston Marathon Campaign

The Boston Marathon has historically received local, national, and international news coverage. Due to the unprecedented nature of the 2013 bombing incident, it received extensive media airtime, and videos of the actual bombing—full of graphic images of severely injured runners, spectators, and rescue and recovery staff—were repeatedly televised and shared on social media continuously for weeks. Much of this news coverage contravened social rules of privacy and even many journalists' own recommendations for coverage of traumatic events.[1300] This intense and extensive exposure exacerbated the behavioral health risks and concerns for those both directly and indirectly involved in the disaster.[1301]

[1299] Naturale, "Outreach Strategies: An Experiential Description."

[1300] Dart Center, "Resources for Covering Mass Shootings."

[1301] Hopwood and Schutte, "Psychological Outcomes in Reaction."

Figure E-2. Bus and subway campaigns featured real-life stories from New Yorkers who called the disaster hotline

Critical Incident Review: Active Shooter at Robb Elementary School |
Appendix E. Public Communications Supplemental Materials

496

In response in 2015, the Massachusetts Office for Victim Assistance (MOVA) subsequently created a large-scale media and communications plan to provide outreach, information, and education to the overall community—everyone affected by their exposure to the event (see figure E-3).[1302] The campaign's goal was to provide messages of support, hope, recovery, and resiliency and to raise awareness of the long-term impacts of violence on families, first responders, and children. For many, learning that some of their symptoms were common and even expected in a post-disaster environment and being reassured that their symptoms would likely decrease over time was an effective behavioral health support.[1303] MOVA's television ads also encouraged people to call the organization for questions and help. In 2019, AskMOVA rebranded to expand the range of services to cover various types of crimes beyond mass violence.[1304]

Figure E-3. MOVA television commercials featuring bombing victims and their families

Source: Used with permission from the Massachusetts Office for Victim Assistance

---

[1302] CIR Fact Finding.

[1303] Naturale, et al., "Lessons Learned from the Boston Marathon Bombing."

[1304] CIR Fact Finding. For more information, visit www.mass.gov/askmova.

Critical Incident Review: Active Shooter at Robb Elementary School |
Appendix E. Public Communications Supplemental Materials

497

Social Media Coverage

Media and public communication stories are driven by the situation, as well as the prevalence of interest from the public, and social media is one way to track that. Social media is also one tool to track community sentiment and the reach of the story. Starting on May 26, Twitter posts using the word "Uvalde" peaked at 133,535 tweets and then dropped by 42 percent in 48 hours.[1305] The San Antonio Express-News collected 10,000 to 18,000 tweets about Uvalde nearly every hour between May 26 to July 5, with approximately one million messages in the end (see figure E-4).[1306]

Figure E-4. Uvalde-related tweets collected by the Express-News

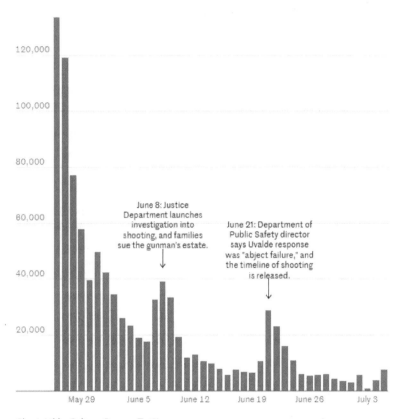

Uvalde-related tweets collected by the Express-News

Chart: Libby Seline • Source: Twitter

Source: San Antonio Express-News/ZUMA Press

[1305] Seline, "So Long 'Thoughts and Prayers.'"

[1306] Seline, "So Long 'Thoughts and Prayers.'"

Critical Incident Review: Active Shooter at Robb Elementary School |
Appendix E. Public Communications Supplemental Materials

498

The most cited person was Texas Governor Greg Abbott at 9,002 tweets, followed by Uvalde native and actor Matthew McConaughy (7,564) and Uvalde Consolidated Independent School District Police Department Chief Pete Arredondo (7,099).[1307] The three most common two-word phrases in order of use were "Uvalde police," "school shooting," and "Uvalde Texas" (see figure E-5), and the top hashtag was #uvalde (see figure E-6 on page 500).[1308]

World leaders—including those from New Zealand, China, Ukraine, Mexico, the United Kingdom, and Canada—commented and expressed condolences via social media or their home news organizations.[1309]

Figure E-5. Top two-word phrases used in Uvalde-related tweets over time between late May and mid-July 2022

Top two-word phrases used in Uvalde-related tweets over time

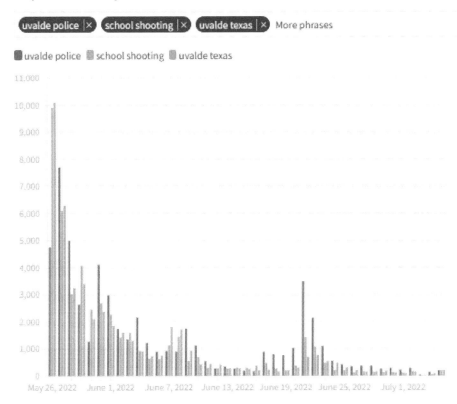

Graph: Libby Seline, Source: Twitter

Source: San Antonio Express-News/ZUMA Press

[1307] Seline, "So Long 'Thoughts and Prayers.'"

[1308] Seline, "So Long 'Thoughts and Prayers.'"

[1309] Treisman and Alex Leff, "How World Leaders Are Reacting to the Uvalde School Shooting."

Figure E-6. Top hashtags used in Uvalde-related tweets over time between late May and mid-July 2022

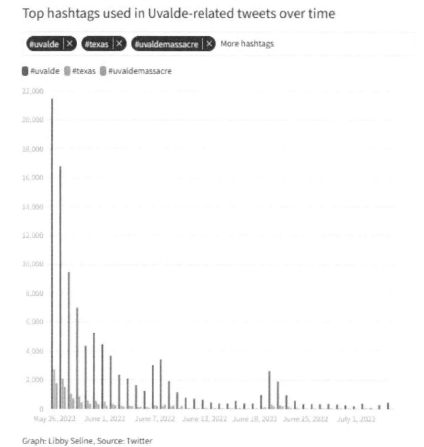

Graph: Libby Seline, Source: Twitter

Source: San Antonio Express-News/ZUMA Press

How Public Communications Impact Outcomes from Traumatic Experiences

A traumatic experience is one that creates a risk of serious injury or death to a person, or to someone they love.[1310] Exposure to the event can inflict psychological harm in varying degrees. The threat and one's proximity to the threat, or even the perception of such a threat, increase the risk of developing a diagnosable mental health condition such as depression, anxiety, or post-traumatic stress disorder (PTSD). This risk is based on other variables that are unique to each victim, including their past trauma history, current mental health concerns, social and economic status, language proficiency, and cultural and ethnic influences. While most people will recover from traumatic events in a reasonable time frame with good coping and social supports, a small but significant percentage of people will go on to develop a diagnosable mental illness as a result of the experience.[1311]

[1310] *Diagnostic and Statistical Manual of Mental Disorders, Fifth Edition.*

[1311] Norris et al., "60,000 Disaster Victims Speak: Part I."

Critical Incident Review: Active Shooter at Robb Elementary School |
Appendix E. Public Communications Supplemental Materials

500

In incidents that are caused by humans with intent to harm, such as mass violence and terrorism, the percentage of those at higher risk of developing a mental illness (20 percent) is twice that of natural disasters or accidents (10 percent).[1312] Additional variables influence whether those impacted actually go on to develop a diagnosable mental illness or recover from their acute stress reactions in a reasonable amount of time. In a large-scale event such as the mass casualty incident at Robb Elementary School, 20 percent of the affected population—as many as 3,000 people—could be at elevated risk of developing a mental illness such as PTSD, depression, or other anxiety disorders.

Mental illness can interrupt a person's ability to engage in a healthy way with others, complete school, succeed at work, have relationships, or be a productive member of the community. While many people who have a mental illness can function well with proper treatment, the rate of unemployment is higher among U.S. adults who have mental illness (7.4 percent) compared to those who do not (4.6 percent).[1313] Of those who are in the public mental health system, almost 80 percent are unemployed.[1314] Additionally, people experiencing the traumatic stress of a mass violence incident can experience more health-related illnesses, such as cardiac problems, immunodeficiency illnesses, and obesity.

Early interventions provided after traumatic events can help mitigate the development of these problems, but many factors inhibit disaster victims, survivors, family members, and responders from receiving the types of services from which they might benefit. Typically, most people do not see themselves in need of mental health services, even in the aftermath of a disaster, emergency, or mass violence event when they are experiencing acute stress and distress. For many people, the stigma surrounding those with mental health concerns and the perception that seeking mental health treatment is a sign of weakness prevent them from identifying themselves as someone in need of or accepting help. Cultural and religious beliefs can also inhibit help seeking, and some lack confidence in health and mental health service providers.

With effective messaging that encourages and normalizes accessing diverse types of support services after a mass violence event, those impacted may be more likely to seek help. Television, radio, and print ads showing everyday people struggling and reaching out for services have been effective in previous mass violence events.[1315] Public awareness and marketing campaigns should be funded as part of a disaster response program. Moreover, planning should include consideration of needs over the long term, which at minimum is considered a three- to five-year period. The negative emotional impacts of mass violence can remain with victims throughout their lives. For many, it takes years to realize that their distress is a result of their exposure to the event, thus it is not unusual for victims to seek services many years after an incident. Communities can help victims understand that reaching out for help months or years later is common and that these disaster-specific supports can help.

[1312] Norris et al., "60,000 Disaster Victims Speak: Part I."

[1313] NAMI, "Mental Health By the Numbers."

[1314] NAMI, "Employment and Mental Illness."

[1315] Naturale, "Outreach Strategies: An Experiential Description;" Naturale et al., "Lessons Learned from the Boston Marathon Bombing."

Critical Incident Review: Active Shooter at Robb Elementary School |
Appendix E. Public Communications Supplemental Materials

501

Another way to combat the stigma is to refrain from referring to recovery and resilience activities as "mental health services." Most interventions related to distress experienced after a disaster or mass violence incident are not traditional mental health treatments.

Psychoeducation

Psychoeducation is an evidence-based therapeutic intervention for victims and their loved ones that provides information and support to help those individuals better understand and cope with traumatic events. Psychoeducation was originally used in the early 1980s to work with patients who had a serious illness, along with their families, but today it is more commonly used to work with anyone experiencing acute stress or distress as a result of a traumatic event.[1316]

Psychoeducation is a recommended intervention offered to victims and family members to help them identify the core, most common distress symptoms they may be at risk of experiencing as a result of a traumatic experience (along with other risk factors) and what they can do to reduce distressing symptoms and mitigate the development of a mental illness as a result. These symptoms can occur in any or all of five domains, often overlapping:

- Physical (heart racing, headaches, stomachaches, exhaustion, sleep problems)

- Behavioral (irritability, shaking, impulsivity)

- Emotional (anger, depressive-like signs such as crying and numbness)

- Cognitive (inability to focus, poor decision-making, poor judgement)

- Spiritual (angry at God, questioning one's faith, loss of a sense of meaning)

The focus is on helping people understand that in the aftermath of a traumatic event (and possibly for an extended period of time, often past the first-year marker of an event), these reactions and symptoms are common, expected, usually short-lived, and can be decreased more quickly with good coping and social supports. Of consideration, too, are external impacts that can increase or decrease distress, such as the economic status of the individual, family, and community; expectations and support or lack thereof (trauma-informed public communications are considered a positive social support that can help in the healing process); social structures, such as racism and inequality; as well as geographic and community-capacity concerns, especially in rural areas and some segments of cities where fewer resources of any kind exist.

[1316] New York State Psychiatric Institute, "Patient and Family Library."

Critical Incident Review: Active Shooter at Robb Elementary School |
Appendix E. Public Communications Supplemental Materials

502

Psychoeducation teaches problem-solving and communication skills and provides education and resources in an empathetic and supportive environment. Psychoeducation can also mean teaching victims and family members specific coping skills that they can use to manage their symptoms (e.g., rest, breathing, and meditation exercises; mild physical exercise like walking and stretching; eating healthy; being with social supports who understand and accept how you feel; reaching out and asking for help). When developing coping skills, victims and family members are more likely to use these skills successfully if they understand why the skills might be helpful and how they work. Results from more than 30 studies indicate that psychoeducation improves well-being, lowers rates of reoccurring symptoms, and improves recovery.[1317] Research in post-disaster situations informs us that victims and family members who have experienced a traumatic event can see a statistically significant decrease in distress symptoms when they are provided with psychoeducational information. Being informed about which acute stress reactions to expect, patterns of recovery, potentially activating events and timelines, and helpful interventions for stress reduction, coping, and self-care can have the effect of decreasing anxiety.[1318]

There were no best practice–based victim/family forums or informational sessions offered to the Robb Elementary victims and family members in the immediate aftermath of the event. Families were not provided details about what happened in the last hour of their loved ones' lives. Nor was any informational meeting arranged that provided psychoeducational information about distress reactions, grief, activating events, coping, or recovery to family members and other victims. Additionally, many responders reported that they were not offered any operational or stress reaction debriefings that could have provided psychoeducation and coping information to help them in their recovery process.

Family and victim forums that are focused on providing psychoeducation regarding what to expect in terms of physical, behavioral, emotional, cognitive, and spiritual impacts; anticipation of activating events and timelines; social supports and good coping vs. negative coping; victim services; and resources and lessons learned from previous events and from peers have become best practices in the aftermath of mass violence events. Holding these events and having victim advocates in attendance with resource and referral information can help victims and family members be informed and feel cared for and cared about in a way that can support their recovery.

[1317] Vreeland, "An Evidence-Based Practice of Psychoeducation for Schizophrenia."

[1318] Hamblen et al., "Cognitive Behavioral Therapy for Postdisaster Distress."

Appendix F. Trauma and Support Services Supplemental Materials

The following sections provide further context and information related to "Chapter 6. Trauma and Support Services."

A Shift in Disaster Mental Health Response

The Oklahoma City Bombing in 1995 was one of the first incidents of mass violence for which a formalized mental health response was launched. In that incident, one of the lessons learned was that not only were the negative mental health impacts felt by victims and family members, but that the effects on responders were also severe. This was found to be related to the expansiveness of the physical destruction, which covered a 16-block radius; the overwhelming numbers of those killed (168) and injured (680); and the responders' exposure to the gruesome deaths of 19 very young children and babies. The impact was so emotionally devastating that the American Red Cross provided counseling to support the Oklahoma City first responders 10 years after the event.[1319]

Six years after the Oklahoma City bombing, the largest U.S. disaster mental health response—which included a multimillion-dollar public communications campaign to promote recovery—would be launched in New York after the 9/11 terrorist attacks.[1320] More than 4,800 crisis counselors spent close to 3 years providing individual, group, and community counseling, psychoeducation, and support services to millions of adults and children, including victims and family members of those killed, the injured, those who escaped but experienced the threat of death in the attacks, responders, and their family members. Most notably, the entire nation was affected by excessive exposure to this violence for years. The exposure came via print media, visual images, and the distressing emotional cries of victims and witnesses repeatedly played on television newscasts and social media platforms. In addition to the event itself, this level of exposure negatively impacted our sense of safety as a nation. For many people, their perspective on their place in the world, as well as their previous sense of meaning and the decisions they made about how to live their lives going forward, was changed significantly. See the "Public Media Campaign Examples" in "Appendix E. Public Communications Supplemental Materials" for more on this public awareness campaign.

The program evaluations from those impacted by mass violence, terrorism, and other community violence/crimes have taught us valuable lessons. We understand the need to mitigate the development of mental health problems in the aftermath of these events. We know that we must attend to

---

[1319] OVC, "Antiterrorism and Emergency Assistance Program (AEAP);" Pfefferbaum et al., "Disaster Mental Health Services Following the 1995 Oklahoma City Bombing."

[1320] Draper, McCleery, and Schaedle, "Mental Health Services Support in Response to September 11th."

Critical Incident Review: Active Shooter at Robb Elementary School |
Appendix F. Trauma and Support Services Supplemental Materials

504

responders and their families in addition to victims and victims' family members.[1321] Helping those exposed to such disasters understand that they can access crisis counseling, learn good coping skills, reach out to social supports, and access their innate strengths to build their resilience can decrease the number of people who go on to develop a mental illness as a result of their exposure to traumatic events and their aftermath. The goal is to return affected individuals and communities to their pre-disaster level of functioning or achieve a sufficient level of adaptation, so they can get back to their lives and back to doing the things they would normally do—working, participating in family and community events, and having moments of joy again.[1322] This is why attention to behavioral health (i.e., mental health and substance use) service delivery matters. It matters to people directly impacted and their families; it matters to those indirectly affected, such as responders and their families; and it matters to the community at large. Crisis intervention and other mental health supports can help mitigate severe emotional distress or the development of a mental illness and allow people to remain productive members of their communities.

While national attention to these incidents usually lasts only until the next event is picked up by the press and public media, for the victims of mass violence events, the experience typically lasts for the rest of their lives. Survivors report that they do not believe in the concept of closure, as they never forget the person they lost and will live with the impact of losing the loved one for the rest of their lives. And as we have learned from mass violence events, the negative mental health impacts of these traumas can be passed on generationally.[1323] Thus, the long-term needs of those who are impacted by incidents of mass violence are becoming a focus of the field, and there is a need for lessons learned as well as formal research on interventions for these populations.

High-Risk Populations Identified in the Literature

The literature shows that exposure to a disaster is the single most important predictor of adverse emotional outcomes. This group includes people:

- Experiencing bereavement (most predictive of PTSD)

- Who sustained an injury or have an injured family member (most predictive of PTSD)

- Whose lives were threatened (most predictive of PTSD)

- Who experienced panic, horror, or feared for their lives

- Who experienced separation from family

[1321] Salston and Figley, "Secondary Traumatic Stress Effects of Working with Survivors of Criminal Victimization."

[1322] Hobfoll et al., "Five Essential Elements of Immediate and Mid-Term Mass Trauma Intervention;" Norris et al., "Toward Understanding and Creating Systems of Postdisaster Care."

[1323] Danieli, Norris, and Engdahl, "Multigenerational Legacies of Trauma;" Danieli et al., "The Danieli Inventory of Multigenerational Legacies of Trauma, Part I;" Healing Collective Trauma, "What Is Collective Trauma?"

- Who experienced an extensive loss of property as a result of the incident/disaster

- Who were relocated or displaced because of the incident/disaster

- Who were responders having experienced a threat to their own lives, risking their lives to help others, suffering from injuries, and witnessing injury to others

Additional factors that contribute to adverse emotional effects post-disaster include:

- *Neighborhood/Community-Level Exposure:* This translates to those in the immediate and nearby communities. In this case of a school shooting incident, this would include those exposed to the alleged perpetrator, those who experienced lockdown, those whose family members/children were at some time, or who would generally have been at the school that day.

- *Gender:* Disasters affect women and girls more adversely than men or boys. Mothers are particularly at risk for substantial distress.

- *Age and Experience:* Middle-aged adults are more adversely affected than other adult age groups. Children can be more negatively affected than adults depending on their developmental level and ability to understand what is happening around them, how their carers respond, and the level of exposure to the event both directly and indirectly.

- *Ethnicity:* Minorities are at greater risk if more severely exposed and/or if beliefs impede help-seeking behavior.

- *Language and Accessibility:* Community members in the United States who do not speak English or for whom English is not their first language are at higher risk for mental health distress especially if language translation is not accessible in the form of a translator or trusted advocates who can act on their behalf.

- *Socioeconomic Status (SES):* Lower SES has been associated with more significant post-disaster distress.[1324]

- *Family Functioning:* Husbands' and wives' partners and significant others' responses affect each other. Marital stress increases after disasters.

  - Parental status can add to post-disaster stress (e.g., single parents can struggle to manage alone; informal guardians worry about being able to access health and mental health care for children they parent without legal status to do so; multiple parents in the form of stepparents and other loved ones may disagree on parenting issues causing conflict and distress for each other and the children).

  - Children are sensitive to familial disaster distress and conflict: Parental responses are the best predictor for children's responses.

[1324] Norris, Friedman, and Watson, "60,000 Disaster Victims Speak: Part II;" Norris et al., "60,000 Disaster Victims Speak: Part I;" Kaniasty and Norris, "In Search of Altruistic Community: Patterns of Social Support Mobilization following Hurricane Hugo."

Critical Incident Review: Active Shooter at Robb Elementary School |
Appendix F. Trauma and Support Services Supplemental Materials

506

- **Pre-Disaster Functioning**: People with higher pre-disaster psychological symptoms are more strongly affected by disasters. A "neurotic" personality increases the likelihood of post-disaster distress.

- **Psychological Resources**: The following can increase resilience and decrease adverse mental health outcomes:

  - Coping skills

  - Beliefs about capabilities to cope

  - Self-efficacy, proficiency, perceived control, self-esteem, hope, and optimism

  - Received and perceived social support-perception of help

- **Resource Deterioration**: The more significant the resource loss, the greater the psychological distress. Resources include loss of facilities such as school buildings and the ability for the community to hold classes, refueling stations and the availability of gasoline for car, truck and bus uses, grocery stores and food distribution centers, office space and the availability of the workforce in the impacted area.

- **Environmental Factors**: The ecological perspective tells us that after traumatic incidents, every aspect of a survivor's environment (familial, social, economic, cultural, educational, physical, intellectual, geographic, spiritual) has the potential to have a strong impact on whether a person develops chronic PTSD or other major mental illnesses such as depression and anxiety. Two of the strongest predictive factors are previous life stress and social support from others.[1325] The most recent research done with trauma survivors of individual trauma (e.g., assault, motor vehicle accidents) has consistently shown that the absence of social support impedes recovery.[1326] Further, negative support reactions such as critical comments about the length of time taken for recovery, from family members in particular, seem to stand in the way of recovery among trauma victims in treatment for PTSD. In disaster studies, the survivor's social network size, vitality, and closeness are also strongly and consistently related to positive mental health outcomes. Disaster survivors who believe that they are cared for by others and that help will be available if needed fare better psychologically than disaster survivors who believe they are unloved and alone.[1327]

[1325] Dunmore, Clark, and Ehlers, "A Prospective Investigation of the Role of Cognitive Factors;" Filipas and Ullman, "Social Reactions to Sexual Assault Victims ;" Zoellner, Foa, and Brigidi, "Interpersonal Friction and PTSD in Female Victims of Sexual and Nonsexual Assault."

[1326] Zoellner et al., "Changes in Negative Beliefs following Three Brief Programs."

[1327] Zoellner et al., "Changes in Negative Beliefs following Three Brief Programs."

Unique Challenges in Addressing Behavioral Health Concerns for Various Responders

There can be differences between fire/emergency medical services (EMS) departments and law enforcement agencies in providing psychological support services, especially after a mass casualty event. While the members of both fire/EMS departments and law enforcement agencies may suffer with trauma and stress from such events, their experiences can be different due to the nature of their work.

Firefighters and EMS providers may face trauma from the physical demands of responding to a mass casualty event. They may also experience stress from the emotional toll of responding to such events, working long hours, and being away from their families for extended periods.

Law enforcement officers may face trauma from the risks involved in responding to a mass casualty event, such as the potential for violence or exposure to hazardous materials. They may also experience stress from managing crowds, securing the scene, performing rescues, and interacting with victims and their families. In the situation at Robb Elementary, law enforcement also faced additional trauma due to the backlash in the community once information about the length of time for the response to the active shooter became known.

Law enforcement behavioral health needs will be related to the different trauma cues, while fire/EMS behavioral health needs will be based on their inability to go in and help, along with the waiting.[1328] This also applies along the responder continuum, which includes hospital staff as well. Thus, it is necessary to tailor the application of services so that the language used and the examples provided of the types of symptoms they may experience are applicable to their unique experiences and roles.[1329]

As a result of these differences, agencies and departments may have different approaches to providing psychological support services after a mass casualty event. Irrespective of the industry, leaders of responder agencies need to recognize the importance of supporting their personnel's mental health and well-being in the aftermath of such events.

Fire/EMS organizations have historically focused on prevention and preparedness, while law enforcement agencies have focused more on response and enforcement. This historical context may contribute to a different approach to stress management and officer wellness. One expert says 95 percent of fire departments across the country have an embedded peer support program.[1330]

[1328] CIR Fact Finding.

[1329] Watson and Westphal, *Stress First Aid for Health Care Workers.*

[1330] CIR Fact Finding.

Critical Incident Review: Active Shooter at Robb Elementary School |
Appendix F. Trauma and Support Services Supplemental Materials

508

Law Enforcement

There are approximately 18,000 law enforcement agencies in the United States, according to the most recent estimate from the Bureau of Justice Statistics.[1331] These agencies include federal, state, local, and tribal law enforcement agencies. Law enforcement agencies are primarily regulated at the state and local level, with each state and local jurisdiction setting its standards and requirements for hiring, training, and certification of law enforcement officers. Although there are no national standards, national guidelines for psychological wellness after a traumatic event are available to law enforcement in the United States.

The Office of Community Oriented Policing Services, in conjunction with St. Petersburg College, developed guidelines for law enforcement agencies to address the mental health needs of their personnel after critical incidents. The guidelines include recommendations for establishing a department-wide crisis response plan, training officers and supervisors on trauma and stress management, and making counseling services available to all personnel.[1332]

Additionally, the International Association of Chiefs of Police (IACP) developed a model policy on officer wellness, which includes recommendations for addressing the mental health needs of officers after a traumatic event. The policy recommends that departments provide access to confidential counseling services, establish peer support programs, and provide education and training on mental health and wellness.[1333]

Furthermore, the Federal Bureau of Investigation (FBI) has developed the National Center for the Analysis of Violent Crime (NCAVC), which supports law enforcement agencies in the aftermath of critical incidents. The NCAVC offers numerous services, including crisis intervention and psychological support for law enforcement personnel.[1334]

Fire Departments

On the fire side, the National Fire Protection Association (NFPA) Standard on Fire Department Occupational Safety, Health, and Wellness Program specifies the minimum requirements for an occupational safety and health program for fire departments and EMS. The standard addresses critical incident stress management and member wellness, along with other areas.[1335]

[1331] Banks et al., "National Sources of Law Enforcement Employment Data."

[1332] Sewell, *Guide for Developing an Effective Stress Management Policy for Law Enforcement.*

[1333] IACP, *Critical Incident Stress Management.*

[1334] FBI, "Investigative Programs Critical Incident Response Group: National Center for the Analysis of Violent Crime."

[1335] *NFPA 1500TM: Standard on Fire Department Occupational Safety, Health, and Wellness Program.*

Critical Incident Review: Active Shooter at Robb Elementary School |
Appendix F. Trauma and Support Services Supplemental Materials

509

The National Volunteer Fire Council (NVFC) is an association representing the interests of volunteer fire, EMS, and rescue services.[1336] The NVFC's Share the Load Program assists individuals seeking help for behavioral health issues, such as anxiety, depression, burnout, and post-traumatic stress disorder. Additionally, the program assists departments looking to implement or enhance a behavioral health program.[1337]

A recent study looked at the differences in psychiatric symptoms and barriers to mental health care between volunteer and career firefighters. Volunteer firefighters generally reported elevated psychiatric symptoms, including depression, post-traumatic stress, and suicide plans and attempts, whereas career firefighters reported elevated levels of problematic alcohol use.[1338] Greater structural barriers to mental health care (e.g., cost and availability of resources) may explain the increased levels of psychiatric symptom observed among volunteer firefighters, which is one of the reasons the study recommended that organizational differences should be considered.[1339] It should be noted that Uvalde's only fire department is a volunteer fire department.

Hospitals

Most hospitals, according to the Center for Disease Control and Prevention, offer workplace wellness programs:

- 83 percent of hospitals in the United States provide workplace wellness programs, compared to 46 percent of all employers.

- 63 percent of hospitals offer health screenings, also known as biometrics, compared to 27 percent of all employers.

- 31 percent of hospitals provide health coaches, compared to 5 percent of all employers.

- 56 percent of hospitals have stress-management programs, compared to 20 percent of all employers.[1340]

[1336] National Volunteer Fire Council, "Home: NVFC."

[1337] National Volunteer Fire Council, "Share the Load Program."

[1338] Stanley et al., "Differences in Psychiatric Symptoms and Barriers to Mental Health Care."

[1339] Stanley et al., "Differences in Psychiatric Symptoms and Barriers to Mental Health Care."

[1340] CDC, "Hospital Employees' Health."

Critical Incident Review: Active Shooter at Robb Elementary School |
Appendix F. Trauma and Support Services Supplemental Materials

510

EMS

The 2020 National EMS Assessment determined that only six states and three U.S. territories recommend health and wellness programs for their EMS professionals. However, in 37 states EMS professionals have access to a critical incident stress management (CISM) resource. The differences lie in the fact that health and wellness programs tend to derive from specific issues addressed by government occupational health and safety agencies, while CISM resources are more regionalized.[1341]

The Texas EMS Alliance has an EMS Peer Referral Program provided by the Texas Health and Human Services Commission.[1342]

Texas First Responders

In September 2017, the Texas Legislature established the Work Group on Mental Health Access for First Responders.[1343] The study, which surveyed Texas police, sheriffs, paid and volunteer firefighters, dispatch/communications, and emergency medical technician (EMT) departments, showed that most paid firefighters (83 percent), paramedics (74 percent), police (66 percent), and EMTs (53 percent) had a formal employee assistance program (EAP) within their departments. Conversely, half of volunteer fire (55 percent), sheriffs' (55 percent), and dispatch/communications (50 percent) departments did not have an EAP. The size of the departments had an impact on whether there was a formal EAP; 78 percent of large departments (>100) had a program, compared to only 42 percent of small departments (<99). There was also a large geographic and demographic discrepancy; only 30 percent of the surveyed first responders in rural departments (<25,000 population) had access to EAPs that addressed mental health needs, compared to 66 percent in urban departments.[1344]

There was an additional disparity by profession in how EAPs were promoted within the first responder departments. When comparing professions, police officers, paid firefighters, and paramedics were more often made aware of their EAP via different avenues (e.g., writing, orientation, newsletter, supervisor), whereas EMTs, staff of sheriffs' departments, volunteer firefighters, and dispatch/communications personnel were least likely to be made aware of their EAP.[1345]

The study concluded that there was a lack of information about mental health resources available and accessible to first responders, especially in smaller departments and rural and frontier areas of the state.[1346]

[1341] NASEMSO, "NASEMSO Releases 2020 National EMS Assessment."

[1342] Texas EMS Alliance, "Peer Assistance."

[1343] HB 1774, Relating to actions and liability associated with certain insurance claims, Texas State Legislature, Legislative Session 85(R).

[1344] *Report on Mental Health Access for First Responders.*

[1345] *Report on Mental Health Access for First Responders.*

[1346] *Report on Mental Health Access for First Responders.*

Critical Incident Review: Active Shooter at Robb Elementary School |
Appendix F. Trauma and Support Services Supplemental Materials

511

Establishing and Maintaining a Responder Support Services Program

Table F-1 provides an overview of key best practices to consider when establishing and maintaining a law enforcement support services and counseling program. However, it is important to adapt and customize these practices based on the specific needs and resources of an agency, as well as any local regulations or guidelines.[1347]

Table F-1. Best practices for establishing and maintaining a law enforcement support services and counseling program

Best Practice	Description
Recruiting, Hiring, and Screening for Mental Wellness	Mental wellness starts in the beginning and should be ingrained in all phases of the selection process for new hires.
Training Academy Resiliency and Self-Care	Training in wellness, stress management, and resiliency should be part of all academy/basic training curricula.
In-Service Training on Mental Wellness	In-service training is another opportunity to train and reinforce the concepts of mental wellness; the agency's trauma services resources, including suicide prevention; and resiliency/self-care.
Supervisors Training as Front-Line Mental Health First Aid	First-line supervisors should be trained in the signs of trauma/stress, ensuring officer health and wellness during challenging times.
Early Warning System	An early warning system can identify officers who may be having problems, including with mental health, and provide appropriate counseling or training.
Chaplaincy Program	A chaplaincy program can provide emotional, moral, and spiritual support to officers, staff, and families.
Psychological Counseling Program	Agency leaders should provide personnel with internal or external psychological counseling.
Employee Assistance Program	An EAP can assist all sworn and civilian employees in resolving problems affecting their job performance or personal life.
Spousal Support, Healthy Families, or Family Day	Agencies should involve the families of agency personnel with communal activities and support.
Leadership Support	Agency leadership should actively support the program, promote its importance, and encourage officers to seek support when needed. Leaders should also lead by example and prioritize their own mental health and well-being.
Creating a Culture of Openness and Support	Agencies should create a culture in which officers feel comfortable seeking help for mental health issues. This can be done by providing regular training on mental health awareness, promoting a stigma-free environment, and making it easy for officers to access counseling services.
Offering Counseling Services	Agencies should offer a variety of counseling services to meet the needs of their officers. This could include individual counseling, group counseling, family counseling, and crisis intervention services.

[1347] Adapted from COPS Office, "Law Enforcement Mental Health and Wellness (LEMHWA) Program Resources."

Critical Incident Review: Active Shooter at Robb Elementary School |
Appendix F. Trauma and Support Services Supplemental Materials

512

Best Practice	Description
Making Counseling Services Accessible	Agencies should make counseling services accessible to their officers. This could include offering services during work hours, providing transportation to appointments, and waiving copays.
Confidentiality	Confidentiality should be protected at all times. Agencies should have clear policies in place regarding confidentiality, and counselors should be trained on how to protect information. Information shared by law enforcement personnel should be treated with strict confidentiality, emphasizing that their privacy will be protected unless there is a risk of harm to themselves or others.
Peer Support Program and Training	Agencies should provide comprehensive training to peer supporters, focusing on active listening, effective communication, crisis intervention, and recognizing signs of stress, trauma, or mental health issues.
Providing Peer Support	Peer support can be an effective way for officers to connect with others who understand what they are going through.
Training on Stress Management and Coping Skills	This training can help officers to manage the stress of their job and to develop healthy coping mechanisms.
Well-Being Initiatives	Agencies should implement well-being initiatives such as stress management programs, mindfulness training, physical fitness activities, and access to mental health resources.
Referral and Resource Network	Agencies should establish a network of mental health professionals, counselors, and support services that officers can access for professional help when needed.
Evaluation and Improvement	Agencies should continuously evaluate the effectiveness of the program through feedback from participants, monitor outcomes, and make necessary improvements to better meet the needs of law enforcement personnel.

Trauma Services and Survivor Support Additional Resources

Trauma Notifications

- Death Notification Policy Center (requires IACP membership) provides guidelines for notifying next of kin of the death of a family member. [IACP] https://www.theiacp.org/resources/policy-center-resource/death-notification

- Death Notification Template is included in the *Law Enforcement-Based Victim Services—Template Package II: Next Steps* and is intended to provide sample language and content to help assess, develop, and refine program and professional victim service standards. [IACP] https://www.theiacp.org/sites/default/files/2023-10/TemplatePackageII.pdf

- We Regret To Inform You . . . is an online training for law enforcement on conducting trauma notifications. [FBI and Pennsylvania State University] https://www.deathnotification.psu.edu/

Resiliency Resources

- Community-Police Engagement: How Law Enforcement Parents Can Talk to Their Children About Current Events provides considerations for parents in law enforcement. [IACP] https://www.theiacp.org/sites/default/files/243807_IACP_OSW_CPE_Talk_to_Children_3%20(1).pdf

- Mental Wellness, Resiliency, and Suicide Prevention Information for Family and Friends of Law Enforcement outlines warning signs, immediate risks, and where to get help. [COPS Office and IACP] https://www.theiacp.org/sites/default/files/2020-03/Officer%20Suicide%20Prev.%20Brochure.pdf

- Officer Safety and Wellness Resources web page includes a collection of resources, trainings, and other publications focusing on officer and family wellness. [U.S. Department of Justice (DOJ)] https://www.justice.gov/asg/officer-safety-and-wellness-resources

- Resilience Strategies for Your Role project page includes resources on resilience strategies. [IACP] https://www.theiacp.org/resources/resilience-strategies-for-your-role

- Supporting Law Enforcement Families in Understanding Trauma is designed to help family and friends of law enforcement identify potential effects of trauma in their loved ones and inform them on how to respond. [Bureau of Justice Assistance (BJA) and IACP] https://www.theiacp.org/sites/default/files/256944_IACP_21_SupportingFamilies_508c_0.pdf

- VALOR Officer Safety App promotes mental and physical preparation to help law enforcement keep safety and wellness at the forefront. [BJA and IACP] https://www.valorforblue.org/VALOR-App

- The Vicarious Trauma Toolkit includes tools and resources tailored specifically to various audiences that provide the knowledge and skills necessary for organizations to address the vicarious trauma needs of their staff. [Office for Victims of Crime (OVC)] https://ovc.ojp.gov/program/vtt/introduction

Suicide Prevention and Intervention

- 988 Suicide & Crisis Lifeline provides 24/7, free, and confidential support for people in distress; prevention and crisis resources; and best practices for professionals in the United States. https://988lifeline.org/

- Comprehensive Framework for Law Enforcement Suicide Prevention is a central resource for law enforcement agencies to use in implementing strategic, holistic, and intentional suicide prevention strategies across the continuum of prevention and intervention and after a suicide loss. [IACP, BJA, Education Development Center, and National Action Alliance for Suicide Prevention] https://www.theiacp.org/sites/default/files/2020-11/_NOSI_Framework_Final%20%28002%29.pdf

Critical Incident Review: Active Shooter at Robb Elementary School |
Appendix F. Trauma and Support Services Supplemental Materials

514

- Messaging About Suicide Prevention in Law Enforcement focuses on the importance of safe messaging and provides information for leadership to use to help promote and support suicide prevention efforts. [IACP]
https://www.theiacp.org/sites/default/files/2021-04/244736_IACP_NOSI_Messaging_p7.pdf

- Preventing Suicide Among Officers highlights resources available from BJA. [BJA]
https://www.bja.ojp.gov/program/law-enforcement-officer-safety-and-wellness/preventing-suicide-among-officers

Victim Compensation

- Help for Victims web page covers victim compensation and assistance by state. [OVC]
https://ovc.ojp.gov/help-for-victims/help-in-your-state

- Law Enforcement's Role in Victim Compensation project page includes training videos and resources to help law enforcement provide a critical connection between the justice system and victim support services. [IACP]
https://www.theiacp.org/LE-Role-in-Victim-Compensation

- National Association of Crime Victim Compensation Boards provides contact information for each state. [National Association of Crime Victim Compensation Boards]
https://nacvcb.org/state-information/

- National Compassion Fund website provides a single, trusted way for the public to give directly to victims of mass casualty crimes. [National Compassion Fund]
https://nationalcompassion.org/

Victims and Loved Ones Tools and Resources

- Coping Tips for Traumatic Events and Disasters web page provides coping strategies, including preparation, self-care, and identifying support systems. [Substance Abuse and Mental Health Services Administration (SAMHSA)]
https://www.samhsa.gov/find-help/disaster-distress-helpline/coping-tips

- Coping With Anger Disaster Technical Assistance Center web page provides tips for self-help and boosting resilience. [SAMHSA]
https://www.samhsa.gov/dtac/disaster-survivors/coping-anger-after-disaster

- Crisis Counseling web page provides access to immediate help. [National Mass Violence Victimization Resource Center (NMVVRC)]
https://nmvvrc.org/survivors/get-help-now/#tab1

- Help for Victims of Terrorism and Mass Violence web page covers victim helplines, compensation, and assistance by state. [OVC]
https://ovc.ojp.gov/help-for-victims/terrorism-and-mass-violence

Critical Incident Review: Active Shooter at Robb Elementary School |
Appendix F. Trauma and Support Services Supplemental Materials

515

- Legal Assistance web page covers agencies and organizations that provide legal assistance. [NMVVRC]
https://nmvvrc.org/survivors/get-help-now/#tab3

- Resources and Support for the Victims in Uvalde, Texas web page includes resources available to help victim service providers, educators, law enforcement, first responders, and community and faith leaders responding to this tragedy. [OVC]
https://ovc.ojp.gov/resources-and-support-victims-uvalde-texas#r4dere

- Resources To Help Youth Cope After a Mass Shooting includes a list of resources to help youth, families, educators, and community members cope with and talk about community trauma, as well as provide psychological first aid. [Youth.gov]
https://youth.gov/feature-article/resources-help-youth-cope-after-mass-shooting

- Restoring a Sense of Safety in the Aftermath of a Shooting: Tips for Parents and Professionals offers parents, caregivers, and professionals guidance for restoring a sense of safety after a mass shooting. [The National Child Traumatic Stress Network (NCTSN)]
https://www.nctsn.org/resources/restoring-sense-safety-aftermath-shooting-tips-parents-and-professionals

- Self-Help web page provides information about the path of recovery and ways to begin the healing process or help a child or someone close to you. [NMVVRC]
https://nmvvrc.org/survivors/self-help/

- Suggestions for Parents—Mass Violence Incidents provides information on talking to your children about mass violence incidents. [NMVVRC]
https://nmvvrc.org/media/0f4p4efn/tipsheet18.pdf

- Taking Care of Your Emotional Health After a Disaster provides information on how to recognize current feelings and tips for taking care of the emotional health of yourself, your family, and your friends. [American Red Cross]
https://www.redcross.org/content/dam/redcross/atg/PDF_s/Preparedness___Disaster_Recovery/General_Preparedness___Recovery/Emotional/Recovering_Emotionally_-_Large_Print.pdf

- Talking to Children About the Shooting provides information on how to talk to children about mass shootings. [NCTSN]
https://www.nctsn.org/resources/talking-children-about-shooting

- Tips for Retaining Staff After a Disaster is a resource for facility executives to consider when trying to retain and care for staff after a disaster or mass casualty incident. [Technical Resources, Assistance Center, and Information Exchange]
https://files.asprtracie.hhs.gov/documents/tips-for-retaining-and-caring-for-staff-after-disaster.pdf

- Tips for Survivors: Coping With Anger after a Disaster or Traumatic Event contains information about anger, the grieving process, and what happens when the process is interrupted and complicated or traumatic grief occurs. [SAMHSA]
https://store.samhsa.gov/sites/default/files/d7/priv/pep19-01-01-002_0.pdf

Critical Incident Review: Active Shooter at Robb Elementary School |
Appendix F. Trauma and Support Services Supplemental Materials

516

- Tips for Survivors: Coping With Grief After a Disaster or Traumatic Event contains information about grief, the grieving process, and what happens when the process is interrupted and complicated or traumatic grief occurs. [SAMHSA]
https://store.samhsa.gov/sites/default/files/d7/priv/sma17-5035.pdf

- Tips for Survivors of a Disaster or Other Traumatic Event: Managing Stress explores stress management techniques for survivors of disasters and other traumatic events by explaining reactions individuals may experience and providing tips for building resilience. [SAMHSA]
https://store.samhsa.gov/sites/default/files/d7/priv/sma13-4776.pdf

- Twelve Self-Help Tips for Coping in the Aftermath of Mass Violence Incidents is a brief tip sheet that offers practical things that can be done to help reduce the distress created by mass violence incidents. [NMVVRC]
https://nmvvrc.org/media/rucl1xdd/twelve-self-help-tips-for-coping-general.pdf

- Resources for the Victims of Recent Mass Violence Incidents web page highlights resources for communities impacted by mass shootings. [OVC]
https://ovc.ojp.gov/news/announcements/view-resources-victims-recent-mass-violence-incidents

Law Enforcement Tools and Resources

- 16 Best Practices for an effective response to criminal mass violence and domestic terrorism incidents provide a framework for planning and preparation. [OVC]
https://icptta.com/16-best-practices/

- Don't Name Them campaign is focused on shifting the media focus from the subjects who commit these acts to the victims, survivors, and heroes who stop them. [Advanced Law Enforcement Rapid Response Training, I Love U Guys Foundation, and FBI]
https://www.dontnamethem.org/

- Employee Mental Health and Wellness document is intended to provide agencies with items for consideration when developing their policies related to employee mental health and wellness, including providing all personnel with access to mental health services and addressing the management of stress resulting from exposure to traumatic incidents. [IACP]
https://www.theiacp.org/sites/default/files/2020-05/Employee%20Mental%20Health%2005-06-2020.pdf

- Identifying and Securing Funding for Victim Response Efforts outlines funding options for law enforcement-based services. [COPS Office and IACP]
https://cops.usdoj.gov/RIC/Publications/cops-w0991-pub.pdf

- Law Enforcement Mental Health and Wellness Act Program Resources web page includes resources for law enforcement agencies addressing the mental health and well-being of their employees, including the report to Congress and case studies. [COPS Office]
https://cops.usdoj.gov/lemhwaresources

Critical Incident Review: Active Shooter at Robb Elementary School |
Appendix F. Trauma and Support Services Supplemental Materials

517

- Mass Fatality Incident Family Assistance Operations Recommended Strategies for Local and State Agencies provides an overview of the components of the family assistance process and family assistance center operations as they relate to transportation and criminal incidents. [FBI and National Transportation Safety Board] https://nmvvrc.org/media/tw5lw23j/mass-fatality-incident-family-assistance-operations.pdf

- Mass Violence Advisory Initiative (MVAI) provides peer-to-peer assistance to law enforcement leaders following a mass violence event to maximize the safety and wellness of officers, other first responders, and the community. [BJA and IACP] https://www.theiacp.org/projects/mass-violence-advisory-initiative

- MVAI Considerations for Law Enforcement Leaders provides a list of recommendations that law enforcement leaders should consider to best support their agencies and communities if they are impacted by tragedy. [BJA and IACP] https://www.theiacp.org/sites/default/files/MVAI/MVAI%20Considerations%20for%20LE%20Leaders%20Booklet.pdf

- MVAI Library of Resources is a searchable database of resources related to preparation, response, and recovery efforts for mass violence and mass casualty events. [BJA and IACP] https://www.myiacp.org/apex/MVAIresource

- Officer Safety and Wellness Resources web page includes a collection of resources, trainings, and other publications focusing on officer and family wellness. [DOJ] https://www.justice.gov/asg/officer-safety-and-wellness-resources

- Psychological First Aid Manual assists people in the immediate aftermath of disasters and terrorism to reduce initial distress and foster short- and long-term adaptive functioning. [U.S. Department of Veterans Affairs (VA)] https://www.ptsd.va.gov/professional/treat/type/psych_firstaid_manual.asp

- Response to Victims of Crime provides a model policy, a concepts and issue paper, and key points for consideration. [IACP] https://www.theiacp.org/sites/default/files/2020-07/Victims%20of%20Crime%20FULL%20-%2007282020.pdf

- 10 Essential Actions To Improve School Safety identifies 10 essential things schools, school districts, and law enforcement agencies can do to mitigate and prevent school violence, as well as to facilitate swift and essential law enforcement assistance when it is necessary. [COPS Office] https://cops.usdoj.gov/RIC/Publications/cops-w0891-pub.pdf

- The Role of Police Executives in Assisting Victims of Mass Violence: Lessons From the Field discusses the immediate aftermath and post-event recovery efforts. [Police Executive Research Forum] https://www.policeforum.org/assets/AssistingVictimsMassViolence.pdf

Critical Incident Review: Active Shooter at Robb Elementary School |
Appendix F. Trauma and Support Services Supplemental Materials

518

Other First and Second Responders Tools and Resources

- Active Shooter Incidents in Health Care Settings web page provides national and state resources for hospitals and health care facilities. [American Hospital Association] https://www.aha.org/hospitals-against-violence/active-shooter-incidents-health-care-settings

- Best Practices in Behavioral Wellness for Emergency Responders provides information on emotional intelligence, resilience, and other behavioral wellness. [International Fire Chiefs Association] https://www.iafc.org/about-iafc/sections/vcos/vcos-resource-detail/vcos-yellow-ribbon-report-update

- Emergency Responders: Tips for Taking Care of Yourself gives important steps responders can take to ensure they are able to do their jobs and cope with challenging situations. [Centers for Disease Control and Prevention (CDC)] https://emergency.cdc.gov/coping/responders.asp

- EMS Safety Practices outlines creating a safety culture within an EMS department. [Federal Emergency Management Agency (FEMA)] https://www.usfa.fema.gov/downloads/pdf/publications/ems-safety-practices.pdf

- Fire Service Behavioral Health Management Guide covers clinical support, peer support, firefighters, and leadership. [National Fallen Firefighters Foundation] https://www.firstrespondercenter.org/wp-content/uploads/2020/09/behavioral-health-mgmt-guide-122017.pdf

- First Responders and Disaster Responders Resource Portal describes signs of stress and stress management, including additional resources and online trainings. [SAMHSA] https://www.samhsa.gov/dtac/disaster-responders

- Mass Violence web page covers resources for health care emergency facilities. [Administration for Strategic Preparedness and Response (ASPR)] https://asprtracie.hhs.gov/mass-violence

- Mass Casualty Trauma Triage Paradigms and Pitfalls provides lessons learned and practices for EMS medical directors, EMS system planners, and hospital emergency planners on responding to mass casualty events. [ASPR] https://files.asprtracie.hhs.gov/documents/aspr-tracie-mass-casualty-triage-final-508.pdf

- Operational Templates and Guidance for EMS Mass Incident Deployment helps EMS prepare and develop response policies for mass care incidents. [FEMA] https://www.usfa.fema.gov/downloads/pdf/publications/templates_guidance_ems_mass_incident_deployment.pdf

Critical Incident Review: Active Shooter at Robb Elementary School |
Appendix F. Trauma and Support Services Supplemental Materials

519

- Responder Peer Support web page discusses issues faced by responders and peer support resources. [SAMHSA]
https://www.samhsa.gov/dtac/disaster-responders/peer-support

- School and Workplace Violence web page covers resources for active shooter incidents, including in recovery. [U.S. Department of Homeland Security]
https://www.dhs.gov/school-and-workplace-violence

Schools and Campuses Tools and Resources

- Active Shooter Situations: After an Active Shooter Incident web page discusses reunification and other recovery aspects. [Readiness and Emergency Management for Schools Technical Assistance Center]
https://rems.ed.gov/IHEAfterAnActiveShooter.aspx

- Best Practice Considerations for Armed Assailant Drills in Schools provides guidance on the crucial factors that schools must take into account when considering and conducting armed assailant drills. [National Association of School Psychologists (NASP), National Association of School Resource Officers, and Safe and Sound Schools]
https://www.nasponline.org/resources-and-publications/resources-and-podcasts/school-safety-and-crisis/systems-level-prevention/best-practice-considerations-for-armed-assailant-drills-in-schools

- Mitigating Psychological Effects of Lockdowns provides best practice guidelines for lockdowns. [NASP]
https://www.nasponline.org/resources-and-publications/resources-and-podcasts/school-safety-and-crisis/systems-level-prevention/mitigating-psychological-effects-of-lockdowns

- The NASSP Principal Recovery Network Guide to Recovery is a collection of best practices and practical advice from principals and assistant principals who led schools in recovery after a shooting. [National Association of Secondary School Principals]
https://www.nassp.org/wp-content/uploads/2022/08/PRN-Guide-FINAL.pdf

- School Violence Resources web page outlines resources for educators and administrators who support students and families in coping with bullying and school violence. [NASP]
https://www.nasponline.org/resources-and-publications/resources-and-podcasts/school-safety-and-crisis/school-violence-resources

Critical Incident Review: Active Shooter at Robb Elementary School |
Appendix F. Trauma and Support Services Supplemental Materials

520

- Teacher Guidelines for Helping Students After Mass Violence offers teachers guidance on helping students after a mass violence event. [NCTSN] https://www.nctsn.org/resources/teacher-guidelines-helping-students-after-mass-violence

- Tip Lines for School Safety describes the prevalence of tip lines, types of schools that are more likely to use tip lines, ways in which tip lines are designed and implemented, challenges of operating tip lines, and perceived effectiveness of tip lines. [RTI International] https://www.theiacp.org/sites/default/files/MVAI/Library%20of%20Resources/Tip%20Lines%20for%20School%20Safety.pdf

Government Leadership Tools and Resources

- Mass Shooting Protocol and Playbook discusses planning and responding to mass violence incidents from a city leadership perspective. [International City/County Management Association (ICMA)] https://icma.org/documents/mass-shooting-protocol-and-playbook-tabletop-exercise

- Mass Shootings in American Cities: Mayors' Experiences and Lessons Learned captures key points from cities that have experienced mass shootings in recent years. [COPS Office and U.S. Conference of Mayors] https://cops.usdoj.gov/RIC/Publications/cops-w0968-pub.pdf

- Robb Elementary School Shootings Response and Recovery Resources highlights relevant resources in both English and Spanish. [Uniformed University Services Center for the Study of Traumatic Stress] https://www.cstsonline.org/resources/resource-master-list/robb-elementary-school-shootings-response-and-recovery-resources

Victim Assistance Professionals Tools and Resources

- After the Death Notification: 10 Guidelines for Assisting Victims and Survivors of Mass Violence focuses on steps that victim assistance professionals can take after the initial death notification has been delivered. [NMVVRC] https://www.nmvvrc.org/media/fmcb5jxo/tipsheet10.pdf

- Attorney General Guidelines for Victim and Witness Assistance, 2022 Edition establishes guidelines to be followed by officers and employees of DOJ investigative, prosecutorial, correctional, and parole components in the treatment of victims of and witnesses to crime. [DOJ] https://ovc.ojp.gov/library/publications/attorney-general-guidelines-victim-and-witness-assistance-2022-edition

- Disaster Technical Assistance Center Supplemental Research Bulletin—Disaster Behavioral Health Interventions Inventory provides an inventory of current intervention options. [SAMHSA] https://www.samhsa.gov/sites/default/files/dtac-disaster-behavioral-health-interventions-inventory.pdf

Critical Incident Review: Active Shooter at Robb Elementary School |
Appendix F. Trauma and Support Services Supplemental Materials

521

- Managing the Finances and Volunteers web page provides resources for organizing and managing volunteers and victim compensation. [NMVVRC] https://nmvvrc.org/community-leaders/rebuild-your-community/managing-the-finances-and-volunteers/

- Mass Violence Initiative Core Compendium includes 26 modules that feature written and audiovisual resources, as well as intensive training strategies, to increase knowledge and build professional and practical skills. [NMVVRC] https://nmvvrc.org/learn/mvi-core-compendium/

- Organizing Support for Victims and Survivors web page provides resources for family assistance centers, how community leaders can support victims and survivors, victim liaisons, and a matrix for providing support. [NMVVRC] https://nmvvrc.org/community-leaders/rebuild-your-community/organizing-support-for-victims-and-survivors/

- Planning and Implementation Guide for Comprehensive, Coordinated Victim Assistance for Mass Violence Incident Trials helps prosecutors, victim services and mental/behavioral health providers, and allied professionals plan for high-profile trials with a focus on victims' and survivors' needs, and effective and coordinate strategies to meet them. [NMVVRC] https://nmvvrc.org/community-leaders/rebuild-your-community/court-planning-guide/

- Planning How To Cope With Commemorations, Special Events, and Timeframes That Activate Trauma Memories describes the signs and risk factors for managing commemorative events, holidays, and other special time frames that may bring distressing memories and reactions from a traumatic event. [OVC] https://cdnsm5-ss8.sharpschool.com/UserFiles/Servers/Server_733753/Image/Mass_Violence_Commemorations_Special_Events_Quick_Tips_Final_508c_09292020%20(002).pdf

- Prepare Your Community toolkit contains information and tools for victim assistance professionals, as well as local, state, and federal government officials, that can be used to prepare communities for mass violence incidents. [OVC and NMVVRC] https://nmvvrc.org/community-leaders/prepare-your-community/

- Psychological Impact of the Recent Shooting describes issues that may be helpful to consider after violence occurs. [NCTSN] https://www.nctsn.org/resources/psychological-impact-recent-shooting

- Responding to a Mass Violence Incident: Developing a Personal "Go Kit" and Victim Assistance Agency/Organization "Go Kit" provide suggestions for victim assistance professionals who may be deployed to a mass violence incident. [NMVVRC] https://nmvvrc.org/media/ix5aamse/individual-go-kit-checklist-for-vaps.pdf; https://nmvvrc.org/media/hdnh0cnu/victim-assistance-agency-go-kit-checklist.pdf

Critical Incident Review: Active Shooter at Robb Elementary School |
Appendix F. Trauma and Support Services Supplemental Materials

522

- <u>Victim List Template</u> allows a community to quickly start to build a database of all victims in an incident. [OVC]
  https://www.myiacp.org/MVAIResourcedetails?id=a4G3s0000009FAEEA2

- <u>Victim Service Professionals</u> web page includes resources and tools for readiness, response, resilience, and recommended reading. [NMVVRC]
  https://nmvvrc.org/vsps-clinicians/vsp-resources/

Communities Tools and Resources

- <u>Active Shooter Safety Resources</u> includes training videos, the role of the FBI, and FBI-produced documentaries. [FBI]
  https://www.fbi.gov/how-we-can-help-you/safety-resources/active-shooter-safety-resources

- <u>Faith Communities and the Disaster Distress Helpline</u> is a tip sheet for U.S. religious leaders responding to disasters. [National Disaster Interfaiths Network]
  https://n-din.org/wp-content/uploads/2021/08/12_NDIN_TS_DisasterDistressHelpline.pdf

- <u>Family Reunification and Support</u> web page provides a collection of resources and guidance documents. [ASPR]
  https://asprtracie.hhs.gov/technical-resources/64/family-reunification-and-support/0

- <u>Incidents of Mass Violence</u> web page provides information about those most at risk for emotional distress from incidents of mass violence and where to find disaster-related resources. [SAMHSA]
  https://www.samhsa.gov/find-help/disaster-distress-helpline/disaster-types/incidents-mass-violence

- <u>Language Access Planning</u> provides resources for those developing a language access program. [DOJ]
  https://www.lep.gov/language-access-planning

- <u>Mass Shooting Protocol and Playbook</u> discusses planning and responding to mass violence incidents from a city leadership perspective. [ICMA]
  https://icma.org/documents/mass-shooting-protocol-and-playbook-tabletop-exercise

- <u>Mass Violence and Terrorism Resources</u> web page includes resources to assist communities and government agencies in planning for and responding to victims of mass violence and terrorism. [OVC]
  https://www.ovcttac.gov/massviolence/?nm=sfa&ns=mvt&nt=resources

- <u>Mental Health: A Guide for Faith Leaders</u> provides information to help faith leaders work with members of their congregations and their families who are facing mental health challenges. [American Psychiatric Association Foundation]
  https://www.psychiatry.org/File%20Library/Psychiatrists/Cultural-Competency/faith-mentalhealth-guide.pdf

- <u>Remembering</u> web page provides resources around remembering tragic events as a community, anniversaries, and permanent memorials. [NMVVRC]
  https://nmvvrc.org/community-leaders/rebuild-your-community/remembering/

Critical Incident Review: Active Shooter at Robb Elementary School |
Appendix F. Trauma and Support Services Supplemental Materials

523

- Resource Guide for Uvalde, TX/Página de Recursos para Uvalde, TX provides resources to help the community and is available in both English and Spanish. [NMVVRC] https://nmvvrc.org/media/4xtjzna0/nmvvrc-resources-for-uvalde.pdf; https://nmvvrc.org/media/51mhs4iw/nmvvrc-resources-for-uvalde-spanish.pdf

- Stress First Aid: Manuals and Resources for Health Care Workers provides a framework to improve recovery from stress reactions, both in oneself and in coworkers. [VA] https://www.ptsd.va.gov/professional/treat/type/stress_first_aid.asp

- Supporting Resilience and Recovery in the Community web page describes ways the community and leadership can support community resilience. [NMVVRC] https://nmvvrc.org/community-leaders/rebuild-your-community/supporting-resilience-and-recovery-in-the-community/

- Transcend NMVC Mobile App was developed to assist those recovering from the psychological and behavioral response that can occur following direct or indirect exposure to mass violence incidents. The app provides information about common reactions to mass violence, crime, and other highly stressful events; guides the user through state-of-the-art self-help strategies to reduce the risk of stress-related behavioral health problems and promote recovery; and connects the user with victim/survivor services and financial, legal, and mental health resources. [NMVVRC] https://nmvvrc.org/survivors/transcend-nmvc/

- Unexpected Challenges for Communities in the Aftermath of a Mass Violence Incident covers some issues that many communities experiencing a mass violence incident say caught them by surprise and suggests solutions for how to manage them. [NMVVRC] https://nmvvrc.org/media/301cm3if/unexpected-challenges-for-communities.pdf

- Unexpected Challenges for Communities in the Recovery Phase of a Mass Violence Incident covers some issues that many communities experiencing a mass violence incident say caught them by surprise in the recovery phase and suggests solutions for how to manage them. [NMVVRC] https://nmvvrc.org/media/00tbio4n/tip-sheet-unexpected-challenges-for-communities-in-recovery-phase.pdf

Critical Incident Review: Active Shooter at Robb Elementary School |
Appendix F. Trauma and Support Services Supplemental Materials

524

Appendix G. Pre-Incident Planning and Preparation Supplemental Materials

The following section provides further context and information related to "Chapter 8. Pre-Incident Planning and Preparation."

Training Providers

Although not the primary focus of the CIR, it became apparent when the team reviewed training materials and observed training delivery methods that training providers, training content, and instructors are vastly different. It is essential that leadership from all agencies and organizations provide quality, vetted, and approved training to employees.

The Texas Commission on Law Enforcement (TCOLE) has 211 "Contract Training Providers" approved to teach TCOLE-approved courses to law enforcement in the state of Texas.[1348] Of those 211, 182 are law enforcement agencies (police departments, sheriffs' offices, training academies) and the balance of 29 are private companies or law enforcement associations (Texas Police Chiefs Association, etc.)

Of the 29 private companies, most have a broad range of courses they offer for TCOLE certification, while a few have specific focus areas they target for instruction (tactics-focused, leadership-focused, etc.). At least 3 of the 29 had course offerings in active shooter response for law enforcement. Additionally, a small number of these 29 private companies have established leadership structures defined on their websites, to include a "President/CEO/Executive Director" or equivalent, "Training Coordinators," and some sort of "Regional Representative." One in particular is run by a single individual with no identified law enforcement experience. This company hosts a central repository of training courses that can be taught across the state; one such course was delivered at UCISD PD.[1349]

[1348] TCOLE, "Training Providers."

[1349] CIR Fact Finding.

TCOLE lists requirements for Training Providers on their website to ensure course participants receive appropriate credit for attending the course, which must include the full lesson plan, learning objectives, instructor(s) biographies and areas of expertise, learning assessment instruments, and course/instructor evaluation.[1350] TCOLE has a curriculum review team embedded in their Training Committee and solicit subject matter experts to consult on this team. To do so, one must submit a letter of interest in the areas of desired instruction, obtain law enforcement agency chief approval, and provide a resume highlighting the desired instruction area and the person's expertise in this area.

More needs to be done to ensure that the highest quality training is being provided to law enforcement agencies across the state of Texas. The International Association of Directors of Law Enforcement Standards and Training (IADLEST) National Certification Program,[1351] which conducts a desk review to ensure the materials include sound learning objectives and practices, is a step in the right direction in ensuring that trainings meet professional standards.

As part of the training provider discussion, the instructors themselves need to be assessed. According to IADLEST, instructors should be evaluated and recertified every 2 years by the entity from which they were originally certified to ensure adherence to course curriculum and so that any modifications to course curriculum are adhered to.[1352]

[1350] TCOLE, "Training Providers."

[1351] IADLEST, "National Certification Program."

[1352] CIR Fact Finding.

About the Team

The Office of Community Oriented Policing Services (COPS Office) led the critical incident review with the support of a team of federal staff, subject matter experts, and other contractual support staff.

COPS Office Leadership Team

- Shanetta Y. Cutlar, Esq., Senior Counsel to the Director
- Robert E. Chapman, Deputy Director

COPS Office Project Management Team

- Nazmia E.A. Comrie, Senior Program Specialist
- George J. Fachner, Senior Program Specialist

Subject Matter Experts

- Rick Braziel, Chief of Police (ret.), Sacramento (California) Police Department
- Gene Deisinger, PhD, Deputy Chief of Police and Director, Threat Management Services (ret.), Virginia Tech (Virginia) Police Department
- Frank Fernandez, Director of Public Safety, Coral Gables, Florida; Deputy Chief (ret.), Miami (Florida) Police Department
- James "Jim" Golden, Deputy Chief (ret.) of School Operations and Chief Safety Executive, School District of Philadelphia
- Albert Guarnieri, Supervisory Special Agent, Federal Bureau of Investigation
- Mark Lomax, Major (ret.), Pennsylvania State Police
- Laura McElroy, Chief Executive Officer, McElroy Media Group
- John Mina, Sheriff, Orange County (Florida) Sheriff's Office
- April Naturale, PhD, Assistant Vice President, Vibrant Emotional Health
- Kristen Ziman, Chief (ret.), Aurora (Illinois) Police Department

Abbreviations and Acronyms

Acronym	Definition
AACR	animal-assisted crisis response
AAR	after action review
ADD	Avoid-Deny-Defend
ALERRT	Advanced Law Enforcement Rapid Response Training
ARC	American Red Cross
ASG	Associate Attorney General
ASPR	Administration for Strategic Preparedness and Response
ATF	Bureau of Alcohol, Tobacco, Firearms and Explosives
BJA	Bureau of Justice Assistance
BORSTAR	Border Patrol Search, Trauma, and Rescue
BORTAC	Border Patrol Tactical Unit
BPA	Border Patrol Agent
BWC	body-worn camera
CBP	U.S. Customs and Border Protection
CCP	casualty collection point
CCTV	closed-circuit television
CDC	Centers for Disease Control and Prevention
CDS	[Church of the Brethren] Children's Disaster Services
CEO	chief executive officer
CERC	Crisis and Emergency Risk Communications
CIR	Critical Incident Review
CIRS	Critical Incident Response Services (TXDPS)
CISM	critical incident stress management
CLEAT	Combined Law Enforcement Associations of Texas
COPS Office	Office of Community Oriented Policing Services
CVC	Crime Victims' Compensation [Program]
DA	district attorney
DBHS	Disaster Behavioral Health Services [Program]
DHS	Department of Homeland Security
DOJ	U.S. Department of Justice

Acronym	Definition
DPS	Department of Public Safety
EAP	Employee Assistance Program
EMC	Emergency management coordinator
EMI	Emergency Management Institute
EMS	emergency medical services
EMT	emergency medical technician
EOC	emergency operations center
EOP	Emergency Operations Plan
ER	emergency room
ERT	Evidence Response Team
FAC	Family Assistance Center
FBI	Federal Bureau of Investigation
FEMA	Federal Emergency Management Agency
FERPA	Family Educational Rights and Privacy Act
FOS	first on scene
FRC	Family Resiliency Center
HHS	[Texas Department of] Health and Human Services
HHSC	(Texas) Health and Human Services Commission
HSPD	Homeland Security Presidential Directive
IACP	International Association of Chiefs of Police
IADLEST	International Association of Directors of Law Enforcement Standards and Training
ICMA	International City/County Management Association
ICP	incident command post
ICS	Incident Command System
JIC	Joint Information Center
JIS	Joint Information System
L-CAN	Location, Conditions, Actions, Needs
LE	law enforcement
LEO	law enforcement officer
LEP	limited English proficiency
LSU	Louisiana State University
MAC Group	Multiagency Coordination Group
MARCH	massive hemorrhage, airway, respiration, circulation, and hypothermia
MCI	mass casualty incident

Acronym	Definition
MMHPI	Meadows Mental Health Policy Institute
MOA	memorandum of agreement
MOU	memorandum of understanding
MOVA	Massachusetts Office for Victim Assistance
MVAI	Mass Violence Advisory Initiative
NASP	National Association of School Psychologists
NCAVC	National Center for the Analysis of Violent Crime
NCF	National Compassion Fund
NCTSN	National Child Traumatic Stress Network
NEP	National Exercise Program
NFPA	National Fire Protection Association
NIMS	National Incident Management System
NMVVRC	National Mass Violence Victimization Resource Center
NQS	National Qualification System
NTOA	National Tactical Officers Association
NVFC	National Volunteer Fire Council
OEM	[Uvalde County] Office of Emergency Management
OPR	Office of Professional Responsibility
OVC	Office for Victims of Crime
PA	public announcement
PBIS·	positive behavior intervention supports
PFA	Psychological First Aid
PII	personally identifiable information
PIO	public information officer
PM-EMT	paramedic–emergency medical technician
POST	Peace Officer Standards and Training
PTSD	post-traumatic stress disorder
RTF	rescue task force
SAMHSA	Substance Abuse and Mental Health Services Administration
SBLE	school-based law enforcement
SBTA	School Behavioral Threat Assessment [policy]
SES	socioeconomic status
START	simple triage and rapid treatment
STRAC	Southwest Texas Regional Advisory Council

Acronym	Definition
SWAT	special weapons and tactics
SWTJC	Southwest Texas Junior College
TAG	Trauma and Grief [Center]
TCOLE	Texas Commission on Law Enforcement
TEA	Texas Education Agency
TGCT	Trauma and Grief Component Therapy
THREAT	Threat suppression, Hemorrhage control, Rapid Extrication to safety, Assessment by medical providers, and Transport to definitive care
TLEPN	Texas Law Enforcement Peer Network
TTAC	Training and Technical Assistance Center
TTX	multiagency tabletop exercises
TXDPS	Texas Department of Public Safety
TXSSC	Texas School Safety Center
UC	Unified Command
UCISD	Uvalde Consolidated Independent School District
UCISD PD	Uvalde Consolidated Independent School District Police Department
UCSO	Uvalde County Sheriff's Office
UEMS	Uvalde Emergency Medical Services
UMH	Uvalde Memorial Hospital
UPD	Uvalde Police Department
USMS	U.S. Marshals Service
UTRC	Uvalde Together Resiliency Center
VESS	Victim and Employee Support Services (TXDPS)
VOAD	Voluntary Organizations Active in Disaster
VOCA	Victims of Crime Act
VSD	Victim Services Division (FBI)
VSRT	Victim Services Response Team
ZCSO	Zavala County Sheriff's Office

Bibliography

"'Loving' Boy Last Texas School Shooting Victim Laid to Rest." KXXV, June 25, 2022. https://www.kxxv.com/news/texas-school-massacre-2022/loving-boy-last-texas-school-shooting-victim-laid-to-rest.

"'That Smile I Will Never Forget': The Victims of the Texas School Shooting" [Image]. *The Guardian,* May 29, 2022. https://www.theguardian.com/us-news/2022/may/25/uvalde-texas-school-shooting-victims.

"Alexandria 'Lexi' Aniyah Rubio Obituary." Rushi-Estes-Knowles Mortuary, 2022. https://www.rekfunerals.com/obituary/AlexandriaLexi-Rubio.

"Alithia Haven Ramirez Obituary." Rushing-Estes-Knowles Mortuary, June 2, 2022. https://www.rekfunerals.com/obituary/Alithia-Ramirez.

"Amerie Jo Garza Obituary." Hillcrest Memorial Funeral Home, 2022. https://www.hillcrestmemorialfuneralhome.com/obituaries/Amerie-Garza.

"As Uvalde Starts School Year, Mistrust Runs High." CBS News, September 6, 2022. https://www.cbsnews.com/news/uvalde-new-school-year-mistrust-high.

"As Uvalde Starts School, One Family Stops to Remember the Little Girl They Lost." *The Today Show,* September 7, 2022. https://www.today.com/parents/parents/uvalde-victims-family-remembers-jackie-cazares-school-starts-rcna46398.

"City of Uvalde Sues DA for 'Concealing Essential Law Enforcement Information.'" CBS Austin, December 1, 2022. https://cbsaustin.com/news/local/city-of-uvalde-sues-da-for-concealing-essential-law-enforcement-information.

"Disney Sends Family of Ellie Garcia a Gift; She Was Days Away from 10th Birthday Party." KENS 5, June 3, 2022. https://www.kens5.com/article/news/special-reports/uvalde-school-shooting/disney-sends-family-of-uvalde-victim-a-gift-she-was-days-away-from-big-birthday-party-news/273-bcb5dfcd-3633-42b6-bb62-8524fdb3be38.

"Eliahna Torres Obituary." Rushing-Estes-Knowles Mortuary, 2022. https://www.rekfunerals.com/obituary/Eliahna-Torres.

"Eliahna Torres." Legacy.com, May 27, 2022. https://www.legacy.com/us/obituaries/name/eliahna-torres-obituary?id=34954567.

"Eva Mireles Obituary." Rushing-Estes-Knowles Mortuary, 2022. https://www.rekfunerals.com/obituary/Eva-Mireles.

"First Interior Image Released in Uvalde School Shooting Shows Officers with More Firepower Than Previously Believed." KVUE, June 20, 2022. https://www.kvue.com/article/news/special-reports/uvalde-school-shooting/interior-images-uvalde-police/269-b1be96cb-aa8a-4edc-aa51-d4cbd41382f4.

"Gov. Abbott Announces DPS Security Measures for Uvalde ISD." KENS 5, August 30, 2022. https://www.kens5.com/article/news/local/gov-abbott-announces-dps-security-measures-for-uvalde-isd-mass-shooting-robb-elementary/273-0ac97491-05bb-4902-ae2a-294e6ae7cc48.

"Hernandez Nears End of Contract." *Uvalde Leader-News,* May 7, 2023. https://www.uvaldeleadernews.com/articles/hernandez-nears-end-of-contract.

"Husband of Teacher Killed at Robb Elementary Resigns from Uvalde CISD Police Department." KENS 5, November 21, 2022. https://www.kens5.com/article/news/special-reports/uvalde-school-shooting/husband-of-teacher-killed-robb-elementary-resigns-from-uvalde-cisd-police-department/273-55a94fcb-595b-4645-b876-b33adfe3e437.

"In Memoriam: 2022 Doodle for Google contestant Alithia Haven Ramirez, 10, 2012–2022." Doodle for Google. https://doodles.google.com/intl/en_us/d4g/honoringalithia.

"Irma Linda Garcia Obituary" [Image]. Rushing-Estes-Knowles Mortuary. https://www.rekfunerals.com/obituary/Irma-Garcia.

"Jailah Nicole Silguero Obituary." Hillcrest Memorial Funeral Home, 2022. https://www.hillcrestmemorialfuneralhome.com/obituaries/Jailah-Silguero/#!/TributeWall.

"Jailah Nicole Silguero." Find a Grave, June 3, 2022. https://www.findagrave.com/memorial/240030599/jailah-nicole-silguero.

"Jayce Carmelo Luevanos" [Image]. Find a Grave, June 3, 2022. https://www.findagrave.com/memorial/240018379/jayce-carmelo-luevanos/photo.

"Layla Marie Salazar Obituary." Rushing-Estes-Knowles Mortuary, 2022. https://www.rekfunerals.com/obituary/Layla-Salazar.

"Maite Yuleana Rodriguez Obituary." Rushing-Estes-Knowles Mortuary, 2022. https://www.rekfunerals.com/obituary/Maite-Rodriguez.

"Makenna Lee Elrod Obituary." Rushing-Estes-Knowles Mortuary, June 4, 2022. https://www.rekfunerals.com/obituary/Makenna-Elrod.

"Maranda Gail Mathis." Legacy.com, May 27, 2022. https://www.legacy.com/us/obituaries/name/maranda-mathis-obituary?id=34946641.

"May 26 Texas Shooting News." Last updated May 27, 2022. https://www.cnn.com/us/live-news/texas-elementary-school-shooting-05-26-22#h_95da3daf9c7951c6ddd986295fb158e8.

"Mayor of Uvalde Sits Down with CNN One Year after School Shooting." May 29, 2023. https://www.cnn.com/videos/us/2023/05/19/uvalde-texas-robb-shooting-actws-accountability-mclaughlin-sot-prokupecz-vpx.cnn.

"New Footage Shows Texas Officer Arrived at Uvalde School Earlier Than Previously Known." July 26, 2022. https://www.cnn.com/videos/us/2022/07/26/uvalde-video-police-response-report-earlier-newday-vpx.cnn.

"Remembering Jacklyn Cazares as a Free Spirit and Always Wanting to Help Others." KENS 5, June 2, 2022. https://www.youtube.com/watch?v=ibwtL0fXV2k.

"Rojelio Fernandez Torres Obituary." Rushing-Estes-Knowles Mortuary, 2022. https://www.rekfunerals.com/obituary/Rojelio-Torres.

"Rojelio Fernandez Torres." Legacy.com, May 28, 2022. https://www.legacy.com/us/obituaries/name/rojelio-torres-obituary?id=34958659.

"SALT Mass Casualty Triage: Concept Endorsed by the American College of Emergency Physicians, American College of Surgeons Committee on Trauma, American Trauma Society, National Association of EMS Physicians, National Disaster Life Support Education Consortium, and State and Territorial Injury Prevention Directors Association." *Disaster Medicine and Public Health Preparedness* 2, no. 4 (2008): 245-246. https://doi.org/10.1097/DMP.0b013e31818d191e.

"Sample Municipal Resolution Adopting NIMS." *Commonwealth of Pennsylvania National Incident Management Implementation Strategy: 2022–2027*, 56. Harrisburg: Pennsylvania Emergency Management Agency, 2022. https://www.pema.pa.gov/Preparedness/NIMS/Pages/default.aspx.

"Surviving Uvalde." The Whole Story with Anderson Cooper. Podcast. May 22, 2023. https://www.cnn.com/audio/podcasts/the-whole-story-with-anderson-cooper/episodes/a714eda3-f1b7-404e-a316-b00800aa9fa4.

"Texas Artists Honor Uvalde Victims with Murals." *The Kelly Clarkson Show*, September 13, 2022. https://www.youtube.com/watch?v=pE1Q_GuQwZQ%29+.

"Texas Gov. Greg Abbott's Statement about Robb Elementary School Shooting in Uvalde on May 24, 2022." KSAT 12, May 24, 2022. https://youtu.be/pjf3VoBiNYk.

"Texas Ranger Suspended Amid Investigation into Uvalde Response." KENS 5, July 5, 2022. https://www.kens5.com/article/news/local/texas/uvalde-shooting-robb-elementary-school-texas-ranger-investigation-dps/273-19d06e62-2a2b-46c6-bf47-0ac6a84254d8.

"Texas Rangers Turns Over Initial Report on Uvalde Shooting to DA." KVUE, January 5, 2023. https://www.kvue.com/video/news/special-reports/uvalde-school-shooting/texas-rangers-turns-over-initial-report-on-uvalde-shooting-to-da/269-2dc17e42-b4c4-40db_8b99_c7ea0577e313.

"Texas School Shooting Victims: Third and Fourth Graders, Beloved Teachers." NBC 5 Dallas–Fort Worth. Last modified May 31, 2022. https://www.nbcdfw.com/news/local/texas-news/uvalde-texas-school-shooting-names-of-victims-begin-to-release/2976993/.

"Two Uvalde CISD Police Officers Leave Department." KSAT 12, February 2, 2023. https://www.ksat.com/video/news/2023/02/02/two-uvalde-cisd-police-officers-leave-department.

"Uvalde District Attorney Gives Update on Investigation into Robb Elementary Mass Shooting." News 4 San Antonio. Last modified May 25, 2023. https://news4sanantonio.com/news/local/uvalde-district-attorney-gives-update-on-investigation-into-robb-elementary-mass-shooting-students-teachers-mayor-rangers-texas-criminal-grand-jury-accountable.

"Uvalde Report Translated to Spanish by USA TODAY Network Journalists." *USA Today,* July 28, 2022. https://www.usatoday.com/videos/opinion/2022/07/28/uvalde-report-translated-spanish-usa-today-network-journalists/10172512002.

"Uvalde School Mass Shooting: What We Know about the Victims." KHOU, May 25, 2022. https://www.khou.com/article/news/local/texas/uvalde-school-shooting-victims/285-496f26a0-7b05-4bcf-9ec6-4c125db8a951.

"Uvalde School Shooting: Call Logs Released between Gov. Abbott, Texas DPS Director." Fox 7 Austin, November 7, 2022. https://www.fox7austin.com/news/uvalde-school-shooting-gov-abbott-texas-dps-director.

"Uvalde Victim's Dream of Sharing Art Comes True." Beeville Art Museum, August 30, 2022. https://www.prnewswire.com/news-releases/uvalde-victims-dream-of-sharing-art-comes-true-301612757.html.

"Uvalde Voters Support Abbott, Suspended Interim Police Chief in Wake of Scrutiny over Robb Massacre." KSAT 12, November 9, 2022. https://www.ksat.com/vote-2022/2022/11/09/uvalde-voters-support-abbott-suspended-interim-police-chief-in-wake-of-scrutiny-over-robb-massacre.

"Uziyah Sergio Garcia Obituary." Gutierrez Funeral Home, 2022. https://www.gutierrezfuneralchapels.com/obituary/Uziyah-Garcia.

"Victim's Father Confronts Uvalde Mayor Over Why He Was Kicked Out of Meeting." July 17, 2022. https://www.cnn.com/videos/us/2022/07/17/father-of-uvalde-victim-confronts-mayor-flores-nr-vpx.cnn.

"Victims of the Texas School Shooting." Reuters, May 26, 2022. https://www.reuters.com/news/picture/victims-of-the-texas-school-shooting-idUSRTS85J5H.

"What to Know about the Allen, Texas, Mall Shooting." *The New York Times*, May 7, 2023. https://www.nytimes.com/article/texas-mall-shooting-allen.html.

"What We Know about the Victims of the Uvalde Shooting." *The New York Times,* June 16, 2022. https://www.nytimes.com/article/uvalde-shooting-victims.html.

"Young Uvalde Victim's Art Displayed in Texas and Paris, Fulfilling Her Stolen Dream." *The Today Show*, September 21, 2022. https://www.today.com/parents/moms/uvalde-victim-alithia-ramirez-art-texas-paris-museums-rcna47352.

1 October: After-Action Review. Las Vegas, NV: Las Vegas Metropolitan Police Department, 2019. https://www.lvmpd.com/en-us/Documents/1_October_AAR_Final_06062019.pdf.

10 U.S.C. § 892 Art. 92, Failure to obey order or regulation (1956). https://www.govinfo.gov/content/pkg/USCODE-2022-title10/html/USCODE-2022-title10-subtitleA-partII-chap47-subchapX-sec892.htm.

42 U.S.C. § 5121, Robert T. Stafford Disaster Relief and Emergency Assistance Act (1974), as amended. https://www.govinfo.gov/content/pkg/USCODE-2021-title42/html/USCODE-2021-title42-chap68-subchapI-sec5121.htm.

Administration for Strategic Preparedness and Response; Technical Resources, Assistance Center, and Information Exchange. *Mass Violence/Active Shooter Incidents: EMS Considerations.* Tip Sheet. Washington, DC: U.S. Department of Health and Human Services, 2022. https://asprtracie.hhs.gov/mass-violence#mass-violence-active-shooter-incident-tip-sheets.

Administration for Strategic Preparedness and Response; Technical Resources, Assistance Center, and Information Exchange. *Mass Casualty Trauma Triage: Paradigms and Pitfalls.* Washington, DC: U.S. Department of Health and Human Services, 2019. https://asprtracie.hhs.gov/technical-resources/resource/7082/mass-casualty-trauma-triage-paradigms-and-pitfalls.

ALERRT (Advanced Law Enforcement Rapid Response Training Center). *Active Shooter Response Level 1 Version 7.2*. San Marcos, TX: Texas State University, 2020.

ALERRT (Advanced Law Enforcement Rapid Response Training Center). *Robb Elementary School Attack Response Assessment and Recommendations.* San Marcos, TX: Texas State University, 2022. https://alerrt.org/reading.

Alfonseca, Kiara, and Ismael Estrada. "Mother of Uvalde Victim Speaks out for 1st Time." ABC News, August 3, 2022. https://abcnews.go.com/US/mother-uvalde-victim-speaks-1st-time/story?id=87824941.

Alfonseca, Kiara, and Nicolas Rothenberg. "Uvalde Shooting Victim Alithia Haven Ramirez Honored with Google Doodle." ABC News, July 22, 2022. https://abcnews.go.com/Technology/uvalde-shooting-victim-alithia-haven-ramirez-honored-google/story?id=87242430.

Alfonseca, Kiara. *Uvalde in Focus: The Kids of Robb Elementary*. ABC News. Accessed August 8, 2023. https://abcnews.go.com/immersive/uvalde?id=90972980.

Allen, Hugh. "Uvalde School District Officials Hold Press Conference 6/09/22 Transcript." Rev. Last modified June 9, 2022. https://www.rev.com/blog/transcripts/uvalde-school-district-officials-hold-press-conference-6-09-22-transcript.

Alliance of Therapy Dogs. "Therapy Dog Certification." Last modified March 23, 2017. https://www.therapydogs.com/therapy-dog-certification.

Alsharif, Mirna. "Inspector Posing as Intruder Slips into Uvalde School during Safety Audit, Superintendent Says." NBC News, December 20, 2022. https://www.nbcnews.com/news/us-news/inspector-posing-intruder-slips-uvalde-school-safety-audit-superintend-rcna62573.

Alvarado, Caroll. "10-Year-Old Shooting Victim Rojelio Torres Was an 'Intelligent, Hardworking and Helpful Person,' His Aunt Says." CNN, May 27, 2022. https://www.cnn.com/us/live-news/texas-elementary-school-shooting-05-27-22/h_f834f699ca617a40e823722b28e48555.

American Humane, *Definition of a Service Dog vs. Emotional Support Animal vs. Therapy Dog*. Washington, DC: American Humane, 2018. https://www.americanhumane.org/initiative/service-dogs-what-you-need-to-know.

Anderson, Nick, Moriah Balingit, Marissa J. Lang, and Ian Shapira. "For Five Years, They Were Co-Teachers. Then They Were Gunned Down." *The Washington Post,* May 25, 2022. https://www.washingtonpost.com/education/2022/05/25/uvalde-teachers-garcia-mireles.

Andreano, Caterina, et al. "Remembering the Victims of the Uvalde School Shooting." *Good Morning America,* April 8, 2022. https://www.goodmorningamerica.com/news/story/remembering-victims-uvalde-school-shooting-85621161.

Aronie, Jonathan, and Christy E. Lopez. "Keeping Each Other Safe: An Assessment of the Use of Peer Intervention Programs to Prevent Police Officer Mistakes and Misconduct, Using New Orleans' EPIC Program as a Potential National Model." *Police Quarterly* 20, no. 3 (2017). https://doi.org/10.1177/1098611117710443.

ATF (Bureau of Alcohol, Tobacco, Firearms and Explosives). "Benefits for Federal Employees." Last modified February 8, 2023.

Atkins, Campbell. "Program Deploys to Uvalde to Provide Support." *Today @Sam*, July 6, 2022. Sam Houston State University. https://www.shsu.edu/today@sam/T@S/article/2022/program-uvalde-support.

ATLS: Advanced Trauma Life Support for Doctors (Student Course Manual), Eighth Edition. Chicago: American College of Surgeons, 2008.

Ball, Andrea. "'They're So Young:' A Grandfather in Uvalde, Texas, Mourns 10-Year-Old Jayce Luevanos." *USA Today,* May 25, 2022. https://www.msn.com/en-us/news/us/they-re-so-young-a-grandfather-mourns-10-year-old-jayce-luevanos-among-the-victims/ar-AAXJra2.

Banks, Duren, Joshua Hendrix, Matthew Hickman, and Tracey Kyckelhahn. "National Sources of Law Enforcement Employment Data." Washington, DC: Bureau of Justice Statistics, 2016. https://bjs.ojp.gov/content/pub/pdf/nsleed.pdf.

Barragan, James, and Zach Despart. "Chief Pete Arredondo Defends Police Response to Uvalde School Shooting." *The Texas Tribune,* June 9, 2022. https://www.texastribune.org/2022/06/09/uvalde-chief-pete-arredondo-interview.

Barragan, James. "House Speaker Dade Phelan Announces Legislative Committee to Investigate Uvalde Shooting." *The Texas Tribune*, June 3, 2022. https://www.texastribune.org/2022/06/03/uvalde-texas-house-investigative-committee.

Basic Emergency Management Plan for Uvalde County, City of Uvalde, and the City of Sabinal, Ver 1.10, 2021–22. Uvalde, Texas: Uvalde County, 2021.

Bennett, Adam. "Uvalde Mayor on Release of Video Showing Response to Shooting." KHOU, July 13, 2022. https://www.khou.com/article/news/special-reports/uvalde-school-shooting/uvalde-community-reacts-hallway-video-robb-elementary-mass-shooting/285-d65d4386-bd64-46f9-940c-f77d13734d10.

BJA (Bureau of Justice Assistance). "Bureau of Justice Assistance National Training and Technical Assistance Center." Accessed December 5, 2023.

Bleiberg, Jake, and Paul Weber. "Texas State Police Launch Internal Review of Uvalde Response." Associated Press, July 19, 2022. https://apnews.com/article/police-shootings-texas-education-a3cab77498a8e9b97ea7d331c1aa5e5d.

Bloom, Adam, Lokesh Reddy, and Eli Kleinman. "Trauma Debrief Prior to Release of Body-Worn Camera Footage." *FBI Law Enforcement Bulletin*, July 11, 2023. https://leb.fbi.gov/articles/featured-articles/trauma-debrief-prior-to-release-of-body-worn-camera-footage.

Braziel, Rick, Frank Straub, George Watson, and Rod Hoops. *Bringing Calm to Chaos: A Critical Incident Review of the San Bernardino Public Safety Response to the December 2, 2015, Terrorist Shooting Incident at the Inland Regional Center*. Washington, DC: Office of Community Oriented Policing Services, 2016. https://portal.cops.usdoj.gov/resourcecenter?item=cops-w0808.

Brinsfield, Kathryn H., and Ernest Mitchell Jr. "The Department of Homeland Security's Role in Enhancing and Implementing the Response to Active Shooter and Intentional Mass Casualty Events." In *Strategies to Enhance Survival in Active Shooter and Intentional Mass Casualty Events: A Compendium*, supplement to the *Bulletin of the American College of Surgeons* 100, no. 1S (2015): 24–27. https://www.stopthebleed.org/media/0svpk45s/hartford_consensus_compendium.pdf.

Briones, Sofia. "Eliahna Amyah Garcia, a Sweet Girl with a Beautiful Soul, Dies at 9." NOWCastSA, 2022. https://nowcastsa.com/obituary/eliahna-amyah-garcia.

Briones, Sofia. "Jose Manuel Flores, Jr., a Baseball Player Who Loved Video Games, Dies at 10."
    NOWCastSA, 2022. https://nowcastsa.com/obituary/jose-manuel-flores-jr.

Briones, Sofia. "Makenna Lee Elrod, a Bright and Caring Natural Born Leader, Dies at 10." NOWCastSA,
    2022. https://nowcastsa.com/obituary/makenna-lee-elrod.

Briones, Sofia. "Maranda Gail Mathis, a Kind Student with a Love for Mermaids, Dies at 11." NowCastSA,
    May 2022. https://nowcastsa.com/obituary/maranda-gail-mathis.

Briones, Sofia. "Nevaeh Alyssa Bravo, an Uvalde Student Who Loved Her Family, Dies at 10."
    NOWCastSA, 2022. https://nowcastsa.com/obituary/nevaeh-alyssa-bravo.

Briones, Sofia. "Tess Marie Mata, an Introverted and Charismatic Girl Who Was Saving Up for a Trip
    to Disney World, Dies at 10." NowCastSA, May 2022.
    https://nowcastsa.com/obituary/tess-marie-mata.

Brooks, David B. *2021 Guide to Texas Laws for County Officials*. Austin, TX: Texas Association of
    Counties, 2021.
    https://www.county.org/TAC/media/TACMedia/Legal/Legal%20Publications%20Documents/2021/2
    021-Guide-to-Laws-for-County-Officials.pdf.

Buch, Jason. "State Police Terminate Another Officer for Response to Uvalde Mass Shooting."
    The Texas Tribune, January 6, 2023,
    https://www.texastribune.org/2023/01/06/texas-ranger-uvalde-shooting-criminal-cases-kindell.

Cabral, Marika, Bokyung Kim, Maya Rossin-Slater, Molly Schnell, and Hannes Schwandt. *Trauma at
    School: The Impacts of Shootings on Students' Human Capital and Economic Outcomes.* Working
    Paper 28311. Revised edition. Cambridge, MA: National Bureau of Economic Research, 2022.
    https://doi.org/10.3386/w28311.

Campoamor, Danielle. "Brett Cross, Dad Of Uvalde Shooting Victim, Protests At District." *The Today
    Show,* October 6, 2022. https://www.today.com/parents/dads/brett-cross-dad-uvalde-shooting-
    victim-protests-district-rcna51033.

Campoamor, Danielle. "Texas Schools Send Parents DNA Kits to Identify Their Kids' Bodies in
    Emergencies." *The Today Show,* October 18, 2022. https://www.today.com/parents/family/texas-
    parents-schools-dna-kits-identify-kids-bodies-rcna52769.

Carey, Bill. "New Uvalde Assistant Chief Looks Forward to Repairing Relationship between Community
    and Officers." Police1. Last modified April 24, 2022. https://www.police1.com/chiefs-
    sheriffs/articles/new-uvalde-assistant-chief-looks-forward-to-repairing-relationship-between-
    community-and-officers-ksDdbGiX2q8w5FFc.

Carlson, Shonna. "Why Prosecutors Need to Understand the Impact of Trauma." *The Crime Report,* March 20, 2020. https://thecrimereport.org/2020/03/20/why-prosecutors-need-to-understand-the-impact-of-trauma.

Carpenter, Michael. "Put It in Writing." *FBI Law Enforcement Bulletin* 69, no. 10 (2000): 1–9. https://leb.fbi.gov/file-repository/archives/oct00leb.pdf/view.

CBP (U.S. Customs and Border Protection). "Employee Assistance Program (EAP)." Last modified July 13, 2023. https://www.cbp.gov/employee-resources/family/employee-assistance-program.

CDC (Centers for Disease Control and Prevention). "Adverse Childhood Experiences (ACEs)." Violence Prevention. Last modified June 29, 2023. https://www.cdc.gov/violenceprevention/aces/index.html#print.

CDC (Centers for Disease Control and Prevention). "CERC Manual." Emergency Preparedness and Response. Last modified January 23, 2018.

CDC (Centers for Disease Control and Prevention). "Training." Emergency Preparedness and Response. Last modified January 23, 2018.

Center for the Study of Traumatic Stress. *Leadership Communication: Anticipating and Responding to Stressful Events.* Bethesda, MD: Uniformed Services University, n.d. https://www.cstsonline.net/resources/resource-master-list/leadership-communication-anticipating-responding-stressful-events.

Centers for Disease Control and Prevention. "Hospital Employees' Health." Workplace Health Promotion. Last updated May 28, 2020. https://www.cdc.gov/workplacehealthpromotion/features/hospital-employees-health.html.

Chappell, Bill, Joe Hernandez, and Rachel Treisman. "What We Know about the Victims of the Uvalde School Shooting." WUSF Public Media, May 31, 2022. https://wusfnews.wusf.usf.edu/2022-05-27/what-we-know-about-the-victims-of-the-uvalde-school-shooting.

Chemical Hazards Emergency Medical Management. "SALT Mass Casualty Triage Algorithm (Sort, Assess, Lifesaving Interventions, Treatment/Transport)." U.S. Department of Health and Human Services. Last modified September 5, 2023. https://chemm.hhs.gov/salttriage.htm.

Chow, Shern-Min. "Texas Police Chiefs Association Responds to Uvalde Shooting Video." KHOU, July 13, 2022. https://www.khou.com/article/news/special-reports/uvalde-school-shooting/texas-police-chiefs-association-president-reacts-to-uvalde-shooting-video/285-c62b2d54-bab6-4709-b90c-2f211e897a0f.

Christenson, Sig, and Claire Bryan. "School Trustee Rushed to Robb Elementary; Now Victims' Families Want Him Booted from Board." *San Antonio Express-News,* October 30, 2022. https://www.expressnews.com/news/local/article/Jesus-Suarez-board-member-17542540.php.

Chute, Nate. "Police Boasted of Heroism after Uvalde Parents Begged for Rescue of Their Children amid School Shooting." *Austin American-Statesman,* September 15, 2022. https://www.statesman.com/videos/news/2022/09/15/uvalde-shooting-parents-children-police-false/8034139001.

Cieciura, Jack. "A Summary of the Bystander Effect: Historical Development and Relevance in the Digital Age." *Inquiries Journal* 8, no. 11 (2016): 1. http://www.inquiriesjournal.com/a?id=1493.

Cohen, Miles. "'I'm not ready': 2 Uvalde Victims Who Texted 'I love you' to Be Buried Next to One Another." *Good Morning America,* June 8, 2022. https://www.goodmorningamerica.com/news/story/im-ready-uvalde-victims-texted-love-buried-85208670.

Cole, Allysa, and Ben Spicer. "Uvalde City Council Approves Updated Memorandum between Police Department, Uvalde CISD." KSAT, March 15, 2023. https://www.ksat.com/news/local/2023/03/15/uvalde-city-council-approves-updated-memorandum-between-police-department-uvalde-cisd.

Collier, Dillon. "Families of Uvalde Shooting Victims Ask Court to Force DPS to Release Records." KSAT, March 15, 2023. https://www.ksat.com/news/local/2023/03/15/families-of-uvalde-shooting-victims-ask-court-to-force-dps-to-release-records.

Collier, Dillon. "Records Detail Secret Council Swearing-In of Uvalde CISD Chief Pete Arredondo." KSAT, June 17, 2022. https://www.ksat.com/news/defenders/2022/06/17/records-detail-secret-council-swearing-in-of-uvalde-cisd-chief.

Combined Law Enforcement Associations of Texas. "Response to Uvalde Mass Shooting." News release, May 31, 2022. https://www.cleat.org/cleat-response-to-uvalde-mass-shooting.

Communicating in a Crisis: Risk Communication Guidelines for Public Officials. Rockville, MD: Substance Abuse and Mental Health Services Administration, 2019.

Contreras, Guillermo. "A 15-Year-Old German Girl Knew the Uvalde Shooter's Plan. She Was Prosecuted for Her Inaction." *San Antonio Express-News,* May 24, 2023. https://www.expressnews.com/news/article/german-teen-uvalde-18116721.php.

COPS Office (Office of Community Oriented Policing Services). "Collaborative Reform Initiative Technical Assistance Center." Accessed December 5, 2023. https://cops.usdoj.gov/cri-tac.

COPS Office (Office of Community Oriented Policing Services). "Law Enforcement Mental Health and Wellness Act (LEMHWA) Program Resources." Accessed December 6, 2023. https://cops.usdoj.gov/lemhwaresources.

COPS Office (Office of Community Oriented Policing Services). "Law Enforcement Agency (LEA) Accreditation." Accessed December 5, 2023. https://cops.usdoj.gov/LEA_accreditation.

COPS Office (Office of Community Oriented Policing Services). "Overcoming Language Barriers in Policing and Building an Effective Language Access Program." https://copstrainingportal.org/project/overcoming-language-barriers-in-policing.

COPS Office (Office of Community Oriented Policing Services). *Guiding Principles for School Resource Officer Programs*. Washington, DC: Office of Community Oriented Policing Services, 2022. https://portal.cops.usdoj.gov/resourcecenter?item=cops-p460.

Cornyn, John. *Opinion No. JC-0125 Re: Authority of County to Provide Law Enforcement Services in a Municipality within its Boundaries*. Office of the Attorney General, State of Texas, October 13, 1999. https://www.texasattorneygeneral.gov/opinions/john-cornyn/jc-0125.

Courts, Jenny Wagnon. "Texas DPS Releases Video of Altercation with Uvalde Victim's Mother." ABC7 Eyewitness News, April 7, 2023. https://abc7chicago.com/texas-dps-releases-video-of-altercation-with-uvalde-victims-mother/13096309.

Covucci, David. "Uvalde Cop Seen with Punisher Lock Screen Goes Viral." *Daily Dot*, July 14, 2022. https://www.dailydot.com/debug/uvalde-police-punisher.

Cowen, Tracie William. "Mother Who Was Cuffed by Marshals Amid Response to Uvalde School Shooting Speaks Out as New Details Emerge." *Complex*, June 2, 2022. https://amp.www.complex.com/life/mother-cuffed-by-marshals-amid-uvalde-shooting-response-speaks-out-new-details-emerge.

Craig, Matthew, and Leigh Waldman. "Scholarship Honors the Life of Robb Elementary Victim Tess Mata." KSAT, February 6, 2023. https://www.ksat.com/news/local/2023/02/07/scholarship-honors-the-life-of-robb-elementary-victim-tess-mata.

C-SPAN. "Governor Abbot News Conference on School Shooting in Uvalde, Texas." Last modified May 25, 2022. https://www.c-span.org/video/?520589-1/governor-abbott-news-conference-school-shooting-uvalde-texas.

Cybersecurity and Infrastructure Security Agency. *National Emergency Communications Plan*. Washington, DC: U.S. Department of Homeland Security, 2019. https://www.cisa.gov/national-emergency-communications-plan.

Danieli, Yael, Fran H. Norris, and Brian Engdahl. "Multigenerational Legacies of Trauma: Modeling the What and How of Transmission." *American Journal of Orthopsychiatry* 86, no. 6 (2016): 639–651. https://psycnet.apa.org/record/2016-02082-001.

Danieli, Yael, Fran H. Norris, Jutta Lindert, Vera Paisner, Brian Engdahl, and Júlia Richter. "The Danieli Inventory of Multigenerational Legacies of Trauma, Part I: Survivors' Posttrauma Adaptational Styles in their Children's Eyes." *Journal of Psychiatric Research* 68 (September 2015): 167–175. https://www.researchgate.net/publication/279070329 The Danieli Inventory of Multigenerational Legacies of Trauma Part I Survivors' Posttrauma Adaptational Styles in their Children's Eyes.

Dart Center for Journalism & Trauma. "Resources for Covering Mass Shootings." Last modified March 15, 2019. https://dartcenter.org/resources/resources-covering-mass-shootings.

DeAngelis, Tori. "The Legacy of Trauma: An Emerging Line of Research is Exploring how Historical and Cultural Trauma Affect Survivors' Children for Generations to Come." *Monitor on Psychology* 50, no. 2 (2019): 36. https://www.apa.org/monitor/2019/02/legacy-trauma.

Despart, Zach, Lomi Kriel, Alejandro Serrano, Joyce Sohyun Lee, Arelis R. Hernandez, Sarah Cahlan, Imogen Piper, and Uriel J. Garcia. "Uvalde Shooting Victims' Care Was Delayed by Medical Response." *The Texas Tribune*, December 20, 2022. https://www.texastribune.org/2022/12/20/uvalde-medical-response.

Despart, Zach, William Melhado, and Lomi Kriel. "Texas State Trooper Who Responded to Uvalde Shooting Fired Amid Investigations into Police Response." *San Antonio Current,* October 22, 2022. https://www.sacurrent.com/news/texas-state-trooper-who-responded-to-uvalde-shooting-fired-amid-investigations-into-police-response-30150004.

DeWolfe, Deborah J. *Training Manual for Mental Health and Human Service Workers in Major Disasters.* Second Edition. Rockville, MD: Substance Abuse and Mental Health Services Administration, 2000. https://eric.ed.gov/?id=ED459383.

Dey, Sneha, et al. "21 Lives Lost: Uvalde Victims Were a Cross-Section of a Small, Mostly Latino town in South Texas." *The Texas Tribune,* May 27, 2022. https://www.texastribune.org/2022/05/25/uvalde-school-shooting-victims/#d37e262a-fa08-4bc1-b639-784afe9900cb.

DHS (U.S. Department of Homeland Security). *Law Enforcement Active Shooter Emergency Response Version 3.1: Instructor Guide.* Washington, DC: U.S. Department of Homeland Security, 2019.

Diagnostic and Statistical Manual of Mental Disorders, Fifth Edition (DSM-5). Washington, DC: American Psychiatric Association, 2013.

DOJ (U.S. Department of Justice). "2015 Language Map App." Accessed August 3, 2023. https://www.lep.gov/maps/lma2015/Final_508.

DOJ (U.S. Department of Justice). "Readout of Associate Attorney General Vanita Gupta's Meeting with Uvalde Families." Press release, April 26, 2023. https://www.justice.gov/opa/pr/readout-associate-attorney-general-vanita-gupta-s-meeting-uvalde-families.

Draper, John, Gerald McCleery, and Richard Schaedle. "Mental Health Services Support in Response to September 11th: The Central Role of the Mental Health Association of New York City." In *9/11: Mental Health in the Wake of Terrorist Attacks*, edited by Yuval Neria, Raz Gross, and Randall D. Marshall, 282–310. New York: Cambridge University Press, 2006.

Dunmore, Emma, David M. Clark, and Anke Ehlers. "A Prospective Investigation of the Role of Cognitive Factors in Persistent Posttraumatic Stress Disorder (PTSD) after Physical or Sexual Assault." *Behavioral Research and Therapy* 39, no. 9 (2001): 1063–1084. https://doi.org/10.1016/S0005-7967(00)00088-7.

Eaton-Stull, Yvonne. "Mental Health Monitor: Animal-Assisted Crisis Response." *Social Work Today* 16, no. 5 (2016): 32. https://www.socialworktoday.com/archive/092116p32.shtml.

Elkins, Faye. "Prepare Today for What Can Happen Tomorrow: Coordinated Active Attack Training for All First Responders." *Community Policing Dispatch* 11, no. 6 (2018). https://cops.usdoj.gov/html/dispatch/06-2018/airr_prepare.html.

Esquivel, Ruben. "Artist's Statement." National Museum of the American Latino, 2022. https://latino.si.edu/exhibitions/healing-uvalde/twenty-one-healing-uvalde-murals/jayce-carmelo-luevanos.

Estrada, Ismael, Jenny Wagnon Courts, and Lucien Bruggeman. "Abbott Meeting with Uvalde Victims, Families Under Scrutiny." ABC News, August 13, 2022. https://abcnews.go.com/US/texas-gov-abbott-meets-uvalde-victims-amid-scrutiny/story?id=88339909.

Everly Jr., George S., and O. Joseph Bienvenu. "'Profiling' School Shooters: Can we tell who will be the next to kill?" *Psychology Today.* Last modified March 29, 2018. https://www.psychologytoday.com/us/blog/when-disaster-strikes-inside-disaster-psychology/201803/profiling-school-shooters.

Everytown for Gun Safety Support Fund. "The Impact of Active Shooter Drills in Schools." Last modified February 20, 2023. https://everytownresearch.org/report/the-impact-of-active-shooter-drills-in-schools.

FBI (Federal Bureau of Investigation). "Finding Solace: FBI Crisis Response Canines Help Victims Cope with Tragedy." Last modified July 15, 2016.

FBI (Federal Bureau of Investigation). "In the Aftermath." YouTube, October 7, 2020. https://www.youtube.com/watch?v=3sKyH68L7OE.

FBI (Federal Bureau of Investigation). "Investigative Programs Critical Incident Response Group: National Center for the Analysis of Violent Crime." Accessed March 19, 2023.

FBI (Federal Bureau of Investigation). "We Regret to Inform You. . . Impact Video." Accessed August 11, 2023. https://www.fbi.gov/video-repository/newss-we-regret-to-inform-you-impact-video/view.

FBI (Federal Bureau of Investigation). *Active Shooter Incidents in the United States in 2021*. Washington, DC: U.S. Department of Justice, 2022. https://www.fbi.gov/file-repository/active-shooter-incidents-in-the-us-2021-052422.pdf/view.

FBI (Federal Bureau of Investigation). *Active Shooter Incidents: 20-Year Review 2000–2019*. Washington, DC: U.S. Department of Justice, 2021. https://www.fbi.gov/file-repository/active-shooter-incidents-20-year-review-2000-2019-060121.pdf/view.

Federspill, Melissa. "UCISD Not Pursuing JPPI Review." *Uvalde Leader-News,* February 5, 2023. https://www.uvaldeleadernews.com/articles/ucisd-not-pursuing-jppi-review.

FEMA (Federal Emergency Management Agency). "About the National Exercise Program." Last modified May 3, 2023.

FEMA (Federal Emergency Management Agency). "Active Shooter | Run (Evacuate): Avoid Shooter." Accessed August 8, 2023. https://community.fema.gov/ProtectiveActions/s/article/Active-Shooter-Run-Evacuate-Avoid-Shooter.

FEMA (Federal Emergency Management Agency). "Command and Coordination." Accessed December 4, 2023.

FEMA (Federal Emergency Management Agency). "Community Recovery Management Toolkit." Last modified February 10, 2023. https://www.fema.gov/emergency-managers/practitioners/recovery-resources/community-toolkit.

FEMA (Federal Emergency Management Agency). "Emergency Management Institute | EMI Courses & Schedules." Last updated December 29, 2021.

FEMA (Federal Emergency Management Agency). "Emergency Management Institute | ICS Resource Center." Accessed August 3, 2023.

FEMA (Federal Emergency Management Agency). "Homeland Security Exercise and Evaluation Program." Last modified August 2, 2023.

FEMA (Federal Emergency Management Agency). "National Incident Management System." Last modified July 14, 2023. https://www.fema.gov/emergency-managers/nims.

FEMA (Federal Emergency Management Agency). "Public Information Awareness and Basics." Accessed December 5, 2023.

FEMA (Federal Emergency Management Agency). "Public Information Officer Advanced Level." Accessed December 5, 2023.

FEMA (Federal Emergency Management Agency). *Developing and Maintaining Emergency Operations Plans.* Washington, DC: U.S. Department of Homeland Security, 2021.

FEMA (Federal Emergency Management Agency). *Local and Elected Appointed Officials Guide: Roles and Resources in Emergency Management*. Washington, DC: U.S. Department of Homeland Security, 2022. https://www.fema.gov/event/fema-releases-local-elected-and-appointed-officials-guide-roles-and-resources-emergency.

FEMA (Federal Emergency Management Agency). *National Incident Management System: Third Edition*. Washington, DC: U.S. Department of Homeland Security, 2017. https://www.fema.gov/sites/default/files/2020-07/fema_nims_doctrine-2017.pdf.

FEMA (Federal Emergency Management Agency). *National Incident Management System Guidance for Public Information Officers*. Washington, DC: U.S. Department of Homeland Security, 2020.

FEMA (Federal Emergency Management Agency). *National Incident Management System Guideline for Mutual Aid*. Washington, DC: U.S. Department of Homeland Security, 2017.

FEMA (Federal Emergency Management Agency). *National Incident Management System Guideline for the National Qualification System*. Washington, DC: U.S. Department of Homeland Security, 2017.

FEMA (Federal Emergency Management Agency). *National Incident Management System Training Program: Summer 2020*. Washington, DC: U.S. Department of Homeland Security, 2020.

FEMA (Federal Emergency Management Agency). *NIMS Implementation Objectives for Local, State, Tribal, and Territorial Jurisdictions*. Washington, DC: U.S. Department of Homeland Security, 2018.

Fetcher, Joshua, and Reese Oxner. "'The Wrong Decision': Texas DPS Says Local Police Made Crucial Error as School Shooting Continued." *The Texas Tribune*, May 27, 2022. https://www.texastribune.org/2022/05/27/uvalde-school-shooting-police-errors.

Fetcher, Joshua, Reese Oxner, and Uriel Garcia. "Authorities Ignore Spanish Speakers at Uvalde Press Conferences." Axios, May 31, 2022. https://www.axios.com/2022/05/31/uvalde-shooting-spanish-speakers-police.

Fetcher, Joshua, Reese Oxner, and Uriel Garcia. "Narratives, and Blame, Shift Again as Dysfunction Engulfs Shooting Probe." *The Texas Tribune,* June 1, 2022. https://www.texastribune.org/2022/05/31/uvalde-school-police-chief-investigation.

Filipas, Henrietta H., and Sarah E. Ullman. "Social Reactions to Sexual Assault Victims from Various Support Sources." *Violence and Victims* 16, no. 6 (2001): 673–692.

FireRescue1 Academy. "NFPA 3000: Preparing and Training Firefighters for Active Shooter Incidents." Last updated August 6, 2019. https://www.firerescue1.com/fire-products/online-training/articles/nfpa-3000-preparing-and-training-firefighters-for-active-shooter-incidents-ebook-B06ex9Lp3fDhJ5YF.

First Responder Guide for Improving Survivability in Improvised Explosive Device and/or Active Shooter Incidents. Washington, DC: U.S. Department of Homeland Security, 2015. https://www.dhs.gov/publication/iedactive-shooter-guidance-first-responders.

Fisher, Andrew D., Max Dodge, Wren Nealy Jr., Eric A. Bank, and Dominic Thompson. "Whole Blood in EMS May Save Lives." *Journal of Emergency Medical Services*. Last modified February 1, 2018. https://www.jems.com/patient-care/whole-blood-in-ems-may-save-lives.

Flores, Rosa. "Uvalde City Council to Investigate Every City Officer Who Responded to School Massacre." CNN. Last modified July 26, 2022. https://www.cnn.com/2022/07/26/us/uvalde-city-council-meeting/index.html.

Florio, Adrian. "What New Footage of the Uvalde Shooting Recording Tells Us About the Police Response." *Morning Edition*. NPR, July 13, 2022. https://www.npr.org/2022/07/13/1111244795/what-new-footage-of-the-uvalde-shooting-recording-tells-us-about-the-police-resp.

Flynn, Brian W., Mary C. Vance, and Joshua C. Morganstein. *Curriculum Recommendations for Disaster Health Professionals: Disaster Behavioral Health, Second Edition*. Bethesda, MD: Uniformed Services University, 2020. https://www.cstsonline.org/whats-new/curriculum-recommendations-for-disaster-health-professionals-disaster-behavioral-health.

Fortenbery, Jay. "Developing Ethical Law Enforcement Leaders: A Plan of Action." *FBI Law Enforcement Bulletin*. Last modified May 5, 2015. https://leb.fbi.gov/articles/featured-articles/developing-ethical-law-enforcement-leaders-a-plan-of-action.

Fraire, Rosanna. "Uvalde Victim Uziyah Garcia Laid to Rest in Hometown of San Angelo." *San Angelo Standard-Times*, June 25, 2022. https://www.gosanangelo.com/story/news/2022/06/25/uvalde-victim-uziyah-garcia-san-angelo-funeral/7736547001.

Friedman, Matthew, and Shimon Prokupecz. "Uvalde Shooting: 2 more Texas DPS Officers to be Investigated Over Actions on Day of Massacre." CNN, September 24, 2022, https://www.cnn.com/2022/09/13/us/uvalde-texas-dps-referrals-massacre/index.html.

Gamboa, Suzanne. "Uvalde Shooter Wrote 'LOL' on Whiteboard in Victims' Blood, Lawmaker Tells Families at Emotional Hearing." NBC News, April 19, 2023. https://www.nbcnews.com/news/latino/uvalde-shooter-wrote-lol-white-board-blood-families-gun-laws-hearing-rcna80287.

Garcia, Ariana. "Family of 10-Year-Old Uvalde Shooting Victim Carries Out Daughter's Wish With Viral TikTok." *Houston Chronical*, June 1, 2022. https://www.chron.com/news/houston-texas/article/Uvalde-shooting-familiy-Tess-Marie-Mata-TikTok-17209650.php.

Garcia, Uriel J., and Lexi Churchill. "Uvalde Families, DA at Odds over Release of Public Records." *The Texas Tribune*, March 8, 2023. https://www.texastribune.org/2023/03/08/uvalde-district-attorney-fights-release-public-records-despite-family.

Garcia-Navarro, Lulu, Sophia Alvarez Boyd, and James Doubek. "Experts Worry Active Shooter Drills in Schools Could Be Traumatic for Students." NPR. Last modified November 10, 2019. https://www.npr.org/2019/11/10/778015261/experts-worry-active-shooter-drills-in-schools-could-be-traumatic-for-students.

Global Programme on Preventing and Countering Violent Extremism. *Crisis Communications Toolkit.* Geneva, Switzerland: United Nations Counter-Terrorism Centre, United Nations Office of Counter-Terrorism, n.d. https://www.un.org/counterterrorism/publication/UNOCT-UNCCT-Crisis-Communications-Toolkit.

Goldman, Robert. "Restorative Justice as a Trauma-Informed Approach." *Psychology Today,* January 17, 2023. https://www.psychologytoday.com/us/blog/building-resilient-minds/202301/the-use-of-restorative-justice-as-a-trauma-informed-approach.

Goldstein, Scott, LeeAnne M. Martin Lee, and Joseph Roarty. *EMS Zones of Care*. Treasure Island, FL: StatPearls Publishing, 2023. https://www.ncbi.nlm.nih.gov/books/NBK436017.

Gomez Licon, Adriana. "Uvalde: Visitations, Funerals and Burials, One after Another." *Albuquerque Journal*, May 31, 2022. https://www.abqjournal.com/2503784/uvalde-visitations-funerals-and-burials-one-after-another.html.

Guerilus, Stephanie. "Uvalde Principal Reinstated at Robb Elementary School Following Suspension." ABC News, July 28, 2022. https://abcnews.go.com/US/uvalde-principal-reinstated-robb-elementary-school-suspension/story?id=87600921.

Hamblen, Jessica L., Fran H. Norris, Siobhan Pietruszkiewicz, Laura E. Gibson, April Naturale, and Claudine Louis. "Cognitive Behavioral Therapy for Postdisaster Distress: A Community Based Treatment Program for Survivors of Hurricane Katrina." *Administration and Policy in Mental Health and Mental Health Services Research* 36, no. 3 (2009): 206–214. https://pubmed.ncbi.nlm.nih.gov/19365725.

Hammer, Alex. "Mother of Girl Shot Dead in Uvalde School Massacre Slams Leak of Security Video." *Daily Mail,* July 13, 2022. https://www.dailymail.co.uk/news/article-11009621/Mother-girl-shot-dead-Uvalde-school-massacre-slams-leak-security-video.html.

Hampton, Daniel. "Texas School Shooting: What We Know about Uvalde Victims." *San Antonio, TX Patch,* May 25, 2022. https://patch.com/texas/sanantonio/texas-school-shooting-what-we-know-uvalde-victims.

Hannah, Jason, and Steve Alsmay. "Uvalde School District Police Chief Pete Arredondo Fired in Unanimous Board Vote." CNN, August 25, 2022. https://www.cnn.com/2022/08/24/us/uvalde-school-police-pete-arredondo/index.html.

HB 1774, Relating to actions and liability associated with certain insurance claims (2017). Texas State Legislature, Legislative Session 85(R). https://capitol.texas.gov/tlodocs/85R/billtext/pdf/HB01774F.pdf.

Healing Collective Trauma. "What Is Collective Trauma?" Accessed August 3, 2023. https://www.healingcollectivetrauma.com.

Helling, Steve. "10-Year-Old Uvalde Victims Who Texted 'I Love You' to Each Other at Bedtime Will be Buried Side by Side." *People,* June 8, 2022. https://people.com/crime/uvalde-victims-texted-i-love-you-buried-side-by-side.

Helping Victims of Mass Violence and Terrorism: Planning, Response, Recovery, and Resources. Washington, DC: Office for Victims of Crime, 2015. https://ovc.ojp.gov/library/publications/helping-victims-mass-violence-and-terrorism-planning-response-recovery-and-0.

Hernandez, Emily. "What is Operation Lone Star? Gov. Greg Abbott's Controversial Border Mission, Explained." *The Texas Tribune*, March 30, 2022. https://www.texastribune.org/2022/03/30/operation-lone-star-texas-explained.

Herron, Daranesha. "Exclusive: Father of Makenna Elrod-Seiler Speaks out for First Time Following Uvalde Mass Shooting That Took His Daughter's Life." KVUE, August 12, 2022. https://www.kvue.com/article/news/special-reports/uvalde-school-shooting/exclusive-makenna-elrod-seiler-father-speaks-uvalde-mass-shooting/269-7a9421d8-8ef5-434e-bc9d-f8fded0adbfe.

HHS (U.S. Department of Health and Human Services). "Bounce Back." Title IV-E Prevention Services Clearinghouse. Accessed August 3, 2023. https://preventionservices.acf.hhs.gov/programs/414/show.

HHS (U.S. Department of Health and Human Services). "Plan and Prepare for Disasters." Accessed August 3, 2023. https://www.dhs.gov/plan-and-prepare-disasters.

HHS (U.S. Department of Health and Human Services). "Program and Service Ratings." Title IV-E Prevention Services Clearinghouse. Accessed August 3, 2023. https://preventionservices.acf.hhs.gov/review-process/psr.

HHS (U.S. Department of Health and Human Services). "Welcome." Title IV-E Prevention Services Clearinghouse. Accessed August 3, 2023. https://preventionservices.acf.hhs.gov.

Hinojosa, Maria. *After Uvalde: Guns, Grief & Texas Politics*. PBS Frontline, 2023. https://www.pbs.org/wgbh/frontline/documentary/after-uvalde-guns-grief-texas-politics.

Hobfoll, Stevan E., Patricia Watson, Carl C. Bell, Richard A. Bryant, Melissa J. Brymer, Matthew J. Friedman, Merle Friedman, et al. "Five Essential Elements of Immediate and Mid-Term Mass Trauma Intervention: Empirical Evidence." *Psychiatry: Interpersonal and Biological Processes* 70, no. 4 (2007): 283–315. https://doi.org/10.1521/psyc.2007.70.4.283.

Homeland Security Presidential Directive 5. Washington, DC: U.S. Department of Homeland Security, 2003. https://www.dhs.gov/publication/homeland-security-presidential-directive-5.

Hopwood, Tanya L., and Nicola S. Schutte. "Psychological Outcomes in Reaction to Media Exposure to Disasters and Large-Scale Violence: A Meta-Analysis." *Psychology of Violence* 7, no. 2 (2017): 316–327. https://psycnet.apa.org/record/2016-22453-001.

Houston, Matt. "Robb Elementary Autopsy Reports Are Done, but a Judge Blocked Their Release." KENS 5, November 7, 2022. https://www.kens5.com/article/news/special-reports/uvalde-school-shooting/robb-elementary-autopsy-reports-done-but-a-judge-blocked-their-release/273-48e42dcc-a72c-448d-a645-68b262b747cd.

Houston, Matt. "Uvalde School Staff Missed Emails Regarding Pete Arredondo Seeking to Upgrade His Discharge Status." KENS 5, February 24, 2023. https://www.kens5.com/article/news/local/texas/pete-arredondo-uvalde-cisd-police-texas-robb-shooting/273-e8035e43-e877-4c91-b3b4-a3ab5de7de3c.

Houston, Matt. "Uvalde Superintendent Explains Why District Nixed Review of School Police Department's Response to Robb Shooting." KENS 5, February 13, 2023. https://www.kens5.com/article/news/special-reports/uvalde-school-shooting/uvalde-superintendent-explains-why-district-nixed-review-school-police-departments-response-to-robb-shooting/273-697b149f-faea-4331-9b06-04d8008ef734.

Hulsman, Sean. "When the Guns Go Silent: How to Manage the Aftermath of a Mass Shooting." EMS1. Last modified August 14, 2019. https://www.ems1.com/mass-shooting/articles/when-the-guns-go-silent-how-to-manage-the-aftermath-of-a-mass-shooting-JcurqDG0NxbeysGc.

Human Resources Division. *Employee Assistance Program Policy Guide*. Washington, DC: Federal Bureau of Investigation, 2022.

Hyde, George E. "Chief Arredono's Attorney Issues Press Statement In Response to Uvalde ISD's Unconstitutional Limitations Placed Upon Name Clearing Hearing and Requested UCISD Read This Statement Out Loud at the Hearing." Statement released by Russell Rodriguez Hyde Bullock LLP, August 24, 2022. https://s3.documentcloud.org/documents/22187659/uvalde-school-police-chief-pete-arredondo-issues-17-page-press-statement-ahead-of-meeting-to-decide-his-fate.pdf.

IACP (International Association of Chiefs of Police). "Law Enforcement Code of Ethics." Accessed December 4, 2023. https://www.theiacp.org/resources/law-enforcement-code-of-ethics.

IACP (International Association of Chiefs of Police). "Law Enforcement-Based Victim Services (LEV) Webinar Series." Accessed August 3, 2023. https://learn.theiacp.org/products/law-enforcement-based-victim-services-lev-webinar-series?_ga=2.96339476.964528332.1679590803-405409729.1651157022#tab-product_tab_contents__79.

IACP (International Association of Chiefs of Police). "Tactical Emergency Medical Training for Law Enforcement Personnel." Resolution adopted at the 120th Annual Conference, October 23, 2013. https://www.theiacp.org/resources/resolution/tactical-emergency-medical-training-for-law-enforcement-personnel.

IACP (International Association of Chiefs of Police). *Critical Incident Stress Management*. Alexandria, VA: International Association of Chiefs of Police, 2011. https://www.theiacp.org/sites/default/files/all/c/CriticalIncidentStressPaper.pdf.

IACP (International Association of Chiefs of Police). *Incident Command Model Policy*. Alexandria, VA: International Association of Chiefs of Police, 2009. https://www.theiacp.org/sites/default/files/2018-08/IncidentCommandPolicy.pdf.

IACP (International Association of Chiefs of Police). *Law Enforcement-Based Victim Services – Template Package IV: Pamphlets*. Alexandria, VA: International Association of Chiefs of Police, 2021. https://www.theiacp.org/sites/default/files/LEV/Publications/TemplatePackageIV_MainDocument_Final-July2021.pdf.

IACP (International Association of Chiefs of Police). *Law Enforcement Oath of Honor*. Alexandria, VA: International Association of Chiefs of Police, n.d. https://www.theiacp.org/sites/default/files/2021-01/246910_IACP_Oath_of_Honor_11x8.5_p1%20%281%29.pdf.

IACP (International Association of Chiefs of Police). *Model Policy on Active Shooter*. Alexandria, VA: International Association of Chiefs of Police, 2018. https://www.theiacp.org/resources/policy-center-resource/active-shooter.

IACP (International Association of Chiefs of Police). *Model Policy on Mutual Aid*. Alexandria, VA: International Association of Chiefs of Police, 2005. https://www.theiacp.org/resources/policy-center-resource/mutual-aid.

IACP (International Association of Chiefs of Police). *Model Policy on Response to Barricaded Individuals*. Alexandria, VA: International Association of Chiefs of Police, 2020. https://www.theiacp.org/sites/default/files/2020-05/Barricaded%20Individuals%2005-26-2020.pdf.

IADLEST (International Association of Directors of Law Enforcement Standards and Training). "National Certification Program." Accessed August 3, 2023. https://iadlest-ncp.org.

Inter-Agency Standing Committee. *IASC Guidelines on Mental Health and Psychosocial Support in Emergency Settings, 2007.* Geneva, Switzerland: United Nations Office for the Coordination of Humanitarian Affairs, 2007. https://interagencystandingcommittee.org/iasc-task-force-mental-health-and-psychosocial-support-emergency-settings/iasc-guidelines-mental-health-and-psychosocial-support-emergency-settings-2007.

Investigative Committee on the Robb Elementary Shooting. *House Investigative Committee on the Robb Elementary Shooting Interim Report 2022.* Austin: Texas House of Representatives, 2022. https://house.texas.gov/committees/reports.

Jacobo, Julia, and Nadine El-Bawab. "Timeline: How the Shooting at a Texas Elementary School Unfolded." ABC News. Last modified December 12, 2022. https://abcnews.go.com/US/timeline-shooting-texas-elementary-school-unfolded/story?id=84966910.

Jimenez, Stephanie. "From Her 'Love of Animals and Pizza,' Maranda Mathis, 11, Remembered as Sweet Girl." KSAT, December 6, 2022. https://www.ksat.com/news/local/2022/12/06/from-her-love-of-animals-and-pizza-maranda-mathis-11-remembered-as-sweet-girl.

Johnson, Phillip M. "Effects of Groupthink on Tactical Decision-Making." Monograph. Leavenworth, KS: School of Advanced Military Studies, 2001. https://apps.dtic.mil/sti/pdfs/ADA387009.pdf.

Justice Technology Information Center. *Law Enforcement Vehicle Lighting and Reflectivity Studies: An Overview.* Washington, DC: National Institute of Justice, 2019. https://www.ojp.gov/library/publications/law-enforcement-vehicle-lighting-and-reflectivity-studies-overview.

Kaniasty, Krzysztof, and Fran H. Norris. "In Search of Altruistic Community: Patterns of Social Support Mobilization following Hurricane Hugo." *American Journal of Community Psychology* 23, no. 4 (1995): 447–477. https://doi.org/10.1007/BF02506964.

Kantor, Wendy Grossman. "14 Months After Uvalde School Shooting, Survivors' Mom Shares His Mental Health Battle: 'Lives with His Scars Daily.'" *People,* July 23, 2023. https://people.com/uvalde-school-shooting-survivor-ptsd-mental-health-struggles-7564236.

Kantor, Wendy Grossman. "Boy Killed in Texas Shooting Wanted to Be Police Officer. Now Uncle Says Cops 'Didn't Even Protect Him.'" *People*, May 28, 2022. https://people.com/crime/boy-killed-texas-shooting-wanted-to-be-police-officer.

Kilander, Gustaf. "New Video from Uvalde Massacre Shows Police Officers Vomiting and Sobbing after Discovering Victims." *The Independent*, May 23, 2023. https://www.independent.co.uk/news/world/americas/crime/uvalde-shooting-video-police-texas-b2343635.html.

King, Cody, Leigh Waldman, Gavin Nesbitt, Andrew Wilson, and Adam Barraza. "Senator Calls for Investigation after Video Shows DPS Officer Shoving Parent of Uvalde Shooting Victim." KSAT, April 5, 2023. https://www.ksat.com/news/local/2023/04/06/senator-calls-for-investigation-after-video-shows-dps-officer-shoving-parent-of-uvalde-shooting-victim.

King, Cody. "'It's Been 4 Months and Nothing's Changed,' Uziyah Garcia's Legal Guardian Calls For Action, Accountability After Robb Elementary Shooting" [Image]. KSAT News, September 25, 2022. https://www.ksat.com/news/local/2022/09/25/its-been-four-months-and-nothings-changed-father-of-uziyah-garcia-calls-for-action-4-months-after-robb-elementary-shooting.

Kochi, Sudiksha. "Fact Check: No Truth to Conspiracy Labeling Uvalde a 'False Flag'." *USA Today,* June 2, 2022. https://www.usatoday.com/story/news/factcheck/2022/06/02/fact-check-no-truth-conspiracy-labeling-uvalde-false-flag/9975616002.

Korrs, Ivan. "Ex-Robb Elementary Principal Takes New Position on Uvalde District School Board | Who's Replacing Her?" *Latin Post,* August 8, 2022. https://www.latinpost.com/articles/156271/20220808/ex-robb-elementary-principal-takes-new-position-uvalde-district-school.htm.

Korrs, Ivan. "Texas Department of Public Safety Facing Legal Heat Over Alleged Withholding of Uvalde Shooting Docs." *Latin Post,* August 1, 2022, https://www.latinpost.com/articles/156176/20220801/texas-department-public-safety-facing-legal-heat-over-alleged-witholding.htm.

La Greca, Annette M., Wendy K. Silverman, Eric M. Vernberg, and Michael C. Roberts, eds. *Helping Children Cope with Disasters and Terrorism.* Washington, DC: American Psychological Association, 2002.

Lass-Hennemann, Johanna, Sarah K Schäfer, Sonja Römer, Elena Holz, Markus Streb, and Tanja Michael. "Therapy Dogs as a Crisis Intervention after Traumatic Events? – An Experimental Study." *Frontiers in Psychology* 9 (2018): 1627. https://doi.org/10.3389/fpsyg.2018.01627.

Lerner, E. Brooke, Richard B. Schwartz, Phillip L. Coule, Eric S. Weinstein, David C. Cone, Richard C. Hunt, Scott M. Sasser, et al. "Mass Casualty Triage: An Evaluation of the Data and Development of a Proposed National Guideline." *Disaster Medicine and Public Health Preparedness* 2, no. S1 (2008): S25–S34. https://doi.org/10.1097/DMP.0b013e318182194e.

Linehan, Patrick, and Olivia Osteen. "Acting Police Chief During Uvalde School Shooting Quits in Wake of Criticism." ABC News, November 17, 2022. https://abcnews.go.com/US/mariano-pargas-acting-police-chief-uvalde-school-shooting/story?id=93507538.

Linehan, Patrick. "Uvalde Police Chief Wins Appeal to Upgrade Termination Record." ABC News, February 21, 2023. https://abcnews.go.com/US/uvalde-police-chief-wins-appeal-upgrade-termination-record/story?id=97372289.

Linehan, Patrick. "Uvalde School District Hires New Police Officers, While Keeping Report from Public." ABC7 Los Angeles, February 14, 2023. https://abc7.com/uvalde-school-district-hires-new-police-officers-while-keeping-rep/12816805.

Lopez, Victoria, Kolten Parker, and Rebecca Salinas. "Uvalde Police Department's Acting Police Chief Placed on Leave After Report Outlines Failed Response." KSAT 12, July 17, 2022. https://www.ksat.com/news/local/2022/07/17/uvalde-police-departments-acting-police-chief-placed-on-leave-after-report-outlines-failed-response.

Lunenburg, Fred C. "Group Decision Making: The Potential for Groupthink." *International Journal of Management, Business, and Administration* 13, no. 1 (2010): 1–6. http://www.nationalforum.com/Journals/IJMBA/IJMBA.htm.

Madden, Monica. "No More DPS Officers Will Be Disciplined for Uvalde Shooting Response, Director Says." KXAN, February 10, 2023. https://www.kxan.com/news/texas/uvalde-school-shooting/uvalde-accountability-dps-director-says-2-employees-to-be-disciplined.

Maldonado, Monica. "Jackie Jaylen Cazares." National Museum of the American Latino, 2022. https://latino.si.edu/exhibitions/healing-uvalde/twenty-one-healing-uvalde-murals/jackie-jaylen-cazares.

Maldonado, Monica. "Makenna Lee Elrod." National Museum of the American Latino, 2022, https://latino.si.edu/exhibitions/healing-uvalde/twenty-one-healing-uvalde-murals/makenna-lee-elrod.

Maldonado, Monica. "Nevaeh Alyssa Bravo." National Museum of the American Latino, 2022. https://latino.si.edu/exhibitions/healing-uvalde/twenty-one-healing-uvalde-murals/nevaeh-alyssa-bravo.

Maldonado, Monica. "Uziyah Sergio Garcia." National Museum of the American Latino, 2022. https://latino.si.edu/exhibitions/healing-uvalde/twenty-one-healing-uvalde-murals/uziyah-garcia.

Margolin, Josh, Jenny Wagnon Courts, Kate Holland, Alex Hosenball, and Hannah Prince. "'I Am Suffering Mentally,' Uvalde Educator Says After False Blame in Shooting Aftermath." ABC News, October 24, 2022. https://abcnews.go.com/US/suffering-mentally-uvalde-educator-false-blame-shooting-aftermath/story?id=91886661.

Marshall, Randall D. "Learning from 9/11: Implications for Disaster Research and Public Health." In *9/11: Mental Health in the Wake of Terrorist Attacks*, edited by Yuval Neria, Raz Gross, and Randall D. Marshall, 617–630. New York: Cambridge University Press, 2006.

Martaindale, M. Hunter, and J. Pete Blair. "The Evolution of Active Shooter Response Training Protocols Since Columbine: Lessons From the Advanced Law Enforcement Rapid Response Training Center." *Journal of Contemporary Criminal Justice* 35, no. 3 (2019): 342–356. https://doi.org/10.1177/1043986219840237.

Martinez, Gina. "Two Best Friends at Uvalde Elementary School Who Texted Each Other 'I Love You' Nightly Before Being Killed in Mass Shooting Will Be Buried Next to Each Other." *Daily Mail,* June 8, 2022. https://www.dailymail.co.uk/news/article-10897749/Two-best-friends-killed-Texas-school-shooting-buried-other.html.

Matkin, Holly. "Ex-Uvalde School Police Chief Won't Have 'Dishonorable' Discharge After School District Failed to Show Up at Hearing." *The Police Tribune,* February 22, 2023. https://policetribune.com/ex-uvalde-school-police-chief-wont-have-dishonorable-discharge-after-school-district-failed-to-show-up-at-hearing.

McElroy, Laura. *Developing a Crisis Communication Plan: 5 Important Strategies.* Body-Worn Camera Training & Technical Assistance Program. Washington, DC: Bureau of Justice Assistance, n.d. http://bwctta.com/bwcs-and-crisis-communication.

McGee, Kevin, and Chris Reilly, "Terrorism and Homeland Security: Hot, Warm and Cold Zones." International Association of Fire Chiefs. Last modified November 8, 2018. https://www.iafc.org/membership/iCHIEFS/iCHIEFS-article/terrorism-and-homeland-security-hot-warm-and-cold-zones.

McNeel, Bekah. "On the Day of the Uvalde Shooting, Her School Bus Became a Makeshift Ambulance." *The Texas Tribune,* December 20, 2022. https://www.texastribune.org/2022/12/20/uvalde-shooting-bus-ambulance.

Medina, Dani. "Cop Leading Uvalde Shooting Investigation Quietly Retires." News Radio 1200 WOAI, October 27, 2022. https://woai.iheart.com/content/2022-10-27-cop-leading-uvalde-shooting-investigation-quietly-retires.

Medina, John Henry. "Tejano Community Attend Funeral of Eliahna 'Ellie' Garcia, One of the Victims of the Uvalde School Shooting." Tejano Nation, June 7, 2022. https://tejanonation.net/2022/06/06/tejano-community-attend-funeral-of-eliahna-ellie-garcia-one-of-the-victims-of-the-uvalde-school-shooting.

Menchaca, Megen. "Texas Politicians Respond to Video of Uvalde Shooting Police Response." *Austin Statesman,* July 13, 2022. https://www.statesman.com/story/news/politics/2022/07/13/uvalde-shooting-video-texas-politicians-respond-police-action/65372606007.

Méndez, María. "Almost 100 Texas School Districts Have Added Their Own Police Departments since 2017, but Not Everyone Feels Safer." *The Texas Tribune*, June 15, 2022. https://www.texastribune.org/2022/06/15/uvalde-school-officers-texas-shootings.

Mental Health Technology Transfer Center. *After a School Tragedy . . . Readiness, Response, Recovery, & Resources.* Rockville, MD: Substance Abuse and Mental Health Services Administration, 2019. https://mhttcnetwork.org/centers/mhttc-network-coordinating-office/product/after-school-tragedyreadiness-response-recovery.

Mercedes, Cheryl. "Uvalde Mass Shooting Families to See Hallway Video." KHOU, July 15, 2022. https://www.khou.com/article/news/special-reports/uvalde-school-shooting/uvalde-victim-families-robb-elementary-hallway-video/285-251a989c-ef05-41af-92f4-04a628227fcf.

Miles, J.D. "Uvalde Victim Alithia Ramirez Remembered for Her Kind Heart." CBS News, May 26, 2022. https://www.cbsnews.com/texas/news/alithia-ramirez-uvalde.

Miller, Laurence. "Law Enforcement Traumatic Stress: Clinical Syndromes and Intervention Strategies." American Academy of Experts in Traumatic Stress, 2020. https://www.aaets.org/traumatic-stress-library/law-enforcement-traumatic-stress-clinical-syndromes-and-intervention-strategies.

Milliard, Beth. "Utilization and Impact of Peer-Support Programs on Police Officers' Mental Health." *Frontiers in Psychology* 11 (2020): 1686. https://doi.org/10.3389/fpsyg.2020.01686.

Mitchell, Taiyler S. "CNN Provides Footage Of Uvalde Shooting to Parents a Year after the Massacre." *Huffpost.* Last modified May 22, 2023. https://www.huffpost.com/entry/cnn-uvalde-video_n_646a787ae4b0ab2b97e85a44.

Montgomery, David, et al. "'She Was My Sweet Girl': Remembering the Victims of the Uvalde Shooting." *The New York Times,* June 5, 2022. https://www.nytimes.com/2022/06/05/us/uvalde-shooting-victims.html.

Moody, Joe (@moodyforelpaso). "This is the husband of teacher Eva Mireles, who contacted him on his phone from her classroom while he was on-scene to say that she'd been shot and was dying. 1/2 #txlege #Uvalde." X (formerly known as Twitter), July 13, 2022, 2:48 pm. https://twitter.com/moodyforelpaso/status/1547291847332069376.

Moreno, Julie, and Leigh Waldman. "Parents Block Entrance at Uvalde CISD Headquarters Demanding Action Against District Officers." KSAT 12, September 27, 2022. https://www.ksat.com/news/local/2022/09/27/parents-block-entrance-at-uvalde-cisd-headquarters-demanding-action-against-district-officers.

Moreno, Julie, and Leigh Waldman. "Uvalde CISD Assistant Superintendent is 4th in Central Office to Retire After Robb Elementary Massacre." KSAT 12, October 26, 2022. https://www.ksat.com/news/local/2022/10/26/uvalde-cisd-assistant-superintendent-is-4th-in-central-office-to-retire-after-robb-elementary-massacre.

Moreno-Lozano, Luz. "Color del dolor: 21 Uvalde Murals of Robb Elementary Victims Use Paint to Heal Pain." *Austin American-Statesman*, October 25, 2022. https://www.statesman.com/in-depth/news/2022/10/25/healing-uvalde-21-murals-memorialize-tell-story-robb-elementary-victims/69520352007.

Morgan, Jack. "Texas Artists Honor the Uvalde Victims with 21 Murals They Hope Will Help Healing." NPR, August 20, 2022. https://www.npr.org/2022/08/20/1118439845/texas-artists-honor-the-uvalde-victims-with-21-murals-they-hope-will-help-healin.

Morris, Cheryl. "The Importance of Leading by Example." *American Police Beat.* Last modified October 31, 2021. https://apbweb.com/2021/10/the-importance-of-leading-by-example.

Morrissey, Jim. "EMS Response to Active-Shooter Incidents." *EMS World.* Last modified July 2011. https://www.hmpgloballearningnetwork.com/site/emsworld/article/10279321/ems-response-active-shooter-incidents.

MPD (Metropolitan [D.C.] Police Department). *After Action Report, Washington Navy Yard, September 16, 2013: Internal Review of the Metropolitan Police Department, Washington, D.C.* Washington, DC: July 2014. https://mpdc.dc.gov/publication/mpd-navy-yard-after-action-report.

NAMI (National Alliance on Mental Illness). "Employment and Mental Illness: Investing in Programs that Work." July 14, 2014. https://www.nami.org/Blogs/NAMI-Blog/July-2014/Employment-and-Mental-Illness-Investing-in-Program.

NAMI (National Alliance on Mental Illness). "Mental Health By the Numbers." Last modified April 2023. https://nami.org/mhstats.

NASEMSO (National Association of State EMS Officials). "NASEMSO Releases 2020 National EMS Assessment." April 9, 2020. https://nasemso.org/news-events/news/news-item/nasemso-releases-2020-national-ems-assessment-2.

NASEMSO (National Association of State EMS Officials). *National Model EMS Clinical Guidelines: Version 2.2.* Falls Church, VA: National Association of State EMS Officials, 2019. https://nasemso.org/projects/model-ems-clinical-guidelines.

National Association of School Psychologists. *Best Practice Consideration for Armed Assailant Drills in Schools.* Bethesda, MD: National Association of School Psychologists, 2021. https://www.nasponline.org/resources-and-publications/resources-and-podcasts/school-safety-and-crisis/systems-level-prevention/best-practice-considerations-for-armed-assailant-drills-in-schools.

National Association of School Psychologists. *Mitigating Psychological Effects of Lockdowns.* Bethesda, MD: National Association of School Psychologists, 2018. https://www.nasponline.org/resources-and-publications/resources-and-podcasts/school-safety-and-crisis/systems-level-prevention/mitigating-psychological-effects-of-lockdowns?te=1&nl=debatable&emc=edit_db_20200805.

National Center for PTSD. "Stress First Aid: Manuals and Resources for Health Care Workers." U.S. Department of Veterans Affairs. Last modified July 6, 2023. https://www.ptsd.va.gov/professional/treat/type/stress_first_aid.asp.

National Center for PTSD. "Types of Debriefing Following Disasters." Last updated October 6, 2022. https://www.ptsd.va.gov/professional/treat/type/debrief_after_disasters.asp.

National Center for PTSD. *Stress First Aid (SFA) for Law Enforcement*. Police Officer Toolkit. U.S. Department of Veterans Affairs, 2016. https://ptsd.va.gov/PTSD/professional/treat/care/toolkits/police/resourcesHandouts.asp.

National Child Traumatic Stress Network. "Mass Violence Resources." Accessed August 8, 2023. https://www.nctsn.org/what-is-child-trauma/trauma-types/terrorism-and-violence/mass-violence?page=1.

National Institute for Health and Care Excellence. "Post-Traumatic Stress Disorder." Last modified December 5, 2018. https://www.nice.org.uk/guidance/ng116/chapter/recommendations#disaster-plan.

National Museum of the American Latino. "Healing Uvalde: Community Healing and Resiliance." Accessed August 3, 2023. https://latino.si.edu/exhibitions/healing-uvalde.

National Threat Assessment Center, U.S. Secret Service. *Averting Targeted School Violence: A U.S. Secret Service Analysis of Plots Against Schools*. Washington, DC: U.S. Department of Homeland Security, 2021. https://www.secretservice.gov/sites/default/files/reports/2021-03/USSS%20Averting%20Targeted%20School%20Violence.2021.03.pdf.

National Threat Assessment Center, U.S. Secret Service. *Mass Attacks in Public Spaces: 2016–2020*. Washington, DC: U.S. Department of Homeland Security, 2023. https://www.secretservice.gov/sites/default/files/reports/2023-01/usss-ntac-maps-2016-2020.pdf.

National Volunteer Fire Council. "Home: NVFC." Accessed December 6, 2023. https://www.nvfc.org.

National Volunteer Fire Council. "Share the Load Program." Accessed June 22, 2023. https://www.nvfc.org/programs/share-the-load-program.

Naturale, April J. "Outreach Strategies: An Experiential Description of the Outreach Methodologies Used in the September 11, 2001, Disaster Response in New York." In *Interventions Following Mass Violence and Disasters*, edited by Elspeth Cameron Ritchie, Patricia J. Watson, and Matthew J. Friedman, 365–386. New York: Guilford Press, 2007.

Naturale, April, Liam T. Lowney, and Corina Sole Brito. "Lessons Learned from the Boston Marathon Bombing Victim Services Program." *Clinical Social Work Journal* 45, no. 4 (2017): 99–188. https://www.researchgate.net/publication/316525844_Lessons_Learned_from_the_Boston_Marathon_Bombing_Victim_Services_Program.

Navarro, Marian. "Uvalde Asks Public for Private Space as One-Year Mark of Robb Elementary Shooting Looms." Texas Public Radio, May 15, 2023. https://www.tpr.org/news/2023-05-15/uvalde-asks-public-for-private-space-as-one-year-mark-of-robb-elementary-shooting-looms.

Neria, Yuval, Sandro Galea, and Fran H. Norris, eds. *Mental Health and Disasters*. Cambridge, UK: Cambridge University Press, 2010. https://doi.org/10.1017/CBO9780511730030.

New York State Psychiatric Institute. "Patient and Family Library." Archived July 1, 2007. https://web.archive.org/web/20070701061820/http:/www.nyspi.org/Kolb/nyspi_pf_library/index.html.

NFPA 1500TM : Standard on Fire Department Occupational Safety, Health, and Wellness Program. Quincy, MA: National Fire Protection Association, 2021. https://www.nfpa.org/codes-and-standards/all-codes-and-standards/list-of-codes-and-standards/detail?code=1500.

Norris, Fran H., Jessica L. Hamblen, Patricia J. Watson, Josef I. Ruzek, Laura E. Gibson, Betty J. Pfefferbaum, Jennifer L. Price, Susan P. Stevens, Bruce H. Young, and Matthew J. Friedman. "Toward Understanding and Creating Systems of Postdisaster Care: A Case Study of New York's Response to the World Trade Center Disaster." In *Interventions Following Mass Violence and Disasters*, edited by Elspeth Cameron Ritchie, Patricia J. Watson, and Matthew J. Friedman, 343–364. New York: Guildford Press, 2006.

Norris, Fran H., Laurie B. Slone, Charlene K. Baker, and Arthur D. Murphy. "Early Physical and Health Consequences of Disaster Exposure and Acute Disaster-Related PTSD." *Anxiety, Stress, and Coping: An International Journal* 19, no. 2 (2006): 95–110. https://doi.org/10.1080/10615800600652209.

Norris, Fran H., Matthew J. Friedman, and Patricia J. Watson. "60,000 Disaster Victims Speak: Part II. Summary and Implications of the Disaster Mental Health Research." *Psychiatry: Interpersonal and Biological Processes* 65, no. 3 (2002): 240–260. https://doi.org/10.1521/psyc.65.3.240.20169.

Norris, Fran H., Matthew J. Friedman, Patricia J. Watson, Christopher M. Byrne, Eolia Diaz, and Krzysztof Kaniasty. "60,000 Disaster Victims Speak: Part I. An Empirical Review of the Empirical Literature, 1981–2001." *Psychiatry* 65, no. 3 (2002): 207–239. https://doi.org/10.1521/psyc.65.3.207.20173.

NTOA (National Tactical Officers Association). *Tactical Response and Operations Standard for Law Enforcement Agencies.* Colorado Springs, CO: National Tactical Officers Association, 2023. https://www.ntoa.org/tros.

O'Callaghan, Erin, ed. "What is Generational Trauma and How Long Can it Last?" Brightside.com. Accessed August 3, 2023. https://www.brightside.com/blog/what-is-generational-trauma-and-how-long-can-it-last.

Office of Senator Robert Nichols. "Nichols Named Chair of Senate Special Committee to Protect All Texans." Press release, June 2, 2022. https://www.senate.texas.gov/members/d03/press/en/p20220602a.pdf.

Office of the Texas Attorney General. "Costs Covered by the Crime Victims' Compensation Program." Accessed August 3, 2023. https://www.texasattorneygeneral.gov/crime-victims/crime-victims-compensation-program/costs-covered-crime-victims-compensation-program.

Office of the Texas Governor. "Governor Abbott Announces New Chief of School Safety and Security." Press release, October 3, 2022. https://gov.texas.gov/news/post/governor-abbott-announces-new-chief-of-school-safety-and-security.

Office of Transportation Disaster Assistance. *Federal Family Assistance Framework for Aviation Disasters*. Washington, DC: National Transportation Safety Board, 2008. https://www.ntsb.gov/tda/er/Pages/tda-fa-aviation.aspx.

Ohlheiser, Abby. "Malcolm Gladwell's Cockpit Culture Theory and the Asiana Crash." *The Atlantic*, July 13, 2013. https://www.theatlantic.com/national/archive/2013/07/malcolm-gladwells-cockpit-culture-theory-everywhere-after-asiana-crash/313442.

Olidepo, Gloria. "Principal of Uvalde Elementary School Suspended in Wake of Deadly Shooting." *The Guardian,* July 26, 2022. https://www.theguardian.com/us-news/2022/jul/26/uvalde-shooting-texas-robb-elementary-principal-suspended.

Orrick, W. Dwayne. *Best Practices Guide: Developing a Police Department Policy-Procedure Manual*. Alexandria, VA: International Association of Chiefs of Police, n.d. https://www.theiacp.org/sites/default/files/2018-08/BP-PolicyProcedures.pdf.

Ortiz, Abel. "Eliahna 'Ellie' Amyah Garcia." National Museum of the American Latino, 2022. https://latino.si.edu/exhibitions/healing-uvalde/twenty-one-healing-uvalde-murals/eliahna-ellie-amyah-garcia.

Osteen, Olivia, Patrick Linehan, Josh Margolin, and Lucien Bruggeman. "Uvalde Residents Confront School Board Over Response to Shooting." ABC News, August 9, 2022. https://abcnews.go.com/US/uvalde-residents-confront-school-board-response-shooting/story?id=88145074.

OVC (Office for Victims of Crime) Training and Technical Assistance Center. "About Us." Last modified August 1, 2023. https://www.ovcttac.gov/views/index.cfm?nm=au.

OVC (Office for Victims of Crime) Training and Technical Assistance Center. "Helping Victims of Mass Violence and Terrorism: How to Design and Implement a Community Resiliency Center." Webinar, June 28, 2021. https://www.ovcttac.gov/massviolence/?nm=sfa&ns=mvt&nt=webinars.

OVC (Office for Victims of Crime). "Antiterrorism and Emergency Assistance Program (AEAP)." Accessed August 3, 2023. https://ovc.ojp.gov/program/antiterrorism-and-emergency-assistance-program-aeap/overview.

OVC (Office for Victims of Crime). "Mass Violence and Terrorism Death Notification." Webinar, January 21, 2020. https://ovc.ojp.gov/events/mass-violence-and-terrorism-death-notification-webinar-0.

OVC (Office for Victims of Crime). "Mass Violence: Death Notifications: Best Practices." Accessed August 3, 2023. https://www.ovcttac.gov/videos/dspMV_DeathNotifications.cfm.

OVC (Office for Victims of Crime). "The VOCA Fix." Last modified December 16, 2021. https://ovc.ojp.gov/about/crime-victims-fund/voca-fix.

OVC (Office for Victims of Crime). "Types of Assistance Available Through AEAP." https://ovc.ojp.gov/program/antiterrorism-and-emergency-assistance-program-aeap/ types-assistance.

Pal, Judy, Khadijah Carter, Eric Kowalczyk, and Christine Townsend. *Strategic Communications for Law Enforcement Executives*. Washington, DC: Office of Community Oriented Policing Services, 2023. https://portal.cops.usdoj.gov/resourcecenter?item=cops-r1127.

Parker, Kolten, and Cody King. "Uvalde City Council Denies Leave of Absence from Future Meetings for Pete Arredondo." KSAT 12, June 21, 2022. https://www.ksat.com/news/local/2022/06/21/uvalde-city-council-to-vote-on-a-leave-of-absence-from-future-meetings-for-pete-arredondo.

Parsons, Jim, and Tiffany Bergin. "The Impact of Criminal Justice Involvement on Victims' Mental Health." *Journal of Traumatic Stress* 23, no. 2 (April 2010): 182–188. https://onlinelibrary.wiley.com/doi/10.1002/jts.20505.

Patton, Mary Claire, and Leigh Waldman. "Video Inside Robb Elementary Shows Gunman Enter School, Police Gathering in Hallway for More Than Hour." KSAT 12, July 13, 2022. https://www.ksat.com/news/local/2022/07/12/video-inside-robb-elementary-school-shows-gunman-enter-school-police-gathering-in-hallway-for-more-than-hour.

Patton, Mary Claire. "Uvalde CISD Announces Plans for Displaced Robb Elementary Students." KSAT 12, July 13, 2022. https://www.ksat.com/news/local/2022/07/13/uvalde-cisd-announces-plans-for-displaced-robb-elementary-students.

Pearce, Jimmy, and Scott Goldstein. "EMS Tactical Movement Techniques." *StatPearls*. Treasure Island, FL: StatPearls Publishing, 2022. https://www.ncbi.nlm.nih.gov/books/NBK499869.

Pennardt, Andre, and Richard Schwartz. "Hot, Warm, and Cold Zones: Applying Existing National Incident Management System Terminology to Enhance Tactical Emergency Medical Support Interoperability." *Journal of Special Operations Medicine* Fall 2014: 78–79. https://www.jsomonline.org/JournalArticles/20143.php.

PERF (Police Executive Research Forum). "ICAT: Integrating Communications, Assessment, and Tactics: A Training Guide for Defusing Critical Incidents." Accessed December 4, 2023. https://www.policeforum.org/icat-training-guide.

Pfefferbaum, Betty, Carol S. North, Brian W. Flynn, Fran H. Norris, and Robert DeMartino. "Disaster Mental Health Services Following the 1995 Oklahoma City Bombing: Modifying Approaches to Address Terrorism." *CNS Spectrums* 7, no. 8 (2002): 575–579. https://www.cambridge.org/core/journals/cns-spectrums/article/abs/disaster-mental-health-services-following-the-1995-oklahoma-city-bombing-modifying-approaches-to-address-terrorism/DCB85284D003F6F3DC9DA442C0B0EAE7.

Phelps, Scot. "Why Paramedics Are Qualified Emergency Care Providers." EMS1. Last modified May 6, 2015. https://www.ems1.com/education-and-training/articles/why-paramedics-are-qualified-emergency-care-providers-ze63hPelbZuctOFP.

Pike, Sarah M. "Memorializing in the Aftermath of Disaster." Counterpoint: Navigating Knowledge, April 17, 2019. https://www.counterpointknowledge.org/memorializing-in-the-aftermath-of-disaster.

Planas, Antonio. "Uvalde Commissioners Launch Review of Sheriff's Office, Which Lacked Active Shooter Policy Before Massacre." NBC News, July 25, 2022. https://www.nbcnews.com/news/us-news/uvalde-commissioners-launch-review-sheriffs-office-lacked-active-shoot-rcna39864.

Plohetski, Tony. "Surveillance Video of Uvalde School Shooting Shows Police Response." *Austin Statesman,* July 12, 2022. https://www.statesman.com/story/news/2022/07/12/uvalde-school-shooting-video-of-robb-elementary-shows-police-response/65370384007.

Plohetski, Tony. "Texas Lawmakers Signed NDAs to Obtain Uvalde Shooting Case File." KVUE, December 1, 2022. https://www.kvue.com/article/news/special-reports/uvalde-school-shooting/uvalde-shooting-texas-lawmakers-nda/269-5d43e735-37b3-4a93-b656-f829ef6c05bb.

Pokorny, Douglas M., Maxwell Braverman, Philip M. Edmundson, David M. Bittenbinder, Caroline S. Zhu, Christopher J. Winckler, Randall Schaefer, et al. "The Use of Prehospital Blood Products in the Resuscitation of Trauma Patients: A Review of Prehospital Transfusion Practices and a Description of Our Regional Whole Blood Program in San Antonio, TX." *ISBT Science Series* 14, no. 3 (2019): 332–342. https://doi.org/10.1111/voxs.12498.

Police Organization Providing Peer Assistance. "Mission." Accessed December 4, 2023. https://poppanewyork.org/about/mission.

Pomerantz, Jay. "Can Posttraumatic Stress Disorder Be Prevented?" *Psychiatric Times* 23, no. 4 (2006). https://www.psychiatrictimes.com/view/can-posttraumatic-stress-disorder-be-prevented.

Power DMS. "Writing Effective Policies and Procedures in Law Enforcement." Last modified December 29, 2020. https://www.powerdms.com/policy-learning-center/writing-effective-policies-and-procedures-in-law-enforcement.

Prieb, Natalie. "Last Uvalde Victim Injured in School Shooting Discharged from San Antonio Hospital." *The Hill,* July 30, 2022. https://thehill.com/homenews/3580709-last-uvalde-victim-injured-in-shooting-discharged-from-san-antonio-hospital.

Prince, Hannah, Josh Margolin, and Emily Shapiro. "Uvalde Families Slam Texas DPS Chief, Call for His Resignation at Public Safety Meeting." ABC News, October 27, 2022. https://abcnews.go.com/US/texas-dps-chief-steven-mccraw-give-update-uvalde/story?id=91883125.

Prokupecz, Shimon, Matthew J. Friedman, and Rachel Clarke. "10-Year-Old Trapped with the Uvalde School Shooter Repeatedly Called 911 for Help. It Took Officials 40 Minutes to Act." CNN, November 2, 2022. https://www.cnn.com/2022/11/01/us/uvalde-911-classroom-call-delay/index.html.

Prokupecz, Shimon, Matthew J. Friedman, and Rachel Clarke. "Exclusive: Uvalde Sheriff Had Vital Information about School Shooter That Was Not Shared." CNN, December 7, 2022. https://www.cnn.com/2022/12/07/us/uvalde-sheriff-ruben-nolasco-robb-elementary-massacre/index.html.

Prokupecz, Shimon, Matthew J. Friedman, and Rachel Clarke. "Officer Being Investigated Over Shooting Response Gave Order to Delay Classroom Breach." CNN, October 20, 2022. https://www.cnn.com/2022/10/20/us/texas-uvalde-dps-investigation-betancourt/index.html.

Prokupecz, Shimon, Matthew J. Friedman, and Rachel Clarke. "Uvalde Shooting: New Audio Shows Acting Police Chief Knew That Children Needed Rescuing." CNN, November 14, 2022. https://www.cnn.com/2022/11/14/us/uvalde-investigation-acting-police-chief-mariano-pargas/index.html.

Prokupecz, Shimon, Matthew J. Friedman, and Rachel Clarke. "Uvalde Shooting: School District Fires Officer After CNN Identifies Her as Trooper Under Investigation for Her Response to Massacre." CNN, October 6, 2022. https://www.cnn.com/2022/10/05/us/texas-uvalde-school-officer-investigation/index.html.

Prokupecz, Shimon, Matthew J. Friedman, and Rachel Clarke. "Uvalde Massacre: School Police Chief Told Investigators Why He Didn't Try to Stop Gunman: 'There's Probably Going to Be Some Deceased in There, But We Don't Need Any More from Out Here.'" CNN, January 11, 2023. https://www.cnn.com/2023/01/10/us/uvalde-school-massacre-arredondo-interview/index.html.

Psychology Today. "Bystander Effect." Accessed August 3, 2023. https://www.psychologytoday.com/us/basics/bystander-effect.

Psychology Today. "Groupthink." Accessed August 3, 2023. https://www.psychologytoday.com/us/basics/groupthink.

Rabb, Shaun. "Texas Launches First-of-Its-Kind Mental and Emotional Support Group for Law Enforcement." FOX 4 News Dallas-Fort Worth, September 9, 2022. https://www.fox4news.com/news/texas-launches-first-of-its-kind-mental-and-emotional-support-group-for-law-enforcement.

Ramirez, Marizen, Karisa Harland, Maisha Frederick, Rhoda Shepherd, Marleen Wong, and Joseph E. Cavanaugh. "Listen Protect Connect for Traumatized Schoolchildren: A Pilot Study of Psychological First Aid." BMC Psychology 1, no. 26 (2013). https://doi.org/10.1186/2050-7283-1-26.

Readiness and Emergency Management for Schools. "Readiness and Emergency Management for Schools Technical Assistance Center." Accessed December 5, 2023. https://rems.ed.gov.

Ready.gov. "Emergency Response Plan." Last modified September 7, 2023.
  https://www.ready.gov/business/emergency-plans/emergency-response-plan.

Regional Field Triage Algorithm. San Antonio, TX: Southwest Texas Regional Advisory Council, 2021.
  https://www.strac.org/prehospital.

Report of Governor Bill Owens' Columbine Review Commission. Denver, CO: Columbine Review
  Commission, 2001.

Report on Mental Health Access for First Responders. Carson City, NV: Nevada State Legislature.
  https://www.leg.state.nv.us/Session/80th2019/Exhibits/Assembly/HHS/AHHS848I.pdf.

Riesman, Abraham Josephine. "Why Cops and Soldiers Love the Punisher." *Vulture,* June 2, 2020.
  https://www.vulture.com/article/marvel-punisher-police-cops-military-fandom.html.

Robino, Ariann E., David M. Feldman, Alyssa N. Stein, Melody A. Schmaltz, Hailey A. Fitzpatrick, Jaime L.
  Tartar, Frankie Pizzo, Marah Friedman, and Olivia Feldman. "Sustained Effects of Animal-Assisted
  Crisis Response on Stress in School Shooting Survivors." *Human-Animal Interaction Bulletin* 12, no. 2
  (2022): 65–85. https://doi.org/10.1079/hai.2022.0019.

Ronen, Anat. "Artist Statement." National Museum of the American Latino, 2022.
  https://latino.si.edu/exhibitions/healing-uvalde/twenty-one-healing-uvalde-murals/tess-mata.

Rose, Suzanna C., Jonathan Bisson, Rachel Churchill, and Simon Wessely. *Psychological Debriefing for
  Preventing Post Traumatic Stress Disorder (PTSD).* Cochrane Database of Systematic Reviews, 2002.
  https://doi.org/10.1002/14651858.CD000560.

Ryser, Rob. "Trauma by Association." *GreenwichTime.* Last modified June 19, 2016.
  https://www.greenwichtime.com/printpromotion/article/Trauma-by-association-8312393.php.

Salinas, Rebecca, and Leigh Waldman. "KSAT's 'One Year In: Uvalde' Honors Victims of Robb Elementary
  Shooting, Highlights Impact in Community." KSAT. Last modified May 25, 2023.
  https://www.ksat.com/news/local/2023/05/18/ksats-one-year-in-uvalde-honors-victims-of-robb-
  elementary-shooting-highlights-impact-in-community.

Salinas, Rebecca, Andrew Wilson, Leigh Waldman, and Gavin Nesbitt. "Students in Uvalde Protest Gun
  Violence on National School Walkout Day." KSAT. Last modified April 5, 2023.
  https://www.ksat.com/news/local/2023/04/05/watch-live-students-at-uvalde-walk-out-of-school-
  in-national-protest-of-gun-violence.

Salinas, Rebecca. "Uvalde Officials Told DPS That Police Had 'Zero Hesitation,' 'Each Minute Was Used to
  Save Lives,' Document Shows." KSAT, July 16, 2022.
  https://www.ksat.com/news/local/2022/07/16/uvalde-officials-told-dps-that-police-had-zero-
  hesitation-each-minute-was-used-to-save-lives-document-shows.

Salston, MaryDale, and Charles R. Figley. "Secondary Traumatic Stress Effects of Working with Survivors of Criminal Victimization." *Journal of Traumatic Stress* 16, no. 2 (2003): 167–175. https://doi.org/10.1023/a:1022899207206.

SAMHSA (Substance Abuse and Mental Health Services Administration). "Crisis Counseling Assistance and Training Program (CCP)." Last modified April 14, 2022. https://www.samhsa.gov/dtac/ccp.

SAMHSA (Substance Abuse and Mental Health Services Administration). "Mass Violence and Behavioral Health." *Disaster Technical Assistance Center Supplemental Research Bulletin,* 2017. https://www.samhsa.gov/dtac/disaster-behavioral-health-resources/supplemental-research-bulletin.

SAMHSA (Substance Abuse and Mental Health Services Administration). "Provide Support." Last modified July 18, 2022. https://www.samhsa.gov/workplace/employer-resources/provide-support.

SAMHSA (Substance Abuse and Mental Health Services Administration). "Stress First Aid for Fire and EMS Personnel." Accessed August 3, 2023. https://www.samhsa.gov/resource/dbhis/stress-first-aid-fire-ems-personnel.

Sanchez, Ray. "'We're in Trouble.' 80 minutes of Horror at Robb Elementary School." CNN, May 29, 2022. https://www.cnn.com/2022/05/29/us/uvalde-texas-elementary-school-shooting-week/index.html.

Sandoval, Edgar. "A Son Was Lost, a Daughter Saved." *The New York Times,* May 30, 2022. https://www.nytimes.com/2022/05/30/us/victims-texas-shooting-family.html.

SB 64, Relating to a peer support network for certain law enforcement personnel (2021). Texas State Legislature, Legislative Session 87(R). https://capitol.texas.gov/billlookup/BillStages.aspx?LegSess=87R&Bill=SB64.

Schildkraut, Jaclyn, and Amanda B. Nickerson. "Should We Or Shouldn't We? Arguments for and Against Lockdown Drills." *The MIT Press Reader.* Last modified June 9, 2022. https://thereader.mitpress.mit.edu/arguments-for-and-against-lockdown-drills.

Schlenger, William E., Juesta M. Caddell, Lori Ebert, Kathleen Jordan, Kathryn M. Rourke, David Wilson, Lisa Thalji, J. Michael Dennis, John A. Fairbank, and Richard A. Kulka. "Psychological Reactions to Terrorist Attacks: Findings From the National Study of Americans' Reactions to September 11." *Journal of the American Medical Association* 288, no. 5 (2002): 581–588. https://doi.org/10.1001/jama.288.5.581.

Schonfeld, David J., Marlene Melzer-Lange, Andrew N. Hashikawa, Peter A. Gorski, Steven Krug, Carl Baum, Sarita Chung, et al. "Participation of Children and Adolescents in Live Crisis Drills and Exercises." *Pediatrics* 146, no. 3 (2020). https://doi.org/10.1542/peds.2020-015503.

Schonfeld, Zach. "What We Know about the Uvalde Victims Who Were Hospitalized." Yahoo! News, May 30, 2022. https://news.yahoo.com/know-uvalde-victims-were-hospitalized-032425461.html?guccounter=1.

Schweit, Katherine W. "Addressing the Problem of the Active Shooter." *FBI Law Enforcement Bulletin.* Last modified May 7, 2013. https://leb.fbi.gov/articles/featured-articles/addressing-the-problem-of-the-active-shooter.

Seline, Libby. "So Long 'Thoughts and Prayers:' 4 Months Later, an Analysis of How Twitter Reacted to Uvalde." *San Antonio Express-News*, September 13, 2022. https://www.expressnews.com/news/local/article/Uvalde-shooting-twitter-analysis-17413430.php.

Serrano, Alejandro, and Uriel J. Garcia. "Uvalde School District Suspends its Entire Police Department." *The Texas Tribune,* October 7, 2022, https://www.texastribune.org/2022/10/07/uvalde-school-police-suspended.

Serrano, Alejandro. "DPS Chief Steve McCraw Says His 'Institution Did Not Fail' in Uvalde." *The Texas Tribune,* October 27, 2022. https://www.texastribune.org/2022/10/27/steve-mccraw-dps-response.

Sewell, James D. *Guide for Developing an Effective Stress Management Policy for Law Enforcement: Psychological Support, Training of Agency Personnel, Cardiovascular Disease, and Police Suicide.* Washington, DC: Office of Community Oriented Policing Services, 2021. https://portal.cops.usdoj.gov/resourcecenter?item=cops-w0943.

Shakhnazarova, Nika. "Texas School Massacre Victims Who Exchanged 'I Love You Texts' Will Be Buried Next to One Another." *New York Post,* June 8, 2022. https://nypost.com/2022/06/08/annabell-rodriguez-james-lopez-to-be-buried-next-to-each-other.

Shalchi, Homa. "Psychological Effects of Active Shooter Drills in Schools." Baylor College of Medicine. Last modified August 19, 2019. https://www.bcm.edu/news/psychological-effect-of-active-shooter-drills.

Silver, Ashley. "Uvalde School District Hires New Interim Police Chief." Police1, November 17, 2022. https://www.police1.com/chiefs-sheriffs/articles/uvalde-school-district-hires-new-interim-police-chief-QzrJTMmKLyEUDLNA.

Silverman, W. K., and A.M. La Greca. "Children Experiencing Disasters: Definitions, Reactions, and Predictors of Outcomes." In *Helping Children Cope with Disasters and Terrorism*, edited by Annette M. La Greca, Wendy K. Silverman, Eric M. Vernberg, and Michael C. Roberts, 11–33. Washington, DC: American Psychological Association, 2002.

Smith, Kelli. "Hundreds of Police Officers Have Signed up for Texas Mental-Health Program, Officials Say." *Dallas Morning News*, September 8, 2022. https://www.dallasnews.com/news/public-safety/2022/09/08/hundreds-of-police-officers-have-signed-up-for-texas-mental-health-program-officials-say/.

Sottile, Zoe. "Their Mom Was Killed in Uvalde, Then Their Dad Died of A Heart Attack – Now People Are Donating Millions for Their Family." CNN, May 29, 2022. https://www.cnn.com/2022/05/29/us/uvalde-family-gofundme-trnd/index.html.

Southwest Texas Regional Advisory Council. "About Us." Accessed December 4, 2023. https://strac.org/index.

Stanley, Ian H., Joseph W. Boffa, Melanie A. Hom, Nathan A. Kimbrel, and Thomas E. Joiner. "Differences in Psychiatric Symptoms and Barriers to Mental Health Care between Volunteer and Career Firefighters." *Psychiatry Research* 247 (2017): 236–242. https://doi.org/10.1016/j.psychres.2016.11.037.

Staub, Ervin. *Overcoming Evil: Genocide, Violent Conflict, and Terrorism.* Oxford, UK: Oxford University Press, 2010. https://doi.org/10.1093/acprof:oso/9780195382044.001.0001.

Staub, Ervin. *The Roots of Goodness and Resistance to Evil: Inclusive Caring, Moral Courage, Altruism Born of Suffering, Active Bystandership, and Heroism.* Oxford, UK: Oxford University Press, 2015.

Stein, Robin, and Alexander Cardia. "State Investigation Fueled Flawed Understanding of Delays During Police Response in Uvalde." *The New York Times,* October 12, 2022. https://www.nytimes.com/2022/10/12/us/uvalde-shooting-police-response-investigation.html.

Steinberg, Alan M., Melissa J. Brymer, Soeun Kim, Ernestine C. Briggs, Chandra Ghosh Ippen, Sarah A. Ostrowski, Kevin J. Gully, and Robert S. Pynoos. "Psychometric Properties of the UCLA PTSD Reaction Index: Part I." *Journal of Traumatic Stress* 26, no. 1 (2013): 1–9. https://doi.org/10.1002/jts.21780.

Strategies to Enhance Survival in Active Shooter and Intentional Mass Casualty Events: A Compendium. Supplement to the Bulletin of the American College of Surgeons 100, no. 1S (2015). https://www.stopthebleed.org/media/0svpk45s/hartford_consensus_compendium.pdf.

Straub, Frank, Blake Norton, Jennifer Zeunik, Brett Meade, Ben Gorban, Rebecca Benson, Joyce Iwashita, Alyse Folino Ley, and Michael Johnson. *Recovering and Moving Forward: Lessons Learned and Recommendations Following the Shooting at Marjory Stoneman Douglas High School.* Washington, DC: National Policing Institute, 2019. https://www.policinginstitute.org/publication/recovering-and-moving-forward-lessons-learned-and-recommendations-following-the-shooting-at-marjory-stoneman-douglas-high-school.

Straub, Frank, Jeffrey Brown, Roberto Villaseñor, Jennifer Zeunik, Ben Gorban, Blake Norton, and Eddie Reyes. *Advancing Charlotte: A Police Foundation Assessment of the Charlotte-Mecklenburg Police Department Response to the September 2016 Demonstrations.* Arlington, VA: National Policing Institute (formerly known as the Police Foundation), 2018. https://www.policinginstitute.org/publication/advancing-charlotte-a-police-foundation-assessment-of-the-charlotte-mecklenburg-police-department-response-to-the-september-2016-demonstrations.

Sturdevant, Neil. "Texas 4-H Scholarship Honors Makenna Lee Elrod Seiler." *Uvalde Leader-News,* December 22, 2022. https://www.uvaldeleadernews.com/articles/texas-4-h-scholarship-honors-makenna-lee-elrod-seiler.

TCOLE (Texas Commission on Law Enforcement). "Basic Peace Officer Course 720." Last modified February 17, 2022. http://www.tcole.texas.gov/content/basic-peace-officer-course-720.

TCOLE (Texas Commission on Law Enforcement). "Basic Telecommunicator Licensing Course (2022)." Last modified September 6, 2022. http://www.tcole.texas.gov/content/basic-telecommunicator-licensing-course-2022.

TCOLE (Texas Commission on Law Enforcement). "Legislatively Mandated Training." Memorandum, June 13, 2022. Austin, TX: Texas Commission on Law Enforcement.

TCOLE (Texas Commission on Law Enforcement). "Proficiency Certificates." Accessed August 3, 2023. http://www.tcole.texas.gov/content/proficiency-certificates.

TCOLE (Texas Commission on Law Enforcement). "School Based Law Enforcement Training." *Technical Assistance Bulletin.* August 27, 2019. https://www.tcole.texas.gov/content/technical-assistance-bulletins.

TCOLE (Texas Commission on Law Enforcement). "TCOLE History." Accessed December 5, 2023. http://www.tcole.texas.gov/content/tcole-history.

TCOLE (Texas Commission on Law Enforcement). "TCOLE Mission." Accessed August 3, 2023. http://www.tcole.texas.gov/content/tcole-mission.

TCOLE (Texas Commission on Law Enforcement). "Training Providers." Accessed August 3, 2023. https://www.tcole.texas.gov/content/training-providers.

TCOLE (Texas Commission on Law Enforcement). "Training Requirements." Accessed August 8, 2023. https://www.tcole.texas.gov/content/training-requirements.

TCOLE (Texas Commission on Law Enforcement). *Active Shooter Response for School-Based Law Enforcement: Course #2195.* Austin: Texas Commission on Law Enforcement, 2020. https://s3.documentcloud.org/documents/22046076/active-shooter-sble-2195-course-final-1-30-20.pdf.

Tedeschi, Richard G., Jane Shakespeare-Finch, Kanako Taku, and Lawrence G. Calhoun. "Developmental Research on Posttraumatic Growth." In *Posttraumatic Growth: Theory, Research and Applications,* 199–125. New York: Routledge, 2018.

TEX. ADMIN. CODE § 221.1, Texas Commission on Law Enforcement: Proficiency Certificate Requirements (2011, as amended). https://texreg.sos.state.tx.us/public/readtac$ext.TacPage?sl=R&app=9&p_dir=&p_rloc=&p_tloc=&p_ploc=&pg=1&p_tac=&ti=37&pt=7&ch=221&rl=1.

TEX. ADMIN. CODE § 221.43, Texas Commission on Law Enforcement: School-Based Law Enforcement Proficiency Certificate (2016, as amended). https://texreg.sos.state.tx.us/public/readtac$ext.TacPage?sl=R&app=9&p_dir=&p_rloc=&p_tloc=&p_ploc=&pg=1&p_tac=&ti=37&pt=7&ch=221&rl=43.

TEX. ADMIN. CODE § 392.303(14), Texas Health and Human Services Commission: Definitions—Memorandum of Understanding (MOU) (2015). https://texreg.sos.state.tx.us/public/readtac$ext.TacPage?sl=R&app=9&p_dir=&p_rloc=&p_tloc=&p_ploc=&pg=1&p_tac=&ti=1&pt=15&ch=392&rl=303.

TEX. CRIM. CODE § 2.17, General Duties of Officers: Conservator of the Peace (1965, as amended). https://statutes.capitol.texas.gov/Docs/CR/htm/CR.2.htm#2.17htm.

TEX. EDUC. CODE § 37.103, Enforcement of Rules (1995). https://statutes.capitol.texas.gov/Docs/ED/htm/ED.37.htm#37.103.

TEX. EDUC. CODE § 37.108(g), Multihazard Emergency Operations Plan; Safety and Security Audit (2005). https://statutes.capitol.texas.gov/Docs/ED/htm/ED.37.htm#37.108.

TEX. EDUC. CODE § 37.109, School Safety and Security Committee (2009, as amended). https://statutes.capitol.texas.gov/Docs/ED/htm/ED.37.htm#37.109.

TEX. EDUC. CODE § 37.114, Best Practices for Emergency School Drills and Exercises; Mandatory School Drills (2019, as amended). https://statutes.capitol.texas.gov/Docs/ED/htm/ED.37.htm#37.114.

TEX. EDUC. CODE § 37.115, Threat Assessment and Safe and Supportive School Program and Team (2019). https://statutes.capitol.texas.gov/Docs/ED/htm/ED.37.htm#37.115.

TEX. EDUC. CODE § 37.201, Texas School Safety Center (2001). https://statutes.capitol.texas.gov/Docs/ED/htm/ED.37.htm#37.201.

TEX. GOV. CODE § 418.1015, Emergency Management Directors (2007, as amended). https://statutes.capitol.texas.gov/Docs/GV/htm/GV.418.htm#418.1015.

Texas Department of Criminal Justice. "Definitions and Acronyms." Accessed August 3, 2023. https://www.tdcj.texas.gov/divisions/vs/index.html.

Texas Department of Public Safety. "Human Resource Operations." Accessed August 3, 2023. https://www.dps.texas.gov/section/human-resource-operations.

Texas Department of Public Safety. "Operation Lone Star: In the News." Last modified May 26, 2023. https://www.dps.texas.gov/operationlonestar.

Texas Department of Public Safety. "Resilience Training." Accessed August 3, 2023. https://www.dps.texas.gov/section/training-operations-tod/resilience-training.

Texas Department of Public Safety. "Statement by Director Steven McCraw on Release of Uvalde Video."
News release, July 12, 2022.
https://www.dps.texas.gov/news/statement-director-steven-mccraw-release-uvalde-video.

Texas Division of Emergency Management. *State of Texas Emergency Management Plan: Basic Plan.* Del
Valle, TX: Texas Division of Emergency Management, 2020.
https://www.tdem.texas.gov/preparedness/state-planning.

Texas Education Agency. "Texas Schools." Accessed December 5, 2023.
https://tea.texas.gov/texas-schools.

Texas EMS Alliance. "Peer Assistance." Accessed August 7, 2023. https://txemsa.com/peer-assistance.

Texas Health and Human Services Network. "Texas Critical Incident Stress Management Network."
Accessed August 3, 2023. https://www.hhs.texas.gov/about/process-improvement/improving-
services-texans/behavioral-health-services/disaster-behavioral-health-services/texas-critical-
incident-stress-management-network.

Texas School Safety Center. "About." Texas State University. Accessed August 3, 2023.
https://txssc.txstate.edu/about.

Texas School Safety Center. "Drill Frequently Asked Questions." In *Training, Drilling, and Exercising
Toolkit: 2.1 Drill Requirements.* San Marcos, TX: Texas State University, n.d.
https://txssc.txstate.edu/tools/tde-toolkit/drill-requirements.

Texas School Safety Center. "School Safety Law Toolkit: 86th Session Updates (2019)." Texas State
University. Accessed August 8, 2023. https://txssc.txstate.edu/tools/law-toolkit/updates/86th.

Texas State Association of Firefighters. "TSAFF Peer Support." Accessed August 3, 2023.
https://www.tsaff.org/peer-support.

Texas Tribune. "Uvalde CISD." Accessed August 8, 2023.
https://schools.texastribune.org/districts/uvalde-cisd.

Thomas, Jake. "Uvalde Hallway Video Reignites Fury at Police as Families Condemn Release." *Newsweek,*
July 13, 2022. https://www.newsweek.com/uvalde-hallway-video-reignites-fury-police-families-
condemn-release-1724104.

Tiesman, Hope M., Katherine L. Elkins, Melissa Brown, Suzanne Marsh, and Leslie M. Carson. "Suicides
Among First Responders: A Call to Action." Centers for Disease Control and Prevention, April 6,
2021. https://blogs.cdc.gov/niosh-science-blog/2021/04/06/suicides-first-responders.

Tosone, Carol, John P. McTighe, Jennifer Bauwens, and April Naturale. "Shared Traumatic Stress and the
Long-Term Impact of September 11th on Manhattan Clinicians." *Journal of Traumatic Stress* 24, no.
5 (2011): 546–552. https://doi.org/10.1002/jts.20686.

Tosone, Carol, Orit Nuttman-Shwartz, and Tricia Stephens. "Shared Trauma: When the Professional is Personal." *Clinical Social Work Journal* 40 (2012): 231–239. https://doi.org/10.1007/s10615-012-0395-0.

Trauma and Grief Component Therapy for Adolescents. Los Angeles: The National Child Traumatic Stress Network, 2018. https://www.nctsn.org/interventions/trauma-and-grief-component-therapy-adolescents.

Treisman, Rachel, and Alex Leff. "How World Leaders Are Reacting to the Uvalde School Shooting." NPR, May 25, 2022. https://www.npr.org/2022/05/25/1101256376/leaders-reaction-to-uvalde-school-shooting-texas-zelenskyy-pope-trudeau.

U.S. Census Bureau. "Language Spoken at Home by Ability to Speak English for the Population 5 Years and Over: Uvalde County, Texas." *American Community Survey.* Accessed August 3, 2023. https://data.census.gov/table?q=B16001+&g=050XX00US48463&tid=ACSDT5Y2015.B16001.

U.S. Census Bureau. "QuickFacts: Uvalde city, Texas." Accessed August 8, 2023. https://www.census.gov/quickfacts/uvaldecitytexas.

U.S. Department of Education. "An Eligible Student Guide to the Family Educational Rights and Privacy Act (FERPA)." https://studentprivacy.ed.gov/sites/default/files/resource_document/file/An%20Eligible%20Student%20Guide%20to%20FERPA_0.pdf.

U.S. Department of Education. "Does FERPA Protect the Education Records of Students that are Deceased?" Accessed August 8, 2023. https://studentprivacy.ed.gov/faq/does-ferpa-protect-education-records-students-are-deceased.

U.S. Fire Administration. *Fire/Emergency Medical Services Department Operational Considerations and Guide for Active Shooter and Mass Casualty Incidents.* Washington, DC: Federal Emergency Management Agency, 2013. https://www.usfa.fema.gov/downloads/pdf/publications/active_shooter_guide.pdf.

UCISD (Uvalde Consolidated Independent School District). "U.C.I.S.D. School Board." Accessed August 8, 2023. https://www.ucisd.net/about-ucisd/schoolboard.

Unexpected Challenges for Communities in the Recovery Phase of a Mass Violence Incident. Charleston, SC: National Mass Violence Victimization Resource Center, 2023. https://nmvvrc.org/media/00tbio4n/unexpected-challenges-for-communities-in-recovery-phase.pdf.

University of North Texas at Dallas. "Texas Law Enforcement Peer Network." Accessed August 3, 2023. https://www.untdallas.edu/cpi/tlepn.

Ura, Alexa. "Irma and Joe Garcia, a Teacher and Her Heartbroken Husband, are Buried Together in Uvalde." *The Texas Tribune,* June 1, 2022. https://www.texastribune.org/2022/06/01/garcia-funeral-uvalde-shooting.

Uria, Daniel. "Mourners Gather for Funerals of Student, Teacher Killed in Uvalde Shooting." UPI, June 2, 2022. https://www.upi.com/Top_News/US/2022/06/01/mourners-gather-funerals-student-teacher-killed-Uvalde-shooting/8631654134736.

Usher, Laura, Stefanie Friedhoff, Sam Cochran, and Anand Pandya. *Preparing for the Unimaginable: How Chiefs Can Safeguard Officer Mental Health before and after Mass Casualty Events.* Washington, DC: Office of Community Oriented Policing Services, 2016. https://portal.cops.usdoj.gov/resourcecenter?item=cops-p347.

Uvalde County. "Contact Us: Constables." Accessed August 3, 2023. https://uvaldecounty.com/index.php/county/constables/constables-contact.

Uvalde Municipal Code of Ordinances. Title 2, Chapter 2.56, Police Department. https://library.municode.com/tx/uvalde/codes/code_of_ordinances?nodeId=TIT2ADPE_CH2.56PODE.

Uvalde Region Mental Health Needs Assessment. Hill Country Mental Health & Developmental Disabilities Center, 2022. https://www.hillcountry.org/uvalde-region-mental-health-needs-assessment.

Uvalde Together Resiliency Center. "Participating Organizations." Accessed August 3, 2023. https://uvaldetogether.org/#participating-organizations.

Virgin, Yami. "New Body Camera Video from Uvalde School Tragedy." KEYE, October 26, 2022. https://cbsaustin.com/newsletter-daily/new-body-camera-video-from-uvalde-school-tragedy.

Virgin, Yami. "Top Texas Ranger Suddenly Retires in Middle of Uvalde School Shooting Investigation." NBC News 4 San Antonio, October 25, 2022. https://news4sanantonio.com/news/local/top-texas-ranger-suddenly-retires-in-middle-of-uvalde-school-shooting-investigation-teachers-students-murder-police-troopers-robb-elementary.

Virginia Tech Review Panel. Mass Shootings at Virginia Tech, April 16, 2007: Report of the Review Panel Presented to Governor Kaine, Commonwealth of Virginia. Blacksburg, VA: Virginia Tech, 2007. https://scholar.lib.vt.edu/prevail/docs/VTReviewPanelReport.pdf.

Vreeland, Betty. "An Evidence-Based Practice of Psychoeducation for Schizophrenia: A Practical Intervention for Patients and Their Families." *Psychiatric Times* 29, no. 2 (2012): 34–40. https://www.psychiatrictimes.com/view/evidence-based-practice-psychoeducation-schizophrenia.

Walton, Xavier. "Uvalde CISD Announces Recommendation to Fire Pete Arredondo." KHOU, July 21, 2022. https://www.khou.com/article/news/special-reports/uvalde-school-shooting/uvalde-cisd-plans-termination-pete-arredondo/285-56df553b-7271-4298-902d-c71cfc13125f.

War Trauma Foundation. *Psychological First Aid: Guide for Field Workers.* Geneva, Switzerland: World Health Organization, 2011. https://www.who.int/publications/i/item/9789241548205.

Watson, Patricia J., Vickie Taylor, Richard Gist, Erika Elvander, Frank Leto, Bob Martin, Jim Tanner, et al. *Stress First Aid for Firefighters and Emergency Medical Services Personnel: Student Manual.* Emmitsburg, MD: National Fallen Firefighters Foundation, 2015. https://www.ptsd.va.gov/professional/treat/type/stress_first_aid_asp.

Watson, Patricia, and Richard J. Westphal. *Stress First Aid for Health Care Workers.* Washington, DC: U.S. Department of Veterans Affairs, 2020. https://www.ptsd.va.gov/professional/treat/type/stress_first_aid.asp.

Weber, Paul J. "Statesman, Other News Media Sue Uvalde Officials for Shooting Records." *Austin American-Statesman,* August 30, 2022, https://www.statesman.com/story/news/2022/08/30/uvalde-shooting-records-lawsuit-statesman-other-news-media-sue/65464656007.

Weber, Paul J. "Uvalde Students Go Back to School For 1st time Since Attack." Associated Press, September 6, 2022. https://apnews.com/article/shootings-texas-education-3e0fc3ec61c1135f8bdae5a18f786ef7.

Wertheimer, Tiffany. "Texas shooting: The teachers who sacrificed their lives to protect children." BBC News, May 26, 2022. https://www.bbc.com/news/world-us-canada-61593071.

The White House. "A Proclamation Honoring The Victims Of The Tragedy In Uvalde, Texas." May 24, 2022. https://www.whitehouse.gov/briefing-room/presidential-actions/2022/05/24/a-proclamation-honoring-the-victims-of-the-tragedy-in-uvalde-texas.

The White House. "Remarks by President Biden on Gun Violence in America." June 2, 2022. https://www.whitehouse.gov/briefing-room/speeches-remarks/2022/06/02/remarks-by-president-biden-on-gun-violence-in-america.

The White House. "Remarks by President Biden on the School Shooting in Uvalde, Texas." May 24, 2022. https://www.whitehouse.gov/briefing-room/speeches-remarks/2022/05/24/remarks-by-president-biden-on-the-school-shooting-in-uvalde-texas.

Wiley, Kelly. "Texas School Shooting in Uvalde Prompts DPS to Change Active Shooter Policy." KXAN, September 9, 2022. https://www.kxan.com/news/active-shooter-policy-changed-in-wake-of-uvalde-according-to-dps-emails.

Willis, Dan. "Perspective: Principles of Effective Law Enforcement Leadership." *FBI Law Enforcement Bulletin.* Last modified March 1, 2011. https://leb.fbi.gov/articles/perspective/perspective-principles-of-effective-law-enforcement-leadership.

Wilson, Laura C. "A Systematic Review of Probable Posttraumatic Stress Disorder in First Responders Following Man-Made Mass Violence." *Psychiatry Research* 229, no. 1–2 (2015): 21–26. https://doi.org/10.1016/j.psychres.2015.06.015.

Wolfe, Elizabeth, and Andy Rose. "Texas Department of Public Safety Must Release Documents Related to Uvalde School Shooting, Judge Rules." CNN, June 29, 2023. https://www.cnn.com/2023/06/29/us/uvalde-texas-dps-shooting-response-records-ruling/index.html.

World Health Organization. "Definition of Health." Accessed August 11, 2023. https://www.publichealth.com.ng/world-health-organizationwho-definition-of-health.

Yan, Holly, Harmeet Kaur, Melissa Alonso, Amir Vera, and Sharif Paget. "Remembering What We Know about the Victims at Robb Elementary School." CNN, July 23, 2022. https://www.cnn.com/2022/05/25/us/victims-uvalde-texas-school-shooting/index.html.

Yousef, Odette. "The Texas School Shooting Conspiracies Show Far-Right Misinformation is Evolving." NPR, May 26, 2022. https://www.npr.org/2022/05/26/1101479269/texas-uvalde-school-shooting-misinformation-conspiracy-far-right.

Zoellner, Lori A., Edna B. Foa, and Bartholomew D. Brigidi. 1999. "Interpersonal Friction and PTSD in Female Victims of Sexual and Nonsexual Assault." *Journal of Traumatic Stress* 12, no. 4 (1999): 689–700. https://doi.org/10.1023/A:1024777303848.

Zoellner, Lori A., Norah C. Feeny, Afsoon Eftekhari, and Edna B. Foa. "Changes in negative beliefs following three brief programs for facilitating recovery after assault." *Depression and Anxiety* 28, no. 7 (2011): 532–540. https://doi.org/10.1002/da.20847.

Additional References

CIR Document and Data Review

CIR Training Analysis

Hillcrest Memorial Funeral Home CCTV Footage

Robb Elementary School CCTV Footage

Texas Department of Public Safety Body-Worn Camera Footage

Texas Department of Public Safety Dashboard Footage

Texas Department of Public Safety Radio Traffic

Texas Parks and Wildlife Body-Worn Camera Footage

Uvalde County Constables Body-Worn Camera Footage

Uvalde County Sheriff's Office Body-Worn Camera Footage

Uvalde County Sheriff's Office Radio Traffic

Uvalde Police Department 911 Calls

Uvalde Police Department Body-Worn Camera Footage

Uvalde Police Department Calls for Service

Uvalde Police Department Dispatch Landline

Uvalde Police Department Incident Call Log

Uvalde Police Department Radio Traffic

Made in the USA
Las Vegas, NV
28 February 2024

86450712R00332